60,001+
Best Baby
Names

DIANE STAFFORD

SOURCEBOOKS, INC.
NAPERVILLE, ILLINOIS

Published by Sourcebooks, Inc.
P.O. Box 4410, Naperville, Illinois 60567-4410
(630) 961-3900
Fax: (630) 961-2168
www.sourcebooks.com

Library of Congress Cataloging-in-Publication Data

Stafford, Diane.
  60,001 best baby names / Diane Stafford.
      p. cm.
  Includes bibliographical references and index.
  1. Names, Personal—Dictionaries. I. Title. II. Title: Sixty thousand and one best baby names.

CS2377.S5733 2008
929.4'4—dc22

2007042739

Printed and bound in Canada.
TR 10 9 8 7 6 5 4

To my wonderful daughter, Jennifer, whose loving ways have brought me happiness every day of her life—and to two-year-old London and five-year-old Ben, my precious grandchildren whose spirit, sweetness, affection, and conversations are, for me, pure magic.

Acknowledgments

Sincere thanks to Ed Knappman of New England Publishing Associates, for giving me the opportunity to write this book—and to Elizabeth Frost Knappman, literary agent and friend, who has made my dreams come true time and again.

I also want to thank Sourcebooks' Dominique Raccah, Shana Drehs, Emily Williams, Bethany Brown, Hillel Black, Kelly Barrales-Saylor, Dan Bulla, Kristin Esch, Samantha Raue, and Morgan Hrejsa for their work on *60,001+ Best Baby Names*.

And special appreciation to my family and friends, whose names will always be tops on my list of favorites: Belle, Clinton, Jennifer, Robert, London, Ben, Allen, Christina, Camilla, Richard, Xanthe, Austin, Gina, Curtis, Melinda, Britt, Renee, Lindsay, Josh, Ella, Cameron, David, Dana, Rachel, Clarence, Chris, Donna, Stacey, Lynn, James, Scott, Tessie.

From the bottom of my heart, I thank my loving husband, Greg Munoz—and his wonderful children and grandchildren, Matt, Laura, Mark, Joey, Romano, Isabella, Patrick, Katrina, Amanda, Molly, Dylan, Liliana, Eamon, Joaquin, Cita, Greg, Liam, Ethan, Patrick.

Contents

Introduction

Your name. Those two words should make you smile.

Nothing is more personal. Whether one-of-a-kind (Shawnikwaronda) or most-popular-of-the-century (Jennifer), your name gives you an identity that sets you apart from the twenty other kids in kindergarten and labels you the first day of a new job. If your name is memorable or a perfect fit, people say it more often. But if yours is hard to pronounce or difficult to remember, chances are good that you will go through life rarely hearing your "Daphinola" at all.

Indeed, a name can affect the ebb and flow of your entire existence. That's exactly why parents-to-be often give the baby-naming process numerous hours of list-perusing, head-scratching, and poll-taking.

For a kid who feels "stuck" with an albatross name, life can be long and bumpy. While people with better names seem to glide through social encounters effortlessly, the name-challenged types are more likely to stumble and bungle their way through the jungle.

If you have any doubt, note the baby-naming efforts of a person who grew up as Nyleen or Hortense, Huelett or Drakeston, and you'll probably find that this individual will have offspring named John or Ann. Just having a sibling with a tough moniker will nudge us in the direction of plain when it comes to naming a tiny, innocent baby.

What's the significance of all of this for you, the parent-in-waiting? You are dead-on right in thinking that finding the "right" name constitutes a major responsibility. This occasion is momentous enough to merit lots of discussion and lots of thumbing through the baby-naming book until you finally hit on it—The Right Name.

Whether or not you want to admit it, you really and truly want your child to like his name. No wonder you feel awed by the job! Most parents fret and falter, marvel and malinger, worry and wonder—sometimes for the entire nine months of pregnancy.

And that's because authors and songwriters immortalize names. People in love grow misty-eyed just thinking of them. Names are glorified and mocked, loved and loathed.

You're looking for a name that resonates, one that's memorable and perfect—but not *frighteningly* memorable or overly perfect. You're out to locate a name that is absolutely sure—100 percent guaranteed—to have a positive effect on your little tyke's life. For that reason alone, you're willing to give the baby-naming gig quite a few hours of overanalysis.

We all want great names. We all struggle with the thousands of contenders.

Couldn't that little embryo give us a hint as to what name he would prefer? Is it better to be one of ten Davids in your class at school or is it more of a challenge to try to pull off a quirky Ringo or Crash?

Maybe you're already submitting name-nominees to the acid tests: Is it too cute? Overly hip? Brutally boring? And what's wrong with just going with your gut? This is your baby, after all. So why not tag that little biscuit with the way-cool name you've had squirreled away since your Barbie-and-Ken days?

Have fun with the name game. Approach it with wackiness, high spirits, and good insider information. Stay on task and don't let yourself get sidetracked by relative schmoozing or movie-star mimicking. Carefully assess the pros and cons of your finalists, and you're bound to come up with a winner.

And while you're at it, do weigh the fact that a name can shape personality, career, and self-esteem. (How could a girl named Buzzie be anything other than a cheerleader?) And just as clearly, a person's name can be a lifelong drawback, as in the guy whose parents reversed the letters of their surname, and came up with an unpronounceable humdinger that made kids laugh at the boy all the way through school. So what happens to this kind of nuisance-name? When the man turns twenty-one, he goes to the courthouse and banishes that kookiness forever. What used to be "Enord" becomes the benign letter "E."

Also, consider any nasty connotations. Erica took on a whole new and scary feel after thirty years of being carried around by the malevolent Erica Kane on the soap *All My Children*. And, by a different, somewhat slatternly yardstick, who could in good conscience name an innocent baby girl "Monica" in the post–Bill Clinton era?

At the same time, names can be assets, sources of pride and distinction. Who would bet on anything other than a promising future for a Theodore or a Saul, a Grace or a Claire? Some parents get so confused that they throw up their hands and pick generic names that children can make of what they want. (Think how many times you've met Anne, Patricia, Carol, Michael, Richard, David, and Mark.)

Everyone knows what his own name did for him growing up (and what it didn't do). Maybe your parents envisioned a man being sworn in for President and chose Adlai, 3

John, Roosevelt, or George. Or perhaps your mother had warm, fuzzy feelings about a good old boy she knew growing up, so you were christened Billy Bob, certainly well suited for country-western singing. Or your aunt loved the "artist formerly known as Prince" and made sure your birth certificate registered the eccentric "Purple Rain."

Boggled by input, many parents toss around names for the entire nine months. Adding to the confusion is the steady stream of names offered by well-meaning grandparents, aunts, uncles, cousins, coworkers, employees, repairmen, and friends.

Baby-naming can even become so daunting that perplexed parents-to-be waffle daily. And then, after they have identified a few winners, a couple faces the key issue that often comes into play—finding a name they can agree on. Usually, the result is a rush to judgment on delivery day, when Mom and Dad are finally forced to choose a name in the maternity ward.

Basic attitudes toward baby-naming can range from frivolous and cavalier to serious and tradition-laden. One Houston mother with the surname Palms named her African-American son White so that each time he introduced himself, "I'm White Palms," he was greeted with a grin or a look of disbelief. The same goes for a Texan named King Solomon, whose name is so memorable that this author was introduced to him at age fifteen and, decades later, can still remember the shock of meeting a very confident kid who actually managed to pull off that spectacular name. (Some children can make a traffic-stopping name a big asset; but some can't.) A friend of mine named Jeffrey wore her boy's name like a badge of honor, growing up to be both funny and popular. But another girl whose parents chose the masculine name Christopher struggled with it life-long, forced to live with other children's ridicule.

That brings up a major trend going strong currently, the meshing of names to come up with something brand new. The U.S. Social Security Administration shows growing numbers of "creations" such as Tamikas and Rayshons, but don't mistake the proliferation for anything resembling approval by the kids that bear these names. Most children don't appreciate their parents' inventiveness, because teachers either mispronounce or simply avoid made-up names as they have through the ages, and classmates make a hobby of terrorizing kids with odd names.

Some folks consider the practice of giving an old name a new spelling—Genefur for Jennifer, for example—a very cool way to go, while others scoff at this as downright laughable. Yet plenty of parents still contend that giving new spellings to old names lends them fresh and splashy feels.

In some ethnic groups, a baby's name reflects the mother's pregnancy impressions. One book titled *Narco* tells of a Spanish mother who had a complicated process for naming seven sons. Each long name was a three-pronged affair consisting of a number for the birth order, a word that represented the mother's main obsession during the nine months, and the name of a famous writer. Cuatro Conrad Confabulation was the fourth son—Cuatro, meaning fourth son; Conrad, for the writer Joseph Conrad; and Confabulation, indicating that she spent her pregnancy gossiping with other pregnant women. Cinco Cervantes Cirrus, by the same token, was the fifth child, named for the writer Miguel Cervantes, and Cirrus, a cloud name that represents the mother's daydreaming pregnancy.

On the other end of the spectrum from those parents who dream up bizarre, fanciful names are the families who view baby-naming as a holy act, right up there with baptism. Some societies believe that names hold spiritual and prophetic significance, and that a child's name is sure to have an enormous impact on his future. The people of Ghana, for instance, think that a name is a mark of religious identification that carries honor and respect. A good name is highly treasured in Ghanaian society, and each baby is honored with a naming ceremony.

Obviously, no science has ever been devised to pinpoint the whys and hows of choosing a name. But, in this book, we give you 60,001 names, tips on the selection process, and, most importantly, clues as to how our names affect us. Be sure to read Part II, which features anecdotes from people who reflect on their names and how they were shaped (or weren't) by their names.

NOTE TO READER:

Find within the text the most popular names of 2008 for boys and girls designated by ◐.

Find within the text the top twin names of 2008 for boys and girls designated by ◑.

part one

Tips for Naming Your Baby

Tips for Naming Your Baby

What do most people do? Some of the baby-naming approaches frequently used include the following:

- Mesh two names together to form a new one.
- Pick a name you've always loved.
- Find a name that bodes well for a promising career.
- Go with a name that connotes a trait—honesty, friendliness, savoir faire.
- Use the mother's maiden name for the first name.
- Honor a beloved relative by using his name.
- Stick with something time-honored and safe.
- Make up a name—a practice that some people consider corny and others rate high on the creativity scale.

And while you are dabbling in the name game, be sure to remember these naming taboos:

- Avoid a name that's carrying baggage equivalent to Amtrak, as in Cher, Michael Jackson, Richard Simmons, Billy Joel, or Sting.
- Don't let family members talk you into a "junior" unless you don't mind your child being called "Little John" or "Junior" lifelong. Listen to all the suggestions relatives fling your way, but you make the call.
- Don't be too bothered by existing connotations that you associate with a name ("I knew a Margaret in school, and she was the meanest person in our class," "I sat next to a Stone in college, and he had a million moles," or "I dated a Morgan, and she was the most boring girl I've ever known"). The reason you shouldn't let old associations trip you up is that once you name your child Tasha or Truman, there isn't another person in the world with that name who matters. Trust me on this.

Ten Great Tips for Successful Baby-Naming

A "set of rules" can ratchet up your confidence. If you don't really need a framework, just read the following tips as a fun diversion.

Here are ten steps for naming your baby:

1. Consider the sound—does it work with your last name?

When the full name is said aloud, you want something that has a nice ring, not a tongue-twister or a rhyme. You may find that a long last name jibes best with a short first name; by the same token, put a long first name with a short last name, and you may have a winner.

The union of a first name ending in a vowel paired with a last name that starts with a vowel is not the greatest choice. For example: Ava Amazon. It's just hard to say. Puns aren't good omens for a happy life, either. Look at the infamous Ima Hogg name of a Houston philanthropist. If the poor woman wasn't burdened enough, she also had to deal with life-long rumors of a sister named Ura.

2. Know exactly what happens when you give your baby a crowd-pleaser name.

Give your kid a common name, and she'll probably end up Sarah B. in a classroom with six Sarahs. She may be comfortable with the anonymity that a plain-Jane name lends her—considering it far better than being the class Brunhilda, who gets ridiculed daily. Or she may ask you every other day of her childhood why you weren't more original in naming her: "Why did you give me the same name fifty million other kids have? Why couldn't you have come up with something better? Why didn't you take more time?"

3. Think seriously about the repercussions of choosing a name that's over-the-top in uniqueness.

You are definitely sticking your neck out by giving your child the name Rusty if your last name is Nail. Sure, he may muster up enough swagger to pull it off, but what if he doesn't? Lots of people with unusual or hard-to-spell last names will purposely opt for a simple first name for their child just to ease the load of having two names to spell over and over. Some research suggests that kids with odd names get more taunting from peers and are less well socialized. You can be sure that junior-high kids will make fun of a boy named Stone, but later, as an adult, he may enjoy having an unusual name.

Just make sure you don't choose a "fun" name simply because you like the idea of having people praise your creativity—instead, ask yourself how your child will feel about being a Bark or a Lake.

4. Ponder the wisdom of carrying on that family name.

Aunt Priscilla did fine with her name, but how will your tiny tot feel in a classroom full of Ambers and Britneys? Extremely old-fashioned names sometimes make their way back into circulation and do just fine, but sometimes they don't. (Will we really ever see the name Durwood soar again?)

5. Consider the confusion that is spawned by a namesake.

A kid named after a parent won't like being "Junior" or "Little Al." Ask anyone who has been in that position about the amount of confusion it generates about credit cards and other personal I.D. information. You'll spend half your life unraveling the mix-ups. Psychiatrists (many of them juniors themselves) will tell you that giving a child his very own name is a much better jump-start than making him a spin-off or a mini-me.

At the same time, we have all run across someone who absolutely loves being Trey or a III because the name represents tradition and history.

6. Make your family/background name an understudy (the middle name).

Let's say you want your baby's name to reflect family heritage or religion, but you strongly prefer more mainstream names. You can fill both bills by using the ancestral name as a middle name.

7. Ponder whether the name's meaning matters to you.

For some people, knowing a name's meaning is extremely important—often much more so than its origin. Your child could turn out to be the type who loves investigating such things. So what happens when that offspring of yours finds out that her name, Delilah, means "whimpering harlot guttersnipe"? She may wish you had taken a longer look at the name's baggage.

8. Look at shortened versions of a name and check out initials.
Don't think your child's schoolmates will fail to notice that his initials spell out S.C.U.M. And you can be sure that Harrison will become "Harry" or, occasionally, "Hairy." View the teasing as being as much a given as school backpacks—and think twice about whether you want to give your child's peer group something they can really grab onto. Tread lightly. Naming always starts with good intentions, but you can do your kid a favor by considering each name-candidate's bullying potential.

9. After you've narrowed your list, try out each name and see how it feels.
Say, "Barnabus Higgins, get yourself over here!" Or, "Harrison Higgins, have you done your homework?" Or, "Hannibal Higgins, would you like some fava beans?"

10. Once you and your mate have decided on a name, don't broadcast it.
You may want to keep your chosen name a secret, otherwise relatives and friends are likely to share all of their issues with the name accompanied by a long string of other, "better" options. Another possibility is that people will start calling the unborn baby that name, which will be unfortunate if you happen to find another you like better.

California mom Molly Rigdon also recommends giving your child a name that has few letters so that when she starts school, it's easy to learn to spell. "These things never come to mind until you're helping your preschooler 'Liliana' write her name." In other words, Jill, Kate, or Emma would have been easier.

Bottom line: take the Name Game seriously, but don't be afraid to go with the one that just feels right. That precious infant who will change your life dramatically is sure to be the best thing that has ever happened to you—so choose a name you will love singing and saying every single day a million times over.

part two

How Names Shape Our Lives

Here, twenty-one people share their thoughts on their names:

Camilla Shirley Pierce, homemaker and mother, Houston: "Although I was named for a beloved great aunt, I always felt that carrying around such an unusual name was not great. When I was a child, no one could pronounce it or spell it. It was a source of embarrassment and aggravation. Now, at age sixty-five, when people read my name they still mispronounce it, and I always feel like saying, 'How hard can it be? I could pronounce it at age three!'"

David Nordin, consultant: "I always liked my name because it had more character than other names. David has Biblical history, and it's more elegant and regal than your average name. On the flip side, my odd middle name caused me years of embarrassment. Teachers would call out that name during roll call, and people would laugh and make fun of me … As soon as I was grown, I had it legally changed. Parents should never name their kids anything that could make them objects of ridicule."

Clarence Raymond Chandler, President of Marshall & Winston, Inc., in Midland, Texas: "I was named after my dad's favorite brother, who was a great guy I admired. I was raised in south Texas (Benavides), where my friends were named Roberto, José, Ricardo, Jesus, and Francisco, so being a George, Bill, Jerry, Charles, or Roger never really came up on my 'wish list.' I was content! Today, technology has caused the minor inconvenience of not being able to find enough room on forms to print out my long name, much less my signature." Chandler adds: "I had it easy compared to my dad, who was born in an era when children were named after famous people; he got incessant ribbing, not to mention playground fights, when he was growing up, because his challenge was answering to Napoleon Bonaparte Chandler, which is right up there with the ranks of Johnny Cash's 'how do you do, my name is Sue.' In school, it was common knowledge that you only picked on him once, or you had a real dogfight on your hands. To avoid 'you gotta be kidding' comments, he adopted the name 'Nap' Chandler. He was a great dad, patriot, WWII veteran, ethical businessman, champion for the little guy, and a loving and tough SOB—he was my hero!"

Jennifer Wright, psychiatrist in Atlanta, Georgia: "I've always liked my name. Some of my best friends have been named Jennifer also, and I think it suits our personalities. The benefit of having a 'common' name is that I never have difficulty finding personalized items. Plus, I like the nicknames 'Jen' and 'Jenny.'"

Kristina Kaczmarek Holt, graphic artist: "I have always liked my name because it was unique. I had never come across a Kristina with a 'K' until I was a teenager, and then it was usually a Kristy or Kristine. I liked the sound of my first and last name together (the two Ks)—that seemed to work. My name was a heck of a thing to learn to spell in kindergarten, but it was all mine. They used to tape your name to those thick green pencils you learned to write with, and I was always sharpening my pencil down into my name. It wasn't until I recently had a child of my own (Noah) that my dad told me where he got my name. I assumed he picked it because it was a Polish name, and his family was half Polish. But, instead, he named me after a woman who was especially nice to him when he was young, who must have made a strong impression, because the name stuck with him until I was born."

Homemaker Dana Huggins Chandler: "I like to be just a little different from everyone else around me, so I always loved my name. There are now many people named Dana, but most don't have the same pronunciation. My name rhymes with Anna and Lana. I always tell people I was named after my dad—Dan—which isn't true, but it does help people remember how to pronounce my name."

Houston TV anchor Dominique Sachse: "Considering you can't pick your name at birth, I'm quite pleased with the one my parents chose for me. I think it has a level of sophistication, and it's unique and European, which I am. I've never considered changing it, shortening it, or going by a nickname. It's a name I feel I've had to live up to."

Cari LaGrange, Internet business owner: "I liked my name growing up, but like most kids, I went through a phase when I wished I could change it, the way girls with straight hair want curly hair and vice versa. Thankfully, my name and its spelling were unique in the town where I grew up, so there was no other girl by my name to compare my identity to."

Jane Vitrano, homemaker in Midland, Texas: "My mother named my sister Linda and me Jane because she hated her own name, Lula Mae, and said she would never want her daughters to have anything but plain names—and no middle names."

Donna Pate, technical writer: "I was neutral about my name. It was okay but not too exciting or interesting. At least it didn't lend itself to juvenile humor. There was the chance of being labeled 'Prima Donna,' but that was beyond the vocabulary of most kids. I liked my name better after I learned what it meant, but that wasn't until I was an adult."

Natasha Graf, editor, New York: "My name is pretty special because I was named after a very important woman in my father's life. When I was young and wanted to be like every other girl with an American name, I didn't always like my name because it was unusual at the time, being Russian and all. However, when my father shared with me who I was named after, I came to love it because I feel like I am connected to her somehow. She was a professor at my father's college, and she spoke seven languages—a brilliant woman who had emigrated from Russia. She was his mentor—the first really intellectual person he met during college, and they stayed friends after he went to medical school. It was not an affair—more a meeting of the minds. They wrote to each other. He saved every letter she wrote, and he let me read them. It was so interesting to see my father as a young person through these letters. She died before I was born, before my father was married. I wish I could have met her; I wonder what she would have thought of me. As you can tell, I wouldn't want my name to be anything else."

JoAnn Roberson, counselor, Edna, Texas: "I didn't like my name because it reminded me of a boy's name—Joe. My dad said they were going to name me Jacquelyn, but an uncle said that was too long a name for a little baby, and I would never learn to spell it. I always wished that was my name."

Trey Speegle, former art director for US Weekly, New York City: "I've always appreciated my name, although when I was very young and wanted to fit in, I wished I had a more normal name, like Chris, or a cool name, like Skip. My great-grandmother named me; I was born on her birthday, April 13, and I was her thirteenth great-grandson. Her son (my grandfather) was John Hugh Speegle Sr., and my father is John Hugh Speegle Jr., so she named me Trey John—'the third' John."

Angela Theresa Clark, co-owner of Court Record Research, Inc.: "My mother named me Angela Theresa after two of her favorite Carmelite nuns. I was known as Theresa until sixth grade, when I tired of telling teachers that I didn't go by Angela and just surrendered to being called that. I thought it was stupid to be named something so close to the word 'angel.' Angels are imaginary, soft, and I saw them as easy prey. I was also afraid people might think I was angelic. I thought I had to be tough in my family, with five brothers and two big (mean) older sisters (ha!). I was tomboyish, and Theresa just fit better. Some family members still call me Theresa, although it doesn't fit me anymore because now I'm softer and much more vulnerable. I love my name."

Spiker Davis, dentist, Houston, Texas: "I really liked my name because people always remembered it, and there's no one to get confused with. Also, with a last name like Davis (seventh most common name in the U.S.), you need something to separate you from the crowd."

Cristy Ann Hayes, journalist and mother of two: "My name became a primary focus when I was young and searching for a sense of self, like other preteens. I was disappointed when people would ask what Cristy was short for, and I had to reply 'nothing.' I would wish my mom had taken more time to give me a name as substantial as Christina or Christian. My name also worked well as a taunt for my brother, who insisted I was the only one of the three siblings whose name didn't start with W, so I was not part of the family. Will and Wendy could be rascals that way. My mom thought it was clever to give my name an unconventional spelling, so I have, my entire life, had to take special care in spelling my name, and often people will add an h. My driver's license is incorrect because of this, and many of my in-laws still spell it wrong. But after years of frustration regarding the spelling, I now appreciate the measuring tool it has become for me, showing how attuned someone is to me. I hold in high regard those who actually take the time to recognize the unique spelling and write it correctly. I believe it says something about one's character and approach to life when you take care to get a name right!"

Frank Vitrano, retired petroleum engineer in Midland, Texas: "I was born in Waco, Texas, of a Sicilian father, and I was named for my grandfather, Frank Anthony, which is the Italian custom for the firstborn son. You get your grandfather's name."

Jennifer Colwell, commercial property management, Midland, Texas: "Since I'm in my fifties, there were not very many Jennifers when I was growing up, and I always loved my name. I thought it was pretty and considered it an asset."

Christopher (Chris) Fleming, teacher and consultant, Houston, Texas: "Growing up, I hated my name, Christopher Anne. I was called Christopher Columbus, was sent a draft notice, and was labeled 'effeminate' on an aptitude test in high school. I finally told my mother how much I had hated my name, and she was surprised. In my opinion, parents should choose a name that indicates the child's sex (not one that's androgynous), and that's easy to spell. I don't think it's good to give a baby a name that's bizarre or made up from several words."

Wendy Schnakenberg Corson, EMT, Oklahoma: "I have always hated my name. There were never any other Wendys, and if there were, they certainly weren't popular. My parents said they also liked the name Robin, which is a name I love; I told them how mad I was that they chose such a terrible name for me. Also, my middle name, Anne, is just boring. I was never teased about my name, so I suppose that is a positive. But, of course, kids had my last name—Schnakenberg—to tease me with!"

part three

Choosing Names That Project Success

You think names don't have socioeconomic impact? Well, think again. A survey conducted by Barclays Bank (in the UK) reveals that people with certain names actually earn more money than folks with "lesser" names. In fact, those most likely to bring home a six-figure income are men named David, John, and Michael.

When Barclays's analysts looked at sixty thousand of their high-end customers whose annual salaries topped £100,000 ($180,000), Susans topped the list of female wage earners, and close behind were Elizabeths, Sarahs, and Janes. Other femmes who brought in big bucks were named Alison, Helen, and Patricia.

Remember, though, that these were names that parents gave their kids in the '60s. Making projections based on lists of favored names for 2005, what we'll probably see topping the earners' chart forty years from now are Emmas and Isabellas, Nicks and Joshuas. Note that all these names sound conventional and trustworthy—nothing quirky, trendy, or fanciful. So if you want your offspring to support you when you're quasi-senile, choose substance over flash.

In his bestselling *Freakonomics*, author Steven D. Levitt observes that names first become entrenched with affluent families and then trickle down into lower income strata in subsequent years. So if a CEO names his twins Graham and Taylor, lower income parents will soon take up the Graham-Taylor banner. By the same token, the names Maddox and Zahara (kids of super-hot, mega-rich Angelina Jolie) resonate with starwatchers and gain momentum accordingly.

Sure, we like glitz, we love glamour, and we're fools for snob appeal. But this particular penchant wars with common sense, which tells us that quirky names give children dubious legacies.

Little wonder, then, that today's "made-up" names generate controversy. Some say it's unfair for employers to get a sneak peek at ethnicity before a job candidate steps in the door. The second argument is that made-up names aren't *real* names, while others loudly contend that all names on birth certificates automatically become legitimate.

Research tells us that name connotations certainly can influence the expectations of HR directors, teachers, and society in general. The name "Diamond" may make the personnel director or grad school administrator dismiss the candidate immediately, just like the knee-jerk reaction to a "Shaquille" will be that he's on the fast track for sports, not legal briefs or prescriptions. Name your baby Romeo or Honey, and you can bet that it will take more than a village to raise this kid from the quagmire of serial-dating issues.

Just like clothing, hairstyle, and grooming, a name makes an impression and often leads to unfair assumptions. That's why savvy business types sometimes go so far as to change their names simply to have a better shot at affluence; "Caprice" becomes "Jane," "Panama" morphs into "Mark," and "Canyon" snags Wall Street success as "James."

In the same way that we attribute good qualities to attractive people before we know them, people with "good" names may get a free pass just by virtue of having been named well. Maybe we simply perceive that people named Elizabeth and David are more substantial, and that paves their way to greater success and wealth than Terrell, Brandy, Fifi, or Fluffy.

Names make statements. Images of success come with names like Elizabeth and Michael, Madison and Ethan, whereas people take less seriously the Roxies, Bambis, Roccos, and Bucks of this world.

Lessons learned:
- Don't give your child a name that conveys undesirable qualities.
- Do give your child a name that implies success, attractiveness, depth, intelligence, and compassion.
- Do ask yourself what kind of impression a name will make on people your child comes in contact with.
- Don't choose haphazardly because "that's my favorite sitcom star" or "I like the sound of it" or "that was my aunt's name."

So while you're going through the rigors of baby-naming, why not factor in future earning potential? Ponder who will make more money: Will or Rip? Anna or Lotus? Sonny or Daniel? DeeDee or Sarah?

Sure, weighing a name's financial ramifications goes against the grain because most parents select sentimentally—they "love" a name, want to honor a relative, or think the name is unique, classic, or cool and trendy.

But good names can indeed provide an edge. You absolutely *can* choose a name that will help your child make friends more easily, have more confidence, have fewer psychological hangups, be happier and more successful, and perhaps become the richest guy or girl on the block.

According to the Barclays survey, the top ten high-earning boys' names were:

1. David
2. John
3. Michael
4. Peter
5. Paul
6. Andrew
7. Richard
8. Robert
9. Mark
10. Stephen

And the survey yielded these top ten high-earning girls' names:

1. Susan
2. Elizabeth
3. Sarah
4. Jane
5. Helen
6. Patricia
7. Jacqueline
8. Alison
9. Anne
10. Nicola

part four

222 Fun Lists

Powerful Names		Names That Get Shortened	
Boys	**Girls**	**Boys**	**Girls**
Andrew	Anna	Alexander	Abigail
Angus	Blake	Augustus	Alexandra
Anthony	Campbell	Barnabus	Anastasia
Charles	Candace	Bradford	Angelina
Cole	Elizabeth	Christopher	Cassandra
Colin	Evan	Cornelius	Charmaine
Easton	Grace	Donovan	Constance
Ford	Greta	Emmanuel	Deborah
Grant	Harper	Enrique	Elizabeth
Harrison	Honor	Franklin	Evangeline
Heath	Hope	Frederic	Gabrielle
Jacob	Jessica	Gregory	Guadalupe
James	Julia	Jonathon	Gwendolyn
Jon	Lauren	Nathaniel	Jacqueline
Justice	Madison	Nicholas	Jennifer
Lamar	Margaret	Randolph	Josephine
Louis	Olivia	Roberto	Kimberly
Michael	Pace	Roderick	Lucretia
Nash	Parker	Roosevelt	Magdalena
Nolan	Pilar	Salvador	Nanette
Quentin	Quinn	Samuel	Penelope
Reagan	Reeve	Solomon	Rebecca
Solomon	Rhea	Timothy	Rosalinda
Thomas	Sarah	Wilfredo	Roxanna
William	Wylie	Woodrow	Susannah

Names That Give You a Leg Up in Life		Tomorrow's Slackers	
Boys	**Girls**	**Boys**	**Girls**
Barrett	Anna	Bacchus	Abilene
Benjamin	Ashley	Bo	Aspen
Blake	Bella	Chauncey	Barbie
Burke	Caroline	Diego	Birdie
Daniel	Celeste	Eden	Callie
David	Claire	Edsel	Chesney
Ethan	Danielle	Gino	DeeDee
Graham	Dominique	Kato	Dodie
Gus	Elizabeth	Kyd	Empress
Julian	Emma	Link	Eve
Kyle	Grace	Loki	Felicity
Lance	Isabella	Longo	Fluffy
Liam	Jennifer	Magni	Happy
Logan	Julia	Mohican	Jethra
Mason	Kim	Montana	Lark
Matt	Margaret	Ojay	Lotus
Max	Marion	Pluto	Marvel
Michael	Merit	Rio	Precious
Nathaniel	Michelle	Rip	Roseanne
Patrick	Natalie	Somers	Sissy
Ralph	Nicole	Sonny	Soleil
Samuel	Rose/Rosa	Taos	Summer
Tremayne	Sadie	Tavaris	Sunny
Tyler	Sidney	Tino	Tea
Will	Sophie	Tyson	Trixie

Achievers		Cool Names for Athletes	
Boys	**Girls**	Althea	Johnny
Andrew	Addison	Arnold	Julius
Butler	Emma	Babe	Kareem
Chason	Blythe	Ben	Lance
Dennis	Bonnie	Bill	Larry
Doug	Brittney	Billie Jean	Lou
Ewan	Camille	Bo	Magic
Gavin	Christina	Bonnie	Mark
Hank	Cindy	Carl	Martina
Jeff	Delisa	Craig	Michael
John	Emerey	Cy	Mickey
Kaufman	Emma	Deion	Muhammad
Keane	Erin	Evander	Picabo
Kent	Gaynor	Gale	Red
Kevin	Gina	George	Sandy
Mitchell	Hollyn	Gordie	Serena
Norton	Janiqua	Greg	Stan
Patton	Jessalyn	Hakeem	Sugar Ray
Rance	Leanne	Hank	Ted
Robert	Mallory	Jack	Tiger
Schultz	Phoebe	Jackie	Ty
Scott	Rebecca	Jeff	Venus
Skip	Roxanne	Jerry	Walter
Teague	Shae	Jesse	Wayne
Thorne	Taylor	Jim	Willie
Usher	Tonya	Joe	Wilma
			Wilt

Future "Most Dependable"		Charmers	
Boys	**Girls**	**Boys**	**Girls**
Aaron	Amica	Brad	Ajana
Alton	Amy	Bret	Bead
Barry	Bethany	Chance	Bridget
Brent	Carrie	David	Chandi
Chris	Chandra	Deryn	Coco
Clint	Deb	Devean	Dancy
Cole	Elle	Duncan	Denise
Demarris	Heather	Fernando	Dionne
Derek	Hope	Jaret	Gidget
Devin	Juliet	Jase	Ginzi
Elmer	Larsen	Jeremy	Halea
Forrest	Lemuela	Kobe	Jen
Gary	Lynn	LeBron	Joanna
Hunter	Olena	Lorenzo	Kimana
Jack	Otilie	Luke	Laya
Jeston	Penthea	Nissan	Maryann
Keller	Randie	Rasheed	Mia
Leo	Siaka	Rob	Nicolae
Mack	Sofie	Russ	Rita
Manny	Trella	Sage	Robin
Overton	Tucker	Santino	Roxy
Radu	Varina	Slater	Shauna
Scott	Weslee	Tolbert	Sierra
Werner	Ximena	Tolfe	Tanisha
Will	Zore	Viggo	Torry

Celebrity Names

Boys

Antonio
Ashton
Ben
Booker
Brad
Burt
Casey
Casper
Damon
Denzel
Fabrice
Fernando
Goran
Griffin
Hudson
Keenan
Kiefer
Liam
Marc
Matthew
Mel
Patrick
Russell
Ryan
Tom

Girls

Charlize
Demi
Drea
Drew
Fiona
Halle
Isabella
Jennifer
Jessica
Julia
Kate
Lara
Liv
Natasha
Oprah
Portia
Reese
Renee
Rosanna
Sela
Selma
Sheena
Simone
Thora
Uma

Names Celebrities Give Their Babies

Boys

Atticus *(Daniel Baldwin and Isabella Hoffman)*

Beckett *(Melissa Etheridge and Julie Cypher)*

Barron William *(Donald and Melania Trump)*

Cashel *(Daniel Day-Lewis and Rebecca Miller)*

Cruz David *(Victoria and David Beckham)*

Giacomo *(Sting and Trudie Styler)*

Jayden James *(Britney Spears and Kevin Federline)*

Jett *(John Travolta and Kelly Preston)*

Johan *(Seal and Heidi Klum)*

Julian Kal *(Jerry and Jessica Seinfeld)*

Kal-El *(Nicholas Cage and Alice Kim)*

Kingston *(Gwen Stefani and Gavin Rossdale)*

Levi Roan *(Uma Thurman and Ethan Hawke)*

Liam *(Tori Spelling and Dean McDermott)*

Max Liron *(Christina Aguilera and Jordan Bratman)*

Max Marco *(Jennifer Lopez and Marc Anthony)*

Moses *(Gwyneth Paltrow and Chris Martin)*

Ocean Alexander *(Forest Whitaker and Raye Dowell)*

Pax Thien *(Angelina Jolie and Brad Pitt)*

Phinnaeus Walter *(Julia Roberts and Danny Moder)*

Ronan Cal *(Daniel Day-Lewis and Rebecca Miller)*

Shepherd Kellen *(Jerry and Jessica Seinfeld)*

Stellan *(Jennifer Connelly and Paul Bettany)*

Willem Wolf *(Billy Idol and Perri Lister)*

Zowie *(David and Angela Bowie)*

Names Celebrities Give Their Babies

Girls

Apple (*Gwyneth Paltrow and Chris Martin*)

Ashby Grace (*Nancy O'Dell and Keith Zubulevich*)

Beatrice Milly (*Paul McCartney and Heather Mills*)

Brielle Nicole (*Desiree and Blair Underwood*)

Coco Riley (*Courtney Cox and David Arquette*)

Daisy Boo (*Jamie Oliver and Juliette Norton*)

Delilah Belle (*Harry Hamlin and Lisa Rinna*)

Eden (*Marcia Cross and Tom Mahoney*)

Ella (*Alex and Cynthia Rodriguez*)

Emme (*Jennifer Lopez and Marc Anthony*)

Fiona Eve (*Jennie Garth and Peter Facinelli*)

Harlow Winter Kate (*Nicole Ritchie and Joel Madden*)

Hazel (*Julia Roberts and Danny Moder*)

Heaven Rain (*Brooke Burke and David Charvet*)

Jagger Joseph Blue (*Soleil Moon Frye and Jason Goldberg*)

Lily-Rose Melody (*Johnny Depp and Vanessa Paradis*)

Luca Bella (*Jennie Garth and Peter Facinelli*)

Nahla (*Halle Berry and Gabriel Aubry*)

Nevis (*Nelly Furtado and Jasper Gahunia*)

Poppy Honey (*Jamie Oliver and Juliette Norton*)

Savannah (*Marcia Cross and Tom Mahoney*)

Shiloh (*Brad Pitt and Angelina Jolie*)

Sonnet Noel (*Forest Whitaker and Keisha Nash*)

Valentina Paloma (*Salma Hayek and Francois-Henri Pinault*)

Violet (*Jennifer Garner and Ben Affleck*)

Pistols, Wild Things, and Pieces-of-Work

Boys	Girls
Ajay	Ambelu
Alec	Aundrea
Brush	Brynne
Corbin	Callie
Cuca	Caralyn
Demetrie	Cawana
Derant	Charner
Drake	Concetta
Dyron	Dandra
Enrico	Dorshea
Erold	Dracy
Flint	Emmagene
Harold	Harley-Jane
Kin	Heydee
Lynus	Jacquier
Mandrake	Kisha
Mashawn	Krysia
Rockney	Mallory
Sean	Mireya
Shamone	Moti
Slim	Nevelyn
Steve	Pariann
Storm	Sharell
TeRez	Tangie
Teshombe	Trenna

Future Fashionistas		Names That Are So Over	
Boys	**Girls**	**Boys**	**Girls**
Ant	Anoushka	Al	Bertie
Barkan	Ardythe	Bob	Betty
Blevin	Austene	Dennis	Carla
Calum	Chiara	Donald	Delores
Clarke	Corianna	Douglas	Edith
Clay	Divine	Ernie	Faye
Dario	Dori	Frank	Frances
Harding	Elkie	Garland	Gail
Kamal	Emge	Gary	Hilary
Jean-Luc	Evette	Glanville	Judy
Kelvin	Fabulia	Harold	Loretta
Kenji	Joonypur	Harvey	Louise
Kirklin	Kisha	Jaden	Marilyn
Laranz	Mare	Jason	Maureen
Lear	Misti	Jerry	Minnie
Leon	Roquina	Juwon	Myrna
Massimo	Sasa	Ken	Nancy
Mustafa	Selia	Leon	Nina
Rage	Shawnda	Marvin	Priscilla
Rainier	Shaytella	Morey	Stacy
Robin	Siva	Oscar	Tiffany
Ruben	Tammy	Ottis	Tracy
Tayshaun	Tanis	Randy	Veronica
Wash	Tirsa	Rick	Wanda
Worth	Viviana	Todd	Winona

Future Truck Drivers		Future Computer Techies	
Boys	**Girls**	**Boys**	**Girls**
Butch	Clara	Alcazar	Anna
Carl	Cora	Alexandre	Arye
Cash	Davette	Boleslav	Brana
Derlin	Edna	Brian	Devane
Derrell	Ethelene	Challen	Eva-Marie
Earl	Flo	Cornel	Gert
Hal	Gretchen	Dan	Glenne
Harlan	Irma	Dickey	Jules
Henry	Jody	Don	Kala
Herb	Lacresha	Emeril	Kate
Hugh	Lataisha	Gray	Keira
Joe-Eddy	Latrice	Gurinder	Kim
Johnny	Makula	Jayon	Kitty
Lonnie	Nadine	Jensen	Margot
Mace	Nerline	Jim	Megan
Marvin	Pearlie	Lon	Nell
Milton	Sherlene	Marshall	Rachel
Nate	Sonequa	Matthieu	Ramonda
Norman	Sue	Ned	Ravada
Otis	Usha	Randolph	Shannon
Otto	Vatoya	Saginaw	Skylar
Revill	Veva	Timothy	Sonora
Rylance	Virgia	Todd	Stephanie
Scatman	Wanda	Warren	Talisa
Sorlie	Zennida	Zero	Tania

Burdensome Names		Names Derived from Literature	
Boys	**Girls**	**Boys**	**Girls**
Ambrose	Alfre	Ahab	Alice
Ankoma	Antigone	Ali Baba	Austen
Archibald	Bathsheba	Boswell	Bronte
Bartholomew	Chastity	Cervantes	Browning
Boaz	Clotilde	Chaucer	Cale
Bouvier	Columbine	Cummings	Charlotte
Cord	Cornelia	Cyrano	Colette
Dakarai	Cricket	Dickens	Daisy
Durwood	Edna	Don Quixote	Godiva
Gershom	Elspeth	Dryden	Grisham
Godfrey	Flannery	Emerson	Harper
Hercules	Henrietta	Foster	Jane
Humphrey	Indiana	Grimm	Kipling
Ignatius	Keturah	Hunter	Lara
Kalunga	Majidah	Keats	McMurtry
Lafayette	Millicent	Lowell	Meg
Lazarus	Minerva	Milton	Melanie
Marmaduke	Muriel	Norman	Millay
Mortimer	Priscilla	Pope	Patricia
Percy	Prudence	Rhett	Sadie
Reginald	Purity	Sherman	Scarlett
Thelonius	Thomasina	Spenser	Scout
Vladimar	Ursula	Swift	Simone
Wolfgang	Zona	Wordsworth	Stella
Zacharias	Zuwena	Yeats	Whittier

Nerd/Dork/Wallflower Names	Future Gymnasts	
	Boys	**Girls**
Barney	Antone	Berit
Bruce	Bendell	Chaley
Cheryl	Bourne	Colleen
Chester	Brandon	Dimitra
Dabney	Cam	Emma
Dudley	Chad	Erica
Durwood	Costa	Fabiana
Edgar	Costello	Goldie
Edward	Eric	Grisham
Elwood	Fahren	Jamie
Emory	Harve	Marissa
Engelbert	Kifney	Mary Lou
Estes	Lohan	Nadia
Ethelbert	Markie	Nasha
Eugene	Plato	Natasha
Eustace	Roddick	Olympia
Ewan	Ryan	Oxana
Fagan	Silver	Pamela
Fairfax	Taber	Shannon
Gomer	Tony	Shonna
Pembroke	Varden	Summer
Percy	Wash	Tynisha
Priscilla	Whip	Winter
Ted	Zatuichi	Zina
Warren	Zhano	Zooey

Place Names		Mr. Perfect and Ms. Perfect	
Boys	**Girls**	**Boys**	**Girls**
Aberdeen	Asia	Alex	Alexandra
Albany	Bali	Anthony	Allison
Aleppo	Bonn	Ben	Bailey
Alps	Cairo	Blake	Brittney
America	Cambay	Brent	Celeste
Beaumont	Capri	Christian	Christiane
Bexley	China	Christopher	Courtney
Billings	Dallas	Clint	Danielle
Bradford	Dayton	Fletcher	Elizabeth
Carson	Easter	Giancarlo	Hollyn
Cuba	Egypt	Harrison	Jennifer
Cyprus	Flanders	Hunter	Jill
Dodge	Georgia	James	Leah
Elam	India	Joaquin	Lexi
Gobi	Indiana	Justin	Marissa
Gwent	Ireland	Kirk	Meredith
Hollywood	Jordan	Kyle	Merit
Hull	Kansas	Monty	Mia
Logan	Kentucky	Reese	Miranda
Macon	Kenya	Riley	Natalie
Orlando	Lansing	Robert	Nia
Rainier	Odessa	Rory	Riley
Sydney	Persia	Ryan	Shara
Texas	Savannah	Wells	Sloan
Yukon	Venice	Zack	Trina

Future Cops		Future Televangelists	
Boys	**Girls**	**Boys**	**Girls**
Arlen	Anne	Abbott	Alma
Artie	Becky	Adam	Amanze
Bold	Bristol	Aleksey	April
Bruno	Carni	Alf	Ariel
Buck	Cricket	Brendon	Athena
Cody	Darla	Carl	Autumn
Doug	Darlyn	Cedric	Beate
Frank	Donella	Ceph	Bernadette
Gary	Holly	Coley	Blynthia
George	Jana	Cordell	Capricia
Gray	Janet	Cornelius	Cherlyn
Guard	Jessie	Darius	Danyelle
Justice	Kathy	Dayne	Darice
Ken	Kim	Dayton	Dinah
Ladden	Kyla	Deangelo	Eunicetine
Law	Lori	Erfan	Irma
Mace	Lydia	Felix	Jardene
Mark	Marg	Hamilton	Karolyn
Matt	Micah	Hardman	Palmira
Mike	Moira	Hardy	Sharonda
Rocko	Paige	Jim	Sondra
Seno	Raquel	Malcolm	Tabitha
Stu	Serena	Sean	Tammy
Tom	Tiawanna	Sumpter	Trish
Wayne	Tully	Wyatt	Valorie

Tomorrow's Justin Timberlake and Gwen Stefani		Future Politicians	
Boys	**Girls**	**Boys**	**Girls**
Amadeo	Adora	Ave	Amarosa
Angus	Becca	Bradlee	Annaca
Arturo	Blondelle	Brew	Ceidy
Bart	Bonita	Chant	Consuell
Bonnard	Breanna	Colt	Danal
Carlos	Caitlin	Deshan	Donna
Chyre	Dyana	Elmo	Erica
Diego	Emma	Gagan	Floweret
Fabrizio	Grace	Hec	Ganine
Francisco	Janelle	Hermanse	Heidel
Gabe	Jasmine	Howie	Hillario
Gabino	Julia	Jerrell	Jillianeo
Giancarlo	Kiki	Kib	Kanique
Heath	Liliana	Lobby	Kishey
Jair	Lily	Mazime	Lanetta
Jude	Lisa	Nixon	Luzey
Lonzo	Lourdes	Ogery	Mavis
Mario	Marva	Owelie	Monda
Pierre	Maryann	Real	Ranika
Ransom	Natalie	Rich	Sabrine
Rory	Nicole	Silverio	Shawna
Ruben	Renee	Theodorist	Starret
Sly	Roxanne	Ty	Vernissha
Zach	Shae	Wilbret	Veronica
Zennie	Shyla	Zekel	Yania

Names for Daredevils		Names That Make Kids Feel Weird	
Boys	**Girls**	**Boys**	**Girls**
Andre	Alyx	Arno	Breezy
Avery	Anatasia	Bloo	Charm
Beau	Ardythe	Butler	Chastity
Blevin	Austin	Car	Cherish
Colombo	Bead	Delete	Delite
Dagan	Della	Elmo	Fashion
Emrys	Elkie	Elmore	Glory
Fernando	Emge	Ervin	Harmony
Fico	Kiera	Excell	Lake
Fitz	Kita	Fabio	Leaf
Geronimo	L'Ann	Fable	Liberty
Hector	LaSonya	Fergus	Michelin
Hughey	Latona	Fife	Misty
LeBron	Lena	Forester	Oceana
Matt	Mare	Geronimo	Panther
Mustafa	Paradise	Gomer	Peace
Nissan	Priss	Maverick	Pity
Owen	Raven	Oswald	Precious
Rick	Rocket	Paris	Promise
Rossano	Seneca	Prince	Purity
Santino	Swan	Rebel	Rain
Sergio	Tirsa	Stone	Sweetpea
Slater	Yelana	Stormy	Tree
Tassos	Zabrina	Welcome	True
Tayshaun	Ziz	Ziggy	Vixen

Bad-to-the-Bone, Death Row Names		High-Spirited Kids	
Boys	**Girls**	**Boys**	**Girls**
Adolph	Aileen Carol	Ace	Armey
Clydell	Ana	Demeet	Bianca
David	Andrea	Dezi	Brandi
Excell	Antoinette	Dino	Chris
Henry Lee	Betty	Eddie	Dottie
Jeffrey	Blanche	Grasshopper	Fawn
Jemarr	Caroline	Jaquan	Gia
Jessie	Christa Gail	Jarrup	Jama
John	Darlie Lynn	Jehan	Kawana
John Wayne	Debra	Jerome	KayKay
Leonard	Delores	Jovan	Kendra
Mack	Faye	Kayotae	Latoya
Markum	Frances	Kerry	Mandy
Napoleon	Gail Kirsey	Lance	Pammy
Randy	Jaqueline	Levi	Rochelle
Reginald	Karla Faye	Mikey	Sheilia
Richard	Kerry	Rambabu	Sherin
Ricky	Latasha	Rocky	Suzy
Robert	Maria	Rosheon	Tara
Rodolfo	Marilyn	Tajuan	Tonie
Speck	Mary Ellen	Thad	Tyna
Stanley	Maureen	Tony	Vicki
Ted	Nadine	Troy	Vida
Timothy	Pamela	Vito	Yvette
Toronto	Vernice	Willie	Zorina
Windell			

Future TV Anchors		Names for Playful Personalities
Boys	**Girls**	Babe
Audon	Bai	Bebe
Carland	Calliope	Bliss
Carr	Cerah	Bunny
Chaffee	Dominique	Buzzie
Chazz	Grisham	Chica
Cornel	Jorja	Dusky
Doran	Julia	Fluffy
Gavin	Kaley	Happy
Judson	Kanye	Jandy
Karcher	Kelly	Jinx
Kwame	Lea	Lily
Landon	Livia	Merrilee
Long	Marianela	Miranda
Lundy	Meloni	Pal
Montgomery	Meryl	Pixie
Ran	Pfeiffer	Poppy
Roly	Phia	Precious
Ronan	Shanahan	Queenie
Sammon	Sheanne	Rabbit
Seaton	Star	Schmoopie
Seth	Taft	Skip
Tassilo	Tana	Sunny
Taye	Tessa	Trixie
Trev	Tru	Viveca
Vane	Wyoming	

Names for Vegetarians		Old-Fashioned Names That Are Cute Again	
Boys	**Girls**	**Boys**	**Girls**
A'Dhron	Alula	Atticus	Abby
Binyon	Analisa	Barney	Alma
Biondi	Anita	Casper	Annette
Bruce	Beatrice	Charlie	Arden
Clyde	Bonita	Chester	Arlene
Dorian	Cassie	Clem	Ava
Germain	Connie	Curtis	Belle
Jerrell	Daphne	Dexter	Betsy
Jovan	Detra	Duane	Beulah
Kemper	Donnette	Duke	Corinna
Kent	Fara-Lynn	Elmer	Ethel
Lari	Gerrita	Gill	Flo
Loring	Jaslynne	Harvey	Hazel
Marquis	Jeannie	Homer	Inez
Nolan	Jenette	Luke	Irene
Norm	Jini	Mitchell	Isabel
Ocy	Jolyn	Monty	Kay
Rex	Joyce	Mort	Kyra
Rhys	Justine	Myron	Laverne
Riquee	Kelsi	Ned	Loretta
Rumford	Kimber	Norm	Lorraine
Silas	Rita	Oscar	Lydia
Todd	Sarita	Stanley	Mabel
Trav	Talonna	Wilbur	Polly
Vince	Zhyra	Wyatt	Trudy

Future Inventors		Names for Smart Kids	
Boys	**Girls**	**Boys**	**Girls**
Arnold	Amira	Adam	Allene
Brody	Cate	Allen	Beth
Cain	Clea	Barry	Carolyn
Chew	Connery	Benjamin	Carrie
Clever	Crisiant	Brent	Colby
Deems	Cyd	Byron	Dana
Dov	Delfina	Clarence	Dominique
Gif	Drea	Curtis	Donna
Grail	Fia	David	Elizabeth
Hadwin	Gaudi	Eric	Jamie
Halston	Greer	Gray	Jennifer
Inder	Isolde	Guy	Karen
Isaac	JoBeth	Hillel	Kathleen
John	Joie	Jack	Kristina
Jute	Juanita	Kent	Leticia
Kelvis	LaTanya	Laurens	Maude
Kobi	Madelon	Martin	Micheline
Laphonso	Nicollette	Maximilian	Natasha
Lee	Novela	Peter	Page
Lucan	Olwen	Philip	Shannon
Marvell	Pandora	Richard	Shari
Ola	Rhonwen	Russell	Shaune
Pirney	Robin	Scott	Suzanne
Thanos	Romola	Trevor	Tessie
Tinker	Wendy	William	Zoann

Future Models		Future Doctors	
Boys	**Girls**	**Boys**	**Girls**
Adebayo	Alessandra	Bryant	Ann
Alim	Anise	Charles	Athena
Anka	Bovary	Dimitri	Brenda
Canyon	Camara	Frazier	Bryce
Carswell	Carles	George	Catrice
Dagan	Cinda	Herbert	Claire
Daly	Donella	James	Dana
Eaves	Estelle	John	Donna
Fabron	Heather	Judd	Elaine
Faldo	Imogene	Lister	Elizabeth
Faxan	Gabi	Mark	Freda
Flea	Grazia	Martin	Greta
Franchot	Jonica	Mason	Jane
Friso	Katrine	Murray	Jennifer
Gabor	Lily	Newell	Linda
Hagan	Lizzie	Nick	Lydia
Jory	Madchen	Niles	Lynn
Kipp	Majandra	Peter	Marianne
Tyee	Mirren	Philip	Mary
Tymon	Monet	Ralph	Maureen
Umar	Paulina	Randall	Miriam
Vachel	Rue	Reagan	Sarah
Walmond	Rylance	Rell	Suzanne
Yudel	Sloan	Russell	Tina
Xenos	Zim	Sabin	Victoria

Last Names as First Names		Future Republicans	
Boys	**Girls**	**Boys**	**Girls**
Afton	Abery	Alan	Angie
Besley	Briley	Ambrose	Barbara
Bevil	Campbell	Ari	Bo
Bolin	Childers	Arnold	Condoleezza
Brandt	Cortland	Bill	Diane
Cawley	Fields	Calvin	Elaine
Chatwin	Garson	Charlton	Erika
Coben	Gilmore	Colin	Gale
Corbitt	Gray	David	Heather
Deagan	Harrison	Dennis	Jeane
Given	Holiday	Gary	Jenna
Greer	Keaton	Gerald	Jennette
Halliwell	Jennings	J.C.	Jill
Hutter	Lancaster	Jack	Katherine
Kentlee	Lane	Mitt	Laura
Laskey	Mackenzie	Newt	Lilibet
Mackeane	Maclaine	Norm	Linda
Orton	O'Brien	Orrin	Lindsey
Prescott	Pace	Richard	Lynne
Rollins	Payton	Rudy	Mary
Stadler	Pfeiffer	Rush	Michelle
Tomlin	Rainey	Sean	Mona
Trivett	Reeve	Spiro	Nancy
Vane	Somers	Tony	Peggy
Wingate	Taylor	Trent	Tammy

	Future Democrats		Patriotic Names

Future Democrats

Boys	Girls
Al	Barbara
Barack	Bess
Bill	Carol
Blythe	Chelsea
Bob	Claudia
Carter	Debbie
Delano	Donna
Evan	Edith
Harry	Eleanor
Howard	Geraldine
Jesse	Gloria
Joseph	Jacqueline
Kent	Janeane
Lloyd	Janet
Lyndon	Joycelyn
Max	Kim
Michael	Madeleine
Robert	Molly
Thomas	Patricia
Tim	Rosalynn
Theodore	Ruth
Walter	Sandra
Warren	Susan
Wesley	Teresa
Zell	Tipper

Patriotic Names

America
Amerigo
Asia
Blue
Cherokee
Cheyenne
Columbus
Eagle
Flag
Free
Liberty
Librada
Lincoln
Loyalty
Nation
Pacifika
Patriot
Peace
Red
Sailor
Salute
Spirit
Starr
Utopia
Victory

Overpowering Names		Soap Opera Names	
Boys	**Girls**	**Boys**	**Girls**
Abbott	Antoinette	Blake	Allura
Axelrod	Aunjanue	Carson	Amanda
Baldridge	Bjork	Cyrano	Amber
Balthazar	Calista	Dag	Bianca
Domenico	Colemand	Dante	Brandy
Don Quixote	Deja-Marie	Dario	Brisa
Dontrell	Gwyneth	Dax	Candy
Esmond	Illeana	Dean	Carmen
Gabbana	Ione	Deone	Charmaine
Galbraith	Jowannah	Destin	Cocoa
Huntley	Kallioppe	Diego	Dakota
Hyde	Karalenae	Dom	Desiree
Kensington	Madonna	Duke	Fawn
Lothario	Mariangela	Fabio	Madonna
Montague	Oprah	Harley	Monica
Napoleon	Penelope	Keller	Renee
Ottway	Perabo	Maximilian	Salome
Pluto	Philomena	Rico	Samantha
Quintavius	Russo	Rip	Sasha
Reginald	Sahara	Romeo	Simone
Rochester	Siphronia	Ryan	Tatiana
Ronford	Stockard	Sebastian	Tawny
Roosevelt	Teah	Shiloh	Tish
Thor	Thora	Thor	Treece
Wyclef	Winifred	Wells	Yolie

Future Olympians		Future Lawyers	
Boys	**Girls**	**Boys**	**Girls**
Aaron	Amanda	Atticus	Ann
Alexei	Carly	Bryan	Brianna
Andre	Chris	Caleb	Campbell
Apolo	Dorothy	Carlson	Carlisle
Bart	Fanny	Dick	Charlotte
Bruce	Jill	Gary	Dana
Dan	Joanna	Jack	Emily
David	Katarina	Jacob	Haley
Derek	Kelly	John	Joanna
Dwight	Kerri	Josh	Kate
Gary	Kimberly	Lawrence	Kendra
Greg	Kristi	Noble	Lane
Jeremy	Mariel	Preston	Madison
Justin	Mia	Price	Mariel
Matthew	Michelle	Quinn	Mason
Michael	Misty	Reese	Meg
Paul	Nadia	Roark	Parker
Phil	Nancy	Robert	Rachel
Rulon	Natalie	Rush	Sally
Scott	Peggy	Rusty	Sarah
Shawn	Sarah	Ryder	Serena
Steven	Sasha	Samuel	Sloan
Timothy	Sonja	Sander	Taylor
Todd	Tristan	Sandford	Tekla
Tyler		Tom	Terese

Future Cowboys and Cowgirls		Future Nobel Prize Winners	
Cowboys	**Cowgirls**	**Boys**	**Girls**
Austin	Abilene	Archer	Alva
Beau	Angeline	Baruch	Barbara
Chaparro	Annie	Boyd	Bertha
Cody	Arizona	Cordell	Betty
Cole	Cassidy	Dario	Christiane
Cooper	Cheyenne	Desmond	Dorothy
Dallas	Conroe	Emil	Emily
Dobie	Cydell	Giulio	Gabriela
Doc	Dacey	Hamilton	Gerty
Dustin	Daisy	Jacinto	Grazia
Earp	Dakota	Kenichi	Irene
Emmett	Denton	Kenzaburo	Jane
Gene	Dixie	Linus	Jody
Jesse	Dobie	Niels	Mairead
Jimmydee	Dusty	Peyton	Marie
Justin	Harlee	Renato	Nadine
Kyle	Jessie	Roald	Pearl
Maverick	Johanna	Romain	Rigoberta
Rusty	Luella	Seamus	Rita
Shane	Montana	Simon	Rosalyn
Stetson	Oakley	Sinclair	Selma
Sudbury	Rosita	Susumu	Shirin
Sutter	Ruby	Sydney	Sigrid
Wadell	Sierra	Werner	Teresa
Wyatt	Suellen	Winston	Toni

TV Character Names		Architects	
Boys	**Girls**	**Boys**	**Girls**
Aidan	Blossom	Aaron	Adrianna
Balki	Calleigh	Alan	Alana
Cory	Carla	Alexander	Annie
Dante	Daphne	Art	Beata
Elliot	Dharma	Ed	Candace
Elvin	Elaine	Jack	Deandra
Gil	Fran	Jay	Diana
Grady	Jeannie	Lawrence	Ernestine
Gunther	Krissie	Liam	Fawn
Jack	Laverne	Paul	Fortune
Jordan	Lorelai	Rafael	Grace
Kramer	Lucy	Robert	Hannah
Maxwell	Mallory	Ron	Janna
Niles	Marissa	Royce	Joann
Odafin	Meadow	Sage	Justine
Raymond	Miranda	Sam	Katy
Ricky	Phoebe	Sebastian	Kelly
Sam	Prue	Seth	Landa
Simon	Rayanne	Shaw	Marianne
Vinnie	Rhoda	Smith	Olga
Wilson	Rudy	Sterling	Penelope
	Scully	Taylor	Queen
	Sidney	Theo	Stella
	Tabitha	Victor	Susannah
	Topanga	Walt	Treece

Unforgettable Names	Future Chefs	
	Boys	**Girls**
Allegra	Alton	Angelica
Aura	Baker	Betty
Bai	Basil	Candy
Cocoa	Bobby	Caraway
Hyacinth	Cary	Cassia
Jumbe	Charlie	Ceci
King	Cook	Cicely
Lake	Coriander	Crescent
Leelee	Delmonico	Debbie
Lindberg	Dweezil	Genievre
Madonna	Emeril	Ginger
Momo	Francis	Honey
Montague	George	Ina
Pink	Herb	Jenny
Prince	Hiroyuki	Julia
Rivers	Jamie	Marjolaine
Santeene	Lawson	Martha
Schmoopie	Martin	Nigella
Spirit	Rick	Poppy
Sting	Tamarind	Rosemary
Symphony	Tarragon	Saffron
Talent	Ted	Sandra
Tame	Tyler	Sarriette
Trocky	Wolfgang	Seattle
Wyclef		Verbena

Season/Weather Names

Autumn
Cloudy
Dusky
Easter
Equinox
Fog
Frosty
Grey
Holly
Misty
Noel
Rain
Rainbow
Season
Sky
Snow
Soleil
Spring
Storm
Summer
Sunny
Sunshine
Typhoon
Windy
Winter

Scary/Creepy Names

Boys	Girls
Bigram	Adelaide
Brick	Agnes
Bruno	Arlette
Butcher	Beatrix
Delete	Crispy
Dweezil	Denz
Elmo	Earlene
Graven	Edna
Gruver	Hortense
Horatio	Lakeesha
Izzy	Nunu
Modred	Nyleen
Nada	Peta
Napoleon	Phyllida
Narcissus	Quinceanos
Nellie	Randelle
Neptune	Scylla
Nero	Sharama
Percival	Swoosie
Pontius	Tashanee
Seymour	Uzbek
Sindbad	Winnie
Sisyphus	Wyetta
Socrates	Zeb
Zero	Zulemita

Names for the Handsome and Beautiful

Mythological and Astrological

Boys	Girls	
Allen	Addison	Ajax
Austin	Anabelle	Alala
Benjamin	Annie	Argus
Cal	Ashley	Aries
Cameron	Ava	Bacchus
Chad	Belle	Bran
Cooper	Catrice	Cadmus
Dax	Dominique	Cressida
Dylan	Eden	Evander
Ethan	Gina	Galatea
Fletcher	Jade	Gawain
Gus	Jennifer	Gemini
Hudson	Jessica	Kalliope
Ian	Jinx	Lake
Jan-Erik	Jolie	Lancelot
Jude	Jordan	Merlin
Julian	Liz	Nestor
Kyle	Marisol	Ocean
Logan	Miranda	Penelope
Owen	Natasha	Phoenix
Riley	Petra	Tane
Ryan	Rachel	Terra
Sebastian	Renee	Thor
Shiloh	Sheyn	Venus
Will	Trista	Zeus

Macho Men	Sweetie-Pies	Names for Popular Kids	
		Boys	**Girls**
Bucko	Alicia	Britt	Ava
Butch	Angie	Cam	Britney
Buzz	Annabelle	Cody	Clancy
Cal	Bay	Dylan	Coby
Cash	Brook	Ethan	Coco
Duke	Darcy	Evan	Emma
Esteban	Dolce	Fletch	Gina
Evander	Dove	Gino	Lauren
Hud	Faith	Gus	Lexi
Hugo	Goldie	Heath	Lily
Jock	Greta	Hunter	Lindsay
Judd	Honey	Ian	Lola
Mack	Jenny	Jake	London
Ram	Julianna	Jason	Lyla
Rebel	Kate	Jeremy	Mackenzie
Reem	Laurel	Jerod	Madison
Rip	Lisa	Joshua	Morgan
Rocco	Marina	Julian	Nicole
Sam	Robin	Justin	Piper
Santiago	Rosa	Kyle	Reese
Spike	Roseanne	London	Samantha
Stone	Sarah-Jessica	Max	Skye
Trocky	Tammy	Morgan	Sophie
Waylon	Wylie	Nick	Tara
Zoom	Yolie	Tyler	Taylor

Future Artists		World's Strangest Names
Boys	**Girls**	Adjanys
Ballard	Alexis	Bego
Blaze	Ashantia	Blue
Ceron	Azure	Bucko
Eduardo	Caramia	Bukola
Francesco	Chantal	Car
Francoise	DeeDee	Dix
Frederic	Emelle	Dweezil
Gansta	Eve	Edju
Graham	Janice	Idarah
Hector	Jenna	Kermit
Jean-Claude	Kavita	Kiwa
Jose	Lace	Lovella
Laurent	Lanee	Moon Unit
Lionel	Lavonne	Nimrod
Maximilian	Margina	Oak
Michael	Mary-Catherine	Obey
Octavio	Michaele	Pity
Oscar	Mona	Rudow
Paulo	Neva	Swell
Pash	Prema	Tiago
Pedro	Regine	Tilla
Ronnie	Sisteene	Zap
Sancho	Skyler	Zip
Sebastian	Tallulah	Zone
Stephan	Zora	

Future Workaholics		Wimpy Names	Girly-Girl Names
Boys	**Girls**	Babe	Bebe
Aneel	Abigail	Barney	Bubbles
Archie	Andrea	Bobo	Buffy
Bill	Belva	Brownie	Bunny
Charles	Bette	Brucie	Cherry
D.J.	Brenda	Byrd	Cinderella
David	Carleton	Chubby	Cinnamon
Douglas	Carol	Clydell	Cookie
Edward	Catherine	Corky	Darlie
Franklin	Christa	Denny	Debbie-Jean
Fred	Clara	Dewey	Deedee
Ivan	Dale	Dudley	Dolly
James	Dawn	Dusty	Fluffy
Jerry	Emma	Dwight	Melrose
Lawrence	Judith	Feo	Poppy
Louis	Lucille	Fergie	Posy
Matthew	Macy	Fuddy	Precious
Michael	Marjorie	Perry	Primrose
Miles	Mary Kay	Skeeter	Princess
Pierre	Meg	Skippy	Prissy
Promod	Muriel	Spanky	Sissy
Roger	Nadia	Terry	Sugar
Seth	Oprah	Timmy	Sweetpea
Ted	Shelly	Tippy	Tippie
Thomas	Shirley	Wendell	Trixiebelle
Vernon	Valentina		
William			

Exotic Names		Names Teachers Can't Pronounce	
Boys	**Girls**	**Boys**	**Girls**
Desiderio	Cherokee	Artemus	Aisha
Destin	Cheyenne	Declan	Aleithea
Diego	Chiara	Dionysus	Camilla
Enrique	Kia	Flody	Carenleigh
Enzo	Kimone	Gyth	Chesskwana
Esme	Lakesha	Hamif	Deighan
Francesco	Lani	Hermes	Falesyia
Franco	Laurent	Hieronymos	Gisbelle
Frederic	Pax	Honorato	Gresia
Gabriel	Pepita	Iago	Madchen
Gaston	Phaedra	Ignatius	Maromisa
Genaro	Philomena	Ioannis	Mayghaen
Giancarlo	Phyllida	Isidro	Meyka
Hamlet	Quanda	Jetal	Naeemah
Hansel	Rania	Jovan	Nissie
Hawke	Rasheeda	Larrmyne	Nunibelle
Heinz	Rhiannon	Mihow	Rhonwen
Helio	Saffron	Mischa	Ruthemma
Hermes	Santana	Moey	Sade
Honorato	Sasha	Raoul	Shaleina
Jacques	Sequoia	Revin	Sharrona
Janus	Sheba	Sladkey	Shawneequa
Javier	Shoshana	Slavek	Tanyav
Jean-Paul	Simone	Takeya	Tierah
Johann	Solange		Twyla

Names for Sports Fanatics		Names for Future Authors	
Boys	**Girls**	**Boys**	**Girls**
A.J.	Annika	Albert	Alice
Al	Cammi	Antoine	Amy
Barry	Carol	Anton	Anais
Dick	Chamique	Bertolt	Bobbi Ann
Eddie	Charlotte	Conrad	Djuna
Edwin	Cheryl	Derek	Doris
Elgin	Chris	Ernest	Edith
Gale	Donna	Fenimore	Eudora
Gordie	Florence	Isaac	Flannery
Honus	Glenna Collett	Italo	Harper
Jack	Hazel	James	Helen
Lawrence	Ingrid	Jean-Paul	Isabel
Mario	Janet	John	Jamaica
Maurice	Jeannie	Jorge	Judy
O.J.	Julie	Kurt	Kate
Oscar	Lisa	Miguel	Louisa May
Otto	Manon	Raymond	Maeve
Rafer	Mickey	Samuel	Margaret
Roberto	Paula	T.S.	Marguerite
Rocky	Senda	Thomas	Maryse
Rogers	Sheryl	Umberto	Sandra
Sammy	Steffi	Upton	Simone
Satchel	Susan	Vladimir	Virginia
Willie	Tamara	William	Willa
	Tracy		Zora

Hippie-Sounding Names

Apple
Breezy
Cloud
Dune
Free
Gypsy
Happy
Maverick
Oceana
Peace
Peaches
Rain
Rainbow
River
Sea
Serenity
Sierra
Spring
Star
Summer
Sunny
Tree
True
Willow
Winner

Plain Jane and Joe Schmoe

Joe Schmoe	Plain Jane
Bill	Annabelle
Bob	Betty
Buddy	Carol
Claude	Cindy
Ed	Dana
Floyd	Dawn
Fred	Doris
Guy	Edith
Henry	Jane
Jack	Janet
Joe	Jill
John	Martha
Kevin	Mary
Larry	Nancy
Lloyd	Norma
Mark	Patty
Max	Pauline
Paul	Sally
Ralph	Sarah
Rick	Shirley
Sam	Sue
Scott	Thelma
Tom	Velma
Wally	Vera
Wayne	Wilda

Names That Spawn Nasty Nicknames

Boys	Girls
Adolf	Christopher
Aldred	Cocoa
Alec	Dusky-Dream
Alfonso	Earlene
Apple	Feather
Ash	Fortune
Asher	Gay
Ashley	Harriet
Ashton	Haute
Babe	Hedy
Boris	Hermione
Bucky	Hodge
Butler	Hortense
Byrd	Lesbia
Clement	Monica
Dominic	Rainey
Farley	Romona
Farnham	Ruta
Farr	Scarlett
Ferdinand	Sesame
Flabia	Sigrun
Harry	Sweetpea
Haywood	Taffy
Jericho	Teddi
Titus	Winifred

Androgynous

Andy/Andi
Bailey
Cameron
Carol, Carroll
Chris
Corey
Dakota
Dale, Dell
Darcy
Darryl
Dylan
Gail/Gale
Jamie
Jean, Gene
Jordan
Kat
Kelly
Kerry/Carrie
Lane
Lee
Leslie
Morgan
Pat
Shawn, Sean
Terry

Names That Sound Presidential		Names for Future Poets	
Boys	**Girls**	**Boys**	**Girls**
Abraham	Andrea	Billy	Adrienne
Adam	Ann	Carl	Amy
Adlai	Carolyn	Charles	Anne
Andrew	Claire	David	Audre
Benjamin	Elizabeth	Dylan	Barbara
Blake	Ella	Edgar Allan	Brigit
Calvin	Emily	Ezra	Christina
Charles	Emma	Gary	Denise
Daniel	Evan	Gerard	Dorothy
Dwight	Helen	Henry David	Edna
Earnest	Hillary	John	Elizabeth
George	Isabel	Kahlil	Emily
Hamilton	Julia	Langston	Gertrude
Hampton	Kay	Ogden	Gwendolyn
Harrison	Kelly	Pablo	Hilda
Henry	Kyle	Percy	Jorie
Hudson	Lauren	Philip	Louise
James	Madison	Ralph Waldo	Marge
John	Mia	Robert	Marianne
Reagan	Miriam	Seamus	Maxine
Robert	Parker	Sherman	Maya
Roger	Rachel	Stanley	Nikki
Ronald	Rose	Tennyson	Rita
Winston	Stella	Theodore	Sara
Zachary	Taylor	William	Sylvia

Comfy Names		Over-the-Top Names to Avoid	
Boys	**Girls**	**Boys**	**Girls**
Allen	Allison	Achilles	Aphrodite
Ben	Amber	Adonis	Asp
Brent	Annie	Amadeus	Bijou
Brian	Ashley	Aristotle	Birdie
Casey	Becca	Attila	Blaze
Chad	Callie	Bark	Bless
Daniel	Carrie	Beauregard	Blossom
Dave	Danielle	Brando	Blush
Ethan	Diane	Caesar	Butter
Gavin	Emily	Eagle	Chantilly
Jack	Hailey	Goliath	Chastity
Jake	Heather	Hamlet	Cher
Jason	Isabel	Jock	Cleopatra
Jesse	Jessica	Lancelot	Desire
Josh	Jordan	Laramie	Fantasia
Justin	Justine	Lobo	Fashion
Logan	Kim	Lord	Fawn
Matt	Lauren	Lothario	Fluffy
Max	Liz	Rambo	Honesty
Mike	Maggie	Rip	Jezebel
Nicholas	Nicole	Rocco	Loyalty
Rob	Rachel	Rod	Ophelia
Ryan	Samantha	Stormy	Psyche
Sam	Sarah	Sylvester	Purity
Tyler	Selena	Titan	Tempest

Colors		Future Country-Western Singers	
Boys	**Girls**	**Boys**	**Girls**
Amarillo	Amber	Alan	Allison
Auburn	Azura	Billy Ray	Anne
Brinley	Bionda	Brad	Barbara
Brown	Blanche	Buck	Brenda
Cyan	Burgundy	Cash	Carlene
Forest	Carmine	Chance	Cristy
Hazel	Cerise	Charley	Dolly
Hunter	Ciara	Chet	Emily
Jet	Crimson	Clay	Faith
Kuper	Crystal	Clint	Jo Dee
Laban	Cyanetta	Conway	Kitty
Loden	Fuchsia	Dwight	LeAnn
Odhran	Henna	Garth	Lee Ann
Phoenix	Indigo	George	Loretta
Red	Iona	Hank	Martie
Ross	Jade	Kenny	Martina
Rudd	Jetta	Lyle	Maybelle
Russet	Kelly	Merle	Natalie
Rusty	Lavender	Tex	Pam
Sable	Melina	Tim	Patsy
Sand	Peridot	Toby	Reba
Slate	Saffron	Travis	Shania
Stone	Scarlet	Vince	Tamara
Tyrian	Sienna	Waylon	Trisha
Umber	Xanthe	Willie	Wynonna

Brand-Name Babies

Old Maids and Grumpy Old Men

Boys

(Uncle) Ben
(Mercedes) Benz
Brooks (Brothers)
Calvin (Klein)
Carter (Carter's baby clothes)
Duncan (Hines)
Gianni (Versace)
Giorgio (Armani)
Hamlet (Cigars)
Hiram (Walker)
Hugo (Boss)
Isaac (Mizrahi)
Jack (Daniels)
Jimmy (Dean)
John (Deere)
Johnnie (Walker)
Kenneth (Cole)
Merrill (Lynch)
Morton (Salt)
Samuel (Adams)
Scott (Tissue)
T.J. (Maxx)
Thomas (Cooke)
Todd (Oldham)
Tommy (Hilfiger)

Girls

Anna (Sui)
Anne (Klein)
Betsey (Johnson)
Betty (Crocker)
Campbell (Soup)
Charmin (bath tissue)
Cristal (champagne)
(Little) Debbie
Donna (Karan)
Elizabeth (Arden)
Ellen (Tracy)
Fanta
Gloria (Vanderbilt)
Harley (Davidson)
(Aunt) Jemima
Kimberly (Clark)
Lexus
Liz (Claiborne)
Mercedes (Benz)
Sara (Lee)
Stella (Artois)

Grumpy Old Men

Adolf
Ambrose
Amos
Clifford
Cyrus
Diedrich
Ebenezer
Edwin
Elmer
Engelbert
Felix
Gaylord
Godfrey
Gomer
Henry
Herb
Leander
Lester
Maurice
Maynard
Mortimer
Oscar
Otis
Percival
Sigmund

Old Maids

Amelia
Baptista
Bertha
Clemence
Clotilde
Corliss
Eldora
Ernestine
Estelle
Geraldine
Gladys
Heloise
Hildegard
Hortense
Mabel
Matilda
Maude
Mavis
Mildred
Millicent
Phyllis
Solange
Thelma
Winifred
Zelda

Future Middle Management		Future Composers	Names from Music and Instruments
Boys	**Girls**	Aaron	Allegra
Bob	Ceil	Antonin	Aria
Brent	Celeste	Antonio Lucio	Baird
Buddy	Connie	Belle	Bongo
Chalmers	Darla	Dimitri	Cadence
Davey	Fay	Domenico	Canon
Deke	Fern	Elisabetta	Chantal
Dewey	Florence	Felix	Citare
Dick	Gayle	Francesca	Giritha
Duane	Ingrid	Franz Peter	Gloria
Fabian	Jo-Dee	Fryderyk Franciszek	Harmony
Gareth	Kay	George	Harper
Gene	Lauralee	Johann Sebastian	Kalliope
Howard	Leeanne	Joseph	Kyrie
Irv	Leonora	Leo	Lydia
Leonard	Luna	Ludwig	Lyra
Myron	Marge	Maria	Melody
Newt	Marisol	Melinda	Nicola
Ronnie	Mitzi	Paul	Octavia
Rosco	Myrtle	Rebecca	Odele
Sal	Pearl	Wolfgang Amadeus	Pitch
Sanford	Ruth		Sonata
Skip	Shirley		Tune
Terrance	Trudy		Viola
Ward	Velma		Whistler
Wyatt	Yvonne		

Eccentric Names	International Treasure Names

Eccentric Names

Antigone
Balfour
Bark
Beetle
Bird
Chantilly
Cloudy
Echo
Ecstasy
Flirt
Free
Fudge
Galatea
Gawain
Goliath
Lady
LaRue
Lazarus
Obedience
Orson
Oz
Rambo
Stoli
Webb
Zeus

International Treasure Names

Alexandria (Lighthouse)

Amazon (rainforest, Brazil)

Artemis/Artemesia/ Artemia (Temple, Sardis)

Asmara (capital of Eritrea)

(Magna) Carta

Damascus (capital of Syria)

Delphi

Dover (Cliffs)

Easter (Island)

Euphrates (River)

Giza (pyramid)

Hope (Diamond)

Limoges (French China)

Niagara (Falls)

Nicosia (capital city of Cyprus)

(city of) Olympia

Petra (Ancient City, Jordan)

(The Colossus of) Rhodes

Saffron (Spice)

Santorini (Greece)

Sistine (Chapel, Vatican City)

Names from Works of Art

Adam (Michelangelo) (sculpture)

Ambroise Vollard (Picasso)

Beatrice (Tiepelo)

Cana (Gerard David)

Cindy (Robert Longo)

Danae (Gustav Klimt)

David (Donatello, also Michelangelo)

Fanny (Chuck Close)

Francesco Clemente Pinxit (Francesco) Clemente

Hyacinth (Alphonse Mucha)

Irene (Renoir)

Jackie (Andy Warhol)

Jacob (Gaugin)

Jeremiah (Rembrandt)

Joseph Roulin (Van Gogh)

Madonna (Sanzio Raffaello)

Magdalen (La Tour)

Marcus Aurelius (unknown)

Marie (Rubens)

Mona Lisa (Leonardo da Vinci)

Olympia (Manet)

Salome (Beardsley)

Sarah Bernhardt (Nadar)

Theresa (Bernini)

Venus (Botticelli)

Names from John Hughes Movies

Boys	Girls
Andrew	Allison
Blane	Amanda
Brian	Andie
Bryce	Brenda
Cameron	Caroline
Chet	Claire
Ferris	Kristy
Jake	Lisa
Richard	Samantha
Ted	Sloane

Names Resurrected from the Past

Boys	Girls
Atticus	Annette
Charlie	Ava
Dexter	Belle
Gill	Hazel
Mitchell	Inez
Monty	Isabel
Oscar	Kyra
Stanley	Lydia
Wilbur	Polly
Wyatt	Trudy

Jewish/Hebrew Names

Boys	Girls
Aaron	Anne
Abe	Claire
Barry	Esther
Benjamin	Golda
Daniel	Hannah
David	Ilana
Eli	Jenny
Esau	Johanna
Ethan	Judith
Gabriel	Leah
Ira	Lena
Isaac	Lillian
Jake	Linda
Jay	Mary
Joshua	Miriam
Levi	Naomi
Marvin	Rachel
Milton	Rebekah
Nathan	Ruth
Sam	Sadie
Saul	Sarah
Sheldon	Shara
Solomon	Sophie
Stanley	Sylvia
	Tovah

Arabic/Islamic Names		Biblical and Saintly Names	
Boys	**Girls**	**Boys**	**Girls**
Abdul-Jabbar	Aisha	Abel	Anna
Ahmad, Ahmed	Almira	Adam	Bathsheba
Ali	Asma	Benjamin	Deborah
Amir	Bathsira	Daniel	Delilah
Dawud	Cala	David	Dinah
Fariol	Dhelal	Elijah	Esther
Ghassan	Fatima	Ezekiel	Eve
Habib	Habibah	Isaiah	Joanna
Hakim, Hakeem	Hadil	Jacob	Judith
Hamid	Hajar, Hagir	Jesus	Julia
Hasan	Hayfa	Job	Leah
Ibrahim	Ihab	John	Magdalene
Jabir, Jabbar	Jamila	Jonah	Martha
Jamal	Kalila	Joseph	Mary
Kamal, Kamil	Karima	Joshua	Miriam
Kareem	Laila	Lazarus	Naamah
Khalid	Leila	Luke	Naomi
Mahmud	Malak	Mark	Phoebe
Muhammad,	Nada	Matthew	Rachel
Mohammad	Nima	Moses	Rebekah
Nuri	Rashidah	Noah	Ruth
Rafi	Rida	Paul	Salome
Rashid	Sabah	Peter	Sarah
Salim	Salima	Samuel	Tamar
Sharif	Zulema	Solomon	Zipporah
Yasir			

Scandinavian Names		Italian Names	
Boys	**Girls**	**Boys**	**Girls**
Aksel	Astrid	Aldo	Annamaria
Anders	Birgit	Alessandro	Bella
Anton	Bonnevie	Angelo	Cara
Bjorn	Dufvenius	Arturo	Caramia
Christian	Elsa	Carlo	Carissa
Claus	Erika	Carmine	Carlotta
Dirk	Fia	Ciro	Chiara
Erik	Frida	Cosmo	Donna
Gustav	Gudrun	Dante	Elda
Hendrik	Gunilla	Emilio	Elena
Ingmar	Inge	Enrico	Eliana
Isak	Ingrid	Franco	Elisa
Johannes	Janna	Gianni	Elletra
Karl	Johanna	Gino	Faustina
Knut	Kristina	Giorgio	Fidelia
Krister	Liv	Guido	Gina
Lars	Lotta	Leonardo	Isabella
Matts	Mini	Lorenzo	Maria
Mikael	Sabina	Luciano	Melania
Niels	Sanna	Marco	Nicola
Niklas	Sigrid	Mario	Paulina
Oskar	Sofia	Salvatore	Pia
Per	Sonya	Tomasso	Rosa
Rudolf	Ursula	Vincenzo	Rosamaria
Stellan	Wilhelmina	Vito	Sophia

French Names		German Names	
Boys	**Girls**	**Boys**	**Girls**
Alain	Aimee	Claus, Klaus	Ada
Charles	Amelie	Erik	Anke
Claude	Anais	Folker	Anneliese
Francois	Angelique	Freiderich	Annemarie
Frederic	Antoinette	Garrick	Beata
Gaston	Arianne	Gerhard	Clotilda
Gerard	Chantal	Gunther	Constanze
Germain	Claire	Gustaf	Cordula
Gregoire	Colette	Heinrich	Ebba
Guy	Daniele	Helmut	Elisabeth
Henri	Desiree	Hendrik	Elsa
Isidore	Dominique	Karl	Emma
Jacques	Eliane	Konrad	Felicie
Jean	Elisabeth	Kurt	Gudrun
Jean-Claude	Emmanuelle	Leopold	Heidi
Jean-Michel	Esmee	Max	Hilda
Jean-Paul	Gabrielle	Norbert	Juliana
Laurent	Genevieve	Oswald	Karoline
Louis	Giselle	Otto	Katharina
Luc	Maria	Ralph	Kristina
Marcel	Michele	Roger	Margarite
Maxime	Monique	Rudy	Maria
Phillipe	Simone	Stefan	Martina
Robert	Yvette	Wilhelm	Rosa
Yves	Yvonne	Wolfgang	Ursula

Polish Names

Boys	Girls
Aleksander	Anna
Andrzej	Barbara
Aniol	Cecilia
Anzelm	Celestyna
Bogdan	Gabriela
Boleslaw	Gizela
Czeslaw	Grazyna
Dobromir	Hanna
Helmut	Honorata
Jacek	Iwona
Jozef	Jadwiga
Karol	Kamilia
Kazimierz	Karolina
Krzysztof	Krysta
Marek	Krystyna
Pawel	Lucja
Ryszard	Maria
Slawomir	Marusya
Waclaw	Matylda
Walenty	Mirka
Witold	Monika
Wladymir	Otylia
Wladyslaw	Roksana
Wojtek	Waleria
Zbigniew	Wiktoria

Russian Names

Boys	Girls
Adya	Anastasiya
Alek	Anninka
Aleksei	Dariya
Denis	Dasha
Dmitri	Duscha
Grigori	Elena
Igor	Evelina
Ivan	Inessa
Karl	Irene/Irina
Maksimilian	Ivanna
Mikhail	Kira
Misha	Lara
Nikita	Lia
Nikolai	Masha
Oleg	Nadya
Pavel	Natalia
Sasha	Natasha
Sergei	Oksana
Sidor	Olga
Stanislav	Polina
Valentin	Sasha
Valeri	Sofya
Vlad	Sonya
Vladimir	Svetlana
Vladja	Tatiana

Irish Names		Scottish Names	
Boys	**Girls**	**Boys**	**Girls**
Aidan	Aileen	Ainsley	Alexandra
Art	Amanda	Alan	Alison
Bran	Annie	Angus	Annella
Brendan	Brenda	Bean	Christy
Brian	Briana	Bennett	Dina
Colin	Catherine	Cally	Fiona
Curran	Cathleen	Cameron	Heather
Devin	Ciara	Charles	Jeanie
Farris	Deirdre	Clement	Jenny
Fergus	Dorren	Conall	Lexine
Finn	Eavan	Donald	Lexy
Ian	Eliza	Fergus	Lindsay
James	Emma	Gregor	Lucy
Jamie	Ethnea	Harry	Maidie
John	Karen	Iagan	Maisie
Kevin	Kate	Ian	Margaret
Kieran, Keiran	Kathy	James	Nan
Killian	Maggie	Jock	Netta
Liam	Molly	Jon	Nora
Lochlain	Nancy	Kenneth	Peigi
Owen	Nessa	Peader	Robina
Patrick	Polly	Roddy	Rona
Rowan	Riona	Scott	Rowena
Sean	Sally	Stewart	Sandy
Shay	Sinead	Walter	Tory

English Names		African Names	
Boys	**Girls**	**Boys**	**Girls**
Arthur	Agnes	Addae	Aamori
Charles	Alexandra	Adio	Abayomi
Clinton	Althea	Ayo	Adia
Clive	Amanda	Bakari	Aisha
Colin	Andie	Bomani	Asabi
Earl	Angie	Dalila	Bayo
Edward	Anna/Anne	Dumisani	Eshe
George	Becky	Hamidi	Fatima
Harry	Betty	Harun	Femi
Henry	Carla	Hasani	Habiba
Jay	Connie	Hondo	Hasina
Jeff	Cynthia	Jaja	Jumoke
Max	Elizabeth	Kamal	Kibibi
Michael	Esther	Kamau	Kissa
Nicholas	Georgina	Muhhamad	Lateefa
Nigel	Hayley	Rudo	Maudisa
Norman	Ida	Runako	Nailah
Peter	Jennifer	Saeed	Nomble
Philip	Jill	Salehe	Omorose
Roger	Katherine	Salim	Oni
Roland	Margaret	Sekani	Rufaro
Ronald	Moira	Themba	Salama
Toby	Pippa	Umi	Taliba
William	Rhonda	Zikomo	Tisa
Winston	Wendy	Zuberi	Zahra

Spanish Names		Greek Names	
Boys	**Girls**	**Boys**	**Girls**
Adonis	Angela	Alexandros	Aggie
Alejandro	Beila	Andreas	Andrianna
Alfonso	Beilarosa	Ari	Ariadne
Angel	Bonita	Basil	Athena
Benito	Caliopa	Cletus	Calista
Carlos	Carlotta	Demetri	Calla
Damaso	Carmen	Demetrios	Chloe
Diego	Clementina	Demos	Damalla
Emilio	Consuelo	Flavian	Delos
Enrique	Delfina	Hilarion	Diona
Esteban	Delicia	Jason	Filia
Fiero	Destina	Lucas	Gillian
Francisco	Elena	Markos	Helena
Hector	Flora	Nikos	Iona
Isidoro	Graciela	Paul	Isadora
Javier	Guadalupe	Sander	Kali
Jorge	Honoria	Seth	Kalidas
Jose	Juanita	Socrates	Kori
Juan	Maria	Stephanos	Kynthia
Julio	Mariposa	Theo	Leandra
Miguel	Odelita	Theodoros	Nia
Mundo	Paloma	Theophilos	Phyllis
Raoul	Primalia	Tito	Pia
Roberto	Soledad	Verniamin	Theodora
Tomas		Zeno	Zoe

Asian Names		Future Racecar Drivers
Boys	**Girls**	
An (Chinese)	Bao (Chinese)	A.J.
Chang (Chinese)	Bay (Vietnamese)	Alex
Dong (Chinese)	Cai (Chinese)	Arie
Hiro (Japanese)	Connie-Kim	Bruno
Huang (Chinese)	(Vietnamese)	Buddy
Ibu (Japanese)	De (Chinese)	Dale
Ji (Chinese)	Fang (Chinese)	Dan
Jin (Chinese)	Ha (Vietnamese)	Dario
Jing (Chinese)	Lei (Chinese)	Denny
Ju-Long (Chinese)	Li (Chinese)	Eddie
Kang (Korean)	Lian (Chinese)	Helio
Li (Chinese)	Ling (Chinese)	Jacques
Liang (Chinese)	Mai (Japanese)	Jeff
Pin (Vietnamese)	Min (Chinese)	Jimmy
Quon (Chinese)	Ming (Chinese)	Johnny
Shen (Chinese)	Niu (Chinese)	Juan
Sheng (Chinese)	Nu (Vietnamese)	Jules
Shuu (Japanese)	Pang (Chinese)	Kenny
So (Vietnamese)	Tam (Japanese)	Leo
Tan (Japanese)	Thim (Thai)	Mario
Tung (Chinese,	Veata (Cambodian)	Mauri
Vietnamese)	Yu (Chinese)	Oriol
Yen (Chinese)	Zan (Chinese)	Sam
Yu (Chinese)	Zhi (Chinese)	Scott
Yuan (Chinese)	Zhong (Chinese)	Tony
Zhong (Chinese)	Zi (Chinese)	

Future Chefs		Future Poets	
Boys	**Girls**	**Boys**	**Girls**
Alton	Angelica	Billy	Adrienne
Anthony	Betty	Carl	Amy
Baker	Caraway	Charles	Anne
Basil	Cassia	David	Audre
Bobby	Ceci	Dylan	Barbara
Cary	Cicely	Edgar	Brigit
Charlie	Crescent	Gary	Christina
Cook	Debbie	Gerard	Denise
Coriander	Giada	Henry David	Dorothy
Delmonico	Ginger	John	Edna
Emeril	Honey	Kahlil	Elizabeth
Francis	Ina	Langston	Emily
George	Jenny	Ogden	Gertrude
Grant	Julia	Pablo	Gwendolyn
Jamie	Marjolaine	Percy	Hilda
Lawson	Martha	Philip	Jorie
Mark	Nigella	Ralph	Louise
Martin	Paula	Robert	Marianne
Rick	Poppy	Seamus	Marge
Tamarind	Rachael	Sherman	Maxine
Tarragon	Rosemary	Stanley	Maya
Ted	Saffron	Theodore	Nikki
Tom	Sandra	William	Rita
Tyler	Sarriette		Sara
Wolfgang	Seattle		Sylvia

Most Popular Names of the 1880s

Boys	Girls
1. John	1. Mary
2. William	2. Anna
3. James	3. Emma
4. George	4. Elizabeth
5. Charles	5. Margaret
6. Frank	6. Minnie
7. Joseph	7. Ida
8. Henry	8. Bertha
9. Robert	9. Clara
10. Thomas	10. Alice
11. Edward	11. Annie
12. Harry	12. Florence
13. Walter	13. Bessie
14. Arthur	14. Grace
15. Fred	15. Ethel
16. Albert	16. Sarah
17. Samuel	17. Ella
18. Clarence	18. Martha
19. Louis	19. Nellie
20. David	20. Mabel
21. Joe	21. Laura
22. Charlie	22. Carrie
23. Richard	23. Cora
24. Ernest	24. Helen
25. Roy	25. Maude

Most Popular Names of the 1890s

Boys	Girls
1. John	1. Mary
2. William	2. Anna
3. James	3. Margaret
4. George	4. Helen
5. Charles	5. Elizabeth
6. Joseph	6. Ruth
7. Frank	7. Florence
8. Robert	8. Ethel
9. Edward	9. Emma
10. Henry	10. Marie
11. Harry	11. Clara
12. Thomas	12. Bertha
13. Walter	13. Minnie
14. Arthur	14. Bessie
15. Fred	15. Alice
16. Albert	16. Lillian
17. Clarence	17. Edna
18. Willie	18. Grace
19. Roy	19. Annie
20. Louis	20. Mabel
21. Earl	21. Ida
22. Paul	22. Rose
23. Carl	23. Hazel
24. Ernest	24. Gertrude
25. Samuel	25. Martha

Most Popular Names of the 1900s

Boys	Girls
1. John	1. Mary
2. William	2. Helen
3. James	3. Margaret
4. George	4. Anna
5. Charles	5. Ruth
6. Robert	6. Elizabeth
7. Joseph	7. Dorothy
8. Frank	8. Marie
9. Edward	9. Florence
10. Thomas	10. Mildred
11. Henry	11. Alice
12. Walter	12. Ethel
13. Harry	13. Lillian
14. Willie	14. Gladys
15. Arthur	15. Edna
16. Albert	16. Frances
17. Clarence	17. Rose
18. Fred	18. Annie
19. Harold	19. Grace
20. Paul	20. Bertha
21. Raymond	21. Emma
22. Richard	22. Bessie
23. Roy	23. Clara
24. Joe	24. Hazel
25. Louis	

Most Popular Names of the 1910s

Boys	Girls
1. John	1. Mary
2. William	2. Helen
3. James	3. Dorothy
4. Robert	4. Margaret
5. Joseph	5. Ruth
6. George	6. Mildred
7. Charles	7. Anna
8. Edward	8. Elizabeth
9. Frank	9. Frances
10. Thomas	10. Virginia
11. Walter	11. Marie
12. Harold	12. Evelyn
13. Henry	13. Alice
14. Paul	14. Florence
15. Richard	15. Lillian
16. Raymond	16. Rose
17. Albert	17. Irene
18. Arthur	18. Louise
19. Harry	19. Edna
20. Donald	20. Catherine
21. Ralph	21. Gladys
22. Louis	22. Ethel
23. Jack	23. Josephine
24. Clarence	24. Ruby
25. Carl	25. Martha

Most Popular Names of the 1920s

Boys	Girls
1. Robert	1. Mary
2. John	2. Dorothy
3. James	3. Helen
4. William	4. Betty
5. Charles	5. Margaret
6. George	6. Ruth
7. Joseph	7. Virginia
8. Richard	8. Doris
9. Edward	9. Mildred
10. Donald	10. Frances
11. Thomas	11. Elizabeth
12. Frank	12. Evelyn
13. Harold	13. Anna
14. Paul	14. Marie
15. Raymond	15. Alice
16. Walter	16. Jean
17. Jack	17. Shirley
18. Henry	18. Barbara
19. Kenneth	19. Irene
20. Arthur	20. Marjorie
21. Albert	21. Florence
22. David	22. Lois
23. Harry	23. Martha
24. Eugene	24. Rose
25. Ralph	25. Lillian

Most Popular Names of the 1930s

Boys	Girls
1. Robert	1. Mary
2. James	2. Betty
3. John	3. Barbara
4. William	4. Shirley
5. Richard	5. Patricia
6. Charles	6. Dorothy
7. Donald	7. Joan
8. George	8. Margaret
9. Thomas	9. Nancy
10. Joseph	10. Helen
11. David	11. Carol
12. Edward	12. Joyce
13. Ronald	13. Doris
14. Paul	14. Ruth
15. Kenneth	15. Virginia
16. Frank	16. Marilyn
17. Raymond	17. Elizabeth
18. Jack	18. Jean
19. Harold	19. Frances
20. Billy	20. Beverly
21. Gerald	21. Lois
22. Walter	22. Alice
23. Jerry	23. Donna
24. Joe	24. Martha
25. Eugene	25. Dolores

Most Popular Names of the 1940s

Boys	Girls
1. James	1. Linda
2. Robert	2. Barbara
3. John	3. Patricia
4. William	4. Carol
5. Richard	5. Sandra
6. David	6. Nancy
7. Charles	7. Sharon
8. Thomas	8. Judith
9. Michael	9. Susan
10. Ronald	10. Betty
11. Larry	11. Carolyn
12. Donald	12. Margaret
13. Joseph	13. Shirley
14. Gary	14. Judy
15. George	15. Karen
16. Kenneth	16. Donna
17. Paul	17. Kathleen
18. Edward	18. Joyce
19. Jerry	19. Dorothy
20. Dennis	20. Janet
21. Frank	21. Diane
22. Daniel	22. Janice
23. Raymond	23. Joan
24. Roger	24. Elizabeth
25. Steven	

Most Popular Names of the 1950s

Boys	Girls
1. Michael	1. Mary
2. James	2. Linda
3. Robert	3. Patricia
4. John	4. Susan
5. David	5. Deborah
6. William	6. Barbara
7. Richard	7. Debra
8. Thomas	8. Karen
9. Mark	9. Nancy
10. Charles	10. Donna
11. Steven	11. Cynthia
12. Gary	12. Sandra
13. Joseph	13. Pamela
14. Donald	14. Sharon
15. Ronald	15. Kathleen
16. Kenneth	16. Carol
17. Paul	17. Diane
18. Larry	18. Brenda
19. Daniel	19. Cheryl
20. Stephen	20. Elizabeth
21. Dennis	21. Janet
22. Timothy	22. Kathy
23. Edward	23. Margaret
24. Jeffrey	24. Janice
25. George	25. Carolyn

Most Popular Names of the 1960s

Boys	Girls
1. Michael	1. Lisa
2. David	2. Mary
3. John	3. Karen
4. James	4. Susan
5. Robert	5. Kimberly
6. Mark	6. Patricia
7. William	7. Linda
8. Richard	8. Donna
9. Thomas	9. Michelle
10. Jeffrey	10. Cynthia
11. Steven	11. Sandra
12. Joseph	12. Deborah
13. Timothy	13. Pamela
14. Kevin	14. Tammy
15. Scott	15. Laura
16. Brian	16. Lori
17. Charles	17. Elizabeth
18. Daniel	18. Julie
19. Paul	19. Jennifer
20. Christopher	20. Brenda
21. Kenneth	21. Angela
22. Anthony	22. Barbara
23. Gregory	23. Debra
24. Ronald	24. Sharon
25. Donald	25. Teresa

Most Popular Names of the 1970s

Boys	Girls
1. Michael	1. Jennifer
2. Christopher	2. Amy
3. Jason	3. Melissa
4. David	4. Michelle
5. James	5. Kimberly
6. John	6. Lisa
7. Robert	7. Angela
8. Brian	8. Heather
9. William	9. Stephanie
10. Matthew	10. Jessica
11. Daniel	11. Elizabeth
12. Joseph	12. Nicole
13. Kevin	13. Rebecca
14. Eric	14. Kelly
15. Jeffrey	15. Mary
16. Richard	16. Christina
17. Scott	17. Amanda
18. Mark	18. Sarah
19. Steven	19. Laura
20. Timothy	20. Julie
21. Thomas	21. Shannon
22. Anthony	22. Christine
23. Charles	23. Tammy
24. Jeremy	24. Karen
25. Joshua	25. Tracy

Most Popular Names of the 1980s

Boys
1. Michael
2. Christopher
3. Matthew
4. Joshua
5. David
6. Daniel
7. James
8. Robert
9. John
10. Joseph
11. Jason
12. Justin
13. Andrew
14. Ryan
15. William
16. Brian
17. Jonathan
18. Brandon
19. Nicholas
20. Anthony
21. Eric
22. Adam
23. Kevin
24. Steven
25. Thomas

Girls
1. Jessica
2. Jennifer
3. Amanda
4. Ashley
5. Sarah
6. Stephanie
7. Melissa
8. Nicole
9. Elizabeth
10. Heather
11. Tiffany
12. Michelle
13. Amber
14. Megan
15. Rachel
16. Amy
17. Lauren
18. Kimberly
19. Christina
20. Brittany
21. Crystal
22. Rebecca
23. Laura
24. Emily
25. Danielle

Most Popular Names of the 1990s

Boys
1. Michael
2. Christopher
3. Matthew
4. Joshua
5. Jacob
6. Andrew
7. Daniel
8. Nicholas
9. Tyler
10. Joseph
11. David
12. Brandon
13. James
14. John
15. Ryan
16. Zachary
17. Justin
18. Anthony
19. William
20. Robert
21. Jonathan
22. Kyle
23. Austin
24. Alexander
25. Kevin

Girls
1. Ashley
2. Jessica
3. Emily
4. Sarah
5. Samantha
6. Brittany
7. Amanda
8. Elizabeth
9. Taylor
10. Megan
11. Stephanie
12. Kayla
13. Lauren
14. Jennifer
15. Rachel
16. Hannah
17. Nicole
18. Amber
19. Alexis
20. Courtney
21. Victoria
22. Danielle
23. Alyssa
24. Rebecca
25. Jasmine

Most Popular Names of 2006		Most Popular Names of 2007	
Boys	**Girls**	**Boys**	**Girls**
1. Jacob	1. Emily	1. Jacob	1. Emily
2. Michael	2. Emma	2. Michael	2. Isabella
3. Joshua	3. Madison	3. Ethan	3. Emma
4. Ethan	4. Isabella	4. Joshua	4. Ava
5. Matthew	5. Ava	5. Daniel	5. Madison
6. Daniel	6. Abigail	6. Christopher	6. Sophia
7. Christopher	7. Olivia	7. Anthony	7. Olivia
8. Andrew	8. Hannah	8. William	8. Abigail
9. Anthony	9. Sophia	9. Matthew	9. Hannah
10. William	10. Samantha	10. Andrew	10. Elizabeth
11. Joseph	11. Elizabeth	11. Alexander	11. Addison
12. Alexander	12. Ashley	12. David	12. Samantha
13. David	13. Mia	13. Joseph	13. Ashley
14. Ryan	14. Alexis	14. Noah	14. Alyssa
15. Noah	15. Sarah	15. James	15. Mia
16. James	16. Natalie	16. Ryan	16. Chloe
17. Nicholas	17. Grace	17. Logan	17. Natalie
18. Tyler	18. Chloe	18. Jayden	18. Sarah
19. Logan	19. Alyssa	19. John	19. Alexis
20. John	20. Brianna	20. Nicholas	20. Grace
21. Christian	21. Ella	21. Tyler	21. Ella
22. Jonathan	22. Taylor	22. Christian	22. Brianna
23. Nathan	23. Anna	23. Jonathan	23. Hailey
24. Benjamin	24. Lauren	24. Nathan	24. Taylor
25. Samuel	25. Hailey	25. Samuel	25. Anna

Most Popular Names of 2008

Boys

1. Jacob	26. Jonathan
2. Michael	27. Tyler
3. Ethan	28. Samuel
4. Joshua	29. Nicholas
5. Daniel	30. Gaven
6. Alexander	31. Dylan
7. Anthony	32. Jackson
8. William	33. Brandon
9. Christopher	34. Caleb
10. Matthew	35. Mason
11. Jayden	36. Angel
12. Andrew	37. Isaac
13. Joseph	38. Evan
14. David	39. Jack
15. Noah	40. Kevin
16. Aidan	41. Jose
17. James	42. Isaiah
18. Ryan	43. Luke
19. Logan	44. Landon
20. John	45. Justin
21. Nathan	46. Lucas
22. Elijah	47. Zachary
23. Christian	48. Jordan
24. Gabriel	49. Robert
25. Benjamin	50. Aaron

Girls

1. Emma	26. Anna
2. Isabella	27. Victoria
3. Emily	28. Kayla
4. Madison	29. Lillian
5. Ava	30. Lauren
6. Olivia	31. Kaylee
7. Sophia	32. Allison
8. Abigail	33. Savannah
9. Elizabeth	34. Nevaeh
10. Chloe	35. Gabriella
11. Samantha	36. Sofia
12. Addison	37. Makayla
13. Natalie	38. Avery
14. Mia	39. Riley
15. Alexis	40. Julia
16. Alyssa	41. Leah
17. Hannah	42. Aubrey
18. Ashley	43. Jasmine
19. Ella	44. Audrey
20. Sarah	45. Katherine
21. Grace	46. Morgan
22. Taylor	47. Brooklyn
23. Brianna	48. Destiny
24. Lily	49. Sydney
25. Hailey	50. Alexa

Boys

A

Aabid (Arabic) loyal

Aalam (Arabic) universal spirit

Aarcuus (Greek) rambunctious

Aaron ✪ ⊤ (Hebrew) revered; sharer

Aahron, Aaran, Aaren, Aareon, Aarin,
Aarone, Aaronn, Aarron, Aaryn, Aeron,
Aharon, Ahran, Ahren, Ahron, Aranne,
Aren, Arin, Aron, Arron

Aashiq (Arabic) fights evil

Aasif (Hindi) brash

Aasim (Hindi) in God's grace

Aatiq (Arabic) caring

Abacus (Greek) device for doing
calculations; clever

Abacas, Abakus, Abba

Abaddon (Hebrew) knows God

Abahu (Hindi) hopeful

Abana (Biblical) place name

Abanobi (Mythology) water lover

Abasi (African) strict

Abbas (Arabic) harsh

Ab, Abba

Abbey (Hebrew) spiritual

Abbie, Abie, Abby

Abbott (Hebrew) father; leader

Abbitt, Abott, Abotte

Abdi (African) serves well

Abdiel (Arabic) serving Allah

Abdon (Greek) God's worker

Abdul (Arabic) servant of Allah

Ab, Abdal, Abdeel, Abdel, Abdoul,
Abdu, Abdual, Abul

Abdulaziz (Hindi) servant of a
friend

Abdelazim, Abdelaziz, Abdulazaz,
Abdulazeez

Abdul-Jabbar (Arabic) comforting

Abdullah (Arabic) Allah's servant

Abdalah, Abdalla, Abdallah, Abdualla,
Abdulah, Abdulahi, Abdulla

Abe (Hebrew) form of Abraham:
father of a multitude

Abey, Abie

Abednego (Aramaic) faithful

Abeeku (African) Wednesday-born

Abel (Hebrew) vital

Abe, Abele, Abell, Abey, Abie, Able,
Adal, Avel

Abelard (German) firm

Ab, Abalard, Abbey, Abby, Abe, Abel,
Abelerd, Abelhard, Abilard, Adalard,
Adelard

Abelardo (Spanish) decisive

Abelino (Spanish) from biblical Abel

Abel, Able

Aben (Spanish) diligent

Abercius (Latin) open mind

Aberdeen (Place name) serene

Aber, Dean, Deen

Aberlin (German) ambitious

Abhay (Indian) unafraid

Abhijit (Indian) winner

Abi (Turkish) family's oldest brother

Abiah (Hebrew) child of Jehovah

Abia, Abiel, Abija, Abijah, Abisha,
Abishai, Aviya, Aviyah

Abiasaph (Biblical) loyal to God

Abidan (Biblical) God judges him

Abidla (Arabic) worshipping

Abiezer (Hebrew) father's light

Abihu (Biblical) believer

Abijah (Hebrew) God's gift

Abish

Abilene (Place name) town in Texas;
good old boy

Abalene, Abileen

Abimael (Biblical) loves God

Abimbola (African) destined for
riches

Abimelech (Hebrew) believer

Abinadab (African) tuesday-born

Abioye (African) he loves God

Abir (Hebrew) strong

Abeer

Abisia (Hebrew) God's gift; gifted child

Abixah, Absa

Abisoye (African) believer

Able (French) strong

Abner (Hebrew) cheerful leader

Ab, Abnir, Abnor, Avner, Ebner

Aboo (African) father; wise

Abosi (African) remembered

Abraar (Hebrew) fathers many

Abraham (Hebrew) father of a multitude

Abarran, Abe, Aberham, Abey, Abhiram, Abie, Abrahim, Abrahm, Abram, Bram, Ibrahim

Abram (Hebrew) form of Abraham: father of a multitude

Abe, Abrams, Avram, Bram

Abrasha (Hebrew) father

Abraxas (Spanish) bright

Aba

Abs (Hebrew) form of Absalom: my father is peace

Abe

Absalom (Hebrew) my father is peace

Abe, Abs, Absalon, Avshalom

Absolon (French) form of Absalom: my father is peace

Abundiantus (Latin) plentiful

Abbondanzio, Abbondazio, Abbondio

Abundio (Spanish) living in abundance

Abun, Abund

Acacius (Latin) blameless

Ace (Latin) one; unity

Acer, Acey, Acie

Acencion (Spanish) ascends

Ace-Shane (American) gracious God is first

Achaea (Biblical) good ancestry

Achard (French) dark mind

Achilles (Greek) heroic

Achill, Achille, Achillea, Achillios, Ackill, Akil, Akili, Akilles

Acho (Greek) loud

Acisclo (Spanish) frantic

Acisclus (Greek) from the river god Achelous

Ack (Scandinavian) peaceful

Acker (American) oak tree

Aker

Ackerley (English) born of the meadow; nature-loving

Accerley, Ackerlea, Ackerleigh, Ackersley, Acklea, Ackleigh, Ackley, Acklie

Actium (Biblical) place name

Acton (English) sturdy; oaks

Acten, Actin, Actohn, Actone

Adad (Mythology) stormy

Adael (Hebrew) decorated by God

Adair (Scottish) negotiator

Adaire, Adare, Ade

Adal (German) noble man

Adall, Adel

Adalai (Hebrew) my witness

Adalard (German) brave

Adalberto (Spanish) bright; dignified

Adal, Berto

Adam ✪ (Hebrew) first man; original

Ad, Adahm, Adama, Adamo, Adas, Addam, Addams, Addie, Addy, Adem, Adham

Adamson (Hebrew) Adam's son

Adams, Adamsen, Adamsson, Addamson

Adan (Irish) bold spirit

Aden, Adin, Adyn, Aidan, Aiden

Adar (Hebrew) fire; spirited

Addar

Adarsh (Spanish) first man (Adam)

Adbeel (Biblical) crowned

Add (Greek) steadfast

Addae (African) the sun

Addis (English) form of Addison: Adam's son
  Addace, Addice, Addy, Adis

Addison (English) Adam's son
  Ad, Addis, Adison, Adisson

Addo (Spanish) amazing

Addy (German) awesome; outgoing
  Addey, Addi, Addie, Adi

Ade (German) form ofm of Adel: royal

Adebayo (African) joyfully born

Adeeb (African) twelfth son

Adel (German) royal
  Adal, Addey, Addie, Addy

Adelaido (Latin) adorned

Adelante (Spanish) brave

Adelard (German) brave
  Adalar, Adalard, Addy, Adel, Adelar, Adelarde

Adelmo (German) protects others

Adelpho (Greek) breathes
  Adelfo

Aden (Irish) fiery

Adeniyi (Biblical) believer

Adeone (Welsh) royal
  Addy, Adeon

Adeoye (Latin) God-given

Adewale (Welsh) in flight; soars

Adhinav (Indian) newest

A'Dhron (American) warm

Adi (Arabic) fair

Adigun (American) distinctive

Adilson (Jewish) son of justice

Adin (Hebrew) good-looking
  Adan

Adina (Biblical) slight

Adio (African) devout

Adir (Hindi) lightning

Adit (Sanskrit) bright

Aditya (Sanskrit) sun

Adlai (Hebrew) ornamented
  Ad, Addy, Adlay, Adley, Adlie

Adlay (Hebrew) God's haven
  Adlei, Adley

Adler (German) eagle-eyed
  Ad, Addler, Adlar

Admer (English) noble

Adna (Hebrew) physical

Adnee (English) loner
  Adni, Adny

Ado (American) respected
  Ad, Addy

Adofo (German) sly

Adolf (German) sly wolf
  Ad, Adolfe, Adolph

Adolphus (German) noble wolf
  Adolfus, Adulphus

Adom (African) blessed

Adomas (African) blessed

Adonai (Biblical) my Lord

Adonaldo (Spanish) baby of hope

Adonijah (Hebrew) believer

Adonis (Greek) gorgeous; Aphrodite's love in mythology
  Addonis, Adon, Adones, Adonnis, Adonys, Andonice

Adoren (Hebrew) my Lord

Adorjan (Welsh) birdlike

Adrastos (Mythology) tenacious

Adrian ✪ ⊕ (Latin) wealthy; dark-skinned
  Adarian, Ade, Addie, Adorjan, Adrain, Adreeyan, Adreian, Adreyan, Adriaan, Adriane, Adriann, Adrien, Adrion, Adron, Adryan, Adryon, Aydrien, Aydrienne

Adriano (Italian) wealthy
  Adriannho, Adrianno

Adrie (Hungarian) leader of men

Adriel (Hebrew) God's follower
  Adrial, Adryel

Adrien (French) form of Adrian: wealthy; dark-skinned
  Ade, Adriene, Adrienn

Adya (Russian) man from Adria

Adyn (Irish) manly
  Adann, Ade, Aden, Aidan, Ayden

Adzel (Native American) fruitful

Aedan (Welsh) fire; fiery temperament

Aedron (Welsh) fiery

Aegle (Mythology) light

Aemilios (German) nobility

Aeneas (Greek) worthy of praise
Aineas, Aineias, Eneas, Eneis

Aeolus (Greek) ruler of the winds

Aerin (Welsh) berry

Aeron (Mythology) masculine god

Aesoh (Biblical name spelled
backward) revered

Aeson (Mythology) steady

Afan (Russian) form of Afanasy:
forever

Afanasy (Russian) forever
Afanasi

Afdhaal (Arabic) quiet

Affie (Arabic) pure

Afililio (Hispanic) commentator

Afra (Arabic) pale red hair

Afton (English) dignified
Affton, Aftawn, Aften

Afzal (Arabic) best

Agaf (Greek) martyr

Agamemnon (Greek) slow but sure
Agamem

Agapito (Spanish) loving

Agapius (Greek) love

Agaue (Greek) worker

Aggie (English) works the soil

Aggis (Asian) good

Aglay (Russian) splendid

Agnar (Irish) purity

Agricola (Irish) farms

Agripino (Hispanic) grieves

Agron (Spanish) farmer

Agrona (Celtic) combative

Aguayo (Spanish) smart

Agueda (Spanish) gives

Agueleo (Greek) wise one

Agurs (Spanish) good; often a girl's
name

Agus (Spanish) form of Agustin:
dignified

Agustin (Latin) dignified
Aguste, Auggie, Augustin

Agustive (Spanish) thoughtful

Ahab (Hebrew) father's brother; sea
captain in *Moby Dick*

Ahaziah (Hebrew) beloved

Ahearn (Irish) horse tender
Ahearne, Aherin, Ahern, Aherne, Hearn

Aherin (Hebrew) held on high
Aharon, Ahern, Aherne

Ahimelech (Biblical) religious
support

Ahmad (Arabic) praised man
*Achmad, Achmed, Ahamad, Ahamada,
Ahamed, Ahmaad, Ahmaud, Amad,
Amahd, Amed*

Ahmed (Arabic) praised man

Ahmoz (African) praised

Ahsan (Hindi) gracious; (Arabic)
grateful

Ahti (Mythology) water god

Ahura (Mythology) wise

Aiah (Biblical) shepherd

Aidan ✪ ❶ (Irish) fiery spirit
*Adan, Aden, Adin, **Aiden**, Aydan,
Ayden, Aydin*

Aided (Irish) spirited

Aigars (Russian) content

Aignan (Greek) pure

Aijalon (Biblical) place name

Aiken (English) hardy; oak-hewn
Aicken, Aikin, Ayken, Aykin

Ailbhe (Irish) saint

Ailill (Irish) small; elfin

Ailred (English) spiritual

Aimery (German) leader
*Aime, Aimerey, Aimeric, Amerey,
Aymeric, Aymery*

Aimo (Scandinavian) plenty

Aino (Scandinavian) the best one

Ainsley (Scottish) in a meadow
*Ainslee, Ainslie, Ainsleigh, Ainsli,
Ansley, Aynslee, Aynsley, Aynslie*

Ainsworth (English) joyful

Aiolos (Greek) fleet

Aisha (Arabic) living; typically a
female name

Aiwar (Arabic) form of Anwar: shining

Aiyetoro (African) destined for a peaceful life

Ajani (African) victorious

Ajax (Greek) daring
Ajacks

Ajay (American) spontaneous
A.J., Aj, Ajah, Ajai

Ajmal (African) depressed

Akan (Biblical) blessed

Akando (Asian) smart boy

Akar (Hindi) lightning
Akara

Akash (Indian) of the sky

Akbar (Hindi) Muslim king; giving

Ake (Scandinavian) inherits

Akeem (Arab) form of Hakim: brilliant
Ackeem, Ackim, Akieme, Akim, Hakeem

Akevy (Hebrew) form of Akiva: cunning

Aki (Scandinavian) blameless

Akil (Arabic) intelligent
Ahkeel, Akeel, Akeyla, Akhil, Akiel, Akili

Akilles (Greek) form of Achilles: heroic

Akim (Russian) loved by God
Achim, Ackeem, Ackim, Ahkieme, Akeam, Akee, Akeem, Akiem, Akima, Arkeem

Akinori (Japanese) spring flower

Akins (African) brave

Akira (Japanese) intellectual

Akiva (Hebrew) cunning
Akiba, Kiva

Akram (Arabic) kind

Akren (American) in jeopardy

Aksel (Scandinavian) calm

Akwasi (African) hopes

Akwete (African) second-born twin

Al (Irish) form of Alexander: great leader; helpful; form of Alan: handsome boy

Aladdin (Arabic) believer
Al, Ala, Alaa, Alaaddin, Aladdein, Aladean, Aladen

Alain (French) form of Alan: handsome boy
Alaen, Alainn, Alayn, Allain, Alun

Alair (Gaelic) happy
Alaire

Alan (Irish) handsome boy
Ailin, Al, Aland, Alen, Allan, Allen, Alley, Allie, Allin, Allyn, Alon, Alun

Alander (American) argumentative; cogitative

Alando (Spanish) form of Alan: handsome boy
Al, Alaindo, Alan, Aland, Alano, Allen, Allie, Alun, Alundo, Alyn

Alanson (Celtic) son of Alan; handsome
Alansen, Alenson, Allanson

Alarcon (French) dominant; (German) rules

Alaric (German) ruler
Alarick, Alarik, Aleric, Allaric, Allarick, Alric, Alrick

Alasdair (Scottish) form of Alastair: strong leader
Al, Alaisdair, Alasdaire, Alasdare, Alisdair, Allysdair

Alastair (Scottish) strong leader
Alaistair, Alastaire, Alasteir, Alastere, Alastor, Aleistere, Alester, Alistair, Allaistar, Allastair, Allastir, Alystair

Alaster (American) form of Alastair: strong leader
Alaste, Alester, Allaster

Albair (Welsh) rules

Alban (Latin) white man; from Alba's white hill
Abion, Albain, Albany, Albean, Albee, Albein, Alben, Albi, Albie, Albin, Alby, Auban

Albanse (American) form of Albany: town in New York; restless
Alban, Albance, Albanee, Albany, Albie, Alby

Albany (American) town in New York; restless
Albanee, Albanie

Albe (Latin) from Alba's white hill

Alberic (German) ruler; tough
Albric

Albert (German) distinguished
Al, Alberto, Alberts, Albie, Albrecht, Alby, Ally, Aubert

Alberto (Italian) distinguished
Al, Albert, Bertie, Berto

Albie (German) form of Albert: distinguished
Albee, Albi, Alby

Albion (Greek) old-fashioned
Albionne, Albyon

Albis (Spanish) unaware

Alby (Irish) white

Alcario (Spanish) delight

Alcide (Spanish) spirited

Alcippe (Greek) strong horse

Alcordia (American) in accord with others
Alcord, Alkie, Alky

Alcott (English) cottage-dweller
Alcot, Alkokt, Alkott, Allcot, Allcott,
Allkot, Allkott

Aldee (American) friend

Aldegundo (Spanish) old soul

Alden (English) wise
Al, Aldan, Aldin, Aldon, Elden

Alder (English) revered; kind

Aldest (Last name used as first name) great

Aldo (Italian) older one; jovial
Aldoh

Aldor (Spanish) elder

Aldorse (American) form of Aldo: older one; jovial
Al, Aldorce, Aldors

Aldous (German) wealthy
Aldas, Aldis, Aldus

Aldred (English) advisor; judgmental
Al, Aldrid, Aldy, Alldred, Eldred

Aldren (English) old friend
Al, Aldie, Aldran, Aldrun, Aldryn, Aldy

Aldrich (English) wise advisor
Aldie, Aldric, Aldrick, Aldridge, Aldrige,
Aldrish, Aldritch, Alldric, Alldrich,
Alldrick, Alldridge, Eldridge

Aldrin (English) old ruler

Aldwin (English) old friend

Aldyn (Irish) veteran

Alec (Greek) high-minded
Al, Aleck, Alek, Alic

Alecs (Scandinavian) defends man

Aleden (English) old friend

Alejandro (Spanish) defender; bold and brave
Alejandra, Alejo, Alex, Alexjandro

Alek (Russian) form of Aleksei: defender; brilliant
Aleks

Aleka (Slavic) form of Alex: great leader; helpful

Aleksander (Greek and Polish) defender
Alek, Sander

Aleksei (Russian) defender; brilliant
Alek, Alexi, Alik

Aleksey (Russian) smart

Aleman (Spanish) protects

Alemet (African) world leader

Aleppo (Place name) easygoing
Alepo

Aleric (Scandinavian) rules all
Alarik, Alerick, Alleric, Allerick

Aleron (French) the knight's armor; protected

Alessandro (Italian) helpful; defender
Alessand, Allessandro

Alessio (Italian) defensive

Alex ✪ (Greek) form of Alexander: great leader; helpful
Alax, Alecs, Alix, Allax, Allex

Alexander ✪ ❶ (Greek) great
leader; helpful
*Al, Alec, Alecsander, Aleksandar,
Aleksander, Aleksandur, Alex,
Alexandar, Alexandor, Alexandr, Alexis,
Alexsander, Alexxander, Alexzander,
Alisander, Alixander, Alixandre*

Alexandros (Greek) form of
Alexander: great leader; helpful
Alesandros, Alexandras

Alexdann (Hawaiian) helpful

Alexis (Greek) form of Alexander:
great leader; helpful
*Alexace, Alexei, Alexes, Alexey, Alexi,
Alexie, Alexius, Alexiz, Alexy, Lex*

Alf (Italian) form of Alfonso: bright;
prepared

Alfa (Spanish) first

Alfalfa (Botanical) sprite

Alfeo (Italian) different

Alfeus (Hebrew) follower
Alpheus

Alfie (English) form of Alfred:
counselor
Alf, Alfi, Alfy

Alfon (Spanish) bright

Alfonso (Spanish) bright; prepared
*Alf, Alfie, Alfons, Alfonsin, Alfonso,
Alfonsus, Alfonz, Alfonza, Alfonzo,
Alfonzus, Alphonsus, Fons, Fonzie,
Fonzy*

Alford (English) wise

Alfred (English) counselor
Al, Alf, Alfeo, Alfie, Alfrede, Alfryd

Alfredo (Italian) alf
Alfie, Alfreedo, Alfrido

Algas (English) has spears

Alger (German) hardworking
Algar, Allgar

Algernon (English) man with facial
hair
*Al, Algenon, Alger, Algie, Algin, Algon,
Algy*

Algia (German) prepared; kind
Alge, Algie

Algirdas (Scandinavian) chariot
rider; believer

Algo (American) lovable

Ali (Arabic) greatest
Alee, Aly

Ali-Baba (Literature) from
A Thousand and One Nights; cunning

Alicio (Spanish) noble; dignified

Alick (English) defends

Alim (Arabic) musical

Alipi (Spanish) calm

Alipio (Spanish) place name

Alireza (Hebrew) joyful

Alirio (Spanish) alert

Alisander (Greek) form of
Alexander: great leader; helpful
*Alisander, Alissander, Allisandre,
Alsandair, Alsandare, Alsander*

Alisen (Irish) honest

Allan (Irish) form of Alan:
handsome boy
Allane, Allayne

Allard (English) brave man
Alard, Ellard

Alleem (American) bold

Allegheny (Place name) mountains
of the Appalachian system; grand
Al, Alleg, Alleganie, Alleghenie

Allen (Irish) handsome boy
*Al, Alen, Alley, Alleyn, Alleyne, Allie,
Allin, Allon, Allyn, Alon*

Allett (Biblical) hides

Allie (Arabic) divine

Allington (English) calm

Allward (Polish) brave

Almagor (Hebrew) courageous

Almar (German) strong
Al, Almarr, Almer

Almedia (Spanish) place name

Almee (German) ruler

Almere (American) director

Almer

Almez (Spanish) dependable

Almo (American) form of Elmo:
gregarious

Almodad (Biblical) sturdy

Almon (Biblical) place name

Almund (Botanical) from almond;
wise

Alois (Czech) famous warrior

Aloisio, Aloysius

Alonzo (Spanish) enthusiàstic

Alano, Alanzo, Alon, Alonso, Alonza,
Alonze, Elonzo, Lon, Lonnie

Alouis (French) sun king

Aloys (French) king

Aloysius (German) famed

Alaois, Alois, Aloisio, Aloisius

Alpar (Hindi) champions
downtrodden

Alpheus (Hebrew) form of Alfeus:
follower

Alphaeus

Alphin (German) leads first

Alphonse (German) distinguished

Alf, Alfonse, Alphons, Alphonsa,
Alphonso, Alphonzus, Fonsi, Fonsie,
Fonz, Fonzie

Alpin (Scottish) man from alpine area

Alps (Place name) climber

Alp

Alquince (American) old; fifth

Al, Alquense, Alquin, Alquins, Alquinse,
Alqwence

Alrick (German) leader

Alrec, Alric

Alston (English) serious; nobleman

Allston, Alsten, Alstin

Alsworth (English) from a manor;
rich

Alta (Latin) high; elevated

Al

Altair (Scottish) defender

Altan (Turkish) dawn

Altarius (African American) form of
Altair: defender

Al, Altare, Altareus, Alterius, Alltair

Altemease (Turkish) dawn light

Alter (Hebrew) old; will live to be old

Altilio (Spanish) bright

Altman (German) wise

Altmann, Atman

Alton (English) excellent; kind

Allton, Altawn, Alten, Altyn

Altonio (Spanish) form of Antonio:
superb

Altus (Latin) form of Alta: high;
elevated

Al

Alula (Latin) winged

Alun (Welsh) adored

Alva (Hebrew) intelligent; beloved
friend

Alvah

Alvado (Spanish) fair

Alvah (Biblical) high God

Alvan (Biblical) friend

Alvar (Spanish) careful

Alvaro, Alver

Alvarado (Spanish) peacemaker

Alvaradoh, Alvaro, Alvie, Alvy

Alvaro (Spanish) just

Alvaroh, Alvarro, Alvey, Alvie, Alvy

Alvern (English) old friend

Al, Alverne, Alvurn

Alvim (Slavic) pale friend

Alvin (Latin) light-haired; loved

Alv, Alvan, Alven, Alvie, Alvy, Alvyn

Alvin-Don (American) combo of
Alvin and Don

Alvis (American) form of Elvis:
all-wise

Al, Alviss, Alvy

Alvord (Greek) cautious

Alwin (German) form of Alvin: light-haired; loved
Allwyn, Alwyn, Alwynn, Aylwin

Alzado (Arabic) forlorn

Amaan (African) loyal
Aman, Amman

Amable (French) amiable

Amac (Mythology) wise

Amadayus (Invented) form of Amadeus: God-loving
Amadayes

Amadeo (Italian) blessed by God; artistic

Amadeus (Latin) God-loving
Amad, Amadayus, Amadeaus, Amadei, Amadio, Amadis, Amado, Amador, Amadou, Amedeo, Amodaos

Amado (Spanish) loved
Amadee, Amadeo, Amadi, Amadis, Amadus, Amando

Amadour (French) loved
Amador, Amadore

Amadus (Latin) adores God
Amandus

Amal (Hebrew) hardworking; optimistic
Amahl, Amhall

Amalek (Biblical) place name; works hard

Amancio (Spanish) faithful

Amandeep (Hindi) light of peace
Amandip, Amanjit, Amanjot, Amanpreet

Amando (Spanish) God-loving

Amandor (Spanish) affectionate

Amanus (Biblical) place name

Amar (Arabic) making a home
Amari, Amario, Amaris, Ammar, Ammer

Amaramto (Latin) beauty does not fade

Amarbir (Spanish) forevermore

Amardeep (Indian) loved

Amarillo (Place name) town in Texas; in Spanish
Amarille, Amarilo

Amarion (Hebrew) believes in God

Amasa (Hebrew) carries a heavy load

Amathus (Biblical) place name

Amato (Italian) loving
Amahto, Amatoh

Amaury (Spanish) slanted; power

Amazu (Hebrew) burdened

Ambert (Arabic) golden boy

Amblin (English) of nobility

Ambrel (Spanish) amber

Ambrogia (Italian) everlasting

Ambrose (German) everlasting
Amba, Ambie, Ambroce, Ambrus, Amby

Ambrosio (Spanish) everlasting

Ambrus (Slavic) immortal

Ameer (Arabic) rules

Amer (Spanish) leader

America (Place name) patriotic

Americo (Spanish) patriotic
Ame, America, Americus, Ameriko

Amerigo (Italian) ruler; name of Italian explorer
Amer, Americo, Ameriko

Amery (Arabic) regal birth
Amory

Ames (French) friendly
Aims

Amias (Latin) devoted to God
Amyas

Amichai (Hebrew) my nation lives

Amiel (Hebrew) my people's God
Ameal, Amheel, Ammiel

Amin (Arabic) honorable; dependable
Aman, Ameen

Amine (Arabic) honest

Amir (Arabic) royal; ruler
Ameer, Amire

Amiren (American) leader

Amit (Hindi) forever;
Amitan, Amreet, Amrit

Amiti (Japanese) endless friend

Ammen (Mythology) hides

Ammiel (Biblical) adventurer

Ammon (Irish) hidden
Amnon

Amodeo (Invented) loving

Amol (Hebrew) perseveres

Amon (Egyptian) secretive

Amor (Latin) love
Amerie, Amoree, Amori, Amorie

Amory (German) home ruler
Amery, Amor

Amos (Hebrew) strong
Amus

Ampah (African) certainty

Amparo (Spanish) winding

Ampy (American) fast
Amp, Ampee, Ampey, Amps

Amram (Biblical) uplifted

Amran (Biblical) spirited

Amund (Scandinavian) fearless

Amyas (Latin) lovable
Aimeus, Ameus, Amias, Amyes

An (Chinese) peaceful; safe
Ana

Anah (Biblical) the answer

Anaitis (Mythology) pure

Anamim (Biblical) windy

Anan (Irish) outdoorsy
An, Annan

Ananan (Biblical) hopes

Anand (Hindi) delightful
Ananda, Anant, Ananth

Ananiah (Biblical) place name

Ananias (Biblical) pious

Anant (Indian) forever

Ananta (Sanskrit) forever

Anarolio (Spanish) called forth

Anas (Czech) born again

Anast (Russian) born again

Anastasius (Greek) reborn
*Anas, Anastagio, Anastas, Anastase,
Anastasi, Anastasio, Anastastios,
Anastice, Anasticius, Anastisis,
Athanasius*

Anatole (French) exotic
*Anatol, Anatoli, Anatolijus, Anatolio,
Anatoly, Anitolle*

Anatu (Hebrew) water

Ancel (French) creative
Ance, Ancell, Anse, Ansel, Ansell

Andalf (Norse) leads with staff

Andel (Scandinavian) honored

Ander (English) form of Andrew:
manly and brave

Anders (Swedish) masculine
*Ander, Andersen, Anderson, Andirs,
Andries, Andy*

Ando (Slavic) form of Andrew: manly
and brave

Andrade (Scandinavian) manly

Andrae (Slavic) form of Andrew:
manly and brave

Andras (French) form of Andrew:
manly and brave
*Andrae, Andres, Andrus, Ondrae,
Ondras*

André (French) masculine
*Andra, Andrae, Andre, Andree, Andrei,
Anrecito, Aundré*

Andreas (Greek) masculine
Adryus, Andrieas, Andries, Andy

Andrej (Slavic) masculine; manly

Andren (English) masculine

Andrere (Greek) manly

Andres (Spanish) macho
Andras, Andrés, Andrez, Andy

Andre-Shaun (French) combo of
Andre and Shaun; kind boy

Andretti (Italian) speedy
Andrette, Andy

Andrew ✪ ✟ (Greek) manly and
brave
*Aindrew, Anders, Andery, Andi, Andie,
Andreas, Andres, Andrews, Andru,
Andrue, Andy, Audrew*

Andrick (Scandinavian) masculine

Andromache (Greek) manly

Andronek (Greek) wins

Andronico (Italian) victor

Andronicus (Greek) clever

Andros (Polish) masculine
Andris, Andrus

Andru (Greek) form of Andrew: manly and brave
Andrue

Andrzej (Polish) manly

Andy (Greek) form of Andrew: manly and brave
Andee, Andie

Anekin (Slavic) manly

Aner (Biblical) well-born

Aneurin (Welsh) golden child
Aneirin

Anfanio (Spanish) secretive

Anferny (American) variation of Anthony
Andee, Anfernee, Anferney, Anferni, Anfernie, Anfurny

Angel ✪ (Greek) angelic messenger
Ange, Angele, Angell, Angie, Angy

Angelberto (Spanish) shining angel
Angel, Angelbert, Bert, Berto

Angelo (Italian) angelic
Ange, Angelito, Angeloh, Angelos, Anglo, Anjelo

Angharad (Welsh) loving

Angits (Celtic) divine

Angle (Word as name) spin doctor
Ange, Angul

Anglin (Greek) angelic
Anglen, Anglinn, Anglun

Angra (Mythology) dark spirit

Angus (Scottish) standout; important
Ange, Angos, Aonghas

Anh (Vietnamese) smart

Anibal (Spanish) brave noble

Aniceto (Spanish) invincible

Anick (Hebrew) gracious

Aniello (Italian) risk-taker

Anil (Hindi) air
Aneel, Anel, Aniel, Aniello

Aniol (Polish) angel
Ahnjol, Ahnyolle

Anju (Indian) younger

Anka (Polish) gracious; stems from Anna

Ankoma (African) last-born child

Ankur (Indian) blooms

Annan (African) second; from Annar

Annatto (Botanical) tree; tough
Annatta

Anndo (Scandinavian) protects

Annibale (Phoenician) form of Hannibal: leader

Anniel (Biblical) angel

Annis (English) God's gift

Anok (Slavic) reliable

Anolus (Greek) masculine
Ano, Anol

Anrue (American) masculine
Anrae, Anroo

Ans (Scandinavian) dramatic

Anscom (English) awesome man
Anscomb

Ansel (French) creative
Ancell, Ansa, Anse, Ansell

Anselm (German) protective
Anse, Ansehlm, Ansellm

Anselmo (Spanish) protected by God
Ancel, Ancelmo, Anse, Ansel, Anselm, Anzelmo, Selmo

Ansgar (German) spear of God

Anshel (Hindi) blessed
Anshl

Anskar (German) brusque

Ansley (English) loner
Anslea, Anslee, Ansleigh, Anslie, Ansly, Ansy

Anson (German) divine male
Anse, Ansonn, Ansun

Anssi (Scandinavian) protected

Antal (Latin) princely

Ante (Slavic) flourishes; (Spanish) special

Antero (Greek) moves with grace

Anthonisamy (Indian) form of Anthony: priceless

Anthony ✪ ⊕ (Latin) priceless
Anathony, Anothony, Anth, Anthawn, Anthey, Anthoney, Anthoni, Anthonie, Anthonio, Anthyonny, Anton, Antony, Tony

Antioch (Biblical) place name

Antioco (Spanish) best

Antipas (Greek) father

Antjuan (American) form of
Anthony: priceless

Antoan (Latin) form of Anthony:
priceless

Antoine (French) worthy of praise
Antone, Antons, Antos, Antwan,
Antwon, Antwone

Antolin (Slavic) unusual

Anton (Latin) outstanding
Antan, Antawn

Antonce (African American) form of
Anthony: priceless
Antawnce

Antonio (Spanish) superb
Antinio, Antoino, Antone, Antonello,
Antonino, Antonioh, Antonnio,
Antonyia, Antonyio, Antonyo, Tony

Antony (Latin) good
Antawny, Antini, Antonah, Antone,
Antoney, Antoni, Antonie, Anty, Tone,
Tony

Antran (Spanish) energetic

Antrinell (African American) valued
Antrie, Antrinel, Antry

Antroy (African American) form of
Anthony: priceless
Antroe, Antroye

Antuane (Slavic) first

Antwan (American) form of Antoine:
worthy of praise
Antawan, Antawn, Anthawn,
Antowine, Antown, Antowne, Antwain,
Antwaine, Antwaion, Antwane,
Antwann, Antwanne, Antwaun,
Antwen, Antwian, Antwine, Antwion,
Antwoan, Antwoin, Antwoine, Antwon,
Antwonn, Antwonne, Antwuan,
Antyon, Antywon

Antwone (American) form of
Antoine: worthy of praise
Antwonn

Anubis (Egyptian) royal

Anulf (Scandinavian) royal

Anwar (Arabic) shining
Anouar, Anour, Anwhour

Anwyl (Welsh) beloved
Anwell, Anwyll

Anyon (Latin) form of Anthony:
priceless

Anzelm (Polish) protective
Ahnzselm

Apatin (Slavic) aggressive

Apearen (Native American) armed

Apen (Irish) likes horses

Aplin (American) strong

Apolinar (Spanish) manly and wise
Apollo

Apolinard (Spanish) strong

Apolla (Greek) strong

Apollo (Greek) masculine; a god in
mythology
Apolloh, Apolo, Apoloniah, Applonian,
Appollo

Apolonio (Greek) form of Apollo:
masculine; a god in mythology

Apostle (Greek) follower; disciple
Apos

Apostolos (Greek) disciple
Apos

Apple (American) favorite;
wholesome
Apel

Aquan (Native American) tranquil

Aquila (Spanish) eagle-eyed
Acquilla, Aquil, Aquilas, Aquile,
Aquilla, Aquillino

Aquileo (Spanish) warrior
Akweleo, Aquilo

Ara (Slavic) integrity

Arachne (Greek) spider

Aracin (Latin) ready; heaven's gate

Araldo (German) army leader

Aralis (Hawaiian) godlike

Aralt (Irish) army leader

Aram (Syrian) noble; honorable
Ara, Aramia, Arra

Aramis (French) clever

Airamis, Arames, Aramith, Aramys, Aramyse, Arhames

Arann (Slavic) calm

Arbel (Biblical) prayerful

Arber (American) from arbor; adorned

Arbet (Last name as first name) high

Arb, Arby

Arbogast (German) covered

Arcana (Latin) esoteric wisdom

Arcen (English) virile

Arceneaux (French) friendly; heavenly

Arce, Arcen, Arceno

Arch (English) form of Archibald: bold leader

Arche

Archard (English) bold

Archer (English) athletic; bowman

Arch, Archie

Archibald (German) bold leader

Arch, Archibold, Archie

Archie (English) form of Archibald: bold leader

Arch, Archi, Archy

Arcis (Spanish) from war god Arecio

Ard (Thai) woodsy

Ardan (Latin) passion; eagle

Ardee (American) ardent

Ard, Ardie, Ardy

Ardell (Latin) go-getter

Ardel

Arden (Latin) ball of fire

Ard, Arda, Ardie, Ardin, Ardon, Arrden

Ardley (English) with dedication

Ardmohr (Latin) more ardent than others

Ard, Ardmoor, Ardmore

Ardolph (German) ardent

Ardor (French) loving

Ardouin (French) ardent

Arecin (French) smooth

Areeb (Arabic) passionate

Areeg (Welsh) gold

Arellano (Scandinavian) unique

Arelus (Latin) form of Aurelius: golden son

Aren (Dutch) form of Aaron: revered; sharer

Arenas (Spanish) eager

Arenda (Spanish) eager

Ares (Mythology) combats

Arethuse (Greek) excels

Arfel (Welsh) struggles

Argan (American) leader

Argee, Argen, Argey, Argi, Argie, Argun

Argento (Spanish) silver

Arge, Argey, Argi, Argy

Argeroula (Greek) shines

Argus (Greek) careful; bright

Agos, Arjus

Argyl (Irish) from Ireland; aware

Argyle (English) diamond pattern; planning

Argile

Ari (Greek) best

Ahree, Aria, Arias, Arie, Arih, Arij, Arri

Arian (Welsh) form of Arion: enchanted man

Aribert (German) holy

Aribold (German) holy

Aric (English) leader

Aaric, Arec, Areck, Arick, Arik, Arric, Arrick, Arrik

Arie (English) God's lion

Ariel (Hebrew) God's spirited lion

Airel, Arel, Arell, Ari, Arie, Ariele, Arielle, Ariya, Ariyel, Arrial, Arriel

Aries (Greek) god of war; mythology

Arees, Arie, Ariez

Arik (German) leads; (Welsh) form of Erik: powerful leader

Arild (Hebrew) God's lion

Arimas (Literature) form of Aramis: clever

Arines (Spanish) strong

Ario (Spanish) warring

Ari, Arrio

Arioch (Biblical) dignity

Arion (Greek) enchanted man

Ari, Arian, Ariane, Arie, Arien, Ariohn, Arrian

Arisbe (Spanish) believer

Arisodemos (Greek) best person

Arist (Greek) God-fearing

Aristeo (Spanish) best

Aris, Aristio, Aristo, Ary

Aristeus (Greek) quintessential

Aristides (Greek) son of the outstanding

Ari, Aris, Aristidis

Aristophanes (Greek) playwright

Aristotle (Greek) best man

Ari, Aris, Aristie, Aristito, Aristo, Aristokles, Aristotelis, Aristottle

Ariwin (Spanish) best friend

Arj (Welsh) white

Arjan (Hindi) archer

Arjun

Arkady (Russian) revered

Arkan (Scandinavian) king's baby

Arkell (Scandinavian) of the king

Arki (Greek) ruler

Arkos (Biblical) people's master

Arkyn (Scandinavian) royal offspring

Aricin, Ark, Arkeen, Arken, Arkin

Arle (Irish) sworn

Arlee, Arley, Arly

Arledge (English) lives by a lake

Arleedj, Arles, Arlidge, Arlledge

Arleigh (Irish) sworn

Arly

Arlen (Irish) dedicated

Arl, Arlan, Arland, Arle, Arlend, Arlin, Arlyn, Arlynn

Arley (English) meadow-loving; outdoorsy

Arleigh, Arlie, Arly

Arlindo (Italian) dedicated

Arlis (Hebrew) dedicated; in charge

Arlas, Arles, Arless, Arly

Arliss (English) wise eyes

Arlo (German) strong

Arloh

Arlonn (Irish) sworn; cheerful

Arlan, Arlann, Arlen, Arlon

Arlyn (Irish) form of Arlen: dedicated

Arlys (Hebrew) pledged

Arlis

Arm (English) arm

Arma, Arman, Arme

Arman (German) army man; defender

Armaan

Armand (German) strong soldier

Armad, Armanda, Armando, Armands,

Armanno, Armaude, Arme, Armenta, Armond, Ormand

Armando (Spanish) entertainer

Armand, Arme, Armondo

Armani (Italian) army; disciplined talent

Amani, Arman, Armanie, Armon, Armoni

Armel (French) royal; sturdy

Armen (Spanish) from Armenia

Arme, Arment, Armenta

Armetris (Greek) prepared; armed

Armineh (Armenian) from Armenia

Armino (Teutonic) warrior

Armitage (Last name as first name) safe haven

Armi, Armita, Army

Armon (Hebrew) strong as a fortress

Arman, Arme, Armen, Armin, Armino, Armoni, Armons

Armstrong (English) strong-armed

Arme, Army

Arnaud (French) strong

Arnaldo, Arnauld

Arnborn (Scandinavian) eagle-bear; animal instincts

Arn, Arnborne, Arnbourne, Arne

Arndt (German) strong

Arne, Arnee, Arney, Arni, Arnie

Arne (German) form of Arnold: ruler; strong

Arn, Arna, Arnel, Arnell

Arnell (American) strong

Arnette (Dutch) little eagle

Arnat, Arnet, Arnot, Arnott

Arnic (Scandinavian) eagle-eyed

Arnie (German) form of Arnold: ruler; strong

Arne, Arney, Arni, Arnny, Arny

Arno (German) farsighted

Arn, Arne, Arnoh, Arnou, Arnoux

Arnold (German) ruler; strong

Arnald, Arndt, Arne, Arnie, Arnoll, Arny

Arnome (Invented) powerful

Arnom

Arnon (German) eagle

Arnot (French) form of Arnold: ruler; strong

Arnart, Arnett, Arnott

Arnov (Slavic) resolved

Arnst (Scandinavian) eagle-eyed

Arn

Arnulfo (Spanish) strong

Arne, Arnie, Arny

Arocles (Greek) masterful

Aroldo (German) eagle; strong

Aron (Hebrew) generous

Aaron, Arron, Erinn

Aronon (Welsh) blond

Arpad (Hungarian) prince; sunny

Arper (Slavic) fruitful

Arquimides (Spanish) philosopher

Arran (Scandinavian) form of Aaron: revered; sharer

Arrigo (Italian) ruler

Arsenio (Greek) macho; virile

Arne, Arsen, Arsenius, Arseny, Arsinio, Arsonio

Arshad (Iranian) revered

Arshaq (Arabic) supports

Arsinoe (Biblical) place name

Arslan (Spanish) form of Arsenio: macho; virile

Arson (Greek) masculine

Art (English) bearlike; wealthy

Arte, Artie

Artax (Biblical) rules

Artemus (Greek) gifted

Art, Artemas, Artemio, Artemis, Artie, Artimas, Artimis, Artimus

Arthel (Slavic) royalty

Arthi (Scandinavian) masculine

Arthisus (Origin unknown) stuffy

Arth, Arthi, Arthy

Arthur (Celtic) bear; stone

Art, Arth, Arther, Arthor, Artie, Artor, Artur, Arty, Aurther, Aurthur

Artie (English) form of Arthur: bear; stone

Art, Artee, Arty

Artin (Slavic) form of Arthur: bear; stone

Artra (Scandinavian) bear boy

Arturo (Italian) talented

Art, Arthuro, Artur, Arture, Arturro

Arun (Hindi) the color of the sky before dawn

Aruns

Arund (Hindi) free spirit

Arundel (English) lives with eagles; soars

Arv (Scandinavian) worthwhile

Arvai (Hebrew) roams

Arve

Arvel (German) friendly

Arvid (Hebrew) full of wanderlust

Arv, Arvad, Arve, Arvie, Arvind, Arvinder, Arvydas

Arvin (German) friendly

Arv, Arven, Arvie, Arvind, Arvinder, Arvon, Arvy

Arvo (Spanish) friend

Arwen (German) friend

Arwee, Arwene, Arwhen, Arwy

Arwey (Welsh) priceless

Arwin (American) assertive friend

Ary (Hebrew) lion; fierce

Ari, Arye

Arya (Indian) analytical

Aryan (English) white

Asa (Hebrew) healer
Ase, Aza

As·d (Arabic) happy
Asaad, Asad, Asid, Assad, Azad

Asafa (Biblical) collector

Asbury (Last name used as first name) dignified

Ascencion (Spanish) ascends

Ascot (English) cottage-dweller

Asgar (Scandinavian) God's home

Ash (Botanical) tree; bold
Ashbey, Ashby, Ashe

Asha (Hebrew) fire

Asharious (Mythology) from Ashur, god of war

Ashbel (Hebrew) fiery god

Ashby (Scandinavian) brash
Ashbee, Ashbey, Ashie, Ashy

Asher (Hebrew) joyful
Ash, Ashar, Ashor, Ashur

Ashfaaq (Arabic) honorable

Ashford (English) spunky
Ash, Ashferd, Ashtin

Ashkenaz (Biblical) sincere

Ashley (English) smooth
Ash, Asheley, Ashelie, Ashely, Ashie,
Ashlan, Ashlee, Ashleigh, Ashlen, Ashlie,
Ashlin, Ashling, Ashlinn, Ashlone, Ashly,
Ashlyn, Ashlynn, Aslan

Ashlin (English) form of Ashley: smooth

Ashmon (English) of the ash trees

Ashok (Indian) content

Ashraf (Arabic) honors others

Ashrin (English) of the ash trees

Ashton (English) handsome
Ashteen, Ashtin

Ashtoreth (Biblical) staunch

Ashur (Hebrew) happy

Ashvin (English) ash tree

Asifa (Hebrew) gathers

Askew (Last name used as first name) distinguished

Askia (American) worthy

Aslan (Literature) from CS Lewis's Narnia series; lionlike

Asmer (Last name used as first name) ash tree

Asmus (German) well-known

Asner (Hebrew) giving

Asriel (Hebrew) praised

Asshurim (Biblical) of the ash-tree land

Assir (Biblical) hawk-like

Aston (English) eastern
Asten, Astin

Aswin (English) from the land of ash trees

Atam (American) form of Adam: first man; original
Atame, Atom, Atym

Atanacio (Spanish) everlasting
Atan, Atanasio

Atanase (Spanish) forever

Atch (American) lively

Ateeq (Arabic) affectionate

Athan (Biblical) form of Dathan: fountain of hope

Athanasius (Greek) immortal
Atanas, Atanasio

Athar (English) lives on a farm

Atherton (English) coming from a farm

Athos (Greek) high

Atilano (Greek) strong

Atilio (Spanish) aggressor

Atinuwa (African) aware

Atkins (Last name as first name) linked; known
Atkin

Atlas (Greek) courier of greatness
Atlass

Atley (English) from the meadow
Atlea, Atlee, Atleigh, Atli, Attley

Aton (Egyptian) sun child

Ator (Scandinavian) born of thunder

Atropos (Greek) unbinding

Atsu (African) second-born twin

Atticus (Greek) ethical

Aticus, Attikus

Attila (Gothic) powerful

Atalik, Atila, Atilio, Atiya, Atlya, Att

Attillio (Italian) hero

Atul (German) good

Atwater (English) living by the water

Atwell (English) the well; full of gusto

Atwood (English) the woods; outdoorsy

Atworth (English) farmer

Atyab (Arabic) cultivated

Auberon (German) like a bear; highborn

Aube, Auberron, Aubrey

Aubert (German) leader

Auber, Aubey

Aubin (French) ruler; elfin

Auben

Aubrey (French/German) ruler

Aubary, Aube, Aubery, Aubree, Aubry, Aubury, Bree

Auburn (Latin) brown with red cast; tenacious

Aubern, Aubie, Auburne

Auday (American) strong

Audelon (French) wealthy

Auden (English) old friend

Aude, Audie

Audencio (Spanish) companion

Auden

Audie (German) strong man

Aude, Audee, Audi, Audiel, Audley

Audley (English) rich

Audlea, Audlee, Audleigh, Audly

Audon (Scandinavian) alone

Audran (American) purposeful

Audras (Scandinavian) having wealth

Audres

Audric (French) wise ruler

Audun (Scandinavian) form of Audon: alone

Audwin (English) rich

Augie (Latin) form of Augustus: highly esteemed

Aug, Auggie, Augy

August (Latin) determined

Auge, Augie

Augustine (Latin) serious and revered

Agostino, Agoston, Agustin, Aug, Augie, August, Augustene, Augustin

Augustive (Spanish) serious

Augusto (Spanish) respected; serious

Agusto, Augey, Auggie, Austeo

Augustus (Latin) highly esteemed

Aug, Auge, Augie, August

Aulderay (American) old soul

Aulie (English) form of Audley: rich

Awlie

Aurek (Latin) golden

Aurelius (Latin) golden son

Arelian, Areliano, Aurel, Aurey, Aurie, Auriel, Aury

Aureo (Spanish) gold; pleases

Ausburn (English) reddish-brown

Aust (American) form of Austin: serious and revered

Austin ✪ ♂ (Latin) form of Augustine: serious and revered

Astin, Aust, Austen, Austine, Auston, Austyn

Austreberto (Spanish) austere

Auther (American) form of Arthur: bear; stone

Authar, Authur

Autry (Latin) golden

Avanindra (Hindi) king of the earth

Avan

Avdis (Slavic) providential

Avelino (Spanish) nature-lover

Avenall (English) from the woods; calm

Avenel, Avenell

Avent (French) up-and-coming
Aventin, Aventino

Averill (French) April-born child
Ave, Averel, Averell, Averiel, Averil,
Averyl, Averyll, Avrel, Avrell, Avrill,
Avryl

Avery (English) soft-spoken
Avary, Ave, Aveary, Averey, Averie, Avry

Avi (Hebrew) springlike
Avian, Avidan, Avidor, Aviel, Avion

Aviaz (Hebrew) believer

Aviden (Hebrew) God judges him

Avinoam (Biblical) pleasant brother

Avion (French) flyer
Aveonn, Avyon, Avyun

Avison (Hebrew) believes

Avitol (Hebrew) vital

Aviv (Hebrew) spring; (French)
vibrant

Avner (Hebrew) father of light
Avneet, Avniel

Avniel (Hebrew) God is my rock

Avon (Hebrew) spring birth; (English)
place name

Avram (Hebrew) almighty father
Arram, Avraham, Avrom, Avrum

Avren (Hebrew) uplifts God

Avrum (Yiddish) form of Abraham:
father of a multitude

Avrylle (French) hunter
Avryll

Axel (German) peaceful;
contemporary
Aksel, Ax, Axe, Axil, Axill, Axl

Axie (Scandinavian) peaceful child

Axton (German) town of peace;
peacemaker

Ayal (English) highborn

Ayden (Turkish) knowing

Aydin (Irish) masculine

Aydinus (Slavic) knowing

Ayers (Last name as first) industrious

Aylen (Native American) joy

Aylmer (English) of noble birth

Aylward (English) guards best

Aylwin (Welsh) elf friend

Ayman (Arabic) fortunate

Ayo (African) happy

Ayson (Origin unknown) lucky
Aison

Aytekin (American) friend

Azad (Arabic) lucky

Azael (Spanish) God-loved

Azar (Biblical) form of Azariah: aided
by Jehovah

Azariah (Biblical) aided by Jehovah

Azeem (Arabic) cherished
Aseem, Asim

Azeez (Arabic) strong

Azhar (Arabic) flourishes

Azi (African) a child

Azia (Biblical) powerful

Azim (Arabic) grandiose

Aziz (Arabic) powerful; (African)
adorable

Azizi (African) beloved

Azmon (Biblical) place name

Azrae (Mythology) Azrael

Azriel (Hebrew) the Lord's angel

Azuriah (Hebrew) aided by God
Azaria, Azariah, Azuria

Azzie (Slavic) strong

B

Babak (Iranian) the father

Babar (Turkish) lion
Baber

Babe (American) athlete

Babu (Hindi) fierce

Bacchus (Greek) reveler; jaded
Baakus, Bakkus, Bakus

Bach (Last name as first name)
talented
Bok

Bachar (Hebrew) eldest

Bachir (Hebrew) oldest son; reliable

Bachur

Bacon (English) literary; outspoken

Baco, Bake, Bakon

Badar (Hindi) full moon

Bade (Welsh) wild boar

Baden (German) bathes; cleansed

Badge (American) moon-watcher

Badger (Last name as first name) difficult

Badge, Badgeant, Bage, Bagent

Badget (English) moon-loving

Badr (African) full moon; lucky

Badru (African) full moon; lucky

Baghai (Arabic) form of Bahij: delighted

Bagher (American) magnificent

Bagley (English) boy from the field

Bagor (English) fun

Baha (Arabic) splendid

Bahij (Arabic) delighted

Bahir (Arabic) magnificent

Bai (Chinese) white

Bailey (French) attentive

Baile, Baily, Baley, Baylie

Bainbridge (Irish) bridge; negotiator

Bain, Banebridge, Beebee

Baines (Last name as first name) pale

Baine, Baynes

Bainlon (American) form of Bailey: attentive

Baily

Baird (Irish) singer/poet; creative

Bard, Bayrde

Bairon (Spanish) creative

Baka (Biblical) place name

Bakari (African) promising

Baker (English) cook

Baiker, Baykar

Bal (Hindi) strong

Bala (Hindi) young

Balan (Indian) youthful

Balbino (Italian) mumbler

Baldemar (Spanish) form of Balthasar: God save the king

Baldy

Balder (Scandinavian) good prince

Baldur, Baudier

Baldev (Hindi) strong God

Baldie (German) nickname for Baldwin: brave friend

Baldric (German) leader

Baldrick, Baledric, Bauldric

Baldridge (English) persuasive

Baldwin (German) steadfast friend

Baldwinn, Baldwynn, Bally

Balendin (Place name) balen

Baley (American) form of Bailey: attentive

Baleye

Balfour (Scottish) landowner

Balf, Balfore

Balfre (Spanish) brave

Balin (Hungarian) from Balint: strong and healthy

Balint (Latin) strong and healthy

Ballance (American) courageous

Balance, Ballans

Ballard (German) brave

Ballerd

Balraj (Hindi) strong king

Balthasar (Greek) God save the king

Bath, Bathazar

Balu (Hindi) young

Balun (English) bold friend

Balwin (Last name as first name) friendly; brave

Ball, Winn

Bamboo (Malay) botanical

BaNaire (Slavic) of God's peace

Banan (Irish) white

Bancroft (English) bean field; gardener

Banc, Bankie, Bankroft

Bandy (Origin unknown) gregarious

Bandee, Bandi

Banjo (Word as name)

Banks (Last name as first name) focused
Bank

Banning (Irish) fair-haired
Bannie, Banny, Bannyng

Bao (Chinese) prized boy

Baptist (Latin) one who has been baptized

Barak (Hebrew) lightning; success
Barrak, Barack

Baram (Hebrew) son of the people

Barclay (Scottish) audacious man; birch tree meadow
Bar, Barclaye, Bark, Barklay, Barky

Bard (Irish) singer
Bar, Barr

Barden (English) peaceful; valley-dweller
Bardon

Bardolf (German) wily hero

Bardrick (English) sings ballads
Bardric

Barek (English) flash

Barend (Scandinavian) bearlike

Baret-Carlyle (American) combo of Baret and Carlyle

Bargo (Last name as first name) outspoken
Barg

Bari (Irish) fair-haired

Baris (Slavic) calm

Barison (English) son of peaceful man

Baritta (Last name used as first name) able

Bark (English) form of Barker: handles bark; lumberjack
Birk

Barker (English) handles bark; lumberjack
Bark, Barkker

Barlaam (History) hermit

Barlam (Hebrew) giving

Barlow (English) hardy
Barloe, Barlowe

Barman (Last name as first name) bright; blessed
Barr

Barn (American) word as name; works in barns
Barnee, Barney, Barny

Barnabas (Hebrew) seer; comforter
Barn, Barnaby, Barnebus, Barney, Barnie, Barny

Barnaby (Hebrew) companionable
Baru, Barnabee, Barnabie, Barnie, Barny

Barnali (Last name used as first name) son of the gatekeeper

Barneo (Place name) barn boy

Barner (English) mercurial
Barn, Barnerr, Barney, Barny

Barnes (English) powerful; bear

Barnett (English) leader of men
Barn, Barnet, Barney

Barney (English) form of Barnett: leader of men
Barn, Barni, Barnie, Barny

Barnum (German) safe; barn
Barnham, Barnhem, Barnie

Baron (English) noble leader
Bare, Baren, Barren, Baryne

Barra (Irish) fair-haired

Barragan (Irish) fenced in

Barrance (Last name used as first name)

Barrett (German) strong and bearlike
Bar, Baret, Barett, Barette, Barry

Barrington (English) dignified
Bare, Baring, Berrington

Barry (Irish) candid
Barre, Barrie, Bary

Barryrex (American) combo of Barry and Rex

Bart (Hebrew) persistent
Bartee, Bartie, Barty

Bartelt (English) form of Bartholomew: friendly; earthy

Barth (Hebrew) protective
Bart, Barthe, Barts

Bartholomew (Hebrew) friendly; earthy
Bart, Barthlolmewe, Bartie

Bartlett (Last name as first name) motivated

Bartley (Last name as first name) rural man
Bart, Bartle, Bartlee, Bartli, Bartly

Barto (Spanish) form of Bartholomew: friendly; earthy
Bartelo, Bartol, Bartoli, Bartolo, Bartolomeo

Barton (English) persistent man; Bart's town
Bart, Barty

Bartosz (Slavic) form of Bartholomew: friendly; earthy

Bartoz (Slavic) form of Bartholomew: friendly; earthy

Bartram (English) intelligent
Bart, Barty

Baruch (Hebrew) most blessed
Barry

Baruti (African) teaches

Basant (Arabic) smiling

Basford (American) charming; low-profile
Bas, Basferd, Basfor

Bash (American) party-loving
Bashey, Bashi, Bashy

Basil (Greek) regal
Basel, Basey, Basile, Bazil

Basim (Arabic) smiles
Bassam

Basir (Turkish) smart

Bass (Last name as first name) fish; charmer
Bassee, Bassey, Bassi, Bassy

Bassam (Arabic) smiles

Bassett (English) small man
Baset, Basett, Basey, Basse

Bastete (Egyptian) fiery cat

Bastian (Greek) respected
Bastien, Bastyun

Basye (American) home-based; centered
Base, Basey

Batch (French) from bachelor; unmarried man
Bat, Bats, Batsh

Bates (English) romantic
Bate

Baudelio (Spanish) bold

Baudoin (Latin) winning

Baudouin (French) bold friend

Bauer (French) small

Baul (Gypsy) slow-moving

Baurice (African American) form of Maurice: dark

Bavan (Welsh) Evan's son

Bavol (Gypsy) windblown

Baxley (English) from the meadow; outdoorsy
Bax, Baxlee, Baxli

Baxter (English) tenacious
Bax, Baxey, Baxie, Baxther

Bay (English) hair of russet; vocal
Baye, Bayie

Bayard (English) russet-haired
Bay, Baye, Bayerd

Bay-Atlas (American) combo of Bay and Atlas; seventh from heaven

Baylon (English) from the bay; outdoorsman

Bayro (Spanish) from the barn

Bazel (French) form of Basil: regal

Bazooka (American) fun-loving; unusual
Bazookah

Bazzy (American) loud
Bazzee, Bazzi, Bazzie

Beacan (Irish) small boy
Beag, Bec, Becan

Beach (English) fun-loving
Bee, Beech

Beacher (English) pale-skinned; beech tree
Beach, Beachie, Beachy, Beecher

Beagan (Irish) small
Beagen, Beagin

Beale (French) attractive

Beal, Beally

Beall (English) handsome

Beaman (English) tends bees

Beamann, Beamen, Beeman

Beamer (English) musician

Beam, Beamy, Beemer

Bean (Scottish) lively

Beann

Beanon (Irish) good boy

Beinean, Beineon, Binean

Bear (Scottish) lively

Beara (American) athletic

Bearach (Irish) spearing

Bearchan, Bercnan, Bergin

Beasley (English) nurturing; pea field

Beas, Beasie, Beesly

Beate (German) serious

Bay, Bayahtah, Baye, Beahta, Beahtae

Beattie (Irish) happy

Beau (French) handsome man

Beaubeau, Bo, Boo, Bow

Beauford (French) attractive

Beau, Beauf, Beaufort

Beaumont (French) attractive and strong

Beau, Bo, Bomont, Bowmont

Beauregard (French) a face much admired

Beau, Beauregarde, Beaurigard, Bobo

Beaver (French) tenacious

Beav, Beave, Beever, Bevoh

Bebe (Spanish) baby

Be-Be

Becher (Hebrew) firstborn

Bee

Beck (English) stream; laid-back

Bec, Becc, Becke, Becker, Bek

Becker (English) calm

Bekker

Becket (English) by the brook

Beckett (English) methodical

Beck, Beket, Bekette

Bede (English) prayerful

Bea, Bead, Beda, Bedah

Bedford (Last name as first name) laid-back

Bedrich (Czech) rules peacefully

Bedro (Spanish) form of Pedro: dependable; rock

Bed

Bedros (Spanish) prays

Beebe (English) tending bees; tenacious

B.B., Bee-be, Beebee

Beechum (English) of the trees (beech)

Beeson (Last name as first name) son of beekeeper; wary

Bees

Beggs (Last name as first name) admired

Begg, Begs

Behlin (Spanish) from Bethlehem

Behrad (Indian) form of Bharat: fire

Beig (English) mouth

Beige (American) calm

Bayge

Beinish (Latin) form of Benedict: blessed man

Beircheart (Welsh) spears

Bela (Hawaiian) beauty

Belden (English) plain-spoken

Beld, Beldene, Beldon, Bell, Bellden, Belldon

Beldon (English) pretty valley child

Belen (Greek) following the arrow's straight path

Belizario (Spanish) archer

Bell (French) handsome man

Bellamy (French) beautiful friend

Belamie, Bell, Bellamie, Bellmee, Belmy

Bellindo (German) ferocious; attractive

Balindo, Belindo, Belyndo

Bello (African) advocates Islam

Belman (English) handsome

Belmount (French) gracious

Belmon, Belmond, Belmonde, Belmont, Belmonta

Belosi (Slavic) humble

Belton (English) from a lovely town of bells

Beltan, Belten

Belvin (American) form of Melvin: friendly

Belven

Belvon (Welsh) smart

Bem (African) peaceful

Ben (Hebrew) form of Benjamin: son of the right hand; son of the south

Benjy, Bennie, Benno, Benny

Benaiah (Hebrew) God-built; wars

Benaya, Benayahu

Benammi (Biblical) comes into his own

Bence (American) form of Benson: son of Ben; brave heart

Bens, Bense, Binse

Bend (American) word as name; lithe

Bendell (Last name used as first name) loving

Ben

Bender (American) tweaker; diplomatic

Ben, Bend

Bendo (American) soothing

Ben, Bend

Benedict (Latin) blessed

Ben, Benedik, Benne, Bennie, Benny

Benes (Czech) blessed

Benesh (Yiddish) blessed

Bengt (Scandinavian) blessed

Beni (Slavic) blessing

Beniah (Hebrew) articulate

Benia, Benyah

Benicio (Spanish) adventurous

Benecio, Benito

Benigno (Latin) kind child

Benito (Italian) blessed

Benedo, Beni, Beno

Benjamin ✪ ✝ (Hebrew) son of the right hand; son of the south

Behnjamin, Ben, Benjamen, Benjamine, Benjie, Benjy, Benni, Bennie, Benny, Benyamin

Benjiro (Japanese) promotes peace

Bennell (Last name used as first name) blessed

Benner (English) blessed

Bennett (French) blessed

Ben, Benet, Benett, Bennet, Bennette, Benny

Benno (Italian) form of Ben: son of the right hand; son of the south

Beno

Benny (Hebrew) form of Benjamin: son of the right hand; son of the south

Benge, Benjy, Benni, Bennie

Benoit (French) growing and flourishing

Ben, Benoyt

Benoni (Hebrew) sorrow

Bensey (American) easygoing; fine

Bence, Bens, Bensee

Benson (Hebrew) son of Ben; brave heart

Bensahn, Bensen

Bent (English) form of Benton: formidable

Bynt

Bentley (English) clever

Bent, Bentlee, Leye

Benton (English) formidable

Bentan, Bentawn, Bentone

Benvenuto (Italian) welcomed child

Ben

Benz (German) from carmaker Mercedes-Benz; upscale

Bens

Benzi (Hebrew) blessed

Beowulf (Literature) warrior

Ber (Hebrew) bear

Berar (French) speaks well

Berdy (German) bright

Beresford (English) place of spears
Berresford

Berfit (Origin unknown) farming; outdoorsman
Berf

Berg (German) tall; mountain
Bergh, Berj, Burg, Burgh

Bergen (Irish) little spear man
Bergin, Birgin

Berger (French) watchful; shepherd
Bergher, Bergie

Bergin (Swedish) loquacious; lives on the hill
Bergan, Berge, Bergen, Berger, Bergin, Birgin

Berj (Scandinavian) form of Birger: helpful

Berk (Turkish) rough-hewn

Berkeley (English) idolized; (place name) town in California
Berk, Berkeley, Berki, Berkie, Berklee, Berkley, Berklie, Berkly, Berky

Berko (Hebrew) bear
Ber

Berks (American) adored
Berk, Berke, Berkelee, Berkey, Berkli, Berksie, Berkslee, Berky, Birklee, Birksey, Burks, Burksey

Berlon (German) loyal

Berman (German) steady
Bermahn, Bermen, Bermin

Bermudez (Spanish) place name; battles

Bernabe (German) bold
Bernabee, Bernabey, Bernaby, Bernby, Bernebe, Berns, Bernus, Burnby

Bernal (German) bearlike
Bern

Bernar (Last name used as first name) hardy

Bernard (German) brave and dependable
Bern, Bernarde, Bernee, Bernerd, Bernie, Berny, Burnard

Bernardo (Spanish) brave; bear
Berna, Bernardo, Barnardoh, Berny

Bernave (American) form of Bernard: brave and dependable
Bernav, Bernee, Berneve, Berni

Bernd (German) bearlike
Bern, Berne, Bernee, Berney, Berny

Berndt (German) hardy

Berne (German) courageous
Bern, Berni, Bernie, Bernne, Berny

Berner (English) bearlike

Bernhard (German) brave

Bernie (German) brave boy
Bern, Berni, Berny, Birnie, Burney

Bernstein (Last name used as first name) brave

Berrios (Spanish) the berries

Berry (English) botanical; flourishing

Bert (English) shining example
Berti, Bertie, Berty, Birt, Burt

Berthold (German) bold ruler
Bert, Berthol, Berthuld, Bertolt, Berty

Berthrand (German) form of Bertram: outstanding
Bert, Berthran, Bertie, Bertrand, Berty

Bertil (Scandinavian) bright
Bertel

Bertin (English) form of Burton: protective; town that is well-fortified
Berton, Burtun

Bertoldo (Spanish) ruler
Bert

Berton (American) form of Burton: protective; town that is well-fortified
Bert, Bertan, Berty

Bertram (German) outstanding
Bert, Bertie, Bertrem, Bertrom, Berty

Bertrand (German) bright
Bert, Bertie, Bertran, Bertrund, Birtryn

Bertren (German) smart

Berts (English) bright

Bertus (Last name used as first name) child of Bert

Berty (English) form of Bert: shining example
Bert, Bertie, Burty

Bervick (American) upwardly mobile; brave
Bervey

Berwyn (English) loyal friend
Berrie, Berwin, Berwynd, Berwynne

Besley (Last name as first name) calm
Bes, Bez

Best (American) word as name; quintessential man
Beste

Betel (Biblical) man of God

Bethel (Hebrew) loves the house of God
Bethell

Bethuel (Biblical) religious

Bettis (American) vocal
Bettes, Bettus, Betus

Beuford (Last name as first name) form of Buford: diligent
Beuf, Bu, Bueford

Beval (Welsh) vivacious

Bevan (Welsh) beguiling
Bev, Bevahn, Beven, Bevin

Bevell (Last name used as first name) craftsman

Bever (English) form of Bevis: strong-willed

Beverly (English) from a stream of beavers; natural

Bevil (English) form of Bevis: strong-willed

Bevis (French) strong-willed
Bev, Bevas, Beves, Bevvis, Bevys, Bevyss

Bexal (American) studious
Bex, Bexlee, Bexly, Bexy

Bexley (Place name) distinguished

Bezalel (Biblical) loyal

Bhakati (Hindi) devoted man

Bhanu (Hindi) sun-loving

Bharat (Hindi) fire

Bhaskar (Hindi) shining

Bhupen (Indian) forest

Biaggio (Italian) stutters; unsure
Biage, Biagio

Bialas (Polish) white-haired
Bialy

Bicken (Last name used as first name) boy with ax

Bickford (English) wields an ax; chops

Bickley (Last name used as first name) boy with ax

Biffy (American) popular
Bibbee, Biff

Bigram (Origin unknown) handsome
Bigraham, Bygram

Bijou (French) jewel

Bijoy (Indian) winning

Biju (French) joy

Bilal (Arabic) selected one

Bill (German) form of William: staunch protector
Billi, Billie, Billy

Billings (Place name) sophisticated

Billy (German) form of William: staunch protector
Bilie, Bill, Billee, Billi, Billie, Bily

Binden (Last name used as first name) binds closely

Bindo (Italian) blessed

Bing (German) outgoing
Beng

Bingo (American) spunky
Bengo, Bingoh

Binh (Vietnamese) a part of the whole

Binkie (English) energetic
Bink, Binki, Binky

Binnie (American) devoted son

Bion (Greek) life

Birch (English) white and shining; birch tree
Berch, Bir, Burch

Bird (American) soaring
Byrd

Biren (American) form of Byron: reclusive; small cottage
Biran

Birger (Scandinavian) helpful

Birinder (Indian) devout

Birkett (English) living in birches; calming
Birk, Birket, Birkie, Birkitt, Burkett, Burkette, Burkitt

Birkey (English) from the birch tree isle
Birkee, Birkie, Birky

Birley (English) outdoorsy; meadow
Berl, Birl, Birlee, Birly

Birney (English) single-minded; island
Birne, Birni, Birny, Burney

Birtle (English) from the hill of birds; natural

Bish (Hindi) universal

Bishamon (Mythology) Japanese god of war and luck

Bishop (Greek) supervisor; serving the bishop
Bish, Bishie, Bishoppe

Bix (American) hip
Bicks, Bixe

Bizzo (American) lively

Bjorn (Swedish) athletic
Bjarn, Bjarne, Bjonie, Bjorne, Bjorny

Black (Scottish) dark
Blacke, Blackee, Blackie

Blackburn (Scottish) lives by a brook; dark

Blade (Spanish) prepared; knife
Bladie, Blayd

Blades (American) sporty

Blagden (English) likes the dark valley

Blaine (Irish) svelte
Blain, Blane, Blayne

Blainen (American) pious

Blair (Irish) open
Blaire, Blare, Blayree

Blaise (French) audacious
Blasé, Blayse, Blaze

Blake ✿ (English) dark and handsome
Blaike, Blakey, Blakie

Blakeley (English) outdoorsy; meadow
Blake, Blakelee, Blakely, Blakie

Blame (American) sad
Blaim, Blaime

Blanchard (Last name as first name) white
Blan

Blanco (Spanish) light
Blancoh, Blonco, Blonko

Blandon (American) form of Brandon: hill; high-spirited

Blanford (English) from the gray ford
Blandford

Blank (American) word as name; blank slate; open
Blanc

Blanket (Invented) security
Blank, Blankee, Blankett, Blankey, Blankie, Blanky

Blanton (English) mild-mannered
Blanten, Blantun

Blasio (Spanish) stutterer
Blaseo, Blasios, Blaze

Blaynn (Last name used as first name) form of Blaine: svelte

Blaze (English and American) daring
Blaase, Blaise, Blazey, Blazie

Blazej (Czech) stutters; insecure

Blazer (American) fiery

Bleddyn (Welsh) heroic

Blendan (Last name used as first name) edge

Bliss (English) happy
Blice, Blyss

Blithe (English) merry
Bly, Blye, Blythe

Blitzer (German) adventurous
Blitz, Blitze

Block (English) on the block; engaged

Blocker (Last name as first name) block

Bloc, Block, Blok

Bloo (American) zany

Blue (Color name) hip

Bleu, Blu

Blunt (Last name used as first name) candid

Blye (American) joyful

Blie

Bo (Scandinavian) lively

Beau

Boat (American) word as name; sea-loving

Bo

Boaz (Hebrew) strong; swift

Bo, Boase, Boaze, Boz

Bob (English) form of Robert: brilliant; renowned

Bobbi, Bobbie, Bobby

Bobby (English) form of Robert: brilliant; renowned

Bob, Bobbie, Bobi

Bobo (African) Tuesday-born

Bocko (English) fair-haired

Bodaway (Native American) fire maker

Boden (French) communicator

Bodin, Bodun, Bowden

Bodhi (Chinese) founder of Ch'an Buddhism in China

Bodhee

Bodhi (American) form of Bodie: laid-back

Bodie (American) laid-back

Bodil (Scandinavian) living

Bodua (African) last one

Bodun (Scandinavian) shelter

Bodynam (Scandinavian) flourishes

Boele (Scandinavian) helpful

Bogan (Slavic) godlike

Bogart (German) bold

Bo, Bobo, Bogardte, Boge, Bogert, Bogey, Bogie

Bogdan (Polish) God's gift

Bogdari (Polish) gift from God

Bogdi

Boggle (American) confusing

Bogg

Boghos (Slavic) strong

Bogumil (Polish) loves God

Bohumil (Polish) favored by God

Bohus (Slavic) favored

Bojan (Czech) fighter

Bojesse (American) comical

Boje, Bojee, Bojeesie, Bojess

Bola (American) careful; bold

Bolah, Boli

Bolden (American) bold man

Boldun

Boleslaw (Polish) in glory

Boleslav

Bolin (Last name as first name) bold

Bolen

Bolivar (Spanish) aggressive

Bolley, Bollivar, Bolly

Bolley (American) strong

Bolly

Bolton (English) town of the bold

Bomani (African) fighter

Boman

Bon (French) good

Bonne

Bonam (English) decent

Bonar (French) gentle

Bonarr, Bonnar, Bonner

Bonaventura (Spanish) good fortune: (Italian) good luck

Bona, Bonavento, Buenaventura, Buenaventure, Ventura

Bonaventure (Latin) humble

Bonaventura, Bonnaventura, Buenaventure

Bond (English) farmer; renegade

Bondee, Bondie, Bondy

Bondee (English) close

Bongani (African) thankful

Bongo (American) type of drum; musical
Bong, Bongy

Boni (Latin) fortunate
Bonne

Bonif (American) giving

Bonifacio (Spanish) benefactor
Bona, Boni, Boniface

Bonner (American) good

Bono (Spanish) good
Bonno

Bonocorso (Italian) good path

Bonsi (Italian) good

Bonyer (American) hopeful

Boo (Literature) recluse in *To Kill a Mockingbird*

Booker (English) lover of books
Book, Booki, Bookie, Booky

Boone (French) blessed; good
Boon, Boonie, Boony

Boonen (English) asset

Bootaan (Unknown) deserted

Booth (German) protective *Boot, Boothe, Boothie, Bootsie*

Boots (American) cowboy
Bootsey, Bootsie, Bootz

Booveeay (Invented) form of Bouvier: elegant; sturdy; ox
Boo

Bordan (English) secretive; of the boar
Borde, Bordee, Borden, Bordi, Bordie, Bordy

Border (American) word as name; fair-minded; aggressive
Bord

Borg (Scandinavian) fortified; castle
Borge, Borgh

Borges (Last name as first name) labyrinthine

Borgey (Scandinavian) castle

Borim (Biblical) place name

Boris (Russian) combative
Boras, Bore, Bores

Borka (Slavic) battles

Bornami (Asian) conflicted

Borr (Russian) contentious

Bos (English) woodsman
Boz

Boscoe (English) woodsman

Boseda (African) Sunday-born

Bosley (English) thriving; grove
Bos, Boslee, Boslie, Bosly

Bosor (Biblical) place name

Bosque (Russian) fighter

Bosser (Scandinavian) lively

Bost (Place name) from Boston
Bostt

Boston (Place name) distinctive
Boss, Bost

Bosvely (English) child from the grove

Boswell (English) well near woods; dignified
Bos, Bosswell, Boz, Bozwell

Botan (Japanese) long-living

Botolf (English) wolf; standoffish
Botof

Bouck (Last name used as first name) worldview

Bour (English) loves the stream

Bourbon (Place name) jazzy
Borbon, Bourbonn, Bourbonne

Bourey (Vietnamese) countryman

Bourne (French) planner; boundary
Bourn, Bourney, Bournie, Byrn, Byrne, Byrnie

Bouvier (French) elegant; sturdy; ox
Bouveah, Bouveay, Bouviay

Bovo (Last name as first name) macho
Bovoh

Bowen (Welsh) shy
Bowie, Bowin

Bowie (Irish) brash; western
Booie, Bowen

Bowing (Last name as first name) blond and young
Beau, Bo, Bow, Bowen

Bowlin (Irish) blond

Bowman (Last name as first name) young; archer
Bow

Bowry (Irish) form of Bowie: brash; western
Bowy

Boy (American) boy child of the family

Boyce (French) defender
Boice, Boy, Boyce

Boyd (Scottish) fair-haired
Boide, Boydie

Boydine (French) from the woods
Boyse

Boydine (American) God's gift

Boydon (Last name used as first name)
fair-haired

Boyer (French) woodsman

Boyette (Last name used as first name) joyful

Boyko (Slavic) fearful

Boylingston (Last name used as first name) sedate

Boyne (Irish) cow; grows

Boysey (Last name used as first name) treasured

Bozarth (Last name used as first name) gifted

Bozidar (Polish) God's precious
Bovza, Bovzek

Brack (English) from the plant bracken; fine
Bracke

Bracken (English) plant name; debonair
Brack, Brackan, Brackin, Brackun

Brackson (English) son of Brack

Bracy (Last name used as first name) holding

Brad (English) form of Bradley: prosperous; expansive
Braddie, Braddy

Brada (American) steadfast

Bradan (English) open-minded
Braden, Bradin, Brady, Bradyn, Braedyn, Braid

Bradford (English) mediator
Brad, Brady

Bradley (English) prosperous; expansive
Brad, Bradie, Bradlee, Bradlie, Bradly

Bradshaw (English) broad-minded
Brad, Brad-Shaw, Bradshie

Brady ○ (Irish) high-spirited
Brade, Bradee, Bradey

Brahma (Hindi) worshipful

Braid (English) form of Bradan: open-minded

Brain (Word as name) brilliant
Brane

Brainard (English) princely
Brainerd

Brait (American) in demand

Braith (Welsh) spotted

Brak (American) support

Bram (Hebrew) form of Abraham: father of a multitude
Brahm, Bramm

Bramb (Dutch) form of Abraham: father of a multitude

Bramly (English) brambles

Bran (Irish) raven; blessed
Brann

Brance (Welsh) dark

Branch (Latin) growing
Bran, Branche

Branco (Last name as first name) authentic
Brank, Branko

Brand (English) fiery
Brandd, Brande, Brandy, Brann

Brandeis (Czech) has a charitable nature

Brandell (Last name used as first name) beacon of light

Brando (American) talented
Brand

Brandon ⊙ ⊤ (English) hill; high-spirited
Bradonn, Bran, Brandan, Brandin, Branny

Brandt (English) dignified
Bran, Brandtt, Brant

Brandy (English) firebrand; bold; brandy drink
Brand, Brandee, Brandey, Brandi, Brandie

Brannon (Irish) bright-minded
Bran, Brann, Brannen, Branon

Bransby (Last name used as first name) beacon of light

Branson (English) persistent
Bran, Brans, Bransan, Bransen

Brant (English) hothead
Brandt

Brantley (English) proud child

Brants (English) proud child

Brashier (French) brash
Brashear, Brasheer

Brasil (Irish) disagrees
Brazil, Breasal, Bresal

Bratcher (Last name as first name) aggressive
Bratch

Bratumil (Polish) brother's love

Braulio (Italian) from a meadow

Braunsen (Last name used as first name) son of brown-haired man

Bravillo (Spanish) brave
Braville

Bravo (Italian) top-notch
Bravoh, Bravvo

Brawley (English) meadow man

Brax (Spanish) scrappy

Braxton (English) worldly
Brack, Brackston, Brax, Braxsten, Braxt

Bray (English) vocal
Brae

Brayan (Origin unknown) to yell out
Brayen

Brayd (English) loyal

Brayden ⊙ (English) effective
Braedan, Braedon, Braydon, Braydun

Braylon (English) steadfast

Brayton (English) town of Bray

Braz (American) mysterious

Brazan (American) mystery

Brazil (Portuguese) reddish brown tree

Brecht (Last name as first) playwright

Breck (Irish) fair and freckled
Breckie, Breckle, Brek

Brecken (Irish) freckled

Brede (Scandinavian) glacier; cold heart

Breeahno (Invented) form of Briano: strong man of honor

Breeon (American) strong

Breer (English) fine

Breeson (American) strong
Breece, Breese, Bresen

Breeze (American) happy
Breese, Breez, Breezy

Bref (American) brave

Brekett (Irish) freckled

Brencis (Russian) sad

Brendan (Irish) armed
Brend, Brenden, Brendie, Brendin, Brendon

Brennan (English) pensive
Bren, Brenn, Brennen, Brennon, Brenny

Brennan (Irish) raven

Brenson (Last name as first name) disturbed; masculine
Brens, Brenz

Brent (English) prepared; on the mountain
Bren, Brint

Brenton (English) forward-thinking; hill town boy
Brent, Brenten, Brintin

Breslin (English) land of Bres

Brett (Scottish) man from Britain; innovative
Bret, Breton, Brette, Bretton, Britt

Brettson (American) manly man; Briton

Brett

Brewer (English) brews

Brewster (English) creative; brewer

Brew, Brewer

Breyen (Irish) strong; aggressive

Brey, Breyan

Brian ✪ ✆ (Irish) strong man of honor

Bri, Briann, Brien, Brienn, Bry, Bryan

Briand (English) jolly

Briander (American) inquisitive; rider of waves

Briano (Celtic) form of Brian: strong man of honor

Briant (American) form of Bryant: honest; strong

Briareus (Mythology) giant with one hundred arms; strong

Brice (Welsh) go-getter

Bryce

Brick (English) alert; bridge

Bricke, Brik

Brickle (American) surprising

Brick, Brickel, Brickell, Bricken, Brickton, Brickun, Brik

Brider (English) of the bride

Bridgely (English) coming from the bridge

Bridgeley

Bridger (English) makes bridges

Bridge

Bridges (English) bridge boy

Bridon (English) bright-eyed

Brielton (English) Briel town

Brig (English) punished

Brigdo (American) leader

Brigg, Briggy

Brigham (English) place name; mediator

Brigg, Briggie, Briggs, Brighum

Brighton (English) from the shining town

Brike (American) creative

Briley (English) calm

Bri, Brilee, Brilie, Brily

Brill (English) climbs

Brimmer (English) hill

Brinden (English) tawny

Brinell (English) tawny

Brink (English) on the precipice

Brinkley (English) meadow on edge

Brinley (English) of the joyful meadow; sweet

Brindley, Brinly, Brynley, Brynly

Briscoe (Last name as first name) forceful

Brisco, Brisko, Briskoe

Brishen (English) craftsman

Bristol (English) place name

Britt (English) humorous; from Britain

Brit, Britts

Brittin (American) boy from Britain

Britton (English) loyal; from Britain

Brock (English) forceful

Broc, Brocke, Brockie, Brocky, Brok

Brockly (English) aggressive

Brocklee, Brockli, Broklee, Broklie, Brokly

Brockton (English) badger; stuffy

Brock

Brod (English) form of Broderick: broad-minded; brother

Broddie, Broddy

Brodall (Irish) rules

Brode (Irish) broad wall

Broder (Scandinavian) true brother

Brolle, Bror

Broderick (English) broad-minded; brother

Brod, Broddee, Broddie, Broddy, Broderic, Broderik, Brodric, Brodrick

Brodie ✪ (Irish) builder

*Brode, Brodee, **Brody***

Brodny (Irish) falling aside; brash

Brodrick (Last name used as first name) ruler's son

Brogan (Irish) sturdy shoe; dependable
Brogann

Bromley (English) meadow of shrubs; unpredictable
Brom, Bromlee, Bromlie, Bromly

Bron (Irish) sadness

Bronc (Spanish) wild; horse
Bronco, Bronk, Bronko

Bronco (Spanish) wild; spirited
Broncoh, Bronko, Bronnco

Brondo (Last name as first name) macho
Bron, Brond

Brone (Irish) sorrow

Bronick (English) brown

Bronnie (American) brown

Bronson (English) Brown's son
Bron, Brondson, Bronni, Bronnie, Bronny, Bronsan, Bronsen

Bronto (American) from brontosaurus; thunderous
Bront, Brontee, Brontey, Bronti, Bronty

Bronze (Metal) alloy of tin and copper; brown
Bronz

Brook (English) easygoing
Brooke, Brookee, Brookie

Brooker (English) stream boy

Brooks (English) easygoing
Brookes, Brooky

Brosio (Spanish) son of the stream

Brost (Spanish) able

Broughton (English) from a protected place

Brow (American) snob
Browy

Brown (English) tan
Browne, Brownie, Browny

Brownie (American) brown-haired
Brown

Brownlee (English) brown-haired

Brownson (Last name used as first name) son of Brown

Broylon (English) noble

Broze (American) soulful

Brubaker (English) brown-haired

Bruce (French) complicated; from a thicket of brushwood
Bru, Brucie, Brucy, Brue

Bruck (English) brown-haired

Bruder (Last name used as first name)

Bruiser (American) tough guy
Bruezer, Bruser, Bruzer

Brumley (French) smart; scattered
Brum

Brundage (Last name used as first name)

Brundo (Spanish) brown-haired

Brune (German) brown-haired

Bruni (German) brown-haired

Bruno (German) brown-skinned
Brune, Brunne, Brunoh

Brunon (Polish) brown-haired

Brush (American) confident

Bruton (Latin) brutal

Brutus (Latin) aggressive; a bully

Bry (American) form of Bryan: ethical; strong

Bryan ✪ ⊕ (Irish) ethical; strong
Brye, Bryen

Bryand (English) form of Bryan: ethical; strong

Bryant (Irish) honest; strong
Bryan, Bryent

Bryce (Welsh) spunky
Brice, Bry, Brye

Brycen (English) fast

Brychan (Welsh) speckled

Brycy (Welsh) lively

Brydon (American) magnanimous
Bridon, Brydan, Bryden, Brydun

Brydson (American) well-liked

Brylee (American)

Bryn (Welsh) hill-dweller

Brynmor (Welsh) big hill

Bryon (American) form of Byron: reclusive; small cottage

Brys (Welsh) spotted

Brysen (English) son of Brice

Bryson (Welsh) Bryce's son; smart
Briceson, Bry, Bryse

Bryton (Welsh) hill town

Bu (Irish) winner; form of Buagh

Bual (English) son of speed

Bubba (German) a regular guy
Bub, Buba, Bubb, Bubbah

Bub-Joo (Asian)

Buck (English) studly; buck deer
Buckey, Buckie, Bucko, Bucky

Buckingham (Last name used as first name) male deer

Buckley (English) outdoorsy; a meadow for deer
Buckey, Buckie, Bucklee, Bucklie, Bucks, Bucky

Bucko (American) macho
Bukko

Bucky (American) warmhearted
Buck, Buckey, Buckie

Bud (English) courier
Budd, Buddie, Buddy, Budi, Budster

Buddy (American) courier
Bud, Buddi, Buddie, Budi

Budington (English) awakened

Budrys (Spanish)

Buell (German) upward; hill
Bue

Buf (English) castle

Buffalo (American) tough-minded
Buff, Buffer, Buffy

Buffington (Last name used as first name) town of Buffing

Buford (English) diligent
Bueford, Bufe, Buforde

Bulgara (Slavic) hardworking
Bulgar, Bulgarah, Bulgaruh

Bulldog (American) rough-and-tough
Bull, Dawg, Dog

Bullock (Last name as first name) practical

Bulmarck (Spanish)

Bulmaro (Spanish) fair

Bumpus (Last name as first name) humorous
Bump, Bumpey, Bumpy

Bunard (English) good
Bunerd, Bunn

Bune (American) free

Bunyan (English) good and burly
Bunyan, Bunyen

Buran (American) complex
Burann, Burun

Burch (English) strong

Burchard (English) tree trunks; sturdy
Burckhardt, Burgard, Burgaud, Burkhart

Burdell (English) in the dell

Burdette (English) shielded

Burditt (Last name as first name) shy
Burdett, Burdette, Burdey

Burford (Last name as first name) from the water

Burge (English) form of Burgess: businessman
Burges, Burgis, Burr

Burgess (English) businessman
Berge, Burge, Burges, Burgiss

Burhan (Last name as first name) complex

Burke (German) fortified
Berk, Berke, Burk, Burkie

Burl (German) homespun

Burley (English) nature-lover; wooded meadow
Burl, Burlea, Burlee, Burli, Burly, Burr

Burnaby (English) brook man

Burne (English) lives by the brook
Bourn, Bourne, Burn, Byrn, Byrne, Byrnes

Burnell (English) of the brook
Burnel

Burnell (French) brown-haired

Burnett (English) by the small brook
Burnet, Burnitt

Burney (English) loner; island
Burn, Burne, Burnie, Burny

Burnie (American) form of Bernie: brave boy

Burnis (English) by the brook; brown-haired
Burn, Burnes, Burney, Burr

Burr (English) prickly; brusque
Burry

Burrell (American) safe

Burrick (English) townsman
Bur, Burr, Burry

Burrin (English) safe haven

Burris (English) sophisticated; living in the town
Berris, Buris, Burr, Burres

Burston (English) safe haven

Burt (English) shining man
Bert, Bertee, Burtie, Burty

Burtard (English) from the stronghold town

Burton (English) protective; town that is well-fortified
Burt, Burty, Brutie

Busby (Scottish) artist; village
Busbee, Busbi, Buzbie, Buzz, Buzzie

Busher (Last name as first name) bold
Bush

Buster (American) fun
Bustah

Bustos (Spanish) jovial

Butcher (English) worker
Butch, Butchy

Butler (English) directing the house; handsome
Butler, Butlir, Butlyr, Buttler

Buxton (Last name as first name) kind

Buz (Biblical) hateful

Buzz (Scottish) popular
Buzy, Buzzi, Buzzie, Buzzy

Byelo (Slavic) white

Byford (English) leaving the cottage; forever young

Byorn (American) form of Bjorn: athletic

Byram (English) stealthy; yard that houses cattle
Bye, Byrem, Byrie, Byrim

Byrd (English) birdlike
Bird

Byrne (English) loner
Birn, Birne, Byrn, Byrni, Byrnie, Byrny

Byrnett (Last name as first name) stable
Burn, Burnett, Burney, Burns, Byrne, Byrney

Byron (English) reclusive; small cottage
Biron, Biryn, Bye, Byren, Byrom, Byrone, Byryn

C

Cab (American) word as name
Cabby, Kab

Cabbon (Biblical) place name

Cabell (Last name as first name) spontaneous

Cable (French) rope-making boy; crafty
Cabel

Cabot (French) loves the water
Cabbott

Cabral (African) Tuesday's child

Cabree (Irish) rides

Cabrera (Spanish) able
Cabrere

Cacal (Last name used as first name) noisy

Cack (American) laughing
Cackey, Cackie, Cacky, Cassy, Caz, Kass, Kassy, Khaki

Cactus (Botanical) prickly
Cack, Kactus

Cadas (Biblical) place name

Cadby (Norse) spirited heritage

Caddock (Last name as first name) high spirits

Cade (English) stylish; bold; round
Cadye, Kade

Cadel (Welsh) fierce

Caden ⚹ (English) spirited
Cadan, Cade, Cadun, Caiden, Kaden, Kayden

Cadman (Irish) fighter
Cadmann

Cadmar (Greek) fiery
Cadmarr

Cadmus (Greek) one who excels; prince
Cad, Cadmuss, Kadmus

Cadon (American) friendly

Cadou (Welsh) fights

Cady (American) forthright
Cadee, Cadey, Cadie

Cael (Irish) slim

Caesar (Latin) focused leader
Caeser, Caez, Caezer, Cesaro, Cezar, Seezer

Caetan (Irish) slim

Cage (American) dramatic
Cadge

Caglar (American) able

Cagle (Spanish) winner

Cailen (American) gentle
Kail, Kailen, Kale

Cain (Hebrew) aggressive
Caine, Cainen, Cane, Kain, Kane

Cairn (Welsh) stone; sturdy
Cairne

Caj (Scandinavian) from Gaius (Caesar's first name); masculine

Caja (American) close proximity

Cal (Latin) form of Calvin: bald
Callie, Kal

Calah (Scandinavian) outdoors

Calam (Scottish) peaceful

Calbert (American) cowboy
Cal, Calbart, Calberte, Calburt, Callie, Colbert

Calcher (American) peaceful

Calden (English) singer

Calder (English) stream; flowing
Cald, Kalder

Calderon (Spanish) stream; flowing
Cald, Kald, Kalder, Kalderon

Caldwell (English) refreshing; cold well

Cale (Hebrew) slim; good heart
Kale

Caleb ⚹ ⊕ (Hebrew) faithful; brave
Cal, Calab, Cale, Caley, Calie, Calub, Kaleb

Calek (American) fighter; loyal
Calec, Kalec, Kalek

Calen (Irish) slim
Cailun

Calendt (American) slim

Caler (English) promising

Caley (Irish) slender

Calf (American) cowboy
Kalf

Calfray (American) singer

Calhoun (Irish) limited; from the narrow woods
Cal, Calhoon, Calhoune, Callie

Calixto (Spanish) handsome
Calex, Calexto, Cali, Calisto, Calix, Callie, Cally, Kalixto

Call (Native American) flourish

Callahan (Irish) spiritual
Cal, Calahan, Calihan, Callie

Callard (Last name used as first name) thrives

Callie (American) form of Calvin: bald
Cal, Calley, Calli, Cally

Callistua (Greek) most beautiful man

Callo (American) attractive
Cal, Cally, Kallo

Cally (Scottish) peacemaker

Calman (Last name as first name) caring
Cal

Calno (Biblical) place name

Calum (Irish) cal
Callum, Calym, Calyme

Calv (American) form of Calvert: respected; herding

Calvary (American) word as name; herding all
Cal, Kal, Kalvary

Calvert (English) respected; herding
Cal, Calber, Calbert, Calver, Kal, Kalvert

Calvin (Latin) bald
Cal, Calvie, Kal

Cam (Scottish) form of Cameron: mischievous; crooked nose
Camm, Cammey, Cammie, Cammy, Kam

Camara (African) instructs

Cambell (American) form of Campbell: bountiful; crooked mouth
Cam, Cambel, Cammy, Kambell

Camberg (Last name as first name) valley man
Cam

Cambio (Italian) short

Cambridge (Place name) city in England; twisting; mover
Cambrydge

Camden (Scottish) conflicted
Cam, Camdan, Camdon

Camerero (Last name as first name) charismatic

Cameron ✪ (Scottish) mischievous; crooked nose
Cam, Camaron, Camerohn, Cami, Cammy, Camren, Camron

Camiel (Spanish) helps

Camilo (Latin) helpful; (Italian) free
Cam, Camillo

Cammer (Spanish) hall worker

Campbell (Scottish) bountiful; crooked mouth
Cambell, Cammie, Camp, Campie, Campy

Campillo (Spanish) form of Camilo: helpful

Campion (English) champion

Camrin (American) form of Cameron: mischievous; crooked nose

Camron (Scottish) form of Cameron: mischievous; crooked nose
Camren

Can (Turkish) vibrant

Canaan (Biblical) spiritual leanings
Cane, Kanaan, Kanan

Canada (Place name) from Canada

Canal (Word as name) waterway
Kanal

Candelario (Spanish) bright and glowing
Cadelario

Cander (American) candid
Can, Candor, Candy, Kan, Kander, Kandy

Candido (Spanish) pure; candid
Can, Candi, Candide, Candy

Candle (American) bright; hip
Candell

Cangelo (Spanish) vibrant

Canice (Spanish) seamless

Cannon (French) courageous
Canney, Canni, Cannie, Canny, Canon, Canyn, Kannon, Kanon

Cano (Scottish) attractive

Canow (American) like a canon

Canten (American Indian) hunter

Canute (Scandinavian) great
Knut, Knute

Canyon (Nature) hip

Capan (American) bird; jaunty

Capi (American) high energy

Capon (American) bird; captain

Capone (Last name used as first name) risk-taker

Capote (Italian) bright

Cappy (French) breezy; lucky
Cappey, Cappi

Capua (Biblical) place name

Caractacus (Latin) bold

Carad (American) wily
Karad

Caradine (Spanish) birdlike

Caravaggio (Italian) painter

Caravale (Last name used as first name) dear valley girl

Carballo (Spanish) explosive

Card (English) form of Cardan: crafty; carder
Kard

Cardan (English) crafty; carder
Card, Carden, Cardon

Cardente (Spanish) clarity; craftsman

Carder (Last name used as first name) confident

Cardew (Welsh) dark

Cardin (Irish) dark home

Cardoc (Welsh) loved

Cardozo (Spanish) supportive

Cardwell (English) craftsman
Kardwell

Carel (Dutch) free

Carew (Latin) runner
Carrew

Carey (Welsh) masculine; by the castle
Care, Cari, Cary, Karey

Cari (English) masculine
Care, Carie, Cary

Carino (Last name as first name) strong

Carl (Swedish) kingly
Karl

Carland (Last name as first name) land of free men

Carlin (Irish) winning
Carlan, Carle, Carlen, Carlie, Carly

Carlisle (English) strengthens
Carl, Carly, Carlyle

Carlo (Italian) sensual; manly
Carl, Carloh

Carlon (Irish) form of Carl: kingly
Karlon, Carlonn

Carlos ✪ (Spanish) manly; sensual
Carl, Carlo

Carlson (English) son of a manly man
Carls, Carlsan, Carlsen

Carlton (English) leader; town of Carl
Carleton, Carltan, Carlten, Carltown, Carltynne

Carmel (Hebrew) growing; garden
Carmell, Karmel

Carmello (Italian) flourishing
Carm, Carmel, Carmelo, Karmello

Carmi (Biblical) beloved son; (Italian) garden

Carmichael (Scottish) bold; Michael's follower
Car, Kar, Karmichael

Carmine (Italian) carmane
Carmin, Carmyne, Karmen, Karmine

Carmo (Italian) songs

Carmody (French) manly; adult
Carmodee

Carn (English) winner

Carneg (Slavic) horner

Carnell (Irish) victor
Car, Carny, Kar, Karnell, Karney

Carney (Irish) winner
Carn, Carnay, Carnee, Carnie, Carny

Caro (Hungarian) horn boy

Carol (Irish) champion
Carroll, Carrol, Carroll

Carpus (Greek) bountiful

Carr (Scandinavian) outdoorsy
Car, Kar

Carrew (Latin) runner

Carrick (Irish) lives on rocky place

Carrier (Last name used as first name) growth

Carroll (German) masculine; winner
Carall, Care, Carell, Caroll, Carrol, Carrolle, Carry, Caryl

Carson ✪ (English) confident
Carr, Cars, Carsan, Carsen

Carsten (German) a Christian

Carswell (English) diligent

Cart (American) word as name; practical
Cartee, Cartey, Kart

Carter ✪ (English) insightful
Cart, Cartah, Cartie

Cartrell (English) practical
Car, Cartrelle, Cartrey, Cartrie, Cartrill, Kar, Kartrel, Kartrell

Cartwright (English) creative
Cart, Cartright, Kart, Kartwright

Carungay (Spanish) crass

Caruso (Italian) musically inclined
Karuso

Carvell (English) innovative
Carvel, Carvelle, Carver, Karvel

Carver (English) carver
Carve, Carvey, Karver, Karvey

Cary (English) pretty brook; charming
Carey

Casady (English) curly-haired

Casdeen (American) assertive; ingenious
Kassdeen

Case (Irish) highly esteemed
Casey

Caseen (Dutch) together

Casel (English) boisterous

Casen (Last name used as first name) bound

Casey (Irish) courageous
Case, Casi, Casie, Kacie, Kacy, Kase, Kaysie

Cash (Latin) conceited
Casha, Cashe, Cazh

Cashmere (American) smooth; soft-spoken
Cash, Cashmeer, Cashmyre, Kashmere

Cashone (American) cash-loving
Casho

Casiano (Latin) empty

Casimir (Polish) peace-loving
Casmer, Casmir

Casimiro (Spanish) famous; aggressor
Casmiro, Kasimiro

Caslu (Biblical) turmoil

Casper (German) secretive
Caspar, Caspey, Caspi, Caspie, Cass

Caspian (Place name) sea near Iran; daring

Caspin (Biblical) place name

Cass (Irish) form of Cassidy: humorous
Cash, Caz, Kass

Cassell (English) saintly

Cassian (Last name used as first name) thinker

Cassidy (Irish) humorous
Casidy, Cass, Cassadie, Cassidee, Cassidie, Kasidy, Kass, Kassidy

Cassie (Irish) form of Cassidy: humorous
Casi, Cass, Cassy

Cassius (Latin) protective
Cass, Casseus, Casshus

Cast (Greek) form of Castor: eager protector
Casta, Caste, Kast

Castellan (Spanish) adventurer

Caster (English) saint

Castern (Last name used as first name) reliable

Castle (Last name used as first name) sturdy

Casto (Mythology) form of Castor: eager protector; (Spanish) star; (Greek) truthful
Cass, Kasto

Castor (Greek) eager protector
Cass, Caster, Castie

Castulo (Spanish) aggressor
Castu, Kastulo

Cata (American) form of Catarino:
unflawed; perfect

Catarino (Spanish) unflawed; perfect
Catrino

Cathal (Irish) leader

Cather (Last name used as first name)
virile

Cathmor (Irish) brave warrior

Cato (Latin) zany and bright
Catoe, Kato

Catou (French) wise

Cauda (Biblical) place name

Caudell (Last name used as first
name) pure

Caughtry (Welsh) fighter

Cavan (Irish) attractive man
Cavahn, Caven, Cavin

Cavance (Irish) handsome
Caeven, Cavanse, Kaeven, Kavance

Cavell (Last name as first name)
opinionated
Cavil, Cavill

Cavin (Irish) safe; stylish

Cavinal (Irish) not of substance;
hollow

Cawley (Last name as first name)
brash

Cayce (American) form of Casey:
courageous
Cace, Case, Kayce

Caycen (American) of the case

Cayern (Last name used as first
name) makes cases

Cayetano (Spanish) feisty; destiny

Cayeto (Spanish) survivor

Caynce (Invented) form of Cayce:
courageous
Caincy, Cainse, Kaynse

Cayo (American) smart

Cazare (Last name as first name)
daring
Cazares

Ceabron (Last name used as first
name) giving

Cease (American) rowdy

Cebriane (Spanish) form of Cyprus:
island south of Turkey; outgoing

Cebron (Spanish) generous

Cecil (Latin) unseeing; hard-headed;
blind
Cece, Cecel, Cecile, Cecilio, Cicile

Cedar (Botanical) tree name; sturdy
Ced, Sed, Sedar

Cedric (English) leader
Ced, Ceda, Cedrick

Ceferino (Spanish) careful

Celedonio (Spanish) heavenly

Celius (Spanish) celestial

Celso (Italian) heavenly
Celesteno, Celestino, Celesto, Celestyno,
Celsus, Selso

Celsorio (Last name used as first
name) soars

Celum (Spanish) holly berries

Celumiel (Spanish) of the heavens
Celu

Celvan (Slavic) winning

Cemal (Arabic) handsome

Cender (Spanish) articulate; peace

Cened (Slavic) wins

Cengiz (Inventive) weapon

Cenobio (Spanish) shy

Centola (Spanish) tenth child
Cento

Century (Invented) remarkable
Cen, Cent

Cerb (Greek) dark mind

Cerber (Mythology) three-headed

Cerbulo (Spanish) serene

Cerce (Greek) form of Circe; thinker

Ceres (Greek) loving

Cerf (French) buck

Cerlito (Spanish)

Ceron (Greek) thunders

Cerone (French) serene; creative
Serone

Cervacio (Spanish) serves

Cervando (Spanish) fawning

Cervant (Spanish) original

Cervantes (Literature) for the
Spanish author; original
Cervantez

Cesaire (French) form of Caesar

Cesar (Spanish) leader
Cesare, Cezar, Zarr

Cesar-Vega (Spanish) combo of
Cesar and Vega; famed star

Cetrell (Spanish) centered

Chaban (American) form of Chabe:
from Shabe in Bible

Chabe (Biblical) from Shabe in the
Bible

Chacko (Spanish) form of Chico: boy

Chad (English) firebrand
Chadd, Chaddy

Chadburn (English) spirited

Chaden (English) battles

Chadley (English) cautions

Chads (English) aggressive

Chadson (English) son of Chad;
comforts

Chadwick (English) warrior
Chad, Chadwyck

Chaffee (Last name as first name)
bold adventurer

Chaggy (American) cocky
Chagg, Shagg, Shaggy

Chaicus (Biblical) strong

Chaika (Hebrew) life
Chai , Chaikeh, Chaikel, Chaiki

Chaim (Hebrew) life
*Chai, Chayim, Haim, Hy, Hyman,
Hymie, Khaim, Manny*

Chaise (French) chases
Chayse

Chaker (Arabic) best

Chalen (American) strong

Chalfie (American)

Chalfin (Last name used as first
name)

Challen (American) form of Allen:
handsome boy

Chalmer (Scottish) the Lord's son
Chall, Chally, Chalmers

Chalmers (French) chambers;
surrounded; (Scottish) Lord's child
Chalm

Chamara (Asian) diligent

Chamb (American) messenger

Chambers (English) regal boy

Chamblin (American) easygoing
Cham

Chan (Chinese) bright; Vietnamese
truthful

Chanan (Hebrew) filled with God's
compassion

Chance (English) good fortune;
happy
*Chancey, Chanci, Chancy, Chanse,
Chanz, Chauncey*

Chancela (American) dedicated

Chancellor (English) book keeper
Chance, Chancey

Chand (Indian) sun

Chanda (Indian) brightness

Chandell (African American)
innovator
*Chandelle, Chandey, Chandie, Shandel,
Shandell*

Chanderkala (Hindi) luminous

Chandler (English) ingenious;
(French) maker of candles
Chand, Chandey, Chandlor

Chandru (Indian) moon

Chaney (French) strong
Chane, Chanie, Chayne, Chaynee

Chang (Chinese) free; flowing

Chanina (Hebrew) compassionate by
virtue of God

Channing (English) brilliant
Chann, Channy

Chanoch (Hebrew) dedicated; loyal

Chantan (Indian) sparkle

Chante (French) singer
Chant, Chanta, Chantay, Chantie

Chapa (Last name as first name) merchant; spirited
Chap, Chappy

Chaparro (Spanish) from chaparral southern landscape; cowboy
Chap, Chaps

Chapel (Last name used as first name) singer

Chapell (Hindi) spiritual

Chapen (French) clergyman
Chapin, Chapland, Chaplin

Chaplin (Last name used as first name) pious

Chapman (English) businessman
Chap, Chappy

Chappelle (French) of the chapel

Char (French) truthful; spiritual

Charilaos (Greek) giving

Charlem (English) of Charles

Charlemagne (French) historic; King of the Franks "Charles the great"

Charles ☺ (German) manly; well-loved
Charl, Charley, Charli, Charlie, Charly, Chas, Chaz, Chazz, Chuck

Charleston (English) Charles's town; confident
Charlesten

Charlie (German) manly
Charl, Charley, Charli, Charly

Charlie-John (American) combo of Charlie and John

Charlton (English) leader
Charles, Charley, Charlie, Charlt

Charome (American) masculine
Char, Charoam, Charom, Charrone, Charry

Charon (Greek) mythological ferryman of the underworld

Charro (Spanish) wild-spirited cowboy
Charo, Charroh

Charudata (Hindi) beautiful

Charvaka (Hindi) form of Charudata: beautiful

Chas (American) form of Charles: manly; well-loved

Chase ○ (French) hunter
Chace, Chass

Chaskel (Hebrew) strong

Chason (French) hunts
Chansen

Chat (American) happy
Chatt

Chatham (Last name as first name) serious

Chatsworth (English) warrior's place

Chatwin (Last name as first name) thoughtful

Chaucer (Literature) for Geoffrey Chaucer; distinguished
Chauce, Chauser

Chaudray (French) hopeful

Chauncey (English) fair-minded
Chance, Chancey, Chanse, Chaunce

Chausse (English) form of Chauncey: fair-minded

Chavers (English) stern

Chavivi (Hebrew) beloved

Chavlier (French) elegant

Chayne (Scottish) swagger
Chane, Channe, Chay

Chaz (German) form of Charles: manly; well-loved
Chas, Chazz, Chazzie, Chazzy

Ché (Spanish) form of José: asset; favored
Chay, Shae, Shay

Ched (French) form of Shad: joyful

Chee (American) high-energy
Che

Chekhov (Russian) playwright; genius

Chen (Chinese) great

Cheney (French) outdoorsman
Chenay, Cheney

Cheramy (American) form of Jeremy: talkative
Charamie, Cheramee, Chermy

Cheran (Biblical) dearest

Chermon (French) my dear

Cherno (Slavic) black

Chesed (Biblical) difficult

Chesley (American) patient
Ches, Cheslee, Chez, Chezlee

Chesman (Last name used as first name) hard

Chester (English) comfy-cozy
Ches, Chessie, Chessy

Chesterfield (English) field of Rochester; comforting

Chet (English) creative
Chett

Chetan (Indian) vibrant

Chetny (Native American) determined

Chetwin (English) winding road

Chevalier (French) gallant
Chev, Chevy

Chevalle (French) dignified
Chev, Chevi, Chevy

Cheven (Invented) playful
Chevy

Chever (Place name)

Chevery (French) form of Chevy: clever
Chev, Shevery

Chevy (French) clever
Chev, Chevi, Chevie, Chevv

Chew (Chinese) mountain

Chiamaka (African) God is good

Chibale (Hebrew) loving

Chick (English) form of Charles: manly; well-loved
Chic, Chickie, Chicky

Chico (Spanish) boy
Chicoh, Chiko

Chief (Word as name) leader

Chieko (Spanish) boy

Chiel (Hebrew) God lives

Chijoke (African) talented

Chikosi (African) the ruins

Chili (American) appetite for hot food

Chillen (American) form of Chilton: serene; farm

Chilton (English) serene; farm
Chill, Chillton, Chilly, Chilt

Chimanga (African) grain

Chimento (Italian) of the chimes

Chin (Korean) precious boy

Chip (English) chip off the old block; like father
Chipp, Chipper

Chiram (Hebrew) held in high esteem

Chiriga (Indian) lights the way

Chisholm (Place name) from Chisholm Trail: pioneer spirit
Chis, Chishom, Chiz

Chita (Spanish) fiery

Chito (American) fast-food eater; hungry
Cheetoh, Chitoh

Chiura (Italian) light; textured

Chiztam (Hebrew) imbued with God's strength

Chobi (Spanish) buddy

Chogie (Spanish) friendly

Choicey (American) word name; picky
Choicie, Choisie

Chombel (American) birdlike

Chonito (Spanish) friend
Chonit, Chono

Chopo (American) cowhand
Chop, Choppy

Choto (Spanish) kid
Shoto

Chotto (Last name as first name) child

Chovev (Hebrew) companion

Chow (Chinese) everywhere

Chris (Greek) form of Christopher: the bearer of Christ
Cris, Chrissy, Chrys

Christer (Norwegian) religious
Krister

Christian ✪ ❂ (Latin) follower of
Christ
Chris, Christen, Christiaan, Christiane,
Christyan, Cristian, Kris, Krist, Kristian

Christo (Spanish) christian

Christodoulous (Greek)
filled with sweet love for Christ

Christop (Greek) christian

Christophe (French) beloved of
Christ
Cristoph, Kristophe

Christopher ✪ ❂ (Greek) the
bearer of Christ
Chris, Christofer, Crista, Cristopher,
Cristos, Kit, Kristopher

Christopherson (English) son of
Christopher; religious
Christophersen, Cristophersen,
Cristopherson

Christos (Greek) form of
Christopher: the bearer of Christ
Chris, Kristos

Chubby (American) oversized
Chubbee, Chubbey, Chubbi, Chubbie

Chuck (German) rash
Chuckee, Chuckey, Chuckie, Chucky

Chuckles (American) clown

Chucky (German) impulsive
Chuckey, Chucki, Chuckie

Chuey (Spanish) form of Charles:
manly; well-loved

Chuhei (Japanese) shy

Chuna (Hebrew) warm

Chuneh (Hebrew) with the Lord's
grace

Chunky (American) word name; large
Chunk, Chunkey, Chunki

Chur (American) form of Churchian:
spirited

Churchian (American) spirited

Churchill (English) bright
Church

Chutar (Spanish) aiming for goals
Chuter

Chux (American) clear

Chuxin (American) clear

Chuyen (Native American) clear

Cian (Irish) old soul

Ciano (Irish) old

Cibab (German) giving

Cicero (Latin) strong speaker
Cice

Ciceron (Latin) chickpea

Cicil (English) shy
Cecil, Cice

Cid (Spanish) leader; lord
Ciddie, Ciddy, Cyd, Sid

Cielo (Spanish) light

Cieran (Spanish) clarity

Cigler (Last name used as first name)

Cimarron (Place name) city in New
Mexico; cowboy
Cimaronn

Cinco (Spanish) fifth child
Cinko, Sinko

Cione (Italian) Last name used as first
name

Ciprian (Latin) from the island of
Cyprus
Cipriano

Ciriaco (Italian) lordly

Ciriak (Spanish) believer

Ciriako (Italian) lord's child

Cirill (English) form of Cyril: regal

Cirillo (Spanish) lordly
Cirilo

Ciro (Italian) lordly
Ciroh, Cirro, Cyro

Cirrus (Latin) thoughtful; cloud
formation
Cerrus, Cirrey, Cirri, Cirrie, Cirry,
Cirus, Serrus, Serus

Cisco (American) clever
Sisco, Sysco

Cisto (Spanish) form of Francisco:
free spirit; from France

Citlalis (Spanish) star

Citronella (American) oil from
fragrant grass; pungent

Cit, Citro, Cytronella, Sitronella

Cival (English) form of Percival: mysterious

Civille (American) form of Saville: willow town

Clady (French) form of Claude: slow-moving; lame

Claiborn (English) born of earth
Claiborne

Clair (English) renowned
Claire, Clare

Clairon (French) clear

Clamente (Spanish) form of Clemente: pleasant

Clance (Irish) form of Clancy: lively; feisty redhead
Clancy, Clanse, Klance, Klancy

Clancy (Irish) lively; feisty redhead
Clancey, Clancie

Claney (American) form of Clancy: lively; feisty redhead

Clant (American) form of Clancy: lively; feisty redhead

Clanton (Last name used as first name)

Claran (Latin) bright
Clarance, Claranse, Claransi, Clare, Claren, Clarence, Clary, Klarense

Clarence (Latin) intelligent
Clarance, Clare, Clarens, Clarense, Clarons, Claronz, Clarrence, Klarence, Klarens

Clarinett (Invented) plays the clarinet
Clare, Clarinet, Clary, Klare, Klari

Clark (French) personable; scholar
Clarke

Clarkey (Last name used as first name) scholar

Clarson (American) clarity

Clary (English) clear

Clater (English) premier

Claude (Latin) slow-moving; lame
Claud, Claudey, Claudie, Claudy, Klaud, Klaude

Claudemir (Slavic) lame

Claudene (Italian) lame

Claudimir (Slavic) lame

Claudio-Clyde (Slavic) combo of Claudio and Claude

Claus (Greek) victorious
Klaas, Klaus

Clausen (English) form of Nicholas: the people's victory

Claven (English) endorsed
Klaven

Clavero (Spanish) lame

Clavey (Last name used as first name)

Clawdell (American) form of Claude: slow-moving; lame
Clawd

Claxton (English) townie
Clax, Klax

Clay (English) reliable
Claye, Klae, Klay

Claybey (American) southern; earthly
Claybie, Klaybee

Clayborne (English) earthly
Clabi, Claybie, Clayborn, Claybourne, Klay

Claybrook (English) sparkling smile
Claibrook, Clay, Claybrooke, Clayie

Clayeo (Spanish) form of Clay: reliable

Clayton (English) stodgy
Clay, Claytan, Clayten

Claywell (English) by the clay well

Cleadis (American) form of Cletus: creative; selected
Famed

Cleary (Irish) smart
Clear, Clearey, Cleàrie

Cleavon (English) daring
Cheavaughn, Cleavaughn, Cleave, Cleevaughan, Cleevon

Clegg (Last name used as first name)

Clem (Latin) casual
Cleme, Clemmey, Clemmie, Clemmy, Clim

Clemen (American) forgives

Clement (Scottish) gentle
Clem, Clemmyl

Clemente (Spanish) pleasant
Clemen, Clementay

Clements (Latin) forgiving man
Clem, Clement, Clemmants, Clemment

Clemer (Latin) mild
Clemmie, Clemmy, Klemer, Klemmie, Klemmye

Clemmie (Latin) mild
Clem, Klem, Klemmee, Klemmy

Clenzy (Spanish) forgiving; cleansed
Clense, Clensy, Klenzy

Cleofas (African American) brave lion

Cleofe (Greek) famed

Cleon (Greek) famed man
Clee, Cleone, Kleon

Cleophas (Greek) seeing glory; known
Cle, Cleofus, Cleoph, Klee, Kleofus, Kleophus

Clete (Greek) form of Cletus: creative; selected
Cleet, Cleete

Cletus (Greek) creative; selected
Clede, Cledus, Cletis

Cleve (English) precarious
Clive

Cleveland (English) daring
Cleavelan, Cleve, Clevon, Clevy, Cliveland

Clevis (Greek) prolific
Cleviss, Clevys, Clevyss

Cliff (English) form of Clifford: dashing
Clif, Cliffey, Cliffie, Cliffy

Cliffen (American)

Clifford (English) dashing
Cleford, Cliff, Cliffy, Clyford

Clift (American) cliff-dweller
Clifte

Clifton (English) risk-taker
Cliff, Cliffian, Cliffien, Cliffy

Clim (American) form of Clem: casual

Cline (Last name as first name) musical

Clint (English) form of Clinton: town on a hill
Clent, Clynt, Klint

Clinton (English) town on a hill
Clenton, Clint, Clinten, Clynton, Klinten, Klinton

Clipper (American) boatsman

Clive (English) daring; living near a cliff
Cleve, Clyve

Clive-John (English) combo of Clive and John

Cliven (English) cliff boy

Clodagh (Scottish) winning

Clooney (American) dramatic
Cloone, Cloonie, Cloony, Clune, Cluney, Clunie, Cluny

Clotaire (French) famous
Clotie, Klotair, Klotie

Clovis (German) famed warrior
Clove, Cloves, Clovus, Klove, Kloves, Klovis

Clowry (Last name used as first name)

Cloyd (American) form of Floyd: practical; hair of gray
Cloy, Cloye, Kloy, Kloyd

Cloyd (American) form of Clyde: adventurer

Clske (Dutch) dark

Clue (Word as name)

Cluny (American) dramatic

Clwe (Dutch) face of a mountain

Clyde (Welsh) adventurer
Clide, Clydey, Clydie, Clydy, Clye, Klyde, Klye

Clydell (American) countrified
Clidell, Clydel

Clydenestra (Spanish) form of
Clyde: adventurer

Coad (English) form of Coady:
comforted

Coady (English) comforted

Coal (American) word as a name
Coale, Koal

Coat (Native American) snake

Cobalt (Word as name) from the
cottage

Cobb (English) cozy
Cob, Cobbe

Cobbie (American) form of Jacob:
he who supplants

Coben (Last name as first name)
creative
*Cob, Cobb, Cobe, Cobee, Cobey, Cobi,
Coby, Kob, Kobee, Koben, Kobi, Koby*

Cobern (English) stream spot

Cobian (American) form of Jacob: he
who supplants

Coble (English) cobler

Cobo (American) friendly

Cobus (Dutch) friend

Coby (American) friendly
Cob, Cobe, Cobey, Cobie

Coca (American) excitable
Coka, Cokey, Cokie, Koca, Koka

Cochise (Native American) warrior
Cocheece, Cochize

Cochran (Last name used as first
name)

Cocinero (Italian) slippery

Coco (French) brash
Coko, Koko

Coder (Last name used as first
name) form of Cody: comforting

Codrington (Last name used as first
name) form of Cody: comforting

Codryll (Last name used as first
name) form of Cody: comforting

Cody (English) comforting
*Coday, Code, Codee, Codey, Codi,
Codie*

Coe (American) form of Cody:
comforting

Coenraad (Dutch) form of Conrad:
optimist

Coffey (English) Friday's child

Coffie (English) Friday's child

Coffman (Last name used as first
name)

Cog (American) form of Cogdell:
needed
Kog

Cogan (English) form of Kegan: ball-
of-fire

Cogdell (Last name as first name)
needed
Cogdale

Coggin (Last name used as first
name)

Cohn (American) winner
Kohn

Coil (Hebrew) giving

Coitlee (American) silver

Coitoine (French) silver

Cokie (American) bright
Cokey, Coki, Cokki, Kokie

Col (American) the colonel

Colak (Irish) bright

Colbert (English) cool and calm
*Colbey, Colbi, Colbie, Colburt, Colby,
Cole*

Colborn (English) intimidating; cold
brook
Colbey, Colborne, Colburn, Colby, Cole

Colby (English) bright; secretive; dark
farm
Colbey, Colbi, Colbie, Cole, Colie

Colden (English) haunting
Coldan, Coldun, Cole

Cole ✪ (Greek) lively; winner
Coal, Coley, Colie, Kohl, Kole

Colee (American) victor

Coleman (English) lively; peacemaker
Cole, Colemann, Colman, Kohlman

Coley (American) victor

Colgate (English) passway
Colgait, Colgaite, Kolgate

Colier (Last name as first name) sophisticated

Colin (Irish) young and quiet; peaceful; the people's victor
Colan, Cole, Colen, Collin, Collyn

Colis (English) he who delights others

Collan (Irish) farms

Coller (Irish) farms

Collett (English) black hair

Colley (English) dark-haired
Col, Colli, Collie

Collier (English) hardworking; miner
Colier, Collie, Colly, Colyer

Collies (English) delights

Collin (Scottish) shy
Collen, Collie, Collon, Colly

Collins (Irish) shy; holly
Collens, Collie, Collons, Colly, Kolly

Colm (Irish) dove; peaceful

Colorado (Place name) U.S. state; multicolored

Coloss (Biblical) colossal

Colson (English) precocious; son of Nicholas
Cole, Colsan, Colsen

Colster (English) colts

Colston (English) young horse town

Colt (English) frisky; horse trainer
Colty, Kolt, Koltt

Colten ✪ (English) dark town; mysterious
Cole, Collton, Colt, Coltan, Coltawn,
Colton, *Kol*

Colter (English) keeping the colts
Colt, Coltor, Colty

Colum (Latin) peaceful; dove
Colm, Kolm, Kolum

Columba (Latin) dove; calm

Columbus (Latin) peaceful; discovered America
Colom, Colombo, Columbe

Colvint (Spanish) river

Colwen (Irish) peaceful
Colvin, Colwin

Comanche (Native American) tribe; wild-spirited; industrious
Comanch, Komanche

Combs (English) Last name used as first name

Commander (Word as name) leader

Commodore (French) commander

Como (Spanish) similar
Comoh

Comus (Greek) humorous
Comas, Comes, Commus, Komus

Con (Irish) form of Conan: worthy of praise

Conal (Irish) strong; wolflike;
Conall

Conall (Scottish) highly regarded
Conal

Conan (Irish) worthy of praise
Conen, Connie, Conny, Conon

Conant (Irish) top-notch
Conent, Connant

Concini (Italian) Last name used as first name

Concord (English) agreeable
Con, Concor, Conny, Koncord, Konny

Conde (Last name as first name) driven

Cong (Chinese) bright

Conger (Irish) tall

Coniah (Irish) pure
Conias, Conah

Conk (Invented) from conch mollusk of the ocean; jazzy
Conch, Conkee, Conkee, Conky, Kanch, Konk, Konkey

Conkel (Last name used as first name)

Conkey (Last name used as first name)

Conklin (English) Last name used as first name

Conlach (Irish) in accord

Conlan (Irish) winner
Con, Conland, Conlen, Conleth, Conlin, Connie, Conny

Conleth (Welsh) hero

Conley (Celtic) hero

Connable (Last name used as first name)

Connaughton (American) sapient

Connell (Irish) strong
Con, Conal, Connall, Connel, Connelle, Connie, Conny

Connelly (Celtic/Gaelic) Last name used as first name; friendship

Connery (Scottish) daring
Con, Conery, Connarie, Connary, Connie, Conny

Connie (Irish) form of Connor: brilliant; form of Conrad: optimist
Con, Conn, Connee, Connery, Conney, Connie, Conny

Connor ✪ (Scottish) brilliant
Con, Conn, Conner, Conor, Kon, Konnor

Conra (Irish) wise

Conrad (German) optimist
Con, Connie, Conny, Conrade, Konrad

Conrado (Spanish) bright advisor
Conrad, Conrod, Conrodo

Conradt (Welsh) Last name used as first name; bold in counsel

Conreed (Welsh) brave

Conridge (Last name as first name) advisor
Con, Conni, Connie, Conny, Ridge

Conroy (Irish) wise writer
Conrie, Conroye, Conry, Roy, Roye

Conrye (American) form of Conrad: optimist

Considine (Last name used as first name) considerate

Consis (Mythology) flourishing

Constant (French) devotee; loyal

Constantine (Latin) constant; steadfast
Con, Conn, Consta, Constance, Constant, Constantin, Constantyne, Konstantin

Consydin (American) form of Considine: considerate

Conte (Italian) accountable

Conway (Irish) vigilant
Con, Connie, Kon, Konway

Cooke (Latin) cook
Cook, Cookie, Cooky

Cooker (English) cooks

Coolidge (Last name as first name) wary
Cooledge

Cooney (Last name as first name) giving

Cooper ✪ (English) handsome; maker of barrels
Coup, Couper, Koop, Kooper, Kouper

Coos (Dutch) friend

Cope (English) able
Cape

Coptos (Biblical) place name

Coral (Nature) from Hebrew goral; pebble

Corbell (Latin) raven; dark
Corbel

Corbet (Latin) dark
Corb, Corbett, Corbit, Corbitt, Korb, Korbet

Corbie (Latin) raven

Corbin (Latin) dark and brooding
Corban, Corben, Corby

Corbitt (Last name as first name) brooding
Corbet, Corbett, Corbie, Corbit, Corby

Corblee (American) dark

Corby (Latin) dark
Corbey, Korbee, Korby, Korry

Corcoran (Irish) ruddy-skinned
Corkie, Corky

Cord (Origin unknown) soap opera
hunk
Corde, Kord

Cordaro (Italian) roped

Cordel (French) practical
Cordell, Cordelle, Cordie, Cordill,
Cordy

Cordell (Latin) bound; rope

Cordero (Spanish) gentle
Cordara, Cordaro, Cordarro, Kordarro,
Kordero

Cordi (Spanish) makes ropes

Cordry (American) makes ropes

Corentin (French) stormy

Coret (French) stormy

Corey (Irish) laughing
Core, Corie, Corry, Cory, Korey, Korrie,
Kory

Coril (American) coral

Corin (Latin) combative
Coren, Dorrin, Koren, Korrin

Corinth (Biblical) from Corinthians

Cork (Place name) county in Ireland
Corkee, Corkey, Corki, Corky, Kork

Corkeen (American) form of Corky:
casual

Corkel (American) form of Corky:
casual

Corkson (American) son of Corky

Corky (American) casual
Corkee, Corkey, Korky

Corl (English) cheery

Corlan (English) of good cheer

Corlon (American) tasteful

Cormac (Irish) the raven's offspring;
watchful
Cormack, Cormak

Cormic (Irish) raven

Cormick (Last name as first name)
old-fashioned
Cormac, Cormack

Corn (Latin) form of Cornelius: horn;
loquacious
Korn

Cornall (Irish) form of Cornelius:
horn; loquacious

Cornelio (Spanish) horn blower

Cornelius (Greek) horn; loquacious
Coarn, Conny, Corn, Corni, Cornie,
Corny, Kornelius, Neel, Neely, Neil,
Neiley

Cornell (French) fair
Corne, Cornelle, Corny, Kornell

Cornellian (Greek) horn color

Coro (Spanish) form of Coronnel:
colonel

Corodon (Greek) lark

Coronnel (Spanish) colonel

Corrado (Italian) worthy advisor

Corrigan (Irish) aggressive
Coregan, Corie, Correghan, Corrie,
Corry, Koregan, Korrigan

Cors (Spanish) from Corsica

Corso (Spanish) form of Kyros:
masterful
Sun

Cort (German) eloquent
Corte, Court, Kort

Cortal (Last name used as first name)
intellectual

Cortant (Spanish) bitter

Cortazar (Last name as first) creative

Cortell (Spanish) cuts

Cortez (Spanish) victorious; explorer
Cortes

Corum (English) form of Corwin:
heart's delight

Corvey (Greek) crest

Corvin (English) friend
Corwin, Corwynn, Korry, Korvin

Corwen (English) delights the heart

Corwin (English) heart's delight
Corrie, Corry, Corwan, Corwann,
Corwyn, Corwynne

Cory (Latin) humorous
Coarie, Core, Corey, Corrie, Kohry, Kori

Coryell (Greek) lark; devious

Cos (Biblical) place name; orderly

Cosell (French) outgoing

Cosgrove (Irish) winner
Cosgrave, Cossy, Kosgrove, Kossy

Cosimo (Greek) orderly

Cosma (Greek) universal
Cos, Kosma

Cosmas (Greek) universal
Cos, Kosmas, Koz

Cosmedin (Spanish) harmony

Cosmo (Greek) in harmony with life
Cos, Cosimo, Cosimon, Cosme, Cosmos,
Kosmo

Cosner (English) organized;
handsome
Cosnar, Kosner

Costas (Greek) constant
Costa, Costah

Coste (Greek) form of Constantine:
constant; steadfast

Costel (Slavic) constant

Costello (Italian) form of
Constantine: constant; steadfast

Cotledge (Last name used as first
name) by the cottage ledge

Cotrer (Last name used as first name)
contrary

Cotter (American) gregarious

Cottingham (Last name used as first
name) day by day

Cottlings (English) in the cottage

Cotton (Botanical name) casual
Cottan

Cottrell (English) in the cottage

Coty (French) comforter
Cotey, Coti, Cotie, Koty

Coug (American) from cougar; fierce
Cougar, Koug, Kougar

Couland (French) from court land

Coulter (English) dealing in colts;
horseman
Colter, Coult, Kolter, Koulter

Council (French) advisor

Counsel (Latin) advisor
Consel, Council, Kounse, Kounsell

Country (Word as name) cowboy

Court (English) royal

Courtland (English) born in the land
of the court; dignitary

Courtnay (English) sophisticated
Cort, Corteney, Court, Courtney,
Courtny

Covell (English) warm
Covele, Covelle

Covet (American) word as name;
desires
Covett, Covette, Kovet

Covington (English) distinctive
Covey, Coving, Kovey, Kovington

Cowan (Irish) cozy
Cowen, Cowie, Cowy

Cowboy (American) western

Cowden (Irish) cave in the hill

Cowell (English) brash; frank
Kowell

Cowey (Irish) reclusive
Cowee, Cowie, Kowey

Coye (English) outdoorsman
Coy, Coyey, Coyie

Coyle (English) in the woods

Coylie (American) coy
Coyl, Koyl, Koylie

Coyne (French) demure

Coystal (American) bashful
Coy, Koy, Koystal

Crad (American) practical
Cradd, Krad, Kradd

Craddock (Last name as first name)
practical

Crager (Scottish) from the crags

Crago (Last name as first name)
macho
Crag, Craggy, Krago

Craig (Irish) brave climber
Crai, Craigie, Cray, Craye, Crayg, Creg,
Cregge, Kraig

Crain (English) cranes

Crandal (English) open
Cran, Crandall, Crandell, Crane

Crandale (English) from the land of cranes

Crandall, Crandell

Crandan (English) from the cranes

Cranley (English) lives in a field of cranes

Cranston (English) from the town of cranes

Cranyon (English) from the cranes

Craon (Greek) leader

Crawford (English) flowing

Crafe, Craford, Craw, Fordy

Cray (English) place name

Crayton (English) substantial

Craeton, Cray, Creighton

Creach (Scottish) home-loving

Creasy (English) Last name used as first name

Creed (American) believer

Crede, Creede, Creyd, Kreed

Creek (English) word as name

Creigh (English) lives near rocks

Creighton (English) sophisticated

Criton

Crenshaw (Last name as first name) good intentions

Crescin (Latin) expansive

Cresencio (Spanish) integrity

Creshaun (African American) inspired

Creshawn, Kreshaun

Cresp (Latin) man with curls

Crisp, Crispen, Crispun, Crispy, Cryspin, Kresp, Krisp, Krispin, Krispyn

Crever (Irish) sly fox

Crevin (Irish) sly fox

Crew (American) word as name; sailor

Krew

Crey (English) form of Creighton: sophisticated

Craedie, Cray, Creigh, Creydie

Crider (English) creek

Cris (Welsh) form of Crisiant: crystallike

Crisanto (Spanish) anoint

Crisiant (Welsh) crystallike

Crisman (Greek) golden

Crisoforo (Spanish) gold clothing; form of Christopher; bearer of Christ

Crispin (Latin) man with curls

Chrispy, Crespen, Crispo, Crispy, Krispin, Krispo

Crispo (Latin) curly-haired

Crisp, Krispo

Crist (Spanish) Christian

Cristhian (Greek) Christian

Cristian (Greek) form of Christian: follower of Christ

Kristian

Cristino (Greek) christian

Cristo (Spanish) mountain of Christ

Kristo

Cristobal (Spanish) bearing Christ

Cristovo (Greek) serves Christ

Criten (American) form of of Critendon: critical

Critan, Kriten

Critendon (Last name as first name) critical

Crit, Criten, Krit, Kritendon

Crofton (Irish) comforter

Croft, Croften

Crolley (English) Last name used as first name

Cromaci (Greek) decorated

Cromer (English) adorned

Crompton (Last name as first name) giving

Cromwell (Irish) giving

Chromwell, Crom, Crommie

Cronin (German) timely

Cronus (Greek) reigning

Croom (American) giving

Crosby (Irish) easygoing

Crosbee, Crosbie, Cross, Krosbie, Krosby

Crosson (English) of the cross

Croston (English) by the cross

Cro, Croton, Kroston

Croswell (English) cross on the well

Crosy (American) of the cross

Crosz (American) of the cross

Crothers (Scottish) Last name used as first name

Crow (English) crow

Crowson (English) son of Crow

Crue (American) form of Crew: word as name; sailor

Cruo (Spanish) cross

Crutcher (English) fighter

Cruz (Spanish) cross

Cruze (Spanish) cross
Cruise, Cruse, Kruise, Kruze

Cruzon (Spanish) cross

Csaba (Hungarian) shepherd

Ctirad (Czech) long-suffering

Cuauhtemoc (Spanish) eagle

Cuba (Place name) distinctive; spicy
Cubah, Cueba, Kueba, Kuba

Cubbenah (African) Wednesday

Cubby (American) child

Cucuta (Place name) city in North Colombia; sharp
Cucu

Cudjo (Jamaican) Monday

Cuelly (American) wild spirit

Cuernavaca (Place name) city in Mexico; cow horn
Vaca

Cuffy (Jamaican) Friday
Cuffee, Cuffey

Cuke (American) zany
Kook, Kooky, Kuke

Culber (American) woods child

Culbert (Last name as first name) practical

Culkin (American) child actor
Culki, Kulkin

Cull (American) selective
Cullee, Cullie, Cully, Kulley

Cullen (Irish) attractive
Culen, Cull, Cullan, Cullen, Cullie, Cully, Kullen, Kully

Culley (Irish) secretive
Cull, Cullie, Cully, Kull, Kully

Cullom (American) wood

Culver (English) peaceful
Colver, Cull, Culley, Culli, Cully

Culverado (American) peaceful
Cull, Cullan, Culver, Culvey, Kull

Cumal (Native American) thunders

Cummings (Literature) for the poet E.E. Cummings; innovative
Cumming, Kummings

Cuney (Last name as first name) serious
Cune, Kune, Kuney

Cuneyt (Scandinavian) warmth

Cunning (Irish) from surname Cunningham; wholesome
Cuning

Cunningham (Irish) milk-pail town; practical
Cuningham

Cupid (Latin) heart's desire

Curb (American) dynamic
Kurb

Curbey (American) form of Kirby: brilliant
Curby

Curbow (Last name used as first name) stone

Curer (French) helps

Curgus (Greek) cunning

Curie (French) innovator

Curley (American) cowboy
Curly, Kurly

Curo (Spanish) sheltered

Curran (Irish) smiling hero
Curan, Curr, Curren, Currey, Currie, Curt

Currere (French) sheltered

Currey (English) messenger; calm

Currie (English) messenger; courteous
Kurrie

Curro (Spanish) form of Curtis: gracious; kindhearted

Curt (French) form of Curtis: gracious; kindhearted
Kurt

Curtis (French) gracious; kindhearted
Curdi, Curdis, Curt, Curtey, Curtice, Curtie, Curtiss, Curty, Kurt

Cush (American) thrives

Custer (Last name as first name) watchful; stubborn
Cust, Kust, Kuster

Cuthah (Biblical) place name

Cuthbert (English) intelligent

Cutle (English) makes knives

Cutler (English) wily
Cutlar, Cutlur, Cuttie, Cutty

Cutlon (English) knife maker

Cutrer (French) knife dealer

Cutsy (English) form of Cutler: wily
Cutlar, Cuttie, Cutty, Kutsee, Kutsi, Kutsy

Cutter (English) man who cuts gemstones

Cuttino (African American) athletic
Kuttino

Cuyler (American) form of Schuyler: protective
Kuyler

Cy (Greek) shining example
Cye, Si

Cybor (American) leader

Cygan (Last name used as first name) shines

Cyler (Irish) protective chapel
Cuyler, Cyle

Cyll (American) bright
Cyl, Syll

Cynric (Greek) thorn

Cyone (Greek) whirlwind

Cyprien (French) religious
Cyp, Cyprian

Cyprus (Place name) island south of Turkey; outgoing

Cyrano (Greek) shy heart
Cyranoh, Cyre, Cyrie, Cyrno, Cyry

Cyree (Greek) Lord

Cyril (Greek) regal
Ciril, Cyral, Cyrell, Cyrille

Cyrilon (Spanish) lofty

Cyrus (Persian) sunny
Cye, Syrus

Cyrx (American) conniving
Cyrxie

Czech (Slavic) Czech

Czeslaw (Polish) honorable
Slav, Slavek

D

Dablo (Spanish) form of Diablo: devil

Dabney (English) careful; funny
Dab, Dabnee, Dabnie, Dabny

Dabriel (American) teaches

Dacey (Irish) southerner
Dace, Dacian, Dacius, Dacy, Daicey, Daicy

Dacga (Slavic) emotional

Dachary (English) form of Dachry: stream

Dache (Latin) audacious

Dachry (English) stream

Dacias (Latin) brash
Dace, Daceas, Dacey, Dacy, Dayce, Daycie

Dacko (American) zany

Dacosta (Italian) from the coast

Dacus (Last name used as first name)

Dada (African) curly-haired

Dade (Place name) county in Florida; renegade
Daide, Dayde

Dadean (English) curly

Dadley (English) curly

Daedalus (Greek) father of Icarus; inventor
Daidalos, Dedalus

Dag (Scandinavian) sunny
Dagg, Dagget, Daggett, Dagny

Dagan (Hebrew) earthy
Dagon

Dagfinn (Scandinavian) sunshine

Daggan (Scandinavian) day

Daggs (Scandinavian) day

Dagny (Scandinavian) day
Dag

Dagoberto (Spanish) day
Dagbert, Dagobert

Dagwood (English) comic
Dag, Dawood, Woody

Dahryan (Indian) compassionate

Dahy (Irish) lithe
Dahey

Dai (Japanese) great man

Daigle (Last name used as first name) dark

Daiki (Japanese) shining

Dailey (English) form of Dale: valley
Daily, Daley, Daly

Dain (Scandinavian) from Denmark

Dainard (Irish) loved
Dainehard, Dainhard, Daneard, Daneardt, Danehard, Danehardt, Daynard

Dairus (Invented) daring
Daras, Dares, Darus

Daithi (Irish) speedy

Daivat (Hindi) powerful man

Dakarai (African) happy
Dakarrai, Dakk

Dako (American) form of Dakota: friendly

Dakota (Native American) friendly
Daccota, Dack, Dak, Dakoda, Dakodah, Dakoetah, Dakotah, Dekota, Dekohta, Dekowta, Kota

Dakote (Place name) from the Dakotas
Dako

Dalai (Indian) peaceful
Dalee

Dalanee (Invented) form of Delaney: challenging
Dalaney, Dalani

Dalbert (English) man who lives in the valley
Del, Delbert

Dalcher (Last name used as first name) gathers

Dale (English) valley
Dail, Daile, Daley, Dallan, Dalle, Dallin, Day, Dayl, Dayle

Dalen (English) up-and-coming
Dalan, Dalin, Dallen, Dallin, Dalyn

Daley (Irish) organized
Dailey, Daily, Dale

Dalgienuz (Slavic) valor

Dalgus (American) loving the outdoors

Dalhart (Place name) city in Texas
Dal

Dalin (Spanish) proud

Dallard (English) proud

Dallas (Place name) good old boy; city in Texas
Dal, Dall, Dalles, Dallice, Dallis, Dallus, Delles

Dallin (English) valley-born; fine
Dal, Dallan, Dallen, Dallon

Dallin (American) form of Dylan: sea god; creative

Dalphy (French) dolphin

Dalsten (English) smart
Dal, Dalston

Dalt (English) abundant
Dall, Daltey, Daltt

Dalton (English) farmer
Daleton, Dall, Dallton, Daltan, Dalten

Daltrey (English) high river

Dalvis (Invented) form of Elvis: all-wise
Dal, Dalves, Dalvus, Dalvy

Daly (Irish) together
Daley, Dawley

Dalziel (Scottish) from the field

Damacio (Spanish) calm; tamed
Damas, Damasio, Damaso, Damazio

Damarcus (African American)
confident
D'Marcus, Damarkes, Damarkus, Demarcus

Damare (Greek) form of Damario:
tamer of wild things

Damari (Greek) gentle

Damario (Spanish) tamer of wild
things
Damarios, Damarius, Damaro, Damero

Damarion (Greek) form of
Damario: tamer of wild things

Damary (Greek) tame
Damaree, Damarie

Damascus (Place name) capital of
Syria; dramatic
Damas, Damask

Damaskenos (Greek) form of
Damascus: dramatic
Damaskinos

Damaso (Spanish) taming
Damas

Damean (American) form of
Damian: fate
Dama, Daman, Damas, Damea

Dameetre (Invented) form of
Dimitri: fertile; flourishing

Damek (Czech) earth
Adamec, Adamek, Adamik, Adamok, Adha, Damick, Damicke

Dameone (Greek) form of Damian:
fate

Dameron (American) form of
Cameron: mischievous; crooked nose

Damian (Greek) fate
Daemon, Daimen, Daimon, Daman, Dame, Damean, Damen, Dameon, Damey, Damiano, Damianos, Damianus, Damien, Damion, Damon, Damyan, Damyean, Damyen, Damyon, Damyun, Dayman, Daymian, Daymon, Demyan

Damiko (Slavic) gentle

Damin (Greek) comforts

Damon (Greek) dramatic; spirited
Damonn, Damyn

Damron (Greek) comforts

Damyi (American) comforts

Dan (Hebrew) form of Daniel: judged
by God; spiritual
Dahn, Dannie, Danny

Dana (Scandinavian) light-haired
Danah, Dane, Danie, Dayna

Danar (English) from Denmark; dry

Danaus (Mythology) king of Argos
Denaus, Dinaus

Dand (Scottish) form of Andrew:
manly and brave

Dandin (Hindi) holy man

Dandre (American) light
Aiondrae, Dan, Dandrae, Dandray, DeAndrae, DeAndray

Dandrer (French) form of Dandre:
light

Dandridge (English) Last name used
as first name

Dandy (Hindi) form of Dandin: holy
man

Dane (English) man from Denmark;
light
Dain, Daine, Daney, Danie, Danyn, Dayne, Dhane

Daneck (American) well-liked
Danek, Danick, Danik, Danike, Dannick

Danel (Hebrew) God judges

Danely (Scandinavian) Danish
Dainely, Daynelee

Danerin (Slavic) giving

Danez (English) helpful

Danfer (Slavic) faithful

Danford (English) place name; the way
or ford of the Danes

Dang (Vietnamese) worthy

Dangelle (Italian) angelic

Dangelo (Italian) angelic
Danjelo

Danger (American) dangerous
Dang, Dange, Dangery

Danial (Hebrew) form of Daniel:
judged by God; spiritual

Daniel ✪ ✝ (Hebrew) judged by
God; spiritual
*Da, Danal, Dane, Daneal, Danek, Dani,
Danial, Daniele, Danil, Danilo, Danko,
Dann, Dannel, Danney, Danni, Dannie,
Danniel, Danny, Danyal, Danyel,
Danyell, Danyyell, Deiniol*

Danilo (Slavic) form of Daniel:
judged by God; spiritual

Danilon (Slavic) form of Daniel:
judged by God; spiritual

Danne (Biblical) form of Daniel:
judged by God; spiritual
Dann

Danner (Last name as first name)
rescued by God
Dan, Dann, Danny

Danno (Hebrew) kind
Dannoh, Dano

Danny (Hebrew) form of Daniel:
judged by God; spiritual
*Dan, Dann, Dannee, Danney, Danni,
Dannie*

Danon (French) remembered
Danen, Danhann, Dannon, Danton

Danron (American) combo of Dan
and Ron

Dante (Latin) enduring
*Dan, Danne, Dantae, Dantay, Dantey,
Dauntay, Dayntay, Dontae, Dontay,
Donté*

Danter (Latin) form of Dante:
enduring

Dantin (American) form of Daniel:
judged by God; spiritual

Danton (Last name as first name)
Dan's town

Dantre (African American) faithful
*Dantrae, Dantray, Dantrey, Dantri,
Dantry, Don, Dont, Dontre, Dontrey,
Dontri*

Dantrell (African American) spunky
Dantrele, Dantrill, Dantrille

Dantzler (American) form of Daniel:
judged by God; spiritual

Danube (Place name) flowing; river
Dannube, Danuube, Donau

Danut (Slavic) form of Dan: judged
by God; spiritual

Danyo (Hebrew) form of Daniel:
judged by God; spiritual

Danza (English) form of Denzel:
sensual

Daphnis (Greek) attractive

Daquan (African American)
rambunctious
*Dakwan, Daquanne, Dekwan,
Dekwohn, Dekwohnne, Dequan,
Dequanne*

Dar (English) deerlike

Darb (Irish) form of Darby: free spirit

Darbrie (Irish) free man; lighthearted
Dar, Darb, Darbree, Darbry

Darby (Irish) free spirit
*Dar, Darb, Darbee, Darbey, Darbie,
Darre, Derby*

Darce (Irish) dark
D'Arcy, Darcy, Dars, Darsy

Darcel (French) dark
*Dar, Darce, Darcelle, Darcey, Darcy,
Darsy*

Darcell (Irish) dark hair

Darcus (Irish) dark hair

Darcy (French) slow-moving
Darce, Darse, Darsey, Darsy

Dard (Greek) clever

Dardanos (Greek) adored
Dar, Dardanio, Dardanios, Dardanus

Darhen (American) form of Darwin:
dearest friend

Darian (American) inventive
*Dari, Darien, Darion, Darrian,
Darrien, Darrion, Derreynn*

Darin (Irish) great

Daren, Darren, Darrie, Daryn

Dario (Spanish) rich

Darioh, Darrey

Darion (Irish) great potential

Dare, Darien, Darrion, Daryun

Daris (Greek) form of Darius: affluent

Darius (Greek) affluent

Dare, Dareas, Dareus, Darias, Dariess, Dario, Darious, Darrius, Derrius, Derry

Darji (American) rich

Dark (Slavic) form of Darko: macho

Dar, Darc

Darkell (English) brunette

Darko (Slavic) macho

Dark

Darko (English) brunette

Darlen (American) darling

Darlan, Darlun

Darman (English) hidden

Darnell (English) secretive

Dar, Darn, Darnall, Darnel, Darnie, Darny

Darnley (English) sly

Darold (American) clever

Dare, Darrold, Darroll, Derold

Daron (Irish) great

Darren, Dayron

Daros (Greek) loved

Darr (English) loved

Darrah (Irish) dark

Darach, Darragh

Darrel (Aboriginal) blue sky

Darral, Darrell, Darrill, Darrol, Darroll, Darry, Darryl, Darryll, Daryl, Derrel, Derrell, Derril, Derrill, Deryl, Deryll

Darrell (French) loved man

Darel, Darol, Darrel, Darrey, Daryl, Derrel, Derrell

Darren (Irish) great

Daren, Darin, Daron, Darran, Darrin, Darring, Darron, Darryn, Derrin, Derron, Derry

Darrett (American) form of Garrett: brave; watchful

Dare, Darry

Darrick (American) form of Derrick: bold heart

Darrien (Greek) with riches

Darian, Darion, Darrian, Darrion, Darryan, Darryen

Darrien (Irish) greatness

Darris (Greek) rich

Darrti (American) fast; deer

Dart, Darrt

Darryl (French) darling man

Darrie, Daryl, Derrie, Deryl, Deryll

Darshak (Sanskrit) insight

Darshan (African American) pious

Dart (English) decisive

Darte, Dartt

D'Artagnan (French) leader; ostentatious

Darton (English) swift; deer

Darty (American) Last name as first name

Darvin (English) friendship

Darwin (English) dearest friend

Dar, Darwen, Darwinne, Darwon, Darwyn, Derwin, Derwynn

Daryn (American) form of Darin: great

Darynn, Deryn

Darynth (English) form of Darren: great

Dash (American) speedy; dashing

Dashy

Dashawn (African American) unusual

Dashaun, Deshaun, Deshawn, D'Sean, D'Shawn

Dashell (African American) dashing

Dashiell

Dasher (American) dashing; fast

Dash

Dashiell (English) from author Dashiell Hammett

Dasno (Latin) royal

Dassinger (Last name as first name)

Dathan (Biblical) fountain of hope

Dauer (Last name as first name)

Daufen (French) dolphin

Dault (English) valley boy

Davao (Place name) city in the
Philippines; exotic
Davo

Dave (Hebrew) form of David:
beloved
Davey, Davi, Davie, Davy

Daven (American) dashing
Davan

Davender (Hebrew) form of David:
beloved

Davenport (Last name as first name)
of the old school; sea-loving

Davey (Hebrew) form of David:
beloved
Dave, Davee, Davi, Davie, Davy

Davian (Hebrew) dear one
*Daivian, Daivyan, Daveon, Davien,
Davion, Davyan, Davyen, Davyon*

David ✪ ✆ (Hebrew) beloved
*Daffy, Daffyd, Dafydd, Dai, Davad,
Dave, Daved, Davee, Daven, Davey,
Davi, Davide, Davie, Davies, Davin,
Davis, Davon, Davy, Davyd, Davydd*

Davidpaul (American) beloved
David-Paul

Davidson (English) son of David
Davidsen, Davison

Davik (Slavic) form of David: beloved

Davin (Scandinavian) smart
Dave, Daven, Dayven

Davinal (American) form of David:
beloved

Davinno (English) bright

Davins (American) form of David:
beloved
Davens

Davion (American) form of David:
beloved

Davis (Welsh) David's son; heart's
child
*Dave, Daves, Davidson, Davies,
Davison, Daviss, Davy*

Davon (American) sweet
*Davaughan, Davaughn, Dave, Davone,
Devon*

Davonnae (African American) form
of David: beloved
Davawnae, Davonae

Davonne (American) form of Davin:
smart

Davonte (African American)
energetic
Davontay, Devonta, D'Vontay

Daw (English) quiet
Dawe, Dawes

Dawber (Last name as first name)
funny
*Daw, Dawb, Dawbee, Dawbey, Dawby,
Daws*

Dawes (Last name used as first name)
form of David: beloved

Dawk (American) spirited
Dawkins

Dawkins (Last name used as first
name) form of David: beloved

Daws (English) dedicated
Daw, Dawsen, Dawz

Dawson (English) David's son; loved
*Daw, Dawe, Dawes, Dawsan, Dawse,
Dawsen, Dawsey, Dawsin*

Dax (French) unique; water-loving
Dacks, Daxie

Day (English) calm
Daye

Dayanand (Hindi) a loving man

Dayman (Greek) form of Damon:
dramatic; spirited

Daymond (Invented) compassionate

Dayt (Last name used as first name) day

Dayton (English) the town of David;
planner
*Daeton, Day, Daye, Daytan, Daytawn,
Dayten, Deytawn, Deyton*

Dazh (Slavic) giver

Dazo (American) form of David: beloved

Dazon (American) form of David: beloved

Deacon (Greek) giving
Deakin, Decon, Deecon, Deekon, Dekawn, Deke, Dekie, Dekon, Diakonos

Deadon (French) form of Dieudonne: loves a gracious God

Deagan (Last name as first name) capable
Degan

Deak (American) form of Richard: wealthy leader

Dean (English) leader
Deane, Deanie, Deany, Deen, Dene, Deyn, Dino

DeAndré (African American) very masculine
DeAndrae, D'André, DeAndray, Diandray, Diondrae, Diondray

Deangelo (Italian) sweet; personable; angelic
Dang, Dange, DeAngelo, D'Angelo, Deanjelo, Deeanjelo, DiAngelo, Di-Angelo

Deans (English) sylvan; valley
Dean, Deaney, Deanie

Deanthony (African American) rambunctious
Deanthe, Deanthoney, Deanthonie, Deeanthie, Dianth

Deanza (Spanish) smooth
Denza

Dearborn (Last name as first name) endearing; kind from birth
Dearbourn, Dearburne, Deerborn

Dearing (Last name as first name) endearing
Dear

Dearmon (Last name used as first name) man of deer

Dearon (American) dear one
Dear

Deason (Invented) cocky
Deace, Deas, Dease, Deasen, Deasun

Debdan (Indian) God's gift

Debonair (French) with a beautiful air; elegant and cultured
Debonaire, Debonnair, Debonnaire

Debrum (Czech) kindness

Debythis (African American) strange
Debiathes

Decatur (Place name) city in Illinois; special
Dec, Decatar, Decater, Deck

Deccan (Place name) region in India; scholar
Dec, Dek

Decimus (Latin) tenth child
Decio

Deck (Irish) form of Declan: strong; prayerful
Decky

Declan (Irish) strong; prayerful
Dec, Deck, Dek, Deklan, Deklon

Dedal (Greek) artistic

Dedan (Indian) form of Deodan: serving God

Deddrick (American) form of Dedric: leader
Dead, Dedric, Dedrick, Dedrik, Dietrich

Dedeaux (French) sweet
Dede, Dee

Dederic (American) substance

Dedlus (Greek) industrious

Dedric (German) leader
Dedrick, Deidrich

Dee (American) form of names that start with D
D, De

Deek (American) form of Deacon: giving
Deke

Deeley (Irish) assembly

Deems (English) merits

Deepak (Sanskrit) light of knowledge

Depak, Depakk, Dipak

Dees (Slavic) desires

Deeter (American) friendly

Deter

DeForest (French) of the forest

Defforest

DeFoy (French) child of Foy

Defoy, Defoye

Degner (Slavic) of the day

Degraf (French) child of Graf

DeGraf

Dehlin (American) form of Dylan:
sea god; creative

Deicy (Latin) God-loving

Deidric (German) rules

Deidrich (German) leader

*Dedric, Dedrick, Deed, Deide,
Deidrick, Diedrich*

Deinol (Greek) form of Daniel:
judged by God; spiritual

Deinorus (African American)
vigorous

Denorius, Denorus

Deion (Greek) form of Dion: joyous
celebrant; god of wine

Dee

Dejanee (Slavic) action-oriented

Dejuan (African American) talkative

*Dajuan, Dajuwan, Dejuane, Dejuwan,
Dewaan, Dewan, Dewaughan, Dewon,
Dewonn, Dewuan, Dwon, Dwonn,
Dwonne*

Dejuon (American) form of Dejuan:
talkative

Deke (Hebrew) form of Dekel: palm
tree

Deek

Dekel (Hebrew) palm tree

Del (English) valley; laid-back and
helpful

Dail, Dell, Delle

DeLane (Irish) form of Delaney:
challenging

Delaney (Irish) challenging

*Del, Delaine, Delainey, Delainie,
Delane, Delanie, Delany, Dell*

Delano (Irish) dark

Del, Delaynoh, Dell

Delanoy (Irish) darkness

Delayme (American) form of
Delaney: challenging

Delber (English) daylight

Delbert (English) sunny

*Bert, Bertie, Berty, Dalbert, Del,
Delburt, Dell, Dilbert*

Deleon (Spanish) Last name used as
first name

Delete (Origin unknown) ordinary

Delette

Delfino (Spanish) dolphin; sea-loving

Define, Fino

Delgado (Spanish) slim

Delin (English) of the sea

Delius (Greek) from the island Delos

Deli, Delia, Delios, Delos

Delk (American) celebrant

Dell (English) from the country;
sparkles

Delley (Scandinavian) fascinates

Dellin (Scandinavian) fascinates

Delling (Norse) shines

Delm (Scandinavian) charismatic

Delman (French) from the mountain

Delmar (Last name as first name)
friendly

Delm

Delmer (American) country

Del, Delmar, Delmir

Delmis (Spanish) friend

Del, Delms

Delmore (French) seagoing

*Del, Delmar, Delmer, Delmor, Delmoor,
Delmoore*

Delmy (American) form of Delmore:
seagoing

Delmi

Delp (Indian) form of Dilip: protests; royal

Delphin (French) dolphin
Delfin, Delfino, Delfinos, Delfinus, Delphino, Delphinos, Delphinus, Delvin

Delrin (English) of the dell

Delroy (French) royal; special
Del, Dell, Dellroy, Delroi, Roi, Roy

Delsen (Native American) of a just God

Delsi (American) easygoing
Delci, Delcie, Dels, Delsee, Delsey, Delsy

Delt (American) fraternity boy
Delta

Delton (English) friend
Delt, Deltan, Delten

DeLuca (Italian) lucky

Delvan (English) form of Delwin: companion
Del, Dell, Delly, Delven, Delvin, Delvun, Delvyn

Delvern (English) proud

Delvie (English) proud

Delwin (English) companion
Dalwin, Dalwyn, Delavan, Delevan, Dellwin, Delwen, Delwins, Delwince, Delwinse, Delwy, Delwyn

Deman (Dutch) man

Demarco (Italian) daring
Deemarko, Demarkoe, Demie, Demmy, Dimarco, D'Marco

Demarcus (American) zany; royal
Damarcus, DaMarkiss, DeMarco, DeMarcus, Demarkes, Demarkess, DeMarko, DeMarkus, Demarkus, DeMarquess, DeMarquez, Demarquiss, DeMarquiss

Demario (Italian) bold
Demarioh, Demarrio, Demie, Demmy, Dimario, D'Mareo, D'Mario

Demarion (American) combo of De and Marion

Demarques (African American) son of Marques; noble
Demark, Demarkes, Demarquis, Demmy

Demarris (American) combo of De and Marris; loud

Demas (Greek) well-liked
Dimas

Dement (French) mountain

Demesio (Italian) treacherous

Demete (American) form of Demetrius: follower of Demeter
Deme, Demetay

Demetrice (Greek) form of Demetrius: follower of Demeter

Demetrick (African American) earthy
Demetrik, Demi, Demitrick

Demetrios (Greek) earth-loving
Demeetrius, Demetreus, Demetri, Demetrious, Demetris, Demi, Demie

Demetrius (Greek) follower of Demeter
Dametrius, Dem, Demetri, Demetrice, Demetris, Demitrios, Demmy, Demos, Dhimitrios, Dimetre, Dimitri, Dimitrios, Dimitrious, Dimitry, Dmitri, Dmitrios, Dmitry

Demian (Slavic) form of Damian: fate

Demin (Spanish) form of Demos: of the people

Deming (English) form of Demos: of the people

Demitree (American) form of Dimitri: fertile; flourishing

Demitri (Greek) fertile; earthy
Demetrie, Demetry, Demi, Demie, Demitry, Dmitri

Democri (Greek) judges

Demond (African American) worldly
Demonde

Demondre (American) of the world

Demos (Greek) of the people
Demas, Demmos

Demosthenes (Greek) orator; eloquent
Demos

Demps (Irish) form of Dempsey: respected; judge
Demps, Dempse, Dempz

Dempsey (Irish) respected; judge
Dem, Demi, Demps, Dempsie, Dempsy

Den (Greek) form of Dennis: reveler

Denali (Hindi) great

Denard (Last name as first name) envied
Den, Denar, Denarde, Denny

Denby (Scandinavian) adventurous
Danby, Denbee, Denbey, Denbie, Denney, Dennie, Denny

Dene (Hungarian) reveler

Deneki (Slavic) star of the day

Denham (Scandinavian) hamlet of Danes

Denholm (Scandinavian) house of Danes

Deni (English) form of Dionysius: joyous celebrant; god of wine
Denni

Denim (French) cotton fabric

Denk (American) sporty
Denky, Dink

Denley (English) dark
Denlie, Denly

Denman (English) dark; valley-dweller
Den, Deni, Denmin, Denney, Denni, Dennie, Dennman, Denny, Dinman

Denmark (Place name) from Denmark

Dennar (English) valley boy

Dennard (English) valley boy

Dennell (English) valley boy

Dennis (Greek) reveler
Den, Denes, Deni, Denies, Denis, Deniss, Dennes, Dennet, Denney, Denni, Dennie, Dennies, Dennison, Denniz, Denny, Dennys, Deno, Denys, Deon, Dino, Dion, Dionisio, Dionysius, Dionysus, Diot

Dennisen (English) Dennis's son; partier
Den, Denison, Dennison, Dennizon, Dennyson, Tennyson

Denno (Greek) form of Dennis: reveler

Denny (Greek) form of Dennis: reveler
Den, Denee, Deni, Denney, Denni

Denoy (Greek) form of Dennis: reveler

Densey (English) place name

Dent (American) form of Denzel: sensual

Denton (English) valley settlement; happy
Denny, Dent, Dentan, Denten, Dentie, Dentin

Denver (Place name) capital of Colorado; climber
Den, Denny

Denzel (English) sensual
Den, Denny, Densie, Denz, Denze, Denzell, Denzelle, Denziel, Denzil, Denzill, Denzille, Denzyl, Denzylle, Dinzie

Denzie (English) place name

Deo (Sanskrit) God

Deodan (Latin) serving God

Deodar (Sanskrit) cedar

Deondray (African American) romantic
Deandre, Deeon, Deondrae, Deondrey, Deone

Deone (Greek) form of Dionysius: joyous celebrant; god of wine
Deion, Deonah, Deonne, Dion

Deonnetaye (American) extrovert

Deonté (French) outgoing
De'On, Deontae, Deontay, Deontie, Diontay, Diontayye

Deordre (African American) outgoing
Deordray

Depp (American) dashing

Dep

Derby (Irish) guileless

Derbey, Derbie

Derek (German) ruler; bold heart

Darrick, Darriq, Derak, Dere, Dereck,
Deric, Derick, Derik, Deriq, Deriqk,
Derk, Derreck, Derrek, Derrick, Derrik,
Derryck, Derryk, Deryk, Deryke, Dirk,
Dirke, Dyrk

Derenzo (Italian) form of Darren:
great

Derett (American) form of Derrick:
bold heart

Derlam (American) form of Derlin;
form of Derland: from the land of deer

Derland (English) from the land of
deer

Durland

Derlin (English) from the land of
deer

Derl, Derlan, Derlen, Derlyn, Durland,
Durlin

Dermod (Irish) form of Dermot:
unabashed; giving

Dermud

Dermond (Irish) unassuming

Dermon, Dermun, Dermund, Derr

Dermot (Irish) unabashed; giving

Der, Dermod, Dermott, Derree, Derrey,
Derri, Diarmid, Diarmuid

Dern (Hebrew) form of Deron: smart

Deron (African American) form of
Darren: smart

Dare, Daron, DaRon, Darone, Darron,
Dayron, Dere, DeRronn

Deronce (American) form of Direnc:
resistance

Derrell (French) form of Darrell:
loved

Dere, Derrel, Derrill

Derrence (American) form of
Direnc: resistance

Derrett (French) form of Darren:
great

Derri (American) breezy

Derree, Derry

Derrick (German) bold heart

Derak, Derick

Derry (Irish) red-haired

Dare, Darry, Derrey, Derri, Derrie

Dervando (Italian) friend

Derward (Last name as first name)
clunky

Der, Derr, Derwy, Dur, Durr, Ward

Derwent (Last name as first name) of
deer

Derwin (English) bookish

Darwin, Darwyn, Derwyn, Derwynn,
Durwen, Durwin

Derya (Slavic) from the ocean

Des (Irish) form of Desmond: from
Munster

Desaro (Spanish) desired

Deseo (Spanish) desire

Des, Desi, Dezi

Deshan (Hindi) patriot

Deshad, Deshal

Deshawn (African American) brassy

Dashaun, Dashawn, Desean, Deshaun,
Deshaune, Deshawnn, Deshon, D'Sean,
D'Shawn

Deshea (American) confident

Desh, DeShay, Deshay, Deshie

Deshon (African American) bold; open

Desh, Deshan, Deshann

Desi (Latin) form of Desmond: from
Munster; form of Desiderio: yearning;
sorrow; desired

Desiderio (Latin) yearning; sorrow;
desired

Deri, Derito, Des, Desi, Desideratus,
Desiderios, Desiderius, Desie, Diderot,
Didier, Dizier

Desidoro (Spanish) desirable

Desire (American) desirable

Des, Desi, Desidero

Desley (American) form of Lesley: strong-willed

Desmee (Irish) form of Desmond: from Munster
Desi, Desmey, Dessy, Dezme, Dezmee, Dezmie, Dezmo, Dezzy

Desmond (Irish) from Munster
Des, Desi, Desmon, Desmund, Dezmond, Dizmond

Desmondae (Irish) loyal Irishman

Desmun (Irish) form of Desmond: from Munster
Dez, Dezmund

Desoto (Spanish) explores

Desperado (Spanish) renegade
Des, Deseperado, Dessy, Dezzy

Dessles (African) happy

Destin (Place name) city in Florida; destiny; fate
Desten, Destie, Deston, Destrie

Detleff (Germanic) decisive
Detlef, Detlev

Detler (German) decides

Detrick (German) rules

Detries (German) form of Dedric: leader

Detroy (African American) outgoing
Detroe

Detry (German) rules

Detton (Last name as first name) determined
Deet, Dett

Deuce (American) two in cards; second child
Doos, Duz

DeUndre (African American) child of Undre
Deundrae, DeUndray, Deundry

Deuter (German) warrior

Dev (Irish) form of Devlin: fearless
Deb, Deo

Deval (Hindi) godlike
Deven

Devann (American) divine child
DeVanne, Deven

Devaughan (American) bravado
Devan, Devaughn, Devonne

Devdan (Hindi) God's gift
Debdan, Deodan

Devend (Indian) from Hindu god Indra Devendra

Devender (American) poetic
Devander, Deven, Devendar

Dever (American) generous

Deverell (American) special
Dev, Devee, Deverel, Deverelle, Devie, Devy

Devereux (French surname) divine
Deveraux

Deverges (French) diverges

Devin ✪ (Irish) poetic; writer
Dev, Devan, Deven, Devinn, Devon, Devvy, Devyn, Devynn

Devine (Latin) divine
Dev, Devinne

Devinson (Irish) poetic
Davin, Dev, Devan, Devee, Deven, Devy

Devland (Irish) courageous
Dev, Devlend, Devlind, Devvy

Devlin (Irish) fearless
Devlan, Devlen, Devlon, Devlyn, Devy

Devo (American) quirky; fun
Divo

Devoe (French) Last name used as first name; lives near beautiful valley

Devon (Irish) writer
Deavon, Dev, Deven, Devin, Devohne, Devond, Devonn, Devy, Devyn

Devonte (African American) form of writer
Devontae, Devontay

Devroy (French) God as royalty

Dew (English) word as name

Dewalt (Last name as first name)

Dewan (American) form of Dejuan: talkative
Dewey

Deward (Spanish) holy*

Deway (American) invented

Dewayne (American) spirited
Dewain, Dewaine, Duwain, Dwain

Dewell (Last name as first name)

Dewey (Welsh) valued
Dew, Dewi, Dewie, Dewy, Duey

DeWhayne (American) form of
Dewayne: spirited

Dewitt (English) fair-haired
Dewie, DeWitt, Dwight, Witt, Wittie,
Witty

DeWittay (African American) witty
Dewitt, DeWitt, Witt, Witty

Dewon (African American) clever
Dejuan, Dewan

Dex (Latin) form of Dexter: skillful;
right-handed
Dexe

Dexee (American) form of Dexter:
skillful; right-handed
Dex, Dexey, Dexi, Dexie

Dexter (Latin) skillful; right-handed
Decster, Dex, Dext, Dextah, Dextar,
Dextor

Dezi (Irish) form of Desi: from
Munster; yearning; sorrow; desired

Dhan (Indian) rich

Dhananjay (Indian) rich

Dhaval (Indian) purity

Dhiaa (African) winning

Dhillon (American) form of Dillon:
devoted

Dhrga (Indian) unreachable

Dhruv (Indian) star

Diablo (Spanish) devil

Dial (Word as name)

Diamon (American) luminous
Diamund, Dimon, Dimun

Diamond (English) bright; gem
Dimah, Dime, Dimond, Dimont

Diante (English) form of Deonte:
outgoing

Diarmid (Irish) happy for others'
successes
Diarmaid, Diarmait, Diarmi

Diaz (Spanish) rowdy
Dias, Diazz

Dice (English) risk-taking
Dicey, Dies, Dize, Dyce, Dyse

Dick (German) form of Richard:
wealthy leader
Dickey, Dicki, Dickie, Dicky, Dik

Dickens (Literature) for Charles
Dickens; articulate

Dickinson (Last name as first name)
poetic

Dickon (Last name as first name)
strong king

Didier (French) desirable

Didionne (French) form of Didier:
desirable

Diedrich (German) form of Dedric:
leader
Dedrick, Deed, Died, Dietrich

Diego ✪ (Spanish) form of James: he
who supplants
Dago, Deago, Deagoh, Dee, Diago

Dierkes (Scandinavian) rules

Dierks (Scandinavian) rules

Diesel (American) rugged
Dees, Deez, Desel, Dezsel, Diezel

Diet (German) form of Dedric: leader

Dieter (German) prepared
Dedrick, Deke, Derek, Detah, Deter,
Diederick, Dirk

Dietmar (German) famous

Dieudonne (French) loves a gracious
God

Digby (Irish) man of simplicity

Diggory (French) lost
Diggery, Diggorey, Digory

Diggs (Last name as first name)

Digna (Scandinavian) worthwhile

Digneo (Latin) worthwhile

Dijon (Place name) city in France;
refined
Dejawn

Dilean (Irish) loyal

Dilip (Hindi) protests; royal
Duleep

Dill (Irish) faithful
Dillard, Dilly

Dilley (Irish) loyal

Dillion (Irish) form of Dillon: devoted

Dillon (Irish) devoted
Dill, Dillan, Dillen, Dilly, Dilon, Dylan, Dylanne, Dyllon, Dylon

Dimas (Spanish) frank

Dimitri (Russian) fertile; flourishing
Demetry, Demi, Demitri, Demitry, Dmitri

Dimitrios (Greek) earth-loving

Dimter (Last name used as first name) form of Dimitri: fertile; flourishing

Dinesh (Hindi) day Lord

Dingo (Animal) wild spirit

Dink (American) from *Dink, the Little Dinosaur* television series

Dino (Italian) form of Dean: leader
Dean, Deanie, Deano, Deinoh, Dinoh

Dinos (Greek) form of Constantine: proud
Dean, Dinohs, Dynos

Dinose (American) form of Dino: leader
Denoze, Dino, Dinoce, Dinoz, Dinoze

Dins (American) climber
Dinse, Dinz

Dinsdale (English) hill protector; innovator

Dinsmore (Irish) guarded
Dinnie, Dinnsmore, Dinny, Dins

Diogenes (Greek) honest man
Dee, Dioge, Dioh

Diogo (Spanish) form of Diego: he who supplants

Diohne (Greek) form of Dion: joyous celebrant; god of wine

Dion (Greek) form of Dionysius: joyous celebrant; god of wine
Deion, Deon, Deonn, Deonys, Deyon, Dio, Dionn

Dionel (Welsh) form of Daniel: judged by God; spiritual
Deinel

Dionisio (Spanish) form of Dionysius: joyous celebrant; god of wine
Dionis, Dioniso, Dionysio

Dionysus (Greek) joyous celebrant; god of wine
Dee, Deonysios, Dion, Dionio, Dioniso, Dionysios, Dionysius, Dionysos,

Diosdado (Spanish) wise; loves God

Direnc (Turkish) resistance

Direnzo (Italian) rules

Dirk (Scandinavian) leader
Derk, Dierck, Dieric, Dierick, Dirck, Dirke, Dirky, Durk,

Diron (American) form of Darin: great
Diran, Dirun, Dyronn

Dishan (Biblical) a threshing

Distan (American) invented

Diven (Last name as first name)

Divina (Spanish) divine

Dix (American) energetic
Dex

Dixen (English) jovial

Dixie (American) southerner
Dix, Dixee, Dixey, Dixi

Dixon (English) Dick's son; happy
Dickson, Dix, Dixie, Dixo

Dizon (Spanish) form of Dixon: Dick's son; happy

D'Marques (American) form of Demarco: daring

Doak (Scottish) St. Cadoc's servant

Doan (English) hills; quiet
Doane, Doe

Dobbs (English) fire

Dobes (American) unassuming
Dobe, Doe

Dobie (American) reliable; southern
Dobe, Dobee, Dobey, Dobi

Dobine (Slavic) goodness

Dobrin (Slavic) goodness

Dobro (Slavic) goodness

Dobromir (Polish) good

Dobe, Dobry, Doby

Dobry (Polish) good

Dobe, Dobree, Dobrey

Dobson (Slavic) goodness

Dodd (English) swaggering; has a small-town sheriff feel

Dod

Dodge (English) swaggering

Dod, Dodds, Dodgson

Dodgen (English) Last name as first name; son of Dodd or Dodda

Dodsworth (English) Last name as first name

Dody (Greek) God's gift

Doe

Dogan (English) Last name as first name

Doherty (Irish) rash

Docherty, Doh, Doughertey, Douherty

Dolan (Irish) dark

Dolen

Dolbin (American) dark

Dolce (Italian) sweet

Dolek (American) doleful

Dolen (Irish) dark

Dolgen (American) tenacious

Dole, Dolg, Dolgan, Dolgin

Dollester (Last name as first name) dark

Dollus (American) dark

Dolon (Irish) brunette

Dole, Dolen, Dolton

Dolph (German) form of Rudolph: wolf

Dolf, Dolfie, Dollfus, Dollfuss, Dollphus, Dolphus

Dolson (Last name as first name) son of Dolan; dark

Dom (Latin) form of Dominic: child of the Lord; saint

Dome, Dommie, Dommy

Domaneke (Latin) loves the Lord; dynamic

Domasz (Slavic) form of Thomas: twin; look-a-like

Domenico (Italian) confident

Dom, Domeniko

Domero (Spanish) courageous

Dominador (Latin) seeks love

Domingo (Spanish) Sunday-born boy

Demingo, Dom, Domin, Dominko

Dominic ✪ (Latin) child of the Lord; saint

Demenico, Demingo, Dom, Domenic, Domenico, Domenique, Domingo, Domini, Dominick, Dominie,

Dominik, Dominique, Domino, Dominy, Nick

Dominiel (American) form of Dominic: child of the Lord; saint

Dominique (French) spiritual

Dom, Dominick, Dominike, Domminique

Domino (Latin) winner

Domeno, Dominoh, Domuno

Domizio (Italian) form of Dominic: child of the Lord; saint

Dommond (Latin) form of Dominic: child of the Lord; saint

Domon (Latin) form of Dominic: child of the Lord; saint

Domy (Italian) of the Lord

Don (Scottish) form of Donald: world leader; powerful

Dahn, Doni, Donn, Donney, Donni, Donnie, Donny

Donaciano (Spanish) dark

Dona, Donace, Donae, Donase

Donahue (Irish) fighter

Don, Donahoe, Donohue

Donald (Scottish) world leader; powerful

Don, Donal, Donaldo, Donall, Donalt, Donaugh, Donel, Doneld, Donelson, Donild, Donn, Donnel, Donnell, Donney, Donni, Donnie, Donny

Donat (French) gives

Donatello (Italian) giving

Don, Donatelo, Donetello, Donny, Tello

Donatien (French) generous

Don, Donatyen, Donn, Donnatyen

Donato (Italian) donates; giving

Donatus (Greek) giving

Donav (Irish) form of Donovan:
combative

Donaway (Last name as first name)

Donder (Dutch) thunder

Donegan (Last name as first name)

Dong (Chinese) from the east

Donker (African) modest

Donley (American) generous

Donnan (Irish) brown-haired;
popular

Donne (Irish) brave

Donnel (Irish) brave

Donnell (Irish) courageous

*Dahn, Don, Donel, Donell, Donhelle,
Donnie, Donny*

Donnelly (Irish) righteous

*Donalee, Donally, Donelli, Donely,
Donn, Donnell, Donnellie, Donnie*

Donnis (American) form of Donald:
world leader; powerful

Don, Donnes, Donnus

Donny (Irish) fond leader

Donney, Donni, Donnie

Donovan (Irish) combative

*Don, Donavan, Donavon,
Donavaughn, Donavyn, Donevin,
Donevon, Donivin, Donny, Donoven,
Donovon*

Dont (American) dark; giving

Don, Dontay

Dontae (African American)
capricious

Dontay, Donté

Dontave (African American) wild spirit

Dontav, Donteve

Dontavious (African American)
giving

Dantavius, Dawntavius, Dewontavius

Donté (Italian) lasting forever

*Dantae, Dantay, Dohntae, Dontae,
Dontay, Dontey*

Donton (American) confident

Don, Donnee, Dont, Dontie

Dontrell (African American) jaded

*Dontray, Dontree, Dontrel, Dontrelle,
Dontrey, Dontrie, Dontrill*

Donyale (African American) regal;
dark

Donyel, Donyelle

Donyell (African American) loyal

Danyel, Donny, Donyal

Donzell (African American) form of
Denzel: sensual

Dons, Donsell, Donz, Donzelle

Doocey (American) clever

Dooce, Doocee, Doocie, Doos

Dool (American) form of Dooley: shy
hero

Dooley (Irish) shy hero

Doolee, Dooli, Dooly

Dop (American) form of Dophy: wise
one

Dophy (French) wise one

Dor (Aboriginal) energetic

Doram, Doriel, Dorli

Doran (Irish) adventurer

Dore, Dorian, Doron, Dorran, Dorren

Dorcel (French) fleet

Dore (Greek) form of Isidore: special
gift

Dorell (Scottish) brave

Dorgan (American) form of Dragan:
dragon

Dorian (Greek) the sea's child;
mysterious; youthful forever

*Dora, Dore, Dorean, Dorey, Dorie,
Dorien, Dorrian, Dorrien, Dorryen,
Dory*

Doriano (Spanish) thriving

Dorin (Romanian) form of Dorian: the sea's child; mysterious; youthful forever

Dorman (Last name as first name) practical
Dor, Dorm

Dorn (Slavic) form of Dorin: the sea's child; mysterious; youthful forever

Doro (Greek) God's gift

Doron (Greek) unlimited passion
Doran, Doroni

Dorral (Last name as first name) vain
Dorale, Dorry

Dorset (Place name) county in England
Dorsett, Dorzet

Dorsey (French) sturdy as a fortress
Dorsee, Dorsie

Dorum (American) form of Dorian: the sea's child; mysterious; youthful forever

Dorval (Irish) poet

Doss (Latin) wealthy

Dotan (African) hardworking
Dotann

Dothan (Biblical) obeys

Dotson (Last name as first name) loquacious; son of Dot
Dotsen, Dottson

Doug (Scottish) form of Douglas: powerful; dark river
Dougie, Dougy, Dug, Dugy

Dougal (Irish) dark
Dougall, Doyle, Dugal, Dugald, Dugall

Douglas (Scottish) powerful; dark river
Doug, Douggie, Dougie, Douglace, Douglass, Douglis, Dugaid

Dougray (Irish) dwells by the dark stream

Dov (Hebrew) bear

Dovan (Asian) village in Himalayas (Nepal)

Dovie (American) peaceable
Dove, Dovee, Dovey, Dovi, Dovy

Dow (Irish) brunette
Dowan, Dowe, Dowson

Dowd (American) serious
Doud, Dowdy, Dowed

Dowden (Irish) dark

Dowding (American) dark

Dowell (Welsh) Last name as first name; dark

Dowen (Irish) dark

Downie (American) form of surname Downey

Dowrick (Last name as first name)

Dox (American) form of Dax: unique; waterloving

Doxey (American) form of Dox: unique; water-loving

Doy (American) form of Douglas: powerful; dark river

Doyal (American) form of Doyle: deep; dark
Doile, Doyl

Doyle (Irish) deep; dark
Doil, Doy, Doyal, Doye, Doyl

Doylton (Last name as first name) pretentious
Doyl, Doyle

Dozier (German) Last name as first name

Draco (Italian) dragon

Dracy (American) form of Stacey: hopeful
Dra, Drace, Dracee, Dracey, Draci, Drase, Drasee, Drasi

Dradell (American) serious
Drade, Dray

Dragan (Slavic) dragon

Drake (English) dragonlike; fire-breathing
Drago, Drakie, Drako

Draper (English) precise; maker of drapes
Draiper, Drape

Draphus (English) draper

Draven (American) capable; cool

Dravey (American) groovy

Dravee, Dravie, Dravy

Dravis (American) form of Travis: conflicted

Dray (Hindi) ambient light

Dren (Scandinavian) courage

Drew (Welsh) wise; well-liked

Dru, Druw

Drexel (American) thoughtful

Drex

Drexie (American) thinker

Dries (Dutch) brave

Dre

Drigger (English) Last name as first name

Driscoll (Irish) pensive

Driscol, Drisk, Driskell

Driver (English) driver

Dru (English) wise; popular

Drew, Drue

Drulon (English) adoring

Drummar (English) drums

Drummon (English) drums

Drummond (Scottish) practical

Drum, Drumon, Drumond

Drurius (American) form of Darius: affluent

Drury (French) loving man

Drew, Drewry, Dru, Drure, Drurey, Drurie

Dryden (English) writer; calm

Driden, Drydan, Drydin

Drystan (Welsh) form of Tristan: sad; wistful

Drestan, Dristan, Drystyn

Dua (Arabic) prays

Dual (American) two

Duan (English) form of Dwayne: swarthy

Duane (Irish) dark man

Dewain, Dewayne, Duain, Duwain, Duwaine, Duwayne, Dwain, Dwaine, Dwayne

Duarte (Spanish) rich

Dub (Irish) form of Dublin: city in Ireland; trendy

Dubby

Dubai (Arabic) place name

Dubak (African) eleventh child

Dubi (Slavic) dark

Duble (Slavic) dark

Dublin (Place name) city in Ireland; trendy

Dubray (English) dark

Duc (Vietnamese) honest

Ducio (Italian) docile

Ducy (Spanish) leads

Dude (American) cool guy

Dudley (English) compromiser; rich; stuffy

Dud, Dudd, Dudlee, Dudlie, Dudly

Dueart (American) kind

Art, Duart, Due, Duey

Duff (Scottish) dark

Duf, Duffey, Duffie, Duffy

Duffin (Last name as first name) dark

DuFrane (French) of the frame

Dugal (Irish) dark

Dugan (Irish) dark man

Doogan, Dougan, Douggan, Duggan, Duggie, Duggy, Dugin

Dugar (French) dark

Dugas (French) dark

Duke (Latin) leader of the pack

Dook, Dukey, Dukie

Dulay (African) works cloth

Duleep (Indian) protects

Dulio (Italian) combative

Dulley (American) popular

Dumah (Biblical) in the mist

Dumas (French) Last name as first name

Dumisani (African) leader

Dumont (French) monumental

Dummont, Dumon, Dumonde, Dumonte, Dumontt

Dunbar (Irish) castle-dweller

Dunbarr

Dunbaron (American) dark

Baron, Dunbar

Duncall (American) form of Dunkle: handsome

Duncan (Scottish) spirited fighter
Dunc, Dunk, Dunkan, Dunn, Dunne

Dunce (English) hill

Dundee (Australian) spunky

Dune (English) word as name

Dunham (Last name as first name) dark

Dunia (American) dark
Dunya

Dunk (Scottish) form of Duncan: spirited fighter
Dunc, Dunk

Dunlap (Scottish) hill

Dunlavy (English) sylvan
Dunlave

Dunley (English) meadow-loving
Dunlea, Dunlee, Dunleigh, Dunli, Dunlie, Dunly, Dunnlea, Dunnleigh, Dunnley

Dunlop (English) sylvan

Dunmore (Scottish) guarded
Dun, Dunmohr, Dunmoore

Dunn (Irish) neutral
Dun, Dunne

Dunney (Scottish) hill

Dunnigan (Scottish) hill

Dunning (Scottish) hill

Dunnson (Scottish) son of Donald

Dunphy (American) dark; serious
Dun, Dunphe, Dunphee, Dunphey

Dunstan (English) well-girded
Dun, Duns, Dunse, Dunsten, Dunstin, Dunston

Dunstand (English) form of Dunstan: well-girded
Dunsce, Dunse, Dunst, Dunsten, Dunstun

Dupree (French) smooth

Durand (Latin) form of Durant: lasting; alluring
Duran, Durayn

Durango (Spanish) place name; Basque durango; fertile lowland surrounded by elevations

Durant (Latin) lasting; alluring
Dante, Duran, Durand, Durante, Durr, Durrie, Durry

Duray (American) endures

Durban (Place name) city in South Africa
Durb, Durben

Durbon (Last name as first name)

Duren (Latin) lasts

Durg (Hindi) out of reach

Durham (Last name as first name) supportive
Duram

Durke (American) form of Dirk: leader

Durmot (French) has no malice

Durnford (English) Last name as first name

Duro (Place name) palo Duro Canyon; enduring
Dure

Duron (American) form of Doran: adventurer

Durrell (English) protective
Durel, Durell, Durr, Durrel, Durry

Durward (English) gatekeeper

Durwin (English) dear friend
Derwin, Derwyn, Durwen, Durwinn, Durwyn

Durwood (English) vigilant; home-loving
Derrwood, Derwood, Durr, Durrwood, Durward, Durwould

Duryea (Hindi) invincible

Duskin (German) form of Dustin: bold and brave

Dusky (English) born at dusk

Dussen (Dutch) energetic

Duster (American) form of Dusty: bold and brave
Dust, Dustee, Dustey, Dusti, Dusty

Dustin (German) bold and brave
Dust, Dustan, Dusten, Duston, Dustie,
Dusty, Dustyn

Dusty (German) form of Dustin:
bold and brave
Dust, Dustee, Dustey, Dusti, Dustie

Dusty-Joe (American) cowboy
Dustee, Dusti, Dusty, Dustyjoe

Dutch (Dutch) from Holland;
optimistic
Dutchie, Dutchy

Duth (Dutch) boy from the
Netherlands

Duthrie (American) form of Guthrie:
windy; heroic

Duval (French) valley; peaceful
Dovahl, Duv, Duvall, Duvalle

Duvin (French) of the wine

Dwain (American) form of Dwayne:
swarthy
Dwaine

Dwan (African American) fresh
Dewan, D'wan, D'Wan, Dwawn,
Dwon

Dwanae (African American) dark;
small
Dwannay

Dwayne (Gaelic) swarthy
Duane, Duwain, Duwane, Duwayne,
Dwain, Dwaine

Dweezel (American) creative
Dweez, Dweezil

Dwight (English) intelligent; white
Dwi, Dwite

Dwighton (English) Dwight's town

Dwyer (Irish) wise
Dwire, Dwyyer

Dwyke (American) form of Dwight:
intelligent; white

Dyam (Native American) eagle

Dybry (Slavic) good

Dyer (English) creative
Di, Dier, Dyar, Dye

Dykins (English) near the dike

Dylan ♂ ⚧ (Welsh) sea god; creative
Dill, Dillan, Dillon, Dilloyn, Dilon,
Dyl, Dylahn, Dylen, Dylin, Dyllan,
Dylon, Dylonn

Dyle (Welsh) form of Dylan: sea god;
creative

Dylion (Welsh) form of Dylan: sea
god; creative

Dym (Russian) form of Dimitri:
fertile; flourishing

Dynell (African American) seaman;
gambler
Dinell, Dyne

Dyre (Scandinavian) dearest

Dyron (African American) mercurial;
sea-loving

Diron, Dyronn, Dyronne

Dyron (Scandinavian) dearest

Dyson (English) sea-loving
Dieson, Dison, Dysan, Dysen, Dysun,
Dyzon

Dyvet (English) worker; dyes
Dye

E

Eagan (Irish) form of Egan: spirited
Egon

Eagle (Native American) sharp-eyed
Eagal, Egle

Eagul (American) eagle

Eamon (Irish) form of Edmond:
protective
Amon, Eamen, Emon

Ean (English) form of Ian: believer;
handsome

Earl (English) promising; noble
Earle, Earley, Earlie, Early, Eril, Erl

Earldon (English) noble

Earlen (Irish) form of Earl:
promising; noble

Early (English) punctual
Earl, Earlee, Earley

Earnest (English) genuine

Earn, Earnie, Ern, Ernie

Earon (American) form of Aaron: revered; sharer

Earonn

Earvin (English) sea-loving

Dervin, Ervin

Easau (Biblical) equivocates

Easey (American) easygoing

Easy, Ezey

East (English) from the East

Easte

Easter (English) born on Easter day

Eastland (English) boy from the East

Easton (English) outdoorsy; east town

Easten

Eaton (English) wealthy

Eaten, Etawn, Eton

Eaves (English) edges by

Eb (Hebrew) form of Ebenezer: base of life; rock

Ebal (Biblical) merciful

Ebbe (Scandinavian) brave

Ebby (Hebrew) form of Ebenezer: base of life; rock

Ebbey, Ebbi

Eben (Hebrew) helpful; loud

Eban

Ebenezer (Hebrew) base of life; rock

Eb, Ebbie, Ebby, Eben, Ebeneezer, Ebeneser

Eberhardt (German) brave

Eb, Eber, Eberhard

Ebert (French) bright

Ebo (African) Tuesday-born

Ebun (Hebrew) rock solid

Eckhardt (German) iron-willed

Eck, Eckhard, Eckhart, Ekhard

Ecklee (Last name as first name) strong

Ector (Slavic) dedicated

Ed (English) form of Edward: prospering; defender

Edd, Eddie, Eddy, Edy

Eda (Scottish) fiery

Edan (Scottish) fiery

Edon

Eday (Irish) fiery

Edbert (German) courageous

Ediberto

Edcell (English) focused; wealthy

Ed, Edcelle, Eds, Edsel

Eddie (English) form of Edward: prospering; defender

Eddee, Eddey, Eddy

Edel (German) of noble birth

Adel, Edelmar, Edelweiss

Edeltraud (German) young

Eden (Hebrew) delight

Eadon, Edin, Edon, Edye, Edyn

Edenir (Hebrew) delights

Edenson (Hebrew) son of Eden; delight

Edence, Edens, Edensen

Edgar (English) success

Ed, Eddie, Edghur, Edgur

Edgard (English) spear thrower

Ed, Eddie, Edgarde

Edgardo (English) successful

Edgar, Edgard, Edgardoh

Edge (American) cutting edge; trendsetter

Eddge, Edgy

Edgin (Last name as first name)

Edilberto (Spanish) noble

Edilbert

Edison (English) Edward's son; smart

Ed, Eddie, Edisen, Edyson

Ediwon (Slavic) form of Edward: prospering; defender

Edmond (English) protective

Ed, Edmon, Edmund

Edmun (Polish) rich

Edmundo (Spanish) wealthy protector

Ed, Eddie, Edmond

Edor (Spanish) snowy

Edrick (English) rich leader

Ed, Edri, Edrik, Edry

Edsel (English) rich

Ed, Eddie, Edsil, Edsyl

Edson (English) form of Edison: Edward's son; smart

Eduar (Spanish) form of Edward: prospering; defender

Eduardo (Spanish) flirtatious

Ed, Eddie, Edwardo

Eduviges (Italian) contentious

Edward (English) prospering; defender

Ed, Eddey, Eddi, Eddie, Eddy, Edwar, Edwerd

Edwards (English) Last name as first name; prospers

Edwiges (Spanish) contentious

Edwin (English) prosperous friend

Ed, Edwinn, Edwynn

Edzel (English) affluent

Efemy (Greek) eloquent

Efrain (Hebrew) form of Ephraim: fertile

Efren

Efrat (Spanish) brave

Efremel (Russian) cheerful

Efrim (Hebrew) form of Ephraim: fertile

Ef, Efrem, Efrum

Efton (American) form of Ephraim: fertile

Ef, Eft, Eften, Eftun

Egan (Irish) spirited

Eggie, Egin, Egon

Egbert (English) bright sword

Egber, Egburt, Eggie, Eggy

Egborn (English) ready; born of Edgar

Eg, Egbornem, Egburn, Eggie

Eger (English) form of Edgar: success

Egerton (English) town of a spearman

Edgarton, Edgartown, Edgerton, Egeton

Egeus (American) protective

Aegis, Egis

Eggleston (Last name as first name) town of Edgar

Eghert (German) smart

Eghertt, Eghurt

Egil (Scandinavian) the sword's edge

Eigil

Egmon (German) protective

Egmond, Egmont, Egmun, Egmund, Egmunt

Egon (Irish) passionate

Egypt (Place name) mysterious; majestic

Ehab (Irish) vibrant

Ehren (Hebrew) form of Aaron: revered; sharer

Ehrlich (Last name as first name) aware

Eikki (African) strong

Eilam (Hebrew) form of Elam: eternal

Einar (Scandinavian) lone fighter

Eirene (American) peaceful

Eiton (Hebrew) strong

Ejuan (Spanish) form of Ewan: youthful spirit

Ekels (Last name as first name) Echols variant

Eklund (Last name as first name) honored

Ekon (African) muscular

Ekul (Last name as first name) honored

El (English) old friend

El Fego (Spanish) bird; articulate

El Mahdi (Spanish) loved

Elam (Hebrew) eternal

Elan (French) finesse

Elann, Elen, Elon, Elyn

Elbis (American) exalted

Elb, Elbace, Elbase, Elbus

Elbridge (American) presidential

Elb, Elby

Elcim (Spanish) dignified

Eldaah (Biblical) battles

Eldan (Biblical) God loves

Eldemar (Slavic) old soul

Elder (English) older sibling
El, Eldor

Eldon (English) charitable
Edwin, El, Elden, Eldin

Eldorado (Place name) city in
Arkansas
El, Eld, Eldor

Eldread (English) wise advisor
El, Eldred, Eldrid

Eldridge (English) supportive
Eldredge

Eleazar (Hebrew) helped by God
*Elazar, Eleasar, Eliasar, Eliazar,
Elieser, Elizar*

Elegy (Spanish) memorable
Elegee, Elegie, Elgy

Elendor (Invented) special
Elen, Elend

Eleuter (Greek) freedom of integrity

Eleuterio (Greek) freedom of
integrity

Elex (American) form of Alex: great
leader; helpful

Elger (German) of noble birth
Ellgar, Ellger

Elgin (English) elegant
Elgen

Elham (English) Last name as first
name; place name

Eli ✪ (Hebrew) faithful man; high priest
El, Elie, Eloy, Ely

Elian (Spanish) spirited
Eliann, Elyan

Elias (Greek) spiritual
El, Eli, Eliace, Elyas

Eliason (Greek) form of Elias:
spiritual

Eliazar (Hebrew) God assists him

Elic (American) form of Alec: high-
minded

Eliel (Hebrew) religious

Eliett (Spanish) form of Elliott: God-
loving

Eliezer (Origin unknown) of God
Elieser, Elyeser

Elige (Latin) God has chosen him

Elighie (American) form of Elijah:
religious; Old Testament prophet

Elihu (Hebrew) true believer
Elih, Eliu, Ellihu

Elijah ✪ ⊕ (Hebrew) religious;
Old Testament prophet
El, Elie, Elija

Elik (Hawaiian) form of Eric:
powerful leader

Eliniod (American) God helps him

Eliphaz (Biblical) the endeavor of
God

Elis (Hebrew) form of Eliseo: darling

Eliseo (Spanish) darling
Elizeo

Elisha (Hebrew) of God's salvation
Elishah, Elysha, Elyshah

Elkanah (Biblical) obedient to God

Elkin (Hebrew) obedient to God

Ellard (German) brave man
Ell, Ellarde, Ellee, Ellerd

Ellery (English) dominant
El, Ell, Ellary, Ellerie, Ellie

Ellezer (English) believer

Ellion (American) form of Elliott:
God-loving

Elliott (English) God-loving
Elie, Elio, Ell, Elliot

Ellis (English) form of Elias: spiritual
Ellice, Ells

Ellison (English) circumspect
Ell, Ellason, Ellisen, Ells, Ellyson

Ellkan (Hawaiian) saved by God
Elkan, Elkin

Ellory (Cornish) graceful swan
Elory, Elorey, Ellorey

Ellsha (Hebrew) saved by the Lord
Elljsha, Elisee, Elish, Elishia, Elishua

Elman (American) protective
El, Elle, Elmen, Elmon

Elmer (English) famed
Ell, Elm, Elmar, Elmir, Elmo, Elmoh

Elmerre (English) form of Elmer: famed

Elmito (Spanish) form of Elmer: famed

Elmo (Greek) gregarious
Ellmo, Elmoh

Elmore (English) radiant; sassy; royal
Elm, Elmie, Elmoor, Elmor

Elmot (American) lovable
Elm

Elof (Swedish) the one heir
Loff

Elohim (Hebrew) chosen

Eloi (French) chosen one
Eloie, Eloy

Elois (Spanish) chosen

Elonzo (Spanish) sturdy; happy
El, Elon, Elonso

Elrad (Hebrew) God rules his life

Elran (Spanish) God directs him

Elreno (Spanish) God directs him

Elrette (Spanish) God directs him

Elrid (Hebrew) God directs him

Elrin (American) God helps him

Elroy (French) giving
Elroi, Elroye

Elsden (English) spiritual
Els, Elsdon

Elson (English) form of Elston: sophisticated
Elsen

Elster (Scottish) form of Alastair: strong leader

Elston (English) sophisticated
Els, Elstan, Elsten

Elsworth (Last name as first name) pretentious
Ells, Ellsworth

Elton (English) settlement; famous
Ell, Ellton, Elt, Eltan, Elten

Elusha (Slavic) treasured

Eluteria (Russian) believer

Eluye (Spanish) integrity

Elvie (Spanish) fair

Elvin (English) friend of elves
El, Elv, Elven

Elvind (American) form of Elvin: friend of elves
Elv

Elvis (Scandinavian) all-wise
El, Elvyse, The King

Elvy (English) elfin; small

Elwell (English) born in the old-well area

Elwen (English) friend of elves
Elwee, Elwin, Elwy, Elwyn, Elwynn, Elwynt

Elwond (Last name as first name) steady
Ellwand, Elwon, Eldwund

Elwood (English) old wood; everlasting
Ell, Elwoode, Elwould, Woodie, Woody, Woodye

Elwyne (English) elf-friend

Ely (Hebrew) lifted up
Eli

Elyden (English) from the hill

Elyus (Hebrew) form of Elias: spiritual

Elzaphan (Biblical) God assists him

Emanuel (Hebrew) with God
Em, Eman, Emanuele

Embers (Spanish) fiery

Emberto (Italian) pushy
Berty, Embert, Emberte

Embree (American) fiery

Emerick (German) form of Emery: hardworking leader

Emerit (German) form of Emery: hardworking leader

Emeritus (Latin) having fully earned

Emerson (German) Emery's son; able
Emers, Emersen

Emery (German) hardworking leader
Em, Emeri, Emerie, Emmerie, Emory, Emrie

Emig (Greek) brown

Emigdio (Greek) brown

Emil (Latin) ingratiating
Em, Emel, Emele

Emiliano (Italian) charms

Emilio (Italian) competitive; (Spanish) excelling
Emil, Emile, Emilioh, Emlo

Emjay (American) reliable
Em-J, Em-Jay, M.J., MJ

Emmanuel (Hebrew) with God
Em, Eman, Emmannuel, Emmanuele, Manny

Emmaus (Biblical) place name; safe in God

Emmett (Hebrew) truthful; sincere
Emit, Emmet, Emmit, Emmitt, Emmyt, Emmytt

Emory (German) industrious leader
Emery, Emmory, Emorey, Emori, Emorie

Emre (Turkish) bond of brothers
Emra, Emrah, Emreson

Emress (Spanish) proud

Emric (Slavic) form of Emery; hardworking leader

Emrick (Welsh) immortal
Emryk

Emser (American) hard worker

Emuel (Hebrew) form of Emmanuel: with God
Emanuel, Imuel

Enam (Biblical) place name

Enan (Welsh) hard

Encarnacion (Spanish) embodiment

of life

Enda (Slavic) masculine

Ender (Slavic) form of Andrew: manly and brave

Eneas (Hebrew) much-praised
Ennes, Ennis

Engel (German) angel

Engelbert (German) angel-bright
Bert, Bertie, Berty, Engelber, Inglebert

Engen (American) smart

Enger (Scandinavian) angel

England (English) from England

Englun (American) from England

Engram (English) angelic

Engus (Irish) form of Angus: standout; important

Enlai (Chinese) thankful

Enlow (Last name as first name)

Ennis (Irish) reliable

Enno (Hebrew) form of Enos: mortal

Enny (American) form of Enos: mortal

Enoch (Hebrew) dedicated instructor
En, Enoc, Enok

Enos (Hebrew) mortal
Enoes

Enosh (Biblical) man

Enrick (Spanish) cunning
Enric, Enrik

Enrico (Italian) ruler

Enrike, Enriko, Enryco

Enrique (Spanish) charismatic ruler
Enrika, Enrikae, Enriqué, Enryque, Quiqui

Enrsto (Spanish) form of Ernesto: sincere

Ensor (Slavic) form of Ernest: sincere

Enver (Turkish) brightest child

Enzi (African) strong boy

Enzo (Italian) fun-loving

Eodis (Biblical) good

Epher (Biblical) plenty

Ephesian (Biblical) gifted

Ephraim (Hebrew) fertile
Eff, Efraim, Efram, Efrem, Ephraime, Ephrame, Ephrayme

Epifanio (Spanish) showing intelligence

Eppey (Spanish) smart

Eran (Hebrew) watchful

Erasmus (Greek) beloved
Eras, Erasmas, Erasmis

Erastus (Greek) loved baby

Erazmo (Spanish) loved
Erasmo, Eraz, Ras, Raz

Erbert (German) form of Herbert: famed warrior
Ebert, Erberto

Erby (German) aggressive

Ercell (Italian) the gift*

Ercole (Italian) glorious God's child

Ereb (Greek) dark

Erebus (Greek) nether darkness

Ergo (Latin) word as name; therefore; consequently

Erhardt (German) strong-willed
Erhar, Erhard, Erhart, Erheart

Eric ✪ (Scandinavian) powerful leader
Ehrick, Erek, Erick, Erik, Eryke

Erie (Place name) one of the Great Lakes; vast

Erikson (Scandinavian) Erik's son; bold man
Ericksen, Eriksen, Erycksen, Eryksen, Erykson

Erin (Irish) peace-loving
Aaron, Arin, Aron, Eryn

Eris (Greek) hard life

Erlan (English) aristocratic
Earlan, Earland, Erland, Erlen, Erlin

Erling (English) highborn

Ermitt (English) form of Kermit: droll

Ermot (French) form of Ernest: sincere

Ernest (English) sincere
Earnest, Ern, Ernie, Erno, Ernst, Erny, Ernye

Ernesto (Spanish) sincere

Ernie, Nesto, Nestoh

Ernie (English) form of Ernest: sincere
Ernee, Erney, Erny

Erno (Slavic) form of Ernest: sincere

Ernold (English) sincere

Ernst (Dutch) form of Ernest: sincere

Ernulfo (Spanish) sincere

Erol (American) noble
Eral, Eril, Errol

Erold (Welsh) form of Errol: noble

Erolden (English) wanders

Eronlon (American) form of Aaron: revered; sharer

Eros (Greek) sensual
Ero

Erose (Greek) form of Eros: sensual
Eroce

Errett (American) form of Aaron: revered; sharer

Errick (American) form of Eric: powerful leader

Errin (American) form of Aaron: revered; sharer

Errington (Last name as first name) Aaron's town

Errol (German) noble
Erol, Erold, Erroll, Erryl

Ershcel (American) form of Herschel: deer; swift

Erskine (Scottish) high-minded
Ers, Ersk, Erskin

Erst (Scottish) cliff

Erv (English) good-looking

Ervin (English) sea-loving
Earvin, Erv, Ervan, Erven, Ervind, Ervyn

Ervine (English) sea-lover
Ervene, Ervin

Erving (Scottish) good-looking

Erwey (American) form of Irving: attractive

Erwin (English) friendly
Erwyn

Esau (Hebrew) rough-hewn; raw
Es, Esa, Esauw, Esaw

Escobar (Spanish) swept up

Escobedo (Spanish) Last name as first name

Escoto (Spanish) shy

Esdras (Biblical) form of Ezra: helpful; strong

Eshban (Biblical) fire of discernment

Eshcol (Hebrew) the grapes

Eshter (Indian) form of Eshwar: Hindu god

Eskew (English) Last name as first name

Eskil (Scandinavian) divine

Esmaeil (Spanish) loved

Esmaiel (Spanish) outcast son

Esmail (Indian) God listens

Esmé (French) beloved
Es, Esmae, Esmay

Esmer (Slavic) affluent

Esmond (French) handsome
Esmand, Esmon, Esmund

Esmun (American) kind
Es, Esman, Esmon

Esos (Irish) godlike

Espen (German) bear of God;
(Danish) the bear

Esperanza (Spanish) hopeful
Esper, Esperance, Esperence

Espie (Scandinavian) big

Espy (Scandinavian) of God

Esraa (Hebrew) form of Ezra: helpful;
strong

Esser (Spanish) reassuring

Essex (English) dignified
Ess, Ez

Estanisiao (Spanish) glorified

Este (Spanish) form of Esteban: royal;
friendly

Esteban (Spanish) royal; friendly
Estabon, Estebann, Estevan, Estiban,
Estyban

Estel (American) from the East

Esterlin (Last name as first name)
Easterner

Estes (English) Eastern; open
Estas, Este, Estis

Estevan (Spanish) crowned
Estivan, Estyvan

Estridge (Last name as first name)
fortified
Es, Estri, Estry

Esvin (English) friend of Esser

Etam (Biblical) place name

Etan (Irish) watchful

Etano (Italian) form of Ethan: firm
will

Etereo (Spanish) heavenly; spiritual
Etero

Ethan ✪ ❂ (Hebrew) firm will
Eth, Ethen, Ethin, Ethon

Ethaniel (Italian) form of Gaetano:
from the city of Gaeta; Italian man

Etheal (English) of good birth
Ethal

Ethelbert (German) principled
Ethelburt, Ethylbert

Etren (American) form of Ethan: firm
will

Ettore (Italian) loyal; steadfast
Etor, Etore

Etwin (American) friend of Ethan;
resolved

Eual (Jewish) form of Eyal: deer-like

Euclid (Greek) brilliant
Euclide, Uclid

Eudin (Greek) leads

Eufronio (Greek) bright

Eugene (Greek) blue-blood
Eugean, Eugenie, Ugene

Eural (American) from Ural
Mountains; upward
Eure, Ural, Ury

Eurby (Last name as first name) sea
Erby, Eurb

Eurskie (Invented) dorky
Ersky

Eurus (Greek) form of Eros: sensual

Eusebio (Spanish) devoted to God
Eucebio, Eusabio, Eusevio, Sebio, Usibo

Eustace (Latin) calming
Eustice, Eustis, Stace, Stacey, Ustace

Eustacio (Spanish) calm; visionary
Eustacio, Eustase, Eustasio, Eustazio,
Eustes, Eustis

Eustorgio (Greek) beloved

Euxinus (Greek) highborn

Evagelos (Greek) form of Andrew:
manly and brave
Evaggelos, Evangelo, Evangelos

Evan ✪ ❂ (Irish) warrior
Ev, Evann, Evanne, Even, Evin

Evander (Greek) manly; champion
Evand, Evandar, Evandir

Evans (Welsh) believer in a gracious God
Evens, Evyns

Evanus (American) form of Evan: warrior
Evin, Evinas, Evinus

Evar (Scandinavian) courageous

Evaristo (Spanish) form of Evan: warrior
Evariso, Evaro

Eve (Invented) form of Yves: honest; handsome
Eeve

Evelle (American) vibrant

Evelyn (American) writer
Ev, Evlinn, Evlyn

Even (Latin) does well

Ever (German) strong wild boar

Everard (German) tough
Ev, Evrard

Everest (Place name) highest mountain peak in the world

Everestin (American) everlasting

Everett (English) strong
Ev, Everet, Everitt, Evret, Evrit

Everette (English) brave

Everhart (Scandinavian) vibrant
Evhart, Evert

Everly (American) singing
Everlee, Everley, Everlie, Evers

Evert (Dutch) of the wild boars

Everton (English) from the town of boars; fearless

Every (English) word as name

Evetier (French) good

Evett (American) bright
Ev, Evatt, Eve, Evidt, Evitt

Evince (American) invincible

Evitt (American) invincible

Evodio (Spanish) righteous

Evon (Welsh) form of Evan: warrior
Even, Evin, Evonn, Evonne, Evyn

Evre (American) form of Everett: strong

Evres (American) form of Everettt: strong

Evret (American) form of Everettt: strong

Evzek (Slavic) brave

Ewald (Polish) fair ruler

Ewan (Scottish) youthful spirit
Ewahn, Ewon

Ewand (Welsh) form of Evan: warrior
Ewen, Ewon

Ewanell (American) form of Ewan: youthful spirit
Ewanel, Ewenall

Ewart (English) shepherd; caring
Ewar, Eward, Ewert

Ewen (Scottish) form of Eugene: blue-blood

Ewing (English) law-abiding
Ewin, Ewyng

Excell (American) competitive
Excel, Exsel, Exsell

Exek (American) God gives strength

Exia (Spanish) demanding
Ex, Exy

Exios (Spanish) finds a way

Exiquio (Spanish) exacting

Exod (Spanish) his exodus

Exzel (American) form of Edsel: rich

Eyal (American) form of Eagle: sharp-eyed

Eydis (Scandinavian) island god

Eytin (American) form of Ethan: firm will

Eza (Hebrew) form of Ezra: helpful; strong
Esri

Ezekiel (Hebrew) God's strength
Eze, Ezek, Ezekhal, Ezekial, Ezikiel, Ezikyel, Ezkeil, Ezykiel, Zeke

Ezequiel (Spanish) devout

Ezer (Hebrew) helpful boy

Ezion (Biblical) place name

Ezira (Hebrew) helpful
Ezirah, Ezyra, Ezyrah

Ezno (Spanish) humble

Ezra (Hebrew) helpful; strong
Esra, Ezrah

Ezri (Hebrew) my help
Ezrey, Ezry

Ezron (American) created

Ezzie (Hebrew) form of Ezra: helpful;
strong
Ez

F

Faakhir (Arabic) proud

Faber (German) grower
Fabar, Fabir, Fabyre

Faberto (Latin) form of Fabian:
grower
Fabe, Fabey, Fabien, Fabre

Fabian (Latin) grower
*Fab, Fabe, Fabean, Fabeone, Fabiano,
Fabie, Fabien,*

Fabio (Italian) seductive; handsome
Fab, Fabioh

Fabish (American) form of Fabrice:
skilled worker

Fable (American) storyteller
Fabal, Fabe, Fabel, Fabil

Fablo (American) form of Fabio:
seductive; handsome

Fabrice (French) skilled worker
*Fabriano, Fabricius, Fabritius, Fabrizio,
Fabrizius*

Fabrizio (Italian) fabulous

Fabron (French) blacksmith

Fabryce (Latin) crafty
Fab, Fabby, Fabreese, Fabrese, Fabrice

Fabulous (American) vain
Fab, Fabby, Fabu

Fachan (Last name as first name)
precocious

Factor (English) entrepreneur

Facundo (Last name as first name)
profound

Faddis (American) loner; deals in beans
Faddes, Fadice, Fadis

Faddy (American) faddish
Fad, Faddey, Faddi

Fadi (Arabic) saved by grace

Fadil (Arabic) giving

Faeus (Biblical) form of Alfeus:
follower

Fagan (Irish) fiery
Fagane, Fagen, Fagin, Fegan

Fahd (Arabic) fierce; panther; brave
Fahad

Faheem (Arabic) brilliant

Fahim (Arabic) intelligent

Fahren (American) form of Faran:
sincere

Fahrer (French) leader

Faino (American) the start

Fair (English) blond

Fairbairn (Scottish) fair-haired child

Fairbanks (English) bank along the
pathway
Fairbanx, Farebanks

Fairchild (English) fair-haired child

Fairfax (English) full of warmth
Fairfacks, Farefax, Fax, Faxy

Faisal (Arabic) authoritative
Faisel, Faizal, Fasel, Fayzelle

Faizon (Arabic) understanding

Fakhr (Arabic) proud

Faladrick (Origin unknown) form of
Frederick: plainspoken leader; peaceful
Faldrick, Faldrik

Falcon (American) bird as name;
dark; watchful
Falk, Falkon

Falcone (Latin) of the falcons

Faldo (Last name as first) brassy

Falguni (Indian) Hindi for month
Falgun

Faline (Hindi) fertile

Falk (Hebrew) falcon
Falke

Falkner (French) handles falcons
Faulkner, Fowler

Fallows (English) inactive
Fallow

Falvey (English) of the falcons

Fam (American) family-oriented
Fammy

Famous (American) ambitious
Fame

Fane (English) exuberant
Fain, Faine

Fanlie (American) free

Fannin (English) happy
Fane

Fant (Latin) guileless

Fantroy (French) naive, royal

Fany (Spanish) freedom

Faolan (Irish) wolf; sly
Felan, Phelan

Far (English) traveler
Farr

Faraji (African) he who comforts
others

Faralito (Spanish) comforts

Faramond (English) protected
Faramund, Farrimond, Farrimund,
Pharamond, Pharamund

Faran (American) sincere
Fahran, Faren, Faron, Feren, Ferren

Fardan (Arabic) unique

Fareed (Arabic) special

Fargo (American) jaunty
Fargouh

Farhad (Arabic) unusual

Faris (Arabic) knighted

Farkas (Last name as first name)
strong man

Farley (English) open
Farl, Farlee, Farleigh, Farlie, Farly,
Farlye

Farmer (English) he farms

Farnall (Last name as first name)
strong man
Farnell, Fernald

Farnham (English) windblown; field
Farnhum, Farnie, Farnum, Farny

Farnley (English) from a place of ferns

Farno (Italian) in ferns

Farold (Invented) lively

Farolito (Spanish) little ferns

Farouk (Arabic) knowing what's true
Faruq, Faruqh

Farquar (French) masculine

Farr (English) adventurer
Far

Farrar (French) distinguished
Farr

Farre (English) wanders

Farrell (Irish) brave
Farel, Farell, Faryl

Farren (English) mover
Faran, Faron, Farrin, Farron

Farris (Arabic) rider; (Irish) rock;
reliable
Fare, Farice, Faris

Farro (Italian) grain
Farron, Faro

Farrow (English) tends the pigs

Fasta (Spanish) offering

Fattah (Arabic) conqueror

Faughn (Italian) raven

Faulkner (English) disciplinarian
Falcon, Falconner, Falkner, Falkoner

Faunus (Latin) god of nature
Fawnus

Fausatino (Spanish) lucky

Faust (Latin) lucky
Fauston

Faustino (Italian) lucky

Favero (French) insightful

Favian (Latin) knowing
Fav, Favion

Favor (French) gives

Fawad (Arabic) victorious

Fawcett (American) audacious
Fawce, Fawcet, Fawcette, Fawcie,
Fawsie, Fowcett

Faxan (Anglo-Saxon) outgoing
  Faxen, Faxon

Faxon (German) lush hair

Fay (Irish) raven-haired
  Faye, Fayette

Fayne (English) happy

Faysal (Arabic) judgmental

Fazio (Italian) diligent

Fe (Latin) shining

Fearon (American) keen

Febronio (Spanish) bright

Fedde (Dutch) ruler

Federico (Spanish) peaceful and
  affluent
  Federik

Fedil (French) excellence

Fedor (German) form of Theodore:
  God's gift; a blessing
  Faydor, Feodor, Fyodor

Fedrick (American) form of Cedric:
  leader
  Fed, Fedric, Fedrik

Feeney (Irish) Last name as first
  name; soldier

Feibush (Last name as first name)
  particular

Feivel (Hebrew) bright

Feixon (Hebrew) helped by God

Feldronio (Spanish) from the field

Felimy (Irish) good

Felipe (Spanish) horse-lover
  Felepe, Filipe, Flippo

Felix (Latin) joyful
  Felixce, Filix, Phelix, Philix

Felker (English) Last name as first
  name

Fellini (Last name as first)
  carnivalesque

Felman (Last name as first name)
  smart
  Fel, Fell

Felton (English) farming the field

Fenimore (Last name as first name)
  creative

Fenner (English) capable
  Fen, Fenn, Fynner

Fennessey (English) form of
  Phineas: farsighted

Fenris (Scandinavian) fierce

Fenton (English) nature-loving
  Fen, Fenn, Fennie, Fenny

Fentress (English) natural
  Fentres, Fyntres

Fenwick (English) from the marsh
  village; able

Feo (Native American) confident
  Feeo, Feoh

Ferdinand (German) adventurer
  Ferdie, Ferdnand, Ferdy, Fernand

Ferenc (Hungarian) free

Ferg (Irish) strong

Fergall (Irish) bravest man
  Fearghall, Forgael

Fergonn (French) strong

Fergus (Irish) man of strength
  Feargus, Ferges, Fergie, Fergis, Fergy

Ferguson (Irish) bold; excellent
  *Fergie, Fergs, Fergus, Fergusahn,
  Fergusen, Fergy, Furgs, Furgus*

Ferlin (American) countrified
  Ferlan

Ferll (Irish) strong

Fermin (Spanish) strong-willed
  Fer, Fermen, Fermun

Fernan (Spanish) risk-taker

Fernando (Spanish) bold leader
  *Ferd, Ferdie, Ferdinando, Ferdy,
  Fernand*

Fernao (Spanish) form of Fernando:
  bold leader

Fernley (English) from the fern
  meadow; natural
  *Farnlea, Farnlee, Farnleigh, Farnley,
  Fernlea, Fernlee, Fernleigh*

Feroza (Persian) lucky

Feroze (Persian) lucky

Ferrand (French) gray-haired
  Farrand, Farrant, Ferrant

Ferraro (Italian) fiery

Ferrell (Irish) hero
Fere, Ferrel, Feryl

Ferret (English) star

Ferris (Irish) rock
Farris, Farrish, Ferriss

Ferylin (Irish) hero

Festatus (Irish) raven; dark

Festive (American) word as name;
joyful
Fest, Festas, Festes

Festus (Latin) happy
Festes

Feven (Russian) sees God

Fhoki (Japanese) discriminating

Fiachra (Irish) raven; watchful

Fico (Italian) form of Frederick:
plainspoken leader; peaceful

Fidel (Latin) faithful
Fidele, Fidell, Fydel

Fideles (Latin) loyal

Fidencio (Spanish) confidence
Fidens, Fido

Fides (Greek) calms

Field (English) outdoorsman
Fields

Fielding (English) outdoorsman;
working the fields

Fien (American) elegant
Fiene, Fine

Fiero (Spanish) fiery

Fierro (Spanish) fiery

Fife (Scottish) bright-eyed
Fyfe, Phyfe

Fifel (Scottish) form of Fife: bright-
eyed

Fiji (Place name) Fiji Islands; islander
Fege, Fegee, Fijie

Fikry (American) industrious
Fike, Fikree, Fikrey

Filbert (English) genius
Fil, Filb, Bert, Phil

Filemon (Greek) loves horses

Filetus (Biblical) beloved

Filinto (Spanish) friendly

Filip (Greek) horse-lover; (Belgium)
form of Philip: outdoorsman
Fil, Fill

Filmer (English) form of Filmore:
famed
Fill, Filmar

Filmore (English) famed
Fill, Fillie, Fillmore, Filly, Fylmore

Filomelo (Spanish) friend

Filson (Last name as first name) son
of Phil; meanders

Fimy (African) loved by God

Finbar (Irish) blond

Finbarr (Irish) blond

Finch (Last name as first name)
birdlike

Fineas (Egyptian) dark

Finell (Irish) blond

Finesse (English) word as name;
extreme delicacy or subtlety in action

Finian (Irish) fair
Fin, Finean, Finn, Fynian

Finis (Latin) finished

Finlan (Irish) blond

Finlay (Irish) blond soldier
Finley, Findlay, Findley

Finley (Irish) magical
Fin, Finny, Fynn, Fynnie

Finn (Scandinavian) fair-haired; from
Finland
Fin, Finnie, Finny

Finna (Scandinavian) blond

Finnegan (Irish) fair
Finegan, Finigan, Finn, Finny

Finnian (German) from Finland

Finoch (Scottish) blond

Fintan (Irish) small blond man

Finton (Irish) magical
Finn, Finny, Fynton

Fiorello (Italian) flowering

Firdaus (Arabic) from the garden of
paradise

Firman (French) loyal
Farman, Farmann, Fermin, Firmin

Firoozeh (Arabic) succeeds

Fishel (Hebrew) fish

Fish, Fysh

Fisher (English) he fishes

Fish, Fischer, Fisscher, Visscher

Fisk (Scandinavian) fisherman

Fiske

Fitch (French) throws spears

Fito (Spanish) little

Fitz (French) bright young man; son

Fitzy

Fitzgerald (English) bright young

man; Gerald's son

Fitzhugh (French) Hugh's son; big-

hearted

Fitzmorris (Last name as first name)

son of Morris

Fitz, Morrey, Morris

Fitzpatrick (French) Patrick's son;

noble

Fitzroy (French) son of Roy; lively

Fitzsimmons (English) bright

young man; Simmons's son

Five (Word as name)

Fiven (American) five

Flabia (Spanish) light-haired

Flavia

Flag (American) patriotic

Flagg

Flame (Last name as first name)

confident

Flaminio (Spanish) priest; thoughtful

Flamino

Flann (Irish) red-haired

Flainn, Flannan, Flannery

Flannan (Irish) red-haired

Flannigan (Last name as first name)

red-haired

Flappan (Last name as first name)

Flass (Last name as first name)

Flaubert (French) fame, bright

Flavean (Greek) form of Flavian:

blond

Flavian (Greek) blond

Flovian

Flavio (Italian) shining

Flav, Flavioh

Fleada (American) introvert

Flayda

Fleetwood (English) from the

woods

Flemmer (English) a native of

Flanders

Flemming (English) a native of

Flanders; confident

Fleming, Flyming

Fletcher (English) kindhearted;

maker of arrows

Fletch, Fletchi, Fletchie, Fletchy

Flimmel (Last name as first name)

Flint (English) stream; nature-lover

Flinn, Flintt, Flynt, Flynnt

Flintlee (English) of the stream

Flip (English) loves horses; wild

movements

Flippin (Spanish) form of Felipe:

horse-lover

Floan (American) form of Flynn:

brash

Floran (Spanish) flourishing like a

flower garden

Florante (Spanish) flowers

Florecio (Spanish) flowering

Florencione (Italian) flowering

Florentin (Italian) blooming

Florencio

Florian (Latin) flourishing

Florean, Florie

Floyd (English) practical; hair of gray

Floid

Flux (Middle English) flowing

Flynn (Irish) brash

Flin, Flinn, Flinnie, Flinny, Flyne

Flynt (English) flowing; stream

Flint, Flinte, Flinty, Flynte

Fobbs (Last name as first name)

flourishing

Fobo (Greek) fearful

Fogle (Last name as first name)

Folan (Last name as first name) of the folks

Foley (Last name as first name) creative
Folee, Folie

Folke (German) of the people

Folker (German) watchful
Folke, Folko

Follis (Last name as first name) of the folks

Fonseca (Italian) form of Alphonse: distinguished

Fontayne (French) giving; fountain
Font, Fontaine, Fontane, Fountaine

Fontenot (French) fountain

Fonzie (German) form of Alphonse: distinguished
Fons, Fonsi, Fonz, Fonzi

For (American) representative
Fore

Foran (American) derivative of foreign; exotic
Foren, Forun

Forbes (Irish) wealthy
Forb

Ford (English) strong
Feord, Forde, Fyord

Fordan (English) river crossing; inventive
Ford, Forday, Forden

Foreign (American) word as name; foreigner
Foran

Foreman (Last name as first name) leader

Forend (American) forward
Fore, Foryn, Forynd

Forest (French) nature-loving
Forrest, Fory, Fourast

Forester (English) protective; of the forest
Forrester, Forry

Forge (English) crosses stream

Foros (Greek) carries forward

Forsey (Scottish) Last name as first name; man of peace

Fortino (Spanish) fortune

Fortney (Latin) strength of character
Fortenay, Forteney, Forteny, Fortny, Fourtney

Fortune (French) fortunate man
Fortounay, Fortunae

Fortuno (Spanish) lucky man
Fortunio

Fost (Latin) form of Foster: worthy
Foste, Fostee, Fosty

Foster (Latin) worthy
Fauster, Fostay

Fotis (Greek) light

Fouad (Arabic) good heart
Fuad

Fowler (English) hunter; traps fowl
Fowller

Foy (American) foible

Frace (American) fragile

Fraime (Anglo-Saxon) newcomer

Fraine (English) ash tree; tall
Frayne, Freyne

Fralin (Last name as first name) frail

Francesco (Italian) flirtatious
Fran, Francey, Frankie, Franky

Franchot (French) free

Francis (Latin) free spirit; from France
Fran, Frances, Franciss, Frank, Franky, Frannkie, Franny, Frans

Francisco (Spanish) form of Francis: free spirit; from France
Chuco, Cisco, Francisk, Franco, Frisco, Paco, Pancho

Francista (Spanish) Frenchman; free
Cisco, Cisto, Francisco, Franciscus, Fransico

Franckie (German) dynamic

Franco (Spanish) defender; spear
Francoh, Franko

Francois (French) smooth; patriot; Frenchman
Frans, Franswaw, French, Frenchie, Frenchy

Frank (English) form of Franklin: outspoken; landowner
Franc, Franco, Frankee, Frankie, Frankey, Franko, Franky

Frankel (German) free

Franklin (English) outspoken; landowner
Francklin, Franclin, Frank, Frankie, Franklinn, Franklyn, Franklynn, Franky

Franqueli (Italian) free

Frantisek (Czech) free man

Franz (German) man from France; free
Frans

Frasher (English) curls

Frasier (English) attractive; man with curls
Frase, Fraser, Fraze, Frazer

Frayley (English) of the ash meadow

Frayne (English) foreigner
Fraine, Frayn, Frean, Freen, Freyne

Fraze (English) curls

Fred (German) form of Frederick: plainspoken leader; peaceful
Fredde, Freddo, Freddy, Fredo

Fredder (German) form of Fred: plainspoken leader; peaceful

Freddie (German) form of Frederick: plainspoken leader; peaceful
Freddee, Freddey, Freddi, Freddy

Freddis (German) form of Frederick: plainspoken leader; peaceful
Freddus, Fredes, Fredis

Fredell (German) form of Frederick: plainspoken leader; peaceful

Frederic (French) peaceful king
Fred, Freddy

Frederick (German) plainspoken leader; peaceful
Fred, Freddy, Frederic, Fredrich, Fredrik, Fryderyk

Freeborn (English) born free

Freed (English) free boy
Fried

Freedom (American) loves freedom

Freedy (English) free

Freeman (English) free man
Free, Freedman, Freman

Fremont (German) protective; noble

Fren (Spanish) form of Francisco: free

French (English) boy from France

Francisco (Spanish) free

Fres (Spanish) fresh air

Fresco (Spanish) open

Freslev (American) freshness

Frewen (Anglo-Saxon) free
Frewin

Frey (Scandinavian) fertility god

Frick (English) brave man

Frid (German) peaceful

Fridmann (Last name as first name) free man

Fridolf (Scandinavian) relishes peace
Freydolf, Freydulf, Friedolf, Fridulf

Fridolin (German) free

Frieder (German) peaceful leader
Frie, Fried, Friedrick

Friederich (German) form of Frederick: plainspoken leader; peaceful
Fridrich, Friedrich

Friedhelm (German) peaceful helmet
Friedelm

Frisco (American) form of Francisco: free spirit; from France
Cisco, Frisko

Friso (Anglo-Saxon) best self

Fritz (German) form of Frederick: plainspoken leader
Firzie, Firzy, Frits, Fritts, Fritzi, Fritzie, Fritzy

Fritzie (German) peaceful

Fritzon (Norse) peacemaker

Frode (Scandinavian) intellectual

Froilan (German) popular leader

Fromel (Hebrew) outgoing

Frosino (Italian) merry

Frost (English) cold; freeze

Frosten (American) of the winter

Froyim (Hebrew) kind

Fructuoso (Spanish) fruitful
Fru, Fructo

Fry (English) new sprout; growing
Frye, Fryer

Fu (Japanese) form of Fudo: the god of fire and wisdom

Fuddy (Origin unknown) bright-eyed
Fuddie, Fudee, Fudi

Fudo (Japanese) the god of fire and wisdom

Fukuda (Japanese) field

Fulbright (German) brilliant; full of brightness
Fulbrite

Fulgentius (Latin) full of kindness; shines
Fulgencio

Fulke (English) folksy
Fawke, Fowke, Fulk

Fuller (English) tough-willed
Fuler

Fullerton (English) strong
Fuller, Fullerten

Fulton (English) fresh mind; field by the town

Funge (Last name as first name) stodgy
Funje, Funny

Furlo (American) macho
Furl

Furman (German) form of Firman: loyal
Fuhrman, Fuhrmann, Furmann

Fursey (Irish) spiritual

Fyfe (Scottish) craftsman
Fife, Fyffe, Phyfe

Fyodor (Russian) divine
Feodor, Fyodr

G

Gabae (Biblical) loves God

Gabaldon (English) Last name as first name

Gabata (Biblical) place name

Gabbana (Italian) creative
Gabi

Gabe (Hebrew) form of Gabriel: God's hero; devout
Gabbee, Gabbi, Gabbie, Gabby, Gabi, Gabie, Gaby

Gabino (Spanish) strong believer
Gabby, Gabi

Gable (French) dashing

Gablen (American) form of Gabriel: God's hero; devout

Gabor (Last name as first name) believer; colorful

Gabriel ✪ ✤ (Hebrew) God's hero; devout
Gabby, Gabe, Gabi, Gabreal, Gabrel, Gabriele, Gabrielle, Gabryel

Gad (Hebrew) lucky; audacious
Gadd

Gaddi (Arabic)

Gaddiel (Hebrew) fortunate; loves God
Gadiel

Gaddis (American) hard to please; picky
Gad, Gaddes, Gadis

Gadi (Hebrew) form of Gaddiel: fortunate; loves god
Gadish

Gael (English) speaks Gaelic; independent

Gaetano (Italian) from the city of Gaeta; Italian man
Gaetan, Geitano, Guytano

Gaffar (Arabic) from the stream

Gagan (French) form of Gage: dedicated

Gage (French) dedicated

Gager (French) dedicated

Gaghe (American) jaunty

Gaham (Biblical) searches

Gahuj (African) hunts

Gailen (French) healer; physician
Galan, Galen, Galun

Gain (Word as name) gainful

Gaines (English) increase in wealth
Ganes, Gaynes

Gair (Irish) little boy
Gaer, Geir

Gaither (French) victor

Gaius (Latin) joyful
Gal

Galatian (Biblical) bible book
Galatians

Galavis (Greek) white

Galax (Spanish) of the galaxy

Galbraith (Irish) sensible
Gal

Galbreath (Irish) practical man
Galbraith, Gall

Galdin (American) calm

Galdino (Spanish) calm

Gale (English) cheerful
Gael, Gail, Gaile, Gaille, Gayle

Galegina (Native American) lithe; deer

Galen (Greek) calming; intelligent
Gaelin, Gailen, Gale, Galean, Galey, Gaylen

Galene (Spanish) shining

Galfrid (Last name as first name) uplifted
Galfryd

Gali (Spanish) shining

Galileo (Italian) from Galilee
Galilayo

Gallagher (Irish) helpful
Galagher, Gallager, Gallie, Gally

Gallant (American) savoir-faire
Gael, Gail, Gaila, Gaile, Gayle

Gallman (Last name as first name) lively
Gallway, Galman, Galway

Galloway (Irish) outgoing
Gallie, Gally, Galoway, Galway

Galo (Spanish) enthusiastic
Gallo

Galt (German) empowered

Galton (English) landowner; reclusive

Galvin (Irish) sparrow; flighty
Gallven, Gallvin, Galvan, Galven, Galway

Gamal (Arabic) camel; travels long distances

Gamaliel (Hebrew) rewarded by God
Gamaleel, Gamalyel

Gamba (African) warring

Gamberro (Spanish) hooligan
Gami

Gamble (Scandinavian) mature wisdom
Gam, Gamb, Gambel, Gambie, Gamby

Gamel (Hebrew) God rewards him

Gamliel (Arabic) camel; wanders
Gamaliel

Gammon (Last name as first name) game
Gamen, Gamon, Gamun

Gan (Chinese) wanders wide

Gandy (American) adventurer

Ganesh (Hindi) Lord of all

Ganit (American) leader

Ganon (Irish) fair-skinned
Gannon, Ganny

Ganso (Spanish) goose; goofy
Gans, Ganz

Ganya (Russian) strong

Gar (English) form of Garbin: pure

Garai (African) settled

Garbhan (Irish) rough boy

Garbin (Spanish) pure

Garbini (Spanish) pure

Garcia (Spanish) strong
Garce, Garcey, Garsey

Gard (English) guard
Garde, Gardey, Gardi, Gardie, Gardy, Guard

Gardner (English) keeper of the garden
Gar, Gard, Gardener, Gardie, Gardiner, Gardnyr, Gardy

Garee (English) form of Gary: strong man

Garek (Polish) brave boy
Garreck, Garrik, Gerek

Gareth (Irish) kind
Gare

Garfiel (English) form of Garfield: armed

Garfield (English) armed
Gar, Garfeld

Gariana (Hindi) shout

Garin (American) form of Darin: great
Gare, Gary

Garis (Biblical) place name

Garl (French) form of Garland: adorned

Garland (French) adorned
Gar, Garlan, Garlend, Garlind, Garlynd

Garlando (Spanish) wreath

Garlon (French) wreath

Garmon (German) man who throws spears
Garmen

Garn (American) prepared
Gar, Garnie, Garny, Garr

Garner (French) guard
Gar, Garn, Garnar, Garnir

Garnett (English) armed; spear
Gar, Garn, Garnet, Garny

Garnock (Welsh) from the alder-tree place; outdoor spirit

Garoa (Spanish) morning dew

Garold (American) form of Harold: leader of an army

Garon (American) gentle
Garonn, Garonne

Garonzick (Last name as first name) secure
Gare, Garon, Garons, Garonz

Garr (English) form of Garrett: brave; watchful; form of Garth: sunny; gardener
Gar

Garrad (English) form of Gerard: brave

Garren (American) kind

Garreth (German) brave
Gareth, Garryth, Garyth

Garrett (Irish) brave; watchful
Gare, Garet, Garitt, Garret, Garritt, Gary, Gerrot

Garrick (English) ruler with a spear; brave
Garey, Garic, Garick, Garik, Garreck, Gary, Gerrick, Gerrieck

Garridan (English) form of Gary: strong man

Garrison (French) prepared
Garris, Garrish, Garry, Gary

Garrist (English) form of Garrison: prepared

Garroway (English) throws spears; physical presence
Garraway

Garson (English) son of Gar; fort home; industrious

Garth (Scandinavian) sunny; gardener
Gar, Gare, Garry, Gart, Garthe, Gary

Garthay (Irish) form of Gareth: gentle
Garthae

Garton (English) place of spear man; rowdy

Garv (English) peaceful
Garvey, Garvy

Garvan (English) throws spears; athletic

Garver (English) friend

Garvy (Irish) peacemaker
Garvey

Garwin (English) friend who struggles

Garwood (English) natural
Garr, Garwode, Garwoode, Woody

Gary (English) strong man
Gare, Garrey, Garri

Garyle (German) form of Gary: strong man

Gask (American) form of Gaskill

Gaskill (Last name as first name)

Gasos (Greek) form of Pegasus: horse; rider

Gaspard (French) holds treasure
Gaspar, Gasper

Gaspare (Italian) treasure-holder
Casper, Gasp, Gasparo

Gassia (Slavic) treasure

Gaston (French) native of Gascony; stranger
Gastawn, Gastowyn

Gat (American) form of Gatam: their lowing; their touch

Gatam (Biblical) their lowing; their touch

Gataz (Spanish) open-minded

Gatch (American) jaunty

Gate (English) open
Gait, Gates

Gath (Biblical) place name

Gathen (American) form of Gath: place name

Gathrir (American) form of Gath: place name

Gatlin (Last name as first name)

Gatsby (Literature) from Fitzgerald's *The Great Gatsby*; ambitious; tragic

Gaudencio (Spanish) content

Gaudy (American) word as name; colorful
Gaudin

Gauge (French) form of Gage: dedicated

Gauran (French) form of George: land-loving; farmer

Gaurav (Hindi) proud

Gauri (Indian) white

Gautier (French) form of Walter: army leader
Gauther, Gauthier

Gavard (Last name as first name) creative
Gav, Gaverd

Gavin ✪ (English) alert; hawk
Gav, Gaven, Gavinn, Gavon, Gavvin, Gavyn

Gavine (French) hawk

Gavino (Italian) hawk

Gavra (Hebrew) dedicated to God

Gavri (Hebrew) form of Gavriel: filled by God's strength

Gavriel (Herbew) filled by God's strength
Gavryel

Gavril (Hebrew) strong
Gavrill, Gavryl, Gavryll

Gawain (Hebrew) archangel
Gawaine, Gawayne, Gwayne

Gawath (Welsh) form of Gawain: archangel

Gawin (Scottish) watchful; wise
Gawyn

Gayathri (Russian) God-fearing

Gaylin (Greek) calm
Gaelin, Gayle, Gaylen, Gaylon

Gaylord (French) high-energy
Gallerd, Galurd, Gaylar, Gayllaird, Gaylor

Gaynor (Irish) spunky
Gainer, Gaye, Gayner

Gayton (Irish) fair
Gayten, Gaytun

Gaza (Arabic) place name; strong

Gazara (Biblical) place name

Gean (American) form of Gene: noble

Gearld (English) changes

Gearn (English) changes

Geary (English) flexible
Gearey

Gebby (German) gifted

Gedaliah (Hebrew) great in
Jehovah's love
Gedalia, Gedaliahu, Gedalya,
Gedalyahu

Gedion (French) form of Gideon:
power-wielding

Gedor (Biblical) place name

Geer (German) spearman
Geere

Gefaniah (Hebrew) vineyard of the
Lord; grows
Gefania, Gefanya, Gephania,
Gephaniah

Geibe (American) bright

Geir (Biblical) shining

Geka (Scandinavian) armed

Gelo (Russian) nobility

Gemini (Astrology) zodiac twins;
intelligent

Gen (Slavic) family man

Genaro (Latin) dedicated
Genaroe, Genaroh

Gene (Greek) noble
Geno, Jene, Jeno

General (American) military rank as
name; leader

Genio (Spanish) blue blood

Gennaro (Latin) devout

Geno (Italian) spontaneous

Genoah (Place name) city in Italy
Genoa, Jenoa, Jenoah

Genoris (Italian) giving

Genovese (Italian) spontaneous;
from Genoa
Genno, Geno, Genovise, Genovize

Gent (American) from gentleman;
mannerly
Gynt, Jent, Jynt

Gentil (Spanish) charming
Gentilo

Gentry (American) high breeding
Genntrie, Gent, Gentree, Gentrie

Genty (Irish) man of snow; changes

Geo (Greek) form of George: land-
loving; farmer
Gee

Geoff (English) form of Geoffrey:
peaceful
Jeff

Geoffrey (English) peaceful
Geffry, Geoff, Geoffie, Geoffry, Geoffy,
Geofry, Jeff

Geordan (Scottish) from the hill

Georg (German) works with the earth

George (Greek) land-loving; farmer
Georg, Georgi, Georgie, Georgy, Jorg,
Jorge

George-Hamilton (American) star
quality

Georgio (Italian) earth-worker
Giorgio, Jorgio, Jorjeo, Jorjio

Georgios (Greek) land-loving

Georgy (Greek) form of George:
land-loving; farmer
Georgee, Georgi, Georgie

Geraint (English) old

Gerald (German) strong; ruling with
a spear
Geralde, Gerrald, Gerre, Gerry

Gerant (Welsh) eldest

Gerar (French) brave

Gerard (French) brave
Gerord, Gerr, Gerrard

Gerardus (American) brave

Gerben (Dutch) spear-wielder

Gerber (Last name as first name)
particular
Gerb

Gerbold (German) bold with a spear
Gerbolde

Gerdano (Italian) descends

Gere (English) spear-wielding; dramatic
Gear

Gereon (German) old soul

Gerhard (German) forceful; (French)
finds
Ger, Gerd

Gerico (American) form of Jericho:
nocturnal

Gerlach (German) athlete with spears; musical

Gerlie (Spanish) wins

Germain (French) growing; from Germany
Germa, Germaine, Germane, Germay, Germayne, Jermaine

German (German) from the country of Germany

Gerod (English) form of Gerard: brave
Garard, Geraldo, Gerarde, Gere, Gererde, Gerry, Gerus, Giraud, Jerade, Jerard, Jere, Jerod, Jerott, Jerry

Gerodi (Italian) form of Gerod: brave

Gerold (Danish) rules with spears
Gerrold, Gerry

Geronimo (Italian) sacred name
Geronimoh

Gerrist (Slavic) strong

Gerrit (Dutch) protective

Gerry (English) form of Gerald: strong; ruling with a spear
Gerr, Gerre, Gerree, Gerrey, Gerri, Gerrie

Gersh (Biblical) form of Gershon: his banishment; the change of pilgrimage
Gershe, Gursh, Gurshe

Gershom (Hebrew) exile

Gershon (Biblical) his banishment; the change of pilgrimage

Gerson (English) Gary's son

Gerton (English) town of Gary

Gervaise (French) man of honor
Geru, Gervase, Gervay

Gervasio (Spanish) aggressive
Gervase, Gervaso, Jervasio

Gervis (German) honored
Geru, Gervace, Gervaise, Gervey, Jervaise, Jervis

Gerwyn (Welsh) fair and lovely

Geshem (Hebrew) raining

Geter (Origin unknown) hopeful
Getterr, Getur

Gether (Biblical) in the dark

Gethin (Welsh) dark skin

Gevariah (Hebrew) strength
Gevaria, Gevarya, Gevaryah, Gevaryahu

Ghalby (Origin unknown) winning
Galby

Ghalib (Arabic) wins

Ghassan (Arabic) in the prime of life

Ghayth (Arabic) victor
Ghaith

Gheorgh (Welsh) form of George: land-loving; farmer

Ghorm (American) form of Gorm: blue-eyed

Ghoshal (Hindi) the speaker
Ghoshil

Ghulam (Arabic) slave; servant

Gi (Italian) form of Giann: believer in a gracious God

Giacomo (Italian) replacement; musical
Como, Gia

Giann (Italian) believer in a gracious God
Ghiann, Giahanni, Gian, Gianni, Giannie, Gianny

Gianni (Italian) calm; believer in God's grace
Giannie, Gianny

Gibbon (Scottish) strong
Gibben, Gibbons

Gibbs (English) form of Gibson: smiling
Gib, Gibb, Gibbes

Gibeah (Biblical) a hill

Gibeon (Biblical) place name

Giblen (English) Last name as first name

Gibor (Hebrew) strong one

Gibson (English) smiling
Gib, Gibb, Gibbie, Gibbson, Gibby, Gibsan, Gibsen, Gibsyn

Gid (Hebrew) form of Gideon: power-wielding

Gidd, Giddee, Giddi, Giddy

Gideon (Hebrew) power-wielding

Giddy, Gideone, Gidion, Gidyun

Gidney (English) strong

Gidnee, Gidni

Gidon (Biblical) form of Gideon: power-wielding

Gif (English) giver

Giff

Giffin (English) giving

Giffyn

Gifford (English) generous-hearted

Giff, Gifferd, Giffie, Giffy, Giford

Gig (English) man in the carriage

Giggs (English) carriage man

Gil (Hebrew) form of Gilam: joyful people

Gill

Gilad (Hebrew) testimonial hill; outspoken

Giladi, Gilead

Gilam (Hebrew) joyful people

Gilbert (English) intelligent

Gil, Gilber, Gilburt, Gill, Gilly

Gilberto (Spanish) bright

Bertie, Berty, Gil, Gilb, Gilburto, Gillberto, Gilly

Gilboa (Biblical) place name

Gilbran (Spanish) thinker

Gilby (Irish) blond

Gilbie, Gill, Gillbi

Gilchrist (Irish) open

Gill

Gildardo (German) excellent

Gildea (Irish) God's servant

Gildo (Italian) macho

Gil, Gill, Gilly

Giles (French) protective

Gile, Gyles

Gilesp (Irish) form of Gillespie: humble

Gilford (English) kindhearted

Gill, Gillford, Guilford

Gilgal (Biblical) place name

Gill (Hebrew) happy man

Gil, Gilli, Gillie, Gilly

Gillanders (Scottish) serves

Gillean (Scottish) able server

Gillan, Gillen, Gillian

Gillent (French) form of Gilbert: intelligent

Gilles (French) miraculous

Geal, Zheal, Zheel

Gillespie (Irish) humble

Gilespie, Gill, Gilley, Gilli, Gilly

Gillett (French) hospitable

Gelett, Gelette, Gillette

Gilley (American) countrified

Gill, Gilleye, Gilli, Gilly

Gillian (Irish) devout

Gill, Gilley, Gilly, Gillyun

Gillor (American) serves well

Gilman (Irish) serving well

Gilley, Gilli, Gillman, Gillmand, Gilly, Gilmand, Gilmon

Gilmer (English) riveting

Gelmer, Gill, Gillmer, Gilly

Gilmi (Irish) devout

Gilmore (Irish) riveting

Gill, Gillmore, Gilmohr

Gilo (Hebrew) joyful

Gilon (Hebrew) joyful

Gill

Gilroy (Irish) king's devotee

Gilderoy, Gildray, Gildrey, Gildroy, Gillroy

Gilson (Irish) devoted son

Gilus (Scottish) Jesus's servant

Gimarrai (Biblical) place name

Gimzo (Biblical) place name

Ginnesar (Biblical) place name

Gino (Italian) of good breeding; outgoing

Geeno, Geino, Ginoh

Gins (Greek) life-giving

Ginton (Hebrew) garden

Giona (Italian) form of Giovanni: jovial; happy believer

Giordano (Italian) delivered
Giorgie, Jiordano

Giorgio (Italian) earthy; creative
George, Georgeeo, Georgo, Jorge, Jorgio

Giovanni (Italian) jovial; happy believer
Geovanni, Gio, Giovani, Giovannie, Giovanny, Vannie, Vanny, Vonny

Gipsy (English) travels widely

Girioel (Welsh) Lord

Girolamo (Italian) form of Jerome: holy name; blessed

Giron (American) form of Garon: gentle

Girvin (Irish) tough-minded
Girvan, Girven, Girvon

Gisbert (French) aggressor

Gisli (French) loyal

Gitel (Hebrew) good

Gittaim (Biblical) place name

Gitte (Scandinavian) celebrated

Gittel (Hebrew) good

Giulio (Italian) youth

Giuseppe (Italian) capable
Beppo, Giusepe, Gusepe

Given (Last name as first name) gift
Givens, Gyvan, Gyven, Gyvin

Givon (Hebrew) boy of heights

Gizmo (American) playful
Gis, Gismo, Giz

Gizon (Spanish) morning

Glad (American) happy
Gladd, Gladde, Gladdi, Gladdie, Gladdy

Gladspell (Last name as first name) happy

Gladston (Last name as first name) happy

Gladstone (English) cheering

Gladus (Welsh) lame; rueful

Gladwyn (English) friend who has a light heart
Glad, Gladdy, Gladwin, Gladwynn

Glaisne (Irish) serene
Glasny

Glancy (American) form of Clancy: lively; feisty redhead
Glance, Glancee, Glancey, Glanci

Glanville (French) serene

Glasgow (Place name) city in Scotland

Glasson (Scottish) from Glasgow, Scotland

Glause (Spanish) blue eyes

Glen (Irish) natural wonder
Glenn

Glenard (Irish) from a glen; nature-loving

Glen, Glenerd, Glenn, Glennard, Glenni, Glennie

Glendon (Scottish) fortified in nature
Glen, Glend, Glenden, Glenn, Glynden

Glendower (Welsh) water valley boy

Glenmore (English) valley boy

Glenn (Irish) natural wonder
Glen, Glenni, Glennie, Glenny, Glynn, Glynny

Glennon (Last name as first name) living in a valley
Glenen, Glennen, Glenon

Glenward (Last name as first name)

Gloster (Place name) from Gloucester

Glyndwr (Welsh) water valley life
Glyn, Glynn, Glynne

Glynn (Welsh) lives in a restful glen
Glin, Glinn, Glyn

Gobi (Place name) desert in Central Asia; audacious
Gobee, Gobie

Gobind (Sanskrit) the name of a Hindu deity
Govind

Gockley (Last name as first name) peaceful
Gocklee

Goddard (German) staunch in
spirituality
Godard, Godderd, Goddird

Godfred (German) peaceful; God's
child

Godfrey (Irish) peaceful
Godfree, Godfrie, Godfry

Godfried (German) imbued with
God's peace
Godfreed

Godinez (Spanish) loves God

Godofredo (Spanish) form of
Godfrey: peaceful

Godric (English) man of God
*Godrick, Godrik, Godryc, Godryck,
Godryk*

Godridge (Last name as first name)
place of God

Godwin (English) close to God
Godwinn, Godwyn, Godwynn

Goel (Hebrew) redeemed

Goethe (Last name as first name) poet

Goforth (English) peace wish

Gofraidh (Irish) God's peace child
Gothfraidh, Gothraidh

Goger (Last name as first name)
paternal

Gohn (African American) spirited
Gon

Golan (Biblical) place name

Golding (English) golden boy

Goldo (English) golden
Golo

Goliath (Hebrew) large
Goliathe

Gombos (Last name as first name)
thorough

Gomda (Native American) wind's
moods

Gomer (English) famed fighter
Gomar, Gomher, Gomor

Gomorr (Place name) the battle

Gong (American) forceful

Gonz (Spanish) form of Gonzalo:
feisty wolf
*Gons, Gonz, Gonza, Gonzales,
Gonzalez*

Gonzales (Spanish) feisty
Gonzalez

Gonzalo (Spanish) feisty wolf
Gonz, Gonzoloh

Goode (English) good
Good, Goodey, Goody

Goodman (Last name as first name)
a good man
Goodeman

Goodreau (French) good

Goodrich (Last name as first name)
giving; good
Goodriche

Gopin (Indian) cow song

Gor (Last name as first name) hill

Goran (Croatian) good

Gordion (Biblical) place name

Gordo (American) jovial guy

Gordon (English) nature-lover; hill
*Gord, Gordan, Gorden, Gordi, Gordie,
Gordy*

Gordy (English) form of Gordon:
nature-lover; hill
Gordee, Gordi, Gordie

Gore (English) practical;
pie-shaped land

Gorgey (Latin) gorge

Gorgonio (Greek) trouble

Gorham (English) sophisticated;
name of a silver company
Goram

Gorky (Place name) Russian
amusement park in the novel *Gorky
Park*; mysterious
Gork, Gorkee, Gorkey, Gorki

Gorm (Irish) blue-eyed

Gorman (Irish) small man
Gormann, Gormen

Gormlee (Irish) blue-eyed

Goro (Japanese) fifth son

Goron (Welsh) handsome

Gosheven (Native American) leaps
well; athletic

Goss (English/German) Last name as first name

Gotam (Hindi) best cow; cherished
Gautam, Gautoma

Gottfried (German) form of Godfried: imbued with God's peace

Gotzon (German) angel

Goulet (French) Last name as first name

Gouriet (French) charming

Govannon (Welsh) craftsman

Gower (Welsh) unblemished

Gowon (African) rainmaking

Gozal (Hebrew) baby bird; trying his wings

Gozan (Biblical) place name

Gradin (Irish) diligent

Grady (Irish) hardworking
Grade, Gradee, Gradey

Grae (Scottish) grand

Graem (Scottish) homebody
Graeme

Graffen (Last name as first name) distinguished

Graffin (American) form of Griffin: unconventional

Graham (English) wealthy; grand house
Graeham, Graeme, Grame

Graig (American) form of Craig: brave climber

Grail (Word as name) desired; sought after
Grale, Grayle

Grajeda (Spanish) crow

Gram (American) form of Graham: wealthy; grand house

Granace (American) gray

Granados (Spanish) grand

Granbel (Last name as first name) grand and attractive
Granbell

Granberry (English) farms berries

Granderson (Last name as first name) grand
Grand, Grander

Grange (French) lonely; on the farm
Grainge, Granger, Grangher

Granicus (Biblical) place name

Granison (Last name as first name) son of Gran; grandiose
Gran, Grann

Granit (English) great

Granite (American) rock; hard
Granet

Grant (English) expansive
Grandt, Grann, Grannt

Grantland (French) tall

Grantly (French) tall; lithe
Grantlea, Grantleigh, Grantley

Granvar (English) grand

Granville (French) grandiose
Grann, Granvel, Granvelle, Gravil

Grarol (English) gray

Grasshopper (American) lively

Gratton (Last name as first name) God loved

Graven (English) gray

Gravette (Origin unknown) grave
Gravet

Gravitt (English) gray

Gray (English) hair of gray
Graye, Grey

Grayce (English) gray hair

Graydon (Last name as first name) graceful

Grayer (English) gray

Graylon (English) gray-haired
Gray, Grayan, Graylan, Graylin

Grayson (English) son of man with gray hair
Gray, Grey, Greyson

Graz (Place name) city in Austria

Grazi (Italian) gracious

Graziano (Italian) dearest
Graciano, Graz

Greco (Italian) kind

Gredy (Last name as first name)

Greek (American) Greek

Greeley (English) careful

Grealey, Greel, Greely

Greenlee (English) outdoorsy

Green, Greenlea, Greenly

Greenwood (English) untamed;
forest

*Greene, Greenwoode, Greenwude,
Grenwood*

Greer (Last name as first name) sly

Greere, Grier

Greerzen (American) son of Greer

Greg (Latin) form of Gregory: careful

Gregg, Greggie, Greggy

Greger (Scandinavian) form of
Gregory: careful

Gregoire (French) watchful

Gregorie

Gregor (Greek) cautious

Greger, Gregors, Greig

Gregorio (Greek) careful

Gregory (Greek) careful

*Greg, Greggory, Greggy, Gregori,
Gregorie, Gregry*

Gregson (Last name as first name)
son of Greg; careful

Greggsen, Greggson, Gregsen

Grekel (American) vigilant

Grenville (New Zealand) outdoorsy

Granville, Gren

Gresham (English) of pasture village;
sylvan

Grisham

Greville (English) thoughtful

Grey (Last name as first name) quiet;
grey-haired

Greyson

Griden (Norse) peacemaker

Griffaw (Latin) ruddy

Griffin (Latin) unconventional

*Greffen, Griff, Griffee, Griffen,
Griffey, Griffie, Griffon, Griffy*

Griffith (Welsh) able leader

Griff, Griffee, Griffey, Griffie, Griffy

Grigg (Welsh) vigilant

Grigori (Russian) watchful

Grig, Grigor

Grimbald (Last name as first name)
dark

Grimbold

Grimes (English) spunky

Grimm (English) grim; dark

Grim, Grym

Grimshaw (English) from a dark
forest; quiet

Grindon (Last name as first name)

Gris (German) gray

Griz

Grischa (German) form of Gregory:
careful

Griswald (German) bland

Greswold, Gris, Griswold

Grogan (Last name as first name)

Grosvenor (French) hunts well

Grover (English) thriving

Grove

Gruver (Origin unknown) ambitious

Gruever

Gualberto (Spanish) believer

Gualter (Spanish) form of Walter:
army leader

Guanjone (Spanish) strong

Guapo (Spanish) looker

Guard (American) protects

Guasparre (Italian) values

Gudy (German) good

Guenter (German) warrior

Guerdon (English) combative

Guerino (Italian) protects

Guerry (English) aggressive

Guido (Italian) form of Guy: wood

Guidoh, Gwedo, Gweedo

Guilford (English) from a ford with
yellow flowers; nature-lover

Gilford, Guildford

Guillerm (German) form of William:
staunch protector

Guillermo (Spanish) attentive

Guilermo, Gulermo

Gull (Scandinavian) godlike

Gullen (Scandinavian) godlike

Gullet (Latin) throat

Gulshan (Hindi) gardener; flourishes

Gultekin (Turkish) Last name as first name

Gulzar (Arabic) thrives

Gumecindo (Spanish) excellent

Gunder (Scandinavian) form of Gunnar: bold

Gundy (American) friendly
Gundee

Gunion (Last name as first name)

Gunn (Scandinavian) macho; gunman
Gun, Gunner

Gunnar (Scandinavian) bold
Gunn, Gunner, Gunnir

Guntersen (Scandinavian) macho; gunman
Gun, Gunth

Gunther (Scandinavian) able fighter
Gunn, Gunnar, Gunner, Guntar, Gunthar, Gunthur

Gunvor (Scandinavian) watchful

Gunyon (American) tough; gunman
Gunn, Gunyun

Gur (Hindi) from guru; teacher

Gurd (Scandinavian) guards

Gurjeet (Indian) at the feet of the guru

Gurley (Last name as first name) leads

Gurmot (German) speared

Gurpreet (Hindi) devoted follower

Guryon (Hebrew) lionlike
Garon, Gorion, Gurion

Gus (Scandinavian) form of Augustus: highly esteemed; form of Gustaf: armed; vital
Guss, Gussi, Gussy, Gussye

Gustachian (American) pretentious
Gus, Gussy, Gust

Gustaf (German) armed; vital
Gus, Gusstof, Gustav, Gustovo

Gustavo (Spanish) vital; gusto
Gus, Gustaffo, Gustav

Gustin (Spanish) serious

Gusto (Spanish) pleasure
Gusty

Gustus (Scandinavian) royal
Gus, Gustaf, Gustave, Gustavo

Guth (Irish) form of Guthrie: windy; heroic
Guthe, Guthry

Guthrie (Irish) windy; heroic
Guthree, Guthry

Gutierre (Spanish) form of Walter: army leader

Guto (Welsh) royal; tired

Guy (French) wood
Guye

Guyon (French) leads

Guzet (American) bravado
Guzz, Guzzett, Guzzie

Gwandoya (African) miserable fate

Gweedo (Invented) form of Guido: wood

Gwent (Place name) city in Wales

Gwill (American) dark-eyed
Gewill, Guwill

Gwynedd (Welsh) fair-haired
Gwyn, Gwynfor, Gwynn, Gwynne

Gwynn (Welsh) fair
Gwen, Gwyn

Gyan (Hindi) knowledgeable
Gyani

Gyanee (Italian) form of Gianni: calm; believer in God's grace

Gyasi (African) terrific man

Gye (American) knowing

Gylfi (Scandinavian) king; stealthy

Gyllen (Last name as first name) young

Gylmar (German) loyal

Gyorgy (Italian) form of George: land-loving; farmer

Gyronne (Hindi) wise

Gysen (Hindi) wise

Gysley (English) excellent

Gyth (American) capable

Gith, Gythe

Gyuri (Slavic) form of George: land-loving; farmer

H

Haadee (Arabic) leader

Haafiz (Arabic) protector

Haakon (Scandinavian) chosen son

Haaris (Arabic) good man

Haas (Last name as first name) good

Habakkuk (Hebrew) embrace

Habby (Hebrew) loved

Habib (Arabic) well-loved

Habeeb

Habie (Origin unknown) jovial

Hab

Habimama (African) believer in God

Habor (Biblical) place name

Hachiro (Japanese) eighth son

Hachman (Last name as first name) chops

Hachmann, Hachmin

Hackett (Last name as first name) chops

Hackman (German) fervent; hacks wood

Hackmann

Hadad (Arabic) calm; blacksmith

Hadar (Hebrew) respected

Hadaram, Hadur, Heder

Hadaway (English) from the heather hill

Hadden (American) bright; natural

Haddan, Haddin, Haddon, Haden, Hadon

Haddy (English) form of Hadley: lover of nature; meadow with heather

Had, Haddee, Haddey, Haddi

Hade (Arabic) leads in the right way

Hades (Mythology) Greek god of the dead

Hadi (Arabic) guide

Hadle (English) from the meadow of heather

Hadley (English) lover of nature; meadow with heather

Haddleye, Hadlee, Hadlie, Hadly

Hadran (Latin) dark

Hadrian (Roman) from Hadria

Hadriel (Hebrew) blessed

Hadwin (Last name as first name) natural man

Hadwyn

Haffey (Indian) protects

Haffi (Indian) protects

Hafiz (Arabic) guards others

Hafeez, Hapheez, Haphiz

Hagan (German) defender

Hagen, Haggan, Haggin

Hagar (Hebrew) wanders

Hagen (German) chosen one

Hagan, Haggen

Haggai (Biblical) festive

Haggerty (Irish) Last name as first name; unjust

Hagins (German) strong

Hagit (Last name as first name) defends

Hagley (Last name as first name) defensive

Hahn (Last name as first name) asks

Haidar (Hindi) lionlike

Haider, Haydar, Hyder

Haig (Armenian) strong ancestry

Haike (Asian) of the water

Hailen (Irish) clever

Haim (Hebrew) alive

Hayim, Hayyim

Haines (Last name as first name) confident

Hanus, Haynes

Hajile (Arabic) wanders

Hajir (Arabic) powerful

Hakan (Arabic) fair

Hakim (Arabic) brilliant

Hakeam, Hakeem, Hakym

Hako (Japanese) honorable

Hakon (Scandinavian) chosen son

Haaken, Haakin, Haakon, Hacon,
Hagan, Hagen, Hakan, Hako

Hal (English) home ruler

Haland (Last name as first name)
island

Halland

Halbert (Last name as first name)
island

Bert, Hal

Haldane (German) fierce; person
who is half Danish

Haldayn, Haldayne

Haldas (Last name as first name)
dependable

Halden (German) man who is half
Dane

Haldan, Haldane, Haldin, Halfdan

Haldin (Scandinavian) half-Danish

Haldor (Scandinavian) thunderous
rock

Hale (English) heroic

Hal, Halee, Haley, Hali

Halen (Swedish) portal to life

Hailen, Hale, Haley, Hallen, Haylen,
Haylin

Haley (Irish) innovative

Hail, Hailee, Hailey, Hale, Halee,
Hayley

Halford (Last name as first name)
kind

Hali (Greek) loves the sea

Hall (English) solemn

Hallahan (Last name as first name)

Hallam (African) gentle

Hallberg (English) comes from a
town of valleys

Halberg, Halburg, Hallburg

Halle (Scandinavian) rocklike
dependability

Hallen (Scandinavian) from the hall

Halley (English) holy man

Halliwell (Last name as first name)
sea-loving

Hallman (English) his hall

Hallmark (English) stalwart

Hallward (English) guards the hall;
wily

Halward, Halwerd, Hawarden

Halmer (English) robust

Halos (Greek) halo

Halse (English) on the island

Halce, Halsi, Halsy, Halzee, Halzie

Halsey (English) isolated; island

Halstead (Last name as first name)
home on the rock

Halsted

Halston (Origin unknown)
fashionable

Halton (English) town on a hill;
country boy

Hallton, Halten

Halvard (Scandinavian) staunch

Halvor, Hallvard

Halver (Scandinavian) protects

Halwell (English) special

Hallwell, Halwel, Halwelle

Halyna (Slavic) calm

Ham (Last name as first name)
praising

Hamaker (Last name as first name)
industrious

Ham

Hamal (Arabic) lamb

Hamar (Scandinavian) hammer

Hamath (Biblical) place name

Hamby (Last name as first name)

Hamid (Arabic) grateful

Hameed

Hamidi (Arabic) ham

Hamedi, Hameedi, Hamm, Hammad

Hamil (English) rough-hewn

Hamel, Hamell, Hamill, Hamm

Hamilton (English) benefiting

Hamelton, Hamil, Hammilton

Hamish (Irish) form of James: he
who supplants

Hamlet (German) ham

Hamlette, Hamlit, Hamm

Hamlin (German) homebody

Hamaline, Hamelin, Hamlen, Hamlyn

Hamm (English) Last name as first name; low-lying land by a stream

Hammer (German) works with a hammer; able

Hammar, Hammur

Hammond (English) ingenious

Ham, Hamm, Hammon, Hamond

Hamon (Scandinavian) leader

Hamo

Hamor (Hebrew) organized

Hamp (American) fun-loving

Ham, Hampton

Hampden (English) distinctive; valley home

Hampton (English) distinctive

Ham, Hamm, Hamp, Hampt

Hamza (Arabic) endures

Han (Arabic) form of Hani: happy

Hanan (Arabic) forgiving

Hanani (Arabic) merciful

Hancock (English) has a farm; practical

Handel (German) form of John: God is gracious

Haneef (Arabic) believer

Hanford (Last name as first name) forgiving

Hamford

Hani (Arabic) happy

Hanif (Arabic) Islam believer

Hanisi (African) Thursday-born

Hank (English) form of Henry: leader

Hankey, Hanks, Hanky

Hanley (English) natural; meadow high

Han, Hanlee, Hanleigh, Hanly

Hannelore (Scandinavian) combo of Hanne and Lore

Hannes (Scandinavian) form of Johannes: God is gracious

Hahnes

Hannibal (Slavic) leader

Hanibal, Hanibel, Hann

Hannon (Hebrew) boy of gracefulness

Hanoch (Hebrew) loyal

Hanry (American) form of Henry: leader

Hans (Scandinavian) believer; warm

Hahns, Hanz, Hons

Hansa (Scandinavian) traditional; believer in a gracious Lord

Hans

Hansel (Scandinavian) gullible; open

Hans, Hansie, Hanzel

Hansen (Scandinavian) warm; Hans's son

Han, Handsen, Hans, Hansan, Hanson, Hanssen, Hansson, Hanz

Hans-Joachim (Scandinavian) combo of Hans and Joachim

Hansonn (Scandinavian) son of Hans

Hansraj (Hindi) king of swans; smooth

Hany (Arabic) happy

Haon (Hawaiian) relaxed

Hap (American) form of Hapney: happenstance

Hapney (English) happenstance

Haqq (Arabic) truth

Haran (Biblical) place name; Abraham's brother

Harbin (English) optimist

Harcourt (English) loves nature

Hardeep (Indian) God-loving

Hardell (German) bold

Hardeman (German) bold

Hardesty (German) brave

Hardin (English) lively; valley of hares

Hardee, Harden

Harding (English) fiery

Harden, Hardeng

Hardwick (English) castle boy

Harwyck

Hardwin (English) keeps hares

Hardy (American) fun-loving; substantial

Harday, Hardey, Hardie, Harding

Harean (African) aware

Harel (Scandinavian) ruler

Harence (English) swift

Harford (English) jolly

Harferd

Hargis (English) Last name as first name; baptismal name of son of Agace

Hargrave (Saxon) Last name as first name; provider or commissary of an army

Hargrove (English) fruitful

Hari (Hindi) brownish-orange

Harim (Arabic) above all

Harish (Indian) generous

Harjit (Indian) lights the way

Hark (American) word as name; behold

Harko

Harkin (Irish) red-faced

Harkan, Harken

Harlan (English) army land; athletic

Hal, Harl, Harlen, Harlon, Harlynn

Harland (English) strong fighter's land

Harld (Scandinavian) form of Harold: leader of an army

Harlemm (African American) dancer

Harl, Harlam, Harlem, Harlems, Harlum, Harly

Harley (English) wild-spirited

Harl, Harlee, Harly

Harlow (English) bold

Harlo, Harloh

Harmon (German) dependable

Harm, Harman, Harmen

Harmony (Mythology) from Harmonia; in harmony with life

Harmonio

Harness (English) word as name

Harod (Biblical) king

Harrod

Harold (Scandinavian) leader of an army

Hal, Harald, Hareld, Harry

Haron (Arabic) praiseworthy

Harper (English) artistic and musical; harpist

Harp

Harpo (American) jovial

Harpoh, Harrpo

Harpreet (Indian) God-loving

Harreal (Indian) happy

Harrell (Hebrew) likes the mountain of God; religious

Harrington (English) comes from the town of Harry; old-fashioned

Harris (English) dignified

Haris, Harriss

Harrison (English) Harry's son; adventurer

Harrey, Harri, Harrie, Harris, Harrisan, Harrisen, Harry

Harrod (Hebrew) victor

Harod, Harry

Harry (English) home ruler

Harree, Harrey, Harri, Harrie, Harye

Harshad (Hindi) evokes joy

Harshal (Indian) delight

Harsho (Hindi) joy

Harshul (Indian) deer

Hart (English) giving

Harte

Hartley (English) wilderness wanderer

Hartlee, Hartleigh, Hartly

Hartly (English) boy from the deer field

Hartman (German) strong-willed

Hart, Hartmann, Harttman

Hartmut (German) strong

Hartsey (English) lazing on the meadow; sylvan

Harts, Hartz

Hartwell (English) good-hearted

Harwell, Harwill

Hartwig (German) strong

Haruki (Japanese) child of the spring

Harun (Arabic) highly regarded

Harv (German) able combatant

Har

Harve (French) strong fighter

Harvey (German) fighter

Harv, Harvi, Harvie, Harvy

Harwin (American) safe

Harwen, Harwon

Harwood (English) from the deer wood; artistic

Harewood

Hasan (Arabic) attractive

Hasani (African) good

Hasees (Arabic) good

Hashim (Arabic) force for good

Hasheem

Hashum (African) crushes

Heshum

Hasin (Arabic) handsome

Hasen, Hassin

Hask (Hebrew) form of Haskell: ingratiating

Haske

Haskell (Hebrew) ingratiating

Hask, Haskel, Haskie, Hasky

Haslett (English) land of hazel trees; worthy

Haslit, Haslitt, Hazel, Hazlett, Hazlitt

Hassan (Arabic) good-looking

Hasan

Hasso (German) sun

Hasson

Hastings (English) leader

Haste

Haswell (English) dignified

Has, Haz

Hattan (Place name) from Manhattan; sophisticate

Hatt

Hauran (Biblical) place name

Haval (Biblical) waste

Havard (Scandinavian) guardian of the home

Hav

Havelock (Czech) form of Paul: small; wise

Haven (English) sanctuary

Haiv, Hav

Haward (English) guards the hedge; border man

Hawarden

Hawes (English) stays by the hedges

Haws

Hawke (English) watchful; falcon

Hauk, Hawk

Hawley (English) boy from the hedge

Hawthorne (English) observer

Hay (English) hedge

Hayde (English) hedge

Hayden ✪ ⊕ (English) respectful

Haden, Hadon, Hay, Haydon, Haydyn, Hayton

Haye (English) open

Hayes (English) open

Haies, Hay, Haye

Hayman (English) hedging

Hay

Haymo (Last name as first name) good-natured

Hayne (English) working outdoors

Haine, Haines, Haynes

Hayres (English) aware

Hayward (English) creative; good work ethic

Hay, Heyward

Hayword (English) open-minded

Haword, Hayward, Haywerd

Haz (Hebrew) sees God

Hazael (Old English) hazel tree

Hazaiah (Hebrew) believes God's decisions

Hazard (Origin Unknown) hazzard

Hazen (English) form of Hayes: open

Hazin

Hazleton (English) from woods of hazel trees

Hazlewood (English) from woods of hazel trees

Hearn (English) optimistic

Hearne, Hern

Heath (English) open space; natural

Heathe, Heith, Heth

Heathcliff (English) mysterious

Heaton (English) high-principled

Heat, Heatan, Heaten

Heber (Hebrew) partner; togetherness

Hebor

Hebron (Biblical) friend

Hector (Greek) loyal

Hec, Heck, Heco, Hect, Hectar, Hecter,
Hekter, Tito

Heddwyn (Welsh) peaceful; fair-
haired

Hedwin, Hedwyn, Hedwynn

Hedeon (Russian) woodsman

Hedgardo (Spanish) vigilant

Hedley (English) natural

Hedwig (German) combative

Hedwin (German) peaceful ally

Hefastus (Greek) clear

Heffington (Last name as first name)

Heike (Welsh) peaceful

Heiko (Dutch) rowdy

Heimdall (Scandinavian) white god

Heiman, Heimann

Hein (German) advising

Heiiri, Heiner, Heini, Heinlich

Heinrich (German) form of Henry:
leader

Hein, Heine, Heinrick, Heinrik

Heinz (German) advisor

Heinze

Heladio (Spanish) boy born in
Greece; ingenious

Eladio, Elado, Helado

Heleph (Biblical) place name

Helger (Slavic) holy

Helgi (Scandinavian) happy

Helge

Helio (Hispanic) bright

Heliodor (Greek) sun's adoration

Heliodoro (Greek) sun's adoration

Helios (Greek) sun

Heller (German) brilliant

Hellerson (German) brilliant one's
son; smart

Helley

Helm (German) bravery

Helmand (German) helmet;
protected

Helmar (German) protected; smart

Helm, Helmer, Helmet, Helmut

Helmut (German) courageous

Helon (Biblical) window; grief

Heman (Last name as first name)
direct

Hemant (Indian) season

Hemin (Hebrew) loyal

Heman

Hender (German) ruler; illustrious

Hend

Henderson (English) reliable

Hender, Hendersen, Hendersyn

Hendrik (German) home ruler

Heinrich, Hendrick, Henrick, Hindrick

Hendtrax (Hebrew) gifted

Henech (Last name as first name)
leading the pack

Henach

Henley (English) surprising

Henlee, Henly, Henlye, Hinley

Henning (Scandinavian) ruler

Henrik (Norwegian) leader

Henric, Henrick

Henry ✪ (German) leader

Hal, Hank, Harry, Henny, Henree,
Henri

Hensarling (Last name as first
name)

Henshaw (Last name as first name)

Henson (Last name as first name)
son of Hen; quiet

Heraldo (Spanish) divine

Herb (German) energetic

Herbi, Herbie, Herby, Hurb

Herber (French) valiant

Herbert (German) famed warrior

Bert, Herb, Herbart, Herberto, Herbie, Herbirt, Herby, Hurb, Hurbert

Herbertson (German) famed soldier's son

Hercule (French) strong

Harekuel, Hercuel, Herkuel

Hercules (Greek) grand gift

Herc, Herk, Herkules

Heriberto (Spanish) form of Herbert: famed warrior

Heribert

Herkamer (Last name as first name)

Herman (Latin) fair fighter

Heremon, Herm, Hermahn, Hermann, Hermie, Hermon, Hermy

Hermangildo (Spanish) combative

Hermes (Greek) courier of messages

Hermez

Hermod (Scandinavian) greets and welcomes

Hermosillo (Spanish) fighter

Hernand (Spanish) form of Hernando: bold

Hernando (Spanish) bold

Hernan

Herndon (English) nature-loving

Hern, Hernd

Herne (English) from the bird heron; inventive

Hearne, Hern

Hernley (English) from the heron meadow; easygoing

Hernlea, Hernlee, Hernlie, Hernly

Herodotus (Greek) the father of history

Heroico (Spanish) hero

Herol (American) form of Harold: leader of an army

Herrick (Last name as first name) never alone

Herris (German) rules

Herrod (Biblical) king

Herod

Herron (Latin) heroic

Herschel (Hebrew) deer; swift

Hersch, Hersh, Hershel, Hershell, Hershelle, Herzl, Hirchel, Hirsch, Hirshel

Hershall (Hebrew) deer; swift

Hersch, Herschel, Hersh, Herzl, Heshel, Hirschel, Hirsh, Hirshel

Hertzel (Hebrew) form of Herschel; deer; swift

Hert, Hertsel, Hyrt

Herve (French) ready for battle

Hervey (American) form of Harvey: fighter

Herv, Herve, Hervy

Herzon (American) fast

Herz, Herzan, Herzun

Hesed (Hebrew) sweet

Hesperos (Greek) evening star

Hesperios, Hespers

Hess (Last name as first name) bold

Hes, Hys

Hessel (Dutch) bold man

Heston (Last name as first name) star quality

Hetrick (Last name as first name)

Hevel (Hebrew) alive

Hewis (German) smart

Hewitt (German) smart

Hew, Hewet, Hewett, Hewie, Hewit, Hewy, Hugh

Hewney (Irish) smart

Owney

Hewson (Irish) son of Hugh; smart; giving

Heywood (Last name as first name) thoughtful

Haywood

Hezekiah (Biblical) strong man

Hezeklah, Zeke

Hezron (Biblical) strength

Hiawatha (Native American) Iroquois chief

Hia

Hibah (Arabic) the gift

Hickam (English) Last name as first name; enclosed dwelling

Hickok (American) from Wild Bill Hickok

Hidalgo (American) westerner

Hidde (Japanese) excellent

Hideaki (Japanese) cautious

Hideo (Japanese) excellent

Hideyo

Hieremias (Greek) God lifts him up

Hieronymos (Greek) alternate of Jerome

Heronymous

Hifz (Arabic) memorable

Higinio (Hispanic) forceful

Hilaire (French) happy child

Hilarion (Greek) cheery; hilarious

Hilary, Hill

Hilary (Latin) joyful

Hilaire, Hill, Hillarie, Hillary, Hillery, Hilly, Hilorie

Hildebrand (German) combative; sword

Hill, Hilly

Hill (English) lives on a hill; dreamy

Hillard (German) wars; diligent

Hilliard, Hillier, Hillyer

Hillel (Hebrew) praised; devout

Hilel, Hill

Hillery (Latin) happy; cheerful

Hill

Hilliard (German) brave; settlement on the hill

Hill, Hillard, Hillierd, Hilly, Hillyerd, Hylliard

Hills (Last name as first name) brave; from the hills

Hilton (English) sophisticated

Hillten, Hillton, Hiltan, Hiltawn, Hiltyn, Hylton

Himesh (Hindi) snow king

Hines (Last name as first name) strong

Hine, Hynes

Hipolito (Spanish) man who rides horses

Hippocrates (Greek) philosopher

Hipp

Hippolyte (Greek) frees horses

Hippolit, Hippolitos, Hippolytus, Ippolito

Hiram (Hebrew) most admired; highly praised

Hi, Hirom, Hirym

Hiramatsu (Japanese) exalted

Hiranya (Indian) rich

Hiresh (Indian) treasured

Hiro (Japanese) giving

Hirsh (Hebrew) deer; swift

Hersh, Hershel, Hirschel, Hirshel

Hirza (Hebrew) lithe; deer

Hisham (Arabic) generous nature

Hitchcock (English) creative; spooky

Hitch

Hixon (Last name as first name) high-energy

Hjalmar (Scandinavian) protective warrior

Hjalamar, Hjallmar, Hjalmer

Ho (Chinese) good

Hoan (Asian) complete child

Hoashis (Japanese) God

Hobart (German) haughty

Hobb, Hobert, Hoebard

Hobbes (English) form of Robert: brilliant; renowned

Hob, Hobbs

Hobe (German) hill child

Hobert (German) studious

Hobson (English) helpful backer

Hobb, Hobbie, Hobbson, Hobby, Hobsen

Hock (Asian) smart

Hockley (English) high meadow boy
Hocklea, Hocklee, Hocklie, Hockly

Hockney (English) from a high island
Hockny

Hodge (English) form of Roger: famed warrior
Hodges

Hodgie (English) short for Hodge: famed warrior
Hodgy

Hodgson (English) boy born to Roger; up-and-coming
Hodge, Hodges

Hoffman (Last name as first name) sophisticated

Hogan (Irish) high-energy; vibrant
Hogahn, Hoge, Hoghan

Hogue (Last name as first name) youth
Hoge

Hojar (American) wild spirit
Hobar, Hogar

Hoke (Origin unknown) popular

Hoken (American) liked

Holbert (German) capable
Hilbert

Holbrook (English) educated
Brooke, Brookie, Brooky, Holb, Holbrooke

Holcomb (Last name as first name) bright

Holday (American) form of Holiday: born on a holy day

Holden (English) quiet; gracious
Holdan, Holdin, Holldun

Holder (English) musical
Hold, Holdher, Holdyer

Holdern (Last name as first name)

Holegario (Spanish) superfluous
Holegard

Holger (Last name as first name) devoted

Holiday (English) born on a holy day
Holliday

Holling (English) holly

Hollis (English) flourishing
Holl, Hollace, Hollice, Hollie, Holly

Holloway (Last name as first name) jovial
Hollo, Hollway, Holoway

Hollywood (Place name) city in California; showoff
Holly, Wood

Holm (English) natural; woodsy
Holms

Holmes (English) safe haven; from the river; natural home
Holmm, Holmmes

Holmfrid (Last name as first name) prefers home-and-hearth

Holon (Biblical) place name

Holt (English) shaded view
Holte, Holyte

Homain (Last name as first name) homebody
Holman, Holmen

Homarl (Greek) form of Homer: secure

Homaros (Greek) form of Homer: secure

Homer (Greek) secure
Hohmer, Home, Homere, Homero

Honda (African) form of Hondo: warrior

Hondo (African) warrior

Honesto (Spanish) truthful
Honesta, Honestoh

Hong (Vietnamese) pink; tasteful

Honorato (Spanish) full of honor
Honor, Honoratoh

Honoré (Latin) man who is honored
Honor, Honoray

Hood (Last name as first name) easygoing; player
Hoode, Hoodey

Hooker (English) shepherd

Hoolihan (American) hooligan
Hool, Hoole, Hooli

Hoop (American) ball player

Hooper, Hoopy

Hoover (Last name as first name)

Hopkins (Welsh) Robert's son;

famous

Hopkin, Hopkinson, Hopkyns, Hopper,

Hoppner

Hopper (Last name as first name)

creative

Hoppy (American) lively

Horace (Latin) poetic

Horaace, Horase, Horice

Horatio (Latin) poetic; dashing

Horate, Horaysho

Horeb (Biblical) place name

Horgan (Last name as first name)

Hori (Biblical) prince; freeborn

Hornal (German) gardens

Horsley (English) calm field of

horses; keeper

Horslea, Horsleigh, Horslie, Horsly

Horst (German) deep; thicket

Hurst

Horstman (German) profound

Horst, Horstmen, Horstmun

Horstmar (German) from the

thicket; emphatic

Horston (German) thicket; sturdy

Horst

Horton (English) brash

Horten, Hortun

Horus (Egyptian) kind

Hosa (Native American) crow

Hosaam (Arabic) handsome

Hosea (Hebrew) prophet

Hoshea (Hebrew) saved

Hosie (Hebrew) form of Hosea:

prophet

Hosaya, Hose

Hosni (Arabic) excellent

Houchan (English) spirited

Houghton (English) boy from the

town on high

Houston (English) Texas city; rogue;

hill town

Houst, Hust, Huston

Hovannes (Hebrew) form of

Johannes: God is gracious

How (American) word as a name

Howe, Howey, Howie

Howard (English) well-liked

How, Howerd, Howie, Howurd, Howy

Howart (Origin unknown) admired

Howar

Howden (English) careful

Howe (German) high-minded

How, Howey, Howie

Howell (Welsh) outstanding

Howel, Howey, Howie, Howill

Howent (English) distinctive

Howerd (English) form of Howard:

well-liked

Howlan (English) living on a hill;

high

Howland (American) well-known

Howlend, Howlond, Howlyn

Howze (American) form of Howard:

well-liked

Hoyt (Irish) spirited

Hoit, Hoye

Hrothgar (Literature) king

Huang (Chinese) rich

Hubbard (German) fine

Hubberd, Hubert, Hubie

Huber (German) intelligent

Hubert (German) intellectual

Bert, Bertie, Burt, Hubart, Huberd,

Hue, Huebert, Hugh

Hubie (English) form of Hubert:

intellectual

Hube, Hubee, Hubey, Hubi

Huck (Literature) from *Huckleberry*

Finn

Huckleberry (American) glossy

black berry; from *Huckleberry Finn*;

mischevious

Hud (English) charismatic cowboy

Hudd

Hudson (English) Hugh's son; charismatic adventurer
Hud, Hudsan, Hudsen

Hudspeth (English) form of Hud: charismatic cowboy

Hudya (Arabic) going the right way

Huelett (American) bright; southern
Hu, Hue, Huel, Hugh, Hulette

Huey (French) hearty

Hugh (English) intelligent
Hue, Huey, Hughey, Hughi, Hughie, Hughy

Hughes (English) smart

Hughie (English) intelligent; lucky in parentage
Hughee, Hughi, Hughy

Hugo (Latin) spirited heart

Huitt (English) smart

Hul (Biblical) pain; infirmity

Huland (English) bright
Hue, Huel, Huey, Hugh

Hulbard (Last name as first name) singing; bright
Hulbert, Hulburt

Hull (English) spirited; confident

Hulsey (English) wise eye

Humbert (German) famous giant; renowned warrior

Humberto (Spanish) brilliant
Hum, Humb, Humbie

Hume (Last name as first name) daunting

Humphrey (German) strong peacemaker
Hum, Humfry, Hump, Humphry, Humprey

Hundy (Last name as first name)

Hunghui (Asian)

Hunn (German) combative
Hun

Hunt (English) active

Hunter ♂ ♀ (English) hunter; adventurer
Hunt

Hunting (English) hunter
Huntyng

Huntington (Last name as first name) town of hunters

Huntler (English) hunter
Huntt

Huntley (English) hunter
Hunt, Hunter, Huntlea, Huntlee, Huntlie, Huntly

Huon (Hebrew) form of John: God is gracious

Hur (Biblical) liberty; whiteness; hole

Hurd (Last name as first name) tends the herd

Hurlbert (English) shining army man
Hulbert, Hurlburt, Hurlbutt

Hurley (Irish) the tide; flowing
Hurlea, Hurlee, Hurli, Hurly

Hurst (Last name as first name) entrepreneurial

Hurston (English) boy from town of thickets

Husham (Biblical) good-looking

Husky (American) big
Husk, Huskee, Huskey, Huski

Huss (American) small

Hussein (Arabic) attractive man; handsome
Husain, Husane, Husein, Hussain

Hust (American) form of Houston: Texas city; rogue; hill town

Huston (English) form of Houston: Texas city; rogue; hill town

Hutch (American) safe haven; unique
Hut, Hutchey, Hutchie, Hutchy

Hutner (Last name as first name) child of the house

Hutter (Last name as first name) tough
Hut, Hutt, Huttey, Huttie, Hutty

Hutton (English) sophisticated
Hutt, Huttan, Hutten, Hutts

Huxford (Last name as first name) outdoorsman

Huxley (English) outdoorsman

Hux, Huxel, Huxle, Huxlee, Huxlie

Hwang (Japanese) yellow

Hyacinthe (French) flowering

Hyacinthos, Hyacinthus, Hyakinthos

Hyatt (English) secure

Hy, Hye, Hyett, Hyut

Hyde (English) special; a hyde is 120

acres

Hide, Hy

Hyden (English) tans hides

Hyghner (Last name as first name)

lofty goals

High, Highner, Hygh

Hylan (Asian) hopeful

Hyll (Origin unknown) open-minded

Hy, Hye, Hyell

Hyman (Hebrew) life

Hy, Hymen, Hymie

Hyo (Vietnamese) optimist

I

Iagan (Scottish) fire

Iago (Spanish) feisty villain

Iagoh, Jago

Iah (Egyptian) moonlike

Iain (Scottish) believer

Ian ✪ (Scottish) believer; handsome

Iain, Ean, Eon, Eyon

Iathan (Spanish) form of Nathan:

God's gift to mankind

Ib (Arabic) joy

Ibrahim (Arabic) fathering many

Ibraham, Ibrahem

Ibu (Japanese) creative

Icarus (Mythology) ill-fated

Ikarus

Ich (Hebrew) form of Ichabod: glory

in the past; slim

Ick, Ickee, Ickie, Icky

Ichabod (Hebrew) glory in the past;

slim

Ich, Icha, Ickabod, Ika, Ikabod, Ikie

Idelfonso (Spanish) ready

Idi (Swahili) born during the Idd

festival

Idris (Welsh) impulse-driven

Idriss, Idriys

Idwal (Welsh) known

Iefan (Welsh) form of John: God is

gracious

Ieuan (Welsh) form of Ivan: believer

in a gracious God; reliable one

Ifan (Welsh) form of John: God is

gracious

Ifor (Welsh) archer

Igal (Biblical) redeemed; defiled

Iggy (Latin) form of Ignatius:

firebrand

Iggee, Iggey, Iggi, Iggie

Ignace (French) fiery

Iggy, Ignase

Ignash (Latin) form of Ignatius:

firebrand

Ignasha (Latin) form of Ignatius:

firebrand

Ignatius (Latin) firebrand

Ig, Iggie, Iggy, Ignacius, Ignashus,

Ignatious, Ignnatius

Igor (Russian) warrior

Igoran (Russian) army boy

Ihsan (Arabic) charitable

Ijon (Biblical) place name

Ike (Hebrew) form of Isaac: laughter

Ika, Ikee, Ikey, Ikie

Ilan (Hebrew) tree

Illan

Ilesh (Indian) earth king

Illtyd (Welsh) from the well-

populated homeland

Illtud

Ilmar (Scandinavian) airy

Ilom (Welsh) happy

Immanuel (Hebrew) with God

Emmanuel, Imanuel

Imran (Arabic) host

Imre (Slavic) form of Emery: hardworking leader

Inder (Hindi) the Lord of sky gods is Indra; ethereal
Inderjeet, Inderjit, Inderpal, Indervir, Indra, Indrajit

Indiana (Place name) U.S. state; rowdy; dashing
Indio, Indy

Indore (Place name) city in India
Indor

Indra (Hindi) Lord of sky gods

Ing (Scandinavian) he who is foremost
Inge

Ingan (Scandinavian) prolific

Ingeborg (Scandinavian) fertile

Ingelbert (German) combative
Ing, Inge, Ingelbart, Ingelburt, Inglebert

Inger (Scandinavian) fertile
Ingemar, Ingmar

Ingmar (Scandinavian) famous son
Ing, Ingamar, Ingamur, Inge, Ingemar, Ingmer

Ingra (English) form of Ingram: angelic; kind
Ingie, Ingrah, Ingrie

Ingram (English) angelic; kind
Ing, Ingraham, Ingre, Ingrie, Ingry

Ingvar (Scandinavian) fertility god
Ingevar

Inigo (Spanish) form of Ignatius: firebrand

Iniko (Japanese) serves

Innis (Irish) isolated
Ines, Inis, Innes, Inness, Inniss

Innocencio (Spanish) innocent

Inteus (Native American) proud

Into (Scandinavian) excitable

Ioan (Slavic) believer

Ionel (Slavic) believer

Ior (Welsh) form of Iorwerth: worthy Lord

Iorgos (Greek) outgoing

Iorwerth (Welsh) worthy Lord

Ira (Hebrew) cautious
Irae, Irah

Irakli (Slavic) athletic

Iram (English) smart
Irem, Irham, Irum

Iranga (Sri Lankan) special

Irfan (Arabic) grateful child

Irind (American) peaceful

Irineo (Spanish) peaceful

Irish (English) boy from Ireland

Irmtraud (German) strong soldier

Irv (English) form of Irving: attractive

Irvin (English) attractive
Irv, Irvine

Irving (English) attractive
Irv, Irve, Irveng, Irvy

Irwin (English) practical
Irwen, Irwhen, Irwie, Irwinn, Irwy, Irwynn

Isa (African) saved

Isaac ✪ ✝ (Hebrew) laughter
Isaak, Isack, Izak, Ize, Izek, Izzy

Isadore (Greek) special gift
Isador, Isedore, Isidore, Issy, Izzie, Izzy

Isai (Hebrew) believer

Isaiah ✪ ✝ (Hebrew) saved by God
Isa, Isay, Isayah, Isey, Izaiah, Izey

Isak (Scandinavian) laughter
Isac

Isam (Arabic) protector

Isamu (Japanese) bravery

Isas (Japanese) worthwhile

Isham (Last name as first name) athletic

Ishan (Hindi) sun

Ishbak (Biblical) protector

Ishmael (Hebrew) God hears
Hish, Ish, Ishmel, Ismael

Ishtar (Mythology) goddess of fertility and love

Isidore (Greek) gift of Isis
Izzie

Isidoro (Spanish) gift
Cedro, Cidro, Doro, Izidro, Sidro, Ysidor

Isidro (Greek) gift

Isydro

Israel (Hebrew) God's prince;
conflicted

Israyel, Issy, Izzy

Israj (Hindi) king of gods

Issa (Hebrew) laughing

Issachar (Biblical) reward

Isser (Slavic) creative

Ithamar (Biblical) island of the palm
tree

Ithiel (Biblical) with God beside him

Itil (Welsh) has a giving nature

Itlus (Roman) from Italy

Itsik (Hebrew) form of Isaac: laughter

Itzak (Hebrew) form of Isaac: laughter

Itzik

Iuri (Slavic) form of Yuri: dashing

Ivan (Russian) believer in a gracious
God; reliable one

Ivahn, Ive, Ivey, Ivie

Ivanore (Scandinavian) child of God

Ivar (Scandinavian) Norse god

Ive (English) able

Ivee, Ives, Ivey, Ivie

Ives (American) musical

Ive

Ivo (Polish) yew tree; sturdy

Ivar, Ives, Ivon, Ivonnie, Yvo

Ivon (Slavic) believer

Ivor (Scandinavian) outgoing; ready

Ifot, Ivar, Ive, Iver, Ivy

Izaak (Polish) full of mirth

Izacz (Slavic) spicy; happy

Isaac, Izak, Izie, Izze, Izzee

Izador (Spanish) gift

Dorrie, Dory, Isa, Isador, Isadoro,
Isidoros, Isodore, Iza, Izadoro

Izaiah (Czech) form of Isaiah: saved
by God

Izaith (Spanish) form of Isaiah: saved
by God

Izan (Slavic) asks

Izedin (Spanish) gives

Izhar (Indian) serves well

Izrail (American) form of Isaiah:
saved by God

Izzy (Hebrew) friendly

Issie, Issy, Izi, Izzee, Izzie

J

Ja (Korean) gorgeous

Jaak (Scandinavian) form of Jack:
God is gracious

Jaan (Scandinavian) form of John:
God is gracious

Jabal (Place name) form of Japalpur;
a city in India: attractive

Jabari (African American) brave

Jabbar (Arabic) comforting

Jaber (American) form of Jabir:
supportive

Jabar, Jabe

Jabez (Hebrew) sorrow

Jabezz

Jabin (Hebrew) God's own

Jabir (Arabic) supportive

Jabbar

Jabon (American) wild

Jabonne

Jabot (French) shirt ruffle

Jace (American) audacious

Jase, Jhace

Jacek (Polish) hyacinth; growing

Jack, Yahcik

Jacen (Greek) form of Jason: healer;
the Lord is salvation

Jacett (Invented) jaunty

Jaycett

Jachin (Biblical) ready

Jachym (Hebrew) form of Jacob: he
who supplants

Jach

Jacinto (Spanish) hyacinth; fragrant

Jacint

Jack ✪ (Hebrew) form of John: God is gracious
Jackee, Jackie, Jacko, Jacky, Jax

Jackal (Sanskrit) wild dog; betrays
Jackel, Jackell, Jackyl, Jackyll

Jackie (English) personable
Jackee, Jackey, Jacki, Jacky, Jaki

Jackie-Lee (American) combo of Jackie and Lee

Jackson ✪ (English) Jack's son; full of personality
Jackee, Jackie, Jacks, Jacsen, Jakson, Jax, Jaxon

Jacksonville (Last name as first name) town of Jack's son; sturdy
Jacsonville, Jaksonville

Jaclo (Spanish) combo of Jack and Lo

Jacob ✪ ⊕ (Hebrew) he who supplants
Jaccob, Jacobe, Jacobee, Jake, Jakes, Jakey, Jakob

Jacoben (American) replaces; friend

Jacobo (Spanish) warm
Jake, Jakey

Jacobs (Biblical) replacing
Jakey, Jakobs

Jacobus (Latin) form of Jacob: he who supplants
Jakobus

Jacoby (Hebrew) form of Jacob: he who supplants
Jacobey, Jakobey, Jakoby

Jacquard (French) class act
Jackard, Jackarde, Jacquarde, Jaqard, Jaquard, Jaquarde

Jacques (French) romantic; ingenious
Jacquie, Jacue, Jaques, Jock, Jok

Jacy (American) form of Jacob: he who supplants

Jadaan (Last name as first name) content

Jadall (Invented) punctual
Jada, Jade

Jade (Spanish) valued jade stone
Jadee, Jadie, Jayde

Jaden ✪ ⊕ (Hebrew) Jehovah has heard
Jade, Jadin, Jadon, Jadun, Jadyn, Jaiden, Jaydie, Jaydon

Jadney (Last name as first name) pleased
Jad

Jadran (Slavic) form of Adrian: wealthy; dark-skinned

Jae (French) form of Jay: colorful

Jaegel (English) salesman
Jaeg, Jaeger, Jael

Jaeger (German) outdoorsman
Jaegir, Jagher, Jagur

Jael (Hebrew) climber

Jaewon (African American) form of Juwon: devout; lively
Jaewan, Jaywan, Jaywon

Jaeyel (Hebrew) form of Jael: salesman

Jafar (Arabic) from the stream
Gafar, Jafari

Jafeth (Hebrew) handsome

Jaffar (Arabic) directs

Jaffe (Hebrew) beautiful

Jaffey (English) form of Jaffe: beautiful
Jaff

Jaffiel (Spanish) loves the water

Jafon (Dutch) growth

Jagan (English) confident
Jagen, Jago, Jagun

Jagannath (Indian) Hindi god Vishnu; world leader

Jagger (English) brash
Jagar, Jager, Jaggar, Jagir

Jaggerton (English) brash
Jag, Jagg

Jagit (Invented) brisk
Jaggett, Jaggit, Jagitt

Jago (English) self-assured

Jaguar (Spanish) fast
Jag, Jagg, Jaggy, Jagwar, Jagwhar

Jahan (Sanskrit) worldly

Jaheim (Hindi) worldly

Jahi (African) runs well; dignity

Jahlel (Biblical) God helps

Jahmal (Arabic) beautiful
Jahmaal, Jahmall

Jahmil (Arabic) beautiful
Jahmeel, Jahmyl

Jai (American) adventurer
Jay

Jaidev (Hindi) God's victory

Jaidov (Indian) winning

Jailo (Hindi) worldwise

Jaime (Spanish) follower
Jaimey, Jaimie, Jamee, Jaymie

Jaimini (Hindi) winner

Jaimo (Asian) form of James:
he who supplants

Jair (Hebrew) teacher
Jairo

Jairaj (Hindi) Lord's victor

Jairam (Slavic) God informs him

Jaircineo (Spanish) enlightened

Jairemaine (French) form of
Germain: growing; from Germany

Jairo (Spanish) God enlightens
Jaero, Jairoh

Jairus (Biblical) faithful

Jaison (American) form of Jason:
healer; the Lord is salvation
Jaizon

Jaja (African) praise-worthy

Jakar (Place name) from Jakarta
Jakart, Jakarta, Jakarte

Jake ☻ (Hebrew) form of Jacob: he
who supplants
Jaik, Jakee, Jakey, Jakie, Jayke

Jakeem (Arabic) has been lifted

Jakey (American) nickname for Jake;
friendly
Jaky

Jakin (Biblical) form of Jachin: ready

Jakiren (American) playful

Jakob (Hebrew) form of Jacob: he
who supplants
*Jakab, Jake, Jakeb, Jakey, Jakie, Jakobe,
Jakub*

Jal (English) wanderer

Jalal (Hindi) glory

Jalam (Biblical) victor

Jaleel (Arabic) handsome
Jalil

Jalen (American) vivacious
Jalon, Jaylen, Jaylin, Jaylon

Jalenal (American) wins

Jaliseo (Spanish) modest

Jallen (American) winner

Jalmar (Scandinavian) soldier

Jamail (Arabic) good-looking
*Jahmil, Jam, Jamaal, Jamahal, Jamal,
Jamil, Jamile, Jamy*

Jamaine (Arabic) good-looking

Jaman (American) wonder

Jamar (American) form of Jamail:
good-looking
Jamarr, Jemar, Jimar

Jamari (African American) attractive

Jamarr (African American) attractive;
formidable
Jam, Jamaar, Jamar, Jamel, Jammy

Jamerson (English) son of James

James ✿ ☻ (English) form of Jacob:
he who supplants
*Jaimes, Jamsey, Jamze, Jaymes, Jim,
Jimmy*

James-Bolton (American) musical

Jameson (English) able; James's son
*Jamesan, Jamesen, Jamesey, Jamison,
Jamsie*

Jamie (English) form of James: he
who supplants
*Jaimey, Jaimie, Jamee, Jamey, Jay,
Jaymey, Jaymsey*

Jamil (Arabic) beautiful
Jameel, Jamyl

Jamile (Arabic) handsome

Jamin (Hebrew) favored son
Jamen, James, Jamie, Jamon, Jaymon

Jamisen (American) form of James:
he who supplants
Jami, Jamie, Jamis, Jamison

Jan (Dutch) form of John: God is gracious
Jaan, Jann, Janne

Janardan (Indian) helper

Jance (Scandinavian) form of John: God is gracious

Janesh (Hindi) thankful

Janier (French) form of John: God is gracious

Janis (Slavic) devout

Janko (Slavic) happy

Janon (Hebrew) chosen

Janson (Scandinavian) Jan's son; hardworking
Jan, Janne, Janny, Jansahn, Jansen, Jansey

Jantz (Scandinavian) form of Jantzen: God is gracious
Janson, Janssen, Jantzon, Janz, Janzon

Jantzen (Scandinavian) form of John: God is gracious

Janus (Latin) Roman god of beginnings and endings; optimistic; born in January
Jan, Janis

Januson (Scandinavian) son of Janus; year's gateway

Japheth (Hebrew) grows
Japhet

Jaquanace (American) growth

Jaquawn (African American) rock
Jacquon, Jakka, Jaquan, Jaquie, Jaqwen, Jequon, Jock

Jaquier (French) form of Jacques: romantic; ingenious

Jarah (Hebrew) sweet

Jarat (American) form of Jared: descendant; giving

Jaraus (American) form of Jaran: sings

Jard (American) form of Jared: descendant; giving
Jarra, Jarrd, Jarri, Jerd, Jord

Jareb (Hebrew) contender
Jarib, Yarev, Yariv

Jared (Hebrew) descendant; giving
Jarad, Jarod, Jarode, Jarret, Jarrett, Jerod, Jerrad, Jerrod

Jarek (Slavic) fresh
Jarec

Jarell (Scandinavian) giving
Jare, Jarelle, Jarey, Jarrell, Jerrell

Jaren (Hebrew) vocal
Jaron, Jayrone, J'ron

Jarenal (American) form of Jaren: vocal
Jaranall, Jaret, Jarn, Jaronal, Jarry, Jerry

Jarenn (American) form of Jaran: sings

Jarent (French) sings

Jares (Biblical) form of Jairus: faithful

Jareth (American) open to adventure
Jarey, Jarith, Jarth, Jary

Jariath (American) sings

Jarib (Hebrew) competes

Jaribon (American) laughs

Jario (Hebrew) believer

Jarius (Spanish) generous

Jarkko (Finnish) form of George: land-loving; farmer

Jarl (Scandinavian) noble

Jarles (Scandinavian) noble

Jarman (German) stoic
Jerman

Jarmuth (Biblical) place name

Jarnigan (German) German boy

Jaro (Polish) spring child

Jaroe (American) form of Gerald: strong; ruling with a spear

Jarol (English) form of Gerald: strong; ruling with a spear

Jarold (Polish) form of Gerald: strong; ruling with a spear

Jaromil (Czech) spring love
Jarmil

Jaron (Hebrew) spirited singer

Jarons (Hebrew) spirited singer

Jarred (Hebrew) form of Jared: descendant; giving
Jere, Jerod, Jerred, Jerud

Jarrell (English) jaunty
Jare, Jarell, Jarrel, Jarry, Jerele, Jerrell

Jarrett (English) confident
Jare, Jaret, Jaritt, Jarret, Jarrit, Jarritt, Jarry, Jarryt, Jarrytt, Jerot, Jerret, Jerrett, Jurett, Jurette

Jarrod (Hebrew) form of Jared: descendant; giving
Jare, Jarod, Jarry, Jerod

Jarvett (American) form of Jarrett: confident

Jarvey (German) celebrated
Garvey, Garvy, Jarvee, Jarvi, Jarvy

Jarvis (German) athletic
Jarv, Jarvee, Jarves, Jarvey, Jarvhus, Jarvie, Jarvus, Jarvy

Jary (Spanish) form of Jerry: strong; ruling with a spear
Jaree

Jaryn (Hebrew) sings

Jasdeep (Indian) bright light

Jase (American) hip

Jaskarn (Indian) praises

Jason ✪ (Greek) healer; the Lord is salvation

Jaspal (Pakistani) pure

Jasper (English) guard
Jasp, Jaspur, Jaspy, Jaspyr

Jasraj (Indian) famous

Jassel (Spanish) form of Jason: healer; the Lord is salvation

Jasson (American) form of Jason: healer; the Lord is salvation

Jaster (English) form of Jasper: guard
Jast

Jasvir (Indian) famous

Jatauan (American) joker

Jatin (American) form of Gaetano: from the city of Gaeta; Italian man

Jattir (Biblical) place name

Jaumet (French) foremost

Jaun (American) form of John: God is gracious

Javan (Biblical) righteous
Javin, Javon

Javaris (African American) prepared
Javares, Javarez

Javas (Sanskrit) bright eyes

Jave (American) form of Jove: Roman sky god

Javed (American) form of Jove: Roman sky god

Javen (Hebrew) form of Javan: righteous

Javier (Spanish) affluent; homeowner
Havyaire, Javey, Javiar

Javion (American) form of Javan: righteous

Javon (Hebrew) hopeful
Javan, Javaughn, Javen, Javonn, Javonte

Javonte (African American) jaunty
Javaughantay, Javawnte, Ja-Vonnetay, Ja-Vontae

Javor (Slavic) sturdy tree

Javy (American) form of Javaris; prepared
Javey, Javie

Jawahir (Arabic) gems

Jawdat (Arabic) excellent
Gawdat

Jawhar (Arabic) gem

Jawon (African American) shy
Jawan, Jawaughn, Jawaun, Jawuane, Jewan, Jewon, Jowon

Jax (American) form of Jackson: Jack's son; full of personality
Jacks, Jaxx

Jaxon (English) form of Jackson: Jack's son; full of personality

Jaxson (English) form of Jackson: Jack's son; full of personality

Jay (English) form of a name starting with J; colorful
Jai, Jaye

Jaya (American) jazzy
Jay, Jayah

Jayan (Indian) wins

Jayant (Hindi) winner

Jayashree (Indian) victor

JayC (American) combo of Jay and C

Jayden ✪ ⊕ (American) bright-eyed
Jayde, Jaydey, Jaydi, Jaydie, Jaydon, Jaydun, Jaydy

Jayes (English) form of Jay: form of a name starting with J; colorful

Jayesh (Indian) victor

Jaylon ⊕ (American) combo of Jay and Lon
Jaylen

Jayme (English) form of Jamie: he who supplants

Jaymee (English) form of Jamie: he who supplants

Jaymes (American) form of James: he who supplants
Jaimes

Jaymz (American) form of James: he who supplants

Jayson (Greek) form of Jason: healer; the Lord is salvation

Jaz (American) form of Jazz: jazzy

Jazeps (Latvian) God will increase

Jazer (American) form of Jazz: jazzy

Jazon (Polish) heals

Jazz (American) jazzy
Jazze, Jazzee, Jazzy

Jean (French) form of John: God is gracious
Jeanne, Jeannie, Jene

Jeanis (French) form of John: God is gracious

Jean-Marc (French) combo of Jean and Marc

Jean-Pierre (French) combo of Jean and Pierre

Jean-Sebastien (French) combo of Jean and Sebastian

Jeardo (Polish) form of Jerard: confident

Jearoslav (Polish) glory

Jeb (Hebrew) jolly
Jebb, Jebby

Jebben (Hebrew) form of Jebediah: close to God

Jebediah (Hebrew) close to God
Jeb, Jebadiah, Jebby, Jebedyah

Jebus (Biblical) place name

Jecori (American) exuberant
Jekori

Jed (Hebrew) helpful
Jedd, Jeddy, Jede

Jediah (Hebrew) God's help
Jedi, Jedyah

Jedidiah (Hebrew) close to God
Jed, Jeddy, Jeddyah, Jedidyah

Jedrek (Polish) virile
Jedrick, Jedrus

Jedwog (Polish) manly

Jeeps (French) jaunty

Jeevan (African American) form of Jevan: spirited(Hebrew) religious
Jevaughn, Jevaun

Jeevik (Indian) water

Jeff (English) form of Jeffrey: peaceful; form of Jefferson: dignified
Geoff, Jeffie, Jeffy

Jeffers (English) form of Jeffrey: peaceful

Jefferson (English) dignified
Jeff, Jeffarson, Jeffersen, Jeffursen, Jeffy

Jeffery (English) form of Jeffrey: peaceful
Jeffrie, Jeffry, Jefry

Jeffrey (English) peaceful
Geoffrey, Jeff, Jeffree, Jeffrie, Jeffry, Jeffy, Jefree

Jehan (French) form of John: God is gracious

Jehu (Hebrew) true believer

Jela (African) honors

Jelani (African American) trendy
Jelanee, Jelaney, Jelanne

Jem (English) form of James: he who supplants
Jemmi, Jemmy, Jemmye, Jemy

Jemarr (African American) worldly
Jemahr

Jemonde (French) man of the world
Jemond

Jenda (Czech) form of John: God is gracious

Jenkins (Last name as first name) God is gracious
Jenkin, Jenks, Jenky, Jenkyns, Jenx, Jinx

Jennett (Hindi) heavenly
Jennet, Jennit, Jennitt, Jennyt, Jennytt, Jinnat

Jennings (Last name as first name) attractive
Jennyngs

Jensi (Hungarian) noble
Jenci, Jens

Jenson (English) son of Jen; blessed
Jensen, Jenssen, Jensson

Jep (American) easygoing
Jepp

Jephtha (Biblical) judges others; outgoing

Jerald (English) form of Gerald: strong; ruling with a spear
Jere, Jereld, Jerold, Jerrie, Jerry

Jeramy (Hebrew) exciting
Jeramah, Jeramie, Jere, Jeremy

Jerard (French) confident
Jerrard

Jere (Hebrew) form of Jeremy: talkative
Jeree, Jerey

Jeremiah ☺ (Hebrew) prophet uplifted by God; farsighted
Jeramiah, Jere, Jeremyah, Jerome, Jerry

Jeremie (Hebrew) loquacious
Jeremee, Jeremy

Jeremy ♂ (English) talkative
Jaramie, Jere, Jeremah, Jereme, Jeremey, Jerrey, Jerry

Jeriah (Hebrew) form of Jeremiah: prophet uplifted by God; farsighted

Jericho (Arabic) nocturnal
Jerako, Jere, Jerico, Jeriko, Jerycho, Jerycko, Jeryco, Jeryko

Jerick (American) form of Jericho: nocturnal
Gericho, Jereck, Jerik, Jero, Jerok, Jerrico

Jeril (American) form of Jarrell: leader
Jerill, Jerl, Jerry

Jerma (American) form of Germaine: growing; from Germany
Jermah, Jermane, Jermayne

Jermain (French) from Germany
German, Germane, Germanes, Germano, Germanus, Jermaine, Jerman, Jermane, Jermayn, Jermayne

Jermaine (German) form of Germaine: growing; from Germany
Germain, Germaine, Jere, Jermain, Jermane, Jermene, Jerry

Jermey (American) form of Jermaine: growing; from Germany
Jermy

Jermon (African American) dependable
Jermonn

Jerney (Hebrew) exalted of the Lord

Jernigan (Last name as first name) spontaneous
Jerni, Jerny

Jero (American) jaunty
Jeroh, Jerree, Jerri, Jerro, Jerry

Jerod (Hebrew) form of Jared: descendant; giving

Jerold (English) merry
Jerrold, Jerry

Jerome (Latin) holy name; blessed
Jarome, Jere, Jerohm, Jeromy, Jerree, Jerrome, Jerry, Jirome

Jerone (English) hopeful
Jere, Jerohn, Jeron, Jerrone

Jeronimo (Italian) form of Geronimo: sacred name
Gerry, Jero, Jerry

Jerral (American) form of Jerald:
strong; ruling with a spear
Jeral, Jere, Jerry

Jerram (Hebrew) God has uplifted
Jeram, Jerem, Jerrem, Jerrym, Jerym

Jerrell (American) exciting
Jarell, Jerre, Jerrel, Jerrie, Jerry

Jerrett (Hebrew) form of Jarrett:
confident
Jeret, Jerete, Jerod, Jerot, Jerret

Jerry (German) form of Gerald:
strong; ruling with a spear
Gerry, Gery, Jerre, Jerri, Jerrie, Jerrye

Jerse (Place name) calm; rural
Jerce, Jercey, Jersey, Jersy, Jerzy

Jervis (Greek) honorable
Gervase

Jesmar (American) form of Jesse:
wealthy
Jess, Jessie, Jezz, Jezzie

Jesper (American) easygoing
Jesp, Jess

Jess (Hebrew) wealthy
Jes

Jesse (Hebrew) wealthy
Jess, Jessee, Jessey, Jessi, Jessye

Jessup (Last name as first name) rich
*Jesop, Jesopp, Jess, Jessa, Jessie, Jessopp,
Jessupp, Jessy, Jesup, Jesupp*

Jesuan (Spanish) devout

Jesus ✪ (Hebrew) saved by God
Hesus, Jesu, Jesuso, Jezus

Jet (English) black gem

Jetal (American) zany
Jetahl, Jetil, Jett, Jettale, Jetty

Jethro (Hebrew) fertile
Jeto, Jett, Jetty

Jeton (French) a chip for gamblers;
wild spirit
Jet, Jetawn, Jets, Jett, Jetty

Jett (American) free
Jet, Jets, Jetty, The Jet

Jettie (American) form of Jett: free
Jette, Jettee, Jetti

Jetty (American) form of Jett: free
Jettey

Jevan (African American) spirited
Jevaughn, Jevaun, Jevin, Jevon

Jex (American) form of Jack: God is
gracious

Jhonatan (African) spiritual
Jhon, Jon

Ji (Chinese) organized; orderly

Jibben (American) form of Jivon:
living; vibrant

Jibri (Arabic) angel

Jie (Chinese) wonderful

Jiggins (English) lost

Jiles (American) form of Giles:
protective

Jilve (American) form of Jiles:
protective

Jim (Hebrew) form of James: he who
supplants
Jem, Jihm, Jimi, Jimmee, Jimmy

Jimbo (American) cowhand;
endearment for Jim
Jim, Jimb, Jimbee, Jimbey, Jimby

Jimbob (American) countrified
Gembob, Jim Bob, Jim-Bob, Jymbob

Jimere (Biblical) from Gemar

Jimmy (English) form of James: he
who supplants
Jim, Jimi, Jimmey, Jimmi, Jimmye, Jimy

Jimmy-John (American) country boy
*Jimmiejon, Jimmyjohn, Jimmy-Jon,
Jymmejon*

Jimoh (African) Friday's child

Jin (Chinese) golden

Jinan (Place name) city in China
Jin

Jindrich (Czech) ruling
Jindra, Jindrik, Jindrisek, Jindrousek

Jing (Chinese) unblemished; capital

Jinghua (Asian) ruler

Jinkon (American) vibrant

Jiri (Czech) working the earth
Jira, Jiricek

Jiro (Japanese) second boy born

Jiten (Indian) conquers

Jivon (Hindi) living; vibrant
Jivan

Joab (Hebrew) praising God; hovering
Joabb

Joachim (Hebrew) a king of Judah; powerful; believer
Akim, Jakim, Yachim, Yakim

Joah (Greek) form of Jonah: peacemaker

Joanus (German) form of Johann: God is gracious

Joao (Spanish) form of John: God is gracious

Joaquin (Spanish) bold; hip
Joakeen, Joaquim, Juakeen, Jwaqueen

Joar (Biblical) form of Jair: teacher

Job (Hebrew) patient
Jobb, Jobe, Jobi, Joby

Jobab (Biblical) sorrowful

Jobin (Biblical) perceives

Jobo (Hebrew) patient

Jobse (American) patient

Jobson (English) son of Job; patient

Joby (Hebrew) patient; tested
Job, Jobee, Jobi

Jochen (German) established

Jock (Hebrew) grace in God; athlete
Jockie, Jocky

Joda (Hebrew) devout

Jodbin (Hebrew) combo of Jod and Bin

Jody (Hebrew) believer in Jehovah; (American) combination of Joe and Dee
Jodee, Jodey, Jodie, Jodye, Joe

Joe (Hebrew) form of Joel: prophet in the Bible; form of Joseph: He will add
Jo, Joey, Joeye, Joie

JoeGee (American) combo of Joe and Gee

Joel (Hebrew) Jehovah is the Lord
Joelie, Joell, Jole, Joly

Joerd (Dutch) guards

Joergen (Scandinavian) earth worker

Joest (Scandinavian) just

Joey (Hebrew) form of Joel: prophet in the Bible; form of Joseph: He will add
Joee, Joie

Joffre (German) form of Jeffrey: peaceful

Johann (German) form of John: God is gracious
Johan, Johane, Yohann, Yohanne, Yohon

Johannes (Hebrew) form of John: God is gracious
Johan, Jon

Johar (Hindi) gem

John ☺ ☻ (Hebrew) God is gracious
Jahn, Jhan, Johne, Johnne, Johnni, Johnnie, Johnny, Johnnye, Jon

Johnny (Hebrew) form of John: God is gracious
Gianni, Johnie, Johnnie, Jonni, Jonny

Johnny-Dodd (American) country sheriff
Johnniedodd, Johnny Dodd

Johnny-Ramon (Spanish) renegade
Johnnyramon, Johnny Ramon

Johnson (English) John's son; credible
Johnsen, Johnsonne, Jonsen, Jonson

Joji (Japanese) form of John: God is gracious

JoJo (American) friendly; popular
Jo-Jo

Jokel (American) form of Joachim: king of Judah; powerful; believer

Jokshan (American) form of Jackson: Jack's son; full of personality

Joktan (Biblical) small

Jole (American) jolly

Jolly (American) jolly

Jolon (Native American) oak valley dweller

Joloyd (American) combo of Jo and Lloyd

Jomar (African American) helpful
Joemar, Jomarr

Jomei (Japanese) lightens

Jomo (American) grows crops

Jon (Hebrew) alternative for John
Jonni, Jonnie, Jonny, Jony

Jonah (Hebrew) peacemaker
Joneh

Jonald (Hebrew) combo of Jon and Ronald

Jonas (Hebrew) capable; active
Jon

Jonathan ✪ (Hebrew) gift of God
Johnathan, Johnathon, Jonathon

Jonavon (Hebrew) calm

Jonaz (Hebrew) form of Jonas: capable; active

Jones (American) saucy

Jonnie (Hebrew) form of John: God is gracious

Jonnley (American) form of John: God is gracious
Jonn, Jonnie

Jonte (American) form of John: God is gracious
Johatay, Johate, Jontae

Jools (English) form of Julius: attractive

Joplin (Place name) city in Montana; sings
Joplyn

Joppa (Biblical) place name

Joram (Biblical) giving

Joran (Scandinavian) dependable

Jord (Scandinavian) strong

Jordahno (Invented) form of Giordano: delivered

Jordan ✪ ⚥ (Hebrew) downflowing river
Jorden, Jordon, Jordun, Jordy, Jordyn

Jordane (Hebrew) form of Jordan: downflowing river

Jordan-Michael (American) athletic

Jordison (American) son of Jordy; glowing
Jordisen, Jordysen, Jordyson

Jordy (Hebrew) form of Jordan: downflowing river
Jordey, Jordi, Jordie

Jorge (Spanish) form of George: land-loving; farmer
Jorje, Quiqui

Jorgen (Scandinavian) farmer
Jorgan

Jorger (Scandinavian) form of George: land-loving; farmer

Jorget (French) mutinous

Jorine (French) form of George: land-loving; farmer

Joris (Dutch) form of George: land-loving; farmer

Jory (Hebrew) descendant
Jorey

Jos (Place name) city in Nigeria

Josa (Hebrew) God judges him

José ✪ (Spanish) asset; favored
Joesay, Jose, Pepe, Pepito

Joseph ✪ ⚥ (Hebrew) He will add
Jodie, Joe, Joey, Josef, Josep, Josephe, Jozef, Yusif

Josh (Hebrew) form of Joshua: devout
Joshuam, Joshyam, Josue, Jozua

Josha (Hebrew) form of Joshua: devout

Joshua ✪ ⚥ (Hebrew) devout

Josia (Hebrew) form of Josiah: supported by the Lord
Josea

Josiah ✪ (Hebrew) supported by the Lord
Josyah

Joson (English) form of Jason: healer; the Lord is salvation

Joss (English) form of Joseph: He
will add
Josslin, Jossly

Josue (Spanish) devout

Jotham (Biblical) a king of Judah;
believer in perfect Jehovah
Jothem, Jothym

Jour (French) form of Jourdain:
flowing

Jourdain (French) flowing
Jordane, Jorden

Jourdyun (Slavic) form of Jourdain:
flowing

Jovan (Slavic) gifted
Jovahn, Jovohn

Jovani (Italian) form of Jove: Roman
sky god
Jovanni, Jovanny, Jovany

Jove (Mythology) Roman sky god

Jovi (American) sky

Jovito (Spanish) jubilant

Joza (Czech) form of Joseph: He will
add

Jozef (Polish) supported by Jehovah;
asset
Joe, Joze

Jozo (Slavic) little Joe

Juan ✪ (Spanish) devout; lively
Juann, Juwon

Juanie (Spanish) form of John: God
is gracious

Jubal (Hebrew) celebrant

Jubilo (Spanish) rejoicing; jubilant
Jube

Judah (Biblical) praised
Juda

Judas (Latin) praised

Judd (Latin) secretive
Jud

Jude (Latin) form of Judas: praised
Judah

Judge (English) judgmental
Judg

Judges (Biblical) judgmental

Judson (Last name as first name)
mercurial
Juddsen, Juddson, Judsen, Judssen

Judule (American) form of Judah:
praised
Jud, Judsen, Judsun

Juhi (Indian) flowers

Julan (American) attractive

Jules (Greek) young Adonis
Jewels, Jule

Julian ✪ (Greek) gorgeous
Juliane, Julien, Julyon, Julyun

Julias (Biblical) place name

Julio (Spanish) handsome; youthful
Huleeo, Hulie, Julie

Julius (Greek) attractive
Juleus, Jul-yus, Jul-yuz

Ju-Long (Chinese) powerful

Jumaane (African) Tuesday-born

Jumah (African) born on Friday
Juma

Jumahl (African) form of Jumah:
born on Friday

Jumbe (African) strong
Jumbey, Jumby

Jumble (American) awry

Jumoke (African) beloved

Jun (Japanese) follows the rules

Jund (Arabic) soldier

Juneau (Place name) capital of Alaska
Juno, Junoe

Junior (Latin) young son of the father
Junnie, Junny, Junyer

Junius (Latin) youngster
Junie, Junnie, Junny

Junny (Asian) honest

Juper (German) form of Joseph: He
will add

Jupiter (Roman) god of thunder and
lightning; guardian
Jupe

Jur (Czech) form of George: land-
loving; farmer

Jura (Place name) mountain range between France and Switzerland
Jurah

Juraj (Slavic) form of George: land-loving; farmer

Jurass (American) from Jurassic period of dinosaurs; daunting
Jurases, Jurassic

Jurate (Slavic) forgives

Jurg (Dutch) form of Jurgen: working the earth

Jurgen (Scandinavian) working the earth

Jurgin (Dutch) form of Jurgen: working the earth

Jurgs (Dutch) form of Jurgen: working the earth

Juri (Slavic) farms

Juric (Slavic) form of George: land-loving; farmer

Jus (French) just
Just, Justice, Justis

Juste (French) law-abiding
Just, Zhuste

Juster (American) fair and honest

Justice (Latin) just
Jusees, Just, Justiz, Justus, Juztice

Justie (Latin) honest; fair
Jus, Justee, Justey, Justi

Justin ✪ ⊕ (Latin) fair
Just, Justan, Justen, Justun, Justyn, Justyne

Justinian (Latin) ruler; Roman emperor
Justinyan

Justino (Spanish) fair
Justyno

Justiz (American) judging; fair
Justice, Justis

Justo (Scandinavian) handsome

Justus (German) fair

Jute (Botanical) practical

Juven (Latin) youthful

Juvenal (Latin) young
Juve

Juventino (Spanish) young
Juve, Juven, Juvey, Tino, Tito

Juver (Spanish) form of Javor: sturdy tree

Juwon (African American) form of Juan: devout; lively
Jujuane, Juwan, Juwonne

Jvon (American) form of Juan: devout; lively

Jyles (American) form of Giles: protective

Jyree (Scandinavian) form of George: land-loving; farmer

K

Kaar (American) form of Kar: bold; Michael's follower

Kaarlo (American) form of Carlo: sensual; manly

Kabir (Hindi) spiritual leader
Kabar

Kabonero (African) symbol

Kabonesa (African) born in hard times

Kacancu (Rukonjo) firstborn

Kacy (American) happy
K.C., Kace, Kacee, Kase, Kasee, Kasy, Kaycee

Kadar (Arabic) empowered
Kader

Kade (American) exciting
Cade, Caden, K.D., Kadey, Kaid, Kayde, Kydee

Kadeem (Arabic) servant
Kadim

Kaden ✪ (American) exciting
Cade, Caden, Caiden, Caidin, Caidon, Caydan, Cayden, Caydin, Caydon, Kadan, Kadon, Kadyn, Kaiden

Kading (Last name as first name) powerful

Kadir (Hindi) talented
Kadeer, Qadeer, Qadir

Kadjaly (African) born from God

Kadmiel (Hebrew) God-loving

Kado (Japanese) through life's gate

Kaelan (Irish) strong
Kael, Kaelen, Kaelin, Kaelyn

Kaemon (Japanese) happy

Kaeto (American) form of Cato: zany and bright
Cayto, Caytoe, Kato

Kafele (African) supreme

Kafus (American) laughing boy

Kaha (Hawaiian) domesticated

Kahale (Hawaiian) homebody

Kahane (Egyptian) brave

Kahil (Turkish) ingenue; (Arabic) friend; (Greek) handsome
Cahill, Kaleel, Kalil, Kayhil, Khalil

Kaholo (Hawaiian) boy who runs

Kai (Hawaiian) kay
Keh

Kaid (English) round; happy
Caiden, Cayde, Caydin, Kaden, Kadin, Kayd

Kaihe (Hawaiian) spear

Kailey (Hawaiian) religious

Kailin (Irish) sporty
Kailyn, Kale, Kalen, Kaley, Kalin, Kallen, Kaylen

Kaine (Irish) handsome

Kainen (Irish) handsome

Kaipo (Hawaiian) embraces

Kairo (Arabic) from Cairo; exotic

Kaiser (German) title that means emperor

Kaiyan (Indian) place name

Kaj (Scandinavian) earthy

Kajah (Biblical) form of Caja: close proximity

Kal (Hawaiian) born of the sun

Kala (Hawaiian) sun boy

Kalama (Hawaiian) source of light
Kalam

Kalani (Hawaiian) of one sky
Kalan

Kalb (Hawaiian) studies

Kale (American) healthy; vegetable
Kail, Kayle, Kaylee, Kayley, Kaylie

Kaleb (American) form of Caleb: faithful; brave

Kalebbe (Hebrew) form of Caleb: faithful; brave

Kalen (Hawaiian) young

Kalgan (Place name) city in China
Kal

Kali (Polynesian) comforts

Kalidas (Indian) creative

Kalil (Arabic) best friend
Kahil, Kahleel, Kahlil, Kaleel, Khaleel, Khalil

Kalin (Arabic) young

Kalkin (Hindi) tenth child

Kallahan (American) form of Callahan: spiritual

Kallen (Greek) handsome
Kallan, Kallin, Kallon, Kallun, Kalon, Kalun, Kalyn

Kalman (Irish) slim

Kalogeros (Greek) beautiful in aging

Kalonn (Irish) strong

Kalunga (African) watchful; the personal god of the Mbunda of Angola

Kalvim (Latin) form of Calvin: bald

Kalvin (Latin) form of Calvin: bald
Kal

Kalyan (Indian) handsome

Kama (Sanskrit) perfection

Kamaka (Hawaiian) pretty face

Kamal (Arabic) perfect; (African) lotus child
Kameel, Kamil

Kamari (African) moonlight child

Kamau (African) quiet soldier
Kamall

Kamden (Scottish) form of Camden: conflicted

Kameron (Scottish) form of Cameron: mischievous; crooked nose
Kameren, Kammeron, Kammi, Kammie, Kammy, Kamran, Kamrin, Kamron

Kammer (African) moon; pained

Kamon (American) alligator; (Biblical) place name
Cayman, Caymun, Kame, Kammy, Kayman, Kaymon

Kamran (American) form of Cameron: mischievous; crooked nose

Kamrino (Italian) form of Cameron: mischievous; crooked nose

Kamyar (Indian) handsome

Kan (American) good-looking

Kana (Japanese) strength of character

Kanah (Biblical) form of Elkanah: obedient to God

Kanak (Indian) golden child

Kanan (Hindi) forest

Kandall (American) form of Kendall: shy

Kane (Gaelic) warlike; honor; tribute
Cahan, Cahane, Cain, Kaince, Kaine, Kaney, Kanie, Kayne

Kang (Korean) healthy

Kaniel (Hebrew) confident; supported by the Lord; hopeful
Kane, Kan-El, Kanel, Kanelle, Kaney

Kano (Place name) city in Nigeria
Kan, Kanoh

Kant (German) philosopher
Cant

Kantu (Hindi) joyous

Kany (Australian) stone

Kanye (American) unbreakable

Kanzler (German) Last name as first name

Kaori (Japanese) scented

Kaper (American) capricious
Cape, Caper, Kahper, Kape

Kapila (Hindi) foresees
Kapil

Kapono (Hawaiian) anointed one

Kapp (Greek) form of the surname Kaparos
Kap, Kappy

Kapple (English) Last name as first name; from Cable; son of Cabel

Kar (American) form of Carr: outdoorsy

Karan (Hindi) listens

Karau (English) loyal

Karcher (German) beautiful blond boy

Kare (Scandinavian) large
Karee

Kareem (Arabic) generous
Karam, Karehm, Karem, Karim, Karreem, Krehm

Karekin (Scandinavian) large

Karel (Slavic) form of Carl: kingly

Karey (Greek) form of Cary: pretty brook; charming; form of Carey: masculine; by the castle
Karee, Kari, Karrey, Karry

Kari (Scandinavian) hair curls

Kariah (Biblical) form of Zechariah: Lord remembers

Karif (Arabic) fall-born
Kareef

Karime (Arabic) distinctive

Karimen (Scandinavian) big

Karkor (Biblical) place name

Karl (German) manly; forceful
Carl, Kale, Karel, Karlie, Karll, Karol, Karoly

Karlen (Slavic) form of Carl: kingly

Karmel (Hebrew) red-haired
Carmel, Carmelo, Karmeli, Karmelli, Karmelo, Karmello, Karmi

Karmmer (Hebrew) form of Carmel: growing; garden

Karnaim (Biblical) place name

Karney (Irish) wins
Carney

Karolek (Polish) form of Charles: manly; well-loved
Karol

Karp (Russian) abundant; (Greek) fruitful

Karr (Scandinavian) curly hair
Carr

Karst (Greek) anointed

Karstell (Last name as first name)

Karsten (Greek) chosen one

Kartik (Indian) hopes

Karu (Hindi) cousin
Karun

Karyim (Arabic) divisive

Kaseem (Arabic) divides
Kasceem, Kaseym, Kasim, Kazeem

Kaseko (African) ridiculed

Kasem (Asian) joyful

Kasen (Spanish) helmet; protected

Kasey (Irish) form of Casey: courageous
Kasi, Kasie

Kasi (Egyptian) form of Kasiya: leaving
Kasee, Kasey, Kasie

Kasim (Hindi) shining

Kasimir (Arabic) serene
Kasim, Kazimir, Kazmer

Kasin (Slavic) wolf; safety

Kasiya (Egyptian) leaving

Kason (Spanish) safe

Kasper (German) reliable
Caspar, Casper, Kasp, Kaspar, Kaspy

Kass (German) standout among men
Cass, Kasse

Kassidy (Irish) form of Cassidy: humorous
Kass, Kassidi, Kassidie, Kassie

Kastor (Greek) wins

Katell (Scandinavian) pure

Kato (African) second of twins

Katzir (Hebrew) reaping
Katzeer

Kauai (Place name) Hawaiian island; breezy spirit
Kawai

Kaufman (Last name as first name) serious
Kauffmann, Kaufmann

Kauri (Scandinavian) blessed

Kaushal (Indian) smart

Kavan (Irish) good-looking
Cavan, Kaven, Kavin

Kavi (Hindi) poetic

Kavin (Irish) form of Kevin: handsome; gentle

Kawai (Hawaiian) form of Kauai: Hawaiian island; breezy spirit

Kay (Greek) joyful
Kai, Kaye, Kaysie, Kaysy, Keh

Kayin (African) desired baby

Kayle (Hebrew) faithful
Kail, Kayl

Kaylen (Irish) form of Kellen: strong-willed
Kaylan, Kaylin, Kaylon, Kaylyn

Kayo (Sanskrit) wordsmith

Kayode (African) joy-giver

Kayven (Irish) handsome
Cavan, Kavan, Kave

Kaz (Greek) creative

Kazan (Greek) creative
Kazann

Kazar (Slavic) kind

Kazimierz (Polish) practical
Kaz

Kazuo (Japanese) peace-loving; good son

Kealoha (Hawaiian) bright path

Keane (German) attractive
Kean, Keen, Keene, Kiene

Keanu (Hawaiian) cool breeze over mountains
Keahnu

Kearn (Irish) outspoken
Kearny, Kern, Kerne, Kerney

Kearney (Irish) sparkling
Karney, Karny, Kearns, Kerney, Kirney

Kearon (Irish) form of Kieran: handsome brunette

Keary (Irish) form of Kerry: dark

Keat (English) hawk

Keatal (English) hawk

Keaton (English) nature-lover

Keaten, Keatt, Keatun, Keton

Keats (Literature) for poet John Keats; melancholy

Keatz

Keawe (Hawaiian) lovable

Keb (Egyptian) loves the earth

Kecalf (American) inventive

Keecalf

Kechel (African American) kach

Kachelle

Keda (Hindi) form of Kedar: powerful

Kedar (Hindi) powerful

Kadar, Keder

Kedding (English) Last name as first name

Kedem (Hebrew) old soul

Kedemah (Biblical) old

Kedrick (American) form of Kendrick: heroic

Ked, Keddy, Kedric, Kedrik

Kedron (Biblical) place name; King

Kee (Irish) from Keefe: handsome

Kee-Bun (Taiwanese) good news

Keebun

Keefa (Irish) loved and lovely

Keefe (Irish) handsome

Keaf, Keafe, Keef, Keeffe, Kief

Keegan (Irish) ball-of-fire

Keagan, Keagin, Kegan, Kege, Keghun

Keelan (Irish) slim

Kealan, Keallan, Keallin, Keilan, Keillan, Kelan

Keeley (Irish) handsome

Kealey, Kealy, Keelee, Keelie, Keely, Keilie

Keen (German) smart

Kean, Keane, Keene, Keeney, Kene

Keenan (Irish) bright-eyed

Kenan

Keeney (American) incisive

Kean, Keane, Keaney, Keene, Kene

Keesen (Dutch) adored

Keever (Irish) form of Kevin: handsome; gentle

Keevin (Irish) form of Kevin: handsome; gentle

Keffry (American) form of Jeffrey: peaceful

Kefil (African) given by God

Kefir (Hebrew) young lion; high spirits

Kefiwy (African) loyal

Kehlor (American) friend

Keir (Irish) brunette

Keirer (Irish) dark

Kerer

Keiron (Irish) dark

Keiren, Keronn

Keitaro (Japanese) blessed baby

Keita

Keith (English) witty

Keath, Keeth, Keithe

Keithen (Scottish) gentle

Keith

Keizo (American) spice

Keko (Hawaiian) bold

Kekoa (Hawaiian) one warrior; (Asian) brave

Kel (Irish) fighter; energetic

Kell

Kelby (English) snappy; charming

Kel, Kelbey, Kelbi, Kelbie, Kelbye, Kell, Kellby, Kelly

Kelcy (English) helpful

Kelci, Kelcie, Kelcye, Kelsie

Kele (Hawaiian) watches like a hawk

Kelemen (Hungarian) soft-spoken

Kell (English) fresh-faced

Kel, Kelly

Kellagh (Irish) hardworking

Kellach

Kellam (Scottish) calm

Kelle (Scandinavian) springlike

Kellen (Irish) strong-willed

Kel, Kelen, Kelin, Kell, Kellan, Kellin, Kelly, Kelyn

Keller (Last name as first name) bountiful
Kel, Keler, Kelher, Kell, Kylher

Kellins (Irish) strong

Kelly (Irish) able combatant
Keli, Kellee, Kelley, Kelli, Kellie

Kelmen (Hungarian) form of Kelemen: soft-spoken

Kelsen (English) port town child

Kelsey (Scandinavian) unique among men
Kel, Kells, Kelly, Kels, Kelsi, Kelsie, Kelsy, Kelsye, Kelzie, Kelzy

Kelto (Greek) unrequited love

Kelton (Irish) energetic
Keldon, Kelltin, Kellton, Kelten, Keltin, Keltonn

Kelts (Origin unknown) energetic
Kel, Kelly, Kelse, Kelsey, Keltz

Kelvin (English) goal-oriented
Kellven, Kelvan, Kelven, Kelvon, Kelvun, Kelvynn, Kilvin

Kemal (Turkish) honored infant; generous

Kemmer (American) ethical

Kemp (English) champion

Kemper (American) high-minded
Kemp, Kempar

Kempton (American) takes the high road

Kemuel (Hebrew) God's advocate

Ken (Scottish) form of Kenneth: good-looking
Kenn, Kenny, Kinn

Kenan (Irish) strong

Kenaz (Hebrew) bright

Kendall (English) shy
Ken, Kend, Kendahl, Kendal, Kendoll, Kendy, Kenney, Kennie, Kenny, Kindal

Kendan (English) strong; serious
Ken, Kend, Kenden

Kendrick (English) heroic
Kendricks, Kendrik, Kendryck, Kenric, Kenrick, Kenricks, Kenrik

Kenel (Invented) form of Kendall: shy
Kenele

Kenelm (English) handsome boy
Kenhelm, Kennelm

Kenitsu (Asian) many summers

Kenix (American) form of Kenneth: good-looking

Kenji (Asian) careful

Kenley (English) distinguished
Kenlea, Kenlee, Kenleigh, Kenlie, Kenly

Kenn (English) river; flowing

Kennard (English) courageous; selfless; (Irish) bold leader
Ken, Kenard, Kennaird, Kennar, Kenny

Kennavy (Irish) brave

Kennean (Scottish) little Ken

Kennedy (Irish) leader
Canaday, Canady, Kennedey, Kennedie, Kennidy

Kenner (English) capable
Kennard

Kennern (American) able

Kennet (Scandinavian) form of Kenneth: good-looking
Kenet, Kennete

Kenneth (Scottish) good-looking
Ken, Keneth, Kenith, Kennath, Kennie, Kenny

Kenny (Scottish) form of Kenneth: good-looking
Kennee, Kenney, Kenni, Kennie

Kenric (English) bold

Kenrick (English) heroic boy

Kensil (English) form of Kenneth: good-looking

Kent (English) fair-skinned
Kennt, Kentt

Kentaro (Japanese) large baby boy

Kentlee (Last name as first name) dignified
Ken, Kenny, Kent, Kentlea, Kentleigh, Kently

Kentley (English) meadow boy

Kenton (English) form of Kent: fair-skinned
Kentan, Kentin

Kentos (American) form of Quintus: fifth child

Kentrell (English) white

Kenward (Last name as first name) bold

Kenway (Last name as first name) bold

Kenyatta (African) from Kenya; patriotic

Kenyon (Irish) dear blond boy
Ken, Kenjon, Kenny, Kenyawn, Kenyun

Kenzel (Scottish) wise

Kenzie (Scottish) form of Kinsey: affectionate; winning
Kensie

Kenzo (American) form of Ken: good-looking

Keola (Hawaiian) vibrant

Keon (American) unbridled enthusiasm
Keion, Keonne, Keyon, Kion, Kionn

Keontay (African American) outrageous
Keon, Keontae, Keontee

Kepler (German) loves astrology; starry-eyed
Kappler, Keppel, Keppeler, Keppler

Kepner (German) Last name as first name

Kerbie (American) form of Kirby: brilliant

Kerel (African) forever young

Kerem (Hebrew) works in vineyard

Keren (Hebrew) of the horns

Kerey (Irish) dark

Kerm (Irish) form of Kermit: droll
Kurm

Kermit (German) droll
Kerm, Kermee, Kermet, Kermey, Kermi, Kermie, Kermy

Kern (Irish) dark; musically inclined
Curran, Kearn, Kearne, Kearns

Kernaghan (Last name as first name) dark
Carnahan, Kernohan

Kernis (Invented) dark; different
Kernes

Kerr (Scandinavian) serious; (Scottish) surname
Karr, Kerre, Kurr

Kerrick (English) rules

Kerrins (English) of the horns

Kerry (Irish) dark
Keary, Kere, Keri, Kerrey, Kerrie

Kers (Indian) an Indian plant

Kersen (Indonesian) cherry bright

Kerstie (American) spunky
Kerstee, Kersty

Kert (American) form of Curt/Curtis: gracious; kindhearted

Kerwyn (Irish) energetic
Kerwen, Kerwin, Kerwun, Kir, Kirs, Kirwin

Keshawn (African American) friendly
Kesh, Keshaun, Keyshawn, Shawn

Keshet (Hebrew) rainbow; bright hopes

Keshon (African American) sociable
Kesh

Kesin (Hindi) needy

Kesley (American) derivative of Lesley: active
Keslee, Kesli, Kezley

Kesse (American) attractive
Kessee, Kessey, Kessi, Kessie

Kester (Scottish) form of Christopher: the bearer of Christ

Kestrel (English) soars

Ketchum (Place name) city in Idaho
Catch, Ketch, Ketcham, Ketchim

Keth (Irish) form of Keith: witty

Kettil (Scandinavian) self-sacrificing
Keld, Ketil, Ketti, Kjeld

Keung (Chinese) universal spirit

Kevann (Irish) good-looking

Kevin ✪ (Irish) handsome; gentle
Kev, Kevahngn, Kevan, Keven, Kevvie,
Kevvy

Kevis (Irish) form of Kevin:
handsome; gentle
Handsome

Kevontay (American) combo of
Kevon and Tay

Kevork (English) noble

Key (English) key
Keye, Keyes

Keylor (Irish) friend

Keyon (Irish) form of Ewan: youthful
spirit

Keyshawn (African American)
clever; believer

Keyth (Welsh) form of Keith: witty

Keyvan (American) form of Kevin:
handsome; gentle

Khaalis (Greek) beauty

Khadijah (Arabic) premature baby

Khadim (Hindi) forever
Kadeem, Kadeen, Kahdeem, Khadeem

Khak (American) form of Khaki:
laughing

Khaldoun (Arabic) everlasting

Khaldun (Arabic) everlasting

Khalid (Arabic) everlasting
Khalead, Khaled, Khaleed

Khalil (Arabic) good friend

Khaliq (Arabic) ingenious
Kaliq, Khalique

Khambrel (American) articulate
Kambrel, Kham, Khambrell,
Khambrelle, Khambryll, Khamme,
Khammie, Khammy

Khan (Turkish) shares; prince

Khayrat (Arabic) good

Khayru (Arabic) giving
Khiri, Khiry, Kiry

Khevin (American) form of Kevin:
handsome; gentle
Khev

Khiam (American) old

Khosrow (Slavic) denies

Khouri (Arabic) spiritual
Couri, Khory, Khourae, Kori

Khyber (Place name) pass on border
of Pakistan and Afghanistan
Kibe, Kiber, Kyber

Kibbe (Nayas) nocturnal bird

Kibo (Place name) mountain peak;
highest peak of Kilimanjaro;
spectacular
Kib

Kibwy (African) God blesses

Kidd (Last name as first name)
adventurous

Kidder (Last name as first name)
brash; confident

Kidron (English) youthful

Kiefer (Irish) loving
Keefer, Kiefert, Kieffer, Kieffner, Kiefner,
Kuefer, Kueffner

Kiel (Place name) city in North
Germany; (Irish) form of Kyle: serene

Kien (Irish) form of Keenan: bright-
eyed

Kier (Icelandic) large vat or tub

Kieran (Scottish) dark-haired; (Irish)
handsome brunette
Keiran, Keiren, Keiron, Kern, Kernan,
Kier, Kieren, Kierin, Kiernan, Kieron,
Kiers, Kyran

Kiet (Asian) respected

Kiev (Place name) capital city of
Ukraine

Kiho (Hawaiian) moves carefully

Kilbane (English) Last name as first
name

Kilgore (Scottish) Last name as first
name

Killam (Irish) slim

Killi (Irish) form of Killian:
effervescent
Killean, Killee, Killey, Killyun

Killian (Irish) effervescent
Kilean, Kilian, Killean, Killee, Killi,
Killie, Killyun, Kylian

Killion (Irish) slim

Kilroy (Irish) royal

Kilyun (American) form of Killion: slim

Kim (Vietnamese) gold

Kimmie, Kimmy, Kimy, Kym

Kimball (Greek) inviting

Kim, Kimb, Kimbal, Kimbie, Kimble, Kymball

Kimberly (English) bold

Kim, Kimbo, Kimberleigh, Kimberley

Kin (Japanese) golden

Kincaid (Scottish) vigorous

Kincaide, Kinkaid

Kincannon (Scottish) Last name as first name; I'll defend

Kinch (Last name as first name) knife blade

King (English) royal leader

Kingman (Last name as first name) gracious man

Kingsley (English) royal nature

King, Kings, Kingslea, Kingslee, Kingsleigh, Kingsly, Kins

Kingston (English) gracious

King, Kingstan, Kingsten

Kingswell (English) royal; king

Kinnard (Last name as first name) leaning

Kinnaird

Kinnel (Gaelic) dweller at the head of the cliff

Kinney (English) simplifies

Kinsey (English) affectionate; winning

Kensey, Kinsie

Kinton (Hindi) adorned

Kioshi (Japanese) thoughtful silence

Kip (English) focused

Kipp, Kippi, Kippie, Kippy

Kipling (Literature) for writer Rudyard; adventurous

Kiplen, Kippling

Kipp (American) hill; upward bound

Kip, Kyp

Kipster (English) boy from the hill

Kirabo (African) treasured

Kiral (Greek) Lord

Kiran (Hindi) light

Kirann (American) purehearted

Kirby (English) brilliant

Kerb, Kirb, Kirbee, Kirbey, Kirbie, Kyrbee, Kyrby

Kiri (Vietnamese) like mountains

Kiril (Russian) Lord

Cyril, Cyrill, Kirill, Kirillos, Kyril, Kyrill

Kirk (Scandinavian) believer

Kerk, Kirke, Kurk

Kirkan (Scandinavian) of the church

Kirkland (Last name as first name) church land

Kirkley (Last name as first name) church wood

Kirklea, Kirklee, Kirklie, Kirkly

Kirkor (English) of the church

Kirkson (English) church son

Kirkwell (Last name as first name) wood; giving of faith

Kirkwood (English) heavenly

Kirkwoode, Kurkwood

Kirton (English) from the town of churches

Kirvin (American) form of Kevin: handsome; gentle

Kerven, Kervin, Kiru, Kirvan, Kirven

Kishore (Indian) little colt

Kit (Greek) mischievous

Kitt

Kitchell (American) form of Mitchell: optimistic

Kito (African) precious

Kiva (Hebrew) form of Akiva: cunning

Kizza (African) child born after twins' birth

Kjeld (Scandinavian) form of Carl: kingly

Kjell-Ake (Scandinavian) form of Carl: kingly

Kjetil (Scandinavian) form of Carl: kingly

Klaus (German) wealthy
Klaas, Klaes, Klas, Klass

Klausen (German) victor

Klay (English) form of Clay: reliable
Klaie, Klaye

Kleber (Last name as first name) serious
Klebe

Kleef (Dutch) boy from the cliff; daring

Kleigh (American) form of Clay: reliable

Klein (Last name as first name) bright
Kleiner, Kleinert, Kline

Klemens (Latin) gentle
Klemenis, Klement, Kliment

Kleng (Scandinavian) claw; struggles

Klev (Invented) form of Cleve: precarious
Kleve

Knight (English) protector
Knighte, Nighte

Knightley (English) protects
Knight, Knightlea, Knightlee, Knightlie, Knightly, Knights

Knoll (American) flamboyant
Noll

Knollie (English) form of Knowles: outdoorsman

Knossos (Biblical) place name

Knoten (Native American) windy

Knowah (American) form of Noah: peacemaker

Knowles (English) outdoorsman
Knowlie, Knowls, Nowles

Knowlton (English) from the grassy knoll

Knox (English) bold

Knud (Scandinavian) ruler

Knut (Scandinavian) aggressive
Canute, Cnut, Knute

Kobi (Hebrew) cunning; smart
Cobe, Cobey, Cobi, Cobie, Coby, Kobe, Kobee, Kobey, Kobi, Kobie, Koby

Kobin (African) Tuesday's child

Kobus (Dutch) form of Jacob: he who supplants

Kodiak (American) bear; daunting

Kody (English) brash
Kodee, Kodey, Kodi, Kodie, Kodye

Kofi (African) Friday-born

Kohana (Hawaiian) best

Kohath (Biblical) congregation

Kohl (English) form of Cole: lively; winner

Kohler (German) coal

Koji (African) Monday's baby

Kojo (African) Monday-born

Koka (Hawaiian) man from Scotland; strategist

Kolby (American) form of Colby: bright; secretive; dark farm
Kelby, Kole, Kollby

Kole (English) form of Cole: lively; winner

Kolen (Irish) beautiful; light

Kolibar (American) form of Colbert: cool and calm

Kolton (English) coal town

Kombs (American) from catacombs

Komic (Invented) funny
Com, Comic, Kom

Konane (Hawaiian) spot of moonlight

Kondo (African) fights

Kone (Word as name) cone

Kong (Chinese) heavenly

Konnor (Irish) another spelling of Connor; brilliant
Konnar, Konner

Kono (African) industrious

Konrad (German) bold advisor
Khonred, Kon, Konn, Konny, Konraad, Konradd, Konrade, Kord, Kort

Konsa (American) form of Constantine: constant; steadfast

Konstandin (Slavic) steadfast

Konstantin (Greek) loyal
Kon, Konny, Kons, Konstance, Konstantine, Konstantyne

Konstantinos (Greek) loyal
Constance, Konstance, Konstant, Tino, Tinos

Koralion (Greek) coral

Korb (German) form of Korbel: black raven

Korbel (German) black raven

Kore (Greek) pure

Koren (Greek) strong-willed

Korent (English) form of Corentin: stormy

Koresh (Hebrew) farms
Choresh

Korey (Irish) lovable
Kori, Korrey, Korrie

Korling (American) bold

Kornel (Czech) horn; communicator
Kornelisz, Kornelius, Kornell

Kornelius (Latin) form of Cornelius
Korne, Kornellius, Kornelyus, Korney, Kornnelyus

Korrigan (Irish) form of Corrigan
Koregan, Korigan, Korre, Korreghan, Korri, Korrigon

Kort (German) talkative

Korten (German) of the court

Kory (Irish) hollow
Kori, Korre, Korrey, Korrye

Kosana (African) prince

Kosey (African) temperamental; lionlike

Koshua (American) form of Joshua: devout

Koshy (American) jolly
Koshee, Koshey, Koshi

Kosmo (Greek) likes order
Cosmos, Kosmy

Kostas (Russian) form of Konstantin: loyal

Koster (American) spiritual
Kost, Kostar, Koste, Koster

Kosumi (Native American) fishes with a spear; smart

Kosyantyn (Slavic) leader

Kovit (Asian) talented

Krael (Slavic) form of Kyryl: Lord's child

Kraig (Irish) form of Craig: brave climber
Krag, Kragg, Kraggy

Kramer (German) shopkeeper; humorous

Krater (American) form of the word crater

Krause (German) outdoorsy

Krayton (Russian) kind

Kreig (Irish) form of Craig: brave climber

Kres (Slavic) peaceful

Kreso (Slavic) peaceful

Kricker (Last name as first name) reliable
Krick

Krikor (Armenian) form of Gregory: careful

Kris (Greek) form of Kristian: follower of Christ; form of Kristopher: the bearer of Christ
Krissy, Krys

Krishna (Hindu) pleasant
Krishnah

Krispin (Irish) form of Crispin: man with curls

Krissel (German) curly-haired

Krister (Scandinavian) religious

Kristian (Greek) form of Christian: follower of Christ
Kris, Krist, Kristyan

Kristiyan (Slavic) Christian

Kristo (Greek) form of Kristopher: the bearer of Christ

Kristoffer (Scandinavian) form of Christopher: the bearer of Christ

Kristopher (Greek) form of Christopher: the bearer of Christ
Kris, Krist, Kristo, Kristofer

Kroenen (Polish) form of Cronin: timely

Kronos (Greek) black

Kruz (Spanish) delight

Krystyn (Polish) Christian
Krys, Krystian

Krzysztof (Polish) bearing Christ
Kreestof

Kubrick (Last name as first name) creative
Kubrik

Kueng (Chinese) of the universe; fine

Kugonza (African) in love

Kumar (Hindi) boy

Kundayo (African) joy

Kunig (Dutch) clever

Kuno (German) courageous

Kunyo (African) brave

Kuper (Hebrew) copper

Kurt (Latin) wise advisor
Curt, Kurty

Kurtis (Latin) form of Curtis: gracious; kindhearted
Kurt, Kurtes, Kurtey, Kurtie, Kurts, Kurtus, Kurty

Kuster (American) form of Custer: watchful; stubborn

Kutrer (Last name as first name) form of Cutrer: knife dealer

Kutter (American) form of Cutter:

man who cuts gemstones

Kutty (English) knife-wielding
Cutty

Kwadjo (African) Monday-born

Kwako (African) Wednesday-born

Kwame (African) Saturday's child
Kwamee, Kwami

Kwan (Korean) bold character

Kwasi (African) born on Sunday
Kweisi, Kwesi

Kwintyn (Polish) fifth child
Kwint, Kwintin, Kwynt

Ky (Irish) form of Kyle: serene

Kyan (Place name) village in Japan
Kyann

Kylan (Irish) form of Kyle: serene

Kyland (Irish) calm

Kyle ☮ ⚤ (Irish) serene
Kiel, Kiyle, Kye, Kyl, Kyley, Kylie, Kyly

Kyler (English) peaceful
Cuyler, Kieler, Kiler, Kye, Kylor

Kylerly (English) unusual

Kylerton (American) form of Kyle: serene
Kylten

Kymond (American) brave

Kynan (Welsh) leads

Kynaston (English) serene

Kyne (English) blue-blooded

Kyran (Irish) form of Kieran:

handsome brunette

Kyriacos (Greek) masterful

Kyriak (Greek) loves God

Kyros (Greek) masterful

Kyryl (Slavic) Lord's child

Kyston (American) form of Constantine: constant; steadfast

Kyzer (American) wild spirit
Kaizer, Kizer, Kyze

L

La Var (American) combo of La and Var

Laasch (Scandinavian) forward-thinking

Laban (Hebrew) white
Lavan

Labarne (American) form of Laban: white
Labarn

Labaron (French) the baron
LaBaron, LaBaronne

Labhras (Irish) form of Lawrence: honored
Lubhras

LaBryant (African American) son of Bryant; brash
Bryant, La Brian, La Bryan, Labryan, Labryant

Lachean (Scottish) from place of lakes

Lachlan (Scottish) feisty
Lachlann, Lacklan, Lackland, Laughlin, Lock, Locklan

Lachman (Scottish) prospers

Lachtna (Irish) gray; aging with grace

Lacido (Spanish) bright

Lacy (Scottish) warlike
Lacey

Ladan (Hebrew) having seen; aware

Ladd (English) helper; smart
Lad, Laddee, Laddey, Laddie, Laddy

Ladden (American) athletic

Laddie (English) youthful
Lad, Ladd, Laddee, Laddey, Laddy

Laden (English) from Layton: musical

Ladisiao (Spanish) helpful
Laddy

Ladislav (Czech) form of Walter: army leader

Lado (Spanish) artistic

Lael (Hebrew) belonging to Jehovah
Lale

Laertes (Literature) from Shakespeare's Hamlet; action-oriented

Lafaye (American) cheerful
Lafay, Lafayye, Laphay, Laphe

Lafayetta (Spanish) form of Lafayette: ambitious
Lafay

Lafayette (French) ambitious
Lafayet, Lafayett

Lafe (American) punctual
Laafe, Laife, Laiffe

Lafen (English) dearest friend

Lafett (French) form of Lafayette: ambitious

Lafi (Polynesian) shy

Lagos (Place name) city in Nigeria
Lago

Lagrand (African American) the grand
Grand, Grandy, Lagrande

Lahahana (Hawaiian) warm as sunshine

Laionela (Hawaiian) lion boldness

Laird (Scottish) rich
Layrd, Layrde

Lais (Indian) leonine

Laish (Biblical) place name

Laizer (French) form of Lazarus: helped by God

Lajos (Hungarian) famed

Lake (English) tranquil water

Lakista (African American) bold man

Laksen (Scandinavian) lucky son

Lakshman (Hindi) promising; (Indian) rich

Lal (Hindi) beloved

Lalit (Indian) handsome

Lalo (Latin) singer of a lullaby
Laloh

Lam (African) picks lemons

Lamalcom (African American) son of Malcolm; kingly
LaMalcom, LaMalcom, Mal, Malcolm, Malcom

Lamar (Latin) renowned
Lamahr, Lamarr, Lemar, Lemarr

Lamber (German) form of Lambert: bright
Lambur

Lambert (German) bright
Lamb, Lamber, Lambie, Lamburt, Lammie, Lammy

Lamberto (Spanish) bright

Lamech (Biblical) to lower

Lamek (Biblical) form of Lamech: to lower

Lament (Biblical) from Lamentations

Lamis (Arabic) speaks softly

Lamond (French) worldly
Lammond, Lamon, Lamonde, Lemond

Lamont (Scandinavian) lawman
Lamon

Lamonte (French) mountain

Lan (Chinese) orchid

Lance (German) confident
Lanse, Lantz, Lanz

Lancelot (French) romantic
Lance, Lancelott, Launcelot, Launcey

Land (English) form of Landon:
plain; old-fashioned

Landan (English) from the plains;
quiet

Lander (English) landed
Land, Landor

Landers (English) wealthy
Land, Landar, Lander, Landor

Landis (English) owning land; earthy
*Land, Landes, Landice, Landise,
Landly, Landus*

Lando (American) masculine
Land

Landon ♂ ♀ (English) plain; old-
fashioned
Land, Landan, Landen

Landry (French) entrepreneur
Landré, Landree

Lane (English) secure
Laine, Laney, Lanie, Lanni, Layne

Lang (English) top
Lange

Langdon (English) long-winded
Lang, Langden, Langdun

Langen (English) tall

Langerson (Scandinavian) long

Langford (English) healthy
Lanford, Langferd

Langham (Last name as first name)
long
Lang

Langilea (Polynesian) loud as
thunder

Langiloa (Polynesian) stormy; moody

Langley (English) natural
Lang, Langlee, Langli, Langly

Langston (English) long-suffering
Lang, Langstan, Langsten

Langton (English) long
Lange

Langundo (Polynesian) graceful

Langward (Last name as first name)
long

Langworth (Last name as first
name) of long worth

Lani (Hawaiian) lithe

Lanie (Scandinavian) son of tall man

Laning (Last name as first name)

Lanndson (English) Last name as
first name

Lanny (American) popular
Lann, Lanney, Lanni, Lannie

Lansing (Place name) city in
Michigan
Lance, Lans

Lanty (Irish) lively
*Laughun, Leachlainn, Lochlainn,
Lochlann*

Lantz (American) form of Lance:
confident

Lanu (Native American) circular

Lanzo (Italian) lance

Laoghaire (Irish) caretaker of cows

Laoiseach (Place name) from the
county Leix in Ireland

Lap (Vietnamese) independent

Laphonso (African American)
prepared; centered

Lapidos (Greek) cologne
Lapidus

Laramie (French) pensive
Laramee

Lare (American) wealthy
Larre, Layr

Laredo (Spanish) place name

Larence (English) form of Lorenzo:
honored

Largel (American) intrepid
Large

Lari (American) form of Larry: extrovert

Lariat (American) roper
Lare, Lari

Larios (Spanish) form of Lawrence: honored

Larkin (Irish) brash
Lark, Larkan, Larken, Larkie, Larky

Larndell (American) generous
Larn, Larndelle, Larndey, Larne

Larne (Place name) district in Northern Ireland
Larn, Larney, Larny

Larnell (American) giving
Larne

Laron (American) outgoing
Larron, Larrone

Laroyce (French) royal

Larrimore (Last name as first name) loud
Larimore, Larmer, Larmor

Larrmyne (American) boisterous
Larmie, Larmine, Larmy, Larmyne

Larry (Latin) extrovert
Lare, Larrey, Larri, Larrie, Lary

Lars (Scandinavian) form of Lawrence: honored
Larrs, Larse, Larsy

Larsa (Biblical) ancient Babylonian city

Larson (Scandinavian) son of Lars

Lasha (Biblical) place name (east of the Dead Sea); fissure

Lashaun (African American) enthusiastic
Lashawn, La-Shawn, Lashon, Lashond

Lashe (Scandinavian) form of Lasse: winner; the people's victory

Laskey (Last name as first name) jovial
Lask, Laski

Lasse (Scandinavian) form of Nicholas: winner; the people's victory

Lassen (Place name) a peak in California in the Cascade Range
Lase, Lasen, Lassan, Lassun

Lassit (American) broad-minded
Lasset, Lassitte

Lassiter (American) witty
Lassater, Lasseter, Lassie, Lassy

Laszlo (Hungarian) famous leader
Laslo, Lazuli

Lateef (Arabic) a gentle man

Lath (Scandinavian) boy from the barn

Latham (Scandinavian) farmer; knowing
Lathe, Lay

Lathrop (English) home-loving
Lathe, Lathrap, Latrope, Lay, Laye, Laythrep

Latif (Arabic) nice

Latimer (English) interprets; philanthropic
Latymer

Latorris (African American) notorious
LaTorris

Latoure (French) torn

Latravious (African American) healthy
Latrave

Latty (English) giving
Lat, Latti, Lattie

Laughlin (Irish) servant

Laurence (Latin) form of Lawrence: honored
Larence, Laurance, Laurans, Laure, Lorence

Laurens (German) brilliant
Larrie, Larry, Laure, Laurins, Lorens, Lors

Laurent (French) martyred
Laurynt

Laurie (Latin) form of Lawrence: honored

Lavan (Latin) pure

Lavaughn (African American) perky
Lavan, Lavon, Lavonn, Levan, Levaughn

Lavaughor (African American) laughing

Lavaugher, Lavawnar

Lavay (Italian) form of Livia: place name

Lavega (French) eagle star

Laven (Hebrew) white

Lavesh (Hindi) little piece; calm

Lavi (Hebrew) uniter

Lavunn (American) form of Levon: forward-thinking

Law (American) feisty

Lawerence (Latin) form of Lawrence: honored

Lawford (English) dignified

Laford, Lauford, Lawferd

Lawler (Last name as first name) honoring; teacher

Lawlor, Lollar, Loller

Lawrence (Latin) honored

Larrie, Larry, Laurence, Lawrance, Lawrunce

Lawrie (Latin) form of Lawrence: honored

Lowrie

Lawson (English) Lawrence's son; special

Law, Laws, Lawsan, Lawsen

Lawton (Last name as first name) honored town

Laylan (English) from land of Leigh

Layneln (English) form of Lane: secure

Layshaun (African American) merry

Laysh, Layshawn

Laysy (Last name as first name) sophisticated

Lay, Laycie, Laysee

Layt (American) fascinating

Lait, Laite, Late, Layte

Layte (English) meadow boy

Layton (English) musical

Laytan, Laytawn, Layten

Laz (Spanish) form of Lazarus: helped by God

Lazar (Hebrew) form of Lazarus: helped by God

Lazare, Lazaro, Lazear, Lazer

Lazaro (Italian) form of Lazarus: helped by God

Lazarus (Greek) helped by God

Eleazer, Lasarus, Lazerus, Lazoros

Lazo (Spanish) form of Lazarus: helped by God

Leal (Spanish) form of Lael: belonging to Jehovah; (Greek) self-assured

Leamon (American) powerful

Leamm, Leamond, Leemon

Leand (Greek) form of Leander: ferocious; lionlike

Leander (Greek) ferocious; lionlike

Anders, Leann, Leannder

Leandro (Spanish) of Leander

Lear (Greek) royal

Leare, Leere

Learly (Last name as first name) terrific

Learley

Leary (Irish) herds; high goals

Leather (American) word as name; tough

Leath

Leavery (American) giving

Leautree, Leautri, Leautry, Levry, Lo, Lotree, Lotrey, Lotri, Lotry

Leben (Last name as first name) small; hopeful

Lebna (African) soulful

Lebrun (French) brown-haired

Lebron, Labron

Lechoslaw (Polish) glorious Pole; envied

Lech, Leslaw, Leszek

Lecil (American) form of Cecil: unseeing; hard-headed; blind

Leckto (Greek) everlasting

Lectoy (American) form of Leroy: king; loyal

Lec, Lecto, Lek

Lee (English) loving

Lea, Leigh

Leeander (Invented) form of Leander: ferocious; lionlike

Legario (Spanish) cheerful

Leger (French) sent to earth

Leggett (Last name as first name) able

Legate, Leggitt, Liggett

Lei (Hawaiian) wreath; decorative

Leibel (Hebrew) lion

Leif (Scandinavian) loved one

Laif, Leaf, Leife

Leigh (English) smooth

Leighton (Last name as first name) hearty

Laytan, Layton, Leighten, Leightun

Leith (Scottish) broad

Lel (Gypsy) taker

Leland (English) protective

Leeland, Leighlon, Leiland, Lelan, Lelond

Leldon (American) form of Eldon: charitable

Leldun

Lem (Hebrew) form of Lemuel: loves God

Lemar (American) form of Lamar: renowned

Lemarr

Lemmy (Hebrew) loves God

Lemon (American) fruit; tart

Lemonn, Lemun, Limon

Lemuel (Hebrew) loves God

Lem, Lemmie, Lemmy, Lemy

Lemus (Spanish) loves God

Len (German) form of Leonard: courageous

Lennie, Lynn

Lenard (American) form of Leonard: courageous

Lenerd

Lencio (Spanish) valiant; gentle

Leni (Polynesian) lives for today

Lenjun (Dutch) helps

Lennan (Irish) gentle

Lennart (Scandinavian) brave

Lenn, Lenne

Lenno (Italian) brave

Lennon (Irish) renowned; caped

Lenin, Lenn, Lennan, Lennen

Lennor (Last name as first name) brave

Lennox (Scottish) authoritative

Lennix, Lenocks, Lenox, Linnox

Lenny (German) form of Leonard: courageous

Lenn, Lenney, Lenni, Lennie, Leny, Linn

Lensar (English) stays with parents

Lentin (English) summery

Lenton (American) religious

Lent, Lenten, Lentun

Lenvil (Invented) typical

Lenval, Level

Leny (German) form of Leonard: courageous

Leo (Latin) lionlike; fierce

Leobardo (Italian) lionlike

Leocadio (Spanish) lionhearted

Leo

Leolin (Polynesian) watchful

Leoline, Llewelyn

Leon (Greek) tenacious

Lee, Leo, Leone, Leonn

Leonard (German) courageous

Lee, Leo, Leonar, Leonerd, Leonord, Lynar, Lynard, Lynerd

LeOnarda (Spanish) form of Leonardo: lionhearted

Leonardo (Italian) lionhearted

Leo

Leoncio (Spanish) lionhearted

Leon, Leonce, Leonse

Leondras (African American) leonine

Leon, Leondre, Leondrus, Leonid

Leondus (Spanish) lion

Leone (Spanish) lion

Leonel (American) form of Lionel: fierce

Leonidus (Latin) strong
Leon, Leone, Leonidas, Leonydus

Leontes (German) lion's courage

Leonzo (Spanish) lion's courage

Leopold (German) brave
Lee, Leo

Leor (Latin) listens

Leoti (American) outdoorsy
Lee, Leo

Leovardo (Spanish) form of Leonardo: lionhearted
Leo, Leovard

Leovigildo (Spanish) lion heart

Lepern (Italian) leonine

Lepoldo (Spanish) form of Leopold: brave
Lee, Lepold, Poldo

Lepolo (Polynesian) handsome

Lerby (French) circular life

Lerett (Last name as first name) gentle

Lerey (American) form of Larry: extrovert
Lerrie, Lery

Leroy (French) king; royal
Leeroy, Leroi, Le-Roy, Roy, Roye

Leroye (French) royal

Les (English) form of Leslie: fortified
Lez, Lezli

Leshawn (African American) cheery
Lashawn, Leshaun, Le-Shawn

Leslie (Scottish) fortified
Lee, Les, Lesley, Lesli, Lezlie, Lezly

Lesner (Last name as first name) serious
Les, Lez, Lezner

Lester (American) large persona
Les, Lestor

Letian (Spanish) happy

Leto (Latin) happy

Letrae (French) joyful

Letushim (Biblical) hammermen; filemen

Leuk (Irish) form of Lake: tranquil water

Leumas (Biblical) name spelled backward

Leummim (Biblical) countries, without water.

Lev (Russian) lionine

Levar (American) soft-spoken
Levarr

Levega (French) star

Leven (Hebrew) heart's child

Leveratto (Italian) organized

Leverett (Last name as first name) planner
Lev, Leveret, Leverit, Leveritt

Leverton (Last name as first name) town of Lever; organized

Levesque (French) gatekeeper

Levi (Hebrew) harmonious
Lev, Levey, Levie, Levy

Levonne (African American) forward-thinking
Lavonne, Leevon, Levon

Lew (Polish) form of Louis: famous warrior
Leu

Leward (French) contentious
Lewar, Lewerd

Lewie (French) form of Louis: famous warrior
Lew, Lewee, Lewey, Lewy

Lewin (Last name as first name) lionlike

Lewis (German) form of Louis: famous warrior
Lewey, Lewie, Lewus, Lewy

Lewy (Irish) giving

Lex (English) form of Alexander: great leader; helpful
Lexa, Lexe, Lexi, Lexie, Lexy

Lexonne (American) form of Alexander: great leader; helpful

Leyland (Last name as first name) protective

Leyth (Scottish) river

Li (Chinese) strong man

Liam ○ (Irish) protective; handsome
Leam, Leeam, Leeum

Liang (Chinese) good man

Libardo (Spanish) free

Liber (Roman) freedom

Liberio (Spanish) liberated
Libere, Lyberio

Liberty (American) freedom-loving
Lib

Libni (Slavic) love

Libor (Czech) free

Licien (French) form of Lucian: soothing

Lidio (Greek) pleasant man

Lidon (Hebrew) judge

Liem (Vietnamese) truthful

Lienad (Biblical) name spelled backward

Lif (Scandinavian) full of life

Lifen (Dutch) beloved

Lige (Spanish) form of Ligia: clear

Ligi (Spanish) form of Ligia: clear

Ligia (Spanish) clear

Lihau (Hawaiian) cool; fresh

Like (Asian) soft-spoken

Liko (Hawaiian) budding; flourishing

Lillo (American) triple-threat talent
Lilo

Limo (Invented) from limousine; sporty
Lim

Limu (Polynesian) seaweed; natural

Linc (English) form of Lincoln: leader; lake colony
Link, Links

Lincoln (English) leader; lake colony
Link

Lindberg (German) linden-tree mountain
Lin, Lind, Lindburg, Lindie, Lindy, Lyndberg, Lyndburg

Lindell (Last name as first name) in harmony with nature
Lindall, Lindel, Lyndall, Lyndell

Linden (Botanical) tree
Lindun

Lindoh (American) sturdy
Lindo, Lindy

Lindsay (English) natural
Lind, Lindsee, Lindsey, Linz, Linzee, Lyndsey, Lyndzie, Lynz, Lynzie

Lindy (German) form of Lindberg: linden-tree mountain
Lind

Linford (Last name as first name) bold man
Lynford

Linfred (Last name as first name) proactive

Linley (English) open-minded
Lin, Linlee, Linleigh, Lynlie

Linnard (German) form of Leonard: courageous
Linard, Lynard

Lino (American) form of Linus: blond

Linos (Spanish) praised

Linton (English) lives near lime trees
Lintonn, Lynton, Lyntonn

Linus (Greek) blond
Linas, Line, Lines

Linvel (English) from flax town

Linwood (American) open

Lionel (French) fierce
Li, Lion, Lionell, Lye, Lyon, Lyonel, Lyonell

Liron (Hebrew) my song
Lyron

Lisiate (Polynesian) courageous

Lisimba (African) attacked by lion; victim

Lister (Origin unknown) intelligent

Littlejoe (Spanish) small

Litton (English) centered
Lyten, Lyton, Lytton

Liu (Asian) quiet

Liuz (Polish) light

Livias (Biblical) place name

Livingston (English) comforting

Liv, Livey, Livingstone

Liwanu (Asian) released

Llano (Place name) river in Texas; flowing

Lano

Llewellyn (English) fiery; fast

Lew, Lewellen, Lewellyn

Lleyton (Slavic) of the garden

Lloy (Welsh) holy

Lloyd (English) spiritual; joyful

Loy, Loyd, Loydde, Loye

Lobo (Spanish) wolf

Loboe, Lobow

Loc (English) of the forest

Lochan (Irish) lively

Lochlain (Irish) assertive

Lochlaine, Lochlane, Locklain

Lock (English) natural

Locke

Lod (Biblical) place name

Lodewuk (Scandinavian) warrior

Ladewijk, Ludovic

Lodge (English) safe haven

Lodi (American) place name

Lodovico (Italian) famous

Lodur (Scandinavian) vivid

Loey (American) daring

Loie, Lowee, Lowi

Lofton (Last name as first name) lofty

Loften

Logan ○ ❶ (Irish) eloquent

Logen, Loggy, Logun

Lohan (Last name as first name) capable

Lokela (Hawaiian) famed spear-thrower

Lokene (Hawaiian) form of Rodney: open-minded

Lokesh (Indian) hindu god Brahma

Lokie (Mythology) chaotic

Loknath (Indian) world leader

Lokni (Hawaiian) red rose

Loman (Irish) bare

Lomas (Spanish) good man

Lomax (English) Last name as first name

Lombain (French) peaceful (from the name Colombain)

Lombard (Teutonic) long-beard

Lombardi (Italian) winner

Bardi, Bardy, Lom, Lombard, Lombardy

Lon (Irish) intense

Lonata (Spanish) bravery

Lonato (Native American) flint stone; calm

Loncel (French) gentle

Lond (English) form of London: ethereal; capital of great Britain

London (English) ethereal; capital of great Britain

Londen

Long (Last name as first name) Chinese dragon; methodical

Lonnie (Spanish) form of Alonzo: enthusiastic

Lonney, Lonni, Lonny

Lono (Hawaiian) god of peace and agriculture

Loocho (Invented) form of Lucho: lucky; light

Loomis (American) young

Loramie (American) form of Laramie: pensive

Loran (American) form of Lauren: laurel-crowned

Lorance (Latin) form of Lawrence: honored

Lorans, Lorence

Lorca (Last name as first) poet

Lorcan (Irish) fiery

Lord (English) regal

Lorde

Lordlee (English) regal

Lordly, Lords

Lordson (English) Lord's son

Loredo (Spanish) smart; cowboy
Lorado, Loredoh, Lorre, Lorrey

Loren (Latin) hopeful; winning
Lorin, Lorrin

Lorens (Scandinavian) form of
Lawrence: honored

Lorenzo (Spanish) form of Lawrence:
honored
Larenzo, Loranzo, Lore, Lorence,
Lorenso, Lorentz, Lorenz, Lorrie, Lorry

Loreto (Italian) form of Lawrence:
honored

Loriano (Italian) form of Lorenzo;
form of Lawrence: honored

Lorimer (Last name as first name)
brash
Lorrimer

Loring (German) brash; (Greek) son
of soldier
Looring, Lorrie, Louring

Lorl (English) laurel plant

Lorne (Latin) grounded
Lorn, Lorny

Lorry (English) form of Laurie:
honored
Lore, Lorri, Lorrie, Lorry, Lory

Loryn (Latin) praised

Lot (Hebrew) furtive
Lott

Lotan (Biblical) secret

Lothario (German) lover
Lotario, Lothaire, Lotherio, Lothurio

Lou (German) form of Louis: famous
warrior
Lew

Loudin (German) from low valley;
blessed child

Loudon (American) enthusiastic
Louden, Lowden, Lowdon

Louie (German) form of Louis:
famous warrior
Louey

Louis (German) famous warrior
Lewis, Lou, Louie, Lue, Luie, Luis

Louks (Dutch) mysterious

Loundis (American) visionary
Lound, Loundas, Loundes, Lowndis

Louvain (English) city in Belgium;
wanderer

Love (Swedish) form of Louis: famous
warrior

Lovell (English) brilliant
Lovall, Love, Lovelle, Lovie

Lovett (Last name as first name)
loving
Lovat, Lovet

Low (American) word as a name; low-
key
Lowey

Lowell (English) loved
Lowall, Lowel

Lowry (Last name as first name)
leader
Lowree, Lowrey

Loy (English) loyal

Loyal (English) true to the word
Loy

Loys (American) loyal
Loyce, Loyse

Loza (Spanish) form of Louis: famous
warrior

Lozano (Spanish) Last name as first
name

Luas (Slavic) combative

Lubin (Slavic) loving

Lubomil (Polish) loves grace

Lubomir (Slavic) loves peace

Lubos (Slavic) loving

Luboslaw (Polish) loves glory

Luc (French) light; laidback
Lucca, Luke

Luca (Italian) lighthearted
Louca, Louka, Luka

Lucan (Irish) light

Lucas ✪ ✿ (Greek) patron saint of
doctors/artists; creative
Lucca, Luces, Luka, Lukas, Luke, Lukes,
Lukus

Lucason (German) son of Lucas; light

Lucho (Spanish) lucky; light

Lucian (Latin) soothing
Lew, Luciyan, Lushun

Luciano (Italian) lighthearted
Luca, Lucas, Luke

Lucious (African American) light; delicious
Luceous, Lushus

Lucius (Latin) sunny
Lucca, Luchious, Lushus

Lucky (American) lucky
Luckee, Luckey, Luckie

Lud (Biblical) warring

Luddey (Scandinavian) warring

Ludger (Scandinavian) wielding spears

Ludie (English) glorious
Ludd

Ludim (Biblical) warring

Luding (English) warrior

Ludington (English) warrior

Ludlow (German) respected
Ludlo, Ludloe

Ludolf (English) form of Rudolf: wolf

Ludomir (Polish) of well-known ancestry

Ludoslav (Polish) of glorified people

Ludovic (Slavic) smart; spiritual
Luddovik, Lude, Ludovik, Ludvic, Vick

Ludrie (Last name as first name) respected

Ludwig (German) talented
Ludvig, Ludweg, Ludwige

Ludwin (English) friend of Ludwig

Lugus (Irish) shining

Luigi (Italian) famed warrior
Lui, Louie

Luis ✪ (Spanish) outspoken
Luez, Luise, Luiz

Luisito (Spanish) form of Louis: famous warrior

Luister (Irish) form of Louis: famous warrior

Lujo (Spanish) luxurious
Luj

Luka (Italian) form of Luca: lighthearted
Luke

Lukae (Slavic) form of Luke: worshipful

Lukah (Invented) form of Luca: lighthearted

Lukas (Greek) lighthearted; creative
Lucus

Luke ✪ ⊕ (Latin) worshipful
Luc, Lucc, Luk, Lukus

Lukman (Last name as first name) vivacious

Lulani (Hawaiian) light sky

Lullo (American) form of Luke: worshipful

Lumer (American) light
Lumar, Lume, Lumur

Luna (Spanish) moon

Lund (Scottish) island grove child

Lundy (Scandinavian) island-lover

Lunell (Irish) light

Lunn (Irish) smart and brave
Lun, Lunne

Lunt (Scandinavian) grove-dweller

Luo (Hawaiian) light

Luong (Vietnamese) from the land of bamboo

Lusk (Last name as first name) hearty
Lus, Luske, Luskee, Luskey, Luski, Lusky

Lussier (French) Last name as first name

Lutalo (African) bold fighter

Lute (Polynesian) pigeon; inconspicuous

Luther (German) reformer
Luthar, Luth, Luthur

Luthus (American) form of Luther: reformer
Luth, Luthas

Luto (Greek) from Pluto

Lux (English) light

Lyal (English) form of Lyle: unique

Lye

Lyall (Scottish) faithful

Lycur (Greek) sly

Lydan (Irish) gray

Lyfe (American) life

Lyle (French) unique

Lile, Ly

Lyleon (Scottish) of the isles

Lyles (English) of the isles

Lyman (English)

meadow-man; sportsman

Leaman, Leyman

Lyndall (English) nature-lover

Lynd, Lyndal, Lyndell

Lyndles (English) of nature

Lyndon (English) verbose

Lindon, Lyn, Lynd, Lyndonn

Lynge (Scandinavian) sylvan nature

Lynn (English) water-loving

Lin, Linn, Lyn, Lynne

Lynton (English) town of nature lovers

Linton

Lynus (Greek) flax

Lynusse (American) form of Lynus:

flax

Lynwood (English) forest

Lyon (Place name) city in France

Lyone

Lyr (Welsh) sea god

Lyron (Hebrew) my song

Lysande (Greek) freewheeling

Lyse

Lysander (Greek) lover

Lysand

Lyulf (German) haughty; combative

Lyulfe, Lyulff

M

Maarten (Welsh) form of Martin:

warlike; god of war

Mablevi (African) do not deceive

Mac (Irish) mack

Mackee, Macki, Mackie, Macky

Macabee (Biblical/Hebrew) hammer

MacAdam (Scottish) son of Adam;

first

Macadee (Scandinavian) headstrong

Macaffie (Scottish) charming

Mac, Mack, Mackey, McAfee, McAffee,
McAffie

Macario (Spanish) blessed

Macareo, Makario

Macarlos (Spanish) manly

Carlos

Macarthur (Irish) arthur's son

Macaru (Spanish)

Macaul (Scottish) form of Macaulley:

devout son

Macauley (Scottish) righteous;

dramatic

Mac, Macaulay, McCauley

Macauliffe (Last name as first name)

bookish

Macaulif, Macauliff

Macaulley (Scottish) devout son

Macbey (American) form of Mackie:

friendly

Mackbey, Makbee, Makbi

Macdowell (Last name as first

name) giving

Macdowl

Mace (French) club

Macedonio (Spanish) from

Macedonia; travels

MacEgan (Last name as first name)

son of Egan; capable

Maceo (Spanish) form of Macedonio:

from Macedonia; travels

Maceson (French) son of Mace

Macgowan (Irish) able; gallant

Macgowen, Macgowyn

Machen (Slavic) winner

Mackay (Scottish) form of Mackie:

friendly

Mackeane (Last name as first name) attractive
Mackeene

Macken (Scottish) from Mackay

Mackenna (Irish) giving; leader
Mackena

Mackenzie (Irish) giving
Mack, Mackenzy, Mackinsey, Makinzie, McKenzie

Mackeon (Last name as first name) smiling

Mackie (Irish) friendly
Mackey

MacKinley (Irish) son of Kinley; educated

Mackinney (Last name as first name) good-looking
Mackinny

Macklin (Irish) good-humored

Maclain (Irish) natural wonder
McLain, McLaine, McLean

Maclean (Irish) dependable
Macleen

MacMurray (Irish) loves the sea

Macnair (Scottish) practical

Macon (Place name) city in Georgia; creative
Makon

Macy (French) lasting; wealthy
Mace, Macee, Macey, Macye

Madai (Biblical) of the Medes (ancient Persians)

Madan (Hindi) god of love; loving

Madden (Pakistani) planner
Maddin, Maddyn, Maden, Madin, Madyn

Maddock (Welsh) generous
Maddoc, Maddox, Madocock, Madox

Maddok (Welsh) form of Maddock: generous

Maddox (English) giving
Maddocks, Maddy, Madox

Madeo (Italian) form of Mateo: God's gift

Madhav (Hindi) sweet
Madhu

Madhavi (Indian) sweet as honey

Madison (English) good
Maddison, Maddy, Madisan, Madisen, Son

Madock (American) giving
Maddock, Maddy, Madoc

Madon (Irish) giving

Madras (Place name) city in India

Madu (African) manly

Madzimoyo (African) nourished by water; simple

Magaidi (African) last

Magalirio (Spanish) charming

Magee (Irish) practical; lively
Mackie, Maggy, McGee

Magellan (Spanish) explorer

Magene (Latin) creative

Magglio (Hispanic) athletic

Magic (American) magical
Majic

Magick (American) magical

Magli (Icelandic) magnanimous

Magne (Latin) great

Magni (Latin) greatness

Magno (Latin) greatness

Magnus (Latin) outstanding
Maggy, Magnes

Magog (Biblical) son of Gog; place name

Maguire (Irish) subtle
Macky, Maggy, McGuire

Mahadev (Indian) omnipotent

Mahali (Biblical) unhealthy

Mahan (American) cowboy
Mahahn, Mahand, Mahen, Mayhan

Maharba (Biblical) name spelled backward

Mahatma (Sanskrit) spiritually elevated

Maheshkumar (Indian) son of Lord Shiva

Mahir (Arabic) skilled

Mahler (Last name as first) famous composer; sweeping

Mahli (Hebrew) brilliant

Mahlon (English) astute

Mahluli (African) conqueror

Mahmud (Arabic) remarkable

Maikan (Welsh) calm

Maimon (Arabic) of good fortune

Main (Place name) river in Germany; leader
Mainess, Mane, Maness

Maisel (Persian) warrior
Meisel

Maitland (English) of the meadow; fresh ideas

Maj (Arabic) form of Majid: glorious

Majeed (Arabic) majestic
Majid

Majid (Arabic) glorious

Major (Latin) leading
Mage, Magy, Majar, Maje, Majer

Makale (Invented) form of Mikhail: godlike

Makaz (Biblical) place name

Makhi (American) form of Mikhail: godlike

Makio (Hawaiian) great

Makoto (Japanese) sincere; honest

Maks (Russian) form of Maksimilian: competitor

Maksimilian (Russian) competitor
Maksim

Makya (Native American) hunter

Mal (Hindi) gardens; flourishes

Mala (Indian) necklace

Malachi (Hebrew) angelic; magnanimous
Malachy, Malakai, Malaki, Maleki

Malachil (Hawaiian) angel

Malack (American) form of Malakai: God's angel

Malakai (Hebrew) God's angel

Malaki (Hebrew) God's angel

Malakinn (African) lordly

Malawa (African) flowering

Malcolm (Scottish) peaceful
Mal, Malkalm, Malkelm, Malkolm

Maldon (French) strong and combative
Maldan, Malden

Malfred (German) feisty
Malfrid, Mann

Malidan (English) meets

Malik (Arabic) angelic; masterful
Malic

Malikah (Hindi) royalty

Malise (French) masterful

Malk (Hindi) royal

Malla-Ki (Invented) form of Malachi: angelic; magnanimous

Malley (German) form of Mallory: wild spirit

Mallin (English) rowdy; warrior
Malen, Malin, Mallan, Mallen, Mallie, Mally

Mallory (French) wild spirit
Mal, Mallie, Malloree, Mallorie, Mally, Malory

Mallun (English) soldier's strength

Maloney (Irish) religious
Mal, Malone, Malonie, Malony

Malta (Biblical) place name

Malvin (English) open-minded
Mal, Malv, Malven, Malvyne

Mamre (Biblical) rebellious; bitter; set with trees

Mamun (Arabic) trustworthy

Manahath (Biblical) among men

Manasseh (Hebrew) cannot remember
Manases

Manchester (English) dignity; (Place name) city in England

Manchu (Chinese) unflawed

Mandar (Indian) flower

Mandell (German) tough; almond
Mandee, Mandel, Mandela, Mandie, Mandy

Mandla (African) powerful

Mandy (Latin) lovable

Mandey

Manfred (English) peaceful

Manferd, Manford, Mannfred, Mannie,
Manny, Mannye

Manfredo (Italian) strong
peacefulness

Mani (Spanish) God's gift

Manila (Place name) capital of
Philippines

Manilla

Maninder (Hindi) masculine; potent

Manish (Indian) mind god

Manjuk (Arabic) lightness

Manley (English) virile; haven

Man, Manlee, Manlie, Manly

Mann (German) masculine

Mannes, Manning

Manning (English) heroic

Man, Maning, Mann

Mannis (Irish) great

Manish, Manus

Mannix (Irish) spiritual

Manix, Mann, Mannicks

Mannon (French) exciting

Manny (Spanish) form of Manuel:
with God

Manney, Manni, Mannie

Manoj (Sanskrit) cupid

Manolito (Spanish) God loves

Manolo (Spanish) from Spanish shoe
designer Manolo Blahnik; cutting-edge

Manpreet (Indian) beloved; calm

Manriquez (German) brave

Manse (English) winning

Mansfield (English) outdoorsman

Manesfeld, Mans, Mansfeld, Mansfielde

Manshel (English) of the house;
domestic

Mansel

Mantel (English) formidable

Mantell, Mantle

Manton (English) man's town; special

Manu (Hindi) father of people;
masculine

Manuel (Hebrew) form of
Emmanuel: with God

Mannuel, Manny, Manual, Manuelle

Manus (American) strong-willed;
(Slavic) daybreak

Manes, Mann, Mannas, Mannes,
Mannis, Mannus

Manvel (French) great town;
hardworking

Mann, Manny, Manvil, Manville

Manzo (Japanese) third-born

Mao (Chinese) hair

Maquinn (Native American)
generous

Marat (Russian) desirable

Marathon (Biblical) place name

Marathus (Biblical) place name

Marble (English) word as name

Marc (French) combative

Markee, Markey, Markeye, Markie
Mark, Marko, Marky

Marcel (French) singing God's praises

Marcell, Mars, Marsel

Marceli (French) form of Marcellus:
romantic; persevering

Marcellin (French) combative

Marc-Elliott (French) combination
of Marc and Elliott

Marcellus (Latin) romantic;
persevering

Marcel, Marcelis, Marcey, Marsellus,
Marsey

Marcelno (Slavic) combative

Marcelo (Italian) combative

March (English) fruitful month

Marche

Marchand (French) merchant

Marchell (English) has limits

Marcial (Spanish) martial; combative

Mars

Marciano (Italian) manly; macho

Marcyano

Marciel (French) warring

Marcin (Polish) form of Martin:
warlike; god of war

Marcio (Italian) warring

Marcion (Italian) warring

Marcionne (Italian) form of Martin: warlike; god of war

Marco (Italian) tender
Marc, Mark, Markie, Marko, Marky

Marconi (Italian) inventive; tough

Marcos (Spanish) outgoing
Marco, Marko, Markos, Marky

Marco-Tulio (Spanish) fighter; substantial
Marco Tulio, Marcotulio

Marcoux (French) aggressive; manly
Marce, Mars

Marcus (Latin) combative
Marc, Mark, Markus, Marky

Marcus-Anthony (Spanish) valuable; aggressive
Marc Anthony, Marc-Antonito, Marcus-Antoneo, Marcusantonio, Markanthony, Taco, Tonio, Tono

Marduk (Hindi) bothered

Mardy (Jewish) competitive

Marek (Polish) masculine

Marekel (Slavic) form of Marcus: combative

Marett (Greek) pearl

Margarito (Italian) pearl

Marguez (Spanish) noble
Marguiz

Mariano (Italian) combative; manly
Mario

Marico (Italian) reasonable

Marin (French) ocean-loving
Maren, Marino, Maryn

Mariner (Greek) form of Myron: aromatic oil

Mario (Italian) masculine
Marioh, Marius, Marrio, Morio

Marion (Latin) suspicious
Mareon, Marionn

Marios (Italian) combative

Marius (German) masculine; virile
Marrius

Marjuan (Spanish) contentious
Marhwon, Marwon, Marwond

Mark ✪ (Latin) form of Marcus: combative

Markan (Latin) form of Marcus: combative

Markay (American) manly

Markee (Polish) warring

Markel (Latin) form of Mark: combative

Markell (African American) personable
Markelle

Marker (American) form of Mark: combative

Markham (English) homebody
Marcum, Markhum, Markum

Markos (Greek) warring; masculine

Markys (French) form of Marcus: combative

Marl (English) rebel
Marley, Marli

Marley (English) secretive; boy of the woods
Marlee, Marleigh, Marly

Marlin (English) opportunistic; fish
Marllin

Marlo (English) hill by a lake; optimistic
Mar, Marl, Marlow, Marlowe

Marlon (French) wizard; strange
Marlan, Marlen, Marlin, Marly

Marlones (French) form of Marlon: wizard; strange

Marlous (English) boy from lake

Marlowes (English) boy from lake

Marmaduke (English) haughty
Duke, Marmadook, Marmahduke

Marmion (French) famed
Marmeonne, Marmyon

Marnin (Hebrew) ebullient

Maroulis (Greek) dark

Marq (French) noble
Mark, Marque, Marquie

Marque (French) noble; smart
Marcqe, Marcque, Marqe

Marquel (French) nobleman

Marques (African American) noble
Marqes, Marqis, Marquez, Marquis

Marquise (French) noble
Mark, Markese, Marky, Marq,
Marquese, Marquie, Marquis

Marquison (Last name as first
name) capable

Mars (Latin) warlike; god of war
Marrs, Marz

Marsdon (English) comforting
Marr, Mars, Marsden, Marsdyn

Marsh (English) handsome
Marr, Mars, Marsch, Marsey, Marsy

Marshall (French) giving care
Marsh, Marshal, Marshel, Marshell,
Marsy

Marson (English) Mark's son

Marston (English) personable
Mars, Marst, Marstan, Marsten

Martand (Indian) sunny

Marte (English) warring

Martial (French) form of Mark:
combative

Martim (Latin) form of Martin:
warlike; god of war

Martin (Latin) form of Mars: warlike;
god of war
Mart, Marten, Marti, Martie, Marton,
Marty

Martone (French) form of Martin:
warlike; god of war

Marty (Latin) form of Martin:
warlike; god of war
Mart, Martee, Martey, Marti, Martie,
Martye

Martyn (French) form of Martin:
warlike; god of war

Marv (English) form of Marvin:
steadfast friend
Marve, Marvy

Marvell (French) marvelous man
Marvel, Marvil, Marvill, Marvyl,
Marvyll

Marvie (English) form of Marvin:
steadfast friend

Marvin (English) steadfast friend
Marv, Marven, Marvy

Marvous (American) marvelous

Marwood (English) forest man

Masa (African) centered

Masaaki (Japanese) correct
brightness

Masada (Hebrew) stronghold

Masajiro (Japanese) integrity
Masahiro, Masaji

Masamba (African) departs

Masamitsu (Japanese) feeling

Masanao (Japanese) good

Masayuki (Japanese) problematic

Mash (African) delights

Mashael (Invented) form of
Michael: like the Lord

Mashane (English) form of Maxime:
greatest

Mashawn (African American)
vivacious
Masean, Mashaun, Mayshawn

Maslen (American) promising
Mas, Masline, Maslyn

Mason ♂ ⚦ (French) ingenious;
reliable; stone mason
Mace, Mase

Masood (Iranian) helpful

Massa (Biblical) a burden; prophecy

Massey (English) doubly excellent
Maccey, Masey, Massi

Massiel (Slavic) best; from Massimo

Massim (Italian) best; from Massimo

Massimo (Italian) great
Masimo, Massey, Massimmo

Masson (French) stone mason

Master (English) masterful

Masura (Japanese) fated for good life

Mate (Spanish) form of Mateo: God's
gift

Matej (Polish) form of Matthew: God's gift

Mateo (Italian) God's gift

Mateus (Italian) God's gift

Mathan (Hebrew) fine gift

Mathau (American) spunky
Mathou, Mathow, Mathoy

Mather (English) leader; army; strong
Mathar

Matheson (English) son of God's gift
Mathesen, Mathisen, Mathison, Mathysen, Mathyson

Matheu (French) form of Matthew: God's gift
Matt, Matty

Mathias (German) form of Matthew: God's gift
Mathies, Mathyes, Matt, Matthias, Matty

Mathieson (German) son of Mathias

Mathieu (French) form of Matthew: God's gift

Matias (Spanish) form of Matthew: God's gift
Mathias, Matios, Mattias

Matin (Hebrew) gift

Matine (French) kind

Matisse (French) gifted

Matland (English) mat's land; homesteader

Matlock (American) rancher
Lock, Mat, Matt

Mato (Native American) bear; brawler

Matson (Hebrew) son of Matthew
Matsan, Matsen, Matt, Matty

Matt (Hebrew) form of Matthew: God's gift
Mat, Matte

Matteo (Spanish) God's gift

Matteson (English) son of Matt; God's gift

Matthew ☼ ☥ (Hebrew) God's gift
Math, Matheu, Mathieu, Matt, Mattie, Mattsy, Matty

Matthewson (Last name as first name) son of Matthew; devout
Mathewsen, Mathewson, Matthewsen

Matthias (Scandinavian) form of Matthew: God's gift

Matti (Scandinavian) form of Mathias: God's gift
Mat, Mats

Mattison (Last name as first name) son of Matti; worldly
Matisen, Matison, Mattysen, Mattyson, Matysen, Matyson

Matts (Swedish) form of Matthew: God's gift

Matty (Hebrew) form of Matthew: God's gift
Mattey, Matti

Matun (Biblical) treasure

Matunde (African) form of Matthew: God's gift

Matus (Czech) form of Matthew: God's gift

Mauli (Hawaiian) spirited

Maurice (Latin) dark
Maur, Maurie, Maurise, Maury, Moorice, Morice, Morrie, Morry

Mauricio (Italian) dark
Mari, Mauri, Maurizio

Mauricion (Latin) dark

Maurizio (Italian) dark
Marits, Miritza, Moritz, Moritza, Moritzio

Mauro (Latin) form of Maurice: dark

Maury (Latin) form of Maurice: dark
Mauree, Maurey, Mauri

Maven (American) dramatic

Maverick (American) unconventional
Mav, Mavarick, Mavereck, Mavreck, Mavvy

Mavis (French) bird; thrush; free
Mavas, Mavus

Mawali (African) vibrant

Mawulol (African) thanks God

Max (Latin) best
Mac, Mack, Macks, Maxey, Maxie, Maxx, Maxy

Maxcy (Slavic) form of Maximilian: most wonderful

Maxence (French) excellent

Maxfield (English) of the great field; lives large

Maxime (French) greatest
Max, Maxeem, Maxim

Maximeen (French) best

Maximilian (Latin) most wonderful
Max, Maxemillion, Maxie, Maxima, Maximillion, Maxmyllyun, Maxy

Maximino (Spanish) maximum; tops
Max, Maxem, Maxey, Maxi, Maxim, Maxy

Maximinole (Italian) best

Maximus (Greek) best

Maxinen (Spanish) maximum
Max, Maxanen, Maxi

Maxwell ♂ (English) full of excellence
Maxe, Maxie, Maxwel, Maxwill, Maxy

Mayer (Hebrew) smart
Mayar, Maye, Mayor, Mayur

Mayfield (English) grace

Maynard (English) reliable
Mayne, Maynerd

Mayne (English) power figure

Mayner (English) form of Maynard: reliable

Mayo (Irish) nature-loving
Maio, Maioh, May, Mayes, Mayoh, Mays

Mayon (Place name) volcano in the Philippines
May, Mayan, Mays, Mayun

Mays (English) of the field; athlete

Mayz (Arabic) form of Mazin: mannered

Maz (Hebrew) aid
Maise, Maiz, Mazey, Mazi, Mazie, Mazy

Mazaca (Biblical) place name

Mazal (Arabic) sedate

Mazin (Arabic) mannered

McCoy (Irish) jaunty; coy
Coye, MacCoy

McDonald (Scottish) open-minded
Mac-D, Macdonald

McFarlin (Last name as first name) son of Farlin; confident
Far, Farr

McGill (Irish) tricky

McGowan (Irish) feisty
Mac-G, Mcgowan

McGregor (Irish) philanthropic
Macgregor

McKay (Scottish) connives

McKinley (Last name as first name) son of Kinley; holding his own
Kin, Kinley, McKinlee

McLean (Scottish) stays lithe

McLin (Irish) careful
Mac, Mack

Mead (English) outdoorsman
Meade, Meede

Meadey (English) child of the meadow

Meallan (Irish) sweet
Maylan, Meall

Meant (American) closed

Mearl (French) form of Merlin: clever

Mechell (French) strong ancestry

Medad (Hebrew) loves

Medan (Biblical) judgment; process

Medardo (Spanish) power figure

Medford (French) natural; comical
Med, Medfor

Medgar (German) strong

Medina (Spanish) place name

Medwin (German) friendly

Megiddo (Biblical) place name

Mehmet (Sanskrit) royal

Mehrdad (Persian) sun

Mehul (Indian) rainy

Meindert (German) hearty boy
Meinhard, Meinrad

Meir (Hebrew) teacher

Mayer, Myer

Mek (Scandinavian) spiritual

Mekhi (Asian) vision

Mel (Irish) form of Melvin: friendly

Mell

Melanio (Spanish) royal

Melar (English) mill man; pleases

Melbourne (Place name) city in Australia; serene; (English) from the mill stream

Mel, Melborn, Melbourn, Melburn, Melburne

Melburn (English) sylvan; outdoorsy

Mel, Melbourn, Melburne, Milbourn, Milburn

Melch (Hebrew) royalty

Melchor (Polish) city's king

Meldon (English) destined for fame

Melden, Meldin, Meldyn

Meldric (English) leader

Mel, Meldrik

Melech (Jewish) king

Melecio (Spanish) cautious

Melesio, Melezio, Mesio

Meletius (Greek) ultra-cautious

Meletios, Meletus

Melford (English) boy from mill ford

Melito (Spanish) small and calm

Meliton (Greek) malta child

Melle (English) masculine form of Mary: star of the sea; sea of bitterness

Melos (Greek) favorite

Milos

Melquiades (Spanish) gypsy

Melroy (American) form of Elroy: giving

Mel

Melton (English) nature; natural

Mel, Meltan

Melvan (Irish) form of Melvin: friendly

Melville (French) mill town

Mel, Mell, Melvil, Melvill

Melvin (English) friendly

Mel, Melvine, Melvon, Melvyn, Milvin

Melvis (American) form of Elvis: all-wise

Mel, Melv

Melvo (American) form of Melvin: friendly

Memphis (Place name) city in Tennessee

Memphus

Menas (Hebrew) forgets

Mendel (English) methodical

Mendl, Menka, Menke, Menla, Menlin

Menes (Egyptian) first king of the 1st Egyptian Dynasty

Menlus (Greek) endures

Menno (Dutch) strong

Mensa (African) third son; genius

Mensah

Ment (Greek) teaches

Menter (Greek) helper; mentor

Merari (Biblical/Hebrew) bitter

Merce (English) merchant

Mercer (English) affluent

Merce, Mercur, Murcer

Merch (English) merchant

Merchant (English) merchant

Mercury (Latin) mercurial

Mercutio (Literature) from Shakespeare's Romeo and Juliet; mercurial

Merdyth (Welsh) form of Meredith: protector

Meredith (Welsh) protector

Merdith, Mere, Meredyth, Meridith, Merrey

Mereld (Irish) form of Merrill: renowned

Merika (Slavic) sea child

Merlin (English) clever

Merl, Merlan, Merle, Merlinn, Merlun, Murlin

Merlot (Word as name) wine

Merrical (American) miracle

Merrick (English) bountiful seaman

Mere, Meric, Merik, Merrack, Merrik

Merrie (English) giving

Merey, Meri, Merri

Merrill (French) renowned

Mere, Merell, Merill, Merrell, Merril, Meryll

Merritt (Latin) worthy

Merid, Merit, Merret, Merrid

Merson (Irish) son of the sea

Merv (Irish) form of Mervin: bold

Murv

Mervin (Irish) bold

Merv, Merven, Mervun, Mervy, Mervyn, Murv, Murvin

Merwin (Irish) friend of the sea

Merzian (American) sea child

Meshach (Hebrew) fortunate

Meeshak, Meshack, Meshak

Meson (Spanish) of the house

Mesquite (American) rancher; spiny shrub

Meskeet

Messiah (Biblical) delivered the Jews

Metheus (Greek) form of Prometheus: friend of man; bringer of fire

Methuse (Biblical) from Methuselah

Metin (Turkish) dominant

Metzger (Last name as first name)

Meyer (Hebrew) brilliant

Maye, Meier, Mye, Myer

Meyshaun (African American) searching

Maysh, Mayshaun, Mayshawn, Meyshawn

Mibsam (Biblical) smelling sweet

Micah (Hebrew) prophet; sees all

Mica, Micha, Michah

Mican (Hebrew) form of Michael: like the Lord

Michael ✪ ✝ (Hebrew) like the Lord

Mical, Michaelle, Mickey, Mikael, Mike, Mikey, Mikiee, Miko

Michel (French) fond

Mich, Michelle, Mike, Mikey

Michelangelo (Italian) God's angel/messenger; artistic

Michel, Michelanjelo, Mikalangelo, Mike, Mikel, Mikelangelo

Michitt (American) form of Michael: like the Lord

Michon (French) form of Michel: fond

Mich, Michonn, Mish, Mishon

Mick (Hebrew) closest to God

Mic, Mik

Mickel (American) form of Michael: like the Lord

Mick, Mikel

Mickey (American) enthusiastic

Mick, Micki, Mickie, Micky, Miki, Myck

Mickey-Lee (American) friendly

Mickey Lee, Mickeylee, Mickie-Lee

Miga (Spanish) persona; essence

Migdol (Biblical) place name

Migio (Spanish) form of Remigio: from Rheims

Migron (Biblical) place name

Miguel (Spanish) form of Michael: like the Lord

Megel, Migel, Migelle

Miguelangel (Spanish) angelic

Miguelanjel

Mihir (Hindi) sunny

Mika (Hebrew) form of Micah: prophet; sees all

Mikah, Mikie, Myka, Mykie, Myky

Mikael (Scandinavian) warrior

Michael, Mikel, Mikkel

Mikahael (Slavic) form of Michael: like the Lord

Mikaile (Scandinavian) form of Michael: like the Lord

Mikas (Russian) form of Mikhail: godlike

Mike (Hebrew) form of Michael: like the Lord

Meik, Miik, Myke

Mikel (Slavic) form of Mikhail: godlike

Mikelis (Slavic) form of Michael: like the Lord

Mikhail (Russian) godlike
Mika, Mikey, Mikkail, Mykhey

Mikolaj (Polish) form of Michael: like the Lord

Mikolas (Greek) form of Nicholas: winner; the people's victory
Mick, Mickey, Mickolas, Mik, Miko, Mikolus, Miky

Mil (Slavic) loved

Milagros (Spanish) miracle
Milagro

Milam (Last name as first name) uncomplicated
Mylam

Milan (Place name) city in Italy; smooth
Milano

Milburn (Scottish) volatile
Milbyrn, Milbyrne, Millburn

Miles (German) forgiving
Mile, Miley, Myles, Myyles

Miletus (Biblical) loved

Miley (American) reliable; forgiving
Mile, Miles, Mili, Mily, Myles, Myley

Milford (English) from a calm mill setting; country
setting; country, Milferd, Milfor

Milid (Biblical) place name

Milko (Czech) form of Michael: like the Lord

Millard (Latin) old-fashioned
Milard, Mill, Millerd, Millurd, Milly

Miller (English) practical
Mille, Myller

Milli (English) miller

Millian (English) miller

Millo (German) form of Miles: forgiving

Mills (English) safe
Mill, Milly, Mylls

Milo (German) soft-hearted
Miles, Milos, Mye, Mylo

Milos (Slavic) kind
Mile, Miles, Myle, Mylos

Milou (French) mill man

Milton (English) innovative
Melton, Milt, Miltey, Milti, Miltie, Milty, Mylt, Mylton

Mimi (Greek) outspoken
Mims

Miner (Last name as first name) hardworking; miner
Mine, Miney

Mingo (American) flirtatious
Ming-O, Myngo

Minnow (American) beachcomber

Minter (Last name as first name) dull

Mirko (Slavic) glory in peace

Mirlam (American) great
Mir, Mirsam, Mirtam

Mirsab (Arabic) judicious

Misa (Slavic) form of Michael: like the Lord

Misael (Hebrew) godlike

Misha (Russian) form of Mikhail: godlike; graceful

Mishael (Hebrew) form of Michael: like the Lord

Mishma (Biblical) hearing; obeying

Mitch (English) form of Mitchell: optimistic

Mitchell (English) optimistic
Mitch, Mitchel, Mitchelle, Mitchie, Mitchill, Mitchy, Mitshell, Mytchil

Mitchum (Last name as first name) dramatic; known
Mitchem

Mithun (Indian) Gemini; couple; soft

Mitul (Indian) basic

Mizzah (Biblical/Hebrew) despair

Moab (Biblical) of his father; son of Lot; place name (east of Dead Sea)

Modein (Biblical) place name

Modesto (Spanish) modest
Modysto

Modi (Norse) son of Thor

Modred (Greek) unafraid
Modrede, Modrid

Moe (American) form of names beginning with Mo or Moe; easygoing
Mo

Moey (Hebrew) easygoing
Moe, Moeye

Moges (Dutch) power

Mohammad (Arabic) praiseworthy
Mohamad, Mohamid, Mohammed, Mohamud, Muhammad

Mohan (Hindi) compelling; riveting

Mohana (Sanskrit) handsome
Mohann

Mohawk (Place name) river in New York

Mohit (Indian) seeks beauty

Mohsen (Persian) one who does good deeds
Mosen

Mois (Hebrew) humble

Moises (Hebrew) drawn from the water
Moe

Mojave (Place name) desert in California; towering man
Mohave, Mohavey

Mokei (Hawaiian) Moses child

Molim (African) softspoken

Moline (American) narrow
Moleen, Molene

Momo (American) rascal

Monaco (Place name) unique, alone

Monahan (Irish) believer
Mon, Monaghan, Monehan, Monnahan

Mondo (Spanish) world

Money (American) word as name; popular
Muney

Monico (Spanish) player
Mon

Monroe (Irish) delightful; presidential
Mon, Monro, Munro, Munroe

Montague (French) forward-thinking
Mont, Montagew, Montagu, Montegue, Monty

Montana (Spanish) mountain; (Place name) U.S. state; (American) sports icon
Mont, Montane, Montayna, Monty

Monte (Spanish) form of Montgomery: wealthy; form of Montague: forward-thinking
Mont, Montee, Monti, Monts, Monty

Montero (Spanish) mountain

Montes (French) discriminating

Montford (English) of the mount

Montgomery (English) wealthy
Mongomerey, Monte, Montgomry, Monty

Montoi (French) mountain

Montrae (French) ostentatious

Montraie (African American) fussy
Mont, Montray, Montraye, Monty

Montrel (African American) popular
Montrell, Montrelle, Monty

Montrese (American) form of Montgomery: wealthy

Montrose (French) high and mighty
Mont, Montroce, Montros, Monty

Monty (English) form of Montgomery: wealthy; form of Montague: forward-thinking
Monte, Montee, Montey, Monti

Moody (American) expansive
Moodee, Moodey, Moodie

Moon (African) dreamer

Mooney (American) dreamer
Moon, Moonee, Moonie

Moore (French) dark-haired
Mohr, Moores, More

Mooring (Last name as first name) centered
Moring

Moose (American) large guy

Moos, Mooz, Mooze

Moray (Scottish) place name

Mordchai (Hebrew) combative

Mordecai (Hebrew) combative

Mord, Morde, Mordekai, Morducai, Mordy

Mordechay (American) form of Mordecai: combative

Moreland (Last name as first name) of wealth

Mooreland, Moorland, Moorlande, Morland, Morlande

Morell (French) secretive

More, Morelle, Morey, Morrell, Mourell, Murell

Moretti (Italian) desired child

Morey (Latin) dark

Morrie, Morry

Morgan (Celtic) confident; seaman

Morg, Morgen, Morghan

Moriah (Hebrew) Jehovah is my teacher

Moric (Slavic) form of Maurice: dark

Morland (English) from the land of moors

Morlen (English) outdoorsy

Morlan, Morlie, Morly

Morones (Spanish) joyful

Moroni (Place name) city in Comoros; joyful

Maroney, Maroni, Marony, Moroney, Morony

Morph (Greek) changing

Morpheus (Greek) god of dreams; shapes

Morrell (French) dark

Morris (Latin) dark

Maurice, Moris, Morse, Mouris

Morrison (Last name as first name) son of Morris; dark

Morrisen, Morrysen, Morryson

Morrley (English) outdoors-loving

More, Morlee, Morley, Morly, Morrs

Morrow (Last name as first name) follower

Morrowe

Morry (Hebrew) taught by God; old friend

Morey, Morrey, Mory

Morse (English) bright; code-maker

Morce, Morcey, Morry, Morsey

Mortimer (French) deep

Mort, Mortemer, Mortie, Morty, Mortymer

Morton (English) town of moors; dark

Mort, Mortan, Mortun, Morty

Mos (American) special

Moschi (Jewish) form of Moses: appointed for special things

Moses (Hebrew) appointed for special things

Mosa, Mose, Mosesh, Mosie, Mozes, Mozie

Moshe (Hebrew) special

Mosh, Moshie

Mosi (African) firstborn

Moss (Irish) giving

Mossy

Mostin (Welsh) settler

Mostyn (Welsh) mossy

Motaz (Slavic) form of Matthew: God's gift

Motor (American) word as name; speedy; active

Mote

Mottel (Hebrew) form of Max: best

Moushegh (Welsh) form of Moses: appointed for special things

Moylan (American) lights in the sky

Mozam (Place name) from Mozambique

Moze

Mudge (Last name as first name) friendly

Mud, Mudj

Muhammad (Arabic) form of
Mohammad: praiseworthy
Muhamed, Muhammed

Mukul (Hindi) bird; beginnings

Mulder (American) of the dark

Muldoon (Last name as first name)
different
Muldoone, Muldune

Muna (Arabic) wished for

Munday (English) Monday's child

Mundo (Spanish) form of Edmundo:
wealthy protector
Mun, Mund

Mungo (Scottish) loved; congenial
Mongo, Mongoh, Munge, Mungoh

Munir (Arabic) shines strongly

Munnin (Scandinavian) memorable

Murcia (Place name) region in Spain
Mursea

Murdoch (Scottish) rich
*Merdock, Merdok, Murd, Murdock,
Murdok, Murdy*

Murfain (American) bold spirit
*Merfaine, Murf, Murfee, Murfy,
Murphy*

Murff (Irish) form of Murphy: fighter
Merf, Murf

Murk (Slavic) content

Murl (English) nature-lover; sea

Murli (Hindi) flute

Murlie (Hindi) form of Murli: flute

Murphy (Irish) fighter
Merph, Merphy, Murfie, Murph

Murray (Scottish) sea-loving; sailor
Mur, Muray, Murrey, Murry

Murrell (English) nature-lover; sea

Murrill (English) nature-loving

Murt (American) happy

Murthy (American) form of Murphy:
fighter

Murtough (Irish) of the sea
Murtagh, Murrough

Murugan (Last name as first name)

Musa (African) forgiving

Mushi (Biblical) giving

Mushki (Biblical) place name

Muslim (Arabic) religious

Musri (Biblical) place name

Mustafa (Arabic) chosen one;
Turkish
ingenious

Mustapha (Arabic) the right one

Mutka (African) New Year's baby

Mycheal (African American) devoted
Mysheal

Myle (Latin) soldier

Myles (German) form of Miles:
forgiving

Mylie (German) form of Miles:
forgiving

Mylik (Slavic) form of Miles:
forgiving

Mylos (Slavic) kind
Milos

Mynor (Latin) form of Miner:
hardworking; miner

Mynton (English) town of miners

Myrden (Irish) fragrant

Myren (Greek) form of Myron:
aromatic oil

Myreon (Greek) aromatic oil
Myron

Myrle (American) able
Merl, Merle, Myrie, Myryee

Myron (Greek) aromatic oil
Mi, Miron, My, Myrayn

Myrzon (American) humorous
Merzon, Myrs, Myrz

Mystikal (American) musician;
mystical

Mystry (American) mysterious

N

Nabil (Arabic) of noble birth;
honored
Nabeel, Nobila

Nabor (Hebrew) light of the future

Nachman (Last name as first name) unique
Menachem, Menahem, Nacham, Nachmann, Nahum

Nachson (Last name as first name) son of Nach; up-and-coming

Nachum (Hebrew) comforts others

Nad (Biblical) name spelled backward

Nada (Arabic) morning dew; giver
Nadah

Nadab (Biblical) free and voluntary gift; prince

Nader (Arabic) dearest

Nadim (Arabic) fellow celebrant
Nadeem

Nadir (Arabic) rare man
Nadeer, Nadeir

Naeem (Arabic) happy

Nafis (Hebrew) struggles

Naftali (African) runs in woods
Naphtali, Neftali, Nefihali, Nephtali, Nephthali

Nag (Indian) form of Nagesh: Hindi serpent god

Nagel (English) smooth
Naegel, Nageler, Nagelle, Nagle, Nagler

Nagesh (Indian) Hindi serpent god

Nagid (Arabic) regal

Nahath (Biblical) rest; a leader

Nahbi (Biblical) very secret

Nahir (Hebrew) light
Naheer, Nahor

Nahshon (Biblical) that foretells; that conjectures

Nahum (Arabic) content; (Biblical) comforter; penitent
Nemo

Naim (Arabic) content
Naeem

Naima (arabic) comforting

Nain (Biblical) place name

Nairi (Biblical) place name

Nairn (Last name as first name) born again
Nairne

Nairobi (Place name) city in Kenya; starting out

Naissus (Biblical) place name

Najib (Arabic) noble
Nageeb, Nagib, Najeeb

Naldo (Italian) form of Reynaldo: knowledgeable tutor

Nalin (Hindi) lotus; pretty boy
Naleen

Namir (Hebrew) leopard; fast
Nameer

Nana (African) king

Nanda (Indian) achiever

Nando (Spanish) form of Fernando: bold leader

Nandor (Hungarian) form of Ferdinand: adventurer

Nandy (Hindi) from the god Nandin; destructs

Nano (Hawaiian) springtime

Nanson (American) spunky
Nance, Nanse, Nansen, Nansson

Nansor (Indian) defiant

Napier (French) mover
Neper

Napoleon (German) lion of Naples; domineering
Nap, Napo, Napoleone, Napolion, Napolleon, Nappy

Narayana (Indian) secure

Narciso (Latin) lily; daffodil
Narcis

Narcissus (Greek) self-loving; vain
Narciss, Narcissah, Narcise, Nars

Nardino (Spanish) kind

Naren (Hindi) best

Narendar (Indian) king

Narendra (Indian) king

Narithier (Indian) king

Narjis (Indian) lord

Narmad (Indian) delights

Nartan (Indian) dancing

Nasario (Spanish) dedicated to God
Nasar, Nasareo, Nassario, Nazareo,
Nazarlo, Nazaro, Nazor

Nash (Last name as first name)
exciting
Nashe, Nashey

Nashe (Arabic) soothing advisor

Nashua (Native American)
thunderous

Nasir (Arabic) wins

Nason (Biblical) perseveres

Nasser (Arabic) winning
Naser, Nasir, Nasr, Nassar, Nasse,
Nassee, Nassor

Nat (Hebrew) form of Nathaniel:
God's gift to mankind
Natt, Natte, Nattie, Natty

Natal (Hebrew) gift of God
Natale, Natalino, Natalio, Nataly

Natan (Hebrew) magnanimous

Natchio (Spanish) form of Nathan:
God's gift to mankind

Nate (Hebrew) form of Nathan and
Nathaniel: God's gift to mankind
Natey

Nath (Hebrew) form of Nathan:
God's gift to mankind

Nathan ○ ⊙ (Hebrew) form of
Nathaniel: God's gift to mankind
Nat, Nate, Nathen, Nathin, Natthaen,
Natthan, Natthen, Natty

Nathaniel ○ (Hebrew) God's gift to
mankind
Nat, Nate, Nathan, Nathaneal,
Nathanial, Nathe, Nathenial

Nation (American) patriotic

Natividad (Spanish) a child born at
Christmastime

Nato (American) gentle
Nate, Natoe, Natoh

Navarro (Spanish) wild spirit
Navaro, Navarroh, Naverro

Naveed (Hindi) wishing you well
Navid

Naveen (Hindi) new

Navnit (Indian) smooth

Nayan (Hebrew) form of Nathan:
God's gift to mankind

Naylor (English) likes order
Nailer, Nailor

Nazaire (Biblical) from Nazareth;
religious boy
Nasareo, Nasarrio, Nazario, Nazarius,
Nazaro, Nazor

Neal (Irish) winner
Neale, Nealey, Neall, Nealy, Neel,
Neelee, Neely, Nele

Nebaioth (Biblical) firstborn

Nebo (Mythology) Babylonian god of
wisdom

Nebraska (Place name) U.S. state
Neb

Nebulous (Word as name)

Nectarios (Greek) sweet nectar;
immortal man
Nectaire, Nectarius, Nektario,
Nektarios, Nektarius

Ned (English) form of Edward:
prospering; defender
Neddee, Neddie, Neddy

Nedrun (American) difficult
Ned, Nedd, Neddy, Nedran, Nedro

Neely (Scottish) winning
Neel, Neels

Negasi (African) destined for royalty

Negeb (Arabic) well-known

Nehemiah (Hebrew) compassionate
Nechemia, Nechemiah, Nechemya,
Nehemyah, Nemo

Neiel (Biblical) place name

Neil (Scottish) victor
Neal, Neale, Neall, Nealle, Nealon,
Neel, Neile, Neill, Neille, Neils, Nels,
Nial, Niall, Niel, Niles

Neirin (Irish) light

Nekane (Spanish) saddened

Nellie (English) form of Nelson: broad-minded
Nell, Nellee, Nelli, Nells, Nelly

Nelo (Spanish) form of Daniel: judged by God; spiritual

Nels (Scandinavian) victor

Nelson (English) broad-minded
Nell, Nels, Nelsen, Nelsun, Nilsson

Nemesio (Spanish) justice
Nemo

Nemo (Literature) from Jules Verne's *Twenty Thousand Leagues Under the Sea*; courageous

Neo (Greek) new

Nepheg (Biblical) weak; slacked

Neptune (Latin) god of the sea
Neptoon, Neptoone, Neptunne

Ner (Hebrew) light

Neral (Greek) of the sea

Nereus (Greek) of the sea
Nereo

Neris (Greek) of the sea

Nero (Latin) unyielding
Neroh

Nery (Spanish) daring
Neree, Nerey, Nerrie, Nerry

Nesbit (Last name as first name) man who wanders
Naisbit, Naisbitt, Nesbitt, Nisbet, Nisbett

Ness (English) form of Nesbit: man who wanders

Nesto (Greek) adventurer
Nestoh, Nestoro

Nestor (Greek) wanderer
Nest, Nester, Nestir, Nesto, Nesty

Netar (African American) bright
Netardas

Nethanel (Hebrew) form of Nathaniel: God's gift to mankind

Nets (American) athletic

Netuno (Spanish) form of Neptune: god of the sea

Netzer (American) form of Nestor: wanderer
Net

Nevada (Place name) U.S. state
Nev, Nevadah

Nevardo (Spanish) masculine

Never (English) word as name

Neville (French) innovator
Nev, Nevil, Nevile, Nevvy, Nevyle, Niville

Nevin (Irish) small holy man
Nev, Nevan, Neven, Nevins, Nevon, Niven

Nevins (Irish) devout

Newbie (American) novice
New, Newb

Newbury (Last name as first name) renewal
Newbery, Newberry

Newcomb (Last name as first name) renewal
Newcombe

Newell (English) new hall
New, Newall, Newel, Newy, Nywell

Newland (Last name as first name) of a new land

Newlin (Welsh) able; new pond
Newl, Newlynn, Nule

Newman (English) attractive young man
Neuman, Neumann, New, Newmann

Newport (Last name as first name) from a new seaport

Newt (English) new

Newton (English) bright; new mind
New, Newt

Neyman (American) son of Ney; bookish
Ney, Neymann, Neysa

Nezer (Arabic) winning boy

Nezib (Biblical) place name

Nga (Asian) herb

Niall (Irish) winner
Nial

Niambi (African (Swahili)) melody

Niaz (Hindi) gift

Nibshan (Biblical) place name

Nicah (Greek) victorious
Nik, Nike

Nicandro (Spanish) a man who excels
Nicandreo, Nicandrios, Nicandros, Nikander, Nikandreo, Nikandrios

Nicasio (Spanish) winning

Nicholas ♂ ♀ (Greek) winner; the people's victory
Nichelas, Nicholus, Nick, Nickee, Nickie, Nicklus, Nickolas, Nicky, Nikolas, Nyck, Nykolas

Nichols (English) kindhearted
Nicholes, Nick, Nicky, Nikols

Nick (English) form of Nicholas: victorious; winner; the people's victory
Nic, Nik

Nickel (English) word as name

Nicklaus (Greek) form of Nicholas: winner; the people's victory
Nicklaws, Niklus

Nickleby (Last name as first name) betting on the odds

Nickler (American) fleet-footed; perspicacious

Nicko (Greek) form of Nico: victors

Nicky (Greek) form of Nicholas: winner; the people's victory
Nick, Nickee, Nickey, Nicki, Nik, Nikee, Nikki

Nico (Italian) victor
Nicos, Niko, Nikos

Nicodemus (Greek) people's victory
Nicodemo, Nikodema

Nicol (Scottish) form of Nicholas: winner; the people's victory

Nicolas (Italian) form of Nicholas: winner; the people's victory
Nic, Nico, Nicolus

Nicomedes (Greek) thinking of victory
Nicomedo, Nikomedes

Nieblas (Spanish) winner

Niels (Scandinavian) victorious
Neels

Nigel (English) champion
Nigie, Nigil, Nygelle

Night (American) nocturnal

Nike (Greek) winning
Nykee, Nykie, Nyke

Nikhil (Russian) form of Nicholas: winner; the people's victory

Nikita (Russian) not yet won
Nika

Niklas (Scandinavian) winner
Niklaas, Nils, Klaas

Nikolai (Russian) winning
Nika

Nikolas (Greek) form of Nicholas: winner; the people's victory
Nik, Nike, Niko, Nikos, Nyloas

Nikolaus (Greek) form of Nicholas: winner; the people's victory

Nikom (Greek) winning

Nikon (Greek) victorious

Nikos (Greek) victor
Nicos, Niko, Nikolos

Nikostratos (Greek) the army's victory
Nicostrato, Nicostratos, Nicostratus

Niles (English) smooth
Ni, Nile, Niley, Nyles, Nyley

Nimro (American) form of Nimrod: renegade

Nimrod (Hebrew) renegade
Nimrodd, Nymrod

Ninad (Indian) gentle noise

Ninian (Gaelic) name given in honor of a fifth-century Irish saint

Nino (Spanish) child; young boy

Ninus (Biblical) place name

Ninyun (American) spirited
Ninian, Ninion, Ninyan, Nynyun

Niran (Indian) everlasting

Nissan (Hebrew) omen
Nisan, Nissyn

Nissim (Hebrew) Nisan is seventh Jewish month; believer

Nitin (Indian) attractive

Nito (Italian) form of Benito: blessed

Nivea (Spanish) reborn

Niven (Last name as first name) smooth

Nix (American) negative
Nicks, Nixy

Nixon (English) audacious
Nickson, Nixen, Nixun

Nizam (Arabic) leader

Njord (Scandinavian) man of the north
Njorth

Noah ☼ ⚤ (Hebrew) peacemaker
Noa, Noe, Nouh

Noam (Hebrew) sweet man; pleases others
Noahm, Noe

Nob (Biblical) place name

Noble (Latin) regal
Nobe, Nobee, Nobel, Nobie, Noby

Noblen (American) protected

Nocona (Native American) leads man

Nod (Biblical) vagabond; fugitive

Noden (Native American) windy day

Noe (Spanish) quiet;
Noeh, Noey

Noean (Spanish) calm

Noel (French) born on Christmas
Noelle, Noelly, Nole, Nollie

Noey (Spanish) form of Noah: peacemaker
Noe, Noie

Nofri (Italian) ancestor

Nolan (Irish) outstanding; noble
Nole, Nolen, Nolline, Nolun, Nolyn

Nolden (American) noble
Nold

Noll (Scandinavian) form of Oliver; loving nature

Nolly (Scandinavian) hopeful
Nole, Noli, Noll, Nolley, Nolleye, Nolli, Nollie

Nonan (Latin) superb

Noon (English) word as name, from Latin nona: ninth hour

Noor (Hindi) light
Nour, Nur

Noph (Biblical) place name

Norb (Scandinavian) innovative
Noberto, Norbie, Norbs, Norby

Norberito (Spanish) form of Norbert: bright north

Norbert (German) bright north
Norb, Norbie, Norby

Norberto (Spanish) form of Norbert: bright north

Nordin (Nordic) handsome
Nord, Nordan, Norde, Nordee, Nordeen, Nordi, Nordun, Nordy

Noriel (Spanish) hero

Norin (French) from the north

Norka (Scandinavian) charming

Norman (English) sincere; man of the north
Norm, Normen, Normey, Normi, Normie, Normon, Normun, Normy

Norrell (French) from the north

Norris (English) from the north

Norrison (French) northerner

Norriston (French) northern town

Norse (English) scandinavian boy

Norshell (African American) brash
Norshel, Norshelle

North (American) directional
Norf, Northe

Northcliff (English) from the north cliff
Northcliffe, Northclyff, Northclyffe

Northrop (English) northerner
Northrup

Norton (English) dignified man of the north
Nort, Nortan, Norten

Norval (English) from the north
Norvan

Norvell (French) northern town

Norville (French) resident of a northern village; warmhearted

Norval, Norvel, Norvil, Norvill, Norvyl

Norward (English) going north

Norwerd

Norwell (English) northward bound

Norwin (English) friendly

Norvin, Norwen, Norwind, Norwinn

Norwood (English) of the north woods

Novae (Biblical) place name

Novak (Slavic) Last name as first name

Novio (Spanish) boyfriend

Nowell (Last name as first name) dependable

Nowe

Nowey (American) knowing

Nowee, Nowie

Nuad (Welsh) tolerant

Nueces (Place name) river in Texas

Nuell (American) form of Newell: new hall

Nuel

Numa (Arabic) nice

Nun (Biblical) from the ocean

Nuncio (Spanish) messenger; informant

Nunzio

Nunry (Last name as first name) giving

Nunri

Nuri (Arabic) light

Noori, Nur, Nuriel, Nuris

Nuriel (Hebrew) light of God

Nooriel, Nuriya, Nuriyah, Nurya

Nuys (Place name) from Van Nuys

Nies, Nyes, Nys

Nye (Welsh) focused

Ni, Nie, Nyee

Nyle (American) form of Niles: smooth

Nyl, Nyles

Nyron (English) form of Neil: victor

Nyx (American) humorous

O

Oak (English) sturdy

Oake, Oakes, Oakie

Oakes (English) sturdy oak

Oakley (English) sturdy; strong

Oak, Oakie, Oaklee, Oakleigh, Oakly, Oklie

Oat (English) word as name

Oba (Hebrew) form of Obadiah: serving God

Obadiah (Hebrew) serving God

Obadyah, Obediah, Obee, Obie, Oby

Obal (Biblical) leader

Obasi (African) God-loving

Obataiye (African) world leader

Obayana (African) king by the fire

Obba (African) form of Obi: big heart

Obbie (Biblical) form of Obadiah: serving God

Obey, Obi, Obie

Obed (Hebrew) serves

Obedience (American) strict

Obie

Ober (Scandinavian) famed

Oberon (German) strong-bearing

Auberon, Auberron, Obaron, Oberahn, Oberone, Oburon

Obert (German) rich man

Obey (American) form of Obadiah: serving God

Obe, Obee, Obie, Oby

Obi (African) big heart

Obie (Hebrew) form of Obadiah: serving God

Obbie, Obe, Oby

Obike (African) loved by his family

Oboth (Biblical) place name

Ocean (Greek) ocean;
child born under a water sign
Oceane, Oceanus

Ocie (Greek) form of Ocean: ocean;
child born under a water sign
Osie

O'Connor (Irish) son of Connor

Octavio (Latin) eight; able
*Octave, Octavian, Octavien, Octavioh,
Octavo, Ottavio*

Oda (Scandinavian) precise

Odakota (Native American) has
many friends

Ode (Greek) poetry as a name; poetic
Odee, Odie

Oded (Hebrew) supportive

Odegard (Scandinavian) powerful
guard

Odell (American) musical
Dell, Odall, Ode, Odey, Odyll

Oder (Place name) river in Europe
Ode

Odessus (Biblical) place name

Odhran (Irish) green; creative
Odran, Oran

Odie (English) form of Odell: musical

Odilon (German) rich

Odin (Scandinavian) Norse god of
magic; soulful
Odan, Oden

Odinan (Hungarian) rich; powerful

Odion (African) the first twin

Odisoose (Invented) form of
Odysseus: wanderer
Ode

Odissan (African) wanderer

Odolf (Japanese) from the field of
deer; lithe

Odom (African) the oak; strong

Odysseus (Greek) wanderer
Ode, Odey, Odie

Oelen (Spanish) giving

Oescus (Biblical) place name

Ofer (Hebrew) deer

Og (Aramaic) king

Ogano (Japanese) wise

Ogdon (English) literate
Og, Ogdan, Ogden

Ogen (German) invincible

Oghe (Irish) horse rider
Oghie, Oho

Ogle (American) word as name; leer;
stare
Ogal, Ogel, Ogll, Ogul

Ogun (Japanese) undaunted

Ohad (Biblical) praising; confessing

Ohanko (Japanese) invincible

Ohanzee (Native American)
shadowy figure

Ohin (Japanese) wanted child

Oisin (Irish) fawn; gentle

Oistin (Latin) much revered

Ojas (Indian) shiny

Ojay (American) brash
O.J., Oojai

Ojo (African) he came of a hard birth

Okan (Turkish) horse
Oke

Okapi (African) graceful

Okechuku (African) God's blessing

Okello (African) child after twins
were born

Okemos (African) advises

Okie (American) man from
Oklahoma
Okey, Okeydokey

Oko (Japanese) evoker; charming

Okon (Japanese) from the darkness

Okoth (African) sad child;
born during rainfall

Okpara (African) first son

Oktawian (African) eighth child

Ola (African) child much honored

Olabisi (African) rich

Oladele (African) honored at home

Olaf (Scandinavian) watchful
Olay, Ole, Olef, Olev, Oluf

Olafemi (African) lucky child

Olafur (Scandinavian) forunate

Olajuwon (Arabic) honorable
Olajuwan, Olujuwon

Olakeakua (Hawaiian) living for God

Olamina (African) rich of spirit

Olan (Scandinavian) royal ancestor
Olin, Ollee

Olaniyan (African) honored all around

Olav (Scandinavian) traditional
Ola, Olov, Oluf

Oldrich (Czech) leader; strong
Olda, Oldra, Oldrisek, Olecek, Olik, Olin, Olouvsek

Ole (Scandinavian) watchful
Olay

Oleg (Russian) holy; religious
Olag, Ole, Olig

Olegario (Spanish) aggressor

Olek (Scandinavian) holy

Olin (English) holly; jubilant
Olen, Olney, Olyn

Olindo (Latin) sweet fragrance

Oliver (Latin) loving nature
Olaver, Olive, Ollie, Olliver, Olly, Oluvor

Olivier (French) eloquent
Oliveay

Oliwa (Hawaiian) from an army of elves

Ollie (English) form of Oliver: loving nature
Olie, Ollee, Olley, Olly

Olliem (Scandinavian) form of William: staunch protector

Olmos (Spanish) altruistic

Olney (English) lonely field

Olo (Spanish) form of Orlando: famed; distinctive

Olorun (African) blessed; counsels others

Olsen (Scandinavian) Last name as first name

Olubayo (African) full of happiness

Olufemi (African) God's loved child
Olviemi

Olugbala (African) the people's God

Olujimi (African) hand in hand with God

Olumide (African) God has come

Olumoi (African) blessed by God

Olushegun (African) marches with God

Olushola (African) blessed

Oluwa (African) believer

Oluyemi (African) man full of God

Olvera (Spanish) form of Oliver: loving nature

Olvery (English) draws others near

Omaha (Place name) city in Nebraska

Omanand (Hindi) joyful thinker

Omar (Arabic) spiritual
Omahr, Omarr

Omari (African) in high esteem

Ombre (Spanish) man

Omedes (Greek) ponders

Omer (Arabic) form of Omar: spiritual

Omie (Italian) homebody
Omey, Omi, Omye

Omri (Hebrew) Jehovah's servant; giving

On (African) desirable

Onacona (Native American) white owl; watchful

Onam (Biblical) success

Onan (Turkish) rich

Onaney (African) sees all

Onani (Asian) sweet

Onaona (Hawaiian) fragrant

Onder (Scandinavian) form of Andrew: manly and brave

Ondraze (Scandinavian) form of Andrew: manly and brave

Ondrej (Czech) masculine
Ondra, Ondravsek, Ondrejek, Ondrousek

Onesimo (Spanish) number one;
important
Onie

Onkar (Hindi) purest one

Ono (Biblical) place name

Onofrio (German) smart
Ono, Onofreeo, Onofrioh

Onorato (Spanish) honored

Onslow (Arabic) climbing passion's
hill
Ounslow

Onur (Turkish) promising boy

Onwoachi (African) God's world

Ophel (Biblical) place name

Ophir (Hebrew) loyal

Ophlas (Biblical) place name

Oqwapi (Native American) red cloud

Oracio (Spanish) oracle

Oral (Latin) eloquent

Oran (Irish) pale
Orin, Orran, Orren, Orrin

Orangel (Greek) angel of truth

Oranos (Greek) universal

Orban (Hungarian) city man;
sophisticated

Orbie (Slavic) sophisticated

Orchard (English) botanical name

Ordell (Latin) the start

Oregon (Place name) state

Oren (Hebrew) form of Owen:
wellborn; high-principled

Orenthiel (American) sturdy as a pine
Ore, Oren

Orenthiem (American) sturdy as a
pine
Orenth, Orenthe

Orest (Greek) form of Orestes: leader

Orestes (Greek) leader
Oresta, Oreste, Restie, Resty

Orestis (Greek) form of Orestes:
leader

Orev (Hebrew) raven; observing

Orford (Last name as first name)
noble

Ori (Hebrew) flame of truth

Orie (English) form of Orrin: river boy

Oriol (Spanish) best
Orioll

Orion (Greek) fiery hunter
Oreon, Ori, Orie, Ory

Orji (African) sturdy tree

Orlando (Spanish) famed; distinctive
Orl, Orland, Orlie, Orlondo, Orly

Orlay (Spanish) famed

Orlean (Latin) gold

Orleans (Latin) the golden boy
Orlins

Orlis (English) bearlike

Orman (Latin) noble
Ormand, Ormond, Ormonde

Orme (English) kind
Orm

Ormond (English) kindhearted
*Ormand, Ormande, Orme, Ormon,
Ormonde, Ormund, Ormunde*

Orn (Latin) form of Oren: well born;
high-principled

Oro (Spanish) golden child

Oron (Hebrew) light spirit

Orontes (Biblical) place name

Orpheus (Greek) darkness of night;
mythological musician

Orr (English) form of Orrick: sturdy as
an oak

Orran (Irish) green-eyed
Ore, Oren, Orin

Orrent (Greek) excites

Orrial (Latin) form of Uriel: light;
God-inspired

Orrick (English) sturdy as an oak
Oric, Orick, Orreck, Orrik

Orrie (American) form of Orson:
strong as a bear
Orry

Orrin (English) river boy

Orris (Latin) form of Horatio: poetic;
dashing
Oris, Orriss

Orry (Latin) oriental; exotic
Oarrie, Orrey, Orrie

Orso (Latin) form of Orson: strong as a bear

Orson (Latin) strong as a bear
Orsan, Orsen, Orsey, Orsun

Orth (English) honest
Orthe

Orton (English) town on the shore; reaching

Orturo (Spanish) form of Arturo: talented

Ortwin (English) shore friend

Orunjan (African) god of the noon-time sun

Orval (American) form of Orville: brave; (Scandinavian) eagle-eyed
Orvale

Orven (English) spears

Orville (French) brave
Orv, Orvelle, Orvie, Orvil

Orvin (Last name as first name) fated for success
Orwin, Orwynn

Orway (American) kind
Orwaye

Osai (Afghanistan) deerlike

Osakwe (Japanese) good destiny

Osanmwesr (Japanese) leaving

Osayaba (Japanese) wonders

Osbert (English) smart

Osborne (English) strong-spirited
Osborn, Osbourne, Osburn, Osburne, Ossie, Oz, Ozzie, Ozzy

Osburt (English) smart
Osbart, Osbert, Ozbert, Ozburt

Oscar (Scandinavian) divine
Ozkar

Oscard (Greek) fighter
Oscar, Oskard

Osceola (Native American) black drink

Osciel (Spanish) gracious

Osei (African) gracious

Osgood (English) good man
Osgude, Ozgood

Oshea (Hebrew) kind spirit

Osileani (Polynesian) talking forever

Osin (Irish) small deer

Osk (Scandinavian) spears

Oslo (Place name) capital of Norway
Os, Oz

Osman (Spanish) verbose
Os, Osmen, Osmin, Ossie, Oz, Ozzie

Osmar (English) amazing; divine

Osmenio (Spanish) talkative

Osmond (English) singing to the world
Os, Osmonde, Osmund, Ossie, Oz, Ozzy

Ospe (Russian) form of Joseph: He will add

Osrec (Scandinavian) leader
Os, Ossie

Osred (Scandinavian) leads mankind

Osric (Scandinavian) leader
Osrick

Ossie (Hebrew) powerful
Os, Oz, Ozzy

Osten (Last name as first name) religious leader
Ostin, Ostyn

Osval (Slavic) form of Oswald: divine power

Osvaldo (German) divine power
Osvald, Oswaldo

Oswald (English) divine power
Oswalde, Oswold, Oswuld, Oszie, Oz

Oswin (English) God's ally
Osvin, Oswinn, Oswyn, Oswynn

Ota (Czech) affluent

Otadan (Native American) abundance

Otey (Slavic) wealthy

Othar (Slavic) leader

Othell (African American) thriving
Oth, Othey, Otho

Othello (Spanish) bold
Otello, Othell

Othman (Last name as first name) man of bravery

Othnel (Biblical) God's lion

Othniel (Hebrew) rendered brave by God's love

Othon (German) rich

Otik (German) lucky

Otis (Greek) intuitive
Oates, Odis, Otes, Ottes, Ottis

Otokar (Czech) prudent in wealth

Otoniel (Spanish) fashionable
Otonel

Otskai (Native American) leaving

Ottah (African) thin boy

Ottar (Scandinavian) warring
Otomars, Ottomar

Otto (German) wealthy
Oto, Ott, Ottoh

Ottokar (German) can-do spirit; fighter
Otokars, Ottocar

Ottway (German) fortunate
Otwae, Otway

Otu (Native American) industrious

Oukounaka (Asian) from the surf

Ouray (Native American) arrow man

Oved (Hebrew) serving
Obed

Overton (Last name as first name) leader

Ove, Overten

Ovidio (Spanish) from Roman poet Ovid; creative
Ovido

Ovido (Spanish) tends sheep

Owen ✪ (Welsh) wellborn; high-principled
Owan, Owin, Owwen

Owney (Irish) old one
Oney

Ox (American) animal; strong
Oxy

Oxford (English) scholar; ox crossing
Fordy, Oxferd, Oxfor

Oya (African) vocal

Oz (Hebrew) courageous; unusual

Ozais (Hebrew) strong in God

Ozden (Hebrew) good in God

Ozeas (Italian) strong

Ozell (English) strong
Ozel

Oziel (Spanish) strong

Ozni (Hebrew) knows God

Ozuru (Japanese) stork; lively hope

Ozzie (English) form of Oswald: divine power
Oz, Ozzee, Ozzey, Ozzy

P

Paal (Scandinavian) form of Paul: small; wise

Pablo (Spanish) strong; creative
Pabel, Pabo, Paublo

Pace (English) peace

Pacian (Spanish) peaceful
Pacien, Pace

Packer (Last name as first name) orderly
Pack

Paco (Spanish) energetic
Pak, Pakkoh, Pako, Paquito

Padden (English) form of Patton: warrior's town
Paddin, Paddyn

Paddy (Irish) form of Patrick: noble
Paddey, Paddi, Paddie, Padee

Paden (English) form of Patrick: noble

Padget (French) learning; growing
Padgett, Pagas

Padraic (Irish) form of Patrick: noble
Padraick, Padraik, Padrayc, Padrayck, Padrayk

Padre (Spanish) father; cajoles
Padrae, Padray

Paeter (Scandinavian) form of Peter: dependable; rock

Page (French) helpful
Pagey, Paige, Payg

Pageman (Last name as first name) sharp

Pagiel (Hebrew) worships

Pago (Place name) for Pago Pago
Pay

Pagolo (Italian) placid

Pahan (Native American) summons

Paine (Latin) countryman
Payne

Paki (African) has seen the truth

Palani (Slavic) long-suffering

Pall (Scandinavian) form of Paul: small; wise

Palladin (Greek) confrontational; wise
Palidin, Palladyn, Palleden, Pallie, Pally

Pallaton (Native American) tough; fighter
Palladin

Pallav (Indian) new growth

Pallu (Biblical) distinct

Palma (Latin) successful

Palmer (English) open; grows palms
Pallmar, Pallmer, Palmar, Palmur

Palti (Hebrew) getaway

Pampa (Place name) city in Texas

Pan (Greek mythology) god of forest and shepherds
Pann

Panama (Place name) canal connecting North and South America; rounder
Pan

Pancho (Spanish) form of Francisco: free spirit; from France
Panchoh, Ponchito

Pancrazio (Italian) all-powerful
Pankraz

Pandy (English) from Panda

Panfilo (Spanish) loving all nature

Pankaj (Hindi) lotus flower

Panos (Greek) rock; sturdy

Pantaleon (Spanish) pants; trousers; manly
Pant, Pantalon

Pantias (Greek) philosophical

Pao (Italian) form of Paul: small; wise

Paolo (Italian) form of Paul: small; wise
Paoloh, Paulo

Paphos (Biblical) place name

Papillion (French) butterfly

Paquito (Spanish) dear Paco

Parah (Biblical) place name

Paran (Biblical) place name

Parindra (Indian) lion

Paris (English) lover; France's capital
Pare, Paree, Parris

Parish (French) priest's place; lovely boy
Parrish, Parrysh, Parysh

Park (English) calming
Parke, Parkey, Parks

Parker (English) manager
Park, Parks

Parley (Scottish) reluctant
Parly

Parnell (French) ribald
Parle, Parne, Parnel, Parnelle, Perne

Parnelli (Italian) frisky
Parnell

Parnes (French) form of Peter: dependable; rock

Paros (Place name) Greek island; charming
Par, Paro

Parr (English) protective
Par, Parre

Parris (French) priest's place; lovely boy
Paris, Pariss, Parriss, Parrys, Parryss

Parrish (French) separate and unique; district

Parry (Welsh) young son
Parrie, Pary

Parryth (American) up-and-coming
Pareth, Parre, Parry, Parythe

Parson (English) clergyman
Parsen

Parthik (Greek) virginal

Partholon (Irish) form of
Bartholomew: friendly; earthy
Parlan

Parvati (Indian) best

Pascal (French) boy born on Easter
or Passover; spiritual
Pascalle, Paschal, Pasco, Pascual,
Paskalle, Pasky

Pascasio (Spanish) Easter baby

Pasko (English) form of Pascal: boy
born on Easter or Passover; spiritual

Pasquale (Italian) spiritual
Pask, Paskwoll, Pasq, Pasquell, Posquel

Pass (Russian) form of Paul: small;
wise

Pastor (English) clergyman
Pastar, Paster

Pat (English) form of Patrick: noble
Pattee, Pattey, Patti, Patty, Pattye

Patcher (American) unusual

Pate (Latin) form of Patrick: noble
Pait, Payte

Patek (Latin) form of Patrick: noble
Patec, Pateck

Pater (Greek) father

Paterno (Spanish) fatherly

Paterson (Last name as first name)
intelligent father

Patricio (Spanish) form of Patrick:
noble
Patricyo

Patricius (Latin) noble

Patrick (Irish) noble
Paddy, Partric, Patric, Patrik,
Patriquek, Patryk, Pats, Patsy

Patriot (American) patriotic

Patterson (English) intellectual
Paterson, Pattersen, Pattersun,
Pattersund

Pattison (English) son of Pat; noble
Pattisen, Pattysen, Pattyson, Patysen,
Patyson

Patton (English) warrior's town
Patten, Pattun, Patun, Peyton

Paul (Latin) small; wise
Pauley, Paulie, Pauly

Paul-Erik (Scandinavian)
combination of Paul and Erik

Pauli (Italian) dear Paul
Paulee, Pauley, Paulie, Pauly

Paulin (German) form of Paul: small;
wise
Paulyn

Paulis (Latin) form of Paul: small;
wise
Pauliss, Paulys, Paulyss

Paulo (Spanish) form of Paul: small;
wise

Paulos (Greek) form of Paul: small;
wise

Paulus (Latin) small
Paul, Paulie, Paulis, Pauly

Paun (American) form of Paul: small;
wise

Pavan (Indian) wind

Pavel (Russian) inspired
Pasha

Paviter (Indian) pure

Pavlof (Last name as first name)
reactive; small
Pavel

Pavol (Slavic) form of Paul: small; wise

Pavun (Indian) belonging to the
middle

Pawel (Polish) believer
Pawl

Pax (Latin) peace-loving
Paks, Paxy

Paxon (German) peaceful
Packston, Packton

Paxton (English) from a town of peace; gentle boy
Paxten

Payam (Slavic) message

Payan (Indian) ornamented

Payne (Latin) countryman
Paine, Payn

Payton ♂ (English) soldier's town
Pate, Paton, Payten, Paytun, Peyton

Peabo (Irish) rock

Peader (Scottish) rock or stone; reliable
Peder, Peter

Peak (English) word as name

Peale (English) bell-ringer in a church; religious
Peal, Peel, Peele

Pearson (English) dark-eyed
Pearse, Pearsen, Pearsun, Peerson

Peat (English) form of Pete: dependable; rock

Peck (American) peaceful

Pecos (Place name) Texas river; cowboy
Peck, Pekos

Pedaias (Biblical) God loves
Pedaiah

Peder (Scandinavian) form of Peter: dependable; rock

Pederson (Scandinavian) form of Peterson: son of Peter
Pedersen

Pedram (Indian)

Pedro (Spanish) form of Peter: dependable; rock
Pedra, Pedrin, Pedroh

Peer (Scandinavian) rock

Peerson (English) son of Peter; smart
Peersen

Pegasus (Mythology) horse; rider

Peili (Spanish) joyful

Peirano (Italian) form of Peter: dependable; rock

Peleg (Greek) the sea

Pelle (Swedish) for Peter; rock
Pele, Pelee

Pelly (English) happy
Peli, Pelley, Pelli

Pelon (Spanish) joyful

Pelton (Last name as first name) town of Pel; respectful

Pembroke (French) sophisticated
Brookie, Pemb, Pembrooke, Pimbroke

Pender (Last name as first name) loves music

Penley (Last name as first name) strong

Penn (German) strong-willed
Pen, Pennee, Penney, Pennie, Penny

Penrod (German) respected leader

Penrose (Last name as first name) liked

Pentecost (Religion) pious person
Penticost, Pentycost

Pentige (Last name as first name) worthy

Pentz (Last name as first name) visionary

Penuel (Hebrew) face of God

Pepic (German) perseveres

Pepin (German) ardent
Pepen, Pepi, Pepp, Peppi, Peppy, Pepun

Pepper (Botanical) live wire
Pep, Pepp, Peppy

Peppino (Spanish) energetic

Per (Scandinavian) secretive

Peralta (Italian) pearl

Percival (French) mysterious
Parsival, Perc, Perce, Perceval, Percey, Percy, Perseval, Purcival, Purcy

Percy (French) form of Percival: mysterious
Percee, Percey, Perci, Percie

Peregrino (Italian) bird; ordinary

Perfecto (Spanish) perfect
Perfek

Peri (English) form of Perry: tough-minded

Perick (French) form of Peter: dependable; rock

Pericles (Greek) fair leader
Periklees, Perikles, Perry

Perine (Latin) adventurer
Perrin, Perrine, Perry, Peryne

Perk (American) perky
Perkey, Perki, Perky

Perkin (English) opinionated
Parkin

Perkins (English) political
Perk, Perkens, Perkey

Pernell (French) form of Parnell: ribald; form of Peter: dependable; rock
Pernel

Peron (Last name as first name) leader

Perre (English) form of Peter: dependable; rock

Perrin (Latin) traveler
Perrine, Pero, Per

Perrince (American) form of Terrence: calm

Perris (Greek) legendary kidnapper of Helen of Troy; daring
Paris, Peris, Periss, Perrys, Perys

Perry (English) tough-minded
Parry, Perr, Perrey, Perri, Perrie

Perryman (Last name as first name) nature-lover
Perry

Perseus (Greek) destroyer; mythological hero

Persis (Biblical) place name

Perth (Place name) capital of Western Australia
Purth

Perun (Slavic) thunder; god of lightning

Pete (English) form of Peter: dependable; rock
Petey, Petie

Peter (Greek) dependable; rock
Per, Petar, Pete, Petee, Petey, Petie, Petur, Pyotr

Peterson (Scandinavian) son of Peter
Petersen

Pethuel (Aramaic) God's vision

Petra (Place name) city in Arabia; dashing

Petre (Slavic) form of Peter: dependable; rock

Petru (Slavic) form of Peter: dependable; rock

Petrus (Scandinavian) dependable

Petter (Scandinavian) form of Peter: dependable; rock
Petya

Peverel (Latin) peverell
Peveril

Peyman (English) form of Peyten: soldier's town

Peyton (English) form of Payton: soldier's town
Pey, Peyt

Pharaton (Biblical) place name

Pharis (Irish) heroic
Farres, Farrus, Pharris

Pharo (Latin) ruler

Pharpar (Biblical) place name

Pharrington (Last name as first name)

Phasael (Biblical) place name

Phelan (Irish) the small wolf; fierce

Phelgen (Last name as first name) stylish
Phelgon

Phelim (Irish) wolfish; fierce
Phelym

Phelps (English) droll
Felps, Filps

Phex (American) kind
Fex

Phil (Greek) form of Philip: outdoorsman; horse-lover
Fill, Phill

Philander (Greek) lover of many;
infidel
Filander, Phil, Philandyr, Philender

Philemon (Greek) showing affection;
(Biblical) loves others
Filemon, Philamon, Philo

Philetus (Greek) collector

Philip (Greek) outdoorsman; horse-
lover
*Felipe, Filipp, Flippo, Phil, Phillie,
Phillip, Phillippe, Philly*

Philippe (French) form of Philip:
outdoorsman; horse-lover
Felipe, Filippe, Philipe

Philo (Greek) lover
Filo

Phineas (English) farsighted
Fineas, Finny, Pheneas, Phineus, Phinny

Phoenix (Greek) bird of immortality;
everlasting
Fee, Feenix, Fenix, Nix

Photius (Greek) scholarly

Picardus (Hispanic) adventurous

Pickford (Last name as first name)
old-fashioned

Pico (Spanish) the epitome; peak

Pier (Dutch) for Peter

Pierce (English) insightful; piercing
*Pearce, Peerce, Peers, Peersey, Percy,
Piercy, Piers*

Piero (Italian) form of Peter:
dependable; rock
Pierro

Pierre (French) socially adroit
Piere

Pierrepont (French) social
Pierpont

Pierre-Yves (French) combination
of Pierre and Yves

Pierrick (English) form of Pier: for
Peter

Piers (English) form of Philip:
outdoorsman; horse-lover

Pierson (English) son of Pier; rock
Pearson, Peirsen

Pietro (Italian) reliable
Pete

Pike (English) word as name

Pilar (Spanish) basic
Pilarr

Pildash (Biblical) biblical relative of
Abraham

Pilgrim (English) a traveler
Pilgrym

Pillion (French) excellence
Pilion, Pillyon, Pilyon

Pilot (French) excellence

Pim (Dutch) precise

Pin (Vietnamese) joyful

Pincus (American) dark

Pincas, Pinchas, Pinchus, Pinkus

Pinechas (Hebrew) form of Paul:
small; wise

Pineda (Spanish) Last name as first
name

Pinero (Spanish) springtime

Piney (American) living among pines;
comfortable
Pine, Pyney

Pinkston (Last name as first name)
different
Pink, Pinky

Pinky (American) familiar form of
Pinchas

Pinya (Hebrew) loyal

Pio (Italian) pious

Piotr (Slavic) form of Peter:
dependable; rock

Pip (German) ingenious
Pipp, Pippin, Pippo, Pippy

Pippin (English) shy

Pippo (Italian) gift

Pirney (Scottish) from the island

Pirro (Greek) red hair

Pitch (American) musical

Pithom (Biblical) place name

Piton (Spanish) form of Felix: joyful

Pitt (English) swerving dramatically

Pittman (English) blue-collar worker

Pius (Polish) pious

Placid (Latin) calm

Plasid

Placido (Italian) serene songster

Placeedo, Placidoh, Placydo

Placidon (Spanish) serene

Plan (American) word as name; organized

Plash (American) splashy; zany

Plat (French) from the flatlands; landowner

Platt

Platinum (English) worthwhile

Plato (Greek) broad-minded

Plata, Platoh

Playtoh (Invented) form of Plato: broad-minded

Plicerio (Spanish) capable

Plinio (Spanish) talented

Pluck (American) audacious; plucky

Plutarco (Greek) nefarious

Po (Biblical) place name

Poe (Last name as first name) dark spirit

Poet (American) writer

Poe

Pola (Biblical) place name

Polemos (Greek) warlike

Policarpo (Greek) with much fruit

Polja (Russian) creative

Polk (Last name as first name) political

Pollard (German) closed-minded

Polard, Pollar, Pollerd, Polley

Pollock (Last name as first name) creative

Pollux (Last name as first name) underdog

Polo (Greek) adventurer

Poloe, Poloh

Polonice (Polish) respects

Polygnotos (Greek) lover of many

Pomeroy (Last name as first name) polite

Pomposo (Spanish) pompous

Ponce (Spanish) fifth; wanderer

Poncey, Ponciano, Ponse

Ponciano (Spanish) of the sea

Poncio (Spanish) of the sea

Ponipake (Hawaiian) good luck

Pons (Spanish) fifth; explores

Ponse

Pontius (Latin) the fifth

Pontias, Pontus

Pontos (Greek) sea

Pony (Scottish) dashing

Poney, Ponie

Poogie (American) snuggly

Poog, Poogee, Poogi, Poogs, Pookie

Poole (Place name) area in England

Pool

Pope (Greek) father

Po

Porfirio (Spanish) audacious

Port (Latin) gatekeeper

Porte

Porter (Latin) decisive

Poart, Port, Portur, Porty

Portnoy (Latin) gate

Potiphar (Biblical) bull of Africa; a fat bull

Poul (Scandinavian) small

Powder (American) cowboy

Powd, Powe

Powell (English) ready

Powers (English) wields power

Pragedis (Spanish) prays

Prairie (American) rural man or rancher

Prair, Prairey, Prairi, Prairy

Prakash (Indian) light

Pramad (Indian) happy

Pranav (Indian) om (syllable)

Prasanna (Indian) happy

Prashant (Indian) calm

Pratt (Last name as first name) talkative

Pravat (Indian) leads

Pravin (Indian) talented

Praxedes (Last name as first name) prayerful

Preemoh (Invented) form of Primo: top-notch

Prentice (English) learning
Prenticce, Prentis, Prentiss, Printiss

Prescott (Last name as first name) sophisticated

Presley (English) songbird; meadow of the priest
Preslee, Preslie, Presly

Prest (English) priest

Preston (English) spiritual
Prestyn

Preston (Last name as first name) village of a priest; religious home

Pretio (Spanish) prays

Pretivo (Spanish) prays

Preto (Latin) important

Priamos (Greek) saved

Price (Welsh) vigorous
Pricey, Pryce

Priestley (English) cottage of the priest
Priestlea, Priestlee, Priestly

Primerica (American) from America; patriotic
Prime

Primitivo (Spanish) primitive
Primi, Tito, Tivo

Primitivus (Spanish) first

Primo (Italian) top-notch
Preemo, Primoh, Prymo

Prince (Latin) regal leader
Preenz, Prins, Prinz, Prinze

Prine (English) prime

Priore (Italian) first

Prisciliano (Spanish) wise old man

Procopio (Greek) progressive

Procter (Last name as first name) leads
Proctor

Prometheus (Mythology) friend of man; bringer of fire

Promiz (Slavic) first

Prop (American) word as name; fun-loving
Propp

Prospen (French) prospers

Prosper (Italian) having good fortune
Pros

Proteus (Greek) first

Prudencio (Spanish) wise

Prusa (Biblical) place name

Pry (Latin) before

Pryor (Latin) spiritual director
Pry, Prye

Publias (Greek) thinker
Publius

Puck (Literature) vibrant

Pullman (English) train man; motivator
Pulman, Pulmann, Pullmann

Pullum (Greek) song

Puneet (Indian) purest

Punon (Biblical) place name

Pura (Spanish) pure of heart

Pureza (Spanish) pure

Purley (Welsh) caring

Pursey (American) form of Percy: mysterious

Purvin (English) helpful
Pervin

Purvis (French) provider
Pervis, Purviss

Pushkin (Last name as first) poet; playful

Puskar (Indian) fountain

Putiel (English) inquiring mind

Putnam (English) fond of water
Puddy, Putnum, Puttie, Putty

Pyke (English) a spear

Pynchon (Last name as first) brilliant; inventive

Pyre (Latin) fire; excitable

Q

Qabil (Arabic) capable

Qadim (Arabic) able

Qadir (Arabic) talented

Qadar, Qadeer, Qadeer, Quadir

Qamar (Arabic) moon; dreamy

Qasim (Arabic) generous

Qidri (Biblical) place name

Qimat (Hindi) valued

Quaashie (African American) ambitious

Quaddus (African American) bright

Quadrees (Latin) fourth

Kwadrees, Quadrhys

Quais (American) form of Qusay: rough hewn

Quan (Vietnamese) dignified

Quanah (Native American) good-smelling

Quan

Quannell (African American) strong-willed

Kwan, Kwanell, Kwanelle, Quan, Quanelle, Quannell

Quant (Latin) knowing his worth

Quanta, Quantae, Quantal, Quantay, Quantea, Quantey, Quantez

Quanza (Spanish) giving

Quaronne (African American) haughty

Kwarohn, Kwaronne, Quaronn

Quashawn (African American) tenacious

Kwashan, Kwashaun, Kwashawn, Quasha, Quashie, Quashy

Qudamah (Arabic) courage

Quebrado (Spanish) broken

Qued (Native American) decorated robe

Quelatikan (Native American) blue horn

Quenby (English) giving

Quenbee, Quenbie, Quenbey

Quennell (French) strength of an oak

Quenell, Quennel

Quentel (Latin) fifth

Quentin (Latin) fifth

Kwent, Qeuntin, Quantin, Quent, Quenten, Quenton, Quientin, Quienton, Quint, Quintin, Quinton, Qwent, Qwentin, Qwenton

Quention (Latin) fifth

Querubin (Hebrew) fast bull

Quick (American) fast; remarkable

Quico (Spanish) stands by his friends

Paco

Quidem (American) believer

Quiessencia (Spanish) essential; essence

Quiess, Quiessence

Quigley (Irish) loving nature

Quiglee, Quigly, Quiggly, Quiggy

Quilaq (Native American) seal

Quillan (Irish) club; joined

Quill, Quillen, Quillon

Quimby (Norse) woman's house

Quincy (French) fifth; patient

Quensie, Quincee, Quincey, Quinci, Quincie, Quinnsy, Quinsey

Quinlan (Irish) fit physique

Quindlen, Quinlen, Quinlin, Quinn, Quinnlan

Quinlin (Irish) strong

Quinn (Irish) form of Quintin: planner

Kwen, Kwene, Quenn, Quin

Quinnton (Latin) fifth

Quinntone (Latin) fifth

Quintavius (African American) fifth child

Quint

Quintin (Latin) planner

Quenten, Quint, Quinton

Quinto (Spanish) fifth
Quiqui

Quintus (Spanish) fifth child
Quin, Quinn, Quint

Quiqui (Spanish) friend; form of Enrique
Kaka, Keke, Quinto, Quiquin

Quirin (English) a magic spell

Quirinus (Latin) spear; Roman god of war

Quito (Spanish) lively
Kito

Qumran (Biblical) place name

Qunnoune (Native American) tall

Quoitrel (African American) equalizer
Kwotrel, Quoitrelle

Quon (Chinese) bright; light

Qusay (Arabic) rough hewn
Qussay

R

Raamah (Hebrew) thunders

Raashid (Arabic) form of Rashad: wise

Rab (Scottish) form of Raibeart: brilliant; renowned
Rabbie

Rabbaanee (African) easygoing

Rabbi (Hebrew) master

Rabbit (Literature) for John Updike's novels; fast
Rab

Rabul (Hispanic) rich

Race (English) one who races

Racelis (Spanish) of the sky

Racey (English) form of Race: one who races

Rachins (Hebrew) merciful

Racine (French) Last name as first name; root

Racqueab (Arabic) homebody

Rad (Scandinavian) helpful; confident
Radd

Radbert (English) intelligent
Rad

Radborne (English) born happy
Radbourne, Radburn

Radcliff (English) from the bright cliff; able

Raddy (Slavic) cheerful
Rad, Radde, Raddie, Radey

Radford (English) helpful
Rad, Raddey, Raddie, Raddy, Radferd

Radimir (Polish) joyful

Radko (Slavic) happy child

Radley (English) sways with the wind
Radlea, Radlee, Radleigh

Radnor (English) boy of the bright shore; natural

Radolf (Anglo-Saxon) warrior

Radomir (Slavic) delightful

Radonir (Polish) form of Radomir: delightful

Radovan (Czech) delighted

Rady (Filipino) happy

Raekwon (African American) proud
Raykwonn

Raenn (American) form of Rain: helpful; smart

Raeshawn (American) brainy

Raeshon (American) form of Raeshawn; brainy
Rayshawn, Rashone, Reshawn

Raf (Spanish) healed by God

Rafael (Hebrew) rafaelle
Rafayel, Rafayelle, Rafe, Raphael, Raphaele

Rafe (Irish) tough
Raff, Raffe, Raif

Rafeeq (Arabic) gregarious

Rafferty (Irish) wealthy
Rafarty, Rafe, Raferty, Raff, Raffarty, Raffertie, Raffety

Raffin (Hebrew) form of Raphael: God has healed

Rafi (Arabic) musical; friend
Rafee, Raffy

Rafik (Arabic) friendly

Rage (American) trendsetter

Raghib (Arabic) rapturous

Ragin (Biblical) in God's circle

Ragnar (Scandinavian) power fighter

Ragu (Indian) fast

Ragul (Scandinavian) advises

Raheem (Arabic) having empathy
Rahim

Rahime (Arabic) sweet

Rahman (Arabic) full of compassion
Raman, Rahmahn

Rahn (American) form of Ron: kind
Rahnney, Rahnnie, Rahnny

Rahn (American) form of Ron: kind

Rahsaan (Arabic) organized

Rai (Japanese) next child

Raibeart (Gaelic) form of Robert: brilliant; renowned

Raiden (Japanese) storm; thunder god

Railee (American) gregarious

Raimund (German) wise

Rain (English) helpful; smart
Raine, Rainey, Raini, Rains, Raney, Rayne

Rainer (German) advisor
Rainor, Rayner, Raynor

Rainey (German) generous
Rain, Raine, Raney, Raynie

Rainier (Place name) distinguished

Rainy (German) advises

Raj (Sanskrit) with stripes
Rajiv

Raja (Sanskrit) king
Raj

Rajab (Arabic) glorified

Rajan (Pakistani) kingly

Rajendra (Hindi) strong king

Rajendran (Indian) Indra is the king

Rajesh (Hindi) king rules

Rajnish (Indian) night rules

Rake (American) mischief

Rakesh (Hindi) king

Raleigh (English) jovial
Ralea, Ralee, Raleighe, Rawlee, Rawley, Rawlie

Ralf (American) form of Ralph: advisor to all
Raulf

Ralik (Hindi) purified

Ralis (Latin) thin
Rallus

Ralph (English) advisor to all
Ralf, Ralphie, Ralphy, Raulf, Rolf

Ralpheal (American) form of Raphael: God has healed

Ralphie (English) form of Ralph: advisor to all
Ralphee, Ralphi

Ralston (English) Ralph's town; quirky boy
Ralfston, Rolfston

Ralton (Last name as first name) from the rail town

Ram (Sanskrit) compelling; pleasant
Rama, Ramm

Ramah (Indian) pleases

Rambert (German) pleasant kid
Ramburt

Rambo (American) daring; action-oriented
Ram

Ramel (Hindi) godlike
Raymel

Rameshwar (Indian) Rama Lord

Rami (Spanish) form of Ramiro: judicious
Ramiah

Raminz (Indian) charms

Ramiro (Spanish) judicious
Rameero, Ramero, Ramey, Rami

Ramjee (Indian) pleasing

Ramman (Biblical) form of Ram: compelling; pleasant

Rammy (Spanish) charming

Ramone (Spanish) wise advocate; romantic
Ramond, Raymond, Romon

Ramono (Spanish) form of Raymond: strong

Ramp (American) word as name; hyper
Ram, Rams

Rams (English) form of Ramsey: savvy
Ramm, Ramz

Ramsden (English) born in ram valley; loves the outdoors

Ramsey (English) savvy
Rams, Ramsay, Ramsy, Ramz, Ramzee, Ramzy

Ramsis (Egyptian) born

Ramzan (Indian) pleases

Ramzey (American) form of Ramsey: savvy

Ran (Scottish) form of Ronald: kind
Ranald

Rance (American) renegade
Rans, Ranse

Ranceford (English) from the ford of Laurence; rooted in reality

Rancye (American) form of Rance: renegade
Rancel, Rancy

Rand (Place name) ridge of gold-bearing rock in South Africa

Randall (English) secretive
Randahl, Randal, Randel, Randey, Randull, Randy

Randic (American) form of Randall: secretive

Randolph (English) protective
Rand, Randolf, Randolphe, Randy

Randy (English) form of Randall: secretive; form of Randolph: protective
Randee, Randey, Randi, Randie

Ranean (Biblical) from Mediterranean

Ranen (Hebrew) joyful

Rangarajan (Hindi) charming

Ranger (French) vigilant
Rainge, Range, Rangur

Rangini (Polynesian) celestial

Rani (Hebrew) joyful
Ran, Ranie, Rannie

Ranien (American) counsels

Ranjan (Hindi) delightful

Rank (American) top
Ran

Rankin (English) shielded

Rannon (Jewish) renewed

Ransell (English) form of Lawrence: honored; form of Ransom: wealthy
Rancell

Ransford (English) the raven's ford; watchful

Ransley (English) the raven's field; watchful

Ransom (Latin) wealthy
Rance, Ranse, Ransome, Ransum, Ransym

Ranson (English) form of Ransom: wealthy

Rant (English) word as name; from Dutch ranten: to talk foolishly

Rante (American) form of Randy: secretive; protective

Ranteen (Italian) prudent

Ranuel (Hebrew) God's own

Ranulf (English) a Lord chancellor; regal

Rao (French) form of Raoul: advisor to all

Raoul (Spanish) form of Raul: advisor to all
Raulio

Raous (French) form of Raoul: advisor to all

Raphael (Hebrew) God has healed
Rafael, Rafe, Rapfaele

Raphon (Biblical) place name

Raqib (Arabic) glorified

Rascheed (Arabic) giving

Rashad (Arabic) wise

Rachad, Rashaud, Rashid, Rashod, Roshad

Rashard (American) good

Rasheed (Arabic) intelligent

Rashid (Arabic) focused

Rasmus (Greek) form of Erasmus: beloved

Rasool (Arabic) herald

Rasputin (Russian) a Russian mystic

Rasp

Rastus (Greek) form of Erastus: loved baby

Rastas

Rasul (Arabic) brings message

Rathik (Slavic) vengeful

Raudel (African American) rowdy

Raudell, Rowdel

Rauf (Arabic) compassionate

Raul (Spanish) form of Ralph: advisor to all

Rauly, Rawl

Raven (American) bird; dark and mysterious

Rave, Ravey, Ravy, Rayven

Ravenel (English) darkness of ravens

Ravi (Hindi) sun god

Ravee

Ravid (Hebrew) searching

Ravin (Indian) sun

Ravindra (Hindi) a strong sun

Ravis (Sanskrit) sunny

Rawdan (English) hilly; adventurous

Rawden, Rawdin, Rawdon

Rawle (American) form of Raul: advisor to all

Rawleigh (American) jovial; (English) from the dear meadow

Rawlee, Rawli

Rawlins (French) form of Roland: renowned

Ray (French) royal; king

Rae, Raye, Rayray

Rayal (Irish) form of Ray: royal; king

Rayan (Irish) form of Ryan: royal; good-looking

Raybourne (English) from the deer brook; sylvan

Rayburn, Raybin

Rayce (American) form of Raymond: strong

Rays, Rayse

Rayfield (English) woodsy; capable

Rafe, Ray, Rayfe

Rayk (American) form of Rake: mischief

Rayland (English) streamland boy

Rayman (English) form of Raymond: strong

Raymond (English) strong

Rai, Ramand, Ramond, Ray, Raymie, Raymonde, Raymun, Raymund, Raymy

Raynard (French) judge; sly

Ray, Raynaud, Renard, Renaud, Rey, Reynard, Reynaud

Rayner (French) form of Raymond: strong

Ray, Rayne

Rayon (English) word as name; fabric; from "ray" as in "ray of light"

Raypheon (American) form of Raphael: God has healed

Raysh (American) form of Rayshan: inventive

Rayshan (African American) inventive

Ray, Raysh, Raysha, Rayshun

Rayson (American) son of Ray

Razi (Aramaic) secretive

Razus (American) happy

Reace (Welsh) passionate

Reece, Rees, Reese

Read (English) red-haired

Reade, Reed, Reid

Reagan (Irish) kingly

Ragan, Raghan, Reagen, Reegan, Regan

Reaman (Irish) prolific

Reaner (Last name as first name) even-tempered
Rean, Rener

Rearden (Irish) creative

Reaser (Welsh) excitable

Reavis (American) enthusiastic

Rebal (American) variant on Rebel: outlaw

Rebel (American) outlaw
Reb, Rebbe, Rebele

Red (English) man with red hair
Redd, Reddy

Redford (English) handsome man with ruddy skin
Readford, Red, Reddy, Redferd, Redfor

Redin (Last name as first name) red-haired

Redmon (German) protective
Redd, Reddy, Redmond, Redmun, Redmund

Redney (American) form of Rodney: open minded

Reece (Welsh) vivacious
Rees, Reese, Reez

Reed (English) red-haired
Read, Reede, Reid

Reed-Kanan (Scandinavian)

Reef (Nature) water-loving boy

Reem (Hebrew) horned animal or unicorn

Rees (Welsh) form of Rhys: loving
Reece, Reese, Reez, Rez

Reese (Welsh) vivacious
Reis, Rhys

Reesey (Welsh) form of Reese: vivacious

Reeves (English) giving
Reave, Reaves, Reeve

Reez (American) form of Reese: vivacious

Reg (Scandinavian) form of Reginald: wise advisor

Regal (American) debonair
Regall

Regane (Scandinavian) decides

Regen (English) leader

Regent (Latin) royal; grand

Reggie (English) form of Reginald: wise advisor
Reg, Reggey, Reggi, Reggye

Reginald (English) wise advisor
Reg, Reggie, Reginal, Regineld

Reginaldo (Spanish) leader

Regine (French) artistic
Regeen

Regis (Latin) kingly
Reggis

Regney (Slavic) leader

Regulo (Italian) form of Reginald: wise advisor

Rehob (Biblical) place name

Rehoboam (Biblical) son of Solomon

Reid (English) red-haired
Reide

Reidar (Scandinavian) soldier

Reider (Scottish) red-skinned

Reillon (Spanish) realm

Reilly (Irish) daring
Rilee, Riley, Rilie

Rein (German) advises

Reinald (French) judges

Reinder (German) wins

Reine (Scandinavian) victor

Reinhart (German) brave-hearted
Reinhar, Reinhardt, Rhinehard, Rhinehart

Reith (American) shy

Relio (Spanish) gold

Rema (English) form of Remus: fast

Remberto (Spanish) pious

Remeth (Biblical) place name

Remi (French) fun-loving
Remee, Remey, Remmy, Remy

Remiel (Hebrew) saved by God

Remigio (Italian) from Rheims; religious

Reming (English) raven

Remington (Last name as first name) intellectual
Rem, Remmy

Remko (Last name as first name) believes

Remo (Italian) confident

Remuda (Spanish) herd of horses
Rem, Remmie, Remmy

Remus (Latin) fast
Reemus, Remes, Remous

Renaloza (Spanish) reborn

Renard (French) smart; brave; fox
Renardt

Renato (Italian) born again
Renata, Renate

Renaud (English) powerful
Renny

Renba (Biblical) name spelled backward

Render (Dutch) draws

René (French) born again
Renee, Rennie, Renny, Re-Re

Renferd (English) peace-loving
Renfred

Renfro (Welsh) calm
Renfroe, Renfrow, Renphro, Rinfro

Renji (Japanese) truthful

Rennell (Irish) advises

Renny (French) able
Renney, Renni, Rennye

Rennye (Irish) advises

Reno (Place name) city in Nevada
Reen, Reenie, Renoh

Renshaw (English) born in the raven wood

Renson (Last name as first name) son of Ren

Renton (English) born in the town of deer

Renwick (English) born in the village of deer

Renze (Italian) excellence

Renzo (Italian) form of Lorenzo: honored

ReShard (African American) rough
Reshar, Reshard

Reshma (Indian) sun

Resk (American) variant on Rex: kingly

Reslie (American) form of Leslie: fiesty; beautiful and smart

Restes (Greek) form of Orestes: leader

Reston (English) form of Royston: town of Royce

Reth (American) form of Seth: chosen

Reto (German) resides

Rett (Literature) form of Rhett: romantic

Reuben (Hebrew) behold, a son
Rube, Rubey, Rubie, Rubin, Ruby, Rubyn

Rev (Invented) ramped up
Revv

Revera (Spanish) values God

Revin (American) distinctive
Revan, Revinn, Revun

Rex (Latin) kingly
Rexe

Rexel (Latin) king

Rexford (American) form of Rex: kingly
Rexferd, Rexfor, Rexy

Rey (Spanish) form of Reynaldo: knowledgable tutor
Ray, Reye, Reyes

Reymund (French) honored

Reymundo (Spanish) form of Raymond: strong

Reynaldo (Spanish) knowledgeable tutor

Reynard (French) brilliant
Raynard, Rayne, Renardo

Reynaud (French) advisor; judge

Reynold (English) knowledgeable tutor
Ranald, Ranold, Reinold, Renald, Renalde, Rey, Reye, Reynolds

Reza (Iranian) content

Rezeile (Biblical) name spelled backward

Rezeph (Biblical) place name

Rhagae (Biblical) place name

Rhegium (Biblical) place name

Rhene (American) smiley

Reen, Rheen

Rhett (American) romantic

Rhet, Rhette

Rho (Welsh) rose

Rhoden (Greek) rose

Rhodes (Greek) lovely

Rhoades, Rodes

Rhodree (Welsh) ruler

Rodree, Rodrey, Rodry

Rhondel (English) form of Rondel: poetic

Rhoris (Irish) red hair

Rhymen (American) form of Ryan: royal; good-looking

Rhyon (Irish) form of Ryan: royal; good-looking

Rhyan, Rhyen

Rhyph (Welsh) jovial

Rhys (Welsh) loving

Reece, Reese

Rian (Irish) little king

Riano (Italian) king

Riao (Spanish) form of Rio: water-loving

Ribal (American) from ribald; revels

Ribog (Slavic) of God

Ricardo (Spanish) snappy

Recardo, Ric, Riccardo, Ricky

Ricardoph (Spanish) energetic

Riccardio (Italian) brave

Rice (English) rich

Ryes

Rich (English) affluent

Richie, Ritchie

Richard (English) wealthy leader

Rich, Richerd, Richey, Richi, Richie, Rickie, Ricky, Ritchie

Richey (German) ruler

Rich, Richee, Richie, Ritch, Ritchee, Ritchee, Ritchey

Richie (English) form of Richard: wealthy leader

Richey, Richi, Ritchey, Ritchie

Richman (German) has power

Richmond (German) rich and protective

Rich, Richie, Richmon, Richmun, Ricky, Ritchmun

Richshae (English) form of Richard: wealthy leader

Richter (Last name as first name) hopeful

Rick, Ricky, Rik, Rikter

Rick (German) form of Richard: wealthy leader

Ric, Rickey, Ricki, Rickie, Ricky, Rik

Rickard (Scandinavian) form of Richard: wealthy leader

Rick, Rickert, Rickward, Rikkert

Rico (Italian) spirited; ruler

Reco, Reko, Ricko, Rikko, Riko

Ricod (American) form of Rico: spirited; ruler

Ricsi (American) form of Richie: wealthy leader

Riddle (Word as name) perplexes

Riddock (Irish) man of the field

Rider (American) horse rider

Ryder

Ridge (English) on the ridge; risk-taker

Ridglee (English) man of the ridge

Ridgley, Ridglea

Ridhaa (Arabic) delight

Ridley (English) ingenious

Redley, Rid, Ridlie, Ridly, Rydley

Riemer (English) from Rheims

Rien (Dutch) mariner

Rigby (English) high-energy

Rigbie, Rigbye, Rygby

Rigel (Arabic) foot; star in constellation Orion

Rigney (Greek) power

Rigo (Spanish) ridge boy

Rigoberto (Spanish) strong; ridge boy
Bert, Berto, Rigo

Rike (American) form of Nike: winning
Rikee, Rykee, Rykie, Ryky

Rikken (Slavic) form of Rik: hopeful

Rilan (English) land of rye

Rilee (American) form of Riley: brave
Rilea, Rileigh

Rileigh (American) form of Riley: brave
Ryleigh

Riley (Irish) brave
Reilly, Rylee, Ryley, Rylie, Ryly

Rimme (French) form of Remi: fun-loving

Rimmon (Biblical) place name

Rimon (Hebrew) pomegranate

Ringo (English) funny
Ring, Ringgoh, Ryngo

Rinus (American) form of Ryan: royal; good-looking

Rinzel (American) thinker

Rio (Spanish) water-loving
Reeo

Rio Grande (Spanish) a river in Texas
Rio, Riogrande

Rion (American) form of Ryan/Rian: royal; good-looking; little king

Rione (Spanish) flowing
Reo, Reone, Rio

Rionn (Greek) form of Orion: fiery hunter

Riordan (Irish) lordly
Rearden

Riordene (Irish) poetic

Rip (English) serene
Ripp, Rippe

Ripley (English) serene
Riplee

Ris (English) outdoorsman; smart
Rislea, Rislee, Risleigh, Riz, Rizlee

Rise (Welsh) form of Rhys: loving

Rishab (American) form of Rashad: wise

Rishi (Arabic) first; (Indian) wise man

Rishon (Hebrew) first

Risley (English) smart and quiet
Rislee, Risleye, Rizlee, Rizley

Risto (Scandinavian) bears Christ

Ristoffer (American) form of Christopher: the bearer of Christ

Ristoph (German) form of Christopher: the bearer of Christ

Ritch (American) leader
Rich, Richee, Richey, Ritch, Ritchal, Ritchee, Ritchi

Ritchell (English) controller

Ritchie (English) form of Richie: wealthy leader
Ritchee, Ritchey, Ritchy

Rito (American) spunky
Reit

Ritt (German) debonair
Rit, Rittie, Rittly

Ritter (German) debonair
Riter, Rittyr

Rivan (Literature) from Eddings's The Rivan Codex; esoteric

River (English) flowing water; hip
Riv, Ryver

Rivers (English) flowing river

Riverson (English) son of River

Rixus (Greek) excites

Rizal (Spanish) athletic

Rizalino (Spanish) pleased

Rizo (Italian) lively

Roald (Scandinavian) famous ruler

Roam (American) wanderer
Roamey, Roamy, Roma, Rome

Roan (English) form of Rogan: spirited redhead

Roar (Irish) form of Roarke: ruler

Roarke (Irish) ruler
Roark, Rork, Rourke

Rob (English) form of Robert: brilliant; renowned
Robb

Robbie (English) form of Robert: brilliant; renowned
Robbee, Robbey, Robbi, Robby

Robert ✪ (English) brilliant; renowned
Bob, Bobbie, Bobby, Rob, Robart, Robbie, Robby, Roberto, Robs, Roburt

Robert-Lee (American) patriotic
Bobbylee, Robby Lee, Robert-E-Lee, Robert Lee, Robertlee

Roberto (Spanish) form of Robert: brilliant; renowned
Berto, Rob, Robert, Tito

Roberts (Last name as first name) luminous
Rob, Robards, Robarts, Roburts

Robeson (English) Rob's son; bright
Roberson, Robison

Robhert (Welsh) form of Robert: brilliant; renowned

Robin (English) gregarious
Robb, Robbin, Robby, Robyn

Roble (Last name as first name) divine
Robel, Robl, Robley

Roblee (American) patriot

Robles (English) royal

Robson (English) sterling character

Robb, Robbson, Robsen

Roc (Italian) form of Rocco: tough

Rocal (American) form of Rocco: tough

Rocco (Italian) tough
Roc, Rock, Rockie, Rocko, Rocky, Rok, Rokee, Rokko, Roko

Roch (English) form of Rock: hardy

Rochester (English) guarded
Roche

Rocio (Spanish) form of Rocco: tough

Rock (American) hardy
Roc, Rocky, Rok

Rocket (American) word as a name; snappy
Rokket

Rockleigh (English) dependable; outdoorsy
Rocco, Rock, Rocklee, Rockley, Rocky, Roklee

Rockmun (English) man who rests

Rockne (English) form of Rocco/ Rock: tough; hardy

Rockney (American) brash

Rockwell (American) spring of strength
Rock, Rockwelle, Rocky

Rocky (English) hardy; tough
Rocco, Rock, Rockee, Rockey, Rocki, Rockie

Rocquin (Spanish) form of Joaquin: bold; hip

Rod (English) brash
Rodd, Roddy

Rodalfo (Spanish) form of Rudolph: wolf

Rodas (Spanish) Spanish name for the Rhone River in France; of Rhodes
Rod, Roda

Rodden (English) powerful

Roddick (Last name as first name) goes far

Roddy (German) form of Roderick: effective leader
Roddee, Roddi, Roddie

Rodel (American) generous
Rodell, Rodey, Rodie

Rodeo (Spanish) roundup; cowboy
Rodayo, Roddy, Rodyo

Roderick (German) effective leader
Roddy, Roddyrke, Roderic, Roderik, Rodreck, Rodrick, Rodrik

Rodger (German) form of Roger: famed warrior
Rodge, Roge

Rodion (Biblical) form of Herodion: heroic

Rodman (German) hero
Rodmin, Rodmun

Rodney (English) open-minded

Rod, Roddy, Rodnee, Rodni, Rodnie

Rodo (French) wolflike

Rodolfo (Spanish) spark

Rod, Rudolfo, Rudolpho

Rodree (American) leader

Rodrey, Rodri, Rodry

Rodrigo (Spanish) feisty leader

Rod, Roddy, Rodrego, Rodriko

Rodriguez (Spanish) hot-blooded

Rod, Roddy, Rodreguez, Rodrigues

Rodwell (German) renowned

Roe (English) deer

Roel (Dutch) famed hero

Roemello (Italian) form of Romulus: presumptuous

Rogan (Irish) spirited redhead

Rogasiano (Spanish) red hair

Rogelio (Spanish) aggressive

Rojel, Rojelio

Rogell (Dutch) strong

Roger (German) famed warrior

Rodge, Rodger, Roge, Rogie, Rogyer, Rogers

Rognan (Slavic) upward

Rohan (Hindi) going higher

Rohanee (Indian) comes down to earth

Rohit (Hindi) he fishes

Roi (French) form of Roy: king

Roisin (Irish) the rose

Rokee (Slavic) peaceful boy

Rokel (Scandinavian) a ewe

Roland (German) renowned

Rolend, Rollan, Rolland, Rollie, Rollo, Rolund

Rolando (Spanish) famous

Rolan

Roldan (Spanish) leader

Role (American) brash

Roel, Roll

Rolf (German) kind advisor

Rolfee, Rolfie, Rolfy, Rolph

Rolfon (Norwegian) overbearing

Rollan (Russian) from Roland: renowned

Rollie (English) form of Roland: renowned

Rollee, Rolley, Rolli, Rolly

Rollins (German) form of Roland: renowned

Rolin, Rolins, Rollin, Rolyn

Rollo (German) famous

Rolly (English) famous

Rolt (Latin) wolfish

Roly (English) form of Roland: renowned

Roman (Latin) fun-loving

Romain, Romen, Romey, Romi, Romun, Romy

Romano (Italian) from Rome

Romar (English) from Rome

Rombert (Latin) from Rome

Rome (Place name) city in Italy

Romeo

Romedios (Spanish) Roman

Romeo (Italian) romantic lover

Romah, Rome, Romeoh, Romero, Romey, Romi, Romy

Romer (American) form of Rome: city in Italy

Roamar, Roamer

Rommel (Latin) from Rome

Romney (Welsh) roamer

Rom, Romnie

Romo (French) boy from Rome

Romulo (Spanish) man from Rome; of Rome

Romo

Romulon (Mythology) of Rome

Romulus (Latin) presumptuous

Rom, Romules, Romulo

Romy (German) form of Romulus: presumptuous

Ron (English) form of Ronald: kind

Ronn

Ronak (Scandinavian) powerful

Ronald (English) kind

Ron, Ronal, Ronel, Ronney, Ronni, Ronnie, Ronuld

Ronalk (Slavic) form of Ronald: kind

Ronan (Irish) seal; playful

Rond (American) from the word round

Rondel (French) poetic

Ron, Rondal, Rondell, Rondie, Rondy

Ronen (Jewish) joyful

Ronford (English) distinguished

Ronferd, Ronnforde

Rong (Chinese) warring

Roni (Hebrew) joyful

Rone, Ronee

Ronicle (American) form of Ron: kind

Ronit (Jewish) sings

Ronneal (American) leaving

Ronnie (English) form of Ronald: kind

Ronnee, Ronney, Ronni, Ronny

Ronomy (Biblical) from Deuteronomy

Ronson (Scottish) Ron's son; likable

Rook (Spanish) form of Roque: rock

Roon (Scandinavian) form of Rune: secretive

Roone (Irish) distinctive; bright face

Rooney, Roune

Rooney (Irish) man with red hair

Rooni, Roony

Roose (Last name as first name) high-energy

Rooce, Roos, Rooz, Ruz

Roosevelt (Dutch) strong leader

Rooseveldt, Rosevelt, Rosy, Velte

Rooster (American) loud

Roos, Rooz

Roper (American) roper

Rope

Roque (Portuguese) rock

Rorden (Irish) creative

Rorelle (English) red-haired

Rorick (French) red-haired

Rorin (American) form of Rory: strong

Rory (German) strong

Roree, Rorey, Roreye, Rorie

Rosalio (Spanish) rose; charmer

Rosano (Italian) rosy prospects; romantic

Roscoe (English) woods; nature-loving

Rosco, Roskie, Rosko, Rosky

Rosembelt (Spanish) beauty of roses

Rosendo (Italian) rose

Roser (American) redhead; outgoing

Rozer

Roshanek (Slavic) bright flower

Roshaun (African American) loyal

Roshawn

Roshni (Indian) brightness

Rosk (American) swift

Roske

Rosley (English) of the rosary

Rosling (Scottish) redhead; explosive

Roslin, Rosy, Rozling

Ross (Latin) attractive

Rossey, Rossie, Rossy

Rossa (American) exuberant

Ross, Rosz

Rossain (American) hopeful

Rossane

Rossan (French) rose

Rossano (Italian) handsome

Rossell (French) rose

Rossi (Italian) rose red

Roston (English) rusting

Roswell (English) fascinating

Roswel, Roswelle, Rosy, Rozwell, Well

Roteus (Greek) form of Proteus: first

Roth (German) man with red hair

Rauth, Rothe

Rouel (French) form of Rule: emphatic

Roumen (Slavic) Roman

Roupen (American) quiet

Ropan, Ropen, Ropun

Roven (English) wanders

Rover (English) wanderer

Rovar, Rovey, Rovur, Rovy

Roverb (Invented) from Proverb

Rovere (French) travels

Rovonte (French) roving

Rowan (English) red-haired; adorned

Rowe, Rowen

Rowand (Last name as first name) reliable

Rowdy (English) athletic; loud
Roudy, Rowdee, Rowdi, Rowdie

Rowe (English) outgoing
Roe, Row, Rowie

Rowel (English) famed

Rowell (English) rocker
Roll, Rowl

Rowenam (English) red-haired

Rowland (Scandinavian) form of Roland: renowned

Rowley (English) from the rough meadow; spirited

Rown (English) form of Rowan: red-haired; adorned

Roxen (English) precise

Roy (French) king
Roi

Royal (French) king
Roy, Royall, Royalle, Roye

Royalton (French) king
Royal, Royallton

Royce (German) famous
Roy, Royse

Roycell (French) form of Royce: famous

Roycie (American) form of Royce: famous
Rory, Roy, Royse, Roysie

Royd (English) good humor

Roydean (American) combo of Roy and Dean

Roydee (English) natural

Royden (English) outdoors; regal
Roy, Roydin

Royderrick (English) form of Roderick: effective leader

Royelio (Spanish) royal

Royle (English) kingly

Roysell (American) form of Royce: famous

Royst (American) form of Royce: famous

Royston (English) town of Royce

Ruadhan (Hindi) brash

Ruari (Irish) red-haired
Ruairi, Ruaridh

Rube (Spanish) form of Ruben: behold, a son
Rubino

Ruben (Spanish) form of Reuben: behold, a son
Rube, Ruby

Rubens (Dutch) son

Rubi (Hebrew) form of Rubin: behold, a son

Ruchirat (French) rich

Rudder (English) ruddy skin

Ruddy (English) ruddy skin

Rudeger (German) friendly
Rudger, Rudgyr, Rudigar, Rudiger, Rudy

Rudo (African) loving

Rudolf (German) wolf
Rodolf, Rudy

Rudolph (German) wolf
Rodolf, Rodolph, Rud, Rudee, Rudey, Rudi, Rudolpho, Rudy

Rudow (German) lovable

Rudy (German) form of Rudolph: wolf
Rude, Rudee, Rudey, Rudi

Rudyard (English) closed off
Rud, Rudd, Ruddy

Rueban (American) form of Reuben: behold, a son
Ruban

Rued (Spanish) dishonest

Ruel (French) variant on Rule: emphatic

Ruelas (Spanish) ambitious

Rufaro (African) gives happiness

Ruffo (Spanish) form of Rufus: redhead

Rufine (French) red hair

Rufino (Spanish) redhead

Rufus (Latin) redhead
Fue, Rufas, Rufes, Ruffie, Ruffis, Ruffy, Rufous

Rugby (English) braced for contact
Rug, Rugbee, Rugbie, Ruggy

Rugerd (Slavic) famed

Ruggier (French) form of Roger:
famed warrior

Rugo (Italian) famed

Rui (Spanish) powerful fighter

Ruiden (Irish) red-haired

Ruiz (Spanish) chummy

Rujul (Indian) truthful

Rule (English) emphatic

Rulei (French) unit

Rulon (Native American) spirited
Rulonn

Rumford (English) lives at river
crossing; grounded

Rummel (American) form of
Rommel: from Rome

Rumont (French) red mountain

Runa (German) keeps score

Runako (African) attractive

Rune (German) secretive
Roone, Runes

Rupad (Hindi) secretive
Rupesh

Rupchand (Sanskrit) as beautiful as
the moon

Rupert (English) prince
Rupe

Rupin (Indian) handsome

Rurik (Russian) famous

Rush (English) loquacious
Rusch

Rushford (English) from the ford of
rushes; found

Rushon (French) red hair

Rusi (English) red-haired

Rusim (Biblical) traditional

Rusk (Spanish) innovator
Rusck, Ruske, Ruskk

Ruskin (French) red-haired

Ruslan (English) rusty hair

Russ (French) form of Russell: man
with red hair; charmer

Russell (French) man with red hair;
charmer
Russ, Russel, Russy, Rusty

Russo (Italian) russet

Russon (French) red hair

Rustice (French) rusty hair

Rustin (English) redhead
Rustan, Ruston, Rusty

Rusty (French) form of Russell: man
with red hair; charmer
Rustee, Rustey, Rusti

Rutherford (English) dignified
Ruthe, Rutherfurd, Rutherfyrd

Rutil (Spanish) faithful

Rutilio (Spanish) faithful

Rutland (Norse) red land

Rutledge (English) substantial
Rutlidge

Rutley (English) from red country;
fertile

Ruud (Dutch) like a wolf; well-known

Ruvim (Hebrew) meaningful

Ryall (American) capable

Ryan ✪ ❂ (Irish) royal; good-looking
*Rhine, Rhyan, Rhyne, Ry, Ryane,
Ryann, Ryanne, Ryen, Ryun*

Ryander (American) competitive;
obstinate

Ryden (English) form of Ryder:
outdoorsy; man who rides horses

Ryder (English) outdoorsy; man who
rides horses
Rider, Rye

Ryderin (Welsh) caring

Rye (Botanical) grain; basic

Ryerson (English) fit outdoorsman
Rye

Rygel (Spanish) regal

Ryk (American) form of Rick: wealthy
leader

Ryke (Slavic) form of Richard:
wealthy leader

Ryken (Slavic) form of Richard:
wealthy leader

Ryker (English) of the rye land; farms

Rykey (American) easygoing

Ryland (English) excellent
Rilan, Riland, Rye, Rylan

Rylandar (English) farmer
Rye, Rylan, Ryland

Rylant (American) form of Ryland: excellent

Ryle (American) form of Kyle: serene

Ryman (English) man of rye; fundamental

Rymmy (Spanish) form of Romy: presumptuous

Ryne (Irish) form of Ryan: royal; good-looking
Rine, Ryn, Rynn

Ryoun (American) form of Ryan: royal; good-looking

Ryston (English) form of Royston: town of Royce

Ryszard (Polish) courageous leader
Reshard

Ryton (English) from the town of rye; fundamental

Ryvers (American) form of Rivers: flowing river

S

Saad (Aramaic) helping others

Saahdia (Aramaic) helped by the Lord
Saadya, Seadya

Saarik (Hindi) sings like a bird
Saariq, Sareek, Sareeq, Sariq

Sabene (Latin) optimist
Sabe, Sabeen, Sabin, Sabyn, Sabyne

Saber (French) armed; sword
Sabar, Sabe, Sabre

Sabin (Latin) sabine
Sabeeno, Sabino, Savin, Savino

Sable (French) animal; brown-haired child

Sacha (Russian) defends; charms
Sascha, Sasha

Sachar (Hebrew) well-rewarded
Sacar

Sachetan (Indian) logical

Saddam (Arabic) powerful ruler
Saddum

Sadiki (African) loyal
Sadeeki

Sadler (English) practical
Sadd, Saddle, Sadlar, Sadlur

Sae (American) talkative
Saye

Saeed (African) lucky

Safford (English) boy from the river of willows

Saffron (Botanical) spice/plant; orange-haired
Saffran, Saffren, Saphron

Sagar (Indian) ocean

Sagaz (Spanish) clever
Saga, Sago

Sage (Botanical) wise
Saje

Sageal (Spanish) smart

Sagel (Indian) ocean

Sager (American) rewarded; short
Sayger

Sagi (Hebrew) best

Saginaw (Place name) city in Michigan; (Native American) bold
Sag, Saggy

Sagiv (Hebrew) the best
Segev

Saguaro (Botanical) cactus; prickly
Seguaro

Sahak (Slavic) jovial

Sahil (Hindi) leader
Sahel

Sahn (Hindi) held high

Sai (Arabic) sword

Saied (Arabic) fortunate

Sail (American) water; natural

Sailan (American) of the sea

Sainsbury (English) from the home of saints; religious
Sainsberry

Saint (Latin) holy man

Saith (English) to speak
Saithe, Saythe

Sajan (Hindi) beloved

Sakar (Biblical) form of Issachar: reward

Sal (Italian) form of Salvador: savior; spirited; form of Salvatore: rescuer; spirited
Sall, Sallie, Sally

Saladin (Arabic) devout
Saladdin

Salado (Spanish) funny
Sal

Salath (Biblical) generous

Salehe (African) good

Salem (Hebrew) peaceful

Salford (Place name) city in England

Salim (Arabic) safe; peaceful
Saleem

Salisbury (English) born in the willows
Salisbery, Salisberry, Saulisbury, Saulsberry, Saulsbery, Saulsbury

Salm (Biblical) from Psalms

Salman (Arabic) protected

Salom (Biblical) form of Absalom: my father is peace

Salomaa (Spanish) ideal

Salt (American) salt-of-the-earth
Salty

Salustia (Spanish) healthy

Salute (American) patriotic

Salvacion (Spanish) salvation

Salvador (Spanish) savior; spirited
Sal, Sally, Salvadore

Salvatore (Italian) rescuer; spirited
Sal, Sallie, Sally, Salvatori, Salvatorre

Salvio (Latin) saved
Salvian, Salviano, Salviatus

Salvoterre (Spanish) salvation

Sam (Hebrew) form of Samuel: man who heard God; prophet
Samm, Sammey, Sammi, Sammy

Samaga (Biblical) place name

Samal (Biblical) place name

Saman (Hebrew) hears all

Samce (Biblical) form of Samson: strong man

Samed (Arabic) everlasting

Sami (Lebanese) high

Samilo (Italian) upward

Samir (Arabic) special
Sameer, Samere, Samyr

Sammon (Arabic) grocer
Sammen

Sammy (Hebrew) wise
Samie, Sammee, Sammey, Sammi, Sammie, Samy

Samos (Place name) casual

Samrat (Indian) of the emperor

Samson (Hebrew) strong man
Sam, Sampson

Samuel ✚ ✝ (Hebrew) man who heard God; prophet
Sam, Samael, Sammeul, Sammie, Sammo, Sammuel, Sammy, Samual

Samvel (Hebrew) know the name of God
Samvell, Samvelle

Sanborn (English) one with nature
Sanborne, Sanbourn, Sandy

Sancho (Latin) genuine
Sanch, Sanchoh

Sandage (English) form of Sander: savior of mankind; nice

Sandalio (Spanish) wolflike

Sandberg (Last name as first name) writer
Sandburg

Sander (Greek) savior of mankind; nice
Sandor

Sanders (English) kind
Sandars, Sandors, Saunders

Sanderson (Last name as first name) defender
Sandersen

Sandhurst (English) from the sandy thicket; undaunted
Sandhirst

Sandiego (Spanish) place name

Sanditon (English) from the sandy town; perseveres

Sandro (Italian) form of Alexander: great leader; helpful

Sandy (English) personable
Sandee, Sandey, Sandi

Sanford (English) negotiator
Sandford, Sandy, Sanferd, Sanfor

Sangarius (Biblical) place name

Sango (Asian) coral

Sanjay (Sanskrit) wins every time

Sanjiv (Hindi) longlasting

Sanjog (Indian) lucky chance

Sanogo (Spanish) brave

Sanorelle (African American) honest
Sanny, Sano, Sanorel, Sanorell

Sansone (Italian) strong

Santana (Spanish) saintly
Santa, Santanah, Santanna, Santee

Santiago (Spanish) sainted; valuable
Sandiago, Santego, Santiagoh, Santy, Tago

Santino (Italian) sacred
Santeeno, Santyno

Santon (English) sandy home

Santos (Italian) holy; blessed
Sant, Santo

Santosh (Hindi) happy

Sapir (Hebrew) sapphire; jewel
Safir, Saphir, Saphiros

Saral (Indian) straightforward

Sarang (Indian) deer

Sarday (American) extrovert
Sardae, Sardaye

Sardica (Biblical) place name

Sardis (Biblical) place name

Sargent (French) officer/leader
Sarge, Sergeant

Sargis (Slavic) serves

Sargon (Persian) sun king

Sarid (Biblical) place name

Sarkis (Greek) the Lord

Sasan (Hebrew) happy

Sasha (Russian) helpful
Sacha, Sash

Sassacus (Native American) wild soul

Sasso (Hebrew) happy

Sasson (Hebrew) happy

Sastry (Indian) safe

Satchel (American) unique
Satch, Satchell

Saturnin (Spanish) from planet Saturn; melancholy
Saturnino

Satya (Indian) honesty

Saul (Hebrew) gift
Saulie, Sawl, Sol, Solly

Saunder (English) defensive; focused
Saunders

Sava (Slavic) aware

Savage (Last name as first name) wild
Sav

Saverio (Spanish) bright

Saviero (Spanish) form of Xavier: home; shining

Saville (French) willow town
Savelle, Savile, Savill, Seville

Savini (Italian) bright

Savio (Italian) smart

Savone (Italian) form of Savino: sabine

Savoy (Place name) region in France
Savoe

Savyon (Spanish) great attitude

Sawyer (English) hardworking
Saw, Sawyrr

Saxe (English) form of Saxon: sword-fighter; feisty
Sax, Saxee, Saxey, Saxie

Saxon (English) sword-fighter; feisty
Sackson, Sax, Saxan, Saxe, Saxen

Saxton (Place name) stern

Saxten

Sayan (Asian) standing

Sayre (Welsh) skilled

Saye, Sayer, Sayers

Scafell (Place name) mountain in England

Scanlon (Irish) devious

Scan, Scanlin, Scanlun, Scanne

Scant (American) word as name; too little

Scanty

Schae (American) safe; careful

Schay

Schaffer (German) watchful

Schaffur, Shaffer

Schawn (American) form of Shawn/Sean: God is gracious

Schelde (Place name) river in Europe; calm

Shelde

Schelte (German) sheltie

Schmidt (German) hardworking; blacksmith

Schmit

Schneider (German) stylish; tailor

Sneider, Snider

Schubert (German) cobbler

Shubert

Schumann (Last name as first) famous composer; romantic

Schuyler (Dutch) protective

Skylar, Skyler

Scipio (Greek) leader

Scirocco (Italian) warmth of the wind

Cirocco, Sirocco

Scopus (Biblical) place name

Scorpio (Latin) lethal

Scorp, Scorpioh

Scotland (Place name) from Scotland

Scott (English) from Scotland; happy

Scot, Scotty

Scotty (English) happy

Scottee, Scottey, Scotti

Scout (French) hears all; scouts for information

Scribner (English) the one who writes

Scully (Irish) vocal

Scullee, Sculley, Scullie

Scupi (Biblical) place name

Seabert (English) shines like the sea

Seabright, Sebert, Seibert

Seabrook (English) outdoorsy

Seabrooke

Seabury (English) lives by the sea

Seaberry, Seabry

Seaby (American) form of Sebastian: dramatic; honorable

Seaman (English) seafarer

Seamus (Gaelic) replacement; bonus

Seemus, Semus

Sean ✪ (Irish) God is gracious

Seann, Shaun, Shaune, Shawn

Searcy (English) fortified

Searcee, Searcey

Searles (English) fortified

Searl, Searle, Serles, Serls

Seaton (Place name) seaton

Seaten, Seeten, Seeton

Seaver (Last name as first name) safe

Seever

Sebastian ✪ (Latin) dramatic; honorable

Bastian, Seb, Sebashun, Sebastien, Sebastion, Sebastuan, Sebo

Sebbie (American) form of Sebastian: dramatic; honorable

Sebe (Latin) form of Sebastian: dramatic; honorable

Seb, Sebo, Seborn, Sebron, Sebrun

Secondo (Italian) second-born boy

Segundo

Sedgley (American) classy

Sedg, Sedge, Sedgeley, Sedgely

Sedgwick (English) from the place of swords; defensive

Sedgewick, Sedgewyck, Sedgwyck

Seely (Last name as first name) fun-loving
Sealy, Sealey, Seeley

Seerath (Indian) great

Sef (Egyptian) yesterday

Seferino (Spanish) flying in the wind
Cefirino, Sebarino, Sephirio, Zefarin, Zefirino, Zephir, Zephyr

Sefre (Welsh) peace

Sefton (English) from the town in the rushes; safe

Seger (Last name as first name) singer
Seager, Seeger, Sega, Segur

Segundo (Spanish) second child

Seidon (Greek) from Greek mythology Poseidon

Sekani (African) laughing

Sela (Hebrew) from the cliff; dares
Selah

Selby (English) from a village of mansions; rich
Selbey, Shelbey, Shelbie, Shelby

Seldon (English) from the willow valley; swaying
Selden, Sellden, Shelden

Selestino (Spanish) heavenly
Celeste, Celestino, Celey, Sele, Selestyno

Selig (German) blessed boy
Seligman, Seligmann, Zelig

Selim (Turkish) safe haven

Selkirk (Scottish) church home boy; conflicted

Sellers (English) dweller of marshland; sturdy
Sellars

Selmo (Spanish) form of Anselmo: protected by God

Selmy (French) form of Anselme: protective

Selo (Biblical) place name

Selvin (English) from the woods

Selvon (American) gregarious
Sel, Selman, Selv, Selvaughn, Selvawn

Selwyn (English) friend from the mansion; wealthy
Selwin, Selwinn, Selwynn, Selwynne

Semaj (Turkish) named

Semath (American) unites

Semeon (Biblical) form of Simon: good listener; thoughtful

Seminole (Native American) tribe name; unyielding

Semion (Slavic) form of Simon: good listener; thoughtful

Senath (Biblical) belongs

Sender (Hebrew) form of Alexander: great leader; helpful

Seneca (Native American) tribe name; revered

Senen (Irish) wise boy

Senior (French) older
Sennyur, Senyur, Sinior

Sennen (English) aged

Sennett (French) old spirit
Sennet

Sentino (Italian) form of Santino: sacred

Seppel (German) loved

Sepph (Biblical) place name

Septimus (Latin) seventh child; neglected

Sequoia (Native American) tree; sturdy

Serafin (Spanish) form of Seraphim: full of fire

Seraphim (Hebrew) full of fire
Sarafim, Saraphim, Serafim, Serephim

Sereno (Latin) serene
Cereno

Serf (Spanish) serves

Serge (French) gentle man
Serg

Sergeant (French) officer; leader
Sarge, Sargent

Sergei (Russian) good looking
Serg, Serge, Sergie, Sergy, Surge

Sergio (Italian) handsome
Serge, Sergeeo, Sergeoh, Sergyo

Serguej (Slavic) serves well

Sero (Italian) sun

Servacio (Spanish) saved

Servando (Spanish) services

Servas (Latin) saved

Servaas, Servacio, Servatus

Sesame (Botanical) seed; flavors

Sesamey, Sessame, Sessamee

Seth ✪ (Hebrew) chosen

Sethe

Seton (English) from the sea town; loves the water

Sevastian (American) form of Sebastian: dramatic; honorable

Seven (American) dramatic; seventh child

Sevene, Sevin

Several (American) multiplies

Sevral, Sevrull

Severence (French) strict

Severince, Severynce

Severin (Latin) severe

Saverino, Severinus, Seweryn

Severn (English) having boundaries

Severo (Italian) unbending; harsh

Sevester (American) form of Sylvester: forest-dweller; heavy-duty

Seveste, Sevy

Sevrin (Scandinavian) severe

Seward (English) guarding the sea

Sew, Sewerd, Sward

Sewell (Last name as first name) seaward

Seawel, Seawell, Sewel

Sexton (English) church-loving

Sextan, Sextin, Sextown

Sextus (Latin) sixth child; mischievous

Sesto, Sixto, Sixtus

Seymour (French) prayerful

Seamore, See, Seye, Seymore

Shaamar (Biblical) name spelled backward

Shabat (Hebrew) the end

Shabbat

Shachar (Hebrew) the dawn

Shad (African) joyful

Shade (English) secretive

Shadee, Shadey, Shady

Shadman (Hebrew) farm

Shadow (English) mystique

Shade, Shadoe

Shadrach (Biblical) godlike; brave

Shad, Shadd, Shadrack, Shadreck, Shadryack

Shadrie (Biblical) form of Shadrach: godlike; brave

Shaff (American) companion

Shafiq (Arabic) forgiving

Shafeek, Shafik

Shafir (Hebrew) handsome

Shafeer, Shafer, Shefer

Shago (American) casual

Shahzad (Persian) royalty; king

Shai (Hebrew) the gift

Shaikh (French) severe

Shak (Arabic) attracts

Shakil (Arabic) attractive

Shakeel, Shakill, Shakille, Shaqueel, Shaquil, Shaquille

Shakir (Arabic) appreciative

Shakee, Shakeer

Shakunt (Indian) bluebird

Shakur (Arabic) thankful

Shakurr

Shale (Hebrew) form of Shalev: calm

Shaile, Shayle

Shalev (Hebrew) calm

Shalom (Hebrew) peaceful

Sholem, Sholom

Shalu (American) peace

Sham (Biblical) armed

Shaman (Russian) mystical

Shamain, Shamon, Shayman

Shamar (Indian) proud

Shamir (Hebrew) thorn

Shameer

Shammah (Biblical) devout

Shamus (Irish) seizing

Schaemus, Schamus, Shamuss

Shan (Hindi) bright sun

Shanahan (Irish) giving
Shanihan, Shanyhan

Shance (American) form of Chance:
good fortune; happy
Shan, Shanse

Shand (English) loud
Shandy

Shandee (English) noisy
Shandi, Shandy

Shane (Irish) easygoing
Shain, Shay, Shayne

Shani (African) a wonder; (Hebrew)
red

Shanley (Irish) old soul
Shannley

Shannon (Irish) wise
*Shana, Shanan, Shane, Shanen, Shann,
Shannen, Shanon*

Shantam (Hindi) bright sun

Shantan (Sanskrit) peaceful

Shante (American) poised
Shantae, Shantay

Shap (English) form of Shep:
watchful

Shapleigh (English) form of Shepley:
from the sheep meadow; tender

Shaq (Arabic) form of Shaquille:
handsome
Shack, Shak

Shaquille (Arabic) handsome
Shak, Shakeel, Shaq, Shaquil, Shaquill

Sharad (Indian) fall season

Sharif (Arabic) truthful
Shareef, Sheref

Sharkie (American) crafty

Sharman (American) magic man

Sharp (Word as name) bright

Shashee (Indian) moon

Shashhi (Hindi) moon

Shasta (Place name) Oregon
mountain; high hopes

Shaun (Irish) form of Sean: God is
gracious
Seanne, Shaune, Shaunn

Shaw (English) safe; in a tree grove
Shawe

Shawn (Irish) form of Sean: God is
gracious
Shawnay, Shawne, Shawnee, Shawney

Shawnell (African American)
talkative
Shaunell

Shawner (American) form of Shawn:
God is gracious

Shawon (African American)
optimistic
Shawan, Shawaughn, Shawaun

Shay (Irish) form of Shamus: seizing
Shai

Shayan (Native American) from
Cheyenne; tribe; erratic

Shayde (Irish) confident
Shaedy, Sheade

Shaykeen (African American)
successful
Shay, Shaykine

Shea (Irish) vital
Shay

Sheamus (Irish) form of James: he
who supplants

Sheban (Biblical) sworn

Shechem (Biblical)

Sheehan (Irish) clever
Shehan, Shihan

Sheen (English) bright and shining;
talented
Shean, Sheene

Shehzad (Arabic) prince

Shel (Hebrew) mine

Shelah (Biblical) vivacious

Shelby (English) established
*Shel, Shelbee, Shelbey, Shelbie, Shell,
Shelly*

Sheldon (English) quiet
*Shel, Sheld, Shelden, Sheldin, Shell,
Shelly*

Shell (English) form of Sheldon:
quiet

Shelley (English) form of Shelby: established
Shelly

Shelton (English) from the village of ledges

Shem (Hebrew) famous

Shen (Chinese) introspective

Shenandoah (Place name) valley; nostalgic

Sheng (Chinese) winning

Shep (English) watchful
Shepp, Sheppy

Shepal (English) herds sheep

Shepher (English) sheep herder

Shepherd (Last name as first name) vigilant; (English) herds sheep
Shepard, Sheperd, Shephard

Shepho (Biblical) herds sheep

Shepley (English) from the sheep meadow; tender
Sheplea, Shepleigh, Shepply, Shipley

Sherag (Jewish) bright

Sherborn (English) from the bright shiny stream; careful
Sherborne, Sherbourn, Sherburn, Sherburne

Sheridan (Irish) wild-spirited
Sharidan, Sheridon, Sherr, Sherrey, Shuridun

Sheridun (Irish) confident

Sherill (English) from the shining hill; special
Sherrill

Sherlock (English) fair-haired; smart
Sherlocke, Shurlock

Sherm (English) worker; shears
Shermy

Sherman (English) tough-willed
Cherman, Shermann, Shermy, Shurman

Sherrerd (English) from open land; rancher
Sherard, Sherrard, Sherrod

Sherrick (Last name as first name) already gone
Sherric, Sherrik, Sherryc, Sherryck, Sherryk

Sherris (English) herds sheep

Sherwin (English) fleet of foot
Sherwind, Sherwinn, Sherwyn, Sherwynne

Sherwood (English) bright options
Sherwoode, Shurwood, Woodie, Woody

Shevon (African American) zany
Shavonne, Shevaughan, Shevaughn

Shiloh (Hebrew) gift from God; charmer
Shile, Shilo, Shy, Shye

Shimron (Biblical) place name

Shin (Korean) faithful

Shine (American) shines

Shiney (American) luminescent

Shing (Chinese) wins

Shingo (Japanese) clutch

Shipley (English) meadow of sheep
Ship

Shipton (English) from the ship village; sailor

Shire (Place name) English county; humorous
Shyre

Shirely (English) of the shire

Shishir (Indian) season

Shiva (Hindi) of great depth and range; life/death
Shiv

Shlomo (Hebrew) form of Solomon: peaceful and wise
Shelomi, Shelomo, Shlomi

Shmuel (Hebrew) form of Samuel: man who heard God; prophet

Shomer (Hebrew) watches

Shon (American) form of Shawn: God is gracious
Sean, Shaun, Shonn

Shontae (African American) hopeful
Shauntae, Shauntay, Shawntae, Shontay, Shontee, Shonti, Shontie, Shonty

Shorty (American) small in stature
Shortey, Shorti

Shoshone (Native American) tribe; wanderer
Shoshoni

Shoval (Hebrew) on the right path

Shreya (Indian) best

Shuan (Mythology) dark place

Shunem (Biblical) place name

Shur (Biblical) place name

Shura (Russian) protective
Schura, Shoura

Shuu (Japanese) responsible

Shyam (Hindi) dark

Si (Hebrew) form of Simon: good listener; thoughtful
Sy

Sichuan (Place name) Chinese

Sicily (Place name) traveler
Sicilly

Sid (French) form of Sidney: attractive
Cyd, Sidd, Siddie, Siddy, Syd, Sydd

Side (Biblical) place name

Sidel (English) valley child

Sidney (French) attractive
Ciddie, Cidnie, Cyd, Cydnee, Sidnee, Sidnie, Syd, Sydney

Sidon (Biblical) place name

Sidonio (Spanish) form of Sidney: attractive

Sidor (Russian) gifted
Isidor, Sydor

Sidromio (Spanish) form of Sydney: attractive

Sidus (Latin) star
Sydus

Siegbert (German) wins

Siegfried (German) victor
Siegfred, Sig, Sigfred, Sigfrid, Siggee, Siggie, Siggy

Siello (Indian) superb

Sierra (Spanish) dangerous
See-see, Serra, Siexa, Sierrah

Sig (German) form of Sigmund and Siegfried: victor
Siggey, Siggi, Sigi, Syg

Sigga (Scandinavian) form of Siegfried: victor
Sig

Sigge (German) form of Sigmund: victor

Sigmund (German) victor
Siegmund, Sig, Siggi, Siggy, Sigi, Sigmon, Sigmond

Signe (Scandinavian) victor
Signy

Sigoph (Biblical) place name

Sigurd (Scandinavian) winning personality

Sigus (German) winner

Sigwald (German) leader
Siegwald

Sil (Spanish) light

Silar (American Indian) leader

Silas (Latin) saver
Si, Siles, Silus

Sill (English) beam of light
Sills

Silo (Scandinavian) legendary

Siloam (Biblical) place name

Silous (American) form of Silas: saver
Si, Silouz

Silvano (Latin) of the woods; unique
Silvan, Silvani, Silvio, Sylvan

Silvanus (Mythology) woodland

Silver (Latin) silver
Sylver

Silverman (German) works with silver; craftsman

Silverton (English) from the town of silversmiths
Silvertown

Silvester (Latin) from the woods
Silvestre, Silvestro, Sylvester

Silvio (Italian) sylvan

Sim (African) form of Simba: lionlike

Simba (African) lionlike

Simcha (Hebrew) joyful

Siment (Scandinavian) form of Simon: good listener; thoughtful

Simeon (French) listener
Si, Simion, Simone, Simyon, Sy

Simington (English) devout

Simmon (Hebrew) devout

Simms (Hebrew) good listener

Sims

Simon (Hebrew) good listener;
thoughtful

*Si, Siman, Simen, Simeon, Simmy, Sye,
Symon, Syms*

Simpson (Hebrew) simplistic

Simpsen, Simpsun, Simson

Simran (Indian) God loves

Simus (Biblical) form of Onesimus:
profits

Sinc (Native American) leader

Sinclair (French) prayerful

Clair, Sinc, Sinclare, Synclaire

Sinclar (French) prays

Sindbad (Literature) from *The
Arabian Nights*; daring

Sinbad

Sindry (Mythology) shines

Singer (Last name as first name)
vocalist

Synger

Singh (Hindi) lion's courage

Singo (American) genuine

Sinjin (English) form of St. John

Sion (Hebrew) heavenly peak

Zion

Sione (African) believer

Sipher (American) treasure

Siraj (Arabic) shines

Sirion (Biblical) place name

Siris (Egyptian) starlike

Sirius (Greek) shining

Sissel (Greek) difficult

Sisto (American) cowboy

Sisyphus (Greek) in mythology

Sivney (Irish) satisfied

Sivneigh, Sivnie

Six (American) number as name

Syx

Sixto (Greek) well-mannered

Sixtus (Latin) sixth child

Skay (Native American) white

Skeeter (English) fast

Skeater, Skeet, Skeets

Skeetz (American) zany

Skeet, Skeeter, Skeets

Skelly (Irish) bard

Scully

Skerry (Scandinavian) from the
island of stone; pragmatist

Ski (Scandinavian) sends out

Skilling (English) masterful

Skillings

Skinner (English) skins for a living

Skip (American) form of Skipper:
shipmaster

Skipp, Skyp, Skyppe

Skipper (American) shipmaster

Skippy (American) fast

Skippee, Skippie, Skyppey

Skye (Dutch) goal-oriented

Sky

Skylar (Dutch) protective

Skilar, Skye, Skyeler, Skylir

Slade (English) quiet child

Slaid, Slaide, Slayd, Slayde

Sladen (English) valley child

Sladkey (Slavic) glorious

Sladkie

Slam (American) friendly

Slams, Slamz

Slane (Irish) good health

Slap (American) casual

Slater (Last name as first name)
precocious

Slaiter, Slayter

Slatter (English) works on roofs

Slav (Russian) glorified

Slava (Russian) form of Stanislav:
glory in leading

Slavek (Polish) smart; glorious

Slavec, Slavik

Slavin (Irish) mountain man; hermit

Slaven, Slawin

Slawomir (Slavic) great glory; famed

Slavek, Slavomir

Slim (English) nickname for slim guy

Sloan (Irish) sleek
Sloane, Slonne

Slocum (Last name as first name) happy
Slo, Slocom, Slocumb

Slover (Last name as first name) slove

Sly (Latin) form of Sylvester: forest-dweller; heavy-duty

Smedley (English) of the flat meadow
Smedleigh, Smedly

Smerdyakov (Russian) sinister

Smith (English) crafty; blacksmith
Smid, Smidt, Smit, Smitt, Smitti, Smitty

Smithson (Last name as first name) son of Smith; craftsman

Smitty (English) craftsman
Smittey

Smokey (American) smokin'
Smoke, Smokee, Smoky

Snake (Place name) U.S. river

Snead (English) Last name as first name

Snowden (English) from a snowy hill; fresh
Snowdon

Snyder (German) tailor's clothing; stylish
Schneiger, Snider

So (Vietnamese) smart

Socorro (Spanish) helpful
Sokorro

Socrates (Greek) philosophical; brilliant
Socratez, Socratis, Sokrates

Soeren (Scandinavian) sun ray

Sofian (Arabic) devoted

Sofus (Greek) wise
Sophus

Sogane (Biblical) place name

Sohan (Hindi) charmer; handsome

Sohil (Hindi) beautiful

Sol (Hebrew) form of Solomon: peaceful and wise
Solly

Solano (Latin) from the east

Solly (Hebrew) form of Solomon: peaceful and wise
Sollee, Solley, Solli, Sollie

Solomon (Hebrew) peaceful and wise
Salamon, Sol, Sollie, Solly, Soloman

Somerby (English) from the summer village; lighthearted
Somerbie, Somersby, Sommersby

Somerley (Irish) summer sailor
Somerled, Sorley

Somers (English) loving summer
Sommers

Somerset (English) talented
Somer, Somers, Sommerset, Summerset

Somerton (English) from the summer town
Somervile, Somerville

Sommar (English) summer
Somer, Somers, Somm, Sommars, Sommer

Son (English) boy
Sonni, Sonnie, Sonny

Sonny (English) boy
Son, Sonney, Sonni, Sonnie

Sonteeahgo (Invented) form of Santiago: sainted; valuable

Sophocles (Greek) playwright

Sorel (Botanical) form of Sorrel: reddish-brown horse; horse lover

Soren (Scandinavian) good communicator
Soryn

Sorrel (French) reddish-brown horse; horse lover
Sorre, Sorrell, Sorrey

Sorren (Scandinavian) sun ray

Sosimo (Spanish) promise

Sothern (English) from the south; warmhearted
Southern

Sound (American) word as a name; dynamic

Sousan (French) underdog

Southwell (English) living by the southern well

Sovann (Asian) golden

Spanky (American) outspoken; stubborn
Spank, Spankee, Spankie

Sparks (English) happy

Sparky (Latin) ball of fire; joyful
Spark, Sparkee, Sparkey, Sparki, Sparkie

Sparta (Biblical) place name

Spas (Slavic) saved by God

Spaulding (Last name as first name) comic
Spalding, Spaldying, Spauldyng

Specie (American) special child

Speed (English) plucky

Speedy (English) fast

Speers (English) good with spears; swift-moving
Speares, Spears, Spiers

Spence (English) form of Spencer: giver; provides well
Spens, Spense

Spencer (English) giver; provides well
Spence, Spencey, Spenser, Spensor, Spensy

Sperry (Last name as first name) inventive
Sperrey

Spider (American) scary
Spyder

Spidey (American) zany

Spike (American) word as name
Spiker

Spiker (English) go-getter
Spike, Spikey, Spyk

Spillane (American) funloving

Spiridon (Greek) like a breath of fresh air
Speero, Spero, Spiridon, Spiro, Spiros, Spyridon, Spyros

Spiro (Greek) coil; spiral
Spi, Spiroh, Spiros, Spy, Spyro

Sprague (French) high-energy

Springer (English) fresh
Spring

Sprinter (American) runner

Spud (English) energetic

Spunk (American) spunky; lively
Spunki, Spunky

Spurgeon (Botanical) from the shrub spurge; natural
Spurge

Spurs (American) boot devices used to spur horses; cowboy
Spur

Spyros (Greek) round

Squire (English) land-loving
Squirre, Skwyre

Sravanthi (Indian) old soul

Stace (English) optimist
Stayce

Stacey (English) hopeful
Stace, Stacee, Stacy, Stase, Stasi

Stackler (Last name as first name) aligned

Stadler (Last name as first name) staid
Stadtler

Staffan (Slavic) crowned

Stafford (English) dignified
Staff, Staffard, Stafferd, Staffi, Staffie, Staffor, Staffy

Stagio (Italian) of the stage

Stajonne (Slavic) form of Stoyan: loyal

Stamos (Greek) reasonable
Stammos, Stamohs

Stan (Latin) form of Stanley: traveler

Stanbury (English) fortified
Stanberry, Stanbery, Stanburghe, Stansberry, Stansburghe, Stansbury

Stancliff (English) from the stone cliff; prepared
Stancliffe, Stanclyffe, Stanscliff, Stanscliffe

Standa (Slavic) glory

Standish (English) farsighted

Standysh

Standley (English) travels

Stanfield (English) from the stone field; able

Stansfield

Stanford (English) dignified

Stan, Stanferd, Stann

Stanislaus (Latin) glorious

Staneslaus, Stanis, Stanislus, Stann, Stanus

Stanislav (Russian) glory in leading

Slava, Stasi

Stanley (English) traveler

Stan, Stanlea, Stanlee, Stanli, Stanly

Stanmore (English) lake of stones; ill-fated

Stanton (English) stone-hard

Stan

Stanway (English) came from the stone road

Stanaway, Stannaway, Stannway

Stanwick (English) born in village of stone; hard

Stanwicke, Stanwyck

Stanwood (English) stone woods man; tough

Stark (German) high-energy

Starke, Starkey

Starling (English) singer; bird

Starlling

Starr (English) bright star

Star, Starri, Starrie, Starry

Stash (Russian) form of Stanislav: glory in leading

Stavros (Greek) winner

Stavrohs, Stavrows

Stavrus (Greek) cross

Steadman (English) landowner; wealthy

Steadmann, Sted, Stedmann

Steaven (Scottish) form of Steven: victorious

Steed (English) horse of high spirits

Steele (English) hardworking

Steel, Stille

Stefan (Scandinavian) crowned; (German) chosen one

Stefawn, Steff, Steffan, Steffie, Steffon, Steffy, Stefin, Stephan

Stefano (Italian) supreme ruler

Stef, Steffie, Steffy, Stephano, Stephanos

Stehlin (Last name as first name) genius

Staylin, Stealan, Stehlan

Stein (German) stonelike

Steen, Sten, Steno

Steinar (Scandinavian) muse; rock

Steinard, Steinart, Steinhardt

Steinbeck (Last name as first) writer

John

Stelios (Greek) community hero

Stellan (Swedish) star

Sten (Scandinavian) star stone

Stene, Stine

Stennis (Scottish) prehistoric standing stones; eternal

Stepan (English) form of Stephen: victorious

Stepen, Stepyn

Steph (English) form of Stephen: victorious

Stef, Steff, Steffy

Stephan (Greek) form of Stephen: victorious

Stephanos (Greek) crowned; martyr

Stef, Stefanos, Steph, Stephanas

Stephen (Greek) victorious

Stephan, Stephon, Stevee, Steven, Stevey, Stevi, Stevie, Stevy

Stephene (French) form of Stephen: victorious

Stef, Steff, Steph

Stephine (French) wins

Sterl (English) valuable

Sterling (English) worthwhile

Stern (German) bright; serious

Stearn, Sterns

Stetson (American) cowboy

Stetsen, Stetsun, Stettson

Steubing (Last name as first name) stepping

Steuben, Stu, Stuben, Stubing

Steve (Greek) form of Steven or Stephen: victorious

Stevie

Steven (Greek) victorious

Stevan, Steve, Stevey, Stevie

Steveo (American) form of Steve: victorious

Stevie (English) form of Steven: victorious

Stevee, Stevey, Stevi, Stevy

Stevland (English) steve's place

Stewart (English) form of Stuart: careful; watchful

Stewert, Stu, Stuie

Stian (Scandinavian) traveler

Stieran (Scandinavian) wandering

Steeran, Steeren, Steeryn, Stieren, Stieryn

Stig (Scandinavian) upwardly mobile

Stigg, Styg, Stygg

Stiles (English) practical

Stile, Stiley, Styles

Stillman (English) quiet boy

Sting (English) spike of grain

Stoat (English) small mammal also

called ermine; white

Stoate, Stote

Stobart (German) harsh

Stobe, Stobey, Stoby

Stock (American) macho

Stok

Stockard (English) dramatic

Stock, Stockerd, Stockord

Stockdale (English) from meadow with trees

Stocker (English) foundation

Stock

Stockett (English) from meadow with trees

Stockley (English) in a field of tree stumps stock; rooted in reality

Stockton (English) strong foundation

Stockten

Stockwell (English) from the well by tree stumps; grounded

Stoddard (English) caretaker of horses

Stoddart

Stokley (English) stokes the fire

Stoli (Russian) celebrant

Stone (English) athletic

Stonee, Stoney, Stonie, Stony

Stonewall (English) fortified

Stone, Stoney, Wall

Stoney (American) form of Stone: athletic

Stonee, Stoni, Stonie

Stonne (English) stone

Storey (English) one story of a house; storyteller

Story

Storm (English) impetuous; volatile

Storme, Stormy

Stowe (English) secretive

Stow, Stowey

Stoy (Slavic) steadfast

Stoyan (Slavic) loyal

Strahan (Irish) sings stories

Strachan

Stratan (Greek) from the army

Stratford (English) river-crossing boy; happy

Strafford

Strato (Invented) strategic

Strat, Stratt

Stratton (Scottish) home-loving

Straton, Strattawn

Straus (German) ostrich; in disbelief

Strauss

Strausser (Last name as first name)

Stretch (American) easygoing

Stretcher

Strickland (English) field of flax; outdoorsy

Strider (Literature) from Tolkien's *Lord of the Rings*; great warrior

Strike (American) word as name; aggressive
Striker

Stroheim (Last name as first name) great director

Strom (German) water-lover
Strome, Stromm

Strong (English) strength of character

Strother (Irish) strict
Strothers, Struther, Struthers

Struther (Last name as first name) flowing
Strother, Strothers, Struthers

Stu (English) form of Stuart: careful; watchful
Stew, Stue, Stuey

Stuart (English) careful; watchful
Stewart, Stu, Stuey

Studs (American) cocky; (English) wears studs; masculine
Studd, Studds

Sture (Scandinavian) difficult
Sturah

Styles (English) practical
Stile, Stiles, Style

Stylianos (Greek) stylish
Styli

Sudal (Indian) good

Sudarshan (Indian) handsome

Sudbury (English) southern town boy; lackadaisical
Sudbery, Sudberry, Sudborough

Sudhakar (Indian) good; sweet nectar

Suede (Arabic) leader

Suffield (English) man from the south field

Suffolk (English) from southern folks

Sugar-Ray (American) strong; singer
Sugar Ray

Sujay (Hindi) good
Sujit

Sujit (Indian) wins

Sulaiman (Arabic) loves peace
Suleiman, Suleyman

Sullivan (Irish) dark-eyed; quiet
Sullavan, Sullie, Sullivahn, Sully

Sully (Irish) melancholy; hushed
Sull, Sullee, Sulley, Sullie

Sultan (American) bold
Sultane, Sulten, Sultin

Suman (Hindi) ingenious

Sumano (Spanish) smart

Sumarto (Indian) good

Sumit (Indian) measured

Sumner (Last name as first name) honorable; fortified

Sumney (American) ethereal

Summ, Summy, Sumnee, Sumnie

Sunder (Indian) handsome

Sunil (Hindi) blue; sad

Sunny (American) happy baby boy
Sunney, Sunnie

Suresh (Indian) sun

Surian (Sanskrit) sun

Surinder (Indian) believes in Indra

Surya (Indian) sun

Sutcliff (English) from the south cliff; edgy
Sutcliffe

Sutherland (Scandinavian) sunny; southerner
Southerland

Sutter (English) southern
Sutt, Suttee, Sutty

Sutterly (English) southerner

Sutton (English) sunny; southerner

Suvomoy (Indian) religious

Suvrat (Indian) devout

Svatomir (Slavic) known for being spiritual

Svatoslav (Slavic) having the glory of being devout

Sven (Scandinavian) young boy
Svein, Svend, Swen

Svendin (Scandinavian) young

Svere (Scandinavian) untamed

Swahili (Arabic) language of East Africa; verbal

Swain (English) rigid; leading the herd
Swaine, Swayne

Swanton (English) where swans live; sylvan boy

Swapnil (Indian) fantasy

Sween (Irish) ambitious

Sweeney (Irish) hero
Schwennie, Sweeny

Swen (Scandinavian) form of Sven: young boy

Swift (English) fast
Swifty

Swinburne (English) seeing pigs in the stream
Swinborn, Swinbourne, Swinburn, Swinbyrn, Swynborne

Swindell (English) polished
Schwindell, Swin, Swindel

Swinford (English) seeing pigs in the ford
Swynford

Swinton (English) from the town of swine

Swithin (English) swift
Swithinn, Swithun

Sy (Latin) form of Silas: saver
Si, Sylas

Sychar (Biblical) place name

Sydney (French) form of Sidney: attractive
Cyd, Syd, Sydie

Sye (Latin) form of Silas: saver

Syfron (American) form of Saffron: spice/plant; orange-haired

Sylvain (Latin) reclusive
Syl

Sylvan (Spanish) nature-loving
Silvan, Syl, Sylvany, Sylvin

Sylvester (Latin) forest dweller; heavy-duty
Sil, Silvester, Sly, Syl

Symms (Last name as first name) landowner

Symotris (African American) fortunate
Sym, Symetris, Symotrice, Syms

Synklair (American) form of Sinclair: prayerful

Syon (Sanskrit) lucky boy

Syrtis (Biblical) place name

T

Taanach (Biblical) place name

Tab (German) intelligent
Tabbey, Tabby

Tabbai (Hebrew) good boy

Tabbebo (Native American) boy of the sun

Tabib (Turkish) physician
Tabeeb

Tabor (Aramaic) unfortunate
Taber, Taibor, Tayber, Taybor

Tack (American) popular

Taco (Spanish) thoughtful

Tad (Greek) form of Thaddeus: courageous
Tadd, Taddee, Taddey, Taddie, Taddy

Tadashi (Japanese) loyal

Taddeo (Italian) form of Thaddeus: courageous

Taden (Native American) bountiful

Tadeu (Slavic) praised

Tadeusz (Polish) praise-worthy; (Slavic) worthy
Tad, Taduce

Tadhg (Irish) poetic
Taidghin, Teague, Teige

Tadi (Native American) wind child

Tadmor (Biblical) place name

Tadros (Slavic) brave

Tadzi (Polish) praised

Tae (Irish) poetic

Tafar (African) impressive

Taff (American) sweet
Taf, Taffee, Taffey, Taffi, Taffy

Taft (English) flowing
Tafte, Taftie, Taffy

Taggart (Last name as first name) keeps track; singer

Taghee (Native American) chief
Taighe, Taihee, Tyee, Tyhee

Tague (Scandinavian) star of the day

Taha (Polynesian) first
Tahatan

Taher (Arabic) cleansed

Taheton (Native American) like a hawk

Tahi (Polynesian) by the sea

Tahir (African) pure

Tahj (African) crowned

Tahl (Hebrew) rainy

Tahoe (Place name) Lake Tahoe
Taho

Tahoma (Native American) mountain peak; high hopes
Tohoma

Tahti (Scandinavian) shining star

Tai (Vietnamese) talented

Taillam (French) works iron

Taima (Native American) storm baby

Taimah (Native American) thunder

Tair (Arabic) form of Tahir: pure

Taisto (Scandinavian) fighter

Tait (Scandinavian) form of Tate: happy

Taiwo (African) first of twins

Taizo (Japanese) third son

Taj (Sanskrit) royal; crowned

Takao (Asian) strong

Takeshi (Japanese) unbending

Taklishim (Native American) gray-haired

Takoda (Native American) friend

Tal (Hebrew) worrier
Tallee, Talley, Talli, Tally

Talal (Indian) prayerful

Talan (American) opportunistic

Talat (Arabic) prays

Talbot (French) skillful
Tal, Talbert, Talbott, Tallbot, Tallbott, Tally

Talcot (English) lake-cottage dweller; laidback

Tale (African) green; open

Talfryn (Welsh) on the high hill

Talib (African) looking for enlightenment

Taliesin (Welsh) head that shines
Taltesin

Talli (Hebrew) dew; fresh

Talm (Aramaic) hurt

Talmadge (English) natural; living by lakes
Tal, Tally, Tamidge

Talmai (Aramaic) born on a hill

Talman (Hebrew) from my hill
Tallie, Tally, Talmon

Talon (French) wily
Tallie, Tallon, Tally, Tawlon

Talor (French) cutter; tailor

Tam (Hebrew) truthful
Tammy

Taman (Hindi) needed

Tamar (Hebrew) grows dates

Tamarius (African American) stubborn
Tam, Tamerius, Tammy, T'Marius

Tamer (Arabic) tall

Tamir (Arabic) owner

Tammany (Native American) friendly boy
Tamanend

Tammy (English) form of Thomas: twin; look-alike; form of Tamarius: stubborn
Tammee, Tammey, Tammie

Tan (Japanese) high achiever

Tanafa (Polynesian) drumbeat

Tanaki (Polynesian) boy who counts

Tanay (Hindi) son

Tandie (African American) virile

Tandy (English) together

Tane (Polynesian) sky god; fertile
Tain

Tangaloa (Polynesian) gutsy

Tangie (French) battles

Tanh (Vietnamese) having his way

Tani (African American) form of
Tanier: tanner of skins

Tank (American) big; bullish

Tankie (American) large
Tank, Tankee, Tanky

Tanmay (Indian) mesmerizing

Tanner ♂ (English) tanner of skins
Tan, Tanier, Tann, Tannar, Tanne,
Tanney, Tannie, Tannor, Tanny

Tano (Ghanese) named for the river

Tanom (American) creative

Tanton (English) town of tanners

Tanveer (Indian) informed

Taos (Place name) town in New Mexico
Tao, Tayo

Tap (American) light touch
Tapp, Tappi, Tappy

Tapan (Indian) sun

Tarek (Indian) star

Tarem (American) the son

Taren (French) God's gift

Tarentum (Biblical) place name

Tarhe (Native American) strength of a
tree

Tarick (American) form of Tarek: star

Tarik (Arabic) knocks
Taril, Tarin, Tariq

Tariq (African American) conqueror
Tarik

Tarking (Arabic) summons

Tarlach (Hebrew) wild

Tarleton (English) stormy
Tally, Tarlton

Tarm (Scandinavian) energy

Tarmo (Scandinavian) energy

Taro (Japanese) firstborn son

Tarquin (Roman clan) impulsive

Tarrance (Latin) smooth
Terance, Terrance, Terry

Tarrant (Place name) county in Texas;
lawful

Tarri (American) form of Terry: tender
Tari, Tarree, Tarrey, Tarry

Tarso (Italian) dashing

Tarsus (Biblical) place name

Tarum (Indian) young

Tarun (Arabic) knocks

Tarvin (English) on the hill

Tary (American) form of Terry: tender

Taryll (American) form of Terrell:
puller
Tarell

Tas (Place name) from Tasmania
Taz

Tashunka (Native American) horse
lover
Tasunke

Tasi (Greek) on the mark

Taso (Greek) on the mark

Tassilo (Scandinavian) fearless
protector

Tasso (Greek) on the mark

Tassos (Italian) dark

Tatankamimi (Native American) the
buffalo walks

Tate (English) happy
Tait, Taitt, Tatey, Tayt, Tayte

Taten (Scandinavian) happy

Tatlock (English) happy

Tatonga (Native American) deer;
swift

Tatry (Place name) mountains in
Poland
Tate, Tatree, Tatri

Tau (African) leonine

Taufiq (Arabic) wins

Tauney (English) form of Tawny:
tan-skinned

Taurean (African American)
reclusive; quiet
Taureen

Taurino (Italian) reserved

Taurus (Astrological sign) macho
Tar, Taur, Tauras, Taures

Tava (Polynesian) fruit; fertile

Tavares (African American) hopeful
Tavarus

Tavarius (African American) fun-
loving
Tav, Taverius, Tavurius, Tavvy

Tavas (Hebrew) peacock; handsome

Taven (Scandinavian) form of Tavi:
good

Tavi (Scandinavian) form of David:
beloved; (Aramaic) good

Tavish (Scottish) upbeat
Tav, Taven, Tavis, Tevis

Tavium (Biblical) place name

Tavor (Aramaic) unfortunate
Tabor

Taw (African) form of Tau: leonine

Tawa (Native American) sun boy

Tawagahe (Native American)
builder

Tawanima (Native American)
measures the sun
Tewanima

Tawfiq (Arabic) fortunate
Tawfi

Tawl (Arabic) tall
Taweel

Tawno (American) small

Tay (Scottish) river in Scotland; jaunty
Tae, Taye

Tayhan (Last name as first name)

Tayib (Arabic) city in Israel; spiritual

Taylor ⊘ (English) tailor
Tailor, Talor, Tayler, Tayley

Tayton (American) form of Payton:
soldier's town
Tate, Taye, Tayte, Tayten, Taytin

Tayve (Scandinavian) form of David:
beloved

Taz (Arabic) cup; vibrant

Teagu (Irish) poetic

Teague (Celtic) poet
Teaguey, Tege

Teal (English) duck

Tearlach (Scottish) adult man; bold

Techomir (Czech) famed comfort

Techoslav (Slavic) glorious comfort

Tecumseh (Native American)
shooting star; bright

Ted (English) form of Theodore:
God's gift; a blessing
Teddee, Teddey, Teddi, Teddy

Teddy-Blue (American) smiley
*Blu, Blue, Teddie-Blue, Teddy, Teddyblu,
Teddy-Blu, Teddyblue*

Tedmund (American) shy
Tedmond

Tedrick (African American) form of
Cedric: leader
Ted, Tedrik

Tegan (Celtic) doe
Tege, Tegen, Tegun, Teige

Tego (Irish) form of Teague: poetic

Tehaney (English) reddish-brown

Tejomay (Hindi) glorious
Tej

Tejraj (Indian) sharp

Teklad (Slavic) wonder

Tekoa (Biblical) place name

Tekonsha (Native American) caribou

Telamon (Greek) mythological hero

Telek (Polish) ironworker

Telem (Hebrew) their dew; their
shadow

Telemachus (Mythological) son of
Ulysses

Telesforo (Spanish) country boy

Telesphoros (Greek) leading to an
end; centered

Telford (English) cutting iron;
targeted
Telfer, Telfor, Telfour

Teller (English) relates stories;
storytelling
Tellie, Telly

Tello (German) reformed

Telmo (English) works earth

Telvis (American) form of Elvis: all-
wise
Telly

Tem (African) form of Teman:
spiritual

Tema (Biblical) southerner

Teman (Hebrew) spiritual (Temani are Jews from Yemen)

Tempest (French) stormy; volatile
Tempie, Tempy, Tempyst

Templar (Latin) form of Temple: spiritual

Temple (Latin) spiritual; temple
Tempie, Templle, Tempy

Templeton (English) from a religious place
Temp, Tempie, Temple, Temps

Temre (American) spices

Ten (American) tenth

Tendoy (Native American) he who climbs higher
Tendoi

Teneangopte (Native American) bird; flies high

Tennant (American) capable
Tenn

Tennessee (Native American) able fighter; U.S. state
Tenns, Tenny

Tennison (English) creates

Tenny (English) creative

Tennyson (English) storyteller
Tenie, Tenn, Tenney, Tenneyson, Tennie, Tenny, Tennysen

Tensk (Native American) open

Teo (Greek) gift of God

Teodo (Greek) form of Theodore: God's gift; a blessing

Teodoro (Spanish) God's gift
Tedoro, Teo, Teodore, Theo

Teofanes (Spanish) God-loving

Teofilo (Greek) God-loving

Tephon (Biblical) place name

Teppo (Scandinavian) from Stephen: victorious

TeQuarius (African American) secretive
Teq, Tequarius, Tequie

Terach (Hebrew) wild goat; contentious
Tera, Terah

Terak (Biblical) established

Terard (Invented) form of Gerard: brave
Terar, Tererd, Terry

Tercer (Spanish) third baby

Tercero (Spanish) third baby

Terence (Irish) tender
Tarrance, Terencio, Terrance, Terrence, Terrey, Terri, Terry

TeRez (African American) creative

Terhea (American) from the oak tree

Terl (German) ruler

Term (Latin) terminates

Termell (Invented) form of Terrell: puller
Termel

Teron (Greek) hunter; calms

Terrance (Latin) calm
Terance, Terence, Terre, Terree, Terrence, Terrie, Terry

Terrell (French) puller

Terrelle (German) thunderous; outspoken
Terel, Terele, Terell, Teril, Terille, Terral, Terrale, Terre, Terrel, Terril, Terrill, Terrille, Terry, Tirill, Tirrill, Tyrel, Tyril

Terrien (Greek) hunts; calms

Terron (Greek) hunts

Terry (English) form of Terence: tender
Terree, Terrey, Terri, Terrie

Tesher (Hebrew) gift

Teshombe (African American) able

Tet (Vietnamese) Vietnamese New Year

Teunis (Dutch) form of Antonio: superb

Teva (Hebrew) natural
Tevah

Tevaughn (African American) tiger
Tev, Tevan, Tevaughan, Tivan, Tivaughan

Tevey (Hebrew) good
Tev, Tevi, Tevie

Tevin (African American) outgoing
Tev, Tevan, Tivan

Tevis (American) flamboyant
Tev, Tevas, Teves, Teviss, Tevy

Tex (American) from Texas; cowboy
Texas, Texx

Texas (Place name) U.S. state;
cowboy
Tex

Thabiti (African) real man

Thabo (African) joyful

Thad (Greek) form of Thaddeus:
courageous
Thadd, Thaddy

Thaddeous (Greek) form of
Thaddeus: courageous

Thaddeus (Greek) courageous
Taddeo, Tadeo, Tadio, Thad, Thaddaus,
Thaddius, Thaddy, Thadeus, Thadius

Thaddus (African) brave

Thady (Irish) thankful
Thad, Thaddee, Thaddie, Thaddy, Thads

Thai (Vietnamese) winner

Thais (Asian) flourishes

Thalan (Irish) charming

Thamar (Biblical) form of Ithamar:
island of the palm trees

Thamer (American) helpful

Thanatos (Greek) dies

Thandiwe (African) loved

Thane (English) protective
Thain, Thaine, Thayn, Thayne

Thang (Vietnamese) victorious

Thanh (Vietnamese) tops

Thanos (Greek) praiseworthy
Thanasis

Thanus (American) landowner; wealthy
Thainas, Thaines

Thao (American) variant on Theo:
godlike

Thatcher (English) practical
Thacher, Thatch, Thatchar, Thaxter

Thavin (Greek) shows love for God

Thaw (Word as name) cool

Thayer (English) protected; sheltered
Thay, Thayar

Thayle (Jewish) form of Tal: worrier

Thebez (Biblical) place name

Thel (Hebrew) upper story

Themba (African) hopeful

Themis (Greek) lawful

Thena (Greek) honoree

Thenan (Greek) honored

Thenard (American) form of
Leonard: courageous

Theo (Greek) godlike

Theobald (German) brave man
Thebaud, Thebault, Thibault, Thibaut,
Tibold, Tiebold

Theodis (English) spirited

Theodore (Greek) God's gift; a
blessing
Teador, Ted, Tedd, Teddey, Teddie,
Teddy, Tedor, Teodor, Teodoro, Theeo,
Theo, Theodor, Theos

Theodoric (African American) God's
gift
Thierry

Theodoros (Greek) God's gift
Theo, Theodor

Theodorus (Greek) form of
Theodore: God's gift; a blessing

Theophilos (Greek) loved by God
Teofil, Theo, Theophile

Theopoline (Greek) open

Therman (Scandinavian) thunderous
Thur, Thurman, Thurmen

Theron (Greek) industrious
Therron, Theryon

Theseus (Mythology) brave

Thessal (Biblical) martyr

Thiago (Spanish) saint

Thiassi (Scandinavian) wily
Thiazi, Thjazi

Thibaud (French) form of Theobald:
brave man

Thibaut (French) form of Theobald:
brave man

Thierno (American) humble
Therno, Their

Tho (Vietnamese) long-living

Thom (American) form of Thomas: twin; look-alike

Thomas ✪ (Greek) twin; look-alike
Thom, Thomes, Thommy, Thomus, Tom, Tomas, Tommi, Tomus

Thompson (English) prepared
Thom, Thompsen, Thompsun, Thomson, Tom, Tommy

Thor (Scandinavian) protective; god of thunder
Thorr, Tor, Torr

Thorald (Scandinavian) thundering
Thorold, Torald

Thoralf (Scandinavian) thunder

Thorbert (Last name as first name) warring

Thorburn (Last name as first name) warlike

Thord (Scandinavian) thunder

Thorer (Scandinavian) warrior
Thorvald

Thorin (Scandinavian) form of Thor: protective; god of thunder
Thorrin, Thors

Thorley (Last name as first name) warrior
Thorlea, Thorlee, Thorleigh, Thorly, Torley

Thormond (Last name as first name) world of thunder
Thurmond, Thurmund

Thorn (English) thorny; bothersome

Thorndike (Last name as first name) powerful
Thorndyck, Thorndyke

Thorne (English) complex
Thorn, Thornee, Thorney, Thornie, Thorny

Thornley (Last name as first name) empowered
Thornlea, Thornleigh, Thornly

Thornston (Scandinavian) protected
Thornse, Thors

Thornton (English) difficult
Thorn, Thornten

Thorpe (English) homebody
Thor, Thorp

Thrace (Place name) region in southeast Europe
Thrase

Thu (Vietnamese) born in the fall

Thuan (Asian) aware

Thuc (Vietnamese) alert

Thuel (Biblical) form of Bethuel: religious

Thunor (Mythology) thunder

Thuong (Vietnamese) in pursuit

Thurlow (Last name as first name) helping

Thurm (Greek) form of Theron: industrious

Thurman (Last name as first name) popular
Thurmahn, Thurmen, Thurmie, Thurmy

Thurmond (Norse) sheltered
Thurman, Thurmon

Thurso (Scandinavian) thunders

Thurston (Scandinavian) thundering
Thor, Thors, Thorst, Thorstan, Thorstein, Thorsteinn, Thorsten, Thur, Thurs, Thurstain, Thurstan, Thursten, Torstein, Torsten, Torston

Thurstron (Scandinavian) volatile
Thorst, Thorsten, Thorstin, Thurs, Thurstran

Thuy (Vietnamese) kind

Tiago (Hispanic) brave
Ti, Tia

Tiaone (Spanish) form of Tiago: brave

Tiarnach (Irish) lordlike
Tighearnach

Tiber (Biblical) place name

Tiberius (Biblical) place name

Tibor (Czech) artist
Tybald, Tybalt, Tybault

Ticio (Spanish) heroic

Tien (Vietnamese) first and foremost

Tiernan (Irish) regal
Tierney

Tifton (English) Last name as first name

Tige (American) easygoing
Tig, Tigg

Tiger (American) ambitious; strong
Tig, Tige, Tigur, Tyg, Tyge, Tyger, Tygur

Tigny (Irish) poetic

Tigran (Latin) tiger

Tigrano (Biblical) place name

Tiki (Mythology) first man

Tilak (Hindi) leader; troubled; spot on forehead

Tildan (English) man who tills

Tilden (Place name) tilden

Tilene (Slavic) religious

Tilford (Last name as first name) tilling the soil

Till (German) form of Tillman: tiller of soil

Tillery (German) ruler
Till, Tiller

Tillman (German) tiller of soil
Tilman

Tillo (German) devout

Tilon (Hebrew) mound; giver

Tilton (English) prospering
Till, Tillie, Tylton

Tim (Greek) form of Timothy: reveres God
Timmy, Tym

Timber (American) word as name
Timb, Timby, Timmey, Timmi, Timmy

Timenn (Indian) child from the sea

Timin (Irish) honors God

Timmy (Greek) truthful
Timi, Timmee, Timmey, Timmie

Timna (Biblical) place name

Timnah (Biblical) place name

Timo (Finnish) form of Timothy: reveres God; form of Timon: from Shakespeare's *Timon of Athens*; wealthy man

Timon (Literature) from Shakespeare's *Timon of Athens*; wealthy man
Tim

Timothy (Greek) reveres God
Tim, Timathy, Timmie, Timmothy, Timmy, Timo, Timon, Timoteo, Timothe, Timothey, Timothie, Timuthy, Tymmothy, Tymothy

Timur (African) timid; ; (Slavic) conquerer

Timus (Scandinavian) powerful

Tin (Vietnamese) proud; pondering

Tingo (Italian) grateful

Tinks (American) coy
Tink, Tinkee, Tinki, Tinky, Tynks, Tynky

Tino (Spanish) respected
Tyno

Tinsley (English) personable
Tensley, Tins, Tinslee, Tinslie, Tinsly

Tinus (Slavic) leader

Tiombe (African) faith

Tione (American) form of Tyrone: self-starter; autonomous

Tip (American) small boy
Tipp, Tippee, Tippey, Tippi, Tippy, Typp

Tippen (American) Last name as first name

Tippie (Scandinavian) from Stephen: victorious

Tipu (Hindi) tiger

Tiras (Biblical) thoughtful

Tirso (Greek) religious

Tiru (Hindi) pious

Tisa (African) ninth child

Titan (Greek) powerful giant
Titun, Tityn

Tito (Latin) honored
Teto, Titoh

Titon (American) concerned

Titus (Latin) heroic
Titas, Tite, Tites

Tivon (African American) popular

Tizian (Italian) creative

Tjaru (Biblical) place name

Toa (Polynesian) brave-hearted

Toafo (Polynesian) in the wild; spontaneous

Toal (Irish) from strong roots; leader; willful

Tob (Biblical) place name

Tobbar (African American) physical

Tobby (African) excellent

Tobert (French) believer

Tobes (Hebrew) form of Tobias: believing the Lord is good
Tobee, Tobi, Tobs

Tobian (Hebrew) form of Tobias: believing the Lord is good

Tobias (Hebrew) believing the Lord is good
Tobe, Tobey, Tobi, Tobiah, Tobie, Tobin, Toby, Tobyas, Tovi

Tobikuma (Japanese) cloud; misty

Tobin (Hebrew) form of Tobias: believing the Lord is good
Toban, Toben, Tobun, Tobyn

Tobit (Biblical) form of Tobias: believing the Lord is good

Toblin (American) form of Tobias: believing the Lord is good

Toby (Hebrew) form of Tobias: believing the Lord is good
Tobe, Tobee, Tobey, Tobie, Toto

Todd (English) sly; fox
Tod, Toddy

Todor (Slavic) dignity

Todros (Hebrew) gifted; treasure
Todos

Togar (Biblical) place name

Togo (Place name) country in West Africa; jaunty

Tohon (Native American) loves the water

Tokala (Native American) fox; sly

Tokar (German) lucky

Toks (American) carefree

Tokutaro (Japanese) virtuous son

Tolan (American) studious
Tolen, Toll

Tolbert (English) bright prospects
Talbart, Talbert, Tolbart, Tolburt, Tollee, Tolley, Tollie, Tolly

Toledo (Place name) city in Ohio; casual
Tol, Tolly

Tolerence (American) unbiased

Tolero (Spanish) tolerant

Tolfe (American) outgoing

Tolin (American) form of Colin: young; quiet; peaceful; the people's victor

Toliver (American) combo of T and Oliver

Tolome (Spanish) strong

Tolomey (French) planner

Tom (English) form of Thomas: twin; look-alike
Thom, Tommy

Tomaro (Spanish) form of Thomas: twin; look-alike

Tomas (Spanish) form of Thomas: twin; look-alike

Tomasso (Italian) doubter
Maso, Tom

Tomer (Hebrew) tall

Tomi (Spanish) form of Tomas: twin; look-alike

Tomiko (Japanese) born to riches

Tomio (Italian) twin

Tomioson (Italian) son of twin

Tomlin (Last name as first name) ambitious

Tommie (Hebrew)
Tommee, Tommey, Tommi, Tomy

Tomochichi (Hawaiian) seeking truth and beauty
Tomocheeehee

Tomok (Slavic) twin

Tond (Slavic) form of Tony: priceless

Tondeloro (Spanish) loud thunder

Tondy (Slavic) form of Tony: priceless

Tong (Chinese) name of a secret society; keeps a secret

Tongo (Asian) sweet aroma

Toni (Greek)
Tonee, Toney, Tonie, Tony

Tonin (Italian) form of Antonio: superb

Tonion (American) form of Tony or Anthony: priceless

Tonny (Spanish) form of Antonio: superb

Tony (Greek) priceless

Tooling (American) vibrant

Toopweets (Native American) strong man

Toph (Greek) valued

Topher (Greek) form of Christopher: the bearer of Christ

Toppin (English) from the hill

Tops (American) best

Topwe (American) jovial

Tor (Scandinavian) thunder; brash
Thor, Torr, Torri, Torrie, Torry

Torao (Japanese) tiger male; wild

Torb (Scandinavian) form of Tor: thunder; brash

Torben (Scandinavian) form of Tor: thunder; brash

Torbie (Scandinavian) form of Tor: thunder; brash

Torcall (Scandinavian) summoned by thunder

Tord (Dutch) peaceful

Tordin (Scandinavian) form of Tor: thunder; brash

Torell (English) form of Tor: thunder; brash

Toreth (Biblical) from Ashtoreth

Torey (English) form of Tor: thunder; brash

Torger (Scandinavian) Thor's spear
Terje, Torgeir

Torgne (American) form of Tor: thunder; brash

Torial (Irish) form of Tor: thunder; brash

Torian (Irish) form of Torin: like thunder

Toribio (Spanish) strong; bullish

Toril (Hindi) having attitude

Torin (African American) like thunder

Torio (Spanish) fierce

Torkel (Scandinavian) protective
Thorkel, Torkil, Torkild, Torkjell, Torquil

Torless (Literature) from *The Confusions of Young Torless* by Musil

Torm (Scandinavian) armed

Tormod (Scottish) man of the north

Torn (Last name as first name) whirlwind
Torne, Tornn

Toro (Spanish) bull

Toroh (Spanish) bull

Torolf (Scandinavian) wolf of Thor
Thorolf, Tolv, Torolv, Torulf

Toronto (Place name) jaded
Torontoe

Torq (Scandinavian) form of Thor: protective; god of thunder
Tork

Torquil (Scandinavian) a kettle of thunder; trouble

Torr (English) tower; tall
Torre

Torrence (Latin) smooth
Torrance, Torence, Torey, Tori, Torr, Torrance, Torrie, Tory

Torrent (Irish) form of Torrence: smooth

Torri (English) calming
Toree, Tori, Torre, Torree, Torrey, Torry

Torst (Scandinavian) thunders

Toru (Scandinavian) thundering

Torun (Scottish) manly

Tosan (Spanish) bull

Tosh (American) form of Josh: devout

Toshiro (Japanese) smart

Totan (Scandinavian) beloved

Toth (Egyptian) life in balance

Toussaint (French) saints; valued

Tov (Hebrew) good
Tovi, Toviel, Tovya, Tuvia, Tuviah, Tuviya

Tova (Hebrew) good
Tov

Tovar (Hebrew) form of Tova: good

Tovaris (Spanish) good

Tove (Scandinavian) ruling; leads
Tuve

Townie (American) jovial
Townee, Towney, Towny

Townley (Last name as first name)
citified
Townlea, Townlee, Townleigh, Townlie, Townly

Townsend (Last name as first name)
went to town

Toyah (Place name) town in Texas;
saucy
Toy, Toya, Toye

Trace (French) careful
Trayse

Tracy (French) spunky
Trace, Tracee, Tracey, Traci

Traddesus (Greek) form of
Thaddeus: brave

Trae (American) form of Trey: third-
born; creatively brilliant

Trahaearn (Welsh) strong man
Trahern, Traherne

Trahan (English) handsome
Trace, Trahahn, Trahain, Trahane, Trahen

Trai (Vietnamese) pearl in the oyster

Trajan (American) form of Trahan:
handsome

Trakis (American) vibrant

Tram (Scottish) form of Tramaine:
protector

Tramar (Scottish) form of Tramaine:
protector

Trampus (American) talkative
Amp, Tramp, Trampy

Tranis (Irish) thunders

Tranquilino (Spanish) calm

Trap (American) word as name;
masculine
Trapp, Trappy

Trapezus (Biblical) place name

Trau (German) loyal

Trauti (French) believer

Travers (English) helpful

Traverse (French) form of Travers:
helpful

Traves (American) traversing
different roads
Trav, Travus, Travys

Travis (English) conflicted
Tavers, Traver, Travers, Traves, Travess, Travey, Travus, Travuss, Travys

Travo (American) form of Travis:
conflicted

Travon (African American) brash;
(Slavic) happy
Travaughn

Travor (English) form of Trevor: wise

Trawin (English) friend of Trevor

Trayton (English) third
Tray, Trey

Treat (English) pleasing

Treavon (American) form of
Trevon/Trevaughan: studious

Treb (Irish) wise

Treebeard (Literature) from
Tolkien's *The Lord of the Rings*; noble;
strong

Trefor (Welsh) form of Trevor: wise

Treiber (Irish) form of Trevor: wise

Treil (American) form of Terrell:
puller

Treit (American) form of Treat:
pleasing

Tremayne (French) protector
Tramaine, Treemayne, Trem, Tremain, Tremaine, Tremane, Tremen

Tremetrice (American) loved

Trent (Latin) quick-minded
Trente, Trenten, Trentin, Trenton, Trenty, Trint, Trynt

Trento (Spanish) form of Trent: quick-minded

Trenton (Latin) fast-moving
Trent, Trentan, Trenten, Trentin

Trer (Irish) form of Trevor: wise

Trest (Welsh) form of Tristan: sad; wistful

Treton (Welsh) form of Tristan: sad; wistful

Trev (Irish) strong

Treva (Irish) wise
Trevan

Trevan (African American) outgoing
Trevahn, Trevann

Trevelyan (English) from Elyan's home; comforted

Trevey (Irish) strong

Trevin (American) form of Trevon: studious

Trevine (American) strong

Trevis (English) form of Travis: conflicted

Trevon (African American) studious
Trevaughan

Trevor (Irish) wise
Trefor, Trev, Trevar, Treve, Trever, Trevis, Trevur

Trevour (American) form of Trevor: wise

Trex (American) combo of T and Rex (as in the dinosaur)

Trey (English) third-born; creatively brilliant
Trae, Tray, Tre, Treye

Trigg (American) from Trigger; quick-witted
Trig, Trygg

Triman (English) form of Truman: honest man

Trinee (Spanish) musical
Triney, Trini

Trinity (Latin) triad
Trinitie

Trint (American) holy trinity

Trinton (American) town of trinity; holy

Trip (English) wanderer
Tripe, Tripp

Triplett (American) one of the triplets

Tripolis (Biblical) place name

Tripsy (English) dancing
Trippsie, Tryppsi

Tripton (English) town of travelers

Tris (Welsh) form of Tristan: sad; wistful

Tristan ✪ (French) form of Triste: sad; wistful
Trestan, Trestyn, Trist, Tristen, Tristie, Triston, Tristy, Tristyn

Tristannel (Welsh) form of Tristan: sad; wistful

Triste (French) sad; wistful
Tristan

Tristian (English) form of Tristan: sad; wistful

Tristram (Welsh) sorrowful

Trivett (Last name as first name) trinity
Trevett, Triv

Trivin (American) form of Devin: poetic; writer
Trevin

Troas (Biblical) place name

Trocky (American) manly
Trockey, Trockie

Troclus (Greek) glorified

Trond (Scandinavian) from Norway

Trotter (American) quick

Trovillion (English) home-loving

Trowbridge (Place name)
Trowbridge Park

Troy (French) good-looking
Troi, Troye, Troyie

Troyal (Irish) form of Troy: good-looking

Trudell (English) remarkable for honesty
Trude, True

Truitt (English) honest
Tru, True, Truett, Truitte

Truk (Place name) islands in the West Pacific; tough
Truck

Truls (Scandinavian) truth

Truman (English) honest man
Tru, True, Trueman, Trumaine, Trumann

Trumble (Last name as first name) sincere
Trumball, Trumbell, Trumbull

Trusdale (English) truthful
Dale, Tru, True

Truslowe (English) truth

Tryg (Scandinavian) trustworthy

Trygve (Scandinavian) trustworthy

Trym (Scandinavian) new

Trysten (Welsh) form of Tristan: sad; wistful

Trystene (American) laughter

Trystenn (American) laughter

Tsalani (African) says good-bye; leaving

Tsatoke (Native American) hunter on a horse

Tsela (Native American) star

Tsin (Native American) riding a horse

Tsoai (Native American) tree; big

Tu (Vietnamese) fourth

Tuan (Vietnamese) simple

Tuar (Native American) eagle-eyed

Tubal (Biblical) place name

Tucker (English) stylish
Tuck, Tucky, Tuckyr

Tucks (English) form of Tucker: stylish
Tuk

Tuder (Welsh) form of Tudor/Theodore: leader; God's gift

Tudor (Welsh) leader; special

Tue (Danish) form of Thor: protective; god of thunder

Tufe (American) energetic

Tukuli (African) moon child

Tulio (Spanish) energetic

Tullis (Latin) important
Tull, Tullice, Tullise, Tully

Tully (Irish) form of Tullis: important
Tull, Tulley, Tulli, Tullie

Tulsa (Place name) city in Oklahoma; rancher

Tulse (American) from Tulsa (place name)

Tulsi (Hindi) holy

Tumaini (African) optimist

Tune (American) dancer; musical
Toone, Tuney

Tung (Vietnamese) medium

Tunney (Welsh) leader

Tunu (Place name) from Tununak

Tuong (Vietnamese) everything

Tupaar (Welsh) God's child

Tupi (Spanish) a language family with Brazilian roots

Turah (Native American) thyme

Turang (Biblical) wave

Turck (Biblical) place name

Ture (Scandinavian) form of Thor: protective; god of thunder

Turer (Scandinavian) soldier

Turgut (German) believer

Turi (Hindi) growth

Turk (English) tough
Terk, Turke

Turlough (Hebrew) form of Tuvia: good

Turlow (Irish) thunder child

Turn (Latin) turner

Turner (Latin) skilled
Turn

Turone (African American) form of Tyrone: self-starter; autonomous
Ture, Turrey, Turry

Turston (Greek) form of Thurston: thundering

Tushar (Indian) droplets

Tut (Arabic) brave
Tuttie, Tutty

Tuttle (Scottish) strong

Tutts (American) unique

Tuvia (Hebrew) good
Tuvyah, Tuvyeh

Tuwa (Native American) earth-loving

Tuyen (Vietnamese) angelic

Twain (English) dual-faceted
Twaine, Tway, Twayn

Twyford (English) debonair

Twymon (English) double

Ty (English) form of Tyler: industrious
Ti, Tie, Tye

Tybalt (Greek) always right

Tyce (American) lively
Tice

Tycho (Scandinavian) focused
Tyge, Tyko

Tydeus (Mythology) determined

Tyee (African American) goal-oriented

Tyerson (English) son of Tye

Tygie (American) energetic
Tygee, Tygey, Tygi

Tyke (Scandinavian) determined

Tyko (Greek) form of Tycho: focused

Tyler ○ ☉ (English) industrious
Tile, Tiler, Ty, Tye, Tylar, Tyle, Tylir, Tylor

Tylus (Scandinavian) impact

Tyman (Scandinavian) high integrity

Tymon (Polish) honored by God

Tynan (Place name) a town in
Northern Ireland; (Irish) dark

Tyobaldo (Slavic) form of Theobald:
brave man

Tyones (American) form of Tyrone:
self-starter; autonomous

Tyonne (African American) feisty
Tye, Tyon

Tyounes (American) form of Tyrone:
self-starter; autonomous

Typhoon (English) volatile
Tifoon, Ty, Tyfoon, Tyfoonn

Tyr (Scandinavian) Norse god; daring
warrior

Tyran (American) form of Tyrone:
self-starter; autonomous

Tyre (English) thunders
Tyr

Tyree (African American) courteous
Ty, Tyrae, Tyrie, Tyry

Tyreece (African American)
combative
Tyreese

Tyrell (African American) personable
Trelle, Tyrel, Tyrelle, Tyril, Tyrrel

Tyrellon (American) form of Tyrell:
personable

Tyrese (American) form of Tyrone:
self-starter; autonomous

Tyresen (American) form of Tyrese:
self-starter; autonomous

Tyron (African American) self-reliant

Tiron, Tyronn

Tyrone (Greek) self-starter;
autonomous
*Terone, Tiron, Tirone, Tirus, Ty,
Tyronne, Tyron, Tyroon, Tyroun*

Tyroneece (African American) ball
of fire
Tironeese, Tyronnee

Tys (American) fighter
Thysen, Tyes, Tyse, Tysen

Tyson (French) son of Ty
Tieson, Tison, Tyse, Tysen, Tysson, Tysy

Tzach (Hebrew) unblemished
Tzachai, Tzachar

Tzadik (Hebrew) fair
Tzadok, Zadik, Zadoc, Zadok, Zaydak

Tzadkiel (Hebrew) righteous
Zadkiel

Tzalmon (Hebrew) dark
Zalmon

Tzephaniah (Hebrew) man
protected by God
*Tzefanya, Zefania, Zefaniah, Zephania,
Zephaniah*

Tzevi (Hebrew) graceful; deer
Tzeviel, Zevi, Zeviel

Tzuriel (Hebrew) depends on God
Zuriel

U

Ualtar (Irish) strong

Ualtarr

Uan (Irish) form of Owen: well-born; high-principled

Uba (African) rich

Ubald (French) brave one

Ubaldo, Ube

Ubanwa (African) wealth in children

Uben (German) practice

Ubin, Ubyn

Ubiwe (African) of the heart

Ubrig (German) big

Ubrigg, Ubryg, Ubrygg

Ubrigens (German) bothered

Ubrigins, Ubrigyns

Uchtred (English) cries

Uchtrid, Uchtryd, Uctred, Uctrid, Uctryd, Uktred, Uktrid

Udall (English) certain; valley of trees

Eudall, Udahl, Udawl, Yudall

Udeep (Indian) flood

Udeh (Hindi) praised

Udel (English) growing

Udell (English) from a tree grove

Del, Dell, Udale, Udall

Udenwa (African) thriving

Udo (German) shows promise

Udolf (German) stodgy

Ufer (German) dark mind

Ugo (Italian) bright mind

Uhr (German) disturbed

Uilleac (Irish) ready

Uilleack, Uilleak, Uilliac, Uilliack, Uilliak, Uillyac, Uillyack, Uillyak

Uilleog (Irish) prepared

Uilliog, Uillyog

Ukel (American) player

Ukal, Uke, Ukil

Ukraine (Place name) republic

Ulan (Place name) city in Russia

Ulane

Uland (African) firstborn twin

Ulande

Ulas (German) noble

Ulbrich (German) aristocratic

Ulfat (Norse) wolf

Ulff (Scandinavian) wolf; wild

Ulf, Ulv

Ulfred (Norse) noble

Ulgar (German) highborn

Ulhas (Indian) mirth

Ulices (Latin) form of Ulysses: forceful

Uly

Ulick (Irish) for William; up-and-coming

Ulise (Latin) form of Ulysses: forceful

Ulissus (Invented) form of Ulysses: forceful

Ulland (English) noble Lord

Uland, Ullund

Ullock (Irish) nobleman

Ulman (German) the wolf's infamy

Ulmann, Ullman, Ullmann

Ulmer (German) wolf; cagy

Ulriah (German) form of Ulrich: ruling; power

Ulria, Ulrya, Ulryah

Ulrich (German) ruling; power

Ric, Rick, Rickie, Ricky, Ulrek, Ulric, Ulriche, Ulrick, Ulrico

Ulrid (German) leader

Ulster (Scandinavian) wolf

Ultan (Irish) noble

Ultann

Ultar (Scandinavian) wolf

Ultarr

Ultman (Hindi) godlike

Ulton (German) highborn

Ulysses (Latin) forceful

Ule, Ulesses, Ulises, Ulisses

Umang (Indian) excited

Umar (Hindi) doing well

Umbard (German) form of Humbert: famous giant; renowned warrior

Umbarde

Umber (French) brown; plain

Umberto (Italian) earthy

Umed (Hindi) has an aim

Umek (Japanese) blossoms

Umher (Arabic) controlling

Umi (African) life

Unique (American) word as name
Uneek, Unik

Unitas (American) united

Univers (American) universal; man
for all

Unser (Last name as first name)
drives hard and fast

Unten (English) not a friend
Untenn

Unus (Latin) one
Unuss

Unwin (Last name as first name)
modest

Updike (Last name as first name)
from up above

Upjohn (English) creative
Upjon

Upton (English) highbrow writer
Uppton, Uptawn, Upten, Uptown

Upwood (Last name as first name)
upper woods is home

Uranus (Greek) the heavens

Urban (Latin) city dweller
Urb, Urbain, Urbaine, Urbane, Urben,
Urbin, Urbun, Urby

Urho (Scandinavian) courageous

Uri (Hebrew) form of Uriel: light;
God-inspired

Uriah (Hebrew) bright; led by God
Uri, Urie, Uryah

Urian (Irish) from heaven
Urion

Urias (Hebrew) Lord as my light; old-
fashioned
Uraeus, Uri, Uria, Urius

Uriel (Hebrew) light; God-inspired

Urielon (American) form of Uriel:
light; God-inspired

Urien (Mythology) lights life

Urs (Scandinavian) bear; growly
Urso

Ursan (French) form of Orson: strong
as a bear
Ursen, Ursyn

Ursino (Spanish) dark

Urteil (German) judgment
Urteel, Urtiel

Uruk (Slavic) form of Urias: Lord as
my light; old-fashioned

Urv (Biblical) place name

Urvano (Spanish) city boy
Urbano

Urvine (Place name) form of Irvin:
attractive
Urveen, Urvene, Urvi

Ury (Hispanic) God-loving; (Hebrew)
shining

Usaid (Arabic) laughs

Usaku (Japanese) moonlit

Usher (Latin) decisive

Usman (Arabic) friend

Usry (Slavic) cultured

Utah (Place name) U.S. state

Uthman (Arabic) bird
Uthmann

Utz (American) befriends all

Uwe (Welsh) gentle

Uz (Hebrew) passion

Uzal (Hebrew) strong in God

Uziah (Hebrew) believes

Uziel (Hebrew) soothed by God's
strength

Uzondu (African) attracts others

Uzu (Biblical) strength in God

Uzzi (Biblical) place name

Uzziel (Hebrew) powerful in God

V

Vachel (French) keeps cows
Vachell

Vadim (French) creative
Vadeem

Vadin (Hindi) speaks well

Vaduz (Place name) city in Germany

Vahan (Slavic) protected

Vail (English) serene
Bail, Bale, Vaile, Vaill, Vale, Valle

Vaino (Scandinavian) wagonbuilder

Val (Latin) form of Valeri: athletic; mighty; form of Valentine: robust
Vall

Vala (Latin) form of Valentine: robust

Valare (Latin) water-loving

Valdem (Scandinavian) rules

Valdemar (Scandinavian) famous leader
Waldemar

Valensi (Spanish) valiant

Valente (Italian) form of Valentin: valiant

Valenti (Italian) mighty; romantic
Val, Valence, Valentin, Valentyn

Valentin (Russian) valiant
Val, Valeri

Valentine (Latin) robust
Val, Valentijn, Valentin, Valentinian, Valentino, Valentinus, Valentyn, Valentyne, Valyntine

Valentino (Italian) strong; healthy
Val

Valeri (Russian) athletic; mighty
Val, Valerian, Valerio, Valry

Valerian (Russian) strong leader
Valerien, Valerio, Valerius, Valery, Valeryan

Vali (Scandinavian) brave man

Valin (Latin) form of Valentin: valiant
Valen, Valyn

Vallance (Last name as first name) tenacious

Vallie (Romanian) valor

Valmar (Slavic) peaceful

Valu (Polynesian) eight

Van (Dutch) descendant
Vann, Von, Vonn

Vance (English) brash
Vans, Vanse

Vanco (Slavic) form of Vincent: victorious

Vanda (Russian) form of Walter: army leader

Vandan (Hindi) saved

Vander (Greek) form of Evander: manly; champion
Vand

Vandiver (American) quiet
Van, Vand, Vandaver, Vandever

Vandwon (African American) covert
Vandawon, Vandjuan

Vandyke (Last name as first name) educated

Vane (Last name as first name) gifted

Vangle (Greek) brings good news

Vanhue (Armenian) protected

Vannevar (Scandinavian) form of Evander: manly; champion

Vanni (Italian) form of Giovanni: jovial; happy believer

Vanny (Slavic) form of Vanya: right

Vanslow (Scandinavian) sophisticated
Vansalo, Vanselow, Vanslaw

Vanya (Russian) right
Van, Yard, Yardy

Varady (Slavic) fortified

Vardon (French) green hill is home
Varden, Verdon, Verdun

Varen (Hindi) rain god Varun

Varesh (Hindu) God is superior

Varg (American) vigorous

Vargu (Scandinavian) wolf-like

Varick (German) defender
Varrick, Warick, Warrick

Varil (French) faithful

Varkey (American) boisterous

Varlan (American) tough

Varland, Varlen, Varlin

Varma (Hindi) fruitful

Varner (Last name as first name) formidable

Varn

Varo (Last name as first name)

Vartan (Russian) gives roses

Vartkes (History) king of all

Varun (Hindi) water Lord; excellent

Varoun

Vas (Slavic) protective

Vaston, Vastun, Vasya

Vasant (Sanskrit) brings spring

Vasch (Slavic) clarity

Vasco (Hindi) excellent

Vash (Spanish) from Velasco, Texas

Vashon (American) delightful

Vashaun, Vashonne

Vasil (Slavic) form of William: staunch protector

Vasile, Vasilek, Vasili, Vasilis, Vasilos, Vasily, Vassily

Vasile (Greek) form of Vasilis: king

Vasilis (Russian) king

Vasileios, Vasilij, Vasily, Vaso, Vasos, Vassilij, Vassily, Vasya, Wassily

Vasin (Hindi) rules all

Vasken (Slavic) quiet

Vassil (Bulgarian) king

Vass

Vassilios (Greek) king

Vasu (Sanskrit) rich boy

Vatche (Armenian) loving

Vaughn (Welsh) compact

Vaughan, Vaunie, Von

Vea (Vietnamese) form of Veasna: fortunate

Veasna (Vietnamese) fortunate

Vedn (Latin) sees

Vee (Hebrew) ash tree

Veejay (American) talkative

V.J., Vee-Jay, Vejay

Veer (English) form of Vere: springlike

Vegas (Place name) from Las Vegas

Vega

Vejis (Invented) form of Regis: kingly

Veejas, Veejaz, Vejas, Vejes

Velamo (Scandinavian) of the sea

Velle (American) tough

Vell, Velley, Velly, Veltree

Veltry (African American) hopeful

Velvet (American) smooth

Vel, Velvat, Velvit

Venancio (Spanish) glorious

Venard (Spanish) starry

Venaventura (Spanish) hurts

Vencel (Hungarian) king

Vendon (Indian) fortified

Venedict (Greek) form of Benedict: blessed man

Venedikt, Venka, Venya

Venezio (Italian) glorious

Venetziano, Veneziano

Venkat (Hindi) godlike

Venkata (Hindi) godlike

Ventura (Spanish) good fortune

Venturo (Italian) lucky

Venturio

Verdun (French) green knoll

Vere (Latin) springlike

Vered (Hebrew) rose-loving

Vergel (Spanish) writer

Vergele, Virgil

Verile (German) macho

Verill, Verille, Verol, Verrill

Verissimo (Spanish) truthful

Verlan (Latin) flourishes

Verle (American) truthful

Verlie (American) form of Verle: truthful

Verley

Verlyn (African American) growing

Verle, Verlin, Verllin, Verlon, Verlyn, Virle, Vyrle

Vermont (Place name) U.S. state

Vern (Latin) form of Vernon: fresh and bright
Verne, Vernie, Verny

Vernados (Greek) hearty

Verner (German) resourceful
Vern, Verne, Vernir, Virner

Verniamin (Greek) form of Benjamin: son of the right hand; son of the south

Vernie (Latin) form of Vernon: fresh and bright

Vernon (Latin) fresh and bright
Lavern, Vern, Vernal, Verne, Vernen, Verney, Vernin

Verona (Italian) man of Venice or Verona
Verone

Verrier (French) faithful

Verrill (German) manly
Verill, Verrall, Verrell, Verroll, Veryl

Verron (Latin) form of Vernon: fresh and bright

Vesa (Scandinavian) young

Vest (English) church child

Vester (Latin) form of Sylvester: forest-dweller; heavy-duty

Vestin (English) church child

Vesuvio (Place name) mount Vesuvius; spontaneous

Vetch (German) comforts

Vetis (Latin) life

Vettorio (Italian) victor

Vezeleo (Spanish) form of Basil: regal

Vic (Latin) form of Victor: victorious
Vick, Vickey, Vik

Vicason (English) son of Victor

Vicente (Spanish) winner
Vic, Vicentay, Visente

Vicken (Latin) victor

Vico (Italian) form of Victor: victorious; winning

Victen (American) form of Victor: victorious

Victor (Latin) victorious
Vic, Vick, Vickter, Victer, Victorien, Victorin, Vidor, Vikki, Viktor, Vitorio, Vittorio

Victoriano (Spanish) form of Victor: victorious

Vid (Spanish) form of Vidal: full of vitality

Vida (Hebrew) beloved; vibrant

Vidal (Spanish) full of vitality
Bidal, Videl, Videlio

Vidalo (Spanish) energetic
Vidal

Vidar (Scandinavian) soldier

Viddell (Spanish) vital

Vidkun (Scandinavian) gives

Vidor (Hungarian) delightful

Vidya (Indian) smart

Vidyalakshmi (Indian) bright

Viggo (Scandinavian) exuberant
Viggoa, Vigo

Vigile (American) vigilant
Vegil, Vigil

Vihs (Hindu) increase

Vijay (Hindi) winning
Bijay, Vijun

Vikas (Indian) growth

Vila (Czech) form of William: staunch protector
Vili, Ville

Vili (Indian) bright

Viliam (Slavic) form of William: staunch protector

Viliami (Slavic) form of William: staunch protector

Villalvazo (Spanish) home of peace

Villantes (French) valiant

Villard (French) village man

Villen (Russian) form of Lennon: renowned; caped

Villiers (French) kindhearted

Vilmos (Italian) happy
Villmos

Vilnis (Slavic) form of Vilmos: happy

Vilok (Hindu) to see

Vimal (Hindi) unblemished

Vin (Italian) form of Vincent: victorious

Vinn, Vinney, Vinni, Vinnie

Vinay (Hindi) good manners; polite

Vince (English) form of Vincent: victorious

Vee, Vence, Vins, Vinse

Vincent (Latin) victorious

Vencent, Vicenzio, Vin, Vince, Vincens, Vincente, Vincentius, Vincents, Vincenty, Vincenz, Vincenzio, Vincenzo, Vincien, Vinciente, Vinicent, Vinn, Vinnie, Vinny, Vinzenze, Wincenty

Vincenzo (Italian) conqueror

Vincenze, Vinnie, Vinny

Vine (Latin) form of Vin: victorious

Vinicius (Indian) victor

Vinod (Hindi) effervescent; joy

Vinson (English) winning attitude

Venson, Vince, Vinny, Vins

Vinton (English) town of wine; reveler

Vinus (Slavic) ready

Vio (Indian) form of Vijay: winning

Vip (Hindi) bounty

Vir (Indian) large

Viral (Indian) mannered

Virat (Indian) big

Vireo (Latin) brave

Virgil (Latin) holding his own; writer

Verge, Vergil, Vergilio, Virge, Virgie, Virgilio, Virgy

Virginius (Latin) virginal

Virginio

Virrgilio (Spanish) form of Virgil: holding his own; writer

Virtus (Greek) virtuous

Vischer (Last name as first name) longing

Visscher

Vishal (Indian) grand

Vishnu (Indian) pervasive

Vison (Hindi) persuades

Vitale (Italian) important

Vitaliano (Italian) vital

Vitalis (Latin) bubbly; vital

Vitas (Latin) animated

Vidas, Vite

Viticus (Biblical) from Leviticus

Vito (Italian) form of Vittorio: lively; victor

Veto, Vital, Vitale, Vitalis, Vitaly, Vitas, Vite, Vitus, Witold

Vitone (Italian) form of Vitas: animated

Vitrano (Indian) great

Vittorio (Italian) lively; victor

Vite, Vito, Vitor, Vitorio, Vittore

Vittorios (Italian) victor

Vitus (Latin) winning

Vivaldo (Italian) celebrant

Vivar (Greek) alive

Viv

Vivek (Hindi) wise; knowing

Vivian (Latin) lively

Viviani, Vivien, Vivyan, Vyvian, Vyvyan

Vlad (Russian) form of Vladimir: glorious leader

Vladimir (Russian) glorious leader

Vlada, Vladameer, Vladamir, Vlademar, Vladimeer, Vlakimar, Wladimir, Wladimyr

Vladislav (Czech) glorious leader

Vladislava (Slavic) glorious ruler

Vladja (Russian) form of Vladislav: glorious leader

Vodie (Scandinavian) victor

Volf (Hebrew) form of Will: staunch protector

Volkan (Slavic) defends

Volker (German) prepared to defend

Volk

Volney (Greek) hidden

Volun (Latin) flies

Volya (Slavic) hopes

Von (German) bright

Vaughn, Vonn, Vonne

Vong (Scandinavian) tough

Vonko (Slavic) form of Vanco: victorious

Vontaire (French) noisy

Vonzie (American) form of Fonzie: distinguished
Vons, Vonze, Vonzee, Vonzey, Vonzi

Vorris (Latin) versatile

Voshon (Slavic) generous

Vui (African) saves

Vuk (Slavic) wolf-like; eloquent

Vuok (Scandinavian) flower

Vurl (American) form of Verle: truthful

Vusen (Dutch) vain

Vyacheslav (Russian) glorious child

Vyom (American) vocal

Waclaw (Polish) glorified

Wacy (Arabic) knowledgeable

Wade (English) mover; crossing a river
Wadie, Waide, Wayde

Wadell (English) southerner
Waddell, Wade

Waden (American) form of Jaden: Jehovah has heard
Wade, Wedan

Wadley (Last name as first name) by the water
Wadleigh, Wadly

Wadsworth (English) homebody
Waddsworth, Wadswurth

Wady (Slavic) water boy

Wael (English) from Wales

Wagner (German) musical; practical
Wagg, Waggner, Waggoner, Wagnar, Wagnur

Wagon (American) conveyance
Wag, Wagg, Waggoner

Wai (Asian) form of Wei: excellent

Wain (English) industrious

Wainwright (Last name as first name) works hard
Wain, Wainright, Wayne, Wayneright, Waynewright, Waynright, Wright

Waisim (Arabic) attractive

Wait (American) word as name; patient
Waite

Wake (Place name) island in the Marshall Islands

Wakefield (English) the field worker
Field, Wake

Wakely (Last name as first name) wet

Wakeman (Last name as first name) wet
Wake

Wal (Arabic) form of Waleed: newborn

Walbert (German) protective; stodgy

Walcott (Last name as first name) steadfast
Wallcot, Wallcott, Wolcott

Waldemar (German) famous leader
Valdemar, Waldermar, Waldo

Walden (English) calming
Wald, Waldan, Waldi, Waldin, Waldo, Waldon, Waldy, Welti

Waldo (German) form of Oswald: divine power
Wald, Waldoh, Waldy

Waldron (English) leader

Waleed (Arabic) newborn
Waled, Walid

Walenty (Polish) strong

Walerian (Polish) powerful

Wales (English) from Wales
Wael, Wail, Wails, Wale, Waley, Wali, Waly

Walford (English) wealthy; from Wales

Walfred (English) from Wales; loyal

Wali (Arabic) newborn

Walker (English) distinctive
Walk, Wally

Wall (English) from Wales

Wallace (English) from Wales; charming

Wallas, Walley, Walli, Wallice, Wallie, Wallis, Wally, Walsh, Welsh

Waller (English) from Wales; confident

Wallis (English) from Wales; smooth

Walls (American) walled

Walen, Wally, Waltz, Walz

Wally (English) form of Walter: army leader

Wall, Walley, Walli, Wallie

Walmir (Slavic) ruler

Walmond (Last name as first name) laidback

Walsh (English) inquisitive

Walls, Welce, Welch, Wells, Welsh

Walt (German) army leader

Waltey, Waltli, Walty

Walter (German) army leader

Walder, Wallie, Wally, Walt, Walther, Waltur, Walty, Wat

Walther (German) army leader; powerful

Walton (English) shut off; protected

Walt, Walten, Waltin

Waltrau (German) strong leader

Walu (American) form of Wally: army leader

Walworth (English) introvert

Walwyn (English) reticent

Walwin, Walwinn, Walwynn, Walwynne, Welwyn

Waman (American) form of Wymann: contentious

Wang (Chinese) hope; wish

Waqar (Arabic) talkative

Warburton (Last name as first name) still

Ward (English) vigilant; alert

Warde, Warden, Worden

Wardell (English) guarded

Warden (English) watchful

Warde, Wardie, Wardin, Wardon

Wardley (English) careful

Wardlea, Wardleigh

Ware (English) aware; cautious

Warey, Wary

Warfield (Last name as first name) cautious

Warford (Last name as first name) defensive

Waring (English) dashing

Wareng, Warin, Warring

Wark (American) watchful

Warley (Last name as first name) worthy people

Warlito (Spanish) warring

Warner (German) protective

Warne

Warren (German) safe haven

Ware, Waren, Waring, Warrenson, Warrin, Warriner, Warron, Warry, Worrin

Warton (English) defended town

Warvin (American) form of Marvin: steadfast friend

Warwen (American) defensive

Warn, Warwun

Warwick (English) lavish

War, Warick, Warrick, Warweck, Warwyc, Warwyck, Wick

Washburn (English) bountiful

Washbern, Washbie, Washby

Washington (English) leader

Wash, Washe, Washing

Wasim (Arabic) pretty baby

Wason (Arabic) form of Wasim: pretty baby

Wat (English) form of Watkins: able

Watford (Last name as first name) soft-spoken

Watkins (English) able

Watkens, Wattie, Wattkins, Watty

Watson (English) helpful

Watsen, Watsie, Watsun, Watsy, Wattsson

Waulkie (English) form of Wilkie: willful

Wave (American) word as a name
Waive, Wayve

Waverley (Place name) city in New South Wales
Waverlee, Waverli, Waverly

Way (English) landed; smart
Waye

Wayel (English) the road

Wayland (English) from the path land

Wayling (English) the right way
Waylan, Wayland, Waylen, Waylin

Waylon (English) form of Wayland: from the path land
Wallen, Walon, Way, Waylan, Waylen, Waylie, Waylin, Waylond, Waylun, Wayly, Weylin

Wayman (English) traveling man
Way, Waym, Waymon, Waymun

Waymon (American) knowing the way
Waymond

Wayne (English) wheeler and dealer
Wain, Wanye, Way, Wayn, Waynell, Waynne

Wazir (Arabic) minister

Weather (Native American) dark

Webb (English) intricate mind
Web, Webbe, Weeb

Weber (German) intuitive
Webb, Webber, Webner

Webley (English) weaves; intuitive
Webbley, Webbly, Webly

Webster (English) creative
Web, Webstar, Webstur

Weddel (Last name as first name) has an angle

Wedon (Last name as first name) inspired

Weebie (American) wily
Weebbi

Wegner (American) form of Wagner: musical; practical

Wehrle (Last name as first name)

Wei (Chinese) excellent

Weido (Italian) bright; personable
Wedo

Welborne (Last name as first name) where the well is
Welborn, Welbourne, Welburn, Wellborn, Wellborne, Wellbourn, Wellburn

Welby (German) astute; farmer by the well
Welbey, Welbi, Welbie, Wellby

Weld (English) from the well

Weldom (American) form of Weldon: where the well is

Weldon (Last name as first name) where the well is

Welford (English) unusual
Walferd, Wallie, Wally

Wellington (English) nobility
Welling

Wellis (American) form of Willis: youthful

Wells (English) unique
Well, Wellie, Welly

Wel-Quo (Asian) bothered
Wel

Welsh (English) form of Walsh: inquisitive
Welch, Wellsh

Welton (English) spring town

Wen (American) winter baby

Wenceslaus (Polish) glorified king
Wenceslas, Wenczeslaw, Wenzel, Wiencyslaw

Wendell (German) full of wanderlust
Wandale, Wend, Wendall, Wendel, Wendey, Wendie, Wendill, Wendle, Wendull, Wendy

Wendolid (Spanish) form of Wendell: full of wanderlust

Wenford (English) confessing
Wynford

Wenjic (Slavic) wanders

Wenli (American) form of Wendell: wanderlust

Went (American) ambitious
Wente, Wentt

Wentworth (English) Last name as first name

Wenworth (English) adventures

Werley (English) Last name as first name

Werner (German) warrior

Werther (German) worthy

Wes (English) form of Wesley: bland
Wess, Wessie, Wessy

Wesh (German) from the west

Wesley (English) bland
Wes, Weslee, Wesleyan, Weslie, Wesly, Wessley, West, Westleigh, Westley, Westly, Wezlee, Wezley

Wessell (English) westerner

Wessey (English) westerner

Wesson (American) from the west
Wess, Wessie

West (English) westerner
Weste, Westt

Westbrook (Last name as first name) from the west brook; nature-loving
Brook, West, Westbrooke

Westby (English) near the west

Westcott (English) from a western cottage
Wescot, Wescott, Westcot

Westel (English) westerner

Westie (American) capricious
West, Westee, Westey, Westt, Westy

Westleigh (English) western
Westlea, Westlie, Wezlee

Westley (English) from the west fields

Westoll (American) open
West, Westall

Weston (English) good neighbor
West, Westen, Westey, Westie, Westin, Westy

Wesze (English) westerner

Weszel (English) westerner

Wether (English) lighthearted
Weather, Weth, Wethar, Wethur

Wetherby (English) lighthearted
Weatherbey, Weatherbie, Weatherby, Wetherbey, Wetherbie

Wetherell (English) lighthearted

Wetherly (English) lighthearted

Wex (English) the fjord of the flats

Whalen (English) from the woods

Whalley (Last name as first name) predicts

Wharton (Last name as first name) provincial
Warton

Wheat (Invented) fair-haired
Wheatie, Wheats, Wheaty, Whete

Wheatley (Last name as first name) fair-haired; fields of wheat
Whatley, Wheatlea, Wheatleigh, Wheatly

Wheaton (Last name as first name) blond; wheat town

Wheel (American) important player
Wheele

Wheeler (English) likes cars; wheel maker
Weeler, Wheel, Wheelie, Wheely

Wheeless (English) off track
Whelus

Wheelie (American) big-wig
Wheeley, Wheels, Wheely

Whesk (American) self-serving

Whip (American) friendly

Whistler (English) melodic
Whis, Whistlar, Whistle, Whistlerr

Whit (English) form of Whitman: man with white hair
Whitt, Whyt, Whyte, Wit, Witt

Whitby (English) white-haired; white-walled town

Whitcomb (English) light in the valley; shining
Whitcombe, Whitcumb

White (English) white

Whitelaw (English) white
Whitlaw

Whitey (English) fair-skinned

White

Whitfield (English) from a white field

Whitford (English) the light source

Whitley (English) white area is home
Whitlea, Whitlee, Whitleigh

Whitman (English) man with white hair
Whit, Whitty, Witman

Whitmore (English) white
Whitmoor, Whittemore, Witmore, Wittemore

Whitney (English) likes white spaces
Whit, Whitnee, Whitnie, Whitt, Whittney, Widney, Widny, Witt

Whitson (English) son of Whit
Whitt, Witt

Whittaker (English) outdoorsy
Whitaker, Whitt, Witaker, Wittaker

Whitter (English) white

Whittson (English) white son

Wick (American) burning
Wic, Wik, Wyck

Wickham (Last name as first name) living in a hamlet
Wick

Wickley (Last name as first name) coming from a small home
Wicley

Wier (German) famous

Wieslaw (Polish) known

Wijnand (Slavic) form of Wymon; soldier

Wilberforce (German) wild and strong

Wilbert (German) smart
Wilberto, Wilburt

Wilbur (English) fortified
Wilbar, Wilber, Wilburt, Willbur, Wilver

Wilburn (German) brilliant
Bernie, Wil, Wilbern, Will

Wilder (English) wild man
Wildar, Wilde, Wildey

Wildon (Last name as first name) willing support
Wilden, Willdon

Wilee (English) form of Wylie: charmer

Wilen (English) form of William: staunch protector

Wiles (American) tricky
Wyles

Wiley (English) cowboy
Wile, Willey, Wylie

Wilf (English) form of Wilford: willowy; peaceful wishes

Wilford (English) willowy; peaceful wishes

Wilfre (German) peaceful

Wilfred (German) peacemaker
Wilferd, Wilford, Wilfrid, Wilfride, Wilfried, Wilfryd, Will, Willfred, Willfried, Willie, Willy

Wilfredo (Italian) peaceful
Fredo, Wifredo, Willfredo

Wilhelm (German) resolute; determined
Wilhelmus, Wilhem, Willem

Wilke (German) form of Wilkins: affectionate

Wilkie (English) willful

Wilkins (English) affectionate
Welkie, Welkins, Wilk, Wilkens, Wilkes, Wilkie, Wilkin, Willkes, Willkins

Wilkinson (English) son of Wilkin; capable
Willkinson

Will (English) form of William: staunch protector
Wil, Wilm, Wim, Wyll

Willard (German) courageous
Wilard, Willerd

Willeo (Spanish) form of William: staunch protector

Willer (American) form of Willard: courageous

Willerson (English) son of Willard

Willialdo (Spanish) form of William: staunch protector

William ✪ ⊕ (English) staunch protector
Bill, Will, Willeam, Willie, Wills, Willy, Willyum, Wilyam

Williams (German) brave
Williamson

Willie (German) form of William: staunch protector
Will, Wille, Willey, Willeye, Willi, Willy, Wily

Willis (German) youthful
Willace, Willece, Willice, Wills, Willus

Willits (Scandinavian) protective

Willoughby (Last name as first name) lives with grace
Willoughbey, Willoughbie

Wills (English) willful

Wilmer (German) resolute; ambitious
Willmar, Willmer, Wilm, Wilmar, Wilmyr, Wylmar, Wylmer

Wilmot (German) tough-minded

Wilson (English) extraordinary
Willson, Wilsen, Wilsun

Wilt (English) talented
Wiltie

Wilton (English) practical and open
Will, Wilt, Wiltie, Wylten, Wylton

Wiltson (English) son of Will

Wim (Slavic) go-getter

Wimmy (American) form of William: staunch protector

Win (German) flirtatious
Winn, Winnie, Winny

Wincate (English) form of Vincent: victorious

Winchell (English) meandering
Winchie, Winshell

Wind (American) word as name; breezy
Windy

Windell (German) wanderer
Windelle, Windyll

Windsor (English) royal
Win, Wincer, Winnie, Winny, Winsor, Wyndsor, Wynser

Winfield (English) peace in the country
Field, Winifield, Winnfield, Wynfield, Wynnfield

Winfried (English) peaceful

Wing (Chinese) in glory
Wing-Chiu, Wing-Kit

Wingate (Last name as first name) glorified

Wingi (American) spunky

Wings (American) soaring; free
Wing

Wink (American) vigorous

Winkel (American) bright; conniving
Wink, Winky

Winkle (American) vigorous

Winlove (Filipino) winning favor

Winn (English) form of Wyn: gregarious

Winnell (English) fair-haired

Winslone (English) form of Winslow: friendly

Winslow (English) friendly
Winslo, Wynslo, Wynslow

Winsome (English) gorgeous; charming
Wins, Winsom, Winz

Winston (English) dignified
Win, Winn, Winnie, Winny, Winstan, Winsten, Winstonn, Winton, Wynstan, Wynsten, Wynston

Winter (English) born in winter
Win, Winnie, Winny, Wintar, Winterford, Wintur, Wynter, Wyntur

Winthrop (English) winning; stuffy
Win, Winn, Winnie, Winny, Wintrop

Winton (English) winning
Wynten, Wynton

Winward (English) friendly

Wiss (American) carefree
Wissie, Wissy

Wit (Polish) life
Witt, Wittie, Witty

Witek (Polish) form of Victor: victorious

Witha (Arabic) vibrant

Witold (Polish) lively

Witt (Slavic) lively
Witte

Witter (Last name as first name) alive

Witton (Last name as first name) lively

Witty (American) humorous
Wit, Witt, Witte, Wittey, Wittie

Wize (American) smart
Wise, Wizey, Wizi, Wizie

Wladymir (Polish) famous ruler
Vladimir

Wladyslaw (Polish) good leader
Slaw

Wlodek (Polish) rules

Wohn (African American) form of John: God is gracious

Wojciech (Polish) comforts

Wojtek (Polish) comforter; warrior

Wolcott (English) home of wool

Wolf (German) form of Wolfgang: talented; a wolf walks
Wolff, Wolfie, Wolfy

Wolfe (German) wolf; ominous
Wolf, Wolff, Wulf, Wulfe

Wolfgang (German) talented; a wolf walks
Wolf, Wolff, Wolfgans, Wolfy, Wulfgang

Wolfram (Jewish) ominous

Wolley (American) form of Wally: army leader
Wolly

Wolsh (Slavic) form of Walter: army leader

Wolter (Slavic) form of Walter: army leader

Wood (English) form of Woodrow: special
Woode, Woody

Woodery (English) woodsman
Wood, Wooderree, Woodree, Woodri, Woodry, Woods, Woodsry, Woody

Woodfield (Last name as first name) enjoys the woods

Woodfin (English) attractive
Wood, Woodfen, Woodfien, Woodfyn, Woodie, Woody

Woodford (Last name as first name) forester

Woodrow (English) special
Wood, Woodrowe, Woody

Woodruff (Last name as first name) smooth; natural

Woodson (Last name as first name) son of Wood; suave

Woodville (Last name as first name) from the town of trees

Woodward (English) watchful
Wood, Woodie, Woodard, Woodwerd, Woody

Woodwer (Native American) mourning

Woody (American) jaunty
Wooddy, Woodey, Woodi, Woodie

Woolsey (English) leader
Wools, Woolsi, Woolsie, Woolsy

Worcester (English) secure

Word (American) talkative
Words, Wordy, Wurd

Worden (American) careful
Word, Wordan, Wordun

Wordsworth (English) poetic
Words, Worth

Worie (English) cautious

Worsh (American) from worship; religious
Wor

Worth (English) deserving; special
Werth, Worthey, Worthie, Worthington, Worthy, Wurth

Wortham (English) worthy

Worthington (English) fun; worthwhile
Worth, Worthey, Worthing, Worthingtun, Wurthington

Wouter (German) power figure

Wrae (English) corner

Wrangle (American) cowboy; wrangler

Wrang, Wrangler, Wrangy

Wray (American) cornered

Wren (American) leader of men

Ren, Rin, Rinn, Wrenn

Wright (English) clear-minded; correct

Right, Rite, Wrighte, Write

Wrigley (Place name) city in Tennessee

Wrisley (American) smart

Wrisee, Wrislie, Wrisly

Wriston (American) good proportions

Wryston

Wulf (Hebrew) wolf

Wolf

Wunig (Native American) believer

Wurei (Native American) windy

Wyam (American) form of Wyoming

Wyanll (Scandinavian) arises

Wyant (American) strong-willed

Wyatt ✪ (French) ready for combat

Wiatt, Wy, Wyat, Wyatte, Wye, Wyeth

Wybert (Last name as first name) good profile

Wyborn (Last name as first name) wellborn

Wyck (English) light

Wyclef (American) trendy

Wycleff

Wycliff (English) edgy

Cliffie, Cliffy, Wicliff, Wyclif, Wycliffe

Wydee (American) form of Wyatt: ready for combat

Wy, Wydey, Wydie

Wykeum (American) different

Wyland (English) charismatic

Wyler (German) creative

Wylie (English) charmer

Wiley, Wye, Wylee

Wylon (English) charismatic

Wymann (English) contentious

Wimann, Wye, Wyman

Wymel (English) famous

Wymen (English) soldier

Wymer (English) rambunctious; fighter

Wymon (English) soldier

Wyn (Welsh) gregarious

Wyndham (English) from a hamlet

Windham, Wynndham

Wynell (English) companion

Wynne (English) dear friend

Winn, Wyn, Wynn

Wynter (English) born in winter

Wynton (English) winter town child

Wyshawn (African American) friendly

Shawn, Shawny, Why, Whysean, Wieshawn, Wye, Wyshawne, Wyshie, Wyshy

Wystan (English) struggles

Wythe (English) fair

Wythel (English) of willows

Wyton (English) fair-haired; crowd-pleaser

Wye, Wytan, Wyten, Wytin

Wyze (American) sizzle; capable

Wise, Wye, Wyse

X

Xan (Greek) form of Alexander: great leader; helpful

Xander (Greek) form of Alexander: great leader; helpful

Xan, Xande, Xandere, Xandre

Xanthin (Greek) gold hair

Xanthos (Greek) attractive

Xanthus (Greek) golden-haired child

Xaque (American) unique

Xat (American) saved

Xatt

Xaver (Spanish) form of Xavier: home; shining

Xaverius (Spanish) form of Xavier: home; shining
Xaverious, Xaveryus

Xavier ✿ (Arabic) home; shining
Saverio, Xaver, Zavey, Zavier

Xavion (Spanish) form of Xavier: home; shining

Xaxon (American) happy
Zaxon

Xayvion (African American) dwells in new house
Savion, Sayveon, Sayvion, Xavion, Xayveon, Zayvion

Xebec (French) from Quebec; cold
Xebeck, Xebek

Xen (African American) original
Zen

Xenik (Russian) sly
Xenic, Xenick, Xenyc, Xenyck, Xenyk

Xeno (Greek) gracious
Xenoes, Zene, Zenno, Zenny, Zeno, Zenos

Xenon (Greek) gracious

Xenophon (Greek) gracious

Xenos (Greek) with grace
Xeno, Zenos

Xerarch (Greek) dancing
Xerarche

Xeres (Persian) form of Xerxes: leader
Xeries

Xerxes (Persian) leader
Xerk, Xerky, Zerk, Zerkes, Zerkez

Xhosas (African) south African tribe
Xhoses, Xhosys

Xiaoping (Chinese) brightest star

Ximen (Spanish) obeys
Ximenes, Ximon, Ximun

Ximena (Spanish) good listener

Xing-Fu (Chinese) happy

Xi-Wang (Chinese) optimistic

Xochitl (Spanish) flowers

Xuthus (Last name as first name) long-suffering

Xyle (American) helpful
Zye, Zyle

Xylo (Greek) form of Xylon: forester

Xylon (Greek) forester

Xyshaun (African American) zany
Xye, Zye, Zyshaun, Zyshawn

Xyst (English) a portico; systematic
Xist

Xystum (Greek) promenade
Xistoum, Xistum, Xysoum

Xystus (Greek) promenade
Xistus

Y

Yaameen (Hebrew) right hand

Yachna (Hebrew) gracious

Yadid (Hebrew) friend

Yadon (Last name as first name) different
Yado, Yadun

Yadua (Hindi) judged

Yael (Hebrew) teacher
Yail, Yaley, Yalie

Yagil (Hebrew) celebrant

Yagna (Indian) devout

Yahir (Hebrew) enlightened

Yahne (Hebrew) adored

Yahya (Arabic) vital
Yahiya

Yair (Hebrew) strong

Yakar (Hebrew) adored

Yakez (Scandinavian) celestial

Yale (German) producer

Yalen (English) old soul

Yall (English) form of Yalman: old man

Yalman (English) old man

Yalon (English) form of Jalen: vivacious

Yamato (Japanese) mountain; scaling heights

Yamen (Indian) death god

Yan (Slavic) form of John: God is gracious

Yana (Native American) bearlike

Yance (American) from England

Yancy (American) vivacious
Yanci, Yancie, Yanzie

Yanis (Hebrew) God's gift
Yannis, Yantsha

Yank (American) Yankee
Yanke

Yankel (Hebrew) supportive
Yaki, Yakov, Yekel

Yannis (Greek) believer in God; form of John: God is gracious
Yannie

Yanny (Hebrew) learns

Yanto (French) confident

Yanton (Hebrew) form of Jonathan: gift of God

Yao (Chinese) athletic; (African) Thursday's child

Yaphet (Hebrew) form of Japheth: grows
Yapheth, Yefat, Yephat

Yar (English) forest

Yarb (Gypsy) spicy

Yarbon (English) surname

Yarbrough (English) surname

Yarden (Hebrew) flowing
Yard, Yardan, Yarde, Yardene, Yardun

Yardley (English) adorned; separate
Yard, Yarde, Yardie, Yardlea, Yardlee, Yardly, Yardy

Yared (Hebrew) form of Jared: descendant; giving

Yaren (Hebrew) form of Jaren: vocal

Yarkon (Hebrew) green

Yarom (Hebrew) sings
Yaron

Yash (Hindi) famous

Yashy (Indian) wealthy

Yasin (Arabic) seer

Yasir (Arabic) rich

Yasmuji (Asian) flowering

Yassah (Indian) famed

Yasuo (Japanese) calm

Yasutaro (Japanese) peaceful

Yates (English) smart; closed
Yate, Yattes, Yeats

Yati (Indian) beloved

Yave (Hindi) giving

Yavin (Hebrew) believes

Yaw (Akan) Thursday's child

Yawo (African) Thursday's child

Yay (African) Thursday's child

Yazeed (Arabic) growing in spirit

Yeardley (Indian) victor

Yeats (English) gates
Yates

Yeb (English) form of Jeb/Jacob: jolly; one who supplants

Yediel (Hebrew) loved by Jehovah

Yehem (Biblical) place name

Yehoshua (Hebrew) alive by God's salvation

Yehuda (Hebrew) praised
Yehudi

Yemin (Hebrew) guarded

Yemyo (Asian) serene

Yen (Chinese) calming; capable

Yenny (Biblical) place name

Yens (Vietnamese) yen; calm

Yeoman (English) helping
Yeomann, Yo, Yoeman, Yoman, Yoyo

Yered (Jewish) form of Jared: descendant; giving

Yerel (Indian) careful

Yero (African) studious

Yesel (Hebrew) won by God

Yeshaya (Hebrew) treasured

Yesher (Hebrew) God's salvation

Yeshurun (Hebrew) focuses on God

Yeshya (Hebrew) gifted

Yevgeny (Russian) life-giving

Yianni (Greek) creative

Yigal (Turkish) lively

Yimer (Scandinavian) giant**

Yiron (Czech) form of George: land-loving; farmer

Yishai (Hebrew) form of Jesse: wealthy

Yisrael (Hebrew) struggles with God

Yitro (Hebrew) form of Jethro: fertile

Yitzhak (Hebrew) laughing
Yitz, Yitzchak

Yngvar (Scandinavian) god of fertility
Ingvar;

Yo (Vietnamese) truthful

Yoav (Hebrew) form of Joab: praising God; hovering

Yobachi (African) prayerful

Yochanan (Hebrew) form of John: God is gracious
Yohanan

Yoel (Hebrew) form of Joel: Jehovah is the Lord

Yogesh (Hindi) another name for Hindu god Shiva

Yogi (Japanese) yoga practicer

Yoginee (Indian) yoga enthusiast

Yohance (Hebrew) form of John: God is gracious

Yohane (Hebrew) form of Johane: God is gracious

Yohann (German) form of Johann: God is gracious
Yohan, Yohn

Yohanys (German) form of Johane: God is gracious

Yoi (Hebrew) bounty

Yojiro (Japanese) hopes

Yolan (French) generous

Yolander (French) violet

Yonah (Hebrew) form of Jonah: peacemaker

Yonatan (Hebrew) form of Jonathan: gift of God
Yonathan, Yonathon

Yong (Chinese) brave

Yoosef (Hebrew) favorite
Yosef

Yoran (Hebrew) to sing

Yorick (Literature) Hamlet's jester

Yorik (English) farms

York (English) affluent
Yorke, Yorkee, Yorkey, Yorki, Yorky

Yorker (English) rich
York, Yorke, Yorkur

Yosef (Hebrew) form of Joseph: He will add
Yose, Yoseff, Yosif

Yosefu (Hebrew) form of Joseph: He will add

Yosemite (Place name) natural wonder

Yosh (Japanese) son

Yoshe (Hebrew) wise

Yoshiaki (Japanese) attractive

Yoshikatsu (Japanese) good

Yoshinobu (Japanese) goodness

Yoshio (Japanese) giving

Yossel (Hebrew) favored
Yoska, Yossi

Yosuke (Japanese) helps

Yosvani (Slavic) form of Johanne: God is gracious

Younes (Hebrew) form of Jonah: peacemaker

Young (English) fledgling
Jung, Younge

Younger (Scandinavian) young

Yoursie (American) form of Juri: farms

Yov (Russian) reliable

Yovan (Slavic) form of Jovan: gifted

Yri (Hebrew) form of Joseph: He will add

Yu (Chinese) shiny; smart

Yuan (Chinese) circle

Yudel (Hebrew) jubilant
Yudi

Yui (Chinese) moon; universal

Yuji (Japanese) snow

Yuke (American) form of Yukon: individualist

Yuki (Japanese) loves snow

Yukichi (Japanese) lucky snow

Yukien (Japanese) of the snows

Yukio (Japanese) man of snow

Yukon (Place name) individualist

Yul (Chinese) infinity

Yule (English) Christmas-born
Yuel, Yul, Yuley, Yulie

Yuli (Basque) childlike

Yuma (Place name) city in Arizona; cowboy
Yumah

Yunuen (Spanish) seer

Yunus (Turkish) young

Yurcel (Turkish) the best

Yuri (Russian) dashing
Yurah, Yure, Yurey, Yurie, Yurri, Yury

Yurik (Japanese) Yuri's child; (Slavic) form of Yorick: Hamlet's jester

Yuris (Latin) farmer
Yures, Yurus

Yuritzi (Slavic) form of Yuri: dashing

Yursa (Japanese) lily; delicate

Yurza (Slavic) form of George: land-loving; farmer

Yusuf (Arabic) form of Joseph: He will add

Yuta (Native American) hunts

Yutu (African) hunter

Yuval (Hebrew) celebrant

Yuvaraj (Indian) prince

Yux (Spanish) form of Joshua: devout

Yuz (Scandinavian) form of John: God is gracious

Yuzhi (Slavic) form of Joseph: He will add

Yves (French) honest; handsome
Eve, Ives

Yvonn (French) attractive
Von, Vonn, Yvon

Z

Zaavan (Biblical) God hides him

Zab (American) slick
Zabbey, Zabbi, Zabbie, Zabby

Zabel (Biblical) place name

Zac (Hebrew) form of Zachariah: Lord remembers
Zacary, Zach, Zachary, Zachry

Zaca (Hebrew) water movement

Zacary (Hebrew) form of Zachary: spiritual
Zac, Zacc, Zaccary, Zaccry, Zaccury

Zaccheus (Hebrew) unblemished
Zac, Zacceus, Zack

Zace (American) pleasure-seeking
Zacey, Zacie, Zase

Zach (Hebrew) form of Zachary: spiritual
Zac, Zachy

Zachariah (Hebrew) Lord remembers
Zac, Zacaria, Zacarias, Zacary, Zacaryah, Zaccaria, Zaccariah, Zaccheus, Zach, Zachaios, Zacharia, Zacharias, Zacharie, Zachary, Zacheriah, Zachery, Zacheus, Zachey, Zachi, Zachie, Zachy, Zack, Zackariah, Zackerias, Zackery, Zak, Zakarias, Zakarie, Zakariyyah, Zakery, Zechariah, Zekariah, Zeke, Zekeriah, Zhack

Zacharias (Hebrew) devout
Zacharyas

Zachary ✿ (Hebrew) spiritual
Zacary, Zacchary, Zach, Zackar, Zackarie, Zak, Zakari, Zakri, Zakrie, Zakry

Zack (Hebrew) form of Zachary: spiritual
Zacky, Zak

Zade (Arabic) flourishing; trendy
Zaid

Zadok (Hebrew) unyielding
Zadek, Zadik, Zayd, Zaydie, Zaydok

Zafar (Hindi) victor
Zaphar

Zafir (Arabic) wins

Zafeer, Zafyr

Zahavi (Hebrew) golden child

Zaher (American) exceeds

Zahir (Hebrew) bright

Zaheer, Zahur

Zahur (Arabic) flourishes

Zain (American) zany

Zane, Zayne

Zaire (Place name) country in Africa; brash

Zakary (Hebrew) form of Zachary: spiritual

Zakhar (Hebrew) pure of heart

Zakhary (Hebrew) form of Zachary: spiritual

Zaki (Arabic) virtuous

Zak

Zale (Greek) strong

Zail, Zaley, Zalie, Zayle

Zalman (Hebrew) peaceful

Salman, Zaloman

Zalmon (Jewish) form of Solomon: peaceful and wise

Zamar (Hebrew) sings

Zamen (Hebrew) form of Zalman: peaceful

Zamil (German) form of Samuel: man who heard God; prophet

Zameel, Zamyl

Zamir (Hebrew) lyrical

Zameer, Zamyr

Zammet (Slavic) head of household

Zamuel (Hebrew) variant on Samuel: man who heard God; prophet

Zan (Hebrew) well-nourished

Xan, Zander, Zandro, Zandros, Zann

Zanchet (French) homebody

Zand (Greek) form of Zander: great leader; helpful

Zander (Greek) form of Alexander: great leader; helpful

Zande, Zandee, Zandey, Zandie, Zandy

Zandy (American) high-energy

Zandee, Zandi

Zane (English) debonair

Zain, Zay, Zayne, Zaynne

Zano (American) unique

Zan

Zanoni (Unknown) from god Zeus

Zaphon (Biblical) God hides him

Zappa (American) zany

Zapah, Zapp

Zappe (Persian) happy

Zappy (Persian) jovial

Zar (African) watchful

Zared (Arabic) gold

Zarek (Aramaic) light

Zarel (Slavic) watchful

Zarethan (Biblical) helped by God

Zario (Biblical) place name

Zartavious (African American) unusual

Zar, Zarta

Zashawn (African American) fiery

Zasean, Zash, Zashaun, Zashe, Zashon, Zashone

Zasu (Slavic) form of Jose: asset; favored

Zauk (Slavic) form of Zac: Lord remembers

Zaul (American) form of Saul: gift

Zavel (American) youthful

Zavier (Arabic) form of Xavier: home; shining

Zavion (American) smiling

Zavien

Zayn (English) form of Zane: debonair

Zazel (Arabic) handsome

Zbigniew (Polish) free of malice; calming; relinquishes anger

Zeb (Hebrew) form of Zebediah: gift from God

Zebe

Zebby (Hebrew) believer; rambunctious

Zabbie, Zeb, Zebb, Zebbie

Zebediah (Hebrew) gift from God
Zeb, Zebadia, Zebb, Zebbie, Zebby,
Zebedee, Zebi, Zebidiah

Zebul (Hebrew) respected

Zebulon (Hebrew) uplifted
Zebulen, Zebulun, Zevulon, Zevulun

Zebulun (Hebrew) revered

Zechariah (Hebrew) form of
Zachariah: Lord remembers
Zeke

Zed (Hebrew) energetic
Zedd, Zede

Zedediah (Hebrew) form of
Zebediah: gift from God
Zededia, Zedidia, Zedidiah

Zedekiah (Hebrew) believing in a
just God
Zed, Zeddy, Zedechia, Zedechiah,
Zedekias

Zeeman (Dutch) seafaring
Zeaman

Zeevy (American) sly
Zeeve, Zeevi, Zeevie

Zef (Hebrew) wolf

Zeffy (American) explosive
Zeff, Zeffe, Zeffi, Zeffie

Zekarias (Dutch) impulsive

Zeke (Hebrew) friendly; outgoing
Zeek, Zekey, Zeki

Zekel (Hebrew) form of Ezekial:
God's strength

Zeker (Hebrew) form of Ezekial:
God's strength

Zekie (Turkish) bright mind

Zel (American) hearty

Zelalem (Biblical) form of Zel: hearty

Zelbie (Hebrew) delicate

Zelig (Hebrew) holy; happy
Selig, Zel, Zeligman, Zelik

Zelmon (English) man of peace

Zemaraim (Biblical) lion-like

Zen (Japanese) spiritual

Zenas (Greek) form of Zeus:
powerful
Zenios, Zenon

Zenen (Biblical) place name

Zenib (Greek) life of Zeus

Zenith (Word as name) famous

Zeno (Greek) philosophical; stoic
Zeney, Zenie, Zenno, Zeny

Zenobios (Greek) living Zeus; lively
Zenobius, Zinov, Zinovi

Zenon (Greek) form of Xenon:
gracious

Zenotis (Greek) form of Zeus:
powerful

Zenovial (Greek) form of Zeus:
powerful

Zent (American) zany
Zynt

Zeph (Greek) form of Zephyr: breezy

Zephaniah (Hebrew) protected by
God
Zeph, Zephan

Zephariah (Hebrew) Jehovah's light

Zephen (Greek) form of Zephyr:
breezy

Zepho (Greek) form of Zephyr:
breezy

Zephyr (Greek) breezy
Zayfeer, Zayfir, Zayphir, Zefar, Zefer,
Zeffer, Zefir, Zefur, Zephir, Zephiros,
Zephirus, Zephyrus

Zerah (Biblical) light

Zero (Arabic) nothing
Zeroh

Zerond (American) helpful
Zerre, Zerrie, Zerry, Zerund

Zes (Biblical) place name

Zeshon (African American) zany
Zeshaune, Zeshawn

Zeson (Spanish) fair

Zestler (Last name as first name)

Zete (Hebrew) shiny

Zeth (American) form of Seth: chosen
Zethe

Zeus (Greek) powerful
Zues

Zev (Hebrew) form of Zebulon: uplifted
Zevv

Zevediah (Hebrew) form of Zebediah; broken dreams
Zevedia, Zevidia, Zevidiah

Zevi (Hebrew) brisk
Zevie

Zevry (Biblical) place name

Zevulon (Hebrew) form of Zebulon: uplifted
Zevulonn

Zexi (Asian) hopeful

Zhen (Chinese) pure

Zhivago (Russian) dashing; romantic
Vago

Zhobin (Slavic) form of George: land-loving; farmer

Zhong (Chinese) middle brother; loyal

Zia (Hebrew) in motion
Zeah, Ziah

Ziad (Arabic) of the light

Zibeon (Arabic) vibrant growth

Zichri (American) form of Zachary: spiritual

Zie (American) compelling
Zye, Zyey

Ziggy (American) zany

Zigmand (American) form of Sigmund: victor

Zig, Ziggy

Ziklag (Biblical) place name

Zikomo (African) grateful

Zilph (Biblical) place name

Zimran (Hebrew) sacred

Zimri (Hebrew) valued

Zin (Biblical) praised

Zinc (Biblical) place name

Zindel (Yiddish) form of Alexander: great leader; helpful
Zindil

Zingo (American) zany

Zino (Greek) philosopher
Zeno

Zion (Hebrew) sign; omen
Sion, Zeione, Zi, Zione, Zye

Zional (Biblical) place name

Zior (African) sky

Ziph (Biblical) place name

Zipkiyah (Native American) archer

Zirkle (Biblical) place name

Zito (Italian) growth

Ziv (Hebrew) energetic
Zeven, Zevy, Ziven, Zivon

Ziven (Polish) lively
Ziv, Zivan, Zyvan

Ziya (Turkish) light

Ziz (Hebrew) sign

Zlatko (Slavic) gold

Zoan (Biblical) place name

Zoar (Biblical) place name

Zobah (Biblical) place name

Zobel (Biblical) place name

Zober (African) strong

Zocco (American) form of Zach: spiritual

Zochi (Turkish) form of Zekie: bright mind

Zohar (Hebrew) light

Zohreh (Indian) blooms

Zoilo (Greek) life; (Spanish) lively

Zol (American) jaunty
Zoll

Zoltan (Hungarian) lively

Zolten-Penn (Hungarian) lively

Zoma (American) loquacious
Zome

Zook (American) form of Zach: spiritual

Zoran (Slavic) dawn

Zorba (Greek) pleasure seeker
Zorbah, Zorbe

Zorby (Greek) tireless
Sorby, Zorb, Zorbie

Zorshawn (African American) jaded
Zahrshy, Zorsh, Zorshie, Zorshon, Zorshy

Zowie (Greek) life
Zowey, Zowy

Zoy (English) life-giving

Zuad (American) devout

Zuadan (American) invented from
Sudan

Zub (Russian) toothy

Zuba (Iranian) attractive

Zuberi (African) powerful
Zooberi, Zubery

Zubren (African) strength

Zucker (English) penitent

Zuhair (Arabic) shines

Zuhayr (Arabic) flowers
Zuhair

Zuhier (American) shines

Zulfer (American) leads

Zumrud (American) unique

Zuni (Native American) creative

Zuriel (Hebrew) believer

Zurlo (American) zany

Zury (Spanish) believer

Zuzel (Spanish) sweet

Zvon (Croatian) form of Zvonimir:
sound of peace
Zevon, Zevonn

Zvonimir (Croatian) sound of peace

Zwie (Spanish) from Jose

Zygmunt (Slavic) form of Sigmund:
victor

Zyke (American) high-energy
Zykee, Zyki, Zykie, Zyky

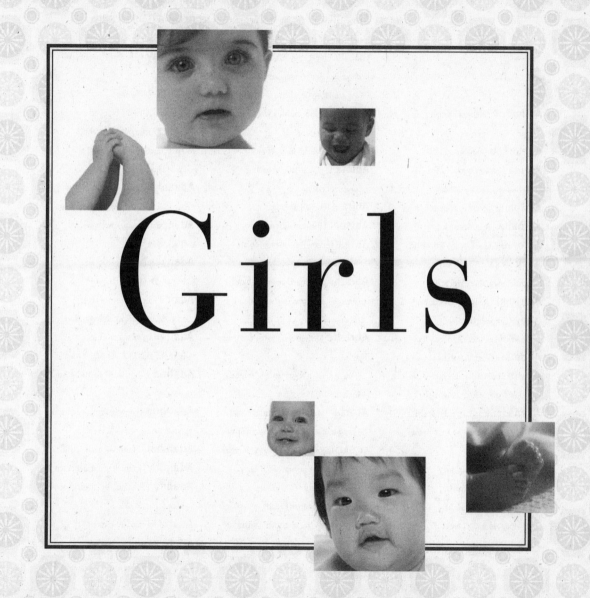

Girls

A

Aaliyah ✪ (Hebrew) moving up
Aliya

Aamori (African) good

Aarika (Welsh) form of Erika:
honorable; leading others

Aarionne (Welsh) knowing

Aaronita (American) knowing

Aaronitia (American) knowing

Abay (Native American) growing
Abai, Abbay, Abey, Abeye

Abayomi (African) giving joy

Abby (English) happy
Abbee, Abbey, Abbi, Abbie, Abbye

Abdulia (Spanish) certain

Abella (French) vulnerable; capable
Abela, Abele, Abell, Bela, Bella

Abena (African) Tuesday's child

Abery (Last name as first name)
supportive
Abby, Aberee, Abrie, Abry

Abha (Hindi) lustrous

Abia (Arabic) excellent
Ab, Aba, Abiah, Abbie

Abida (Arabian) worships

Abigail ✪ ✆ (Hebrew, English, Irish) joyful
Abagail, Abbegayle, Abbey, Abbie, Abby, Abegail, Abey, Abigal, Abigale, Abigayle, Abygail, Abygale, Abygayle, Gail, Gayle

Abilene (Place name) Texas town; southern girl
Abalene, Abi, Abiline, Aby

Abiola (Spanish) God-loving
Abby, Abi, Biola

Abira (Hebrew) strong

Abisael (Biblical) joyful

Abra (Hebrew) example; lesson
Aba, Abbee, Abbey, Abbie, Abby

Abrianna (American) insightful
Abriana, Abryana, Abryanna, Abryannah

Abrielle (American) form of Abigail: joyful
Abby, Abree, Abrey, Abrie, Abriella, Abryelle

Acacia (Greek) everlasting; tree
Akaysha, Cacia, Cacie, Case, Casey, Casha, Casia, Caysha, Kassy, Kaykay

Acadia (Algonquian-Wakashian) place of plenty

Acalena (English) ready

Acantha (Greek) thorny; difficult

Acatia (Greek) forever tree

Accalia (Latin) stand-in
Accal, Accalya, Ace, Ackie

Achantay (African American) reliable
Achantae, Achanté

Ackalin (Greek) beloved nymph

Ackee (American) fall child

Ada (German) noble; joyful
Adah, Addah, Adeia, Aida

Adaani (French) pretty; noble
Adan, Adane, Adani, Daani, Dani

Adaeze (African) prepared
Adaese

Adah (Biblical) decorated
Ada, Adie, Adina, Dina

Adair (Scottish) innovative
Ada, Adare, Adayr, Adayre, Adda

Adalia (Spanish) spunky
Adahlia, Adailya, Adallyuh, Adaylia

Adalind (American) form of Adeline: sweet

Adalinda (French) form of Adelle: giving

Adamina (Hebrew) earth child

Adamita (Spanish) first on earth

Adanna (Spanish) beautiful baby
Adana

Adar (Hebrew) respected

Adara (Greek) lovely
Adarah, Adrah

Addison ✪ ⊺ (English) awesome
Addeson, Addie, Addisen, Addison,
Addy, Addyson, Adeson, Adisen

Addy (English) nickname for
Addison: distinctive; smiling
Addee, Addie, Addye, Adie, Ady

Adea (English) decorative

Adeen (American) decorated
Addy, Adeene, Aden, Adene, Adin

Adekunle (African) crowned at sea

Adela (Polish) peacemaker

Adelaida (Spanish) noble

Adelaide (German) calming;
distinguished
Ada, Adalaid, Adalaide, Adelade,
Adelaid, Laidey

Adelbola (Spanish) brave

Adeline (English) sweet
Adaline, Adealline, Adelenne, Adelina,
Adelind, Adlin, Adline

Adelita (Spanish) form of Adela:
peacemaker
Adalina, Adalita, Adelaina, Adelaine,
Adeleta, Adey, Audilita, Lita, Lite

Adelka (German) form of Adelaide:
calming; distinguished
Addie, Addy, Adel, Adelkah, Adie

Adelle (German) giving
Adel, Adell, Addy

Adelpha (Greek) beloved sister
Adelfa, Adelphe

Adena (Hebrew) precious
Ada, Adenna, Adina, Adynna, Deena,
Dena

Adeniji (Biblical) believer

Adern (Welsh) birdlike
Adyrn

Aderyn (Hebrew) form of Adira:
strong

Adesina (African) threshold child

Adess (Hebrew) decorated

Adhelia (Spanish) of the stars

Adia (African) God's gift

Adiel (African) goat; tough-willed
Adie, Adiell, Adiella

Adil (English) noble born

Adina (Hebrew) high hopes
Addy, Adeen, Adeena, Adine, Deena,
Dena, Dina

Adira (Hebrew) strong

Adisa (Hispanic) friendly
Adesa, Adissa

Aditi (Hindi) free

Adiva (Arabic) gracious

Adjanys (Hispanic) lively
Adjanice, Adjanis

Adline (German) reliable
Addee, Addie, Addy, Adleen, Adlene,
Adlyne

Adolpha (German) noble wolf;
strong girl
Adolpham

Adonia (Greek) beauty
Adona, Adonea, Adoniah, Adonis

Adora (Latin) adored child
Adorae, Adoray, Dora, Dore, Dorey,
Dori, Dorree, Dorrie, Dorry

Adoracion (Spanish) adores

Adoraia (Spanish) adoration

Adoral (Spanish) adored baby

Adoria (Spanish) adored

Adorna (Latin) adorned

Adra (Greek) beauty

Adria (Latin) place name
Adrea

Adrian (English) rich
Adrien, Adryan, Adryen

Adriana ⊺ (Latin) rich; exotic
Addy, Adree, Adrianna, Adrie, Adrin,
Anna

Adrienne (Latin) wealthy
Adreah, Adreanne, Adrenne, Adriah,
Adrian, Adrien, Adrienn, Adrin, Adrina

Aegle (Greek) radiant

Aereale (Hebrew) form of Ariel:
God's lion
Aereal, Aeriel, Areale

Aerena (Welsh) feminine form of
Aaron: revered; sharer

Aeronwenn (Welsh) white; aggressor
Awynn

Affrica (Irish) nice

Afiniti (American) affinity

Afiny (Hebrew) doe

Afra (Arabic) deer; lithe; reddish
Aphra, Aphrah, Ayfara

Africa (Place name) continent
Afrika

Afton (English) confident
Aft, Aftan, Aften, Aftie

Afua (African) baby born on Friday
Afuah

Agafi (Greek) form of Agnes: pure
Ag, Aga, Agafee, Agaffi, Aggie

Agapi (Greek) love
Agapay, Agape, Agappe

Agasha (Greek) form of Agatha:
kindhearted
Agashah, Agashe

Agata (Italian) good girl

Agate (English) gemstone; precious
girl
Agatte, Aget, Aggey, Aggie

Agatha (Greek) kindhearted
*Agath, Agathah, Agathe, Aggey, Aggie,
Aggy*

Agatta (Greek) form of Agatha:
kindhearted
*Ag, Agata, Agathi, Aggie, Agi, Agoti,
Agotti*

Agave (Botanical) strong-spined;
genus of plants
Ag, Agavay, Aggie, Agovay

Agentina (Spanish) form of
Argentina: confident; land of silver
Agen, Agente, Tina

Aggie (Greek) kindhearted
Aggee, Aggy

Aggieth (English) form of Agnes:
pure

Aglae (French) splendid

Aglaia (Greek) goddess of beauty;
splendid

Agnes (Greek) pure
*Ag, Aggie, Aggnes, Aggy, Agnas, Agness,
Agnie, Agnus, Nessie*

Agnesa (Spanish) pure

Aharona (Hebrew) beloved
Arni, Arnina, Arona

Ahimsa (Hindu) virtuous

Ahisa (Spanish) pure

Ahtena (Hebrew) aware

Ahulani (Hawaiian) heavenly place

Ahvanti (African) focused
Avanti

Aida (Arabic) gift
Aeeda, Ayda, Ayeeda, Ieeda

Aidan (Irish) form of the masculine
name Aidan: bold spirit
Aden, Aiden, Aidyn

Aileen (Gaelic) fair-haired beauty
*Aleen, Alene, Alenee, Aline, Allee,
Alleen, Allene, Allie, Ally*

Ailey (Irish) form of Aileen: fair-
haired beauty
Aila, Ailee, Ailie, Ailli, Allie

Ailsa (Irish) noble

Aimee (French) beloved
Aime, Aimey, Aimi, Aimme, Amee, Amy

Aimer (German) leader; loved
Aimery, Ame, Amie

Ainda (American) sure

Aine (Irish) blissful
Ayne

Ainsley (Scottish) meadow;
outdoorsy
*Ainslea, Ainslee, Ainsleigh, Ainslie,
Anes, Anslie, Aynslee, Aynsley*

Aintre (Irish) joyous estate
Aintree, Aintrey, Antre, Antry

Aisha (Arabic) life; lively
*Aaisha, Aaysha, Aeesha, Aiesha,
Aieshah, Ayeesha, Ayisha, Aysha,
Ieashia, Ieeshah, Iesha*

Aisling (Irish) dreamy

Aislinn, Ashling, Isleen

Aislinn (Irish) dreamy

Aisling, Aislyn, Aislynn

Aislinning (Irish) dreamy

Aithne (Irish) fiery

Aine, Eithne, Ena, Ethne

Aja (English) leads

Ajalae (Egyptian) leader

Aka (Hawaiian) regal

Akako (Japanese) red; blushes

Akala (Hawaiian) respected

Akiva (African) morning's baby

Aky (American) lively

Ala (Arabic) excellent

Alla

Alabama (Place name) western

Bama

Alaine (Gaelic) lovely

Alaina, Alaiyne, Alenne, Aleyna, Aleyne,
Allaine, Allayne

Alala (Roman mythology) sister of
Mars; protected

Alalah

Alalia (German) joyful

Alama (American) lovely

Alameda (Spanish) poplar tree;
growth

Alana (Scottish) pretty girl

Alahna, Alahnah, Alaina, Alainah,
Alanah, Alanna, Alannah, Allana,
Allie, Ally

Alanie (Hawaiian) peace

Alanis (French) shining star

Alaniss, Alannis, Alannys, Alanys

Alaoha (American) dear child

Alason (German) form of Allison:
kindhearted

Ala, Alas

Alathea (English) heals and helps

Aleta, Letitia, Letty

Alaula (English) heals and helps

Alaygrah (Invented) form of Allegra:
snappy

Alay, Allay

Alaytheea (Invented) form of
Alethea: truthful

Alay, Thea, Theea

Alba (Italian) white

Alberta (French) bright-eyed

Alb, Albertah, Albie, Albirta, Alburta,
Bertie, Berty

Albertina (Portuguese) bright

Albertine (English) feminine form of
Albert: distinguished

Albertyne, Albie, Albyrtine, Teeny

Albie (American)

Albee, Albey, Alby, Albye

Albina (Italian) white

Albyna

Alcina (Greek) magical; strong-willed

Alcee, Alcie, Als, Alsena, Alsie. Cina,
Seena, Sina

Alda (German) the older child

Aldine (Place name) elder

Aldona (American) sweet

Aldone

Alea (Arabic) excellent

Alaya, Aleah, Aleeah, Alia, Ally

Alechia (Greek) everlasting

Aleeza (Hebrew) joy

Aliza

Alegria (Spanish) beautiful movement

Allegria

Alejandra (Spanish) defender

Alijandra, Alyjandra

Alejandrina (Spanish) defender of
friends

Aleksandra (Russian) form of
Alexandra: defender of mankind

Alencia (German) cleansed

Aleshia (Greek) honest

Aleeshia, Aleeshya, Aleshya, Alyshia,
Alyshya

Alessa (Italian) helper

Alesa

Alessandra (Italian) form of
Alexandra: defender of mankind
Aless, Alessa

Alessia (Italian) nice
Alesha, Allyshia, Alyshia

Alethea (Greek) truthful
*Alathea, Aleethia, Aletha, Aletie,
Altheia, Lathea, Lathey*

Aletta (Greek) carefree
Aleta, Eletta, Letti, Lettie, Letty

Aleviyah (Arabic) helpful

Alex (English) protector

Alexa ✪ (Greek) form of Alexandra:
defender of mankind
*Alecksa, Aleksah, Alex, Alexia, Alixa,
Alyxa*

Alexandra ✪ (Greek) defender of
mankind
*Alejandra, Alejaundro, Alex,
Alexandrah, Alexandria, Alexis,
Alezandra, Allesandro, Ally, Lex, Lexi,
Lexie*

Alexandrine (French) helpful
Alex, Alexandrie, Ally, Lexi, Lexie

Alexcia (English) gracious

Alexi (Greek) form of Alexis: defender
of mankind
*Alexie, Alexy, Alixi, Alixie, Alixy, Alyxi,
Alyxie*

Alexia (Greek) helpful; bright
*Alexea, Alexiah, Alixea, Lex, Lexey,
Lexie, Lexy*

Alexina (Scottish) helper

Alexis ✪ ⊕ (Greek) form of
Alexandra: defender of mankind
*Aleksus, Alexius, Alexus, Alexys, Lex,
Lexey, Lexi, Lexie, Lexis, Lexus*

Alfonsith (German) aggressive
*Alf, Alfee, Alfey, Alfie, Alfonsine, Allfrie,
Alphonsine, Alphonsith*

Alfre (English) form of Alfreda: wise
advisor
Alfree, Alfrey, Alfri, Alfrie, Alfry

Alfreda (English) wise advisor
*Alfi, Alfie, Alfred, Alfredah, Alfrede,
Alfredeh, Freda, Freddy*

Alfreida (English) wisdom

Algorita (Spanish) eager

Ali (Greek) form of Alexandra:
defender of mankind
Aley, Allee, Alley, Ally, Aly

Alia (Arabic) sky girl

Alianet (Spanish) honest; noble
Alia, Aliane

Alice (Greek) honest
*Alece, Alicea, Alise, Alliss, Ally, Allys,
Alyse, Alysse, Lisie, Lisy, Lysse*

Alicea (Spanish) noble

Alicha (Slavic) joy

Alicia (Greek) delicate; lovely
Alisha

Alida (Greek) stylish
*Aleda, Aleta, Aletta, Alidah, Alita, Lee,
Lida, Lita, Lyda*

Alima (Hebrew) strong

Alin (Scottish) lovely

Alina (Slavic) form of Helen:
beautiful; light
*Aleena, Alene, Aline, Allene, Allie, Ally,
Allyne, Alyna, Lena, Lina*

Alinalette (Spanish) noble

Aline (Polish) form of Alina:
beautiful; light
Aleena, Alene, Aline, Allie, Ally

Alisa (Hebrew) happy
Alissa, Allisa, Allissah, Alyssa

Alisha (Greek) happy; truthful
*Aleesha, Alesha, Alicia, Ally, Allyshah,
Alysha, Lesha, Lisha*

Alison (Scottish) noble
Alisen

Alissa (Greek) pretty
*Alesa, Alessa, Alise, Alissah, Allee, Allie,
Ally, Allyssa, Alyssea*

Alita (Native American) sparkling

Alix (Greek) form of Alexandra:
defender of mankind

Aliya (Hebrew) rises; sweetheart
Aleeya, Alya

Aliza (Jewish) joy child

Alka (Polish) distinctive
Alk, Alkae

Alke (English) form of Elke:
distinguished

Allaire (Scottish) open-minded

Allegra (Italian) snappy
Aligra, All, Allagrah, Allie, Alligra, Ally

Allena (Greek) outstanding
Alena, Alenah, Allana, Allie, Ally

Allene (Greek) wonderful
Alene, Alyne

Allesia (English) alyssum flower girl

Allessandra (Italian) kindhearted
Allesandra

Allicent (English) form of Alice:
honest

Allie (Greek) smiling
Ali, Allee, Alli, Ally, Allye

Allison ✪ (English) kindhearted
Alisen, Alison, Allicen, Allie, Allisan, Allisen, Allisun, Ally, Allysen, Allyson, Alysen, Alyson, Sonny

Allura (Hispanic) alluring
Alura

Ally (Greek) pure heart
Allee, Alleigh, Alley, Alli, Allie

Allyson (English) another form of
Allison: kindhearted
Alisaune, Allysen, Allysun, Alyson

Allysse (Greek) smooth
Allice, Allyce, Allyss

Alma (Latin) good; soulful
Almah, Almie, Almy

Almaree (Spanish) smart

Almeida (Spanish) shines; goal-
oriented

Almeria (Arabic) princess
Alma, Almara, Almaria, Almer, Almurea, Als

Almira (Arabic) princess
Allmeerah, Almirah, Elmira, Mira

Alodia (Spanish) thrives; free

Alodie (Origin unknown) thriving
Alodee

Aloha (Hawaiian) love

Aloma (Jewish) form of Alona: sturdy
oak

Alona (Jewish) sturdy oak
Allona

Alonda (Spanish) form of Alexandra:
defender of mankind
Alona

Alondra (Spanish) bright
Alond, Alondre, Alonn

Alouette (French) birdlike
Allie, Allo, Allou, Allouetta, Alou, Alowette

Aloyse (German) renowned
Aloice, Aloise, Aloyce

Alpha (Greek) first; superior
Alf, Alfa, Alfie, Alph, Alphah, Alphia, Alphie

Alphareen (Spanish) first chosen

Alston (English) a place for a noble
Allie, Ally, Alstan, Alsten, Alstun

Alta (Latin) high place; fresh

Altagracia (Spanish) in God's grace

Altea (Polish) healer

Althaea (Greek) pure

Althea (Greek) wholesome
Althe, Althey, Althia, Althie, Althy, Thea, They

Altisha (English) other girl

Alula (Arabic) little maiden girl

Alundey (American) jaunty

Alva (Spanish) fair; bright
Alvah

Alvada (American) evasive
Alvadah, Alvayda

Alverna (English) elf friend
Alver, Alverne, Alvernette

Alvernise (English) form of Alverna:
elf friend
Alvenice

Alvina (English) beloved; friendly
Alvee, Alveena, Alvie, Alvine, Alvy

Alvinetta (English) popular friend

Alvita (Latin) charismatic

Alyasha (Arabic) heaven's child**

Alyda (French) soaring
Aleda, Alida, Alita, Lida, Lyda

Alynn (Dutch) intelligent

Alys (English) noble

Alysea (English) high-born

Alysia (Greek) compelling
Aleecia, Alesha, Alicia, Alish, Alycia

Alyssa ✿ (Greek) flourishing
Alissa, Allissa, Allissae, Ilyssah, Lissa, Lyssa, Lyssy

Alysse (English) form of Alice: honest

Alyx (English) form of Alex: protector

Amaba (African) amiable

Amabe (Latin) loved
Ama

Amabelle (American) loved
Amabel, Amahbel

Amada (Spanish) form of Amanda: fit to be loved
Ama, Amadah

Amal (Arabic) optimistic
Amahl

Amalia (Hungarian/Spanish) industrious

Amalina (German) worker
Am, Ama, Amaleen, Amaline, Amalyne

Amalita (Spanish) hopeful

Amalthea (Greek) perseveres

Amanda (Latin) fit to be loved
Amand, Amandah, Amandy, Manda, Mandee, Mandi, Mandy

Amandra (American) form of Amanda: fit to be loved
Amand, Mandee, Mandi, Mandra, Mandree, Mandry, Mandy

Amara (Latin) everlasting
Am, Amarah, Amareh, Amera, Amura, Mara

Amarillo (Spanish) yellow
Ama, Amari, Amarilla, Amy, Rillo

Amaris (Hebrew) beloved; dedicated
Amares

Amaryllis (Greek) fresh flower
Ama, Amarillis

Amber (French) gorgeous and golden; semiprecious stone
Ambar, Amberre, Ambur, Amburr

Ambike (Hindi) fertile

Amboree (Last name as first name) precocious
Ambor, Ambree

Ambre (French) kinetic energy

Ambree (French) amber color

Ambrin (Greek) long life

Ambrosette (Greek) eternal
Amber, Ambie, Ambro, Ambrosa, Ambrose

Ambrosia (Greek) eternal
Ambroze, Ambrozeah, Ambrozia

Ambrosina (Greek) everlasting
Ambrosine

Amelia ✿ (German) industrious
Amalee, Amaylyuh, Amele, Ameleah, Ameli, Amelie, Amelya, Amilia

Amelina (Spanish) diligent

Ameline (French) diligent

Amelita (Spanish) diligent

Amera (Arabic) of regal birth
Ameera, Amira

America (American) patriotic
Amer, Amerca, Americah, Amerika, Amur

Ameth (Greek) precious gem; amethyst

Amethyst (Greek) precious gem
Amathist, Ameth

Amia (German) loved

Amica (Latin) good friend
Ameca, Ami, Amika

Amici (Italian) friend
Amicie, Amie, Amisie

Amie (French) loved one

Amig (Slavic) loved

Amiga (Spanish) friend
Amigah

Amilla (Slavic) form of Camilla: wonderful

Amina (Arabic) trustworthy

Amena, Amine

Aminta (Latin) protects

Amira (Arabic) nurturer

Amirreza (Spanish) eloquent

Amity (Latin) a good friend

Amitee, Amitey, Amiti

Amiya (Slavic) defense

Amna (Indian) gracious

Amnette (American) haven

Amone (American) harmony

Amor (Spanish) love

Amora, Amore

Amora (Spanish) love

Amorelle (French) lover

Amoray, Amore, Amorel, Amorell

Amoretta (French) little love

Amoreta, Amorreta, Amorretta

Amorette (French) tiny love

Amorrette

Amorita (Spanish) loved

Ampar (Spanish) protected

Amrita (Indian) nectar of immortality

Amvi (Hindi) goddess

Amy ✪ (Latin) loved one

Aimee, Amee, Amey, Ameyye, Ami,
Amie, Amye

Amyrka (Spanish) lively

Amerka, Amurka, Amyrk, Amyrrka

Anabelia (Slavic) well-loved

Anabril (Spanish) merciful; pretty

Anabrelle, Anna, Annabril

Anadare (Hawaiian) graceful

Anahi (Biblical) responsive

Anahita (Hindi) graceful

Anaid (Slavic) kind

Anais (French) form of Anne: loving;
hospitable

Anala (Hindi) fiery

Analae (Hindi) excellent

Analeese (Scandinavian) gracious

Analece, Analeece, Annaleese

Analia (Hebrew) gracious; hopeful

Ana, Analea, Analeah, Analiah, Analya

Analisa (American) lovely

Analy (American) graceful; gracious

Analee, Anali

Anamita (Spanish) enamored

Anand (Hindi) joyful; profound

Anan, Ananda

Anandy (Indian) joy girl

Anapua (Hawaiian) flourishes

Anareli (Spanish) happy

Anastace (Spanish) form of
Anastasia; resurrection

Anastayce, Anestace, Anestayce, Anystace,
Anystayce

Anastasia (Greek) resurrection

Anastasiya, Anastasya

Anastay (Greek) born again;
renewed

Ana, Anastae, Anastie

Anastice (Latin) form of Anastasia:
resurrection

Anasteece, Anesteece, Anestice, Anysteece,
Anystice

Anatola (Greek) from the east

Anatol, Anatole

Anaysis (Latin) form of Anastasia:
resurrection

Anaysys

Anca (Scandinavian) alone

Ancheene (American) creative

Anchoret (Welsh) beloved girl

Ancita (Spanish) favorite

Ancret (Welsh) form of Anchoret:
beloved girl

Ander (Greek) feminine

Anders (Scandinavian) stunning

Andars, Andie, Andurs, Andy

Andes (Greek) feminine

Andee

Andi (English) casual

Andee, Andey, Andie, Andy

Andraa (Greek) feminine

Andrah

Andrea ✪ (Greek) feminine

Andee, Andi, Andie, Andra, Andrae,
Andre, Andreah, Andreena

Andreana (Greek) bold heart
Andreanna, Andriana, Andrianna,
Andryana, Andryanna

Andree (Greek) strong woman
Andrey, Andrie, Andry

Andrenna (Scottish) pretty; gracious
Andreene, Adrena

Andrianna (Greek) feminine
Andree, Andy

Andromeda (Greek) beautiful star
Andromedah

Aneechia (Slavic) pure

Anees (Indian) grace

Aneeta (Indian) grace

Aneith (Slavic) pure

Aneka (Polish) forgiving

Anela (Hawaiian) angelic

Anelica (Spanish) pleasant

Anelka (Slavic) forgives

Anemone (Greek) breath of fresh air

Anetra (Slavic) gracious

Anewk (Invented) form of Anouk:
loving; hospitable

Anganetta (Slavic) angelic

Ange (Greek) form of Angela: angelic;
divine

Angeele (English) lithe angel

Angel (Latin) sweet; angelic
Angelle, Angie, Anjel, Annjell

Angela (Greek) divine; angelic
Angelena, Angelica, Angelina, Angelle,
Angie, Gela, Nini

Angelia (American) angelic
messenger
Angelea, Angeliah

Angelica (Latin) angelic messenger
Angie, Anjeleka, Anjelica, Anjelika,
Anjie

Angelika (Greek) angel
Angelyka, Angilika, Angilyka, Angylika

Angelina ✪ (Latin) angelic
Ange, Angelyna, Angie, Anje, Anjelina,
Anjie

Angeline (American) angelic
Angelene, Angelline

Angelique (French) form of
Angelica: angelic messenger
Angel, Angeleek, Angelik, Angie, Anjee,
Anjel, Anjelique

Angelle (Latin) angelic
Ange, Angell, Anje, Anjell, Anjelle

Angerona (Mythology) angelic

Angha (Hindi) beauty

Angharad (Welsh) graceful
Angahard

Angie (Latin) angelic
Angey, Angi, Angye, Anjie

Aniani (Hawaiian) lovely reflection

Anice (Slavic) form of Anne: gracious

Anick (Hebrew) gracious

Aniece (Hebrew) gracious
Ana, Anesse, Ani, Anice, Annis, Annissa

Aniela (Polish) sent by God
Ahneela

Anika (Hebrew) hospitable
Anec, Anecca, Aneek, Aneeka, Anic,
Anica, Anik, Annika

Anila (Hindi) wind girl

Anina (Aramaic) answer my prayer

Aninda (German) form of Anina:
answer my prayer

Anisha (English) purest one
Aneesha, Anysha

Anissa (Greek) a completed spirit
Anisa, Anise, Anysa, Anyssa, Anysse

Anita (Spanish) gracious
Aneda, Aneeta, Anitta, Anyta

Anitia (Spanish) favored

Anitria (Spanish) favored

Aniyalla (Scandinavian) beloved

Anjali (Hindi) pretty; honored
Anjaly

Anjana (Hindi) merciful; pretty
Anjann

Anjelica (Latin) angelic
Anjelika

Anjeliett (Spanish) little angel
Anjel, Anjeli, Jelette, Jeliett, Jeliette, Jell,
Jelly

Anjul (French) jovial

Angie, Anjewel, Anji, Anjie, Anjool

Anka (Polish) favorite

Anmol (Hindi) valued

Ann (Hebrew) loving; hospitable

Aine, An, Ana, Anna, Anne, Annie,
Ayn

Anna ♥ ☕ (Hebrew) gracious

Ana, Anae, Anah, Annah, Anne, Anuh

Annabella (Italian) lovely girl

Anabela, Anabella, Annabela

Annabelle (English) lovely girl

Anabell, Anabelle, Annabell

Annal (Slavic) form of Anna: gracious

Annalee (English) form of Anne:
gracious

Annalie (Scandinavian) form of
Annalee: gracious

Annaliea (English) form of Annalee:
gracious

Anna-Margarita (Spanish) devout

Ann-Dee (American) courage

Andee, Andey, Andi, Andy, Ann Dee,
Anndi

Anne (English) gracious

Anneka (Scandinavian) form of
Anne: gracious

Anneke

Annelie (German) girl of grace

Anneliese (Scandinavian/German)
form of Anna: gracious, and Liesa:
God is bountiful

Aneliece, Aneliese

Annella (Scottish) graceful

Anell, Anella, Anelle

Annemarie (German) bitter grace

Anmarie, Anne-Marie, Ann Marie,
Annmarie

Annena (Slavic) chosen

Annes (Hebrew) hospitable

Annette (American) vivacious; giving

Anette, Ann, Anne, Annett, Annetta,
Annie, Anny

Anngelite (Slavic) angel

Annice (English) pure of heart

Annie (English) form of Anne:
gracious

Ann, Annee, Anney, Anni, Anny

Annika (Scandinavian) gracious

Anika

Anninka (Russian) gracious;
graceful

Annis (English) pure

Annys

Annissa (Greek) gracious; complete

Anissa, Anni, Annie, Annisa

Annjanette (Mythology) quiet
goddess

Annletta (English) little Ann

Annunciata (Italian) noticed

Anona (Botanical) pineapple; fresh

Anora (Latin) honored

Anouk (French) form of Ann: loving;
hospitable

Anoush (Armenian) sweetness

Anselma (German) helmet of God

Ansley (English) happy in the
meadow

Annesleigh, Ans, Anslea, Anslee,
Ansleigh, Ansli, Anslie

Ansonia (Scandinavian) pure

Anstass (Greek) resurrected; eternal

Ans, Anstase, Stace, Stacey, Stass, Stassee

Anstice (Greek) everlasting

Anst, Steece, Steese, Stice

Answer (Word as name) the answer

Ansylene (English) God protects

Antenise (English) flowering

Anthea (Greek) flowering

Anthia

Antigone (Greek) impulsive; defiant

Antique (Word as name) old soul

Anteek, Antik

Antoinette (French) priceless

Antoine, Antoinet, Antwanett,
Antwonette, Toinette, Tonette

Antonella (French) form of
Antoinette: priceless

Antonetta (Greek) praised

Antoneta

Antonia (Latin) perfect

Antone, Antonea, Antoneah

Antonian (Latin) valuable

Antoinette, Antonetta, Toni, Tonia,

Tonya

Antonine (Greek) praised

Antonyne

Antronette (English) form of

Antoinette: priceless

Antwanette (African American)

prized

Antwan, Antwanett

Anupama (Indian) unusual

Anusha (Armenian) sweet

Anya (Russian) grace

Aoife (Irish) beauty

Apalonia (Greek) girl with strength

and light

Aphra (Hebrew) earthy; sentimental

Af, Affee, Affey, Affy, Afra, Aphree,

Aphrie

Aphrodite (Greek) goddess of love

and beauty

Afrodite, Aphrodytee

Api (Latin) rejoice

Apolinaria (Spanish) form of

Apollonia: sun goddess

Apolinara

Apollonia (Greek) sun goddess

Apolinia, Apolyne, Appollonia

Apple (Botanical) fruit; quirky

Apel, Appell

April (Latin) month; springlike

Aprel, Aprile, Aprille, Apryl

Aptha (Biblical) growing

Aqua (Spanish) colorful

Akwa

Aquanetla (Invented) spontaneous

Aqueelah (Arabic) vigilant

Aquen (Native American) calm

Aquilline (American) eagle eye

Arabella (Latin) answer to a prayer;

beauty

Arabel, Arabela, Arabelle, Arbel,

Arbella, Bella, Belle, Orabele, Orabella

Arabelle (Latin) divine

Arabell

Araceli (Latin) heavenly

Ara, Aracelli, Ari

Aracelle (Spanish) flamboyant;

heavenly

Ara, Aracel, Aracell, Araseli, Celi

Arachne (Greek) weaver; spider

Araiza (Spanish) innovator

Araminta (English) unique; precious

dawn

Ara, Arama, Aramynta, Minta

Araxie (Spanish) creative

Arayalle (English) form of Arielle:

God's lion

Araylia (Latin) golden

Araelea, Aray, Rae, Ray

Arbela (Biblical) place name

Arbra (American) form of Abra:

example; lesson

Arbrae

Arce (Spanish) gift

Arcelia (Spanish) treasured

Arcey, Arci, Arcilia, Arla, Arlia

Arcelious (African American)

treasured

Arce, Arcel, Arcelus, Arcy, Arselious

Archana (Indian) loyal worshipper

Archon (American) capable

Arch, Archee, Archi, Arshon

Ardana (English) ardent

Ardath (Hebrew) ardent

Ardee, Ardie, Ardith, Ardon

Ardele (Latin) enthusiastic; dedicated

Ardell, Ardella, Ardelle, Ardine

Ardelphia (Place name) flourishes

Arden (Latin) ardent; sincere

Ardan, Ardena, Ardin, Ardon, Ardyn

Ardery (English) form of Arden:

ardent; sincere

Ardiana (Spanish) ardent

Ardi, Ardie, Diana

Ardie (American) enthusiastic; special
Ardee, Ardi

Ardienne (American) ardent

Ardina (English) ardent

Ardithan (American) sincere

Ardyss (American) ardent

Areika (Spanish) pure
Areka, Areke, Arika, Arike

Arekah (Greek) virtuous; loving

Arelie (Latin) golden girl
Arelee, Arely, Arlea

Aretha (Greek) virtuous; vocalist
Areetha

Aretta (Greek) virtuous
Arette, Arie

Argelia (Spanish) treasured

Argenta (Latin) silver

Argentina (Place name) confident;
land of silver
Arge, Argen, Argent, Argenta, Argie,
Tina, Tinee

Argosy (French) bright
Argosee, Argosie

Argus (Greek) bright
Arguss

Ari (Hebrew) form of Ariel: God's lion
Aree, Arey, Arie, Ary

Aria (Hebrew) form of Ariel: God's
lion; (English) song
Arya

Ariadna (Slavic) holiest

Ariadne (Greek) holiness
Aryadne

Ariana ☉ (Greek) righteous
Arianna

Arianda (Greek) helper
Ariand

Ariane (Greek) very gracious
Arianne, Aryahn

Arianne (French) kind
Ana, Ari, Ariann

Arianwen (Welsh) form of
Aeronwenn: white; aggressor

Arica (Scandinavian) form of Erica:
honorable; leading others

Aridatha (Hebrew) flourishing
Ar, Arid, Datha

Aridna (English) form of Ariadne:
holiness

Aridne (English) form of Ariadne:
holiness

Ariedsol (Spanish) blessed

Ariel (Hebrew) God's lion
Aeriel, Airey, Arielle

Ariella (French) lioness
Ariela, Aryela, Aryella

Aries (Latin) zodiac sign of the ram;
contentious
Arees

Arin (Arabic) spreads truth
Aryn

Arina (Russian) peaceful

Aris (Greek) best

Arisca (Greek) form of Arista:
wonderful
Ariska, Ariske

Arista (Greek) wonderful

Aristelle (Greek) wonder
Aristela, Aristella

Arith (Hebrew) believes

Aritha (Greek) virtuous
Arete, Aretha

Arizona (Place name) U.S. state;
grand
Zona

Arketta (Invented) outspoken
Arkett, Arkette, Arky

Arlais (Welsh) magical

Arlanda (Slavic) dedicated

Arlea (Greek) heavenly
Airlea, Arlee, Arleigh, Arlie, Arly

Arleana (American) form of Arlene:
dedicated
Arlena, Arlina

Arlen (Irish) devoted
Arlin, Arlyn

Arlena (Irish) dedicated
Arlana, Arlen, Arlenna, Arlie, Arlina,
Arlyna, Arrlina, Lena, Lina, Linney

Arlene (Irish) dedicated

Arlee, Arleen, Arlie, Arline, Arlyne, Arlynn, Lena, Lina

Arlette (French) loyal

Arlet

Arli (English) proactive; girl from rabbit field

Arlind (American) strong; loyal

Arlitra (American) strength of character

Arlyn (Irish) dedicated

Armanda (French) disciplined

Armani (Italian) fashionable

Armanee, Armanie, Armond, Armonee, Armoni, Armonie

Armanth (English) goal-oriented

Armelle (French) armed

Armetrice (Spanish) armed

Armida (Latin) armed; prepared

Armi, Armid, Army

Arminda (Spanish) armed

Armineh (Slavic) defends

Arminell (Latin) nobility

Arminel

Arminta (Slavic) armed

Arna (Slavic) eagle watch

Arnetta

Arnette (English) little eagle; observant

Arn, Arnee, Arnet, Arnett, Ornette

Arnica (American) eagle; intense

Arnite (American) eagle; intense

Arnyx (American) eagle-eyed

Arosa (Spanish) rose

Arosell (Last name as first name) loyal

Arosel

Arpine (Romanian) dedicated

Arpyne

Array (Word as name) colorful

Arrissie (American) the sea

Artemis (Greek) moon goddess

Artemisia (Greek) belonging to Artemis

Arta, Arte, Artema

Arthel (Greek) rich

Arthlese (Irish) rich

Arth, Arthlice, Artis

Arthurena (American) feminine form of Arthur: bear; stone

Arthurene

Artranese (American) hunts

Artriece (Irish) stable

Artee, Artreese, Arty

Artulia (Spanish) high position

Aruna (Hindi) baby of dawn

Arunice (English) silver girl

Arvilla (English) climber

Arvis (American) special

Arvee, Arvess, Arvie, Arviss, Arvy

Arya (Jewish) lioness

Aryana (English) form of Ariana: righteous

Asabi (African) outstanding

Asalia (Spanish) morning child

Asenath (Biblical) possessed of God's spirit

Ash (Hebrew) form of Asha: lucky

Ashe

Asha (Hebrew) lucky

Aasha, Ashah, Ashra

Ashandra (African American) dreamer

Ashan, Ashandre

Ashanti (African) graceful

Ashantay, Anshante

Ashantia (American) outgoing

Ashantea, Ashantiah

Asharaf (Hindi) wishful

Asha, Ashara

Ashby (English) farm of ash trees

Ashbee

Asher (Hebrew) blessed

Ash

Ashla (English) form of Ashley: woodland sprite

Ashland (Irish) dreamlike

Ashelyn, Ashlan, Ashleen, Ashlin, Ashlind, Ashline, Ashlinn

Ashlei (English) form of Ashley: woodland sprite
Ashee, Ashie, Ashly, Ashy

Ashleigh (English) from the ash tree meadow
Ashlynn, Ashton

Ashley ♀ ♂ (English) woodland sprite
Ash, Ashie, Ashlay, Ashlea, Ashlee, Ashleigh, Ashli, Ashlie, Ashly

Ashlyn (English) natural
Ashlin, Ashlinn, Ashlynn

Ashna (Indian) hopeful

Ashonika (African American) pretty
Ashon, Ashoneka, Shon

Ashton (English) from an eastern town; sassy
Ashe, Ashten, Ashtun, Ashtyn

Asia (Greek) sunrise
Ashah, Asiah, Asya, Aysia, Azhuh

Asli (Turkish) authentic

Asma (Arabic) exalted; loyal

Asmay (Origin unknown) special
Asmae, Asmaye

Asmillinda (Spanish) loyal

Asminda (Arabic) loyal

Asoka (Japanese) morning baby

Asp (Greek) form of Aspasia: witty

Aspasia (Greek) witty
Aspashia, Aspasya

Aspen (Place name) city in Colorado; earth mother
Aspin, Aspyn, Azpen

Asphodel (Greek) lily beauty

Asra (Hindi) pure
Azra

Asrika (Slavic) striking

Asta (Greek) star

Astar (Greek) starry-eyed

Astera (Greek) starlike
Asteria, Astra, Astree, Astrie

Astra (Greek) starlike
Astrah, Astrey

Astraea (Greek) starlike

Astrid (Scandinavian/German) fair; beautiful goddess
Aster, Asti, Astred, Astri, Astridd, Astryd, Astrydd, Atty, Estrid

Asusena (Slavic) lovely fragrance

Asysa (Arabic) lively
Aesha, Asha, Aysah

Atalanta (Greek) athletic; fleet-footed
Addi, Atlante, Attie

Atanasia (Spanish) form of the name Anastasia: resurrection

Atara (Hebrew) crowned

Athalet (American) believes

Athalia (Hebrew) ambitious

Athamadia (Greek) believer

Athelean (Greek) eternal; precocious
Athey, Athi

Athena (Greek) wise woman; goddess of wisdom in mythology
Athene, Athenea, Athina, Xena, Zena

Athene (Chinese) wise

Atherine (Spanish) form of Katherine: pure

Athie (Hebrew) wise
Athee, Athey, Athy

Athinoulla (American) praiseworthy

Atianna (American) believer

Atifa (Arabic) compassionate
Ateefah

Atornett (American) off-center

Atropos (Mythology) one of the Greek Fates; cutter

Atu (American) treasured

Aube (French) form of Aubrey: ruler

Auber (French) bright

Aubrey ♀ (French/German) ruler
Aubery, Aubey, Aubrea, Aubree, Aubreye, Aubri, Aubrie, Aubry

Auburne (American) tough-minded
Aubee, Aubern, Auberne, Aubey, Aubi, Aubie, Auburn, Auby

Auden (English) oldest friend

Audia (French) noble

Audie (English) noble strength

Audee, Audey, Audi, Audy, Audye

Audra (English) exciting

Audrah, Audray

Audrea (English) highborn

Audrette (French) highborn

Audrey ○ (Old English) strong and
regal

*Audi, Audie, Audra, Audree, Audreen,
Audreye, Audri, Audrianna, Audrianne,
Audrie, Audrina, Audry*

Augusta (Latin) revered

*Augustah, Auguste, Augustia,
Augustyna, Austina*

Augustene (English) serious

Augustina (Latin) great

*Agustico, Agustin, Augusine, Augustine,
Gusty, Tina, Tino*

Augustine (Latin) dignified;
worthwhile

*Augestinn, Augusta, Augustina,
Augustyna, Augustyne, Austie, Austina,
Austine, Tina*

Aundra (Scandinavian) highborn

Aunjanue (French) sparkling

Aunshaunte (African American)
believer

*Anshauntay, Aunshauntay,
Aunshawntay, Aunshawnte, Shauntae,
Shauntay, Shaunte*

Aunzell (American) magical

Aupra (Slavic) form of Audra:
exciting

Aura (Greek) breeze

Arra

Aurelia (Latin) dawn goddess

*Arelia, Aura, Auralea, Aurel, Aurelie,
Auria, Auriel, Aurielle*

Aurelien (Slavic) golden ornament

Aurian (English) form of Arianne:
kind

Auriel (Latin) gold

Auriol

Auristela (Latin) star

Aurora (Latin) morning glow

Aurorah, Aurore, Rory

Aury (American) golden dawn

Aurysia (Latin) gold

Arys, Arysia, Aurys

Austeena (American) statuesque

Austeenah, Austie, Austina

Austen (Literature) for author Jane
Austen; charming

Austyn

Austine (Latin) respected

Austen, Austene, Austin

Authorea (American) dawning

Autminia (Spanish) child of autumn

Autra (Latin) gold

Autumn ○ ⊙ (Latin) joy of
changing seasons

Autum, Autumm

Ava ○ ⊙ (Latin) pretty; delicate bird

Avah, Eva

Avalon (Celtic) paradise

Avedis (Spanish) welcomes

Avena (Latin) basic; oat field

Avengelica (Spanish) avenging

Angelica, Avenga, Avengele, Gelica

Averil (French) flighty

*Ava, Averile, Averill, Averyl, Averyll,
Aviril*

Avery ○ ⊙ (French) flirtatious

Avary, Averee, Averi, Averie

Aves (Greek) breath of fresh air

Aviana (Latin) fresh

Avianca (Latin) fresh

Avino (Hebrew) believes in God

Avis (Latin) little bird

Avisae (American) springlike

Ava, Avas, Aves, Avi

Aviva (Hebrew) springlike

Avivah

Avivi (Jewish) spring child

Avolonne (African American) happy

*Avalonn, Ave, Avelon, Avlon, Avo,
Avolon, Avolunne*

Avon (English) graceful

Avaughn, Avaugn, Avonn, Avonne

Avonnia (English) graceful; of Avon

Avril (French) April; springlike

Avrit (Hebrew) fresh

Avie, Avree, Avret, Avrie

Awen (Welsh) wise and gentle

Axelle (French) serene

Axel, Axell

Aya (Hebrew) bird in flight

Ayan (Hindi) pure

Ayun

Ayanna (Hindi) innocent

Ayunna

Ayda (Arabic) comes back

Ayeisha (Arabic) feminine

Aeesha, Aieshah, Asha, Ayeeshea, Ayisa,
Iasha, Yeisha, Yeishee, Yisha, Yishie

Ayena (Native American) joyful; pure

Ayesha (Arabic) living

Ayla (Hebrew) strong as an oak

Aylee (Hebrew) light

Ayleen (Hebrew) light-hearted

Aylene

Aylin (Spanish) strong

Aylen

Aylun (Hebrew) strong

Aylwin (Welsh) beloved

Ayle, Aylwie

Aynet (Spanish) grace

Aynona (Hebrew) form of Anne:
gracious

Ayn, Aynon, Aynonna, Aynonne

Ayo (African) joyful

Ayva (American) form on Ava: pretty;
delicate

Azadeth (Biblical) form of Asenath:
possessed of God's spirit

Azalea (Latin) earthy; flowering

Azalee, Azelea

Azalia (Spanish) flower girl

Azami (Japanese) flower

Azenet (Spanish) sun; God's gift

Aza, Azey

Azenett (Spanish) God's child

Azimah (Japanese) Azami: flower

Aziza (African) beloved; vibrant

Asisa

Azriella (Hebrew) form of Ariella:
lioness

Azriela, Azryela, Azryella

Azsure (American) form of Azura:
blue-eyed

Azucena (Spanish) lily pure

Azu, Azuce, Azucina

Azura (French) blue-eyed

Azuhre, Azur, Azure, Azurre, Azzura

B

Baako (Japanese) promising; happy

Baba (American) fun-loving

Babe (Latin) little darling; baby

Babette (French) little Barbara

Babs (American) form of Barbara:
traveler from a foreign land

Baca (Biblical) place name; happy

Bachi (Japanese) happy

Bachee, Bachey, Bachie, Bochee

Bachiko (Japanese) happy

Baden (German) friendly

Boden, Bodey

Baderinwa (African) worthy

Badger (Irish) badger

Badge

Badri (African) moon baby

Badriyyah (Arabic) surprise

Baek (Origin unknown) mysterious

Baffin (Place name)

Bagent (Last name as first name)

baggage

Bage

Bagula (German) enthused

Bahaar (Hindi) spring

Bahama (Place name) islands; sun-loving
Baham

Bahati (African) lucky girl
Baha, Bahah

Bahija (Arabic) excelling
Bahiga

Bahir (Arabic) striking
Bah, Baheer, Bahi

Bahira (Arabic) bright mind

Bai (Chinese) outgoing

Baiben (Irish) sweet; exotic
Babe, Bai, Baib, Baibe, Baibie, Baibin

Bailey ✿ (English) bailiff
Bailee, Baylee, Bayley, Baylie

Bailon (American) form of Bailey: bailiff
Bai, Baye, Baylon

Bain (American) thorn; pale
Baine, Bane, Bayne

Baird (Irish) ballad singer
Bayrde

Bairn (Scottish) child
Bairne

Baka (Hindi) crane; long-legged
Baca

Bakara (African) noble

Bakul (Hindi) flowering
Bakula

Bakura (Hebrew) ripe; prime
Bikura

Balala (Hindi) hopes

Balaniki (Hawaiian) angelic

Balbina (Latin) stammers
Balbine

Baldree (German) brave; loquacious
Baldry

Bali (Place name) island near Indonesia; exotic

Balinda (Slavic) form of Belinda: beautiful

Ballou (American) outspoken
Bailou, Balou

Balvino (Spanish) powerful
Balvene, Balveno

Bambi (Italian) childlike; baby girl
Bambee, Bambie, Bambina, Bamby

Banan (Punjabi) held close

Banht (Hindi) fire

Banita (Hindi) girl; thoughtful

Banjoko (Asian) joy

Banner (Word as name) flamboyant

Bano (Persian) bride
Bannie, Banny, Banoah, Banoh

Bao (Chinese) adorable; creative

Bao-Jin (Chinese) precious gold

Bao-Yo (Chinese) jade; pretty

Baptista (Latin) one who baptizes
Baptiste, Batista, Battista, Bautista

Bara (Hebrew) chosen
Bari, Barra

Barb (Latin) form of Barbara: traveler from a foreign land

Barbara (Greek) traveler from a foreign land
Babb, Babbett, Babbette, Babe, Babett, Babette, Babina, Babita, Babs, Barb, Barbary, Barbe, Barbette, Barbey, Barbi, Barbie, Barbra, Barby, Basha, Basia, Bobbie, Bobi

Barbarette (English) form of Barbara: traveler from a foreign land

Barbrette (English) ill-fated

Barbro (Swedish) extraordinary
Bar, Barb, Barbar

Barcelona (Place name) city in Spain; exotic
Barce, Lona

Barcie (American) sassy
Barsey, Barsi

Bariah (Arabic) does well

Barika (Hebrew) chosen one

Barkait (Arabic) shines
Barkat

Baronetta (English) feminine form of Baron: noble leader

Barran (Arabic) song

Barrent (Last name as first name) hill child

Barrett (Last name as first name) happy girl

Bari, Barret, Barrette, Barry, Berrett

Barrie (Irish) markswoman; candid

Barron (Last name as first name) bright

Bare, Baron, Barrie, Beren, Beron

Barrow (Last name as first name) sharp; sly

Barow

Basey (Last name as first name) beauty

Bacie, Basi

Bashiyra (Arabic) joyful

Basia (Greek) regal

Basha, Basya

Basilia (Greek) regal

Basila, Basilea, Basilie

Basimah (Arabic) smiling

Basima, Basma

Baskama (Biblical) place name; fragrant

Bassen (American) queen

Bastienna (French) form of masculine name Bastien: respected

Bastee, Bastienne

Bat (German) female warrior

Bet

Bathia (German) warrior woman

Basha, Baspa, Batia, Batya, Bitya

Bathilda (German) woman in war

Bathild, Bathilde, Berthilda, Berthilde

Bathsheba (Hebrew) beautiful; daughter of Sheba

Bathseva, Batsheba, Batsheva, Batshua, Sheba

Bathshira (Arabic) happy; seventh

Batia (Hebrew) daughter of God

Batea, Batya

Batice (American) warrior; attractive

Bateese, Batese, Batiece, Batty

Batini (African) ponders much

Batzra (Hebrew) daughter of God

Bay (Vietnamese) Saturday's child; patient; unique

Bae, Baye

Bayani (Indian) joy

Bayla (Indian) young girl

Bala

Baylor (French) of the bay; water-loving

Bayler

Baynes (American) feminine form of Baines: pale

Bain, Baines, Bayne

Bayo (African) bringing joy

Bayonne (Greek) joyful victor

Bay, Baye, Bayonn, Bayonna, Bayunn

Bea (American) form of Beatrice: blessed woman

Beama (English) blessed

Beata (German) blessed

Bayahta, Beate

Beatha (Latin) blessed

Betha

Beatrice (Latin) blessed woman

Beat, Beatrisa, Beatrise, Beattie, Bebe, Bee, Beitris, Beitriss, Bibi, Treece, Trice

Beatrix (Latin) happy

Beatriz (Spanish) form of Beatrice: blessed woman

Bebe (French) baby

Babee, Baby, Bebee

Bebhinn (Irish) sweet girl

Becca (Hebrew) form of Rebecca: loyal

Bekka

Becerra (Spanish) safe haven

Bechira (Hebrew) chosen child

Becky (English) form of Rebecca: loyal

Becki, Beki

Bedelia (Irish) form of Bridget: powerful

Bedriska (Irish) form of Bedelia: powerful

Bee (American) form of Beatrice: blessed woman

Beegee (American) laidback; calm

B.G., Begee, Be-Gee

Beeja (Hindi) the beginning; happy

Beej

Bee-Sun (Filipino) nature-loving; glad

Bee Sun

Bego (Hispanic) spunky

Beago

Begonia (Botanical) flower

Behira (Hebrew) shines

Behorah (Invented) friend

Be, Behi, Behie, Behora

Beige (American) tawny; calm

Bayge

Beige-Dawn (American) clear morning

Bayge-Dawn, Beige Dawn

Beila (Spanish) beautiful

Bejoy (American) filled with joy

Bel (Latin) beauty

Bela (Czech) white

Belah

Belann (Spanish) pretty

Bela, Belan, Belana, Belane, Belanna

Belay (English) white

Belem (Spanish) pretty

Bel, Beleme, Bella

Belems (American) relinquishes

Belen (Latin) beauty

Belgica (American) white

Belgika, Belgike, Belgyke, Bellgica

Belia (Spanish) beauty

Belea, Beliano, Belica, Belicia, Belya, Belyah

Belicia (Spanish) believer

Belia

Belinda (Spanish) beautiful

Belynda

Belita (Spanish) little beauty

Bella (Italian) beautiful

Bellace (Invented) pretty

Bellase, Bellece, Bellice

Belle (French) beautiful

Bela, Bele, Bell, Bella

Bellina (French) beautiful

Bellona (Mythology) strong and lovely

Belva (Latin) beautiful view

Belvia (Invented) practical

Bell, Belva, Belve, Belveah

Bemedikta (Scandinavian) form of Benedicta: blessed

Benedikte

Bena (Native American) pheasant; highbrow

Bendite (Latin) well-blessed

Ben, Bendee, Bendi, Bennie, Benny, Binni

Bene (Latin) blessed

Benecia (Latin) form of Benedicta: blessed

Benedeto (Italian) form of Benedicta: blessed

Benedetto

Benedetta (Latin) form of Benedicta: blessed

Benedicte, Benedikta, Benetta, Benita, Benni, Benoite

Benedicta (Latin) feminine form of Benedict: blessed

Benna, Benni

Benigna (Spanish) kind

Benilda (German) struggles

Bening (Filipino) blessing

Benita (Latin) feminine form of Benedict: blessed

Bena, Benetta, Benitri, Bennie, Binnie

Benneta (Spanish) pretty

Bennetteta (Spanish) blessing

Benni (Latin) form of Benedicta: blessed

Bennie, Binny

Benson (Last name as first name) Ben's child

Benta (Latin) much blessed

Bente (Latin) blessed

Bentley (English) meadow; luxury life

Bentlea, Bentlee, Bentleigh, Bently

Beon (Biblical) place name

Beonn (American) good girl

Bera (German) bearish

Berachan (Hebrew) blessing

Beracha, Berucha, Beruchiya, Beruchya

Berdina (German) bright; robust

Berd, Berdie, Berdine, Berdyne,

Burdine, Burdynne, Dina, Dine

Berdine (German) glows

Berecyntia (Mythology) earth goddess

Berenjena (Spanish) eggplant

Bergen (American) pretty

Berg, Bergin

Berget (Irish) form of Bridget:

powerful

Bergette

Berit (Scandinavian) glorious

Beret, Berette

Berkley (American) smart

Berkeley, Berkie, Berklie, Berkly

Bermuda (Place name) island;

personable

Bermudoh

Bernadette (French) form of

Bernadine: brave

Berna, Bernadene, Bernadett,

Bernadina, Bernarda, Bernardina,

Bernardine, Berneta, Bernetta, Bernette,

Berni, Bernie, Bernita, Berny

Bernadine (German) brave

Bernadene, Berni, Bernie

Bernardita (Spanish) brave little

bear

Berneen (Irish) hearty

Berney (English) brave bear

Bernice (Greek) victorious

Beranice, Berenice, Bernelle, Berneta,

Bernetta, Bernette, Berni, Bernicia,

Bernie, Bernyce

Bernie (American) winning

Bernee, Berney, Berni, Berny

Bernita (Greek) form of Bernice:

victorious

Berry (Botanical) tiny; succulent

Berree, Berri, Berrie

Bersaida (American) sensitive

Bersaid, Bersaide, Bersey, Bersy, Sada,

Saida

Berta (German) bright

Bertel (Slavic) smart

Bertha (German) bright

Barta, Berta, Berte, Berthe, Berti,

Bertie, Bertilda, Bertilde, Bertina,

Bertine, Bertita, Bertuska, Berty, Bird,

Birdie, Birdy, Birtha

Bertie (German) bright

Bert, Bertee, Bertey, Berty

Bertille (German) form of Bertha:

bright

Bertina (German) feminine form of

Bert: shining bright

Bertrice (French) form of Beatrice:

blessed woman

Berule (Greek) bright; pure

Berue, Berulle

Berura (Hebrew) chaste

Beruria

Beryl (Greek) bright and shining gem

Beril, Berlie, Berri, Berrill, Berry,

Beryla, Beryle, Beryn

Bess (Hebrew) form of Elizabeth:

God's promise

Bessie

Bet (Hebrew) daughter

Beta (Greek) from Greek alphabet;

beginning

Betka, Betuska

Beth (Hebrew) form of Elizabeth:

God's promise

Betha (Welsh) devoted to God

Bethah, Bethanne

Bethamie (English) form of

Bethany: God's disciple

Bethann (English) combo of Beth

and Ann; devout

B-Anne, Bethan, Beth-ann, Bethanne

Bethany (Hebrew) God's disciple
Beth, Bethanee, Bethani, Bethania, Bethanie, Bethann, Bethanne, Bethannie, Bethanny, Betheny, Bethina

Bethel (Hebrew) in God's house; holy child

Bethesda (Hebrew) child of a merry home

Bethia (Hebrew) Jehovah's daughter
Betia, Bithia

Beti (English) small woman

Betricia (American) form of Patricia: woman of nobility; unbending

Betriss (Welsh) blessed
Betrys

Bets (Jewish) God's child

Betsayra (Spanish) abundance

Betsy (Hebrew) form of Elizabeth: God's promise
Bet, Betsey, Betsi, Betsie, Betts

Betta (Italian) form of Bettina: God's promise

Bette (French) lively; God-loving

Betty (Hebrew) form of Elizabeth: God's promise
Bett, Betti, Bettye

Betuel (Hebrew) in God's house
Bethuel

Betula (Hebrew) dedicated; religious
Bee, Bet, Bethula, Bethulah, Bett, Betulah

Beulah (Hebrew) married
Bealah, Beula, Bew, Bewla

Beulahma (Biblical) marries

Bev (English) form of Beverly: beavers by the stream; friendly

Beverly (English) beavers by the stream; friendly
Bev, Beverelle, Beverle, Beverlee, Beverley, Beverlie, Beverlye, Bevvy, Verly

Bevina (Irish) vocalist
Beavena, Bev, Beve, Beven, Bevena, Bevin, Bevy, Bovana

Bevinn (Irish) royal
Bevan

Bezetha (Biblical) place name

Bhamini (Hindi) beautiful girl

Bhanumati (Hindi) bright

Bharaati (Hindi) careful

Bhavika (Hindi) devoted girl

Bhuma (Hindi) of the earth

Bian (Vietnamese) hides from life

Bianca (Italian) white
Beanka, Beonca, Beyonca, Biancha, Biancia, Biankah, Bionca, Bionka, Blanca, Blancha

Bibi (Arabic) lady
Bebe, Bibiana, Bibianna, Bibianne, Bibyana

Bibiane (Latin) vibrant

Bice (Last name as first name) axe; sharp talent

Bidelia (Irish) form of Bridget: powerful
Bedilia, Biddy, Bidina

Bienvenida (Spanish) welcomed baby

Bijou (French) jewel
Bejeaux, Bejou, Bejue, Bidge, Bija, Bijie, Bijy

Bik (Chinese) jade

Bikini (Place name) island girl; fun-loving
Bikinee

Bilhah (Biblical) summer's child

Billie (German) feminine form of Bill: staunch protector
Billa, Billee, Billey, Billi, Billy, Billye

Billina (English) feminine form of Bill: staunch protector
Belli, Bill, Billee, Billie, Billy

Billings (American) bright
Billey, Billie, Billing, Billy, Billye, Billyngs, Byllings

Bina (Hebrew) perceptive woman; (Indian) musical instrument
Bena, Binah, Byna

Binali (Hindi) music girl

Binase (Hebrew) bright
Beanase, Benace, Bina, Binah, Binahse

Binti (African) dancer

Binyamina (Hebrew) right hand

Bionda (Italian) black
Beonda, Biondah

Bira (Hebrew) fortified; strong
Biria, Biriya

Bircit (Scandinavian) form of Bridget: powerful

Bird (English) birdlike
Birdy

Birdie (English) bird
Birdee, Birdey, Birdi, Byrdie

Birdron (German) of birds

Birgit (Scandinavian) spectacular
Bergette, Berit, Birgetta, Birgite, Britta, Byrget, Byrgitt

Birgitta (Scandinavian) form of Bridget: powerful
Birgette, Brita, Byrgetta, Byrgitta

Birgitte (Scandinavian) strong

Birte (Scandinavian) form of Bridget: powerful
Berty, Birt, Birtey, Byrt, Byrtee

Birthenne (American) born lucky

Bishop (Last name as first name) loyal
Byshop

Bita (Hebrew) form of Bithia: Jehovah's daughter

Bitha (Biblical) blessed daughter

Bithia (Hebrew) Jehovah's daughter

Bithron (Biblical) resounding

Bitina (Mythology) darkness
Libitina

Bitki (Spanish) form of Beatrix: happy

Bitsie (American) small
Bitsee, Bitzee, Bitzi, Bytsey

Bitta (Scandinavian) form of Bridget: powerful
Bit, Bitt, Bittey

Bittan (Origin unknown) gives joy

Bivona (African American) feisty
BeBe, Biv, Bivon, Bivonne

Bjork (Icelandic) unique
Byork

Blade (English) glorified
Blaide, Blayde

Blaine (Irish) thin
Blane, Blayne

Blair (Scottish) plains-dweller
Blaire, Blayre

Blaise (Latin/French) lisp; stutter
Blaize, Blasé, Blaze

Blake (English) dark

Blakely (English) dark
Blakelee, Blakeley, Blakeli

Blanca (Spanish) white
Blancah, Blonka, Blonkah

Blanche (French) white
Blanca, Blanch, Blancha, Blanchette, Blanka, Blanshe, Blenda

Blanchefleur (French) white flower; pretty

Blanchine (French) white

Blanda (Latin) seductive
Blandina, Blandine

Blanka (Spanish) form of Blanca: white

Blasia (Spanish) form of Blaise; stutter

Blasie (French) blaze; stammering

Blath (Irish) flower

Blaze (Englush) fiery
Blaize, Blayze

Bleinda (American) form of Belinda: beautiful

Blesida (Spanish) blessed

Bless (American) blessed
Blessie

Blessing (English) dedicated

Blessy (American) blessed

Bleu (French) blue
Blue

Blima (Hebrew) blossoming girl
Blimah, Blime

Bliss (English) blissful girl

Blodwen (Welsh) white flower
Blodwyn, Blodyn

Blom (Hebrew) form of Blum: flower

Blonda (English) blonde

Blondelle (French) blonde girl
Blondell, Blondie, Blondy

Blondie (American) blonde
Blondee

Blossom (English) flower

Bluebell (Botanical) pretty
Belle, Blu, Blubel, Blubell, Blue, Bluebelle

Blum (Hebrew) flower
Bluma

Blumelle (English) flowers

Blush (American) pink-cheeked
Blushe

Bly (American) soft; sensual
Blye

Blyde (English) obliging

Blydece (English) obliging

Blythe (English) carefree
Blithe, Blyth

Bo (Chinese) precious girl

Boanah (American) good
Boana, Bonaa, Bonah, Bonita

Bobbi (American) form of Roberta:
brilliant mind
Bobbee, Bobbette, Bobbie, Bobby,
Bobbye, Bobi, Bobina

Bobett (American) form of Roberta:
brilliant mind

Bodil (Polish) heroic
Bothild, Botilda

Bogdana (Polish) gift from God
Boana, Bocdana, Bogda, Bogna,
Bohdana, Bohdana, Bohna

Bogdanka (Slavic) God's gift

Bogumila (Polish) loved by God

Boguslawa (Polish) in God's glory

Boinaiv (Native American) girl in the
grass

Bola (Origin unknown) clever
Bolo

Bolade (African) honored girl

Bolanile (African) rich in spirit

Bolda (Slavic) embolden

Boleslawa (Polish) strong

Bona (Italian) good
Bonah, Bonna

Bonbon (American) goodness

Boncela (Spanish) good

Boncie (Spanish) good

Bonda (Spanish) good
Bona

Bondeau (American) pretty

Bonett (Spanish) pretty

Bonfilia (Italian) good daughter

Bong-Cha (Korean) excellent
daughter

Bonille (Italian) goodness

Bonita (Spanish) good; pretty
Bo, Bona, Boni, Bonie, Bonitah, Nita

Bonn (French) satisfied; good
Bon, Bonne

Bonnefin (Spanish) good end

Bonnevie (Scandinavian) good life

Bonnie (Scottish) fine; attractive;
pretty
Boni, Bonie, Bonne, Bonnebell, Bonnee,
Bonni, Bonnibel, Bonnibell, Bonnibelle,
Bonny

Bonosse (American) generous

Booth (German) from the dwelling;
home-loving
Boothe

Bootsey (American) cowgirl
Boots, Bootsie

Bopelo (African) confident

Borghild (Scandinavian) prepared

Borgny (Scandinavian) fortified;
strong

Bors (Latin) foreign
Borse

Boske (Hungarian) strays

Boston (Place name) city in Massachusetts; courteous
Boste, Bosten, Bostin

Boswell (Last name as first name) intellectual
Boz, Bozwell

Boupha (Vietnamese) flower girl

Boussaina (Arabic) smiles

Bowdy (American) outgoing
Bow, Bowdee, Bowdey, Bowdie

Boxidara (Slavic) divine
Boza, Bozena, Bozka

Bozena (Polish) treasured

Bracha (Hebrew) blessed; sways in wind
Brocha

Bradley (English) girl of the broad meadow; carefree
Bradlee, Bradleigh, Bradlie, Bradly

Brady (Irish) spirited child
Bradee, Bradey, Bradi, Bradie

Braisly (American) cautious
Braise, Braislee, Braize, Braze

Branca (American) form of Blanca: white

Branda (Spanish) brandy

Brandisa (English) brandy

Brandise (English) brandy

Brandy (Dutch) sweet as wine; fun-loving

Bran, Brandais, Brande, Brandea, Brandee, Brandeli, Brandi, Brandye, Brandyn, Brani, Branndea

Branka (Czech) glory
Bran, Branca, Bronca, Bronka

Braxton (English) from town of Brock: safe
Braxten

Brayden (American) humorous
Braden, Brae, Braeden, Bray, Brayd, Braydan, Braydon

Breana (Irish) form of Briana: virtuous; strong
Bre-Anna, Breanne, Breeana, Briana, Briane, Briann, Brianna, Brianne, Briona, Bryanna, Bryanne

Breann (Irish) form of Briana: virtuous; strong
Bre-Ann, Bree, Breean, Breeann

Breathine (English) breath of fresh air

Breck (Irish) freckled

Breckina (Irish) little freckled girl

Bree (Irish) upbeat
Brea, Bria, Brie, Brielle

Breela (Irish) esteemed

Breelya (Irish) popular

Breena (Irish) glowing
Brena

Breene (English) palace child

Breeshonna (African American) happy-go-lucky
Bree, Brie, Brieshona

Breezy (American) easygoing
Breezee, Breezie

Brehea (American) self-sufficient
Breahay, Brehae, Brehay

Breken (English) freckled

Bren (American) form of Brenda: royal; glowing
Breyn

Brena (Irish) strong-willed
Brenna

Brenda (Irish) royal; glowing
Bren, Brendalynn, Brenn, Brenna, Brennda, Brenndah, Brinda, Brindah, Brinna

Brendelle (American) distinctive

Brendette (French) small and royal

Brendie (American) form of Brenda: royal; glowing
Brendee, Brendi

Brenita (Spanish) form of Brenda: royal; glowing

Brenna (Irish) form of Brenda: royal; glowing
Bren, Brenn, Brenie

Brenth (Welsh) hill child

Brenyatta (Welsh) hill child

Brenza (Spanish) quiet

Bresan (American) nice

Brescia (American) nice

Bretislava (Polish) glorious

Breeka, Breticka

Brett (Latin) jolly

Bret, Bretta, Brette

Breyawna (African American) form of Brianna: virtuous; strong

Bryawn, Bryawna, Bryawne

Bria (Irish) form of Brianna: virtuous; strong

Briandi (Irish) honorable

Brianna ✿ (Irish) virtuous; strong

Breana, Breann, Bria, Briana, Briannah, Brie-Ann, Bryanna

Brianne (Irish) strong

Briane, Brienne, Bryn

Briar (French) heather

Brear, Brier

Briar-Rose (Literature) from *Sleeping Beauty*: princess

Briazine (English) honored

Brice (English) quick

Briceidy (English) precocious

Brice, Bricedi, Briceidee, Briceidey

Bricene (American) aware

Bride (Scottish) form of Bridget: powerful

Bridey (Irish) wise

Bredee, Breedee, Bride, Bryde

Bridged (Scottish) has the strength of fire

Bridgid, Briged, Brigid

Bridget (Irish) powerful

Birgit, Birgitt, Birgitte, Breeda, Brid, Bride, Bridge, Bridgett, Bridgette, Bridgey, Bridgitte, Brigantia, Briget, Brigette, Brighid, Brigid, Brigida, Brigit, Brigitt, Brigitta, Brigitte, Brijette, Brygett, Brygida, Brygitka

Brie (French) from the French town Rozay-en-Brie

Bree, Brielle

Brienne (French) honored

Brier (French) heather

Briar

Briesha (African American) giving

Bri, Brieshe

Brigida (Italian) strong

Brigeeda

Brigitta (Romanian) strong

Brigeeta, Brigeetta, Brigita

Bril (American) strong

Brill

Briley (Last name as first name) popular

BeBe, Bri, Brile

Brina (Latin) form of Sabrina: passionate

Breena, Brena, Brinna, Bryn, Bryna, Brynn, Brynna, Brynne

Brindha (Indian) sorrowful

Brindie (American) form of Brenda: royal; glowing

Brindle (Irish) versatile

Bryndle

Brine (Irish) strong

Bryne

Brinkelle (American) independent nature

Binkee, Binky, Brinkee, Brinkel, Brinkell, Brinkie

Brinlee (American) sweetheart

Brendlie, Brenlee, Brenly

Brionna (Irish) happy

Breona, Briona

Brisa (Spanish) beloved

Breezy, Breza, Brisha, Brisia, Brissa, Briza, Bryssa

Brisalle (Spanish) loved

Brisco (American) high-energy woman

Briscoe, Briss, Brissie, Brissy

Briseis (Mythology) prized; loved

Briseyda (Spanish) happy

Brissellies (Spanish) happy

Briselle, Briss, Brisse, Brissel, Brissell, Brissey, Brissi, Brissies

Brit (Latin) British

Britaney (English) girl from Britain
Britanee, Britani, Briteny, Britnee,
Britney, Britni, Brittaney, Brittenie

Brites (Spanish) strong

Britt (Latin) girl from Britain
Brit

Britta (Swedish) strong woman
Brita

Brittany (English) girl from Britain
Brinnee, Britany, Briteney, Britney,
Britni, Brittan, Brittaney, Brittani,
Brittania, Brittanie, Brittannia,
Britteny, Brittni, Brittnie, Brittny

Brittenne (English) girl from Britain

Britty (Irish) form of Brittany: girl
from Britain
Britee, Britey, Briti, Britie, Brittee,
Brittey, Britti, Brittie, Brity

Brizalette (English) beloved

Brody (Irish) girl from the canal
Brodee, Brodey, Brodi, Brodie

Brona (Italian) brown-haired girl

Bronislava (Polish) protective
Brana, Branislava, Branka, Brona,
Bronicka, Bronka

Bronislawa (Polish) protective
Bronya

Bronte (Literature) for authors
Charlotte and Emily Bronte; romantic
Brontae, Brontay

Bronty (American) form of author
surname Bronte: for authors Emily
and Charlotte Bronte; romantic

Bronwyn (Welsh) white-breasted
Bron, Bronwen, Bronwhen, Bronwynn

Brooke ☺ (English) sophisticated
Brook, Brooky

Brookette (American) girl from the
brook

Brooklyn ☺ (Place name)
neighborhood in New York
Brookelyn, Brookelynn, Brooklynn,
Brooklynne

Broolyn (American) form of
Brooklyn: neighborhood in New York

Browning (Literature) for poet
Elizabeth Barrett Browning; pensive

Brucie (French) feminine form of
Bruce: complicated; from a thicket of
brushwood
Brucina, Brucine

Bruenetta (French) brown-haired
Bru, Brunetta

Bruna (Italian) brown-haired girl

Bruneita (German) brown-haired
Broon, Brune, Bruneite, Brunny

Brunella (German) intelligent
Brun, Brunela, Brunelle, Brunetta,
Brunette, Brunilla, Brunne

Brunetta (Slavic) brunette

Brunhilda (German) warrior
Brunhild, Brunhilde, Brunnhilda,
Brunnhilde, Brynhild, Brynhilda, Hilda

Bruni (Spanish) brown hair

Bruno (Italian) brown

Bryanna (Gaelic) powerful female
Breanna, Brianna, Bryana

Bryanta (American) feminine form of
Bryan: ethical; strong
Brianta, Bryan, Bryianta

Bryce (American) happy; (Welsh)
aware
Brice

Bryleigh (English) form of Brittany:
jovial
Brilee, Briley, Brily, Brilye, Brylee, Brylie

Bryn (Welsh) hopeful; climbing a hill
Brenne, Brinn, Brynn, Brynne, Brynnie

Brynn (Welsh) hopeful
Brenn, Brinn, Brynne

Brynna (Welsh) optimistic
Brinn, Brinna

Bryonie (Latin) clinging vine
Breeonee, Brioni, Bryony

Bryony (Latin) vine; clingy
Briony, Bronie, Bryonie

Bua (Vietnamese) fortunate
Boo, Bu

Bubbles (American) perky

Bubb

Buena (Spanish) goodness

Buffy (American) plains-dweller

Buffee, Buffey, Buffie

Bukola (African) wealthy

Bucola

Bule (Biblical) wed

Beul, Beulah

Bunard (American) good

Bunerd, Bunn, Bunny

Bunita (Spanish) wins

Bunmi (Hindi) earth; (Slavic) lady

Bunny (English) little rabbit; bouncy

Bunnee, Bunni, Bunnie

Burcetta (Slavic) sweet

Burgundy (French) red wine; unique

Burgandi, Burgandy

Burke (American) loud

Berk, Burk, Burkie

Burkeley (English) birches;

outdoorsy

Berkeley, Burkelee, Burkeleigh, Burkeli,

Burkelie, Burkely, Burklee, Burkleigh,

Burkley, Burkli, Burklie, Burkly

Burma (Place name)

Burns (Last name as first name)

presumptuous

Bernes, Berns, Burn, Burnee, Burnes,

Burney, Burni, Burny

Buseje (African) interesting

Buthaayna (Arabic) lovely body

Busayna, Buthaynah

Butte (Place name) landscape

Butter (American) smooth

Button (American) sensitive

Buz (Biblical) angry

Buzzie (American) spirited

Buzz, Buzzi

Bwyana (African American) smart

Bwya, Bwyanne

Byhalia (Native American) strong

oak

Byria (Place name)

Byronae (American) feminine form

of Byron: reclusive; small cottage

Byrona, Byronay

Bythia (American) virtuous

C

Cabot (French) fresh-faced

Cabriole (French) adorable

Cabb, Cabby, Cabriolle, Kabriole

Cacalia (Botanical) accommodating

Cachay (African American)

distinctive

Cachet (French) fetching

Cache, Cachee

Cadasa (Biblical) place name

Caddy (American) elusive; alluring

Cade (American) precocious

Kade, Kaid

Cadena (Latin) rhythmic

Cadence (American) musical

Kadence

Cadencia (Spanish) in cadence

Cadenie (American) in cadence

Cadou (French) rhythmic

Cady (English) fun-loving

Cadee, Cadey, Cadye, Caidee, Caidy,

Kadee, Kady

Caesaria (Greek) feminine form of

Caesar: focused leader

Cahara (American) coherent

Cai (Chinese) wealthy; girlish

Cailida (Spanish) passionate

Cailidora (Greek) gifted with a

beautiful face

Cailin (American) happy

Cailyn, Cailynn, Calyn, Cayleen,

Caylin, Caylyn, Caylynne

Caimile (Spanish) helps

Cainwen (Welsh) lovely treasure

Ceinwen, Kayne, Keyne

Cairo (Place name) Egypt's capital;

confident

Kairo, Kayro

Caissa (American) form of
Cassandra: insightful

Cait (Greek) purest
Cate, Kate

Caitlin (Irish) virginal
Cailin, Caitleen, Caitlen, Caitlinn,
Caitlyn, Catlin, Catlyn, Catlynne

Caitrin (Irish) pure of heart

Caitronia (Irish) pure

Cakusola (African) lionhearted

Cala (Arabic) strong
Calla, Callah

Calandra (Greek) lark
Calendra, Calondra, Kalandra

Calanrea (Greek) form of Calantha:
gorgeous flower
Calendrea

Calantha (Greek) gorgeous flower
Calanth, Calanthe, Calanthia,
Callantha, Calli

Calatea (Greek) flowering
Calatee

Cale (Latin) respected
Kale

Caledonia (Latin) from Scotland
Kaledonia

Caleigh (American) beauty
Calleigh

Calenda (Irish) form of Cailin: happy
Calendun

Calent (Irish) form of Cailin: happy

Caley (American) warm
Caleigh, Kaylee

Calhoun (Last name as first name)
surprising

Calia (American) beauty

Calida (Spanish) sincere; warmth

California (Place name) U.S. state;
cool
Callie, Kalifornia, Kallie

Caliopa (Greek) singing beautifully
Kaliopa

Calise (Greek) gorgeous

Calista (Greek) most beautiful
Callista, Calysta, Kali, Kalista, Kalli,
Kallista

Call (American) summoned

Calla (Greek) beautiful
Cala, Callie, Cally

Callen (Irish) loquacious

Callian (Irish) beauty

Callidora (Greek) gift of beauty

Callie (Greek) beautiful
Caleigh, Callee, Calley, Calli, Cally,
Kali, Kallee, Kallie

Calligenia (Italian) beauty's child

Calliope (Greek) poetry muse
Kalliope, Kallyope

Callista (Greek) most beautiful
Calesta, Calista, Callista, Calysta,
Kallista

Callistua (Greek) most beautiful

Callula (Latin) beautiful

Caltha (Latin) gold flower

Calumina (Scottish) calm

Calvina (Latin) has no hair
Calvine

Calypso (Greek) sea nymph

Cam (American) form of Cameron:
popular; crooked nose
Cami, Camie, Cammie

Camaren (American) form of
Cameron: popular; crooked nose

Cambay (American) saucy
Cambaye, Kambay

Cambee (English) of the people

Camber (American) form of Amber:
gorgeous and golden; semiprecious
stone
Cambie, Cambre, Cammy, Kamber

Cambree (Welsh) form of Cambria:
the people
Cambre, Cambrie, Cambry, Kambree,
Kambrie

Cambria (English) the people

Camden (American) glorious face
Cam, Camdon, Cammi, Cammie,
Cammy

Cameka (African American) form of
Tamkia: lively
Cammey, Cammi, Cammy, Kameka,
Kammy

Camelina (American) form of
Camilla: wonderful

Camellia (Italian) flower
Camelia, Kamelia

Camelot (English) elegant
Cam, Cami, Camie, Camy

Cameo (French) piece of jewelry;
singular
Cameoh, Cammie, Kameo

Camera (Word as name) stunning
Kamera

Camerino (Spanish) unblemished
Cam, Cammy

Cameron (Scottish) popular; crooked
nose
Cameran, Camren, Camryn, Kameron,
Kamryn

Cameshia (American) pretty

Cametria (American) pretty

Cami (French) form of Camellia:
flower
Camey, Camie, Cammie, Cammy

Camilla ✿ (Latin/Italian) wonderful
*Cam, Camelia, Camellia, **Camila**,*
Camile, Camille, Camillia

Camille (French) swift runner; great
innocence
Camila, Cammille, Cammy, Camylle,
Kamille

Cammy (American) form of Camilla:
wonderful

Camp (American) outsider
Cam, Campy

Campbell (Last name as first name)
amazing
Cam, Cambell, Camey, Cami, Camie,
Camy

Camrin (American) form of
Cameron: popular; crooked nose
Camren, Camryn

Canace (American) form of Candace:
glowing girl

Canada (Place name) country in
North American; decisive
Cann, Kanada

Canain (Biblical) patient

Candace (Greek) glowing girl
Caddy, Candice, Candis, Candys,
Kandace

Candelara (Spanish) spiritual
Cande, Candee, Candelaria, Candi,
Candy, Lara

Candene (English) glows

Candenza (Italian) form of Candace:
glowing girl

Candice-Rae (American) glows

Candida (Latin) white

Candis (American) form of Candace:
glowing girl

Candlia (American) candlelight

Candra (Latin) she who glows
Candria, Kandra

Candy (American) form of Candace:
glowing girl
Candee, Candi, Candie

Caneadea (Native American) the
horizon; far-reaching goals

Caneeka (American) clever

Canei (Greek) pure

Canela (Spanish) pure

Cannes (Place name) town in France;
selective
Can, Kan

Cannon (American) vital

Cantara (Arabic) bridge
Canta, Kanta, Kantara

Capelta (American) fanciful
Capeltah, Capp, Cappy

Caper (American) mischief

Caplice (American) spontaneous
Capleece, Capleese, Kapleese

Capote (Spanish) cloak; protected

Capri (Place name) island off coast
of Italy
Caprie, Kapri

Caprice (Italian) playful; capricious
Caprece, Capreese, Capricia, Caprise

Caprik (Spanish) capricious

Capucine (French) cloak
Cappy

Car (American) driven
Carr, Kar, Karr

Cara (Latin/Gaelic) beloved friend
Carah, Kara

Caramea (Italian) dear girl

Caramenia (Spanish) dear girl

Caramia (Italian) my dear
Cara Mia, Cara-Mia

Cardea (Mythology) pivotal

Cardia (Spanish) giving
Cardi, Kardia

Careletta (Spanish) smart

Caren (American) dear
Carine, Caryn, Karen, Karyn

Caresse (Greek) well-loved

Carey (Welsh) by a castle; fond
Caree, Cari, Carrie, Cary

Cari (Latin) giving

Caria (Biblical) place name

Caribe (Place name)

Caridad (Spanish) giving; lovng
Cari

Carie (Latin) generous

Carina (French/Italian) pure; darling
Careena, Carena, Carin, Carine, Kareena, Karina

Carinthia (Place name) city in Austria; dear girl

Carissa (Greek) loving
Carisa, Caryssa, Karessa, Karissa

Carita (Latin) giving; loved
Caritta, Carrita, Carritta, Karita

Carla (German) feminine form of Charles: well-loved
Carlah, Carlee, Carli, Carlia, Carlie, Carly, Karla, Karlah

Carlanda (American) darling
Carlan, Carland, Carlande, Carlee, Carlie, Carly, Karlanda

Carle (English) winner

Carleas (American) form of Carlissa: pleasant

Carlee (German) darling
Carleigh, Carley, Carli, Carly, Karlee, Karley

Carlen (English) winner

Carlene (American) sweet
Carleen, Carlina, Carline, Carlyn

Carlett (Spanish) affectionate
Carle, Carlet, Carletta, Carlette, Carley, Carli

Carlice (Spanish) pleases

Carlin (Gaelic) little champion
Caline, Carlan, Carlen

Carlisle (Place name) city on the border of England and Scotland; sharp
Carlile, Carrie, Karlisle

Carlissa (American) pleasant
Carleeza, Carlisse

Carlita (Italian) outstanding

Carlone (Italian) winning

Carlotta (Italian) sensual
Karlotta

Carly (German) darling
Carlee, Carley, Carli, Carlie, Karlee

Carlysle (English) island of Carla

Carm (Italian) garden paradise

Carma (Hebrew) form of Carmel: garden
Car, Carmee, Carmi, Carmie, Karma

Carmel (Hebrew) garden
Carmela, Carmella, Karmel

Carmela (Hebrew) form of Carmel: garden
Carmalla, Carmella, Carmie, Carmilla

Carmen (Hebrew) crimson
Carma, Carman, Carmela, Carmelinda, Carmita, Carmynne, Chita, Mela, Melita

Carmensita (Spanish) dear girl
Carma, Carmens, Carmense, Karmence

Carmi (English) garden

Carmiela (Hebrew) form of Carmel: garden

Carmina (Italian) garden paradise

Carmine (Italian) attractive
Carmyne, Karmine

Carminia (Italian) dearest
Carma, Carmine, Carmynea, Karm, Karminia, Karmynea

Carmiya (Hebrew) form of Carmel: garden

Carmona (Italian) garden paradise

Carmone (Spanish) garden

Carmyle (American) garden

Carna (Latin) horn; sound of joy

Carnation (Botanical) abundant flower
Carn, Carna, Carnee, Carney, Carny

Carnelian (American) gemstone

Carnelle (American) gem

Carnethia (Invented) fragrant
Carnee, Carney, Carnithia, Karnethia

Carni (Latin) horn; vocal
Carna, Carney, Carnia, Carnie, Carniela, Carniella, Carniya, Carny, Karni, Karnia, Karniela, Karniella, Karniya

Carnie (American) happy
Carni, Karni, Karnie

Carody (American) humorous
Caridee, Caridey, Carodee, Carodey, Carrie, Karodee, Karody

Carol (English) feminine; joyful song
Carole, Carroll, Caryl, Karol, Karrole

Carole (French) joyous song
Karol, Karole

Carolena (Italian) happy

Caroli (Last name used as first name) joyous

Carolina (Italian) form of Carla: well-loved
Carrolena, Karolina

Caroline ✪ (German) little; womanly
Caraline, Carilene, Cariline, Caroleen, Carolin, Carrie, Karalyn, Karolina, Karoline, Karolyn, Karolynne

Carolleen (American) form of Carol: feminine; joyful song

Carolye (English) form of Carolina: well-loved

Carolyn (English) womanly
Carilyn, Carilynn, Carolyne, Carolynn, Karolyn

Caron (Welsh) giving heart
Carron, Karon

Caronsy (American) form of Caron: giving heart
Caronnsie, Caronsi, Karonsy

Caroun (Slavic) springtime

Carran (American) generous

Carrell (American) form of Carol: feminine; joyful song

Carrelle (American) lively
Carrele

Carrie (English) form of Caroline: little; womanly
Carey, Cari, Carri, Carry, Kari

Carron (English) form of Karen: purehearted

Carson (Nordic) dramatic
Carse, Carsen, Carsun, Karrson, Karsen, Karson

Carsyn (American) form of Carson: dramatic

Caryn (Danish) form of Karen: purehearted
Caren, Carrin, Caryne, Carynn

Carys (Welsh) love

Casey (Gaelic) alert; watchful
Casie, Cassee, Cassey, Casy, Caysee, Caysie, Caysy, Kasey

Casha (American) radiant

Cashandra (American) form of Cassandra: insightful

Cashonya (African American) monied; lively
Kashonya

Casilda (Latin) from the dwelling

Casilde (Spanish) combative
Casilda, Casill, Cass, Cassey, Cassie

Cason (Greek) seer; spirited
Case, Casey, Kason

Cassandra (Greek) insightful
Casandra, Casandria, Cass, Cassie, Cassondra, Kassandra

Cassia (Greek) spicy; cinnamon

Cassidy (Irish) clever girl
Casadee, Cass, Cassidee, Cassidi, Kassidy

Cassie (Greek) form of Cassandra: insightful
Cassey, Cassi

Cassiopeia (Greek) starry-eyed
Cass, Cassi, Kass, Kassiopia

Cassis (American) form of Carson: dramatic

Cassundra (American) form of Cassandra: insightful

Casta (Spanish) form of Castalina: pure

Castalia (Mythology) ill-fated

Castalina (Spanish) form of Catalina: chaste

Castara (Greek) form of Catherine: pure
Castera, Castora

Castille (Spanish) traditional

Cata (Spanish) pure

Catalina (Spanish) pure
Catalena, Katalena, Katalina

Catalynn (American) form of Catalina: pure

Catarina (Greek) pure
Caterina, Catrina, Katarina

Catava (Greek) uncorrupted

Catesa (American) form of Contessa: pretty

Catharina (Greek) form of Catherine: pure

Cather (Literature) for author Willa Cather; earthy
Kather

Catherine (Greek) pure
Cartharine, Cathrine, Cathryn, Katherine

Catherique (French) pure

Cathleen (Irish) pure; immaculate
Cathelin, Cathelyn, Cathlinne, Cathlyn, Cathy

Cathresha (African American) pure; outspoken
Cathrisha, Cathy, Kathresha, Resha

Cathryn (Greek) form of Catherine: pure

Cathy (Greek) pure; innocent
Cathee, Cathey, Cathie, Kathy

Catima (Greek) pure
Cattima

Catina (Italian) pure
Catin, Catine, Catinean

Catline (Irish) form of Caitlin: virginial
Cataleen, Catalena, Catleen, Catlen, Katline

Catresia (Italian) form of Catima: pure

Catrice (Greek) form of Catherine: pure
Catrece, Catreece, Catreese, Katreece, Katrice

Catrina (Greek) pure
Catreena, Catreene, Catrene, Katrina

Catriona (Greek) form of Catherine: pure
Katriona

Cauda (Biblical) place name

Cavaray (American) celestial

Cavender (American) emotional
Cav, Cavey, Kav, Kavender

Cavinessa (American) form of Kavinli: pretty; gentle

Cawleen (American) vocal

Cayen (American) form of Kay: happy; rejoicing

Cayenne (Word as name) peppery; spice

Cayla (Hebrew) unblemished
Cailie, Calee, Cayley, Caylie, Kayla

Cayley (American) joyful
Caelee, Caeley, Cailey, Cailie, Caylea, Caylee, Cayleigh, Caylie

Cayman (Place name) the islands; free spirit
Caman, Caymanne, Kayman

Cayne (American) generous
Cain, Kaine

Ceanatha (American) form of Ciana: old soul

Ceara (Irish) form of Ciara: brunette

Ceaskarshenna (African American) ostentatious
Ceaskar, Karshenna, Shenna

Cece (Latin) form of Cecilia: blind

Ceci (Latin) form of Cecilia: blind

Cecile (Latin) form of Cecilia: blind
Cecily

Cecilia (Latin) blind
Cacelia, Cece, Cecelia, Ceil, Celia, Cice, Cicilia, Cilley, Secilia, Sissy

Cedrica (English) chief; leader

Cedrice (American) feminine form of Cedric: leader
Ced, Cedrise

Ceil (Latin) blythe
Ceel, Ciel

Ceinwen (Welsh) blessed baby

Ceirra (Irish) clear-eyed
CeAirra, Cierra

Ceiteag (Scottish) purest

Celand (Latin) heavenward
Cel, Cela, Celanda, Celle

Celandine (Greek) wildflower; natural beauty; yellow

Celaya (Spanish) serene

Celebration (American) word as name; celebrant
Cela, Sela

Celena (Greek) form of Selena: like the moon
Celeena, Celene

Celerina (Spanish) moves fast

Celery (Botanical) refreshing
Cel, Celeree, Celree, Celry, Sel, Selery, Selry

Celes (Latin) heavens

Celeslie (Latin) celestial

Celesta (English) celestial

Celeste (Latin) gentle and heavenly
Celest, Celestial, Celestine, Seleste

Celestia (Latin) heavenly
Celeste, Celestea, Celestiah, Seleste, Selestia

Celestina (Spanish) celestial

Celestral (American) celestial

Celestyna (Polish) heavenly
Cela, Celeste, Celesteenah, Celestinah, Celestyne

CeLetha (Spanish) heavenly

Celina (Greek) form of Celena: like the moon
Selina

Celinda (American) lovely

Celine (Greek) lovely
Celeen, Celene

Celisha (Greek) flaming; passionate

Celka (Latin) celestial
Celk, Celkee, Celkie, Selk, Selka

Celkee (Latin) form of Celeste: gentle and heavenly
Celkea, Celkie, Cell, Selkee

Cellene (French) celestial leader

Celnie (French) heavenly

Celosia (Greek) flaming

Celta (American) form of Delta: fourth letter of Greek alphabet

Cena (English) special
Cenna, Sena

Cene' (French) knowing

Cennetta (American) knowing

Cenobia (Spanish) power of Zeus; strong girl
Cenobie, Zenobia, Zenobie

Censey (American) knowing

Ceola (American) clarity

Ceoline (American) clarity

Ceporah (Hebrew) form of Zipporah: bird in flight

Cera (French) colorful; (Spanish) growth

Cerbrenda (American) young raven

Cerea (Greek) thriving
Serea

Cerelia (Latin) spring
Cerallua, Cerellia, Cerelly

Cerella (Latin) springlike

Ceres (Latin) joyful

Ceressa (Spanish) growth

Cerestina (Spanish) growth

Ceridwen (Welsh) poetic; blessed
Ceri, Ceridwyn

Cerina (Latin) form of Serena: calm

Cerise (French) cherry red
Cerese, Cerice, Cerrice, Ceryce

Cerlan (Spanish) growing

Cerrisa (French) cherry red

Cerys (Mythology) harvest goddess
Ceri, Ceries, Cerri, Cerrie

Cesaria (Latin) feminine form of Caesar: focused leader

Cesarina (Latin) strong spirit
Cesarea, Cesarie, Cesarin

Cesary (Polish) outspoken
Cesarie, Cezary, Ceze

Cesia (Spanish) celestial
Cesea, Sesia

Ceylon (Place name)

Chablay (American) wine

Chablis (French) white wine
Chabli

Chabulon (Biblical) place name

Chacita (Spanish) lively girl
Chaca, Chacie, Chaseeta, Chaseta

Chadawndra (African) excitable

Chadee (French) goddess
Shadee

Chadra (Indian) peacock

Chaemarique (Invented) pretty
Chae, Chaemareek, Marique, Shaymarique

Chafin (Last name as first name) sure-footed
Chaffin, Shafin

Chahna (Hindi) she lights the world

Chai (Hebrew) life-giving
Chae, Chaeli

Chaitali (Hindi) light

Chakena (African) energy

Chakra (Sanskrit) energy
Chak, Chaka, Chakara, Chakyra

Chala (African American) exuberant
Chalah, Chalee, Chaley, Chalie

Chalese (French) goblet; toasts life

Chalette (American) good taste
Chalett, Challe, Challie, Shalette

Chalica (American) drinks life fully

Chalice (French) a goblet; toasting
Chalace, Chalece, Chalyse, Chalyssie

Chalina (Spanish) rose; fragrant

Chaline (American) smiling
Chacha, Chaleen, Chalene

Chalis (African American) sunny disposition
Chal, Chaleese, Chalise

Chalissa (African American) optimistic
Chalisa, Chalysa, Chalyssa

Challie (American) charismatic
Challee, Challi, Chally

Chalondra (African American) pretty
Chacha, Chalon, Chalondrah, Cheilonndra, Chelondra

Chalsey (American) variation of Chelsea: safe harbor
Chalsea, Chalsee, Chalsi, Chalsie

Chamania (Hebrew) sunflower; bright
Chamaniya, Hamania, Hamaniya

Chamaran (Hebrew) form of Chamania: sunflower; bright

Chamayne (American) form of Sharmaine; form of Charles: bountiful orchard

Chambray (French) fabric; hardy
Chambree

Chameli (Hindi) jasmine; fragrant

Chamion (American) changes

Champagne (French) sparkling;
luxurious

Chan (Vietnamese) fragrant

Chana (Hindi) moonlike

Chanah (Hebrew) graceful
Chanach, Channah

Chanal (American) moonlike

Chanchall (Hindi) energetic

Chanda (Hindi) moon goddess
Chandi, Chandie, Shanda

Chandani (Hindi) moonbeams
Chandni, Chandree, Chandrika

Chandelle (French) candle-lighter
Chandal, Shandalle, Shandel

Chandi (Sanskrit) goddess

Chandler (English) romantic;
candle-maker
Chandlee, Shandler

Chandra (Hindi) of the moon
Chandre, Shandra, Shandre

Chandrika (Indian) moon

Chanel (French) fashionable;
designer name
*Chan, Chanell, Chanelle, Channel,
Shanel, Shanell, Shanelle*

Chanelle (American) stylish
Shanell, Shanelle

Chaney (English) form of Chandler:
romantic; candlemaker
Chanie, Chaynee, Chayney

Chania (Hebrew) blessed by Lord's
grace
Chaniya, Hania, Haniya

Chanicka (African American) loved
*Chaneeka, Chani, Chanika, Nicka,
Nika, Shanicka*

Chanina (Hebrew) knows a gracious
Lord

Chanise (American) adored
Chanese, Shanise

Chanit (Hebrew) spear; ready for
combat
Chanita, Hanit, Hanita

Channa (Hindi) chickpea; little thing

Channary (Vietnamese) moon girl

Channing (Last name as first name)
clever

Chanon (American) shining
Chanen, Chann, Channon, Chanun

Chansanique (African American)
girl singing
*Chansan, Chansaneek, Chansani,
Chansanike, Shansanique*

Chantal (French) singer of songs
*Chandal, Chantale, Chantalle, Chante,
Chantee, Chantel, Chantell, Chantelle,
Chantile, Chantille, Chawntelle,
Shanta, Shantel, Shawntel, Shontelle*

Chantee (American) singer
*Chante, Chantey, Chanti, Chantie,
Shantee, Shantey*

Chanterelle (French) singer; prized

Chanthoeun (American) chantress

Chanti (American) melodious
Chantee, Chantie

Chantill (French) singer

Chantilly (French) beautiful lace
Chantille, Shantilly

Chantou (French) singer

Chantre (French) singer

Chantrea (Vietnamese) moonlight

Chantrice (French) singer of songs
Shantreece, Treece

Chanya (Hebrew) blessed by
Jehovah's love

Chanyce (American) risk-taker
*Chance, Chancie, Chaneese, Chaniece,
Chanycey*

Chapa (Native American) beaver

Chapawee (Native American) active

Chapin (Last name used as first
name) factual

Chaquanne (African American) sassy
Chaq, Chaquann, Shakwan

Chara (Greek) form of Charis: graceful
Charo

Charbonnet (French) loving and giving
Charbonay, Charbonet, Charbonnay, Sharbonet, Sharbonnet

Charde (French) wine
Charday, Chardea, Shardae

Chardonnay (French) white wine
Char, Chardonee, Chardonnae, Shardonnay

Charelle (French) feminine

Chari (American) cherish

Chariah (Hebrew) God's child

Charian (French) womanly

Charie (Greek) form of Charis: graceful
Chari

Charille (French) form of Charlotte: little woman
Char, Chari, Charill, Shar, Sharille

Charis (Greek) graceful
Charice, Charisse

Charish (American) cherished
Chareesh

Charisma (American) charming
Char, Karismah

Chariss (English) cherish

Charissa (Greek) giving
Char, Charesa, Charisse, Charissey

Charissma (American) magnetic

Charita (Spanish) sweet
Cherita

Charity (Latin) loving; affectionate
Carisa, Charis, Charita, Chariti, Charry, Cherry, Chirity, Sharity

Charla (French) form of Charlotte: little woman
Char

Charlaine (English) form of Charlene: petite and beautiful
Charlane

Charlana (American) form of Charlene: petite and beautiful
Chalanna

Charle (English) feminine form of Charles: well-loved

Charlene (French) petite and beautiful
Charla, Charlaine, Charleen, Charline, Sharlene

Charlesetta (German) feminine form of Charles: well-loved
Charlesette, Charlsetta

Charlesey (American) expansive; generous
Charlesee, Charlie, Charlsie, Charlsy

Charlesia (American) feminine form of Charles: well-loved
Charlese, Charlisce, Charlise, Charlsie, Charlsy, Sharlesia

Charlezet (American) feminine form of Charles: well-loved

Charli (English) feminine

Charlie (American) easygoing
Charl, Charlee, Charley, Charli

Charlize (American) pretty

Charlotee (French) small

Charlotta (French) womanly

Charlotte ✿ (French) little woman
Carly, Charla, Charle, Charlett, Charletta, Charlette, Charlott, Charolot, Char

Charlottie (French) small
Charlotty

Charlsheah (American) happy

Charlsie (French) womanly

Charlton (English) feminine form of Charles: well-loved

Charluce (American) feminine form of Charles: well-loved
Charl, Charla, Charluse

Charlyn (Spanish) feminine

Charm (Greek) form of Charmian: charming; joy-baby
Charma, Charmay, Sharm

Charmaine (Latin) bountiful
orchard
Charma, Charmagne, Charmain,
Charmane, Charmayne, Charmian,
Charmine, Charmyn, Sharmaine,
Sharmane, Sharmayne, Sharmyne

Charmian (Greek) joy baby; charming

Charmine (French) charming
Charmen, Charmin

Charminique (African American)
dashing
Charmineek

Charmonique (African American)
charming
Charm, Charmi, Charmon,
Charmoneek, Charmoni, Charmonik,
Sharmonique

Charna (Slavic) darkness

Charnee (American) effervescent
Charney, Charnie, Charny

Charneeka (African American)
obsessive
Charn, Charnika, Charny

Charneli (Slavic) dark

Charnelle (American) sparkling
Charn, Charnel, Charnell, Charney,
Sharnell, Sharnelle

Charnesa (African American)
noticed
Charnessa, Charnessah

Charnesie (American) dark hair

Charnette (American) little Charna;
dark

Charney (American) dark

Charnise (American) dark

Charo (Spanish) flower
Charro

Charon (Dutch) dreamer

Charra (French) womanly

Charron (African American) form of
Sharon: open heart; desert plain
Charryn, Cheiron

Charry (Spanish) rosary

Charsetta (American) form of
Charlene: petite and beautiful
Charsee, Charsette, Charsey, Charsy

Chartra (American) classy
Chartrah

Chartres (French) planner
Chartrys

Charu (Hindi) gorgeous; beauty

Charudetta (Invented) combo of
Charu and Detta

Charumat (Hindi) lovely and smart

Charvi (Hindi) lovely

Charvonneia (Invented) combo of
Charvon and Vonneia

Charysse (Greek) graceful girl
Charece, Charese, Charisse

Chashmona (Hebrew) princess

Chasia (Hebrew) sheltered
Chasya, Hasia, Hasya

Chasida (Hebrew) religious
Chasidah, Hasida

Chasina (Aramaic) strength of
character

Chasity (Latin) pure
Chassity

Chasmum (Hindi) lovely eyes

Chassie (Latin) form of Chastity:
pure woman
Chass, Chassey, Chassi

Chastaine (English) chaste

Chastity (Latin) pure woman
Chasta, Chastitie

Chateria (Vietnamese) moonlight

Chatie (Spanish) lively

Chatree (Indian) daring

Chau (Aramaic) strength of character

Chaucer (English) demure
Chauser, Chawcer, Chawser

Chava (Hebrew) life-giving
Chavah, Chave, Hava

Chavi (Gypsy) girlish

Chaviva (Hebrew) beloved

Chavon (Hebrew) life
Chavonne

Chaya (Jewish) living

Chayan (Native American) form of Cheyenne: Native American tribe
Chay, Chayanne, Chi, Shayan, Shy

Chazmin (American) form of Jasmine: fragrant; sweet

Chazona (Hebrew) seer

Chea (American) witty
Cheeah

Chedra (Hebrew) happy

Cheer (American) joyful

Cheesa (American) forgiving

Cheifa (Hebrew) enjoys a safe harbor

Chekia (Invented) cheeky
Chekie, Shekia

Chela (Spanish) exuberant
Chelan, Chelena

Cheletha (African American) smiling
Chelethe, Cheley

Chelle (American) form of Chelsea or Michelle: safe harbor; like the Lord
Shell

Chelsea (Old English) safe harbor
Chelcy, Cheli, Chellsie, Chelse, Chelsee, Chelsei, Chelsey, Chelsie, Kelsey, Shelsen

Chemarin (French) fertile; dark

Chemash (Hebrew) servant of God
Chema, Chemesh, Chemosh

Chemda (Hebrew) charismatic

Chemdiah (Hebrew) loves God
Chemdia, Chemdiya, Hemdia,

Hemdiah

Chemelle (American) form of Chanel: fashionable; designer name

Chemikaln (American) hip

Chenchayya (American) responsible

Chenecua (Native American) peace

Chenia (Hebrew) lives by the grace of God
Chen, Chenya, Hen, Henia, Henya

Chenicha (Native American) at odds

Chenille (American) soft
Chenelle, Chenile, Chinille

Chenlei (Asian) wise

Chenoa (American) form of Genoa: playful
Cheney, Cheno

Chenzia (American) peace

Cheops (Egyptian) pyramid builder

Cher (French) dear
Chere, Sher

Cherelle (French) dear
Charell, Cherrelle, Sharelle

Cherian (English) darling

Cherie (French) dear
Cherey, Cheri, Cherice, Cherree, Cherrie, Cherry, Cherye

Cheriel (American) darling

Cherika (French) form of Cherry: cherry red
Chereka, Cherikah

Cherinne (American) happy
Charinn, Cherin, Cherry

Cheris (American) cherished

Cherise (French) cherry
Cherece, Cherice, Cherish, Cherrise

Cherish (French) precious girl
Charish, Cherishe, Sherishe

Cherisha (American) endearing
Cherishah, Cherishuh

Cherita (Spanish) dearest
Cheritt, Cheritta, Cherrita

Cherith (Biblical) place name; charitable

Cheritt (American) charitable

Cheritte (American) held dear
Cher, Cherette, Cheritta

Cherly (American) form of Shirley: bright meadow; cheerful girl
Cherlee, Sherly

Chermelia (American) charm

Chermelle (American) charm

Chermey (American) charm

Chermona (Hebrew) goes to the sacred mountain

Chero (American) dearest

Cherokee (Native American) Indian tribe member

Cherone (Italian) dear

Cherria (American) dear

Cherrill (American) form of Cheryl: beloved

Cherron (American) graceful dancer
Cher, Cheron, Cherronne

Cherry (English/French) cherry red
Cheree, Cherey, Cherrye, Chery

Cheryce (American) cherish

Cheryl (French) beloved
Charyl, Cherel, Cherelle, Cheryll

Chesley (English) pretty; meadow
Ches, Cheslay, Cheslea, Chesleigh

Chesma (Slavic) peace-loving

Chesna (Slavic) peace
Ches, Chesnah

Chesney (English) peacemaker
Chesnee, Chesni, Chesnie, Chessnea

Chessa (Slavic) peace

Chesskwana (African American) evoker
Chesskwan, Chessquana, Chessy

Chessteen (American) needed
Ches, Chessy, Chesteen, Chestene

Chestnut (Botanical) unique

Chet (American) vivacious
Chett

Chevona (Irish) loves a gracious God

Chevy (American) funny
Chev, Chevee

Cheyann (Native American) form of Cheyenne: Native American tribe

Cheye (American) form of Cheyenne: Native American tribe

Cheyenne (Native American) Native American tribe
Chayanne, Cheyan, Cheyanna, Cheyene, Chynne, Shayan, Shayann, Sheyenne

Chezuka (Asian) quiet
Shizuka

Chhaya (Hebrew) life; vibrant; (Indian) shadow

Chi (African) Ibo God; light

Chiante (Italian) wine
Chianti

Chiara (Italian) bright and clear
Cheara, Chiarra, Kiara, Kiarra

Chiarina (Italian) clear

Chiba (Hebrew) love

Chic (Spanish) little; strong

Chica (Spanish) girl
Chika

Chick (American) fun-loving
Chicki, Chickie

Chickadee (American) cute little girl
Chicka, Chickady, Chickee, Chickey, Chicky

Chidi (Spanish) cheerful

Chidori (Japanese) shorebird

Chika (Japanese) dear girl; wise

Chikira (Spanish) dancer
Shakira

Chiku (African) loquacious

Chilali (Native American) snowbird

Childe (American) offspring
Child

Childers (Last name as first name) dignified
Chelders, Childie, Chillders, Chylders

Chillon (American) polished

Chimalis (Native American) snowbird

Chimene (French) self-starter; eager

China (Place name) unique
Chinnah, Chyna, Chynna

Chinadoll (Word as name) delicate
China Doll, China-Doll, Chynadoll

Chinasia (Place name) China and Asia; different

Chinenye (Place name) form of China: unique

Chinesia (Chinese) delicate

Chinnamma (Asian) wonder; summer

Chinnereth (Biblical) place name; God's child

Chinue (African) blessed by Chi

Chionne (Egyptian) kind and obedient

Chipo (African) gift

Chiquida (Spanish) form of
Chiquita: small girl
Chiquide

Chiquita (Spanish) small girl
Chica, Chick, Chickie, Chikita,
Chiquitia, Chiquitta, Shiquita

Chiriga (African) triumphant; capable

Chirline (American) form of
Charline: petite and beautiful
Chirl, Chirlene, Shirl, Shirline

Chislaine (French) loyal

Chita (Spanish) form of Chica: girl

Chitsa (Spanish) form of Carmen:
crimson

Chivonne (American) happy
Chevonne, Chivaughan, Chivaughn,
Chivon, Chivonn

Chiyena (Hebrew) in the Lord's grace

Chiyoko (Japanese) forever

Chizoba (African) well-protected;
strong

Chizu (Japanese) a thousand storks;
bountiful

Chizuko (Japanese) abundant

Chloe ✪ (Greek) flowering
Chloee, Clo, Cloe, Cloee, Cloey, Khloe,
Kloe

Chloris (Greek) pale-skinned
Chloras, Cloris, Kloris

Cho (Japanese) dawn of day
Choko, Choyo

Chofa (Polish) able

Cholena (Native American) birdlike;
sings

Chonzette (English) risk-taker

Chotsani (Asian) adoring

Choye (Asian) pretty

Chris (Greek) form of Christina:
follower of Christ
Chrissie, Chrissy, Kris

Chrisana (American) boisterous
Chris, Chrisanah, Crisane

Chriselda (German) form of
Griselda: patient

Chrissa (Greek) form of Christina:
follower of Christ
Crissa, Cryssa, Krissa

Chrissy (English) form of Christina:
follower of Christ
Chrissie, Chrysie, Krissy

Christa (Latin) anointed one; Christian
Crista, Krista

Christal (Latin) form of Crystal:
clear; open-minded
Christall, Christalle, Christel

Christanda (American) smart
Christandah, Christawnda

Christauna (American) spiritual
Christaun, Christawna, Christown,
Christwan

Christen (Greek) form of Christiana:
follower of Christ
Christan, Christin, Cristen, Kristen

Christiana (Greek) follower of Christ
Christa, Christianna, Christianne,
Christie, Chrystyana, Crystianne,
Crysty-Ann, Kristiana

Christie (Greek) form of Christina:
follower of Christ
Christi, Kristi, Kristie

Christina (Greek) form of
Christiana: follower of Christ
Chris, Chrissie, Christi, Chrystina,
Crista, Kristina

Christine (French/English) form of
Christina: follower of Christ
Christene, Christin, Cristine, Kristine

Christle (German) form of Christina:
follower of Christ
Christian

Christmas (English) Christmas baby

Christopher (Greek) devout
Christian
Kris, Krissie, Krissy, Krista, Kristofer,
Kristopher

Christy (Scottish) Christian
Christee, Christi, Christie

Chrysanthemum (American) flower

Chrys, Chrysanthe, Chrysie, Mum

Chrysanthum (Invented) from flower chrysanthemum; flowering

Chrys, Chrysan, Chrysanth

Chrysolite (American) gemstone

Chuke (African) hopes

Chuki (African) born in a sour time

Chula (Native American) flower; colorful

Chulda (Hebrew) fortune-teller

Hulda, Huldah

Chulisa (Invented) clever

Chully, Ulisa

Chuma (Hebrew) warm

Chumi, Huma, Humi

Chumana (Native American) dew; morning fresh

Chumani (Native American) dewdrop

Chumba (African) darling

Chumina (Hebrew) warmth

Chun (Chinese) springlike

Chyan (American) form of Cheyenne: Native American tribe

Chylene (American) form of Cheyenne: Native American tribe

Chyler (American) feminine form of Kyler: peaceful

Chynna (Chinese) China; wise; musical

Chyna

Ciana (Irish) old soul

Ciandra (Italian) light

Ciani (Irish) old soul

Cianna (Italian) old soul

Ciannait (Irish) an old soul

Ciannata (Latin) old spirit

Ciannedra (Irish) old soul

Ciara (Irish) brunette

Cearra, Ciarah, Ciarra, Ciera, Keera, Keerah

Cicely (Latin) form of Cecilia: blind

Cicelie, Cici, Sicely

Cicylia (English) form of Cicely: blind

Cid (American) fun

Cyd, Syd

Cida (American) form of Cindy: moon goddess

Cidni (American) jovial

Cidnee, Cidney, Cidnie

Cidrah (American) unusual

Cid, Ciddie, Ciddy, Cidra

Cieara (Spanish) dark

CiCi, Ciear, Sieara

Ciemone (American) form of Simone: wise and thoughtful

Ciera (Irish) dark

Ciera, Cia, Cieera, Cierra, Cierre

Cilicia (Biblical) place name

Cilla (Greek) vivacious

Cika, Sica, Sika

Cille (American) form of Lucille: bright-eyed

Ceele

Cilvia (Spanish) form of Sylvia: girl of the forest

Sylvan

Cima (Place name) form of Cimarron: western

Cimarra (Last name used as first name) aware

Cimm (Place name) form of Cimarron: western

Cinderella (French) girl in the ashes

Cinda, Cindi, Cindie, Cindy

Cindy (Greek) form of Cynthia: moon goddess

Cindee, Cindi, Cyndee, Cyndi, Cyndie, Sindee, Syndi, Syndie, Syndy

Cinnamon (English) savory spice

Cenamon, Cinamen, Cinna, Cinnammon, Cinnamond, Cynamon

Cinta (Spanish) mountain of good

Cinthya (American) form of Cynthia: moon goddess

Cinzia (Italian) mountain; reasonable

Ciona (American) steadfast
Cinonah, Cionna, Cyona

Cipriana (Italian) form of Cyprus: island south of Turkey; outgoing
Cipri, Ciprianna, Cipriannah, Cypriana, Cyprianna, Cyprianne, Sipriana, Siprianna

Circe (Greek) sorceress deity; mysterious
Circee, Cirsey, Cirsie

Ciri (Latin) regal
Ceree, Ceri, Seree, Siri

Cirila (Latin) heavenly
Ceri, Cerila, Cerilla, Cerille, Cerine, Ciria, Cirine

Cissy (American) sweet
Ciss, Cissey, Cissi, Sissi

Cita (American) from the musical instrument sitar

Citalin (American) starlike

Citare (Greek) musical;
form of the Indian lute sitar
Citara, Sitare

Citlali (Native American) starry
Citlee

Claire ✪ (Latin/French) form of Clara: clear; bright
Clair, Clairee, Claireen, Claireta, Clairy, Clare, Clarette, Clarry, Klair

Clancey (American) a devil-may-care attitude
Clance, Clancee, Clancie, Clancy

Clara (Latin) clear; bright
Claire, Clare, Clareta, Clarette, Clarie, Clarine, Clary

Claresta (Greek) form of Clarissa: smart; clear-minded

Clareta (Latin) clarity; distinguished
Clarita

Clarice (Latin) form of Clara: clear; bright
Clairece, Claireece, Clairice, Clarece, Clareece, Clariece, Clarise

Clarie (French) clear

Clarieca (Latin) bright
Claire, Clare, Clari, Clarieka, Clary, Klarieca, Klarieka

Clarimond (Latin) shining defender; bright

Clarinda (Latin) form of Claire: clear; bright

Clarion (American) clear

Claris (Italian) insightful

Clarisha (Invented) clarissa

Clarissa (Latin/Greek) smart; clear-minded
Claressa, Clarice, Clarisa, Clarise, Clerissa

Clarissima (Italian) clear

Clarity (Word as name) clear-minded
Clare, Claritee, Claritie

Claronne (French) clear

Clasina (Latin) bright

Classie (American) class act

Claudette (French) persistant
Claude, Claudee, Claudet, Claudi, Claudie, Claudy

Claudia (Latin) lame
Claudelle, Claudie, Claudina, Clodia, Klaudia

Clava (Spanish) earnest; sincere

Clavenna (American) aggressive

Clea (Invented) form of Cleanthe: famed
Clia, Klea, Klee

Cleandrea (American) form of Cleanthe: famed

Cleanthe (English) famed
Clea, Cleantha, Cliantha, Klea, Kleanth

Cleatris (American) form of Cleanthe: famed

Clelia (Latin) glorious girl

Clem (Latin) gentle; vine

Clematia (Greek) winding vine

Clematis (Greek) vine; clings

Clemence (Latin) easygoing; merciful
Clem, Clemense, Clements, Clemmie, Clemmy

Clementina (Spanish) kind; forgiving

Clementas, Clementi, Clementis, Clementyna, Clymentyna, Klementina

Clementine (French/Latin) merciful

Clemencie, Klementine, Klementynne

Cleo (Greek) form of Cleopatra: Egyptian queen

Cleodal (Latin) glory

Cleodel, Cleodell

Cleofe (Greek) glorified

Cleopatra (Greek) Egyptian queen

Cleo, Clee, Kleeo, Kleo

Cleopatrea (American) form of Cleopatra: Egyptian queen

Cleora (American) famed

Cleotilda (French) form of Clotilda: famed fighter

Clerafina (Spanish) clear finish

Cleta (Greek) busy

Cletalline (Greek) busy

Cletenne (Greek) busy

Cleva (English) from the hill

Cliantha (Greek) flower of glory

Cleantha, Cleanthe, Clianthe

Clio (Greek) history muse

Kleeo, Klio

Cliodhna (Irish) dark

Clidna, Cliona

Cliona (Greek) form of Clio: history muse

Clipper (American) topnotch

Cloe (Greek) flourishing

Cloee, Cloey

Cloi (Greek) spins life

Clois (Greek) thrives

Cloise (English) cloissone

Cloreen (American) happy

Clo, Cloreane, Cloree, Cloreene, Corean, Klo, Klorean, Kloreen

Cloressa (American) consoling

Cloresse, Kloressa

Clorinda (Latin) happy

Cloee, Cloey, Clorihde, Clorynda, Klorinda

Cloris (Latin) pale

Chloris

Clory (Spanish) smiling

Clori, Clorie, Kloree, Klory

Closetta (Spanish) secretive

Close, Closette, Klosetta, Klosette

Clotho (Mythology) one of the Greek Fates; spins web of fate

Clotilda (German) famed fighter

Clotilde, Clothilde, Tilda, Tillie, Tilly

Clotilde (French) combative

Cloud (Word as name) airy

Cloudee, Cloudie, Cloudy

Clove (Botanical) distinctive spice

Klove

Clover (Botanical) lucky

Clovah, Clove, Kloverr

Cluette (American) savvy

Clydette (American) feminine form of Clyde: adventurer

Clidette, Clydett, Clydie, Klyde, Klydette

Clymene (Greek) famous

Clytie (Greek) excellent; in love with love

Cly, Clytee, Clytey, Clyty, Klytee, Klytie

Co (American) jovial

Coco, Ko, Koko

Coahoma (Native American) panther; stealthy

Coby (American) glad

Cobe, Cobey, Cobie

Cochava (Hebrew) star girl

Cocheta (Italian) form of Concetta: pure female

Coco (Spanish) coconut

Koko

Cocoa (Spanish) chocolate; spunky girl

Cody (English) softhearted; pillow

Codi, Codie, Kodie

Coffey (American) lovely

Caufey, Cofee

Cofta (Last name used as first name) audacious

Coiya (American) coquettish
Coyuh, Koya

Cokey (American) intelligent
Cokie

Colanda (African American) form of Yolanda: pretty as a violet flower

Colby (English) enduring
Cobie, Colbi, Kolbee

Cole (Last name as first name) laughing
Coe, Colie, Kohl

Colemand (American) adventurer
Colmyand

Colene (American) girl

Coleteen (Invented) created; trusted

Coletta (French) wins

Colette (French) spiritual; victorious
Coey, Collette, Kolette

Colina (American) righteous; girl
Colena, Colin, Colinn

Coline (Greek) victory
Colinette

Colisa (English) delightful
Colissa, Collisa, Collissa

Colleen (Irish) young girl
Coleen, Colene, Coley, Colleene, Collen, Colli, Kolene, Kolleen

Collena (English) girl

Colletta (English) girl

Colley (English) fearful; worrier
Col, Collie, Kolley

Collie (English) female child

Colmbyne (Latin) form of Columbine: dove; flower

Coloma (Spanish) calm
Colo, Colom, Colome

Colossae (Biblical) place name; colossal

Columbia (Latin) form of Columbine: dove; flower
Colombe, Columba

Columbine (Latin) dove; flower

Colure (French) color

Colynne (American) form of Colleen: young girl

Comfort (American) comforting; easygoing
Komfort

Comfortyne (French) comforting
Comfort, Comfortine, Comfurtine, Comfy

Comora (African) moon
Komoria

Comsa (Greek) form of Cosma: of the universe

Concepcion (Spanish) conceived; begins
Conception

Concetta (Italian) pure female

Conchetta (Spanish) wholesome
Concheta, Conchette

Conchie (Latin) conception
Conchee, Conchi, Konchie

Conchita (Spanish) girl of the conception
Chita, Concha, Conchi

Conchiteen (Spanish) pure
Conchita, Conchitee, Connie

Conchobarre (Irish) willful

Concordia (Latin) goddess of peace

Condoleezza (American) smart; with sweetness
Condeleesa, Condilesa, Condolissa

Coneisha (African American) giving
Conisha, Conishah, Conniesha

Conene (American) smart

Conerly (Last name used as first name) worthy

Conesa (American) free-flowing nature
Conisa, Connesa, Konesa

Conita (Dutch) consistent

Conlee (American) form of Connelly: radiant
Con, Conley, Conlie, Conly, Connie, Konlee, Konlie

Conner (American) brave
Con, Coner, Coni, Connie, Connor, Conny, Conor

Connie (English) form of Constance:
loyal
Con, Conni, Conny, Konnie

Connie-Kim (Vietnamese) golden
girl
Conni-Kim

Conradina (German) feminine form
of Conrad: optimist
Connie, Conradine, Conradyna,
Konnie, Konradina

Conroe (Place name) small town in
Texas
Conn, Connie, Konroe

Conroy (Last name as first name)
stately; literary
Conroi, Konroi, Konroy

Conseja (Spanish) advises

Consilletta (Italian) counsels

Consolata (Spanish) consoles others

Constance (Latin) loyal
Con, Connie, Conny, Constantia,
Constantina, Constantine, Constanza

Constantina (Italian) loyal; constant
Conn, Connee, Conni, Connie, Conny,
Constance, Constanteena, Constantinah

Constanza (Hebrew) constant
Constanz, Connstanzah

Constanze (German) unchanging
Con, Connie, Stanzi

Consuelo (Spanish) comfort-giver

Chelo, Consolata, Consuela

Contessa (Italian) pretty
Contesa, Contessah, Contesse

Contina (American) countess

Cookie (American) cute
Cooki

Copeland (Last name as first name)
adaptable
Copelan, Copelyn, Copelynn

Copper (American) redhead
Coppyr

Coppola (Italian) theatrical
Copla, Coppi, Coppo, Coppy, Kopla,
Kopola, Koppola

Coprice (American) form of Caprice:
playful; capricious

Cora (Greek) maid; giving girl
Corah, Corene, Coretta, Corette, Corra,
Correna, Corrie, Corinna, Kora

Coral (Latin) natural; small stone
Corall, Coralle, Coraly, Core, Corel,
Koral, Koraly

Coraline (American) country girl

Coraz (Spanish) form of Corazon:
heart

Corazon (Spanish) heart
Cora, Corrie, Zon, Zonn

Corazonna (Spanish) form of
Corazon: heart

Corby (Latin) raven; dark

Corday (English) prepared; heart
Cord, Cordae, Cordie, Cordy, Korday

Cordelia (Latin) warmhearted
woman
Cordalia, Cordeelia, Cordelie, Cordi,
Cordie, Cordilia, Kordelia, Kordey,
Kordi

Cordelita (Latin/Spanish) heartfelt
Cordelia, Cordelite, Cordella

Cordillera (Latin) form of Cordelia:
warmhearted woman

Cordula (Latin/German) heart; jewel
Cord, Cordie, Cordoola, Cordoolah, Cordy

Corenda (American) derivative of
Dorenda; adored

Corette (Greek) form of Cora: maid;
giving girl

Corey (Irish) perky
Cori, Corree, Corrie, Korey, Korri, Korrie

Corgie (American) funny
Corgi, Korgee, Korgie

Cori (Greek/Irish) caring
Corey, Corri, Corrie, Cory

Coriander (Botanical) seasoning;
simplistic

Corinna (Greek) young girl
Corina, Corrinna, Corryna, Corynna

Corinne (Greek/French) maiden; protective
Coreen, Corina, Corine, Corinna, Corrina, Coryn, Corynn, Koreene, Korinne

Corintha (German) maiden

Corinthian (Place name) a town in Greece; religious

Coris (Greek) singer
Corris, Koris, Korris

Corissa (Greek) kindhearted
Korissa

Corissah (American) mysterious

Corita (Spanish) kind

Corky (American) energetic
Corkee, Corkey, Corki, Corkie, Korkee, Korky

Corliss (English) open-hearted
Corless, Corlise, Corly, Korlis, Korliss

Corlisse (American) cheerful

Corlissen (American) cheerful

Corly (American) active
Corlee, Corli, Corlie, Korli, Korly

Corlyn (American) innovative
Corlin, Corlinn, Corlynn, Corlynne, Korlin, Korlyn

Cormella (Italian) fiery
Cormee, Cormela, Cormelah, Cormellia, Cormey, Cormie

Cornae (Origin unknown) all seeing
Coma, Korna, Kornae

Cornecia (Latin) yellow hair; horn

Corneitha (Latin) horn child

Cornelia (Latin) practical
Carnelia, Corney, Corni

Cornelie (Latin) horn child

Cornelius (Latin) realistic
Corneal, Corneelyus, Corney, Corny

Cornesha (African American) talkative
Cornee, Corneshah, Cornesia

Cornish (English) Cornish

Corona (Spanish) crowned
Corone, Coronna, Korona

Correne (American) musical
Coree, Coreen, Correen, Correna, Korene, Korrene

Corri (English) naive
Corry

Corrianna (American) joyful
Coreanne, Corey, Corianna, Corri, Corriana

Corrie (English) form of Coral: natural; small stone

Corrinda (French) girlish
Corri, Corrin, Korin, Korinda

Corseta (English) unsophisticated

Cortanie (American) form of Courtney: domain of Curtis
Cortanny, Cortany

Cortland (American) distinctive
Cortlan, Courte, Courtland, Courtlin

Cortlinn (American) happy
Cortlenn, Cortlin, Cortlyn, Cortlynn

Corvette (Word as name) speedy
Corv, Corva, Corve, Korvette

Corvina (Latin) raven; brunette

Cosetta (French) pretty thing

Cosette (French) warm
Cossette

Cosima (Greek) universe; harmony
Coseema, Koseema, Kosima

Cosma (Greek) of the universe

Cosmee (Greek) organized
Cos, Cosmi, Cosmie

Cosmiss (American) harmony with the cosmos

Cossette (French) winning
Coss, Cossie, Cossy, Kossee, Kossette

Costanza (Last name as first name) strong-willed; funny

Costner (American) embraced
Cosner, Cost, Costnar, Costnor, Costnur

Cota (Spanish) lively

Cotcha (African American) stylish
Kasha, Katcha, Katshay, Kotsha

Cotia (Spanish) full of vitality

Cotilia (Spanish) vital

Cotrena (American) form of Katrina: melodious

Catreena, Catrina, Catrine, Cotrene, Katrine, Kotrene

Cotton (American) comforting

Cottie

Countess (English) blueblood

Contessa

Courday (French) courteous

Couria (French) courteous

Cournette (American) form of Coronet: regal

Courney, Kournette

Courney (English) form of Courtney: domain of Curtis

Courtney (English) domain of Curtis

Cortney, Courtenay, Courteney, Courtnay, Courtnee, Courtny, Kortnee, Kortney

Covelina (Spanish) cave child

Covin (American) unpredictable

Covan, Cove, Coven, Covyn

Coy (American) sly

Coye, Koi, Koy

Coyah (American) singular

Coya, Coyia

Coyote (American) wild

Coyo, Kaiote, Kaiotee

Cozeth (English) rainbow

Cozetta (English) rainbow

Cozette (French) darling

Cramer (American) jolly

Cramar, Cramir, Kramer

Cramisa (Invented) nice

Cramissa, Kramisa

Creda (English) giving credence

Cree (American) wild spirit

Crea, Creeah

Creed (American) boisterous

Crede, Cree, Kreed

Creesha (English) flower

Creirwy (Welsh) lucky amulet

Cremone (French) wanted

Creola (American) desires

Cresa (English) fickle

Crescena (German) grows

Crescente (American) impressive

Crescent, Cresent, Cress, Cressie

Crescentia (Spanish) crescent-faced; smiling

Crescent, Creseantia, Cressentt

Cresenda (American) explosive

Cressa (Greek) form of Cressida: infidel

Cresa, Cressah, Cress, Cresse, Kressa

Cressell (American) growth

Cressida (Greek) infidel

Cresida, Cresiduh, Cresside

Cressie (American) growing; good

Cress, Cressy, Kress, Kressie

Creston (American) worthy

Crest, Crestan, Creste, Cresten, Crestey, Cresti, Crestie

Cresusa (English) fickle

Cricket (American) energetic

Kricket

Crimson (American) deep

Cremsen, Crims, Crimsen, Crimsonn, Crimsun

Crisanta (American) form of Chrysanthemum: flower

Crisel (English) form of Crystal: clear; open-minded

Criselda (Spanish) wild

Crisselda

Criselle (English) crystal

Crishonna (American) beautiful

Crishona, Crisshone, Crissie, Crissy, Krishona, Krishonna

Crisiant (Welsh) crystal; clear

Cris, Crissie

Crispa (Latin) curly hair

Crispina (Latin) curly-haired girl

Crispy (Invented) fun-loving; zany

Crispee, Krispy

Crista (Italian) form of Christina: follower of Christ

Krista

Cristella (English) crystal

Cristin (Irish) dedicated

Cristen, Crystyn, Kristin, Krystyn

Cristina (Greek) form of Christina: follower of Christ
Kristina

Cristos (Greek) dedicated
Christos, Criss, Crissie

Cristy (English) spiritual
Cristi, Crysti, Kristi, Krystie

Crusitee (Spanish) of the cross

Cruzita (Spanish) of the cross

Cruzitte (Spanish) of the cross

Cryange (Place name)

Crystal (Latin) clear; open-minded
Christal, Chrystal, Cristal, Cristalle, Crys, Crystelle, Krystal

Crystilis (Spanish) focused
Chrysilis, Crys, Cryssi, Cryssie, Crystylis

Csaba (Hungarian) shepherd; wanderer

Csilla (Hungarian) defensive

Cuasha (American) goodness

Cuba (Place name) island; fun-loving girl

Cullen (Irish) attractive
Cullan, Cullie, Cullun, Cully

Cumale (American) open-hearted
Cue, Cuemalie, Cue-maly, Cumahli

Cumthia (American) open-minded
Cumthea, Cumthee, Cumthi, Cumthie, Cumthy

Cupertina (Spanish) covert

Cupid (American) romantic
Cupide

Curine (American) attractive
Curina, Curinne, Curri, Currin

Curisten (Invented) form of Kirsten: follower of Christ

Curry (American) languid
Curree, Currey, Curri, Currie

Cursten (American) form of Kirsten: follower of Christ
Curst, Curstee, Curstie, Curstin

Cushaun (American) elegant
Cooshaun, Cooshawn, Cue, Cushawn, Cushonn, Cushun

Cximara (Spanish) greatness

Cyan (American) colorful
Cyanne, Cyenna, Cyun

Cyanea (Greek) blue-eyed baby

Cyanetta (Greek) little blue
Cyan, Cyanette, Syan, Syanette

Cybele (Greek) conflicted

Cybill (Latin) prophetess
Cybell, Cybelle, Cybil, Sibyl, Sibyle

Cydell (American) country girl
Cydee, Cydel, Cydie, Cydile, Cydy

Cydney (American) perky
Cyd, Cydni, Cydnie

Cylee (American) darling
Cye, Cyle, Cylea, Cyli, Cylie, Cyly

Cylene (American) melodious

Cylena, Cyline

Cyllene (American) sweet

Cyma (Greek) does well

Cymantha (English) form of Simone: wise and thoughtful

Cymbeline (Greek) benevolent ruler
Beline, Cymba, Cymbe, Cymbie, Cyme, Cymmie, Symbe

Cyn (Greek) form of Cynthia: moon goddess
Cynnae, Cynnie, Syn

Cynara (Greek) prickly; particular
Cynarra

Cynder (English) having wanderlust
Cindee, Cinder, Cindy, Cyn, Cyndee, Cyndie, Cyndy

Cynista (English) leader

Cyntanah (American) singer
Cintanna, Cyntanna

Cynthia (Greek) moon goddess
Cindy, Cyn, Cyndee, Cyndy, Cynthea, Cynthee, Cynthie

Cynthiah (American) form of Cynthia: moon goddess

Cyntia (Greek) form of Cynthia: moon goddess
Cyn, Cyntea, Cynthie, Cyntie, Syntia

Cyntrille (African American) gossipy
Cynn, Cyntrell, Cyntrelle, Cyntrie

Cypress (Botanical) swaying
Cypres, Cyprice, Cypris, Cypriss, Cyprus

Cyra (American) willing
Cye, Cyrah, Syra

Cyreen (American) sensual
Cyree, Cyrene, Cyrie

Cyrena (American) form of Serena:
calm

Cyrene (Greek) mythological nymph

Cyrenian (American) bewitching
*Cyree, Cyren, Cyrenean, Cyrey, Siren,
Syrenian*

Cyrenna (American) straightforward
*Cyrena, Cyrennah, Cyrinna, Cyryna,
Cyrynna*

Cyriece (American) artistic
Cyree, Cyreece, Cyreese, Cyrie

Cyrilla (Latin) royal; little minx
Cirila

Cyrise (English) serene

Cytherea (Greek) from the island of
Cythera; celestial

Cyvie (American) clean

Czara (Slavic) leads

Czaree (American) czar-like

Czarina (Russian) royal

D

Daba (Hebrew) kindhearted

Dabaloth (Biblical) angelic

Dabaritta (Biblical) angelic

Daberath (Biblical) angelic

Dabire (Biblical) angelic

Dacey (Irish) a southerner
*Dace, Dacee, Daci, Dacia, Dacie, Dacy,
Daicie, Daycee*

Dacia (Latin) old soul
Dacie, Dachia, Dachi

Dae (English) day
Day, Daye

Daelan (English) aware
*Dael, Daeleen, Daelena, Daelin, Daely,
Daelyn, Daelynne, Dale, Daley, Daylan,
Daylin, Daylind, Dee*

Daevrissa (American) girl of the day

Daeze (African) day

Daffodil (Botanical) flower
Daffy

Dafna (Slavic) form of Daphne:
pretty nymph

Dafnee (Greek) form of Daphne:
pretty nymph
Dafney, Dafnie

Dafo (American) form of Daffodil:
flower

Dagmar (Scandinavian/German)
glorious day
Dag, Dagmara, Dagmarr

Dagny (Scandinavian) day
Dagna, Dagnanna, Dagne, Dagney

Dahlia (Scandinavian) flower
Dahl, Dollie

Dahri (American) form of Dahlia:
flower

Dai (Welsh/Japanese) beloved one of
great importance

Dailah (American) form of Dahlia:
flower

Dainikya (Slavic) form of Danica:
star of the morning

Daira (American) outgoing
*D'Aira, Daire, Dairrah, Darrah,
Derrah*

Daisha (American) sparkling
D'Aisha, Daishe, Dasha, Dashah

Daisy (English) flower; day's eye
*Daisee, Daisey, Daisi, Daisia, Daisie,
Daissy, Daizee, Daizi, Daizy, Dasey,
Dasi, Dasie, Dasy, Daysee, Daysie,
Daysy*

Daisy-Boo (American) frivolous;
flower

Daiton (American) wondrous
Day, Dayten, Dayton

Daja (American) intuitive
Dajah

Dajanae (African American)
persuasive
Daije, Daja, Dajainay, Dayjanah

Dajon (American) gifted
*Dajo, Dajohn, Dajonn, Dajonnay,
Dajonne*

Dakara (American) firebrand
Dacara, Dakarah, Dakarea, Dakarra

Daking (Asian) friendly

Dakota (Native American) tribal
name; solid friend
*Dacota, Dakohta, Dakotah, Dakotha,
Dakotta, Dekoda, Dekota, Dekotah,
Dekotha*

Dalacie (American) brilliant
*Dalaci, Dalacy, Dalasie, Dalce, Dalci,
Dalse*

Dalaina (American) spirited
*Dalana, Dalayna, Delaina, Delaine,
Delayna*

Dalaney (American) hopeful
Dalanee, Dalaynee, Dalayni

Dalaya (English) form of Dahlia:
flower

Dale (English) valley-life
*Daile, Daleleana, Dalena, Dalina,
Dayle*

Daleah (American) pretty
Dalea

Daley (Irish) leader
*Dailey, Dalea, Daleigh, Dali, Dalie,
Daly*

Dali (Spanish) of the day

Dalia (Spanish) flower
*Daliah, Daliyah, Dayliah, Doliah,
Dolliah, Dolya*

Dalian (American) joy
Dalean

Daliana (American) joyful spirit
Daliane, Dalianna, Dilial, Dollianna

Dalice (American) able
Daleese, Dalleece

Dalila (African) gentle
*Dahlila, Dahlilla, Dalia, Dalilah,
Dalilia*

Dalimda (American) form of
Dalinda: beautiful;
honey; sweetheart

Dalin (American) calm
Dalen, Dalenn, Dalun

Dalinda (American) form of Belinda:
beautiful; form of Melinda: honey;
sweetheart

Dalita (American) smooth
*Daleta, Daletta, Dalite, Dalitee,
Dalitta*

Dallas (Place name) city in Texas;
confident
*Dalis, Dalisse, Daliz, Dallice, Dallis,
Dallsyon, Dallus, Dallys, Dalyce, Dalys*

Dallen (American) outspoken
Dal, Dalen, Dalin, Dallin

Dallise (American) gentle
Dalise, Dallece, Dalleece, Dalleese

Dalmar (German) perseveres

Dalmatia (Biblical) place name

Dalondra (Invented) generous
Dalandra, Dalon, Dalondrah, Delondra

Dalonna (Invented) generous
Dalohn, Dalona, Dalonne

Dalphine (French) form of
Delphine: calmness
Dal, Dalf, Dalfeen, Dalfene, Dalphene

Dalton (American) smart
*Dallee, Dalli, Dallie, Dallton, Dally,
Daltawyn*

Daltrey (American) quiet
Daltree, Daltri, Daltrie

Dalva (American) strong

Dalyn (American) smart
Dalin, Dalinne, Dalynn, Dalynne

Dama (Hindi) temptress

Damalla (Greek) fledgling; young

Damala, Damalas, Damalis, Damall

Damara (Greek) gentle

Damaris, Damarra

Damaris (Greek) calm

Damalis, Damar, Damara, Damares,
Damaret, Damarius, Damary,
Damarys, Dameress, Dameris, Damiris,
Dammaris, Dammeris, Damrez,
Damris, Demaras, Demarays, Demaris

Damecia (Invented) sweet

Dameisha, Damesha, Demecia,
Demisha, Demeshe

Dami (Greek) form of Damia: spirited

Damee, Damey, Damie, Damy

Damia (Greek) spirited

Damiah, Damya, Damyah, Damyen,
Damyenne, Damyuh

Damianne (Greek) one who soothes

Damiana

Damica (French) open-spirited

Dameeka, Dameka, Damekah,
Damicah, Damie, Damika, Damikah,
Demeeka, Demeka, Demekah, Demica,
Demicah

Damita (Spanish) small woman of
nobility

Dama, Damah, Damee, Damesha,
Dameshia, Damesia, Dametia,
Dametra, Dametrah

Damitte (Irish) small

Damon (American) sprightly

Damoane, Damone

Damone (American) mighty

Dame

D'Amore (Invented) love

Dana (English) bright gift of God

Daina, Dainna, Danae, Danah,
Danai, Danaia, Danalee, Danan,
Danarra, Danayla, Dane, Danean,
Danee, Daniah, Danie, Danna, Dayna,
Daynah

Danae (Greek) bright and pure

Danay, Danayla, Danays, Danea,
Danee, Dannae, Denae, Denee

Danala (English) happy; golden

Dan, Danalla, Danee, Danela, Danney,
Danny

Danay (American) happy

Danaye, D'Nay, D·nay

Dancel (French) energetic

Dance, Dancell, Dancelle, Dancey,
Dancie, Danse, Dansel, Danselle

Dancie (American) from the word
dancer

Dancy

Dandelion (Botanical) flower

Daneaa (Welsh) bright day

Daneen (Greek) blessed

Daneil (Hebrew) judged by God;
spiritual

Daneal, Daneala, Daneale, Daneel,
Daneela, Daneila

Danelle (Hebrew) kindhearted

Danael, Danalle, Danel, Danele,
Danell, Danella, Dani, Dannele,
Danny

Danelly (Spanish) form of Danielle:
judged by God; spiritual

Daneli, Danellie, Dannelley, Dannelly

Danena (Greek) blessed

Danessa (American) dainty

Danesa, Danese, Danesha, Danesse,
Daniesa, Daniesha, Danisa, Danisha,
Danissa

Danessia (American) delicate child

Danesia, Danieshia, Danisla, Danissia

Danette (American) form of
Danielle: judged by God; spiritual

Danetra, Danett, Danetta

Dangela (Latin) form of Angela:
divine; angelic

Angee, Angelle, Angie, Dangelah,
Dangelia, Dangey, Dangi, Dangie

Dani (Hebrew) form of Danielle:
judged by God; spiritual

Danee, Danie, Danne, Dannee, Danni,
Dannie, Danny, Dany

Dania (Hebrew) form of Danielle:
judged by God: spiritual
Daniah, Danya, Danyah

Daniah (Hebrew) judged
Dan, Dania, Danny, Danya

Danica (Latin/Polish) star of the
morning
*Daneeka, Danika, Danneeka, Dannica,
Dannika*

Daniella (Italian) form of Danielle:
judged by God; spiritual
Danilla

Danielle (Hebrew/French) feminine
form of Daniel: judged by God;
spiritual
*Danelle, Daniele, Daniell, Danniella,
Danyel*

Danir (American) fresh
Daner

Danit (Hebrew) judged by God
*Danett, Danis, Danisha, Daniss,
Danita, Danitra, Danitza, Daniz,
Danni*

Danita (English) form of Danielle:
judged by God; spiritual
Danni, Danny, Denita, Denny

Danla (Slavic) form of Danielle:
judged by God; spiritual

D'Anna (Hebrew) special

Danna (American) cheerful
*D'Ana, D'Anna, Dannae, Danni,
Danny*

Danner (American) morning star

Danube (Place name) river; flowing
spirit

Danuta (Polish) God's gift

Danyella (Slavic) form of Danielle:
judged by God; spiritual

Danyiel (Slavic) form of Danielle:
judged by God; spiritual

Danz (Last name used as first name)
trendsetter

Daphiney (Greek) form of Daphne:
pretty nymph
Daff, Daph

Daphne (Greek) pretty nymph
*Daphane, Daphaney, Daphanie,
Daphany, Daphiney, Daphnee,
Daphney, Daphnie, Daphny, Daphonie,
Daphy*

Daphoneel (Greek) form of
Daphne: pretty nymph

Daphyne (Greek) form of Daphne:
pretty nymph

Daquisha (African American)
talkative

Dara (Hebrew) compassionate
Dahra, Dahrah, Darah, Darra, Darrah

Daralice (Greek) beloved
Dara, Daraleese, Daraliece

Daravia (Hebrew) loving

Darby (Irish) a free woman
Darb, Darbee, Darbi, Darbie, Darbye

Darceece (Irish) form of Darci: dark

Darcelle (American) secretive
Darce, Darcel, Darcell, Darcey

Darci (Irish) dark
*Darce, Darcee, Darcie, Darcy, Dars,
Darsey*

Darda (Hebrew) wise

Dare (Hebrew) compassion

Daretha (Slavic) loved

Dari (Czech) rich

Daria (Persian) queenly
*Dare, Darea, Dareah, Dari, Darian,
Darianne, Darria, Darya*

Darian (Anglo-Saxon) precious
Dare, Darien, Darry, Derian

Darice (English) contemporary
*Dareese, Darese, Dari, Dariece, Darri,
Darrie, Darry*

Darielle (French) rich
*Darell, Darelle, Dariel, Darriel,
Darrielle*

Darienne (Greek) great

Darika (Indian) young maiden

Darilyn (American) darling
Darilin, Darilinn, Darilynn, Derilyn

Darina (Greek) rich

Darine (English) feminine form of Darren: great

Darionne (American) adventuresome
Dareon, Darion, Darionn, Darionna

Dariya (Russian) sweet
Dara, Darya

Darla (English) form of Darlene: darling girl
Darl, Darlee, Darley, Darli, Darlie, Darly

Darlee (English) darling
Darl, Darley, Darli, Darlie

Darlene (French) darling girl
Darlean, Darleen, Darlena, Darlenia, Darlin, Darling

Darlenn (French) form of Darlene: darling girl

Darless (French) form of Darlene: darling girl

Darlette (French) form of Darlene: darling girl

Darlina (French) form of Darlene: darling girl

Darling (American) precious
Darline, Darly, Darlyng

Darlonna (African American) darling
Darlona

Darlusz (Slavic) loved

Darlye (French) darling

Darmetra (American) able

Darnelle (Irish) seamstress
Darnel, Darnell, Darnella, Darnyell

Darnette (American) hides

Daroma (American) treasured

Daron (Irish) great woman
Daren, Darun, Daryn

Darquea (American) different

Darr (Slavic) form of Daria: queenly

Darras (Slavic) rules

Darrelle (English) loved

Darrien (Irish) great

Darrow (Last name as first name) cautious
Darro, Darroh

Darryl (French/English) form of Darlene: darling girl
Darel, Darelle, Daril, Darrell, Darrill, Daryl, Daryll, Derel, Derrell

Darsa (American) bright spirit

Darshelle (African American) confident
Darshel, Darshell

Dart (English) tenacious
Darte, Dartee, Dartt

Darva (Invented) sensible
Darv, Darvah, Darvee, Darvey, Darvi, Darvie

Daryn (Greek/Irish) gift-giver
Daryan, Darynn, Darynne

Daryna (Slavic) form of Daria: queenly

Dash (American) fast-moving
Dashee, Dasher, Dashy

Dasha (Russian) darling
Dashah

Dashanda (African American) loving
Dashan, Dashande

Dashawn (African American) brash
Dashawna, Dashay

Dashawntay (African American) careful
Dash, Dashauntay

Dashea (Hebrew) patient

Dasheena (African American) flashy
Dashea, Dasheana

Dashelle (African American) striking
Dachelle, Dashel, Dashell, Dashy

Dashika (African American) runner
Dash, Dasheka

Dashiki (African) loose shirt; casual
Dashi, Dashika, Dashka, Desheka, Deshiki

Dashilan (American) solemn
Dashelin, Dashelin, Dashlinne, Dashlyn, Dashlynn, Dasialyn

Dasmine (Invented) sleek
Dasmeen, Dasmin, Dazmeen, Dazmine

Dassa (Jewish) form of Hadassah: myrtle tree
Dassah, Dasa

Dassia (American) pretty
Dasie, Dassea, Dasseah, Dassee, Dassi, Dassie, Deassiah

Dathema (Biblical) feminine form of David: beloved

Dati (Hebrew) believer

Dativa (Hebrew) believer

Daufenne (French) of the dolphin

Daulette (American) invented

Dauphinais (French) of the dolphin

Daureen (American) darling
Dareen, Daurean, Daurie, Daury, Dawreen

Dauria (American) form of Daria: queenly

Daveena (Scottish) feminine form of David: beloved
Daveen, Davena, Davey, Davina, Davinna

Davianna (English) beloved

Davida (Hebrew) beloved one
Daveeda, Daveisha, Davesia, Daveta, Davetta, Davette, Davika, Davisha, Davita

Davina (Hebrew) believer; beloved
Dava, Daveena, Davene, Davida, Davita, Devina, Devinia, Devinya

Davincia (Spanish) God-loving; winner
Davince, Davinse, Vincia

Davinique (African American) believer; unique
Davin, Davineek, Vineek

Davis (American) boyish
Daves

Davisnell (Invented) vivacious
Daviesnell, DavisNell

Davonna (Scottish) well-loved
Davon, Davona, Davonda

Davonne (African American) splashy
Davaughan, Davaughn, Davion, Daviona, Davon, Davone, Davonn

Davrush (Yiddish) loves others

Daw (Asian) starlike

Dawa (Tibetan) girl born on Monday

Dawanda (African American) righteous
Dawana, Dawand, Dawanna, Dawauna, Dawonda, Dawonna, Dwanda

Dawn (English) daybreak
Daun, Dawna, Dawne

Dawna (English) eloquence of dawn
Dauna, Daunda, Dawn, Dawnah, Dawnna, Dawny, Dawnya

Dawnesha (American) dawn's child

Dawnika (African American) dawn
Dawneka, Dawneeka, Dawnica, Donika

Dawnisha (African American) breath of dawn
Daunisha, Dawnish, Dawny, Nisa, Nisha

Dawntelle (African American) morning bright
Dawntel, Dawnttell, Dontelle

Dawona (African American) smart
Dawonna, Dawonne

Day (English) day; bright

Dayana (American) form of Diana: divine woman; goddess of the hunt and fertility
Dayannah, Dyana

Dayanara (Spanish) form of Deyanira: aggressor
Day, Daya, Dayan, Dianara, Diannare, Nara

Dayita (Indian) loved

Dayla (American) day's joy

Dayle (American) joyful

Daylee (American) calm; reserved
Dailee, Day, Dayley, Dayly

Dayna (English) form of Dana: bright gift of God
Daynah

Daysha (Russian) serene
Dasha, Dayeisha

Dayshanay (African American)
saucy
*Daysh, Dayshanae, Dayshannay,
Dayshie*

Dayshawna (American) laughing
Dayshauna, Dayshona, Dashonah

Dayshay (African American) lovable
Dashae, Dashay, Dashea

Dayton (Place name) town in Ohio;
fast

Daytona (American) speedy
Dayto, Daytonna

Dayvonne (African American)
careful
Dave, Davey, Davonne, Dayvaughn

De (Chinese) virtuous

Deaborah (Spanish) form of Debora:
prophetess

Deacon (Greek) joyful messenger
Deak, Deakon, Deecon, Deke

Dealba (Irish) Irish girl

Dean (English) practical
Deanie, Deanni

Deana (Latin) divine girl
Deane, Deanna

Deandea (English) form of Deanne:
divine woman; goddess of hunt and
fertility

Deandria (American) sweetheart
Deandreah, Deandriah

Deanie (English) feminine form of
Dean: leader
Deanee, Deaney, Deani

Deanna (Latin/English) divine girl
Deana, Deanne, Dee

Deanne (Latin) form of Diana:
divine woman; goddess of hunt and
fertility
Deann, Dee, Deeann

Dearbhail (Welsh) held close

De-Armone (French) girl of the
army

Dearon (American) dear one
Dear, Dearan, Dearen, Deary

Dearoven (American) form of
Dearon: dear one
Derovan, Deroven

Deasa (Spanish) delightful

Deatra (English) form of Deitra:
goddesslike

DeAyn (Dutch) form of Deanne:
divine woman; goddess of hunt and
fertility

Debara (Spanish) form of Deborah:
prophetess

Debarath (Hebrew) bee; busy
Deborath, Daberath

Debbie (Hebrew) form of Deborah:
prophetess
*Deb, Debbee, Debbey, Debbi, Debby,
Debbye, Debee, Debi, Debie*

Deborah (Hebrew) prophetess
*Debbie, Debbora, Debborah, Debor,
Deboreh, Deborrah, Debra*

Deboria (English) form of Deborah:
prophetess

Debra (Hebrew) prophetess
Debbra, Debbrah, Debrah

Debran (American) form of Deborah:
prophetess

Debrani (American) grace

Debray (American) form of Deborah:
prophetess
Dabrae, Deb, Debrae, Debraye

Debrean (Slavic) form of Deborah:
prophetess

Debreka (Slavic) form of Deborah:
prophetess

Dece (Spanish) tenth child

Decena (Latin) form of Decima:
tenth girl
Decia

Deceshia (American) tenth child

D'Echon (French) echo

Decima (Latin) tenth girl

Decole (French) form of Nicole:
winning

Decolia (American) form of Nicole: winning

Decuma (Mythology) one of the Roman Fates; measures

Dedra (American) spirited
Dee, Deeddra, DeeDee, Deedra, Deedrea, Deedrie, Deidra, Deirdre

Dedranay (American) form of Deidra: sparkling

Dee (English/Irish) lucky one
Dea, Deah, DeeDee, Dee-Dee, Dedee, Didee

Deedee (American) form of D names: vivacious
D.D., Dee Dee, DeeDee, Dee-Dee

Deen (English) form of Dean: practical

Deena (American) soothes

Deepa (Hindi) light

DeErica (African American) audacious
Dee-Erica

Deesha (American) dancing
Dedee, Dee, Deesh, Deeshah, Deisha

Deianna (English) form of Deanna: divine girl

Deidra (Irish) sparkling
Deedra, Deidre, Dierdra

Deighan (American) exciting
Daygan, Deigan

Deina (Spanish) soothes

Deiondra (Greek) feminine form of Dionysis: joyous celebrant
Deandrah, Deann, Deanndra, Dee, Deean, Deeann, DeeDee, Deondra

Deirdre (Irish) passionate
Dedra, Dee, Deedee, Deedrah, Deerdra, Deerdre, Didi

Deissy (Greek) form of Desma: oath
Deisi, Deissey, Deissie, Desmee, Desmer, Dessi

Deitra (Greek) goddess-like
Deetra, Detria

Deittra (English) form of Demetria: harvest goddess

Deja (French) already seen
Dejah, D'Ja

Dejan (Slavic) siren

Dejeane (French) born before

Dejoie (French) joy

Dejon (French) she came before
Daijon, Dajan, Dajona

Deka (African) a pleasure
Dekah, Dekka

Dekeidra (American) pleasant

Dela (English) dramatic

Delakate (American) delicate

Delana (German) protective
Dalana, Dalanna, Dalayna, Daleena, Dalena, Dalenna, Dalina, Dalinna, Deedee, Delaina, Delainah, Delena

Delanah (American) wise
Delana, Delano, Dellana

Delandra (American) outgoing
Delan, Delande

Delaney (Irish) bouncy; enthusiastic
Dalanie, Delaine, Delainey, Delane, DeLayney, Dellie, Dulaney

Delaune (English) form of Delaney: bouncy; enthusiastic

Delaura (American) prefix De and Laura

Delcia (Latin) delightful

Delcine (Latin) a delight

Delcy (American) friendly
Del, Delcee, Delci

Dele (American) rash; noble
Del, Dell

Delene (French) dearest girl

Delfin (Spanish) of the dolphin

Delfina (Latin/Italian) flowering
Dellfina, Delphina

Delia (Greek) lovely; moon goddess
Dehlia, Deilyuh, Del, Delea, Deli, Dellia, Dellya, Delya, Delyah

Delicia (English) delights

Delesha, Delice, Delisa, Delise, Delisha, Delisiah, Delya, Delys, Delyse, Delysia

Delieca (Spanish) delight

Delight (French) wonderful

Delilah (Hebrew) beautiful temptress

Dalia, Dalila, Delila, Lilah

Delina (French) dearest

Delinah (American) form of Adeline: sweet

Delinda (American) form of Melinda: honey; sweetheart

Delin, Delinde, Delynda

Delinde (French) dearest

Delise (Latin) delicious

Del, Delice, Delicia, Delisa, Delissa

Delite (American) a pleasure

Delight

Delja (Slavic) form of Deja: already seen

Dell (Greek) kind

Del

Della (Greek) kind

Dee, Del, Dela, Dell, Delle, Delli, Dells

Dellana (Irish) form of Delaney: bouncy; enthusiastic

Delaine, Delana, Dell, Dellaina, Dellane, Dellann

Dellia (American) pretty

Delmee (American) star

Del, Delmey, Delmi, Delmy

Delmys (American) incredible

Del, Delmas, Delmis

Delo (Slavic) form of Delos: beautiful brunette; a small Aegean isle; stunning

Deloise (Italian) combative

Delon (American) musical

Delonn, Delonne

Delora (Spanish) form of Delores: woman of sorrowful leaning

Dellora, Delorita

Delores (Spanish) woman of sorrowful leaning

Del, Delora, Delore, Deloria, Delories, Deloris, Delorise, Dolores

Delos (Greek) beautiful brunette; a small Aegean isle; stunning

Delas

Delpha (Greek) form of Delphine: calmness

Delfa

Delphina (Greek) dolphin; smart

Delphine (Latin) calmness

Delfina, Delfine, Delpha, Delphe, Delphene, Delphi, Delphia, Delphina, Delphinia, Delvina

Delphy (Biblical) place name

Delphia, Delphi

Delta (Greek) fourth letter of the Greek alphabet

Del, Dell, Dellta, Delte, Deltra

Deltrese (African American) jubilant

Del, Delltrese, Delt, Delta, Deltreese, Deltrice

Delwyn (English/Welsh) friend from the valley; neat and fair

Delwen, Delwenne, Delwin

Demareas (Biblical) calf

Demetia (Greek) harvest goddess

Demetress (Greek) form of Demetria: harvest goddess

Deme, Demetra, Demetres, Demetri, Dimi, Tress, Tressie, Tressy

Demetria (Greek) harvest goddess

Deitra, Demeta, Demeteria, Demetra, Demetrice, Demetris, Demetrish, Demetrius, Demi, Demita, Demitra

Demetriase (Greek) harvest goddess

Demi (French) half

Demiah, Demie

Demtrialle (American) regal

Dena (English) laid back; valley

Deane, Deena, Deeyn, Denae, Denah, Dene, Denea, Deney, Denna

Denada (American) calm

Denae (Hebrew) form of Dena: shows the truth

Danay, Denee

Dencie (English) form of Denise: wine-lover

Denda (American) form of Dena: laid back; valley

Deneane (English) form of Denise: wine-lover

Denedra (American) lively; natural
Den, Dene, Denney

Denee (French) robust

Deneen (American) absolved
Denean, Denene

Deneka (Slavic) star

Denes (English) nature-lover
Denis, Denne, Denny

Denesha (American) rowdy

Denetria (Greek) from God
Denitria, Denny, Dentria

Denetrice (African American) optimistic
Denetrise, Denitrise, Denny

Denezia (Turkish) of the sea
Denizia, Deniz

Denise (French) wine-lover
Danice, Daniece, Danise, Denese, Deni, Denica, Deniece, Denni, Denny

Denisha (American) jubilant
Danisha, Deneesha, Denesha, Deneshea, Deniesha, Denishia

Denna (American) lively

Dennice (American) festive

Denovia (American) reveler

Den'tessa (American) form of Contessa: pretty

Denton (Place name) town in Texas; from a holy town
Dent, Dentun, Denty, Dentyn

Denver (English) born in a green valley
Denv, Denvie

Denyse (American) form of Denise: wine-lover

Denz (Invented) lively
Dens

Denza (American) fun-loving

Deo (Scottish) God's grace

Deoniece (African American) feminine
Dee, DeeDee, Deo, Deone, Deoneece, Deoneese

Deonsha (American) form of Deoniece: feminine

Deonta (American) calm valley

Deora (English) adored

Deoran (American) adored

Dephoine (American) form of Delphine: calmness

Dera (Slavic) ocean's child

Derbe (Biblical) place name

Dericka (American) dancer
Derica, Dericca, D'ericka, Derika, Derrica, Derricka, Derrika

Derie (Hebrew) form of Derorah: free
Derey, Drora, Drorah

Derline (American) from land of deer
Derlini

Derneeka (Slavic) of the ocean

Dernise (American) form of Denise: wine-lover

Deronique (African American) unique girl
Deron, Deroneek

Derorah (Hebrew) free
Derora

Derrinda (Spanish) form of Dorinda: loved

Derrisa (American) form of Merissa: ocean-loving

Derrona (American) natural
Derona, Derone, Derry

Derry (Irish) red-haired woman
Deri, Derrie

Deryn (Welsh) birdlike; small
Derren, Derrin, Derrine, Deryne

Desai (African) desired

Desba (African) desired

Desbiene (American) desired

Desdemona (Greek) tragic figure; destined
Des, Desde, Dez

Desena (American) desired

Deshawna (African American)
vivacious
Dashawna, Deshan, Deshanda,
Deshandra, Deshane, Deshaun,
Deshauna, Deshaundra, Deshaune,
Deshawn, Deshawndra, Deshawnna,
Desheania, Deshona, Deshonda,
Deshonna

Deshette (African American) dishy
Deshett

Deshondra (African American)
vivacious
Deshaundra, Deshondrah, Deshondria

Desi (French) form of Desiree: desired
Dezi, Dezzie

Desiah (French) form of Desiree:
desired

Desire (English) desired
Dezire

Desiree (French) desired
Desairee, Desarae, Desaray, Desaraye,
Desaree, Desarhea, Desary, Deseri,
Des'ree, Desree, Des-Ree, Dezaray,
Deziree, Dezray

Desireenah (American) desirable

Desirette (American) desires

Desislav (Slavic) glory girl

Deslin (American) tenth

Desma (Greek) oath

Desna (Hindi) giving

Despina (Greek) ladylike

Desreta (Spanish) desires

Dess (Slavic) tenth

Desta (Slavic) joyful

Destin (American) destiny
Destinn, Destyn

Destina (Spanish) destiny
Desteena, Desteenah

Destiny ✪ (French) fated
Destanee, Destanie, Desteney, Destinay,
Destinee, Destinei, Destini, Destinyi,
Destnay, Destney, Destonie, Destony,
Destyni

Destry (American) well-fated;
western feel
Destrey, Destri, Destrie

Deterrion (Latin) form of Detra:
blessed
Deterr, Deterreyon, Detrae

Detra (Latin) blessed
Detraye

Deva (Hindi) moon goddess; wielder
of power
Devi

Devahuti (Hindi) in mythology,
daughter of Manu

Devaki (Indian) revered mother of
Krishna

Devalca (Spanish) generous
Deval

Devan (Irish) poetic
Devana, Devn

Devashka (Hebrew) honey

Deven (English) dark

Devendra (Indian) dark skin

Devera (Jewish) form of Devorah:
heroine

Devette (American) form of Devera:
heroine

Devi (Hindi) beloved goddess
Devia, Devian, Deviann, Devie, Devri

Devin (Irish) poetic
Devan, Devane, Devanie, Devany,
Deven, Devena, Deveny, Deveyn,
Devine, Devinne, Devn, Devyn,
Devynne

Devina (Irish) divine; creative
Davena, Devie, Devine, Devy, Divine

Devon (English) poetic
Dev, Devaughan, Devaughn, Devie,
Devonne, Devy

Devonna (English) girl from
Devonshire; happy
Davonna, Devon, Devona, Devonda,
Devondra

Devorah (American) heroine
Devora, Devore, Devra, Devrah

Devy (American) poetic

Devyn (English) poetic

Dew (Word as name) misty; fresh

Dewi, Dewie

Dewanna (African American) clingy

Dewana, Dewanne, D'Wana

Dexhiana (Origin Unknown) nimble

Dexter (English) spunky; dexterous

Dex, Dexee, Dexey, Dexie, Dext, Dextar, Dextur, Dexy

Dextra (Latin) skilled

Deyanira (Spanish) aggressor

Deyan, Deyann, Dianira, Nira

Dezelia (American) desired

Dezena (American) desired

Dezra (American) desirable

Dezral (American) desirable

Dharcia (American) sparkler

Darch, Darsha, Dharsha

Dharika (American) sad

Darica, Darika

Dharini (Indian) earth

Dharma (Hindi) morality; beliefs

Darma, Darmah

Dhazalai (African) sweet

Dhaze, Dhazie

Dhelal (Arabic) coy

Dhessie (American) glowing

Dhessee, Dhessey, Dhessi, Dhessy

Dhira (Indian) flow

Dhivia (Indian) heavenly

Dhumma (Hebrew) form of Dumia: quiet

Di (Latin) form of Diane: goddess-like; divine; or form of Diana: divine woman; goddess of hunt and fertility

Didi, Dy

Di Anna (American) form of Diana: divine woman; goddess of hunt and fertility

Dia (Greek) shining

Deah

Diaelza (Spanish) divine; pretty

Diael, Dialza, Elza

Diah (American) pretty

Dia

Diamantina (Spanish) sparkling

Diama, Diamante, Mantina

Diamond (Latin) precious gemstone

Diamin, Diamon, Diamonda, Diamonds, Diamonte, Diamun, Diamyn, Diamynd, Dyamond

Diamondah (African American) glowing

Diamonda, Diamonde

Diamondique (African American) sparkling

Diamondik

Diamony (American) gem

Diamonee, Diamoney, Diamoni, Diamonie

Diamrose (Spanish) diamond rose

Diana (Latin) divine woman; goddess of hunt and fertility

Dee, Di, Diahana, Diahna, Dianah, Diannah, Didi, Dihanna, Dyanna, Dyannah, Dyhana

Diandro (American) special

Diandra, Diandrea, Diandroh

Diane (Latin) goddess-like; divine

Deane, Deanne, Deeann, Deeanne, Deedee, Di, Diahann, Dian, Diann, Dianne, Didi

Dianelle (American) divine

Diange (American) form of Diane: goddess-like; divine

Dianita (Spanish) divine

Diannie (American) divine girl

Diantha (Greek) flower; heavenly

Dianth

Diarah (American) pretty

Dearah, Di, Diara, Diarra, Dierra

Diathe (Biblical) place name

Diathema (Greek) divine

Diavonne (African American) jovial

Diavone, Diavonna, Diavonni

Dica (Slavic) cautious

Dicey (American) impulsive

Di, Dice, Dicee, Dicy, Dycee, Dycey

Dicia (American) wild

Desha, Dicy

Didah (Biblical) of love

Diedre (Irish) form of Deidre:

sparkling

Diedra, Diedré

Diella (Latin) worships

Dielle

Diesha (African American) zany

Diecia, Dieshah, Dieshay, Dieshie

Diethild (German) believer

Difanee (American) form of Daphne:

pretty nymph

Diggs (American) tomboyish

Digs, Dyggs

Dihana (American) natural

Dihanna

Dijan (Slavic) divine goddess

Dijana (Slavic) form of Diana: divine

woman; goddess of hunt and fertility

Dijonnay (American) fun-loving

Dijon, Dijonae, Dijonay, Dijonnae,

Dijonnaie

Dilan (American) form of Dylan:

creative; from the sea

Dillan, Dilon

Dilcia (Spanish) loved

Dileone (Spanish) worships

Dilia (Spanish) worships

Dilly (Welsh) loyal

Dillyana (English) worshipful

Diliann, Dilli, Dillianna, Dilly

Dilsey (American) dependable; one

who endures

Dilva (Slavic) loyal

Dilynn (American) form of Dylan:

creative; from the sea

Di, Dilenn, Dilinn, Dilyn, Lynn

Dilys (Welsh) of the truth

Dima (American) high-spirited

Deemah, Dema

Dimond (American) form of

Diamond: precious gemstone

Dina (Hebrew/Scottish) right; royal

Dinah (Hebrew) fair judge

Dina, Dinna, Dyna, Dynah

Dinavia (American) form of Dinah:

fair judge

Dinesha (American) happy

Dineisha, Dineshe, Diniesha

Dini (American) joyful

Dinee, Diney, Dinie

Dinora (Spanish) judged by God

Dina, Dino, Nora

Dinorah (Spanish) light

Dinorot (American) form of Dinah:

fair judge

Dioma (Greek) form of Diona: divine

woman

Diona (Greek) divine woman

Dee, Di, Dion, Dionah, Dionuh

Dioneece (American) daring

Dee, DeeDee, Deon, Deone, Deonece,

Deoneece, Dioniece, Neece, Neecey

Dionicia (Spanish) vixen

Di, Dione, Dionice, Dionise, Nicia,

Nise, Nisee

Dionis (English) feminine form of

Dion: joyous celebrant

Dionise (English) feminine form of

Dion: joyous celebrant

Dionish (American) feminine form of

Dion: joyous celebrant

Dionndra (American) loving

Diondra, Diondrah, Diondruh

Dionne (Greek) love goddess

Deona, Deondra, Deonia, Deonna,

Deonne, Dion, Dione, Dionna

Dionnesha (American) feminine

form of Dion: joyous celebrant

Dior (French) stylish

Diora, Diorah, Diore, Diorra, Diorre

Diotima (Latin) in the time of God

Dira (Arabic) soft-spoken

Direll (American) svelte

Di, Direl, Direlle

Dirisha (African American) outgoing
Di, Diresha, Direshe

Dirkae (Scandinavian) feminine form
of Dirk: leader

Disa (Scandinavian) goddess

Disano (Italian) wise

Disha (American) fine
Dishae, Dishuh

Dishawna (African American)
special
Dishana, Dishauna, Dishawnah,
Dishona, Dishonna

Dishi (Indian) the right way

Divina (American) divine being

Divine (Italian) divine soul
Divin, Divina

Divinity (American) sweet; devout
Divinitee, Diviniti, Divinitie

Divora (Indian) divine

Divya (Indian) celestial

Divyanah (Hindi) divine

Dix (French) live wire

Dixie (English/French) from the
South in the United States
Dixee, Dixi, Dixy

Diya (Indian) divine

Diyanne (Slavic) form of Diane:
goddess-like; divine

Dizian (American) joyful

Dnisha (African American) rejoicing
Dnisa, Dnish, D'Nisha, Dnishay, Dnishe

Dobie (American) cowgirl
Dobee, Dobey, Dobi

Dobra (Polish) kindness

Docia (Latin) form of Docilla: docile
Docie

Docilla (Latin) docile
Docila, Docile

Dodie (Greek/Hebrew) gift of God
Doda, Dodee, Dodi, Dody

Dodona (Greek) ancient city in Greece

Doe (Polish) kind

Doherty (American) ambitious
Dhoertey, Dohertee, Dohertie

Doina (Slavic) lady
Dojna

Doka (Slavic) dependable

Dolah (Hindi) loved

Dolas (American) sorrows

Dolchil (American) docile

Dolcy (American) a vision
Dolcee, Dolcie, Dolsee

Dollis (American) doleful

Dolly (American) toylike
Dol, Doll, Dollee, Dolli, Dollie

Doloarea (Spanish) sorrows

Dolores (Spanish) woman of
sorrowful leaning
Delores

Dolory (Slavic) form of Dolores:
woman of sorrowful leaning

Domel (American) steadfast; faithful
Domela, Domella

Dometria (American) form of
Demetria: harvest goddess
Dome, Dometrea, Domi, Domini,
Domitra

Domina (Latin) ladylike

Dominga (Spanish) her dominion

Domini (Latin) feminine form of
Dominic: child of the Lord; saint
Dom, Dominee, Domineke, Dominey,
Dominie, Dominika, Domino, Dominy

Dominica (Latin) follower of God
Dom, Domenica, Domenika, Domineca,
Domineka, Domini, Dominika,
Domonica, Domonika

Dominique (French) bright;
masterful
Dom, Domanique, Domeneque,
Domenique, Domino, Domonik

Domitila (Spanish) home-loving

Dona (Latin) always giving
Donail, Donalea, Donalisa, Donay,
Donelle, Donetta, Doni, Donia, Donice,
Donie, Donise, Donisha, Donishia,
Donita, Donitrae

Donalda (Scottish) loves all

Donaldina, Donaleen, Donelda,
Donella, Donellia, Donette, Doni,
Donita, Donnella, Donnelle

Donalie (American) lady

Donata (Italian) celebrating

Donada, Donatah, Donatha, Donatta,
Donni, Donnie, Donny

Donatella (Latin/Italian) gift

Don, Donnie, Donny

Donatilde (Spanish) gift

Donava (African) jubilant

Donavah

Dondra (American) ladylike

Dondranea (Invented) ladylike

Donela (Italian) leader

Donella

Donelda (Spanish) giving

Donia (American) form of Donna:
ladylike and genteel

Donicia (Spanish) feminine

Donika (African American) form of
Donna: ladylike and genteel

Donica

Donisha (African American)
laughing; cozy

Daneesha, Danisha, Doneesha

Donna (Italian) ladylike and genteel

Dom, Don, Dona, Dondi, Donnie,
Donya

Donnata (Latin) giving

Dona, Donata, Donni

Donnelly (Italian) lush

Donally, Donelly, Donnell, Donnelli,
Donnellie, Donni, Donnie, Donny

Donnettella (Italian) giving

Donnis (American) pleasant; giving

Donnice

Donserena (American) dancer;
giving

Donce, Doncie, Dons, Donse, Donsee,
Donser, Donsey

Dontilan (American) donates

Donya (Italian) feminine

Donyale (African American) form of
Danielle: judged by God; spiritual

Donyelle

Donyan (English) feminine

Donyellan (African) upbeat

Dora (Greek) gift from God

Dorah, Dori, Dorie, Dorra, Dorrah

Dorant (American) gifted

Dorat (French) a gift

Doratt, Dorey, Dorie

Dorby (Spanish) devout

Dorcea (Greek) sea girl

Dorcia

Dorcelline (English) fast

Dordea (English) heritage

Dore (Irish) form of Dora: gift from God

Doree (Hebrew) heritage

Doreen (Greek/Irish) capricious

Dorene, Dorine, Dory

Dorei (American) form of Doris: sea-
loving; sea nymph

Dorekka (Slavic) form of Dorika:
God's gift

Dorel (Spanish) adored

Dorenda (American) adored

Dorende (American) adored

Doreneah (American) adored

Dorenee (American) form of
Doreen: capricious

Dorentia (American) adored

Doreth (American) form of Dorit:
God's gift; shy

Doretha (American) form of Dorit:
God's gift; shy

Dori (French) adorned

Dore, Dorey, Dorie, Dorree, Dorri,
Dorrie, Dorry, Dory

Doria (Greek) form of Dorian: happy

Dori, Doriana, Doriann, Dorianna,
Dorianne

Dorial (American) form of Dorit:
God's gift; shy

Dorian (Greek) happy

Dorean, Doreane, Doree, Doriane,
Dorri, Dorry

Dorianna (Greek) of the sea
Dorianne

Dorie (American) faithful

Dorika (Greek) God's gift
Doreek, Dorike, Dory

Dorin (Greek) form of Dorian: happy

Dorina (Hawaiian) loved

Dorind (American) form of Doreen:
capricious

Dorinda (Spanish) loved

Dorinta (American) gift

Doris (Greek) sea-loving; sea nymph
Dor, Dori, Dorice, Dorise, Doriss,
Dorris, Dorrise, Dorrys, Dory

Doriscus (Biblical) place name

Dorisette (American) form of Doris:
sea-loving; sea nymph

Dorit (Greek) God's gift; shy
Dooritt

Dorita (Greek) empress

Dorle (Greek) empress

Dorly (Greek) empress

Dor-Lyn (Invented) combo of Dor
and Lyn; empress

Dornay (American) involved
Dorn, Dornae, Dornee, Dorny

Dorothea (Greek) gift from God
Dorethea, Dorotha, Dorothia,
Dorotthea, Dorthea, Dorthia

Dorothy (Greek) gift of God
Dorathy, Dorthy

Dorren (Irish) sad-faced
Doren

Dorte (Scandinavian) God's gift

Dortha (Greek) God's gift; studious
Dorth, Dorthee, Dorthey, Dorthy

Dorthe (Scandinavian) God's gift

Dorum (American) God's gift

Dory (French) gilded; gold hair
Dora, Dore, Dorie

Doshene (American) shares

Dosia (Russian) happy

Dossey (Last name as first name)
rambunctious
Dosse, Dossi, Dossie, Dossy, Dozze

Dot (Greek) spunky
Dottee, Dottie, Dotty

Dottie (Greek) form of Dorothy: gift
of God

Dottye (English) gift

Dottylene (English) gift

Doubta (Slavic) doubtful

Douce (French) sweet
Doucia, Dulce, Dulci, Dulcie

Douet (French) dew

Dove (Greek) dreamy

Dovie (English) dove of peace

Doxey (American) variant of Moxie
and Dottie

Doxie (Greek) fine
Doxy

Dragana (Slavic) dragon lady

Drahomira (Czech) dearest

Drake (English) dragon

Draleen (American) dragon

Drancine (French) dragon lady

Draven (American) loyal
Dravan, Dravin, Dravine

Draxy (American) faithful
Drax, Draxee, Draxey, Draxi

Draya (Slavic) form of Drake: dragon

Drea (American) adorable

Dream (American) dream girl; misty
Dreama, Dreamee, Dreamey, Dreami,
Dreamie, Dreamy

Dreana (Spanish) spiritual

Dreda (Anglo-Saxon) thoughtful
Drida

Dree (American) soft-spoken

Dreena (American) cautious
Dreenah, Drina

Drelan (Origin Unknown) watches

Drena (Spanish) form of Adriana:
rich; exotic

Drenda (American) form of Dorinda:
loved

Drenea (American) spiritual

Drestell (American) new

Drew (Greek) woman of valor
Dru, Drue

Driana (American) form of Adriana: rich; exotic

Dricea (American) form of Adriana: rich; exotic

Drina (American) form of Adriana: rich; exotic

Drinda (Spanish) form of Dorinda: loved

Drisena (Spanish) strong

Dristi (Indian) insightful

Drover (American) surprising
Drovah, Drovar

Dru (American) bright
Drew, Drue

Druanna (American) bold
Drewann, Drewanne, Druanah; Druannah

Drucelle (American) smart
Druce, Drucee, Drucel, Drucell, Drucey, Druci, Drucy

Druella (Latin) form of Drusilla: strong

Drummond (Last name used as first name) drummer's mountain

Druna (English) leader

Drusa (Latin) form of Drusilla: strong
Drucie, Drusie

Drusi (Latin) strong girl
Drucey, Drucie, Drucy, Drusey, Drusie, Drusy

Drusilla (Latin) strong
Dru, Drucilla

Dryden (Last name as first name) special
Dydie

Duana (Irish) dark
Dwana

Dubethza (Invented) sad
Dubeth

Duchess (American) fancy
Duc, Duchesse, Ducy, Dutch, Dutchey, Dutchie, Dutchy

Ducy (Slavic) purest

Duena (Spanish) chaperones; guards

Duffy (Irish) spunky

Dufvenius (Swedish) lovely
Duf, Duff

Duhnell (Hebrew) kindhearted
Danee, Danny, Nell

Duiene (Spanish) accompanies

Dulce-Maria (Spanish) sweet Mary
Dulce, Dulcey

Dulceria (Spanish) sweet

Dulcibella (Italian) sweet beauty

Dulcie (Latin/Spanish) sweet one
Dulce, Dulcey, Dulcy

Dulcinea (Latin) sweet nature

Dulvio (Italian) helpful

Duma (African) quiet help
Dumah

Dumia (Hebrew) quiet
Dumi

Duna (Spanish) protects

Dune (American) summery
Doone, Dunah, Dunie

Dunesha (African American) warm
Dunisha

Dunning (Last name used as first name) alive

Dupre (American) soft-spoken
Dupray, Duprey

Dura (Biblical) place name

Dureene (Latin) endures

Durice (American) out of reach

Durrah (Hindi) heroine

Dusanka (Slavic) soulful
Dusan, Dusana, Dusank, Sanka

Duscha (Russian) happy
Dusa, Duschah, Dusha, Dushenka

Duse (Slavic) happy

Dusky (Invented) dreamy

Dusky-Dream (Invented) dreamy
Duskee-Dream

Dustine (German) go-getter
Dustee, Dusteen, Dustene, Dusti, Dustie, Dustina, Dusty

Dusty (American) southern

Dustee, Dustey, Dusti, Dustie

Dwanda (American) athletic

Dwana, Dwayna, Dwunda

Dwayna (American) feminine form
of Dwayne: swarthy

Dwyn (Welsh) fairhaired

Dyan (Latin) form of Diane: goddess-
like; divine

*Dian, Dyana, Dyane, Dyani, Dyann,
Dyanna, Dyanne*

Dyandra (Latin) sleek

Diandra, Dianndrah, Dyan, Dyandruh

Dylan (Welsh) creative; from the sea

*Dilann, Dyl, Dylane, Dylann, Dylanne,
Dylen, Dylin, Dyllan, Dylynn*

Dylana (Welsh) sea-loving

Dymea (American) crazed

Dymond (American) form of
Diamond: precious gemstone

Dymahn, Dymon, Dymonn, Dymund

Dymphia (Irish) poetic

Dimphia

Dynasty (Word as name) substantial;
rich

Dynet (American) curious

Dyney (American) consoling others

Diney, DiNey, Dy

Dyonne (American) marvelous

Dyonn, Dyonna, Dyonnae

Dyronisha (African American) fine

Dyron

Dyshaunna (African American)
dedicated

Dyshaune, Dyshawn, Dyshawna

Dyshay (American) healthy

Dywon (American) bubbly

*Diwon, Dywan, Dywann, Dywaughn,
Dywonne*

Dzidzo (African) universal child

E

Eadrianne (American) standout

*Eddey, Eddi, Eddy, Edreiann, Edrian,
Edrie*

Eamina (American) curious

E'ann (Irish) sunny

Eanna (Irish) sunny

Earla (English) leader

Earlah, Erla, Erlene, Erletta, Erlette

Earlean (Irish) dedicated

*Earla, Earlecia, Earleen, Earlena,
Earlene, Earlina, Earlinda, Earline,
Erla, Erlana, Erlene, Erlenne, Erlina,
Erlinda, Erline, Erlisha*

Earlette (American) dedicated

Earlinetta (American) dedicated

Early (American) bright

Earlee, Earlie, Earlye, Erly

Earlyne (American) dedicated

Earnesia (Spanish) sincere

Earth (English) earth child

Eartha (English) earth mother

Earthelen (American) earthy

Earthine (American) of the earth

Easter (American) born on Easter;
springlike

Easton (American) wholesome

Eastan, Easten, Eastun, Eeston, Estynn

Eavan (Irish) beautiful

Eevonne, Evaughn

Ebba (English/Scandinavian) strong

Eb, Eba, Ebbah

Ebban (American) pretty; affluent

Ebann, Ebbayn

Ebbie (English) blessed child

Ebony (Greek) hard and dark

*Eb, Ebanie, Ebbeny, Ebbie, Ebonea,
Ebonee, Eboney, Eboni, Ebonie, Ebonni*

Ebonyishia (American) black

Eboyn (English) form of Ebony: hard
and dark

Ebrel (Cornish) from the month
April

Ebby, Ebrelle, Ebrie, Ebrielle

Echo (Greek) smitten; echo
Eko

Ecia (Slavic) royal

Ecstasy (American) joyful
Ecstasey, Ecstasie, Stase

Eda (Irish) form of Edith: a blessed girl who is a gift to mankind

Edaena (Irish) fiery; energetic
Ed, Eda, Edae, Edana, Edanah, Edaneah, Eddi

Edalene (German) refined
Eda, Edalyne, Edeline, Ediline, Lena, Lene

Edana (Irish) flaming energy
Eda, Edan, Edanna

Eddi (English) form of Edwina: prospering female
Eddie, Eddy, Edy

Edel (German) clever; noble
Edell, Eddi

Eden (Hebrew) paradise of delights
Ede, Edena, Edene, Edin, Edyn

Edessa (Biblical) place name; flourishes

Edia (Hebrew) special

Edie (English) form of Edith: a blessed girl who is a gift to mankind
Eadie, Edee, Edi, Edy, Edye, Eydie

Edieh (American) gifted

Edina (Slavic) affluent

Edith (English) a blessed girl who is a gift to mankind
Eadith, Ede, Edetta, Edette, Edie, Edithe, Editta, Ediva, Edy, Edyth, Edythe, Eydie

Editha (Spanish) blessed

Edithanette (American) blessed

Edju (Origin unknown) giving
Eddju

Edlin (German) noble; sophisticated
Eddi, Eddy, Edlan, Edland, Edlen

Edmea (Scottish) form of Edme: beloved

Edmee (American) spontaneous
Edmey, Edmi, Edmy, Edmye

Edmonda (English) feminine form of Edmond: protective
Edmon, Edmond, Edmund, Edmunda, Monda

Edna (Hebrew) youthful
Eddie, Ednah, Edneisha, Ednita, Eydie

Edreanna (American) merry
Edrean, Edreana, Edreanne, Edrianna

Edrika (Scandinavian) forever

Edrina (American) old-fashioned
Ed, Eddi, Eddrina, Edrena, Edrinah

Edsel (American) plain
Eds, Edsell, Edzel

Edshone (American) wealthy
Ed, Eds, Edshun

Edwina (English) prospering female
Eddi, Eddy, Edina, Edweena, Edwena, Edwenna, Edwine, Edwyna, Edwynna

Efanye (African) respected

Effemy (Greek/German) form of Euphemia: well-spoken
Efemie, Efemy, Effee, Effemie, Effey, Effie, Effy

Effen (English) eloquent

Effie (Greek) form of Euphemia: well-spoken
Effi, Effia, Effy, Ephie

Efigenia (Spanish) form of Eugenia: high-born

Efrat (Hebrew) bountiful
Efrata

Egan (American) wholesome
Egen, Egun

Eglantyne (French) flower

Egypt (Place name) country; exotic
Egyppt

Egzanth (Invented) form of Xanthe: beautiful blonde; yellow

Ehrone (Slavic) peaceful

Eileen (Irish) bright and spirited
Eilean, Eilee, Eileena, Eileene, Eilena, Eilene, Eiley, Eilleen, Eillen, Eilyn, Elene, Ellie

Eireen (Scandinavian) peacemaker
Eirena, Erene, Ireen, Irene

Eires (Greek) peaceful

Eiress, Eres, Heris

Eirianne (English) peaceful

Eirian, Eriann

Ekaja (Hindi) only child

Ekanta (Hindi) loyalty

Ekaterina (Slavic) respected

Ekaterini (Slavic) form of Katherine: pure

Eko (American) form of Echo: smitten; echo

Eks (Slavic) gleans

Ekta (Indian) together

Elaine (French) dependable girl

Elain, Elaina, Elainia, Elainna, Elan, Elana, Elane, Elania, Elanie, Elanna, Elayn, Elayna, Elayne, Ellaine

Elana (Greek) pretty

Ela, Elan, Elani, Elanie, Lainie

Elanja (Slavic) gleeful girl

Elasa (Biblical) place name

Elata (Latin) bright; well-positioned

Ela, Elate, Elatt, Elle, Elota

Elcida (Spanish) elucidate

Elda (Italian) protective

Eldee (American) light

El, Eldah, Elde

Eldora (Spanish) golden girl; golden spirit

Eldoree, Eldorey, Eldori, Eldoria, Eldorie, Eldory

Eldulita (Spanish) protective

Eleacie (American) forthright

Acey, Elea, Eleasie

Eleanor (Greek) light-hearted

Elana, Elanor, Elanore, Eleanora, Elenor, Elenorah, Eleonor, Eleonore, Elinor, Elinore, Ellie, Ellinor, Ellinore, Elynor, Elynore, Lenore

Eleanora (Greek) light

Elenora, Eleonora, Eleora, Ella nora, Ellenora, Ellenorah, Ellora, Elnora, Elora, Elynora

Eleatrice (Greek) free girl

Electra (Greek) shining; brilliant

Elec, Elek, Elektra

Elegy (American) lasting

Elegee, Eleggee, Elegie, Eligey

Elek (American) star-like

Elec, Ellie, Elly

Elelvina (Spanish) resilient

Elena (Greek/Russian/Spanish) form of Helen: beautiful; light

Elana, Eleana, Eleen, Eleena, Elen, Elene, Eleni, Ilena, Ilene, Lena, Leni, Lennie, Lina, Nina

Eleni (Greek) sweet

Elenee

Eleonore (French) form of Helen: beautiful; light

Elenore, Elle, Elnore

Eleovina (Spanish) bright way

Eleri (Welsh) smooth

Elere, Eleree

Elettra (Latin/Italian) form of Electra: shining; brilliant

Elfin (American) small girl

El, Elf, Elfan, Elfee, Elfey, Elfie, Elfun, Els

Elfreda (English) elf strength; good counselor

Elfrida (German) peaceful spirit

Elfie, Elfrea, Elfredda, Elfreeda, Elfreyda, Elfryda

Elgie (Spanish) chosen elegy

Eliana (Hebrew) the Lord answers

Eliane, Elianna, Elianne, Elliana, Ellianne, Ellie, Liana, Liane

Eliane (French) cheerful; sunny

Elicabeth (American) form of Elizabeth: God's promise

Elicia (Hebrew) dedicated

Ellicia

Eliki (Hawaiian) abundant

Elisa (Spanish) dedicated to God
Elecea, Eleesa, Elesa, Elesia, Elisia, Elissa, Elisse, Elisya, Ellisa, Ellisia, Ellissa, Ellissia, Ellissya, Ellisya, Elysa, Elysia, Elyssia, Elyssya, Elysya, Leese, Leesie, Lisa

Elisabet (Hebrew/Scandinavian) form of Elizabeth: God's promise
Bet, Elisa, Elsa, Else

Elisabeth (Hebrew/French/German) form of Elizabeth: God's promise
Bett, Bettina, Elisa, Elise, Els, Elsa, Elsie, Ilsa, Ilyse, Liesa, Liese, Lisbeth, Lise

Elise (French) consecrated to God
Elice, Elisse, Elle, Ellyse, Lisie

Eliseu (Biblical) abundance in God

Elisha (Greek) God-loving
Eleacia, Eleasha, Elecia, Eleesha, Eleisha, Elesha, Eleshia, Elicia, Eliesha, Ellie, Lisha

Elishama (American) loves God

Elishca (American) form of Elizabeth: God's promise

Elisheba (Biblical) form of Elizabeth: God's promise

Elissa (Greek) from the blessed isles
Ellissa, Ellyssa, Elyssa, Ilissa, Ilyssa

Elita (French) selected one
Elida, Elitia, Elitie, Ellita, Ellitia, Ellitie, Ilida, Ilita, Litia

Elite (Latin) best
Elita

Eliza (Irish) sworn to God
Aliza, Elieza, Elize, Elyza

Elizabeth ✪ (Hebrew) God's promise
Beth, Betsy, Elisabeth, Elizebeth, Lissie, Liza

Elizeth (American) form of Elizabeth: God's promise

Elke (Dutch) distinguished
Elki, Ilki

Elken (American) believer

Elkie (Dutch) form of Elke: distinguished
Elk, Elka

Ella ✪ ✆ (Greek) beautiful and fanciful
Ellamae, Elle, Ellia, Ellie, Elly

Ellaina (American) sincere
Elaina, Ellana, Ellanuh

Ellan (American) coy
Elan, Ellane, Ellyn

Elle (Scandinavian) woman
Ele

Ellen (English) open-minded
El, Elen, Elenee, Eleny, Elin, Ellene, Ellie, Ellyn, Ellynn, Elyn

Ellender (American) decisive
Elender, Ellander, Elle, Ellie

Elli (Scandinavian) aged
Ell, Elle, Ellie

Ellice (English) loves God
Ellecia, Ellyce, Elyce

Ellie (English) candid
Ele, Elie, Elly

Ellina (Scandinavian) valuable

Ells (Scandinavian) patient
Els

Ellyce (French) abundance in God

Elm (Botanical) tree

Elma (Turkish) sweet
El

Elmas (Armenian) diamondlike
Elmaz, Elmes, Elmis

Elna (American) light

Elnora (American) sturdy
Ellie, Elnor, Elnorah

Elocile (Spanish) easy child

Elodia (Spanish) flowering
Elodi

Elodie (French) melody

Eloina (Spanish) fulfills destiny

Eloisa (Italian) sun girl

Eloise (German) high-spirited
Eluise, Luise

Elora (American) fresh-faced
Elorah, Flory, Floree

Eloyse (English) form of Eloise: high-spirited

Eloysee (American) form of Eloise: high-spirited

Elpidia (Spanish) shining
El, Elpey, Elpi, Elpie

Elrica (German) leader
Elrick, Elrika, Elrike, Rica, Rika

Elsa (German) form of Elizabeth: God's promise
Ellsa, Ellse, Ellsey, Els, Elsah, Elseh, Elsie, Ellsee

Elsie (German) hard-working
Elsee, Elsi, Elsy

Elsiy (Spanish) God-loving
El, Els, Elsa, Elsee, Elsi, Elsy

Elspeth (Scottish) loved by God
El, Elle, Els

Elspie (Scottish) regal

Elsy (Spanish) form of Elizabeth: God's promise

Elton (American) spontaneous
Elt, Elten, Eltone, Eltun

Eluvia (Spanish) happy

Elva (English) tiny
Elvah, Elvenea, Elvia, Elvie, Elvina, Elvinea, Elvineah

Elverna (American) form of Elvire: truest of all

Elvetta (American) form of Elva: tiny

Elvia (Latin) sunny
Elvea, Elviah, Elvie

Elvira (Latin/German) truth
Elva, Elvie, Elvina, Elwire, Vira

Elvire (French) truest of all

Elyana (Spanish) friend

Elyanna (American) good friend
Elyana, Elyannah, Elyunna

Elyse (English) soft-mannered
Elice, Elle, Elysee, Elysia, Ilysha, Ilysia

Elysia (Latin) joyful
Elyse, Elysee, Elysha, Elyshia

Elyssa (Greek) form of Elissa: from the blessed isles
Elisa, Elysa, Illysa, Lyssa

Elysse (French) God's abundance

Elzada (Polish) form of Elizabeth: God's promise

Emalee (German) thoughtful
Emalea, Emaleigh, Emaley, Emaline, Emally, Emaly, Emmalynn, Emmeline, Emmelyne

Emann (American) soft-spoken
Eman

Emaunuela (Spanish) believes in God

Ember (American) temperamental
Embere, Embre

Emberatriz (Spanish) respected
Emb, Ember, Embera, Emberatrice, Emberatryce, Embertrice, Embertrise

Emberli (American) pretty
Em, Emb, Ember, Emberlee, Emberley, Emberly

Embray (American) form of Emily: industrious; eager

Eme (Hawaiian) loved; (German) form of Emma: universal: all-embracing
Em, Emee, Emm, Emme, Emmee, Emmie, Emmy

Emea (Dutch) competes

Emelle (American) kind
Emell

Emelsa (Spanish) emulates

Emely (German) go-getter
Emel, Emelee, Emelie

Emena (Latin) of fortunate birth
Em, Emen, Emene, Emina, Emine

Emera (Irish) talented

Emerald (French) bright as a gemstone
Em, Emmie

Emerenciana (Spanish) experienced

Emerene (Spanish) experienced

Emerita (Spanish) experienced

Emesa (Biblical) place name; reserved

Emestina (American) form of
Ernestine: sincere spirit
Emee, Emes, Emest, Tina

Emigdea (Spanish) enigmatic

Emika (Slavic) charming

Emilee (American) form of Emily:
industrious; eager

Emilia (Italian) soft-spirited
Emalia, Emelia, Emila

Emilie (French) charmer

Emily ✿ ✆ (Latin) industrious; eager
*Em, Emalie, Emilee, Emili, Emilie,
Emmi, Emmie*

Emma ✿ ✆ (German) universal; all-
embracing
*Em, Emmah, Emme, Emmie, Emmi,
Emmot, Emmy, Emmye, Emott*

Emmaline (French/German) form of
Emily: industrious; eager
*Em, Emaline, Emalyne, Emiline,
Emmie*

Emmanuelle (Hebrew/French)
believer
Em, Emmi, Emmie, Emmy

Emmatha (Biblical) place name;
dedicated

Emme (German) feminine
Em

Emmi (German) pretty
Emmee, Emmey, Emmy

Emoke (Asian) charms

Emperatriz (Spanish) empress

Emroy (American) elegant royal

Emsky (American) fun

Ena (Hawaiian) intense
Eana, En, Enna, Ina

Encetta (Spanish) starts

Enchantay (American) enchanting
Enchantee

Endah (Irish) flighty
Ena, End, Enda

Endia (American) form of India:
woman of India
Endee, Endey, Endie, Endy, Ndia

Endriss (Slavic) endears

Enedelia (Spanish) praiseworthy

Enedina (Spanish) praised; spirited
Dina, Ened

Enesha (American) warmth

Enette (American) warmth

Engracia (Spanish) ingratiates

Enid (Welsh) lively
Eneid

Enideen (American) vibrant

Enka (Scandinavian) gem

Enna (Greek) ninth child

Ennis (Irish) dignity

Enore (English) careful
Enoor, Enora

Enrichetta (French) enriches the home

Enslie (American) emotional
Ens, Enslee, Ensley, Ensly, Enz

Enya (Irish) fiery; musician
Enyah, Nya

Epatha (African) empathy

Epifania (Spanish) proof
*Epi, Epifaina, Epifanea, Eppie, Pifanie,
Piffy*

Epiphania (Biblical) place name;
religious epiphany

Eppy (Greek) lively
Ep, Eppee, Eppey, Eppi, Eps

Equoia (African American) great
equalizer
Ekowya

Era (Slavic) from the windy place

Eranth (Greek) spring bloomer
Erantha, Eranthae, Eranthe

Erasema (Spanish) happy
Eraseme

Erathine (American) earth child

Erato (Mythology) pretty poet

Erba (Spanish) feminine

Ercella (Spanish) earnest

Ercie (Spanish) sincere

Ercilia (American) frank
Erci, Ercilya

Erdell (American) of the earth

Erendia (Spanish) calm

Erendira (Spanish) peaceful

Erene (Irish) Irish child

Eres (Greek) goddess of chaos
Era, Ere, Eris

Eridania (Spanish) rules

Erika (Scandinavian) honorable;
leading others
Erica, Ericah, Ericca, Ericha, Ericka,
Erikka, Errica, Errika, Eryka, Erykka

Erin (Irish) peace-making
Eran, Eren, Erena, Erene, Ereni, Eri,
Erian, Erine, Erinn, Erinne, Eryn,
Erynn, Erynne

Erina (American) peaceful
Era, Erinna, Erinne, Eryna, Erynne

Eriqueta (Spanish) ruling

Erla (Spanish) loyal; (Irish) playful

Erlen (Spanish) loyal

Erlina (Spanish) loyal

Erlind (Hebrew) form of Erlinda: loyal
Erlinde

Erlinda (Spanish) loyal

Erma (Latin) wealthy
Erm, Irma

Ermelinda (Spanish) fresh-faced
Ermalinda, Ermelind, Ermelynda

Ermine (Latin) rich
Erma, Ermeen, Ermie, Ermin, Ermina,
Erminda, Erminia, Erminie

Erminette (Italian) noble

Erna (English) form of Ernestine:
sincere spirit
Emae, Ernea, Ernie

Ernelle (German) earnest

Ernestine (English) sincere spirit
Erna, Ernaline, Ernesia, Ernesta,
Ernestina, Ernestyne

Ernme (Scandinavian) sincere

Erona (Welsh) form of Erin:
peacemaking

Ersemi (Scandinavian) gem

Ertha (English) form of Eartha;
also form of Bertha: earth mother

Erwen (Welsh) blessing

Eryn (Irish) calm

Erynea (English) earnest

Erzsebet (French) form of Elizabeth:
God's promise

Es (American) form of Estella: radiant
star
Esa, Essie

Esbelda (Spanish) black-haired beauty
Es, Esbilda, Ezbelda

Esdey (American) warmhearted
Esdee, Esdy, Essdey

Esenzia (Spanish) essence

Esha (Slavic) vibrant

Eshah (African) exuberant
Esha

Eshe (African) life
Eshay

Eshey (American) life
Es, Esh, Eshae, Eshay

Esiquio (Spanish) child of Sunday

Esmee (French) much loved
Esma, Esme, Esmie

Esmeralda (Spanish) emerald;
shiny and bright
Emelda, Es, Esmerelda, Esmerilda,
Esmie, Esmiralda, Esmirilda,
Ezmerelda, Ezmirilda

Esmirna (Spanish) noble

Esne (English) happy
Es, Esnee, Esney, Esny, Essie

Esperanza (Spanish) hopeful
Es, Espe, Esperance, Esperans, Esperanta,
Esperanz

Essence (American) ingenious
Esence, Essens, Essense

Essene (Slavic) girl of the wind
Essen

Essica (American) form of Jessica:
rich

Essie (English) shining; queenly
Es, Essa, Essey, Essy

Esta (Hebrew) bright star
Es, Estah

Estalyn (English) noble girl

Estana (Slavic) form of Esther:
myrtle leaf

Estee (English) brightest
Esti

Estefani (Spanish) crowned

Estefania (Spanish) crowned

Estelita (Spanish) little queen

Estella (French) radiant star
Es, Estel, Estell, Estelle, Estie, Stell,
Stella

Estelle (French) glowing star
Es, Essie, Estee, Estel, Estele, Estell, Estie

Esterlea (Scandinavian) star queen

Estevina (Spanish) adorned; wreathed
Estafania, Este, Estebana, Estefania,
Estevan, Estevana

Esth (French) star

Esthelia (Spanish) shining
Esthe, Esthel, Esthele, Esthelya

Esther (Persian) myrtle leaf
Es, Essie, Estee, Ester, Esthur

Estherelda (Spanish) form of
Esther: myrtle leaf

Estherita (Spanish) bright
Estereta

Estime (French) esteemed
Es

Estine (German) sweet child

Estrella (Latin) shining star
Estrell, Estrelle, Estrilla

Eta (German) form of Henrietta:
home-ruler
Etah

Etaney (Hebrew) focused
Eta, Etana, Etanah, Etanee

Ethel (English) noble
Ethelda, Ethelin, Etheline, Ethelle,
Ethelyn, Ethelynn, Ethelynne, Ethyl

Ethelen (English) strong

Ethelene (American) form of Ethel:
noble
Ethe, Etheline

Ethne (Irish) blueblood
Eth, Ethnee, Ethnie, Ethny

Ethnea (Irish) kernel; piece of the
puzzle
Ethna, Ethnia

Etosha (African) energetic

Etta (German/English) form of
Henrietta: home-ruler
Etti, Ettie, Etty

Eudlina (Slavic) generous; affluent
Eudie, Eudlyna, Udie, Udlina

Eudocia (Greek) fine
Eude, Eudocea, Eudosia

Eudora (Greek) cherished

Eudore (Greek) treasured

Eudoxia (Spanish) fine

Eufrocina (Spanish) happiness

Eugenia (Greek) regal and polished
Eugeneia, Eugenie, Eugenina, Eugina,
Gee, Gina

Eula (Greek) specific
Eulia

Eulala (Greek) spoken sweetly
Eulalah

Eulalia (Greek/Italian) well-spoken
Eula, Eulia, Eulie

Eulanda (American) fair
Eudlande, Eulee, Eulie

Eunice (Greek) joyful; winning
Euna, Euniece, Eunique, Eunise, Euniss

Eunja (Asian) silver

Eupheme (Greek) form of
Euphemia: well-spoken
Eu, Euphemee, Euphemi, Euphemie

Euphemia (Greek) well-spoken
Effam, Eufemia, Euphan, Euphie,
Uphie

Euphrosyne (Greek) one of the
three Graces; joy

Eureka (Word as name) surpise

Eurydice (Greek) adventurous
Euridice, Euridyce, Eurydyce

Eustacia (Greek) industrious
Eustace, Stacey, Stacy

Eustolia (Spanish) tenacious; moves
well

Euvenia (American) hardworking

Euvene, Euvenea

Eva (Hebrew/Scandinavian) life

Evah, Evalea, Evalee

Evadne (Greek) pleasing; lucky

Eva, Evad, Evadnee, Evadny

Evaline (French) form of Evelyn:
optimistic

Evalyn, Eveleen

Evan (American) bright; precocious

Evann, Evin

Evana (Greek) lovely woman

Evania, Eve, Ivana, Ivanna

Evangelina (Greek) bringing joy

*Eva, Evangelia, Evangelica, Evangeline,
Evania, Eve, Lina*

Evania (Irish) spirited

*Ev, Evana, Evanea, Evann, Evanna,
Evanne, Evany, Eve, Eveania, Evvanne,
Evyan*

Evanka (Slavic) form of Ivanka:
gracious gift from God

Evanthie (Greek) flowering well

Evanthe, Evanthee, Evanthi

Eve (Hebrew) life

Eva, Evie, Evvy

Evegelina (Spanish) lively

Evelina (Russian) lively

Evalina, Evalinna

Evelyn ✪ (English) optimistic

*Aveline, Ev, Evaleen, Evalene, Evalenne,
Evaline, Evalyn, Evalynn, Evalynne,
Eveleen, Eveline, Evelyne, Evelynn,
Evelynne, Evline*

Evelyna (Scandinavian) form of
Evelyn: optimistic

Ever (Word as name) eternal

Ev

Everilda (Spanish) forever

Everilde (Origin unknown) hunter

Everla (English) ever

Everleen (American) evergreen

Everlin (American) forever

Evette (French) dainty

Evett, Ivette

Evgenia (Slavic) form of Eugenia:
regal and polished

Evie (English) vibrant life

Evine (English) alive

Evlesin (American) lives large

Evline (French) nature girl

*Evleen, Evlene, Evlin, Evlina, Evlyn,
Evlynn, Evlynne*

Evolia (Slavic) form of Evelyn:
optimistic

Evonne (French) form of Yvonne:
athletic

Evanne, Eve, Evie, Yvonne

Evonnette (American) form of
Evelyn: optimistic

Ewelina (Polish) life

Eva, Lina

Exee (American) form of Lexie:
helpful; sparkling

Exelda (Spanish) excels

Eydie (American) endearing

Eidey, Eydee

Eyote (Native American) great

Eyotee

Ezra (Hebrew) happy; helpful

Ezrah, Ezruh

Ezza (American) healthy

Eza

F

Faba (Latin) bean; thin

Fabah, Fava

Fabette (Italian) fabulous little girl

Fabi (Italian) generous

Fabia (Latin) fabulous; special

Fabiann, Fabianna, Fabianne

Fabienne (French) fabulous; farming
beans

Fabio (Latin) fabulous

Fabeeo, Fabeo, Fabeoh

Fabiola (Spanish) royalty

Fabrizia (Italian) manual worker
Fabrice, Fabricia, Fabrienne, Fabriqua, Fabritzia

Fadia (Arabic) saved

Fae (English) form of Faye: light-spirited

Fael (English) of the fairies

Faffa (American) frivolity

Fahimah (Arabic) form of Fatima: wise woman

Faida (Arabic) bountiful
Fayda

Faillace (French) delicate beauty
Faill, Faillaise, Faillase, Falace

Faine (English) happy
Fai, Fainne, Fay, Fayne

Fairlee (English) lovely
Fair, Fairlea, Fairley, Fairly

Faith ✪ ✝ (English) loyal woman
Fay, Fayth

Faithette (American) trustworthy

Falesyia (Hispanic) exotic
Falesyiah, Falisyia

Faline (Latin/French) lively
Faleen, Falene

Fall (Word as name) changeable
Falle

Fallon (Irish) fetching; from the ruling class
Falan, Fallen, Fallyn, Falyn

Falsette (American) fanciful
Falcette

Famke (Polish) little girl

Fanchon (French) form of France
Fan, Fanchee, Fanchie, Fanny, Fran, Frannie, Franny

Fancine (French) fancy

Fancy (English) fanciful
Fanci, Fancie

Fandila (Spanish) dancer

Fane (American) strict
Fain, Faine

Fanfara (Last name as first name) fanfare; excitement
Fann, Fanny

Fang (Chinese) pleasantly scented

Fanny (Latin) from France
Fan, Fani, Fannie

Fantasia (American) inventive
Fantasha, Fantasiah, Fantasya, Fantazia

Fantazee (American) fantasy

Fantazie (American) fantasy

Fanteen (English) clever
Fan, Fannee, Fanney, Fanny, Fantene, Fantine

Farah (English) lovely
Farrah

Faray (Arabic) form of Farrah: good-looking; happy

Faredah (Arabic) special
Farida

Farhanah (Arabic) lovely

Farica (German) leader
Faricka, Fericka, Flicka

Farida (Arabic) wanders far

Farina (Latin) flour
Fareena

Faris (American) forgiving
Fair, Farris, Pharis, Pharris

Farrah (English/Arabic) good-looking; happy
Fara, Farah

Farren (American) fair
Faren, Farin

Farrow (American) narrow-minded
Farow, Farro

Faryl (American) inspiring
Farel, Farelle

Farzana (American) wanders

Fashion (American) stylish
Fashon, Fashy, Fashyun

Fatie (Arabic) winning

Fatima (Arabic) wise woman
Fatema, Fatimah, Fatime

Faulk (American) respected
Falk

Fauna (Roman mythology) goddess of nature
Faunah, Fawna, Fawnah

Faunee (Latin) nature-loving
Fauney, Fauneye, Fawnae, Fawni,
Fawny

Fausta (French) desired; (Italian)
lucky

Faustene (French/American) envied
Fausteen, Faustine, Fausty, Fawsteen

Faustiana (Spanish) good fortune
Faust, Fausti, Faustia, Faustina

Faustina (Italian) lucky
Fausta, Faustine, Fawsteena, Fostina,
Fostynna

Favela (Spanish) favored

Favianna (Italian) confident
Faviana

Faviolia (Indian) lucky

Fawn (French) gentle
Faun, Fawne

Fawna (French) soft-spoken
Fawnna, Fawnah, Fawnuh

Fawntae (English) fawn girl

Fawntay (American) fawn girl

Faye (English/French) light-spirited
Fae, Fay, Fey

Fayette (American) southern
Fayet, Fayett, Fayetta, Fayitte

Fayleen (American) quiet
Faylene, Fayline, Falyn, Falynn, Faye,
Fayla

Fayrale (American) wins

Fayth (American) form of Faith: loyal
woman
Faithe, Faythe

Fe (Latin) believer

Feather (Native American) svelte
Feathyr

Febe (Polish/Greek) bright
Febee

February (Latin) icy
Feb

Fedora (Greek) God's gift

Fedyle (American) loyal

Felda (German) field girl

Felder (Last name as first name)
bright
Felde, Feldy

Felice (Latin) form of Felicia: happy
Felece, Felise

Felicia (Latin) happy
Faleshia, Falesia, Felecia, Felisha

Felicie (Latin) form of Felicia: happy
Feliccie, Felicee, Felicy, Felisie

Felicita (Spanish) gracious
Felice, Felicitas, Felicitee, Felisita

Felicity (Latin) form of Felicia: happy
Felice, Felicite, Felicitee, Felisitee

Felisa (Spanish) form of Felicia:
happy

Felise (German) joyful
Felis

Felixae (Slavic) good fortune

Feliza (Spanish) good fortune

Felyn (Spanish) lucky

Femay (American) classy
Femae

Femi (African) love-seeking
Femmi

Femise (African American)
asking for love
Femeese, Femmis

Fena (Scottish) pale

Fenella (Irish) white
Fionola, Fionnuala

Fenia (Scandinavian) gold worker
Fenja, Fenya

Fenn (American) bright
Fen, Fynn

Fennell (Scottish) pale

Feo (Greek) given by God
Fee, Feeo

Feodora (Greek) God-given girl
Fedora

Feodossia (Slavic) influences

Fereda (Spanish) vigorous

Feride (Hawaiian) calm

Ferilen (American) dares

Fern (German/English) fern
Ferne

Fernanda (German) bold
Ferdie, Fernnande

Fernandaline (French) dares

Fernilia (American) successful

Fern, Fernelia, Ferny, Fyrnilia

Fernley (English) from the fern

meadow; nature girl

Feven (American) shy

Fevan, Fevun

Ffion (Irish) pale face

Fi

Fia (Scandinavian) perky

Fiamma (Italian) fiery spirit

Feamma, Fee, Fia, Fiama, Fiammette,

Fifi

Fiammetta (Italian) fiery

Fiby (Spanish) bright

Fidela (Spanish) loyal

Fidele, Fidella, Fidelle

Fidelia (Italian) faithful

Fidele

Fidelity (Latin) loyal

Fidele, Fidelia

Fidelma (Irish) loyal

Fife (American) dancing eyes; musical

Fifer, Fifey, Fyfe

Fifer (Last name used as first name)

fife-player

Fifi (French) jazzy

Fifee

Fifia (African) Friday's child

FeeFee, Fifeea

Filia (Greek) devoted

Feleah, Filea, Filiah

Filipa (Italian) loves horses

Fillis (Greek) form of Phyllis:

beautiful; leafy bough; articulate;

smitten

Filis, Fill, Fillees, Filly, Fillys, Fylis

Filma (Greek) loved

Filomena (Polish) beloved

Fimy (English) form of Femy: regal

and polished

Fina (Spanish) blessed by God

Finch (English) bird; sings

Finelle (Irish) fair-faced

Fee, Finell, Finn, Finny, Fynelle

Finesse (American) smooth

Fin, Finese, Finess

Finette (Scottish) pale

Finley (English) fair

Finn (Irish) cool

Finnian (English) fiery

Finny (Irish) blonde

Finola (Italian) white

Fion (Irish) blonde

Fiona (Irish) fair-haired

Fi, Fionna

Fionnuala (Irish) white

Nuala

Fiorella (Irish) spirited

Fee, Feorella, Rella

Fire (American) feisty

Firey, Fyre

Flair (English) stylish

Flaire, Flairey, Flare

Flame (Word as name) fiery

Flaminia (Latin) flaming spirit

Flana (Irish) red-haired

Flanagh, Flanna, Flannerey, Flannery

Flanders (Place name) region of

Belgium; creative

Fland, Flann

Flannery (Irish) warm; red-haired

Flann

Flavey (French) fun-filled

Flavia (Latin) light-haired

Flavie

Flaviana (Spanish) pale

Flavine (French) fun

Flax (Botanical) plant with blue

flowers

Flacks, Flaxx

Fleming (Last name as first name)

adorable

Flemma, Flemmie, Flemming, Flyming

Flemmi (Italian) pretty

Flemmy

Fleur (French) flower

Fleura, Fleuretta, Fleurette, Fleuronne

Flicky (American) vivacious

Flirt (Word as name) flirtatious
Flyrtt

Flis (Polish) form of Felicity: happy

Flo (American) form of Florence: flowering

Flor (Spanish) blooming
Flo, Flora, Floralia, Florencia, Florencita, Florens, Florensia, Flores, Floria, Floriole, Florita, Florite

Flora (Latin/Spanish) flowering
Floria, Flórie

Floraba (Spanish) flowering

Florangel (Spanish) angel flower

Florcina (Spanish) flowering

Flordeperla (Spanish) pearly blooms

Florella (Latin) girl from Florence; blooming

Florence (Latin) flowering
Flo, Flora, Florencia, Florense, Florenze, Florie, Florina, Florrie, Flos, Flossie, Floy

Florenina (Spanish) flowering

Florens (Polish) blooming; (Latin) thrives
Floren

Florent (French) flowering
Flor, Floren, Florentine, Florin

Florette (French) flowering

Florian (Dutch) flower-like

Florica (Spanish) flowers

Florida (Place name) U.S. state; flowered
Flora, Flory

Florienna (Italian) flowering

Florin (English) floral

Florinda (English) flower of spring

Florine (American) blooming
Flo, Flora, Floren, Floryne, Florynne

Floris (Latin) flowers

Florizel (Literature) Shakespearean name; in bloom
Flora, Flori, Florisel

Florrie (English) blooms

Flossie (English) grows beautifully

Flower (American) blossoming beauty
Flo

Floy (English) blooms

Floya (Slavic) quick

Fluffy (American) fun-loving
Fluff, Fluffi, Fluffie

Flynn (Irish) red-haired
Flenn, Flinn, Flyn

Fog (American) dreamy
Fogg, Foggee, Foggy

Fola (African) honored
Folah

Folfeen (American) direct

Fonda (American) risk-taker
Fond

Fondee (American) fond

Fondice (American) fond of friends
Fondeese, Fondie

Fontaine (French) fountaining bounty
Fontane, Fontanna, Fontanne

Fontella (American) small fountain

Fontenot (French) special girl; fountain of beauty
Fonny, Fontay, Fonte, Fonteno

Ford (Last name as first name) confident
Forde

Forsythia (Botanical) flower girl

Fortney (Latin) strength
Fortnea, Fortnee, Fortneigh, Fortnie, Fortny

Fortuna (Latin) good fortune
Fortunata

Fortune (Latin) excellent fate; prized

Fotine (Greek) light-hearted
Foty, Fotyne

Fowler (Last name as first name) stylish
Fowla, Fowlar, Fowlir

Foxyn (American) perceptive

Foynt (English) fount

Fozyne (American) fortunate

Fracesca (American) form of Francesca: country; French girl

Frachette (French) fresh

Fran (Latin) form of France: country; French girl
Frann, Franni, Frannie

Franca (Italian) free spirit

France (Place name) country; French girl
Frans, Franse

Francena (English) form of France: country; French girl

Francene (French) free
Francine

Frances (Latin) form of France: country; French girl
Fanny, Fran, Francey, Franci, Francie, Franse

Francesca (Italian) form of France: country; French girl
Fran, Francessca, Franchesca, Francie, Frankie, Frannie

Franchelle (French) form of France: country; French girl
Franchelle, Franchey, Franshell

Franchesca (Italian) form of Francesca: country; French girl
Cheka, Chekkie, Francheska, Franchessca

Francina (Italian) form of France: country; French girl

Francine (French) form of France: country; French girl
Fran, Franceen, Francene, Francie

Françoise (French) free

Franicine (American) form of Francine: country; French girl

Franisbel (Spanish) beautiful French girl
Franisbella, Franisbelle

Frankie (American) a form of France: country; French girl
Franki, Franky

Frannie (English) friendly
Franni, Franny

Fransabelle (Latin) form of France: country; French girl
Fransabella, Franzabelle

Fraya (Scandinavian) highborn
Freya

Frayda (Scandinavian) fertile woman
Frayde, Fraydel, Freyda, Freyde, Freydel

Frea (Scandinavian) noble; hearty
Fray, Freas, Freya

Fred (English) form of Elfreda: elf strength; good counselor

Freda (German) serene

Freddie (English) form of Frederica: peacemaking
Fredi, Freddy

Frederica (German) peacemaking
Federica, Fred, Freda, Freddie, Freida, Frida, Fritze, Rica

Frederique (German) serene

Fredesminda (English) girl of peaceful mind

Fredna (American) strength of character

Fredy (American) strong

Free (Word as name) liberated spirit

Freesia (Botanical) fragrant flower

Freida (German) form of Frederica: peacemaking; form of Alfreda: wise advisor
Freda, Frida, Frieda

Frelecia (Slavic) form of Felicia: happy

Frenchie (American) saucy
French, Frenchee, Frenchi, Frenchy

Frenda (Asian) fern

Fresnay (American) place name

Fressia (American) form of the flower freesia

Freya (Scandinavian) goddess; beautiful
Freja, Freyja

Frida (Scandinavian) lovely

Frieda (German) happy
Freda

Friedelinde (German) gentle girl
Friedalinda

Frigg (Scandinavian) loved one

Frigga (Scandinavian) beloved
Fri, Friga, Frigg

Fristell (Last name used as first name) stiff

Fritzi (German) leads in peace

Frona (English) practical

Frond (Botanical) growing

Frosty (Word as name) crisp and cool
Frostie

Fructuose (Latin) bountiful
Fru, Fructuosa, Fruta

Frula (German) hardworking

Fruma (Hebrew) devout

Frythe (English) calm
Frith, Fryth

Fuchsia (Botanical) blossoming pink
Fuesha

Fudge (American) stubborn
Fudgey

Fuensanta (Spanish) holy fountain
Fuenta

Fulgencia (Latin) glowing

Fulki (Hindi) sparks

Fullan (Hindi) flourishing

Fuller (English) clothier

Fulmala (Hindi) wreath

Fulvia (Latin) blonde

Fulvy (Latin) blonde
Full, Fulvee, Fulvie

Fury (Latin) raging anger
Furee, Furey, Furie

Fushy (American) animated; vivid
Fooshy, Fueshy, Fushee

G

Gable (German) farming woman
Gabbie, Gabby, Gabe, Gabel, Gabell, Gabl

Gabor (French) conflicted
Gaber, Gabi

Gabriella ✪ ⊕ (Italian/Spanish) God is her strength
Caby, Gabela, Gabi, Gabrela, Gabriela, Gabryela, Gabryella

Gabrielle ✪ (French/Hebrew) strong
Gabi, Gabraelle, Gabreelle, Gabreille, Gabriele, Gabriella, Gabrilla, Gabrille, Gabryele, Gabryelle, Gaby, Gaebriell, Gaebrielle, Garbreal

Gaby (French) form of Gabrielle: strong
Gabey, Gabi, Gabie

Gada (Hebrew) fortune

Gadar (Armenian) perfect girl
Gad, Gadahr, Gaddie, Gaddy

Gadara (Biblical) place name

Gae (Greek) form of Gaea: earth goddess
Gay, Gaye

Gaea (Greek) earth goddess
Gaia

Gaegae (Greek) form of Gaea: earth goddess
Gae, Gaege, Gaegie

Gaelle (American) of the earth

Gaenor (Welsh) beautiful

Gaetane (Italian) form of Gaeta, Italy

Gagane (American) sky

Gage (American) happy

Gaia (Greek) goddess of earth
Gaea, Gaya

Gail (Hebrew) form of Abigail: joyful
Gaelle, Gale, Gayle

Gaillen (American) joyful

Gaily (American) fun-loving
Gailai, Galhy

Gailya (Russian) serene
Galya

Gailyn (English) form of Galen: decisive

Gaines (Last name used as first name) gainful

Gaitlynn (American) hopeful
Gaitlin, Gaitline, Gaitlinn, Gaitlyn, Gaytlyn

Gala (French) merrymaking; festivity
Gaila, Gailah, Galaa, Galuh, Gayla

Galatea (Greek) sea nymph in mythology
Gal, Gala

Galatia (Biblical) place name; dramatic

Galaxy (American) universal
Gal, Galaxee, Galaxi

Galen (American) decisive
Galin, Galine, Galyn, Gaye, Gaylen, Gaylin, Gaylyn

Galena (Latin) metal; tough
Galyna, Galynna

Galenza (American) calming girl

Galia (Jewish) flows

Galiana (German) vaulted
Galiyana, Galli, Galliana

Galienna (Russian) steady
Galiena, Galyena, Galyenna

Galina (Russian) deserving
Gailina, Gailinna, Galyna, Galynna

Galise (American) joyful
Galeece, Galeese, Galice, Galyce

Gallaine (Last name used as first name) attractive

Galya (Hebrew) redeemed; merry
Galia

Galyan (Hebrew) saved

Gamala (Biblical) place name; lithe; Lovely

Gamin (American) gamine

Ganisia (American) gains

Garcelle (French) flowered
Garcel, Garsell, Garselle

Gardenia (Botanical) sweet flower baby

Gardner (Last name used as first name) gardens

Garetta (American) form of the name Garrett: bashful

Garim (Hindi) warm

Garima (Hindi) sincere

Garland (American) fancy
Garlan, Garlande, Garlinn, Garlynn

Garlanda (French) flowered wreath; pretty girl
Gar, Garl, Garlynd, Garlynda

Garlin (French) form of Garland: fancy
Garlinn, Garlyn, Garlynn

Garner (American) style-setter
Garnar, Garnir

Garnet (English) pretty; semi-precious stone

Garnett (English) red gemstone; valued

Garnetta (French) gemstone; precious
Garna, Garnet, Garnie, Garny

Garrett (Last name as first name) bashful
Garret, Gerrett

Garri (American) energetic
Garree, Garrey, Garry, Garrye

Garrielle (American) competent
Gariele, Garielle, Garriella

Garrison (American) sturdy
Garisen, Garisun, Garrisen, Garrisun

Garrity (American) smiling
Garety, Garrety, Garity, Garritee, Garritie

Gartha (American) feminine form of Garth: sunny; gardener

Garvin (Last name used as first name) craftsperson

Garyn (American) svelte
Garen, Garin, Garinne, Garun, Garynn, Garynne

Gates (Last name as first name) careful
Gate

Gauri (Hindi) golden goddess

Gavin (American) smart
Gave, Gaven, Gavey, Gavun

Gavion (American) daring
Gaveon, Gavionne

Gaviotte (French) graceful
Gaveott, Gaviot, Gaviott

Gavit (French) form of Gabrielle: strong

Gavitt, Gavyt, Gavytt

Gavotte (French) dancer

Gav, Gavott

Gavrielle (French) form of Gabrielle: strong

Gavriele, Gavryele, Gavryelle

Gay (French) jolly

Gae, Gaye

Gayathri (Indian) happy

Gayla (American) planner

Gaila, Gailah, Gala, Gaye, Gaylah, Gayluh

Gayle (Hebrew) rejoicing

Gaylene (English) delighted

Gaynor (American) precocious

Ganor, Gayner, Gaynorre

Gayor (Hebrew) sunny

Gazee (Hebrew) sturdy

Geanna (American) ostentatious

Geannah, Gianna

Geary (Hebrew) form of Jerry: hopeful

Gearee, Gearey, Geari, Gearie, Geeree, Geerey, Geeri, Geery

Gebra (Greek) graceful

Gederah (Biblical) place name

Geena (Italian) form of Gena: wellborn

Gina, Ginah

Geeta (Italian) pearl

Gelacia (Spanish) treasure

Gela, Gelasha, Gelasia

Gelda (American) gloomy

Geilda, Geldah, Gelduh

Gelil (American) smiling

Gem (American) shining

Gemmy, Gim, Jim

Gemesha (African American) dramatic

Gemeisha, Gemiesha, Gemme, Gemmy, Gimesha

Gemilie (American) gem

Gemini (Greek) twin

Gem, Gemelle, Gemmy

Gemma (Latin) gem; jewel

Gem, Gema, Gemmie, Gemmy

Gemmalis (American) gem

Gemmy (Italian) gem

Gemmee, Gemmi, Gimmy

Gems (American) shining gem

Gem, Gemmie, Gemmy

Gemze (American) gem

Gena (French) form of Gina: wellborn

Geena, Gen, Genah, Geni, Genia

Genay (American) form of Gena: wellborn

Genell (American) form of Janelle: exuberant

Genill

Genera (Greek) highborn

Gen, Genere

Generosa (Spanish) generous

Generosah, Generossa

Genesis ✿ (Latin) fast starter; beginning

Gen, Gena, Genesys, Geney, Genisis, Genisys, Genysis, Genysys, Jenesis

Geneva (French) city in Switzerland; flourishing; like juniper

Gena, Geneeva, Genyva, Janeva, Jeneva

Genevera (Spanish) highborn

Genevieve (German/French) high-minded

Gen, Gena, Genavieve, Geneveeve, Geniveeve, Genivieve, Genna, Genovieve, Genyveeve, Genyvieve

Genica (American) intelligent

Gen, Genicah, Genicuh, Genika, Gennica, Jen, Jenika, Jennika

Genie (Greek) of high birth; tricky

Geenee, Geeney, Geeni, Geenie, Geeny, Genee, Geney, Geni, Geny

Genna (English) womanly

Gen, Genny, Jenna

Gennesaret (Biblical) place name

Gennese (American) helpful
Gen, Geneece, Geniece, Genny, Ginece, Gineese

Gennette (American) form of Jeannette: lively

Gennifer (American) form of Jennifer: white wave
Genefer, Genephur, Genifer

Genny (Greek) of high birth; loving
Genney, Genni, Gennie

Genoa (Italian) playful
Geenoa, Genoah, Jenoa

Genova (Place name)

Genovesia (Place name)

Genoveva (American) form of Genevieve: high-minded
Genny, Geno

Gentle (American) kind
Gen, Gentil, Gentille, Gentlle

Gentry (American) sweet
Gen, Gentree, Gentrie, Jentrie, Jentry

Geoma (American) outstanding
Gee, GeeGee, Geo, Geomah, Geome, Gigi, Jeoma, Oma, Omah

Geonna (American) sparkling
Gee, Geionna, Geone, Geonne, Geonnuh

Georgann (English) bright-eyed
Georganne, Jorgann, Joryann

Georganna (English) form of Georgia: farmer
Georgana, Georgeana, Georgeanna

Georgene (English) wandering
Georgeene, Georgena, Georgyne, Jorgeen, Jorjene

Georgenia (Dutch) farm girl

Georgette (French) lively and little
Georgett, Georgitt, Georgitte, Jorgette

Georgia (Greek) farmer
Georgi, Georgie, Georgina, Georgya, Giorgi, Jorga, Jorgia, Jorja

Georgianna (English) gracious farmer
Georganna, Georgeanna, Georgianne, Jorjeana, Jorgianna

Georgie (English) form of Georgia: farmer
Georgee, Georgey, Georgi, Georgy

Georgina (Latin) feminine form of George: land-loving; farmer

Geowanna (African) earthy

Geraldine (German) strong
Geraldyne, Geri, Gerri, Gerry

Geralena (French) leader
Gera, Geraleen, Geralen, Geralene, Gerre, Gerrilyn, Gerry, Jerrileena, Lena

Gerarda (Spanish) feminine form of Gerard: brave

Gerardette (American) feminine form of Gerard: brave

Gerasa (Biblical) place name

Gerda (Scandinavian) fertility goddess

Gerdelle (American) fertile

Gerdellyne (American) form of Geraldine: strong

Gerdi (Scandinavian) guards

Gerdina (Scandinavian) guarded

Gerdnan (German) guards

Gerisa (English) form of Geraldine: strong
Gerry

Gerldine (American) form of Geraldine: strong

Gerly (English) form of Geraldine: strong

Gerlynne (German) tenderness
Gerlind

Germaine (French/German) important
Germain, Germane, Germayne, Jermaine

Gerol (English) rules

Geroldine (American) form of Geraldine: strong

Gerritta (American) strong

Gerry (German) form of Geraldine: strong

Gertrude (German) beloved
Gerdie, Gerti, Gertie

Gertudis (Slavic) form of Gertrude: beloved

Gervaise (French) strong

Gerva, Gervaisa

Gessalin (American) loving

Gessilin, Gessalyn, Gessalynn, Jessalin, Jessalyn

Gessica (American) form of Jessica: rich

Gesica, Gesika, Gessika

Gethsemane (Biblical) peaceful

Geth, Gethse, Gethsemanee, Gethsemaney, Gethsemanie, Gethy

Geynille (American) womanly

Geynel

Gezelle (American) lithe

Gezzelle, Gizele, Gizelle

Gezzi (Asian) believer

Ggana (African) place name

Ghada (Arabic) graceful

Ghad, Ghadah

Ghadeah (Arabic) graceful

Gadea, Gadeah

Ghaeda (Arabic) graceful

Ghandia (African) able

Gandia, Ghanda, Ghandee, Ghandy, Gondia, Gondiah

Ghea (American) confident

Ghia, Jeah, Jeeah

Gherlan (American) forgiving; joyful

Gerlan, Gherli

Ghislaine (French) loyal

Ghita (Italian) pearl

Gita, Gite

Gia (Italian) lovely

Giacinte (Italian) hyacinth; flowering

Gia, Giacin, Giacinta

Giada (Italian) precious jade

Giani (Italian) feminine form of John: God is gracious

Gianina (Italian) believer

Gia, Giane, Giannina, Gianyna, Janeena, Janina, Jeanina

Gianine (American) feminine form of John: God is gracious

Gianna ✿ (Italian) forgiving

Geonna, Giana, Gianne, Gianni, Giannie, Gianny, Ginny, Gyana, Gyanna

Giannelle (American) hearty

Geanelle, Gianella, Gianelle, Gianne

Giannesha (African American) friendly

Geannesha, Gianesha, Giannesh, Gianneshah, Gianneshuh

Giara (Italian) sensual

Gee, Geara, Gia, Giarah

Gidget (American) cute

Gidge, Gidgett, Gidgette, Gydget

Gift (American) blessed

Gifte, Gyft

Gigi (French) small; spunky

Geegee, Giggi

Gila (Hebrew) joyful

Gilla, Gyla, Gylla

Gilala (Jewish) happy

Gila, Gilah

Gilberta (German) smart

Bertie, Gill

Gilberte (German) shining

Gilda (English) gold-encrusted

Gildi, Gildie, Gill

Gilead (Biblical) place name

Gill (American) intelligent

Gillaine (Latin) young

Gilleese (American) funny

Gill, Gillee, Gilleece, Gillie, Gilly

Gillen (American) humorous

Gill, Gilly, Gillyn, Gyllen

Gilli (American) joyful

Gill, Gillee, Gilly

Gillian (Latin) youthful

Gila, Gili, Gilian, Giliana, Gilien, Gilliana, Gilliane, Gillie, Gillien, Gilly, Gillyan, Gillyen, Gilyan, Gilyen, Jillian

Gillis (Last name as first name) conservative

Gilise, Gillice, Gylis, Gyllis

Gillyle (American) smart

Gilma (American) form of Wilma: sturdy
Gee, Gilly

Gilmore (Last name as first name) striking
Gilmoor, Gill, Gillmore, Gylmore

Gina (Italian) wellborn
Geena, Gena, Gin, Ginah, Ginny, Gyna, Gynah, Jenah

Ginae (Biblical) place name

Ginane (French) wellborn
Gigi, Gina, Gine, Jeanan, Jeanine

Ginate (Italian) precious

Giner (English) ginger

Ginet (French) of the earth

Ginette (Italian) flower

Ginevieve (Irish) form of Genevieve: high-minded
Gineveeve, Giniveeve, Ginivieve, Ginyveeve, Ginyvieve

Ginge (English) feminine form of George: land-loving; farmer

Ginger (Botanical) ginger plant
Gin, Ginny, Jinger

Gingerly (American) careful

Ginnifer (American) form of Jennifer: white wave
Gini, Ginifer, Giniferr, Ginifir, Ginn

Ginny (English) form of Virginia: pure female
Ginnee, Ginney, Ginni, Ginnie

Gioconda (Italian) pleasing
Gio, Giocona

Giolla (Italian) helper

Giono (Last name as first name) delight; friendly
Gio, Gionna, Gionno

Giorgio (Italian) feminine form of George: land-loving; farmer
Giorgi, Giorgie, Jorgio

Giovanna (Italian) gracious believer; great entertainer
Geo, Geovanna, Gio, Giovahna, Giovana

Giovanne (Italian) form of Giovanna: gracious believer; great entertainer

Giovannina (Italian) little Giovanna; believes in God

Giritha (Sri Lankan) melodic
Giri, Girith

Girty (English) form of Gertie: graceful; gracious

Gisbelle (American) lovely girl
Gisbel

Gisella (German) pledged for service
Gisela

Giselle (French) a promise
Gis, Gisel, Gisela, Gisele, Gisell, Gissel, Gissell, Gissella, Gisselle, Gissie, Jizele

Gita (Sanskrit) song
Geta, Gete, Git, Gitah

Gitaleen (German) held in high esteem

Gitana (Spanish) gypsy

Gitele (Hebrew) good
Gitel

Githa (Slavic) form of Gita: song
Gytha

Gitika (Sanskrit) little singer
Getika, Gita, Giti, Gitikah

Gitka (Indian) singing

Gitta (German) highly regarded

Giuletta (Italian) tiny girl

Giulia (Italian) little girl

Giva (Sanskrit) form of Gita: song
Givah, Gyva, Gyvah

Givonnah (Italian) loyal; believer
Gevonna, Gevonnuh, Givonn, Givonna, Givonne, Jevonah, Jevonna, Jivonnah, Juvona

Gizela (Polish) dedicated
Giz, Gizele, Gizella, Gizzy

Gizelle (German) pledged to serve
Giselle, Gizel, Gizele, Gizell

Gizmo (American) tricky
Gis, Gismo, Giz

Glad (Welsh) form of Gladys: flower; princess

Gladdies (American) form of Gladys: flower; princess

Gladiola (Botanical) blooming; flower
Glad, Gladdee, Gladdy

Gladyce (Spanish) princess

Gladys (Welsh) flower; princess
Glad, Gladdie, Gladice, Gladis, Gladise, Gladiss

Glafira (Spanish) giving
Glafee, Glafera, Glafi

Glasira (Spanish) uncanny

Gleam (American) bright girl
Glee, Gleem

Glease (American) gleeful

Glee (American) gleeful

Glenda (Welsh) bright; good
Glinda, Glynda, Glynn, Glynnie

Glendora (English) form of Glenda: good; bright

Glenn (Irish) glen; from a sylvan setting
Glen

Glenna (Irish) valley-living
Glena, Glenah, Glenuh, Glyn, Glynna

Glennesha (African American) special
Glenesha, Gleneshuh, Gleniesha, Glenn, Glenneshah, Glenny, Glinnesha

Glennice (American) top notch
Glenis, Glennis, Glenys, Glenysse, Glynnece, Glynnice

Glennish (American) unique

Glensheen (French) from the home by the glen

Glenys (Welsh) holy
Glenice, Glenis, Gleniss, Glenyss

Glikeria (Slavic) cheerful

Gliselda (American) loyal

Glorene (American) form of Gloria: glorious

Gloria (Latin) glorious
Glorea, Glorey, Glori, Gloriah, Glorrie, Glory

Glorielle (American) generous
Gloree, Glori, Gloriel, Gloriele, Glory,

Gloris (American) glorious
Gloreeca, Glores, Gloresa, Glorisa, Glorus, Gloryssa

Glory (Latin) shining
Gloree, Glorey, Glori, Glorie

Gloss (American) showy
Glosse, Glossee, Glossie, Glossy

Glow (American) glowing

Glyde (American) smooth

Glynis (Welsh) from the glen
Glyniss, Glynys, Glynyss

Glynisha (African American) vibrant
Glynesh, Glynn, Glynnecia, Glynnesha,

Glynnie, Glynnisha

Glynn (Welsh) from the glen
Glin, Glinn, Glyn

Glynnis (Welsh) vivacious; glen
Glenice, Glenis, Glennis, Glinice, Glinnis, Glynn, Glynnie, Glynny

Goala (American) goal-oriented
Go, GoGo, Gola

Gobnat (Irish) cuddly

Goddess (American) gorgeous
Godess, Goddesse

Godiva (English) God's gift; brazen
Godeva, Godivah

Golda (English) golden
Goldi, Goldie

Golden (American) shining
Goldene, Goldon, Goldun, Goldy

Goldie (English) bright and golden girl
Goldee, Goldey, Goldi, Goldy

Goliad (Spanish) goal-oriented
Goleade, Goliade

Gomery (Biblical) all there

Gomti (Hindi) river

Goneril (Literature) Shakespearean name; ruthless
Gonarell, Gonarille, Gonereal

Gordie (American) girl who is watchful

Gordyene (Biblical) place name

Gormie (Scottish) lady

Govindi (Sanskrit) devout; faithful

Grable (American) handsome woman
Gray, Graybell

Grace ✪ ✇ (Latin) graceful
Graci, Gracie, Gracy, Graice, Gray, Grayce

Graceann (American) girl of grace
Gracean, Grace-Ann, Graceanna, Graceanne, Gracee, Gracy

Gracell (American) graceful girl

Gracia (Spanish) gracious

Gracie ✪ (Latin) graceful
Gracee, Gracey, Graci, Gracy, Graecie, Gray

Graciela (Spanish) pleasant; full of grace
Chita, Gracee, Gracella, Gracey, Gracie, Graciella, Gracilla, Grasiela, Graziela

Gracilia (Latin) graceful girl
Gracillia, Gracillya, Gracilya

Grady (Irish) hardworking; diligent

Graham (American) sweet
Graehm, Grayhm

Graichen (American) pearl-like

Grainne (Irish) loving girl
Graine, Grayne, Graynne

Grana (Irish) form of Grania: love

Grania (Irish) love
Grainee, Graini

Grant (Last name used as first name) good values

Grantyne (American) generous

Granya (Russian) breech baby

Gratia (Scandinavian) graceful; gracious
Gart, Gert, Gertie, Grasha, Gratea, Grateah, Gratie

Gray (Last name as first name) quiet
Graye, Grey

Graysha (American) gray hair

Grayson (Last name as first) child of quiet one
Graison, Grasen, Greyson

Grazie (Italian) graceful; pleasant
Grasie, Grazee, Grazy

Grazyna (Polish) graceful; pleasant

Grecian (Place name) form of Greece

Greer (Scottish) aware
Grear, Greare, Greere, Grier

Gregory (American) scholarly
Gregge, Greggy, Gregoree, Gregoria, Gregorie

Greshawn (African American) lively
Greeshawn, Greshaun, Greshawna, Greshonn, Greshun

Gresia (American) compelling
Grasea, Graysea, Grayshea, Grecia

Greta (German) pearl
Gretah, Grete, Gretie, Grette, Grytta

Gretchen (German) pearl
Grechen, Grechin, Grechyn, Gretch, Gretchin, Gretchun, Gretchyn, Grethyn

Grete (Dutch) pearl girl

Gretel (German) pearl; fanciful; (Dutch) manipulative
Gretal, Gretell, Gretelle, Grettel

Grethel (Dutch) form of Gretel: manipulative or pearl; fanciful

Grewn (American) supporter

Greyland (American) focused
Grey, Greylin, Greylyn, Greylynne

Gricie (Spanish) form of Griselda: patient

Griffie (Welsh) royal
Griff, Griffee, Griffey, Griffi, Gryffie

Griffin (Welsh) royal
Griff

Griffith (Last name used as first name) confident

Grindelle (American) live wire
Dell, Delle, Grenn, Grin, Grindee, Grindell, Grindy, Renny

Griselda (German) patient
Grezelda, Grisel, Grissy, Grizel, Grizelda, Grizzie

Griselia (Spanish) gray; patient
Grise, Grisele, Grissy, Seley, Selia

Grisham (Last name as first name)
ambitious
Grish

Gritta (German) pearl

Grittith (American) form of Griffith:
.confident

Grizel (Spanish) long-suffering
Griz, Grizelda, Grizelle, Grizzy

Grove (Botanical) child of the
outdoors

Grushenka (Russian) desirable

Guadalupe (Spanish) patron saint;
easygoing
*Guadelupe, Guadylupe, Lupe, Lupeta,
Lupita*

Guadarrama (Spanish) river of
saints

Gubby (Irish) cuddly
Gub, Gubee, Gubbie

Gudrun (Scandinavian) wise
Gudren, Gudrenne, Gudrin, Gudrinne

Guendolen (Welsh) fair born

Guenevere (Welsh) soft; white

Guenna (Welsh) soft
Guena

Guessa (American) kind

Guinevere (Welsh) queen; white
Guenevere, Guenyveere, Guin, Gwen

Gulab (Hindi) darken

Gulanara (Spanish) needy

Gulenia (Spanish) wanted

Gullermina (Spanish) willful
protector

Gumercindo (Spanish) famed

Gunda (German) combative

Gunilla (Scandinavian) warlike
Gun, Gunn

Gunta (German) form of Gunda:
combative

Gunun (German) lively
Gunan, Gunen

Gurlene (American) smart
Gurl, Gurleen, Gurleene, Gurline

Gurshawn (American) talkative
*Gurdie, Gurshauna, Gurshaune,
Gurshawna, Gurty*

Gussie (Latin) form of Augusta:
revered
Gus, Gussy, Gustie

Gusta (German) form of Gustava: royal
Gussy, Gustana, Gusty

Gustava (Scandinavian) royal

Guy (French) guiding; assertive
Guye

Guyette (French) ambitious

Guyla (French) asserts

Guyna (American) aggressor

Gwen (Welsh) form of Gwendolyn:
mystery goddess; bright
Gweni, Gwenn, Gwenna, Gwyn

Gwenda (Welsh) beautiful
Guenda

Gwendolyn (Welsh) mystery
goddess; bright
*Gwenda, Gwendalinne, Gwendalyn,
Gwendelynn, Gwendolen, Gwendolin,
Gwendoline, Gwendolynn, Gwennie,
Gywnne*

Gwenless (Invented) fair
Gwen, Gwenles, Gwenny

Gwenllian (Welsh) lovely

Gwenna (Welsh) beautiful
Gwena

Gwitira (American) fair

Gwladys (Welsh) form of Gladys:
flower; princess

Gwyn (Welsh) form of Gwyneth: blessed
Gwenn, Gwinn, Gwynn, Gwynne

Gwynedd (Welsh) blessed

Gwyneth (Welsh) blessed
*Gwennie, Gwinith, Gwynethe,
Gwynith, Gwynithe, Gwynne,
Gwynneth, Win, Winnie*

Gyanll (African) genuine

Gyda (Scandinavian) celestine

Gygi (French) form of GiGi: small;
spunky

Gylla (Spanish) feminine form of
Guillermo: attentive
Guilla, Gye, Gyla, Jilla

Gynette (American) form of Jeanette:
lively
Gyn, Gynett, Gynnee, Gynnie

Gypsy (English) adventurer
Gippie, Gipsie, Gypsie

Gyselle (German) form of Giselle: a
promise
Gysel, Gysele

Gyta (American) young

Gythae (English) feisty
Gith, Gyth, Gythay

H

Ha (Vietnamese) happy

Haafizah (Arabic) librarian
Hafeezah

Haalah (Arabic) librarian

Haarisah (Hindi) sun girl

Haarithah (Arabic) angel

Habbai (Arabic) well-loved

Habiba (Arabic) well-loved
Habeebah, Habibah

Habika (Arabic) loved and cherished

Hadassah (Hebrew) myrtle tree
*Hadasa, Hadasah, Hadaseh, Hadassa,
Haddasah, Haddee, Haddi, Haddy*

Hadil (Arabic) cooing

Hadlee (English) girl in heather
Hadlea, Hadley, Hadli, Hadly

Hady (Greek) soulful
Haddie, Hadee, Hadie, Haidee, Haidie

Hadyn (American) smart
Haden

Haelee (English) form of Hailey:
natural; hay meadow

Hagai (Hebrew) abandoned; alone
Haggai, Haggi, Hagi

Hagar (Hebrew) stranger
Hager, Haggar, Hagur

Hagen (Last name used as first name)
defender

Hagir (Arabic) wanderer
Hajar

Haidee (Greek) humble
Haydee

Hailey ♀ ⚥ (English) natural; hay
meadow
*Haile, Hailea, Hailee, Hailie, Haily,
Halee, Haley, Halie, Hallie*

Haiti (Place name)

Halalah (Slavic) serenity

Halcyone (Greek) calm
Halceonne, Halcyon

Halda (Scandinavian) half-Danish
*Haldaine, Haldana, Haldane,
Haldayne*

Halden (Scandinavian) half-Danish
girl
Haldin, Haldyn

Haldi (Scandinavian) form of Halda:
half-Danish
Haldie, Haldis

Halea (Hawaiian) halo

Haleemah (Arabic) speaks quietly

Halena (Russian) form of Helen:
beautiful; light
Haleena, Halyna

Halene (Russian) staunch
Haleen, Halyne

Haletta (Greek) little country girl
from the meadow
*Hale, Halette, Hallee, Halletta, Halley,
Hallie, Hally, Letta, Lettie, Letty*

Halfrida (German) peaceful

Hali (English) heroic

Halia (Hawaiian) remembering

Halima (Arabic) gentle

Halimeda (Greek) sea-loving
Hallie, Hally, Meda

Halina (Russian) faithful
Haleena, Halyna

Hall (Last name as first name)
distinguished
Haul

Halle (German) home ruler

Hallela (Hebrew) praiseworthy

Hallie (German) high-spirited
Haleigh, Hali, Halie, Halle, Hallee,
Hally, Hallye

Halona (Native American) lucky baby
Halonna

Halsey (American) playful
Halcie, Halsea, Halsee, Halsie

Halston (American) stylish
Hall, Halls, Halsten

Halzey (American) leader
Hals, Halsee, Halsi, Halsy, Halze, Halzee

Hameedah (Arabic) grateful

Hamilton (American) wishful
Hamil, Hamilten, Hamiltun, Hamma,
Hamme

Hamony (Latin) form of Harmony:
in synchrony

Hana (Arabic) delight

Haneefah (Arabic) true believer

Hanh (Vietnamese) moral

Hani (Hawaiian) sways

Hanifa (Arabic) righteous

Hanna (Polish) grace

Hannabelle (German) feminine
form Hannibal: happy; beauty
Hannabell, Hannahbell, Hannahbelle

Hannah ✪ ☻ (Hebrew) merciful;
God-blessed
Hanae, Hanah, Hanan, Hannaa,
Hanne, Hanni

Hanne (Scandinavian) girl of grace

Hannelore (American) form of
Hannah: merciful; God-blessed

Hannette (American) form of
Jannette: lovely
Hariett, Hann, Hannett

Hannia (Polish) graceful

Hannie (German) believer

Hansa (Indian) swanlike
Hans, Hansah, Hansey, Hanz

Happy (English) joyful
Hap, Happee, Happi

Haralda (Scandinavian) rules the
army
Hallie, Hally, Harelda, Harilda

Hardin (Last name used as first name)
keeps rabbits

Harla (English) country girl from the
fields
Harlah, Harlea, Harlee, Harlen, Harlie,
Harlun

Harlan (English) athletic
Harlen, Harlon, Harlun

Harlene (French) energetic

Harlequine (Invented) romantic
Harlequinne, Harley

Harley (English) wild thing
Harlea, Harlee, Harleey, Harli, Harlie,
Harly

Harlie (English) in the field; dreamy

Harlinne (American) vivacious
Harleen, Harleene, Harline, Harly

Harlow (American) brash
Harlo, Harly

Harmon (Last name as first name)
attuned
Harmen, Harmone, Harmun, Harmyn

Harmonita (Greek) in harmony

Harmony (Latin) in synchrony
Harmonee, Harmoni, Harmonia,
Harmonie

Harolyn (American) form of
Carolyn: womanly

Harper (English) musician; writer
Harp

Harrah (English) rejoicing;
merriment
Hara, Harah, Harra

Harrell (American) leader
Harell, Harill, Harryl, Haryl

Harriet (French) homebody
Harri, Harrie, Harriett, Harriette,
Harrott, Hat, Hatti, Hattie, Hatty

Harrisah (Indian) happy

Harsha (Indian) joyful

Harshita (English) form of Harriet:
homebody

Hart (American) romantic
Harte, Hartee, Hartie, Harty, Heart

Hartley (Last name as first name)
having heart
Hartlee, Hartleigh, Hartli, Hartlie,
Hartly

Hasina (African) beauty

Hassaanah (African) first girl born

Hattie (English) home-loving
Hatti, Hatty, Hettie, Hetty

Hattina (Biblical) place name;
homebody

Haute (French) high
Hautie

Hava (Hebrew) life; lively
Chaba, Chaya, Haya

Havana (Cuban) loyal
Havanah, Havane, Havanna,
Havanuh, Havvanah

Haven (American) safe place; open
Havin, Havun

Havilah (Hebrew) beloved

Haviland (American) lively; talented
Havilan, Havilynd

Hawkins (American) wily
Hawk, Hawkens, Hawkey, Hawkuns

Hawlee (American) negotiator
Hawlea, Hawleigh, Hawlie, Hawley,
Hawly

Haydee (American) capable
Hady, Hadye, Haydie

Haydeeline (English) sweet

Haydell (Last name used as first
name) hill child

Hayden (Last name used as first
name) hill child

Haydon (American) knowing
Hayden, Hadyn

Hayfa (Arabic) slim

Hayla (Arabic) moon's halo

Hayley (English) natural; hay meadow
Hailey, Haley, Haylee, Hayleigh, Hayli,
Haylie

Haze (American) word as a name;
spontaneous
Haise, Hay, Hays, Hazee, Hazey, Hazy

Hazel (English) powerful
Hazell, Hazelle, Hazie, Hazyl, Hazzell

Hazen (Hindi) joyful

Healy (Last name used as first name)
healthy

Heart (American) romantic
Hart, Hearte

Heath (English) open; healthy
Heathe

Heather (Scottish) flowering

Heath, Heathar, Heathor, Heathur

Heaven ○ (English) happy and beautiful
Heavyn, Hevin

Heavenly (American) spiritual
Heaven, Heavenlee, Heavenley,
Heavynlie, Hevin

Heba (Greek) child; goddess of youth
Hebe

Hecate (Greek) goddess of witchcraft

Hedda (German) capricious; warring
Heda, Heddi, Heddie, Hedi, Hedy,
Hetta

Heddalin (Scandinavian) contender

Hedley (Greek) sweet; (German)
excites
Hedlee, Hedleigh, Hedli, Hedlie, Hedly

Hedviga (Scandinavian) excites

Hedy (German) mercurial
Hedi

Hedya (Hebrew) joy girl
Hedia, Hedva

Hedy-Marie (German) capricious

Heidi (German) noble; watchful;
perky
Heide, Heidee, Heidie, Heidy, Hidi

Heidrun (German) form of Heidi:
noble; watchful; perky

Heija (Korean) bright
Hia, Hya

Heilala (Asian) sun child

Heirnine (Greek) form of Helen: beautiful; light

Heirrierte (English) form of Harriet: homebody

Hela (Biblical) olden

Helaine (French) ray of light; gorgeous
Helainne, Helle, Hellyn, Helyna

Helanna (Greek) lovely
Helahna, Helana, Helani, Heley, Hella

Helayne (American) pretty girl

Helbon (Greek) form of Helen: beautiful; light
Helbona, Helbonia, Helbonna, Helbonnah

Held (Welsh) light

Helen (Greek) beautiful; light
Hela, Hele, Helena, Helyn, Lena, Lenore

Helena (Greek) beautiful; ingenious
Helana, Helayna, Heleana, Helene, Hellena, Helyena, Lena

Helene (French) form of Helen: beautiful; light
Helaine, Heleen, Heline

Helenore (Greek) form of Helen: beautiful; light
Hele, Helenoor, Helenor, Helia, Helie, Hellena, Lena, Lennore, Lenora, Lenore, Lenory, Lina, Nora, Norey, Norie

Helfine (Scandinavian) blessed

Helga (Anglo-Saxon) pious
Helg

Helia (Greek) sun
Heleah, Helya, Helyah

Helice (Greek) form of Helen: beautiful; light

Helie (Greek) sunny
Heley, Heli

Helina (Greek) delightful
Helinah, Helinna, Helinnuh

Heliodora (Spanish) loves sun

Helki (Native American) tender
Helkie, Helky

Hella (Greek) form of Helen: beautiful; light
Helle

Helma (German) helmet; well-protected

Helmina (German) form of Wilhelmina: staunch protector

Heloise (German) hearty
Hale, Haley, Heley, Heloese, Heloyse

Helsa (Scandinavian) God-loving
Helse, Helsie

Helynne (French) moon

Hema (Indian) gold child

Henda (English) form of Henna: mehndi
Hende, Hendel, Heneh

Hender (American) embraced
Hendere

Henia (English) form of Henrietta: home-ruler; (Spanish) well-groomed
Henie, Henna, Henye

Henley (American) sociable
Hendlee, Hendly, Henli, Henlie, Hinlie, Hynlie

Henna (Hindi) mehndi
Hena, Hennah, Hennuh, Henny

Henrietta (English/German) home-ruler
Harriet, Hattie, Henny, Hetta, Hettie

Henriette (French) leads the home

Hensley (American) ambitious
Henslee, Henslie, Hensly

Henton (Last name used as first name) open arms

Hera (Greek) wife of Zeus; radiant

Heraclea (Biblical) place name; of Hercules

Herdis (Scandinavian) army woman

Herendira (Invented) tender and dear
Heren

Herise (Invented) warm
Heree, Hereese, Herice

Herleen (American) quiet
Herlee, Herlene, Herley, Herline, Herly, Hurleen

Herliza (Spanish) sweet

Hermaina (Spanish) speedy

Hermelinda (Spanish) earthy

Hermilla (Spanish) fighter
Herm, Hermila, Hermille

Hermina (Greek) of the earth
Hermine

Hermione (Greek) sensual
Hermina, Hermine

Hermosa (Spanish) beautiful
Ermosa

Hernanda (Spanish) feminine form
of Hernando: daring

Herra (Greek) earth girl
Herrah, Hera

Hersala (Spanish) lithe and lovely
Hers, Hersila, Hersilia, Hersy

Hersilia (Spanish) delicate

Hertha (English) earth
Eartha, Erda, Erta, Ertha, Herta

Hertnia (English) earth
Herrntia

Herwena (Slavic) winner

Hesna (Arabic) star

Hesper (Greek) night star
Hespera, Hespira

Hest (Greek) form of Hester: starlike;
literary
Hessie, Hesta, Hetty

Hesta (Greek) starlike
Hestia

Hester (American) starlike; literary
*Esther, Hestar, Hesther, Hett, Hettie,
Hetty*

Hestia (Greek) hearth

Heti (English) form of Henrietta:
home-ruler

Hetta (German) ruler
Hedda, Heta, Hettie, Hetty

Hetty (English) form of Henrietta:
home-ruler

Heven (American) pretty
Hevan, Hevin, Hevon, Hevun, Hevven

Hewaida (Indian) gift

Heydee (German) form of Heidi:
noble; watchful; perky

Heyzell (American) form of Hazel:
powerful
Hayzale, Heyzel, Heyzelle

Hezekiah (Biblical) pleases

Hiah (Korean) form of Heija: bright
Hia, Hy, Hya, Hye

Hiatt (English) form of Hyatt: high
gate; worthwhile
Hi, Hye

Hibernia (Place name) Latin word
for Ireland

Hibiscus (Botanical) pretty

Hicks (Last name as first name) saucy
Hicksee, Hicksie

Hidee (American) form of Heidi:
noble; watchful; perky
Hidey, Hidie, Hidy, Hydee, Hydeey

Hideko (Japanese) excellence

Hidie (German) lively

Hila (Hebrew) angelic

Hilan (Greek) happy

Hilaria (Latin/Polish) merrymaker
Hilarea, Hilareeah, Hilariah

Hilary (Latin) cheerful and outgoing
*Hilaire, Hilaree, Hilari, Hilaria,
Hillarree, Hillary, Hillerie, Hillery*

Hilda (German) protector
Hild, Hilde, Hildi, Hildie, Hildy

Hildar (Scandinavian) feisty

Hildebrand (German) strong

Hildegard (German) battle
*Hilda, Hildagarde, Hildegarde,
Hildred, Hillie*

Hildegunde (Last name as first
name) princess

Hildemar (German) strong

Hildreth (German) struggles

Hilina (Hawaiian) celestial

Hilja (Finnish) silence

Hilma (German) helmet; protects
herself
Helma

Hilmah (Scandinavian) form of Hilja: silence

Hilton (American) wealthy
Hillie, Hilltawn, Hillton, Hilly

Himalaya (Place name) mountain range; upwardly mobile
Hima

Hina (Scandinavian) leads the home

Hinda (Hebrew) held high

Hindal (Hebrew) form of Hinda: held high

Hinton (American) affluent
Hintan, Hinten, Hintun, Hynton

Hirani (Indian) gold child

Hiroko (Japanese) giving; wise

Hisa (Japanese) forever
Hissa, Hysa, Hyssa

Hisaye (Japanese) longlasting

Hoa (Southeast Asian) flowers

Hodalla (Jewish) queenly

Hodel (German) stern
Hodi

Hodge (Last name as first name) confident
Hodj

Hoku (Hawaiian) starlike

Holda (German) secretive

Holden (English) willing
Holdan, Holdun

Holder (English) beautiful voice
Holdar, Holdur

Holiday (American) jazzy
Holidae, Holidaye, Holladay, Holliday, Holly

Holine (American) special
Hauline, Holinn, Holli, Holyne

Hollah (German) hides much

Holland (Place name) expressive
Hollan, Hollyn, Holyn

Hollander (Dutch) form of Holland: expressive
Holander, Holender, Hollender, Hollynder, Holynder

Hollis (English) smart; girl by the holly
Hollice, Hollyce

Hollisha (English) ingenious; Christmas-born; holly
Holicha, Hollice, Hollichia, Hollise

Holly (Anglo-Saxon) Christmas-born; holly tree
Hollee, Holleigh, Holley, Holli, Hollie, Hollye

Holsey (American) laidback
Holsee, Holsie

Holton (American) whimsical
Holt, Holten, Holtun

Holyn (American) fresh-faced
Holan, Holen, Holland, Hollee, Hollen, Holley, Hollie, Holly, Hollyn

Homer (American) tomboyish
Homar, Home, Homera, Homie, Homir, Homma

Honesty (American) truthful
Honeste, Honestee, Honesti, Honestie, Honestye

Honey (Latin) sweet-hearted
Honie, Hunnie

Honeyblossom (American) sweet

Honeylee (American) sweet

Honor (Latin) ethical
Honer, Honora, Honour

Honora (Latin) honorable
Honorah, Honoree, Honoria, Honoura

Honorata (Polish) respected woman

Honoreen (American) has honor

Honoria (Spanish) of high integrity; a saint
Honoreah

Honorina (Spanish) honored
Honor, Honora, Honoryna

Hope ☻ (Anglo-Saxon) optimistic

Hopkins (American) perky
Hopkin

Hopsey (American) lively

Horatia (Latin) keeps time; careful
Horacia

Horiya (Japanese) gardens

Hortencia (Spanish) green thumb

Hartencia, Hartense, Hartensia, Hortence, Hortense, Hortensia

Hortense (Latin) caretaking the garden

Hortence, Hortensia, Hortinse

Hosanna (Greek) time to pray; worshipping

Hosana, Hosanah, Hosannah

Hoshi (Japanese) shines

Houston (Place name) leader

Houst, Houstie, Huston

Hoyden (Last name as first name) having high spirits

Hoydin, Hoydyn

Huberta (German) brilliant

Hud (American) tomboyish

Hudd

Huda (Arabic) the right way

Hoda

Hudalia (Spanish) leads

Hudel (Scandinavian) lovable

Hudi (Arabic) the right way

Hudson (English) explorer; adventuresome

Hud, Huds

Hueline (German) smart

Hue, Huee, Huel, Huela, Huelene, Huelette, Huelyne, Huey, Hughee, Hughie

Huella (American) joyous

Huela, Huelle

Hueretta (American) smart

Huette (German) intellectual

Huetta, Hugette, Hughette

Hulda (Scandinavian) sweetheart

Huldah, Huldie, Huldy,

Hum (Indian) togetherness

Humairaa (Asian) generous

Humla (Polish) humble

Hun (American) form of Honey: sweet-hearted

Hon

Hunni (American) form of Honey: sweet-hearted

Hunter (English) searching; jubilant

Hun, Huner, Hunner, Hunt, Huntar, Huntter

Hunting (English) hunts

Hurd (Last name used as first name) herds cattle

Hurley (English) fit

Hurlee, Hurlie, Hurly

Hutton (English) right

Hutten, Huttun

Huxlee (American) creative

Hux, Huxleigh, Huxley, Huxly

Hyacinth (Greek) flower

Hy, Hyacinthe, Hycinth

Hyatt (English) high gate; worthwhile

Hyat

Hyde (American) tough-willed

Hide, Hydie

Hydia (German) form of Heidi: noble; watchful; perky

Hydie (American) spirited

Hidi, Hydee, Hydey, Hydi

Hylaine (American) form of Elaine: dependable girl

Hypatia (Greek) tops

I

Iadanna (Biblical) place name

Iana (Greek) form of Iantha: flowering

Iann

Ianeke (Hawaiian) believer in a gracious God

Ianete, Iani

Ianthe (Greek) flowering

Ian, Iantha, Ianthina, Ianthiria

Ibeth (Spanish) form of Elizabeth: God's promise

Ibleam (Biblical) place name

Ibsen (Scandinavian) scholarly

Ida (German) heroine; warrior
Idah, Iduh

Idaa (Hindi) earth woman

Idahlia (Greek) sweet
Idali, Idalia, Idalina, Idaline, Idalis

Idalia (Italian) sweet

Idam (American) feminine form of Adam: original

Idarah (American) social
Idara, Idare, Idareah

Idasia (English) joyful

Ide (Irish) thirsty

Ideh (German) form of Ida: heroine; warrior
Idit

Idelle (Celtic) generous
Idele

Idetta (German) serious worker
Ideta, Idettah, Idette

Idil (Latin) pleasant
Idee, Idey, Idi, Idie, Idyll

Idola (German) worker
Idolah, Idolia

Idolina (American) idolizes
Idol, Idolena

Idolyne (Spanish) idolizes

Idoma (American) form of Idona: fresh

Idona (Scandinavian) fresh
Idonah, Idonea, Idonia, Idonna, Iduna

Idonie (Scandinavian) loving

Idony (Scandinavian) reborn

Idoris (Greek) adores

Idowu (African) baby after twins

Idra (Aramaic) rich; fig tree; flourishes

Idriya (Hebrew) duck; rich
Idria

Idumea (Biblical) place name

Iduna (Scandinavian) fresh
Idun

Iduvina (Spanish) dedicated
Iduvine, Iduvynna, Vina

Ieesh (Arabic) feminine
Ieasha, Ieesha, Iesha, Yesha

Ierne (Irish) form of Ireland: vibrant

Iesha (Arabic) feminine

Ieshia (English) form of Iesha: feminine

Ifama (African) well-being

Ife (African) loving

Ifigenia (Spanish) form of Effie: well-spoken

Ignacia (Latin) passionate
Ignacy, Ignatia, Ignatzia

Ihab (Arabic) gift

Iheoma (Hawaiian) lifted by the Lord

Ihsan (Arabic) good will
Ihsana, Ihsanah

Iianena (Slavic) form of Ileana: soaring

Iilia (English) form of Ileana: soaring

Ijada (Spanish) jade; beauty

Ikabela (Hawaiian) form of Isabella: consecrated to God
Ikapela

Ikea (Scandinavian) smooth
Ikeah, Ikee, Ikie

Ikeida (Invented) spontaneous
Ikae, Ikay

Iku (Japanese) nurturing

Ila (Hindi) of the earth; lovely

Ilaisaane (Asian) bright

Ilamay (French) sweet; from an island
Ilamae, Ila May, Ila-May, Ilamaye

Ilana (Hebrew) tree; gorgeous
Elana, Ilaina, Ilane, Ilani, Illana, Lainie, Lanie

Ilaria (Greek) girl with a good attitude

Ilda (German) warring; feisty

Ildiko (Hungarian) contentious; warrior

Ileana (American) soaring
Ileanna, Ileannah, Ilene, Iliana, Ilianna, Illeana, Illiana

Ilena (Greek) regal
Ileena, Ilina

Ilene (American) svelte
Ileen, Ilenia

Ilesha (Hindi) loves the Lord of the earth

Ilfa (American) ecstatic

Ilia (Greek) from ancient city Ilion; traditional

Iliana (Greek) woman of Troy
Ileanai, Illéana

Ilima (Hawaiian) oahu flower

Ilka (Hungarian) beauty

Ilkee (Slavic) form of Ilka: beauty

Ilkka (Slavic) form of Ilka: beauty

Illana (Hebrew) tree

Illiana (Spanish) form of Helen: beautiful; light

Ilma (American) stubborn

Ilon (Biblical) place name

Ilona (Hungarian) form of Helen: beautiful; light

Ilonka (Slavic) lovely

Ilsa (Scottish) glowing
Elyssa, Illisa, Illysa, Ilsah, Ilse, Lissie

Ilse (German) form of Elizabeth: God's promise

Ilyse (English) charms

Ilyssa (English) form of Alyssa: flourishing

Ima (Japanese) now; the present
Imah

Imagine (Word as name) imaginative

Imaine (Arabic) form of Iman: living in the present
Imain, Imane

Imala (Native American) strongwilled

Iman (Arabic/African) living in the present
Imen

Imana (Arabic) faithful; true

Imani (Arabic) faithful

Imanuela (Spanish) faithful

Imara (Hungarian) ruler

Imari (Japanese) today's girl

Imelda (German) contentious
Imalda

Imena (African) dreamy

Imin (Arabic) loyal

Immaculada (Spanish) spotless

Imogen (Gaelic) maiden
Emogen, Imogene

Imperia (Latin) imperial; stately

In (Arabic) generous

Ina (Latin) small
Inah

Inaki (Asian) generous spirit

Inam (Arabic) generous

Inanna (Mythology) goddess

Inas (Arabic) friendly

Inca (Indian) adventurer
Incah

Inda (Place name) lady

India (Place name) woman of India
Indeah, Indee, Indie, Indy, Indya

Indiana (Place name) salt-of-the-earth; U.S. state
Inda, India

Indiece (American) capable
Indeece, Indeese

Indigo (Latin) eyes of deep blue
Indego, Indigoh

Indira (Hindi) ethereal; God of heaven and thunderstorms
Indra

Indra (Hindi) god of thunder and rain; powerful
Indee, Indi, Indira, Indre

Indranee (Hindi) sky God's wife

Indrani (Indian) wife of Indra; excellent

Indray (American) outspoken
Indee, Indrae, Indree

Indre (Hindi) splendor

Indya (Place name) form of India: woman of India

Ineesha (African American) sparkling
Inesha, Ineshah, Inisha

Ineke (Japanese) nurtures

Ines (Spanish) chaste
Inez, Innez, Ynez

Inessa (Russian) pure
Inesa, Nessa

Inessae (Spanish) form of Ines: chaste

Inetha (Slavic) pure

Inez (Spanish) lovely

Ines

Infinity (American) lasting

Infinitee, Infinitey, Infiniti, Infinitie

Inga (Scandinavian) hero's daughter

Ingalill (Scandinavian) fertile

Ingalls (American) peaceful

Inge (Scandinavian) fertile

Inga

Ingeborg (Scandinavian) fertile

Ingegerd (Scandinavian) form of Ingrid: beautiful

Inger (Scandinavian) lovely

Inglesa (Spanish) English girl

Ingrad (American) form of Ingrid: beautiful

Inger, Ingr

Ingrid (Scandinavian) beautiful

Inga, Inge, Inger, Ingred

Ingrida (Scandinavian) form of Ingrid: beautiful

Iniguez (Spanish) good

Ina, Ini, Niqui

Inka (Scandinavian) abundant

Inna (Slavic) little girl

Innocence (American) pure

Innoce, Innocents, Inocence, Inocencia, Inocents

Inoa (Hawaiian) named

Inocencia (Spanish) innocent

Inocenta, Inocentia

Inola (Greek) form of Iola: dawn

Integrity (American) truthful

Integritee, Integritie

Ioannis (Greek) believer

Iola (Greek) dawn

Iole

Iolana (Hawaiian) violet; pretty

Iolanthe (English) violet; delicate

Iole, Iola

Iona (Place name) for the Isle of Iona in Scotland

Ione, Ionia

Ioni (English) place name; innocent

Ionica (Biblical) place name

Iosepine (Hawaiian) form of Josephine: blessed

Ira (Hebrew) contented; watchful

Irah

Ireland (Place name) vibrant

Irelan, Irelande, Irelyn, Irelynn

Irene (Greek) peace-loving; goddess of peace

Irine

Ireta (Greek) serene

Iretta, Irette

Irina (Greek/Russian) comforting

Ireena, Irena, Irenah, Irene, Irenia,

Irenya

Iris (Greek) bright; goddess of the rainbow

Irisal (Greek) form of Iris: bright; goddess of the rainbow

Iriseene (American) iris flower; rainbow

Irish (American) Irish girl

Irma (Latin) realistic

Irmah

Irmaletta (Spanish) noble; complete

Irmgard (Latin) form of Irma: realistic

Irnee (Scandinavian) growth

Irodell (Invented) peaceful

Irodel, Irodelle

Irra (Greek) serene

Irvette (English) friend of the sea

Isa (Spanish) dark-eyed

Isah

Isabel ✿ (Spanish) God-loving

Isabela, Isabella, Isabelle, Issie, Iza

Isabella ✿ ✆ (Spanish/ Italian) consecrated to God

Isabela, Izabella

Isadora (Greek) beautiful; gift of Isis; fertile

Dora, Dori, Dory, Isidora

Isairis (Spanish) lively

Isa, Isaire

Isamu (Japanese) high-energy

Isandra (Spanish) form of Sandra: helpful; protective

Isatas (Native American) snow
Istas

Isaura (Greek) Asian country

Isela (American) giving
Iselah

Iselderine (Invented) loyal

Iseult (Irish) lovely

Isha (Hindi) protected

Ishana (Hindi) sheltered

Ishi (Japanese) rock; safe
Ishie

Ishiko (Japanese) rock; dependable

Ishtar (Biblical) mother-goddess; faithful

Isis (Egyptian) goddess supreme of moon and fertility

Isla (Place name) river in Scotland; flows

Isleana (Latin) sun girl; jolly
Isaeileen, Islean, Isleen

Ismaela (Hebrew) feminine form of Ishmael: God hears
Isma, Mael, Maella

Ismat (Arabic) protective

Ismene (French) form of the name Esme: much loved
Isme, Ismyne

Ismenia (Place name) region of Mars; loyal

Ismey (French) form of Esme: much loved

Isobelette (American) believes in God

Isoka (African) given by God
Isoke, Soka

Isoke (African) God's gift

Isola (Spanish) lovely

Isolde (Welsh) beautiful
Iseult, Isolda, Isolt, Izette, Yseult

Isotta (Irish) princess

Isra (Arabic) night mover

Issa (English) form of Isabel: God-loving
Isa

Issus (Biblical) place name; wise

Istvan (Hungarian) crowned

Ita (Irish) thirsts for knowledge

Italia (Italian) girl from Italy

Iti (Irish) form of Ita: thirsts for knowledge

Itiah (Hebrew) God comforts her
Itia, Itiya

Itica (Spanish) eloquent
Itaca, Iticah

Itidal (Arabic) cautious

Itinsa (Hawaiian) waterfall

Itka (Irish) form of Ita: thirsts for knowledge

Ito (Japanese) thread; delicate

Ituha (Native American) sturdy oak; white stone

Itzel (Spanish) form of Isabel: God-loving
Itz

Itzelle (Native American) earth goddess

Itzy (American) lively
Itsee, Itzee, Itzie

Iuana (Welsh) believes in gracious God

Iudita (Hawaiian) praises; affectionate

Iuginia (Hawaiian) highborn
Iugina

Iulaua (Hawaiian) eloquent

Iulia (Irish) form of Juliana: youthful; Jove's child

Iunia (Hawaiian) good victory

Iusitina (Hawaiian) justice

Iva (Slavic) dedicated
Ivah

Ivania (Russian) feminine form of Ivan: believer in a gracious God; reliable one

Ivaniah (Russian) feminine form of Ivan: believer in a gracious God; reliable one

Ivanna (Russian) gracious gift from God
Iva, Ivana, Ivanka, Ivie, Ivy

Iverem (African) lucky girl

Ives (French) form of Yves: clever

Ivet (Spanish) athletic

Iveta (French) athletic

Ivette (French) clever and athletic
Ivet, Ivett

Ivey (English/American) a climbing evergreen ornamental plant
Ivee, Ivie, Ivy

Iviannah (American) adorned
Iviana, Ivianna, Ivie, Ivy

Ivisse (American) graceful
Ivice, Iviece, Ivis, Ivise

Ivnia (Russian) feminine form of Ivan: believer in a gracious God; reliable one

Ivon (Spanish) light
Ivonie, Ivonne

Ivona (Slavic) gift
Ivana, Ivanna, Ivannah, Ivonah, Ivone, Ivonne

Ivonne (French) athlete
Ivonn

Ivory (Latin) white
Ivoree, Ivori, Ivorie

Ivria (Hebrew) from Abraham's country
Ivriah, Ivrit

Ivrie (English) form of Ivory: white

Ivy (English) growing
Iv, Ivee, Ivey, Ivie

Iwa (Japanese) strong character

Iwalani (Hebrew) heavenly girl

Iwilla (African American) I will rise

Iwona (Polish) archer; athletic; gift
Iwonna

Iyabo (African) her mother is home

Iyana (Hebrew) sincere

Izabella (American) form of Isabella: consecrated to God
Iza, Izabela, Izabell, Izabelle

Izanne (American) calming
Iza, Izan, Izann, Izanna, Ize

Izdihar (Arabic) blossoming

Izebe (African) staunch supporter

Izegbe (African) baby who was wanted

Izena (Slavic) gracious

Izene (Slavic) gracious

Izolde (Greek) philosophical
Izo, Izolade, Izold

Izusa (Native American) white rock; unique

Izzy (American) zany
Izzee, Izzie

J

Jaala (Arabic) seeks clarity

Jabinea (Biblical) sees

Jacalyn (American) form of Jacqueline: supplanter; substitute
Jacelyn, Jacelyne, Jacelynn, Jacilyn, Jacilyne, Jacilynn, Jacolyn, Jacolyne, Jacolynn, Jacylyn, Jacylyne, Jacylynn

Jacey (Greek) sparkling
J.C., Jace, Jacee, Jaci, Jacie, Jacy

Jacinda (Greek) attractive girl
Jacenda, Jacey, Jaci, Jacinta

Jacinta (Spanish) hyacinth; sweet
Jace, Jacee, Jacey, Jacinda, Jacinna, Jacintae, Jacinth, Jacinthia, Jacy, Jacynth

Jacinth (Greek) beauty

Jackalyn (American) form of Jacqueline: supplanter; substitute
Jackalene, Jackalin, Jackaline, Jackalynn, Jackalynne, Jackelin, Jackeline, Jackelyn, Jackelynn, Jackelynne, Jackilin, Jackilyn, Jackilynn, Jackilynne, Jackolin, Jackoline, Jackolyn, Jackolynn, Jackolynne

Jackie (French) form of Jacqueline: supplanter; substitute
Jackee, Jacki, Jacky, Jaki, Jaky

Jacklyn (American) careful
Jacklin, Jackline, Jacklyne, Jacklynn, Jacklynne

Jackquel (French) watchful
Jackquelin, Jackqueline, Jackquelyn, Jackquelynn, Jackquilin, Jackquiline, Jackquilyn, Jackquilynn, Jackquilynne

Jackson (Last name as first name) swaggering
Jacksen, Jaksin, Jakson

Jaclyn (French) form of Jacqueline: supplanter; substitute
Jacalyn, Jackalene, Jackalin, Jackalyn, Jackeline, Jackolynne, Jacleen, Jaclin, Jacline, Jaclyne, Jaclynn

Jacoba (Hebrew) replaces

Jacobi (Hebrew) stand-in
Cobie, Coby

Jacomine (Dutch) best girl

Jacoy (French) form of Jackie: supplanter; substitute

Jacqua (American) replacement

Jacqueline (French) supplanter; substitute
Jacki, Jackie, Jacklin, Jacklyn, Jaclyn, Jacqualin, Jacqualine, Jacqualyn, Jacqualyne, Jacquel, Jacquelyn,

Jacquelynn, Jacqui, Jacquie, Jakie, Jakline, Jaklinn, Jaklynn, Jaqueline, Jaquie

Jacquelyn (French) form of Jacqueline: supplanter; substitute
Jacquelyne, Jacquelynn

Jacquet (Invented) form of Jacqueline: supplanter; substitute
Jackett, Jackwet, Jacquee, Jacquie, Jakkett

Jacquetta (American) replacement

Jacqui (French) form of Jacqueline: supplanter; substitute
Jacquay, Jacque, Jacquee, Jacquie, Jaki, Jakki, Jaquay, Jaqui, Jaquie

Jacynth (Spanish) hyacinth; flower

Jada ✪ ☻ (Spanish) personable; precious
*Jadah, **Jayda***

Jade (Spanish) green gemstone; courageous; adoring
Jada, Jadah, Jadda, Jadea, Jadeann, Jadee, Jaden, Jadera, Jadi, Jadie, Jadielyn, Jadienne, Jady, Jadzia, Jadziah, Jaeda, Jaedra, Jaida, Jaide, Jaiden, Jaiyde

Jaden (Hebrew) God has heard
Jadan, Jadi, Jadie, Jadin, Jadyn, Jaeden, Jaiden

Jadie (Spanish) jade stone

Jadine (Spanish) jade stone

Jadran (American) jade stone

Jadwiga (Polish) religious
Jad, Jadwig, Wiga

Jadwin (American) friend of Jade

Jadza (Spanish) jade

Jae (Latin) small; jaybird
Jaea, Jay, Jayjay

Jael (Hebrew) high-climbing
Jaela, Jaelee, Jaeli, Jaelie, Jaelle

Jaela (Hebrew) bright
Jael, Jaell, Jayla

Jaelyn (African American) ambitious
Jaela, Jaelynne, Jala, Jalyn, Jaylyn

Jaenesha (African American) spirited
Jacey, Jae, Jaeneisha, Jaeniesha, Janesha, Jaynesha, Nesha

Jae-Sun (Japanese) sun's bird

Jaffa (Hebrew) lovely

Jagan (American) form of Jaden: God has heard
Jag, Jagann, Jagen, Jagun

Jagger (English) cutter
Jaeger, Jag, Jager

Jagodah (Slavic) little berry
Jaga, Jagada, Jago, Jagoda

Jaguar (American) runner
Jag, Jaggy, Jagwar, Jagwor

Jahel (Hebrew) moves upward

Jahnea (Scandinavian) feminine form of John: God is gracious
Jahnae, Jahnay, Jahnie, Jahnnee, Jahnney, Jahnnie, Jahny

Jahnika (Scandinavian) believes in God

Jahnny (American) feminine form of Johnny: God is gracious

Jaidan (American) golden child
Jaedan, Jai, Jaide, Jaidee, Jaidi, Jaidon, Jaidun, Jaidy, Jaidyn, Jaydan, Jaydyn

Jaime (French) girl who loves
Jaeme, Jaemee, Jaima, Jaimee, Jaimey, Jaimi, Jaimie, Jaimy, Jamie, Jaymee

Jaime-Day (American) loving

Jaimela (Spanish) lovely

Jainil (English) form of Janel: exuberent

Jairia (Spanish) taught by God's lessons

Jakira (Arabic) warmth

Jakisha (African American) favored
Jakishe

Jakki (American) form of Jackie: supplanter; substitute
Jakea, Jakia, Jakkia

Jalalynne (Combo of Jala and Lynne) important

Jalila (Arabic) excellent
Jalile

Jalit (American) sparkling
Jal, Jalitt, Jalitte, Jallit

Jalona (Spanish) excellence

Jalou (Scandinavian) form of Jaela: bright

Jamaica (Place name) Caribbean island
Jama, Jamaika, Jamaka, Jamake, Jamana, Jamea, Jameca, Jameka, Jamica, Jamika, Jamiqua, Jamoka, Jemaica, Jemika, Jemyka

Jamais (French) ever
Jamay, Jamaye

Jamalita (Invented) feminine form of James: supplanter
Jama

Jamar (African American) strong
Jam, Jamara, Jamareah, Jamaree, Jamarr, Jamarra, Jammy

Jamashia (African American) soulful
Jamash, Jamashea

Jame (Hebrew) feminine form of James: supplanter

Jameah (African American) bold
Jamea, Jameea, Jamiah

Jamecka (African American) studious
Jamecca, Jameeka, Jameka, Jameke, Jamekka, Jamie, Jamiea, Jamieka

Jameelah (Arabic) lovely

Jameia (Arabic) lovely

Jamelae (American) smart

Jamesetta (American) feminine form of James: supplanter
Jamesette

Jamesha (African American) outgoing
Jamece, Jamecia, Jameciah, Jameisha, James, Jamese, Jameshia, Jameshyia, Jamesia, Jamesica, Jamesika, Jamesina, Jamessa, Jamie, Jamisha, Jay

Jami (Hebrew) replacement
Jamay, Jamia, Jamie, Jamy

Jamie (Hebrew) supplants; fun-loving
Jamee, James, Jami, Jaymee

J'Amie (French) friend; form of Jamie: supplants; fun-loving

Jamika (African American) buoyant
Jameeka, Jamey, Jamica, Jamicka, Jamie

Jamila (Arabic) beautiful female
Jahmela, Jahmilla, Jam, Jameela, Jami, Jamie, Jamil, Jamilah, Jamile, Jamilla, Jamille, Jamilya, Jammell, Jammie

Jan (English) form of Janet: small; forgiving
Jani, Jania, Jandy, Jannie, Janny

JaNa (American) form of Jane: believer in a gracious God

Jana (Slavic/Scandinavian) God's
gracious gift
Janna, Janne

Janae (American) giving
Janea, Jannah, Jannay, Jennae, Jenny

Janaina (Arabic) soulful

Janaki (Indian) seeta

Janalyn (American) giving
*Jan, Janalynn, Janelyn, Janilyn,
Jannalyn, Jannnie, Janny*

Janan (Arabic) soulful
*Jananee, Janani, Jananie, Janann,
Jannani*

Janara (American) generous
Janarah, Janerah, Janira, Janirah

Janay (American) forgiving
Janae, Janah, Janai

Janaya (American) form of Janae:
giving

Jancy (American) risk-taker
*Jan, Jance, Jancee, Jancey, Janci, Jancie,
Janny*

Jandy (American) fun
Jandee, Jandey, Jandi

Jane (Hebrew) believer in a gracious
God
*Jaine, Jan, Janelle, Janene, Janeth,
Janett, Janetta, Janey, Janica, Janie,
Jannie, Jayne, Jaynie*

Janeana (American) sweet
Janea, Janean, Janeanah, Janine

Janeer (American) heartfelt

Janel (French) form of Janelle: exuberant
Janell, Jannel, Jaynel, Jaynell

Janelle (French) exuberant
*Janel, Janell, Jannel, Jenelle, J'Nel,
J'nell, Nell*

Janene (American) form of Jane:
believer in a gracious God
Janeen, Janine, Jenean, Jenine

Janessa (American) forgiving
*Janesha, Janeska, Janessah, Janie,
Janiesa, Janiesha, Janisha, Janissa,
Jannesa, Jannesha, Jannessa, Jannisa,
Jannisha, Jannissa, Janyssa*

Janet (English) small; forgiving
*Jan, Janett, Janetta, Janette, Jannet,
Jannett, Janot, Jessie, Jinett, Johnette,
Jonetta, Jonette*

Janeth (American) fascinating
Janith

Jania (American) heart's delight

Janice (Hebrew) knowing God's grace
*Genese, Jan, Janece, Janecia, Janeese,
Janeice, Janiece, Jannice, Janyce, Jynice*

Janida (Spanish) gracious

Janie (English) form of Jane: believer
in a gracious God
Janey, Jani, Jany

Janiece (American) devout; enthusiastic
*Janece, Janecia, Janeese, Janese, Janesea,
Janesse, Janneece, Jeneece, Jeneese*

Janiecia (African American) sporty
*Jan, Janeisha, Janesha, Janeshah,
Janisha, Jannes, Jannesa*

Janielle (English) form of Janelle:
exuberant

Janier (French) gracious

Janika (Scandinavian) form of Jane:
believer in a gracious God
Janica, Janicah, Janik, Janikka, Jannike

Janina (Scandinavian) devout

Janine (American) kind
*Janean, Janeen, Janene, Janey, Janie,
Jannine, Jannyne, Janyne, Jenine*

Janineata (American) form of
Janine: kind

Janique (Scandinavian) believer;
smart

Janis (English) form of Jane: believer
in a gracious God
Janees, Janeesa, Janes, Janise, Jenice, Jenis

Janisse (American) elegant

Janitza (American) form of Juanita:
believer in a gracious God; forgiving

Janiya (American) believer

Janiyah (American) believer

Janiyal (American) pious

Janjan (Last name as first) sweet; believer
Jan Jan, Jange, Janja, Jan-Jan, Janje, Janni, Jannie, Janny

Janke (Scandinavian) believer in God
Jankee, Jankey, Jankie

Janna (Hebrew) form of Johana: believer in gracious God

Janneke (Scandinavian) smart; believer

Jannette (American) lovely
Jan, Janette, Jannett, Jannie, Janny

Jannie (English) form of Jane: believer in a gracious God; form of Jan: small; forgiving
Janney, Janny, Jannye

Janoah (Biblical) place name

Jansen (Scandinavian) smooth
Jan, Jannsen, Jans, Jansie, Janson, Jansun, Jansy

Janteya (Dutch) form of Jantine: giving

Jantine (Dutch) giving
Jantee, Janteen, Jantene, Jantie, Janty

Jantje (Scandinavian) believer

Japana (American) form of Japan

Japha (Biblical) place name

Jaqueline (French) form of Jacquelyn: supplanter; substitute
Jaqlinn, Jaqlyn, Jaqlynn, Jaqua,

Jaquaeline, Jaqualine, Jaqualyn, Jaquelina, Jaquelyn, Jaquelynne, Jaquie, Jaqulene

Jaquonna (African American) spoiled
Jakwona, Jakwonda, Jakwonna, Jaqui, Jaquie, Jaquon, Jaquona, Jaquonne

Jaranescia (Scandinavian) magnificent

Jardana (American) gardener
Jarde, Jardee, Jardy

Jardena (French) gardens
Jardan, Jardane, Jarden, Jardenia, Jardine, Jardyne

Jarenda (American) lovely

Jarene (American) bright
Jare, Jaree, Jareen, Jaren, Jareni, Jarine, Jarry, Jaryne, Jerry

Jariesha (India) clear-headed

Jarita (Arabic) carries water; befriends
Jara, Jari, Jaria, Jarica, Jarida, Jarietta, Jarika, Jarina, Jaritta, Jaritza

Jariya (Arabic) form of Jarita: carries water; befriends

Jarmila (Czech) beautiful spring

Jarone (American) optimistic
Jaron, Jaroyne, Jerone, Jurone

Jaroslava (Czech) glorious spring

Jarren (American) lovable
Jaren, Jarran, Jarre

Jas (American) form of Jasmine: fragrant; sweet
Jass, Jaz, Jazz, Jazze, Jazzi

Jasalin (American) devoted
Jasalinne, Jasalyn, Jasalynn, Jaselyn, Jasleen, Jaslene, Jass, Jassalyn, Jassy, Jazz, Jazzy

Jasia (Slavic) hopeful

Jasira (Polish) form of Jane: believer in a gracious God

Jasmine ✪ (Persian/Spanish) fragrant; sweet
Jasamine, Jasime, Jasimen, Jasimin, Jasimine, Jasmaine, Jasman, Jasme, Jasmie, Jasmina, Jasminah, Jasmine, Jasminen, Jasminne, Jasmon, Jasmond, Jasmone, Jasmyn, Jasmynn, Jasmynne, Jazie, Jazmaine, Jazman, Jazmeen, Jazmein, Jazmen, Jazmin, Jazmine, Jazmon, Jazmond, Jazmyn, Jazmyne, Jazs, Jazsmen, Jazz, Jazza, Jazzamine, Jazzee, Jazzi, Jazzmeen, Jazzmin, Jazz-Mine, Jazzmun, Jazzy

Jasna (American) talented
Jas, Jazna, Jazz

Jasper (French) gemstone

Jaspreet (Punjabi) pure
Jas, Jaspar, Jasparit, Jasparita, Jasper, Jasprit, Jasprita, Jasprite

Jasvina (Spanish) form of Jasmine: fragrant; sweet

Ja-Tawn (African American) tawny
Ja Tawn, Jatawn, J'Tawn

Jatsue (Spanish) lively
Jat, Jatsey

Jatumn (American) form of Autumn: joy of changing seasons

Jautanza (American) creative

Javalin (American) thrower

Javana (Asian) girl from Java; dancer
Javanna, Javanne, Javon, Javonda, Javonna, Javonne, Javonya, Jawana, Jawanna, Jawn

Javette (American) lively

Javiera (Spanish) owns a home
Javeera, Viera

Jawanda (African) bejeweled

Jawara (Arabic) true gem

Jaya (Hindi) winning
Jaea, Jaia, Jay, Jayah

Jayal (Sanskrit) special

Jayanti (Indian) winning

Jayare (African) winner

Jayatissa (Indian) wins

Jayci (American) vivacious
Jacee, Jacey, Jaci, Jacie, Jacy, Jaycee, Jaycey, Jaycie

Jayden (American) enthusiastic
Jaden, Jay, Jaydeen, Jaydon, Jaydyn, Jaye

Jaydie (American) lively
Jadie, Jady, Jay-Dee, Jaydeye

Jaydra (Spanish) treasured jewel; jade
Jadra, Jay, Jaydrah

Jaye (Latin) small as a jaybird
Jae, Jay

Jayla (American) smiling
Jaila, Jaylah, Jayle, Jaylee

Jayleena (English) wins
Jaylena, Jaylenna

Jaylen ♀ (English) wins

Jaylene (American) feminine form of Jay: colorful
Jayelene, Jayla, Jaylah, Jaylan, Jayleana, Jaylee, Jayleen

Jaylynn (American) feminine form of Jay: colorful
Jaelin, Jaeline, Jaelyn, Jaelyne, Jaelynn, Jaelynne, Jalin, Jaline, Jalyn, Jalyne, Jalynn, Jalynne, Jaylin, Jayline, Jaylyn, Jaylyne, Jaylynne

Jayma (English) dedicated

Jayme (English) feminine form of James: supplanter
Jami, Jamie, Jaymee, Jaymi, Jaymia, Jaymie

Jayna (Hindi) winner
Jaynae

Jayne (Hindi) victorious
Jane, Janey, Jani, Jayn, Jaynee, Jayni, Jaynie, Jaynita, Jaynne

Jaynille (American) form of Janelle: exuberent

Jayrette (American) dear

Jazael (American) form of Giselle: a promise

Jazel (American) form of Giselle: a promise

Jazl (American) zany

Jazz (American) rhythmic
Jas, Jassie, Jaz, Jazzi, Jazzie, Jazzle, Jazzy

Jazza (American) quirky

Jazzell (American) spontaneous
Jazel, Jazell, Jazz, Jazzee, Jazzie

Jean (Scottish) God-loving and gracious
Jeana, Jeanie, Jeanne, Jeannie, Jeanny, Jena, Jenay, Jenna

Jeana (American) form of Gina: wellborn
Jeanna

Jeanane (French) religious

Jeanetta (American) impish
Janetta, Jeannet, Jeannette, Jeanney, Jen, Jenett, Jennita

Jeanette (French) lively
*Janette, Jeannete, Jeanett, Jeanetta,
Jeanita, Jeannete, Jeannett, Jeannetta,
Jeannette, Jeannita, Jenet, Jenett, Jenette,
Jennett, Jennetta, Jennette, Jennita,
Jinetta, Jinette*

Jeanie (Scottish) devout; outspoken
Jeani, Jeannie, Jeanny, Jeany

Jeanine (Scottish) peace-loving
*Jeanene, Jeanina, Jeannina, Jeannine,
Jenine, Jennine*

Jeanisha (African American) pretty
*Jean, Jeaneesh, Jeanise, Jeanna, Jeannie,
Jenisha*

Jearlean (American) vibrant
*Jearlee, Jearlene, Jearley, Jearli, Jearline,
Jearly, Jerline*

Jebel (Origin unknown) form of
Jezebel: wanton woman

Jeca (Slavic) untainted
Jeka

Jecelyn (Invented) form of Jocelyn:
joyful
Jece, Jecee, Jeselyn, Jess

Jedid (Biblical) loving

Jeena (American) bold

Jeffrey (German) peaceful; sparkling
personality
*Jef, Jeff, Jeffa, Jefferi, Jeffery, Jeffie, Jeffre,
Jeffrie, Jeffy, Jefry*

Jefjun (Scandinavian) rich

Jekemea (Slavic) my Jeka

Jelana (Russian) form of Helen:
beautiful; light

Jelane (Russian) light heart
Jelaina, Jelaine, Jelanne, Jilane, Julane

Jelani (American) pretty sky
Jelainy, Jelaney, Jelanie, Jelanni

Jele (Slavic) light

Jelee (Slavic) moon child

Jelena (Slavic) moon child

Jelene (Slavic) moon

Jelka (Slavic) sturdy

Jelline (French) robust

Jemiccia (Italian) treasured

Jemima (Hebrew) dove-like
*Jamima, Jem, Jemi, Jemimah, Jemm,
Jemma, Jemmi, Jemmia, Jemmiah,
Jemmy, Jemora*

Jemine (American) treasured
Jem, Jemmy, Jemyne

Jemma (Hebrew) form of Gemma:
gem; jewel
Jem

Jems (American) treasured
Gemas, Jemma, Jemmey, Jemmi, Jemmy

Jena (Arabic) small
*Janae, Jenaa, Jenaeh, Jenah, Jenai,
Jenal, Jenay, Jenna*

Jenaseth (English) bird

Jenavieve (American) form of
Genevieve: generous

Jenaya (African) hospitable

Jene (English) form of Jane: believer
in a gracious God

Jenea (English) form of Jane: believer
in a gracious God

Jenell (American) form of Janelle:
exuberant
*Janele, Jen, Jenaile, Jenalle, Jenel,
Jenella, Jennelle, Jenny*

Jenesia (Latin) newcomer

Jenette (English) form of Jeanette:
lively

Jeniece (American) form of Janice:
knowing God's grace

Jenifer (Welsh) form of Jennifer:
white wave
*Gennefer, Gennifer, Ginnifur,
Ginnipher, Jay, Jenefer, Jenjen, Jenna,
Jenni, Jenny*

Jenika (English) blonde

Jenille (English) believes in gracious
God

Jenis (Hebrew) the start
Jenesis

Jenna (English) form of Jean: God-
loving and gracious
*Jena, Jennah, Jennat, Jennay, Jhenna,
Jynna*

Jennah (English) form of Jennifer: white wave
Genna, Jena, Jenna

Jennell (English) form of Janelle: exuberant

Jennelle (English) form of Janelle: exuberant

Jenni (Welsh) form of Jennifer: white wave
Jeni, Jenica, Jenie, Jenisa, Jenka, Jenne, Jennee, Jenney, Jennia, Jennier, Jennita, Jennora, Jensine

Jennifer ✿ (Celtic) white wave
Gennefur, Ginnifer, Jen, Jenefer, Jenife, Jenifer, Jeniferr, Jeniffer, Jenipher, Jenn, Jenna, Jennae, Jennafer, Jennefer, Jenni, Jenniffe, Jenniffer, Jenniffier, Jennifier, Jenniphe, Jennipher, Jenniphur, Jenny, Jennyfer, Jennypher

Jennings (Last name as first name) pretty
Jen, Jenny

Jennis (American) white; patient
J, Jay, Jen, Jenace, Jenice, Jenis, Jenn, Jennice

Jennison (American) form of Jennifer: white wave
Gennison, Jenison, Jennisyn, Jenson

Jenny (English) form of Jennifer: white wave
Jen, Jenae, Jeni, Jenjen, Jenney, Jenni, Jennie, Jennye, Jeny, Jinny

Jennys (American) white

Jeno (Greek) heavenly

Jenova (Italian) form of Genoa: playful

Jensen (Scandinavian) athletic

Jenvie (American) lovely
Jennvey, Jenvee, Jenvy

Jenz (Scandinavian) feminine form of Johannes: God is gracious
Jen, Jens

Jeolle (American) fair

Jerdin (English) grows a garden

Jeredine (English) grows a garden

Jerett (English) rules well

Jergen (Dutch) earthy

Jeri (American) hopeful
Geri, Jere, Jerhie, Jerree, Jerri, Jerry, Jerrye

Jeriesha (Biblical) owned

Jerikah (American) sparkling
Jereca, Jerecka, Jeree, Jeri, Jerica, Jerik, Jeriko, Jerrica, Jerry

Jerin (American) daring
Jere, Jeren, Jeron, Jerinn, Jerun

Jerina (Slavic) loyal

Jermaina (American) form of Germaine: important

Jermaine (French) form of Germaine: important
Jermain, Jerman, Jermane, Jermanee, Jermani, Jermany, Jermayne

Jernina (English) form of Jemima: dove-like

Jeroen (Scandinavian) strong

Jerrett (American) spirited
Jerett, Jeriette, Jerre, Jerret, Jerrette, Jerrie, Jerry

Jerrica (American) free spirit
Jerrika

Jerusha (Hebrew) wealthy

Jesa (Indian) flowers

Jesaren (English) form of Jessie: casual

Jesenia (Spanish) witty
Jesene, Jess, Jessenia, Jessie, Jisenia, Yesenia

Jessa (American) spontaneous
Jessah

Jessamine (French) form of Jasmine: fragrant; sweet
Jesamyn, Jess, Jessamin, Jessamon, Jessamy, Jessamyn, Jessemin, Jessemine, Jessie, Jessmine, Jessmon, Jessmy, Jessmyn

Jesse (Hebrew) friendly
Jesie, Jessey, Jessi, Jessy

Jessenia (Arabic) flowering
Jescenia, Jesenia

Jessica ✿ (Hebrew) rich

Jesica, Jess, Jessa, Jessie, Jessika, Jessy, Jezika

Jessie (Scottish) casual

Jescie, Jesey, Jess, Jesse, Jessee, Jessi, Jessye

Jessika (Hebrew) rich

Jesika, Jessieka, Jessyka, Jezika

Jesusa (Spanish) loves Jesus;
feminine form of Jesus: saved by God

Jesusita (Spanish) little Jesus

Jett (American) high-flying

Jettie, Jetty

Jetta (English) black gem; knowing

Jette, Jettie

Jette (Dutch) black as coal

Jet, Jeta, Jetia, Jetta, Jette, Jettee, Jettie

Jeudi (French) born on Thursday

Jeune-Fille (French) young girl

Jevae (Spanish) desired

Jevaie, Jevay

Jevonne (African American) kind

Jev, Jevaughan, Jevaughn, Jevie, Jevon, Jevona, Jevonn, Jevvy

Jewel (French) pretty

Jeul, Jewelia, Jewelie, Jewell, Jewelle, Jewels, Juel, Jule

Jewelina (Spanish) jewel

Jezana (Slavic) womanly

Jezbelline (Spanish) form of Jezebel:
wanton woman

Jeze (Biblical) form of Jezebel: wanton

woman

Jezebel (Hebrew) wanton woman

Jessabel, Jessebel, Jessebelle, Jez, Jezabel, Jezabella, Jezabelle, Jeze, Jezebell, Jezel, Jezell, Jezybel, Jezzie

Jezenya (American) flowering

Jesenya, Jeze, Jezey

Jhamesha (African American)
lovely; soft

Jamesha, Jmesha

Jharna (Hindi) springtime

Jhonsi (Scandinavian) feminine form
of John: God is gracious

Jianna (Italian) trusts in God

Jiana, Jianina, Jianine

Jigna (Hindi) intellectual

Jignasa (Hindi) curious

Jila (American) energetic; young

Jilan (American) mover

Jillan, Jillyn, Jilyn, Jylan, Jylann

Jilana (Slavic) moon child

Jilen (American) young girl

Jill (English) form of Jillian: youthful

Jil, Jilee, Jilli, Jillie, Jilly

Jillaine (Latin) young-hearted

Jilaine, Jilane, Jilayne, Jillana, Jillane, Jillann, Jillanne, Jillayne

Jilleen (American) energetic

Jil, Jileen, Jilene, Jiline, Jill, Jillain, Jilline, Jlynn

Jillian (Latin) youthful

Giliana, Jill, Jillaine, Jillana, Jillena, Jilliane, Jilliann, Jillie, Jillion, Jillione, Jilly, Jilyan

Jillit (English) form of Jillian:
youthful

Jills (Scandinavian) young

Jillyn (American) high-energy; young

Jimi (Hebrew) replaces; reliable

Jimae

Jimmi (American) assured

Jayjay, Jim, Jimi, Jimice

Jimmye (English) replaces; in pain

Jimye (English) replaces; in pain

Jin (Chinese) golden; gem

Jinn, Jinny

Jina (Italian) form of Gina: wellborn

Jena, Jinae, Jinan, Jinda, Jinna, Jinnae

Jinger (American) form of Ginger:
ginger plant

Jin, Jinge

Jini (American) form of Jenny: white
wave

Jinkie (American) bouncy

Jinkee, Jinky, Jynki

Jinny (Scottish) form of Jenny: white wave
Jin, Jina, Jinae, Jinelle, Jinessa, Jinna, Jinnae, Jinnalee, Jinnee, Jinney, Jinni, Jinnie

Jinte (Hindi) patient

Jinx (Latin) a spell
Jin, Jinks, Jinxie, Jinxy, Jynx

Jinxia (Latin) form of Jinx: a spell
Jynx, Jynxia

Jirina (Czech) works the earth

Jisola (African) affluent

Jitendea (Indian) good

Jnae (American) darling
Jenae, J'Nay, Jnay, Jnaye

J'Neane (American) form of Jeannine: peace-loving

J'Netta (American) form of Jeanetta: impish
J'netta, J'Nette, Janetta, Janny

J-Nyl (American) flirtatious

Jo (American) form of Josephine: blessed
Joey, Jojo

Joan (Hebrew) heroine; God-loving
Joane, Joane, Joani, Joanie, Joanni, Joannie, Jonie

Joana (Hebrew) kind
Joanah, Joanna, Joannah, Jonah

Joanie (Hebrew) kind
Joanney, Joanni, Joannie, Joanny, Joany, Joni

Jo-Ann (French) believer; gregarious
Joahnn, JoAn, JoAnn, Joann, Joanna, Joanne, Jo-Anne, Joannie

Joanna (English) kind
Jo, Joana, Joananna, Joananne, Joandra, Joannah, Joeanna, Johannah, Josie

Joanne (English) form of Joan: heroine; God-loving
JoAnn, Joann, Jo-Ann, JoAnne, Joeanne

Joannie (Hebrew) forgiving
Joani, Joanney, Joanni, Joany

Joappa (Origin unknown) noisy

Joaquina (Spanish) form of Joaquin: God helps

Jobi (Hebrew) misunderstood; inventive
Jobee, Jobey, Jobie, Joby

Jobina (Hebrew) hurting
Jobey, Jobie, Joby, Jobye, Jobyna

Jobine (Biblical) friend

Jocasta (Italian) light

Jocelyn ✿ (Latin) joyful
Jocelie, Jocelin, Jocelle, Jocelyne, Jocelynn, Joci, Joclyn, Joclynn, Jocylan, Jocylen, Joycelyn

Jochebal (Biblical) glory to God

Joci (Latin) happy
Jocee, Jocey, Jocie, Jocy, Josi

Jocosa (Latin) laughs; jokes

Jocquice (French) blessed

Jodase (American) brilliant
Jo, Jodace, Jodasse, Jodie, Jody

Jode (American) form of Jodie: happy girl

Jodie (American) happy girl
Jo, Jodee, Jodey, Jodi, Jody

Joedy (American) jolly
Joedey, Joedi, Joedie

Joelle (Hebrew) willing
Jo, Joel, Joela, Joele, Joelee, Joeleen, Joelene, Joeli, Joeline, Joell, Joella, Joelle, Joellen, Joelly

Joelly (American) kindhearted
Joelee, Joeli, Joely

Joely (Hebrew) believer; lively
Jo, Joe, Joey

Joey (American) easygoing
Joe, Joeye

Joezee (American) form of Josey: blessed
Jo, Joe, Joes, Joezey, Joezy

Johanna (German) believer in a gracious God
Johana, Johanah, Jonna

Johnay (American) steadfast
Johnae, Jonay, Jonaye, Jonnay

Johnette (Hebrew) feminine form of John: God is gracious

Johnica (American) feminine form of John: God is gracious
Jonica

Johnna (American) upright
Jahna, John, Johna, Johnae, Jonna, Jonnie

Johnnell (American) happy
Johnelle, Jonell, Jonnel

Johnnetta (American) joyful
Johneta, Johnete, Johnetta, Johnette, Jonetta, Jonette, Jonietta

Johnnisha (African American) steady
Johnisha, Johnnita, Johnny, Jonnisha

Johnson (Last name as first name) confident
Johns

Johntell (African American) sweet
Johna, Johntal, Johntel, Johntelle, Jontell

Johntria (Hebrew) believer

Johppa (Origin unknown) different
Johppah

Joi (Latin) joyful
Joicy, Joie, Jojo, Joy

Joice (American) form of Joyce: joyous

Joji (English) form of JoJo: joyful

Jo-Kiesha (African American) vibrant
Joekiesha

Jola (Greek) violet flower

Jolan (Latin) violet

Jolanda (Italian) a violet flower
Jola, Jolan, Jolana, Jolande, Jolander, Jolane, Jolanka, Jolantha, Jolanthe, Joli

Jolanta (Greek) lovely girl

Jolene (American) jolly
Jo, Joeleane, Joeleen, Joelene, Joelynn, Joleen, Joleene, Jolen, Jolena, Joley, Jolie, Joline, Jolyn, Jolynn

Joletta (American) happy-go-lucky
Jaletta, Jolette, Joley, Joli, Jolie, Jolitta

Jolia (English) joyful girl

Jolie (French) pretty
Jo, Jole, Jolea, Jolee, Joleigh, Joley, Joli, Jollee, Jollie, Jolly, Joly

Jolienne (American) pretty
Joliane, Jolianne, Jolien, Jolina, Joline

Jolina (English) joyful girl

Joline (English) blessed

Jolivette (French) jubilant

Jolly (English) jolly

Jolyane (American) sweetheart
Joliane, Jollyane, Jolyan, Jolyann, Jolyanne

Jomonia (American) loyal

Jona (English) peaceful

JonBenet (French) with God's benediction

Jones (American) saucy

Jonette (American) peaceful

Joni (American) form of Joan: heroine; God-loving
Joanie, Jonie, Jony

Jonica (American) sweet soul

Jonice (American) casual
Joneece, Joneese, Jonise, Jonni

Jonille (English) believer

Jonina (Hebrew) sweetheart
Jona, Jonika, Joniqua, Jonita, Jonnina

Jonita (Hebrew) pretty little one
Janita, Jonati, Jonit, Jonite, Jonta, Jontae

Jonna (Scandinavian) believer
Johnna

Jonquill (American) flower
Jonn, Jonque, Jonquie, Jonquil, Jonquille

Jontelle (American) musical
Jahntelle, Jontaya, Jontel, Jontell, Jontia, Jontlyl

Joone (American) form of June: born in June
Joon

Jophery (American) feminine form of Christopher: the bearer of Christ

Joplin (Last name as first name) wild girl

Jorah (Hebrew) fresh as rain
Jora

Jordan ✪ ⓣ (Hebrew) excellent descendant
Johrdon, Jordaine, Jordane, Jorden, Jordenne, Jordeyn, Jordi, Jordie, Jordin, Jordon, Jordyn, Jordynne, Joudane, Jourdan

Jordana (Hebrew) smart; departs; lonely
Giordanna, Jordain, Jordane, Jordann, Jordanna, Jordanne, Jordannuh, Jorden, Jordenne, Jordi, Jordin, Jordine, Jordon, Jordona, Jordonna, Jordyn, Jordyne, Jori, Jorie, Jourdana, Jourdann, Jourdanna, Jourdanne

Jordy (American) quick
Jordee, Jordey, Jordi, Jordie, Jorey

Jorene (American) wanted

Joretta (English) wanted; pretty girl

Jorgina (Spanish) nurturing
Georgeena, Georgina, Jorge, Jorgi, Jorgie, Jorgine, Jorgy

Jorie (Hebrew) form of Jordan: excellent descendant
Joree, Jorey, Jorhee, Jorhie, Jori, Jorre, Jorrey, Jorri, Jory

Jorja (American) smart
Georgia, Jorge, Jorgia, Jorgie, Jorgy

Jorunn (American) loved by God

Josany (American) joyful girl

Joscelin (Latin) happy girl
Josceline, Joscelyn, Joscelyne, Joscelynn, Joscelynne, Joselin, Joseline, Joselyn, Joselyne, Joselynn, Joselynne, Joshlyn

Josee (American) delights
Joesee, Joesell, Joesette, Joselle, Josette, Josey, Josi, Josiane, Josiann, Josianne, Josielina, Josina, Josy, Jozee, Jozelle, Jozette, Jozie

Josefat (Spanish) feminine form of Joseph: he will add
Fata, Fina, Josef, Josefa, Josefana, Josefenna, Josefita, Joseva, Josey, Josie

Josefina (Hebrew) fertile
Jose, Josephina, Josey, Josie

Joselita (Spanish) joyful girl

Joselito (Spanish) joyful girl

Joselyn (German) pretty
Josalene, Joselene, Joseline, Josey, Josiline, Josilyn, Joslyn, Josselen, Josseline, Josselyne, Josslyn, Josslynn, Josylynn

Josephine (French) blessed
Fena, Fifi, Fina, Jo, Joes, Josefina, Josephene, Josie, Jozaphine

Josetta (French) she trusts in God

Josette (French) little Josephine

Josey (American) form of Josephine: blessed
Josee, Josi, Josie, Jozie

Josezaldy (Spanish) joyful girl

Joshi (Hebrew) God loves

Joshlyn (Latin) saved by God
Joshalin, Joshalyn, Joshalynn, Joshalynne, Joshann, Joshanna, Joshanne, Joshleen, Joshlene, Joshlin, Joshline, Joshlyne, Joshlynn, Joshlynne

Josie (American) thrills
Josee, Josey, Josi, Josy, Josye

Josien (American) joy

Josilin (Latin) form of Jocelyn: joyful
Josielina, Josiline, Josilyn, Josilyne, Josilynn, Josilynne, Joslin, Josline, Joslyn, Joslyne, Joslynn, Joslynne

Joslyn (Latin) jocular
Joclyn, Joslene, Joslinn, Josslin, Josslyn, Josslynn

Jossalin (Latin) form of Jocelyn: joyful
Jossaline, Jossalyn, Jossalynn, Jossalynne, Josseline, Jossellen, Jossellin, Jossellyn, Josselyn, Josselyne, Josselynn, Josselynne, Jossie, Josslin, Jossline, Josslyn, Josslyne, Josslynn, Josslynne

Jostin (American) adorable
Josten, Jostun, Josty, Jostyn

Joubyne (American) joy

Joudn (American) diplomatic
Joy

Jour (French) day

Jourbine (French) doer

Journey (Word as name) adventurer

Jovan (Slavic) feminine form of John: God is gracious

Jovana (Slavic) feminine form of John: God is gracious

Jovannah (Latin) regal
Jeovana, Jeovanna, Jouvan, Jouvanna, Jovan, Jovana, Jovanee, Jovani, Jovanie, Jovann, Jovanna, Jovanne, Jovannie, Jovena, Jovon, Jovonna, Jovonne, Jowanna

Joverne (Slavic) challenges

Jovernita (Slavic) challenges

Jovi (Latin) jovial

Jovita (Latin) glad
Joveeda, Joveeta, Jovena, Joveta, Jovetta, Jovi, Jovida, Jovie, Jovina, Jo-Vita, Jovitta, Jovy

Jowannah (American) happy
Jowanna, Jowanne, Jowonna

Joy (Latin) joyful
Joi, Joie, Joya, Joye

Joyalle (American) joy

Joyce (Latin) joyous
Joice, Joy, Joycey, Joyci, Joycie, Joysel

Joyceen (American) form of Joyce: joyous

Joycela (American) form of Joyce: joyous

Joycey (American) form of Joyce: joyous

Joyous (American) joyful
Joy, Joyus

Joyria (American) of the Lord

Joyslyn (American) form of Jocelyn: joyful
Joycelyn, Joyslin, Joyslinn

Joysteen (American) joy

Jozel (American) joy

Jualle (American) young girl

Juandali (African) believer

Juanisha (African American) delightful
Juanesha, Juaneshia, Juannisha

Juanita (Spanish) believer in a gracious God; forgiving
Juan, Juana, Juaneta, Juanika, Juanna, Juanne, Juannie, Juanny, Wanita

Juanitra (Spanish) ill-fated

Juba (Hebrew) ram; strong-willed

Jubal (Biblical) flowing
Jubilant

Jubelka (African American) jubilant
Jube, Jubi, Jubie

Jubilee (Hebrew) jubilant
Jubalie

Jubini (American) grateful; jubilant
Jubi, Jubine

Jucinda (American) relishing life
Jucin, Jucindah, Jucinde

Judalon (Hebrew) merry
Judalonn, Juddalone, Judelon

Jude (French) confident
Judde, Judea, Judee

Judit (Hebrew) Jewish
Jude, Judi, Juditt

Judith (Hebrew) woman worthy of praise
Judana, Jude, Judi, Judie, Judine, Juditha, Judy, Judyth, Judythe

Judy (Hebrew) form of Judith: woman worthy of praise
Joodie, Jude, Judi, Judie, Judye

Juel (American) dependable
Jewel, Juelle, Juels, Juile, Jule

Jueta (Scandinavian) form of Judith: woman worthy of praise
Juetta, Juta

Juiby (Asian) flower girl

Juirl (American) careful
Ju, Juirll

Jula (American) form of Julia: forever young

Juleen (American) sensual
Jule, Julene, Jules

Julenett (American) form of Julia: forever young

Jules (American) brooding
Jewels, Juels

Juleva (Spanish) young

Julia ✪ (Latin) forever young
Jula, Juliann, Julica, Julina, Juline, Julisa, Julissa, Julya, Julyssa

Julian (Latin) effervescent
Jewelian, Julean, Juliann, Julien, Juliene, Julienn, Julyun

Juliana (Latin) youthful; Jove's child
Juleanna, Julianna, Juliannah, Julie-Anna, Jullyana

Julice (American) feminine form of Julius: attractive

Julie (English) young and vocal
Juel, Jule, Julee, Juli, Juliene, Jullie, July, Julye

Juliet (Italian) loving

Juliette (French) romantic
Julie, Jules, Juliet, Julietta

Juling (American) form of Julia: forever young

Julisan (American) young

Julissa (Latin) universally loved
Jula, Julessa, Julisa, Julisha

Julita (Spanish) adorable; young
Juli, Julitte

Juliza (Latin) form of Julia: forever young

Julo (American) form of Julia: forever young

July (Latin) month; warm

Jumoke (African) most popular

Jun (Chinese) honest

Jundt (Scandinavian) hopeful

June (Latin) born in June
Juneth, Juney, Junie, Junieth, Juny

Junelle (American) form of June: born in June

Junia (Biblical) warm

Junieth (Latin) from the month June; heavenly
Juney, Juni, Junie, Juniethe

Junko (American) form of June: born in June

Juno (Latin) queenly
Juna, June

Juntese (American) form of June: born in June

Juokaka (Asian) pure

Juqwanza (African American) bouncy
Jukwanza, Juqwann, Qwanza

Juraj (American) moves fast

Jurgan (Scandinavian)

Jus (American) fair

Justice (Latin) fair-minded
Just, Justise, Justy

Justika (American) dancing-girl
Justeeka, Justica, Justie, Justy

Justille (American) fair

Justina (Latin) honest
Jestena, Jestina, Justeena, Justena, Justinna, Justyna

Justinan (American) fair

Justine (Latin) fair; upright
Jestine, Justa, Juste, Justean, Justeen, Justena, Justene, Justi, Justie, Justina, Justinn, Justinna, Justy, Justyne, Justynn, Justynne, Juzteen

Jutta (American) ebullient
Juta

Juttah (Biblical) place name

Juturna (Mythology) trickling water

Juvelia (Spanish) young
Juvee, Juvelle, Juvelya, Juvie, Juvilia, Velia, Velya

Juven (Mythology) young girl

Juwanne (African American) lively
Juwan, Juwann, Juwanna, Juwon, Jwanna, Jwanne

Jyneice (American) form of Janeese: devout; enthusiastic

Jyneisce (American) form of Janeese: devout; enthusiastic

Jynx (American) form of Jinx: a spell

Jyoti (Indian) bright light

Jyotsna (Indian) moonlight

Jzquelyn (Slavic) form of Jacqueline: supplanter; substitute

K

Kacey (Irish) daring
Casey, Casie, K.C., K.Cee, Kace, Kacee, Kaci, Kacy, Kasey, Kasie, Kaycee, Kaycie, Kaysie

Kachina (Native American) sacred dancer; doll-like
Cachina, Kachena, Kachine

Kacia (Greek) form of Acacia: everlasting; tree
Kaycia, Kaysia

Kacondra (African American) bold
Condra, Connie, Conny, Kacon, Kacond, Kaecondra, Kakondra, Kaycondra

Kaden (American) charismatic
Caden, Kadenn

Kadenza (Latin) cadence; dances
Cadenza, Kadena, Kadence

Kadie (American) virtuous
Kadee

Kady (English) sassy
Cady, K.D., Kadee, Kadie, Kaydie, Kaydy

Kaela (Arabic) sweet
Kaelah, Kayla, Kaylah, Keyla, Keylah

Kaelin (Irish) pure; impetuous
Kaelan, Kaelen, Kaelinn, Kaelyn, Kaelynn, Kaelynne, Kaylin

Kagan (American) form of Keagan: melodious

Kai (Hawaiian) the sea
Kaia

Kailah (Greek) virtuous
Kail, Kala, Kalae, Kalah

Kaileen (American) sweet

Kailey (American) spunky
Kaili, Kailie, Kaylee, Kaylei

Kaimi (American) form of Cammy: wonderful

Kairen (French) pure heart

Kaitlin ✿ (Irish) purehearted
Caitlin, Caitlyn, Kaitlan, Kaitland, Kaitlinn, Kaitlyn, Kaitlynn, Kalyn, Katelyn, Katelynn, Katelynne, Kathlin, Kathlinne, Kathlyn

Kaiulania (Hawaiian) sea and heavens

Kajasa (Asian) forgiving

Kakay (American) pure

Kakiesta (Hawaiian) unblemished

Kala (Hindi) black; royal

Kalan (American) celestial

Kalani (Hawaiian) leader
Kalauni, Kaloni, Kaylanie

Kalavati (Indian) creates

Kalb (German) willful

Kalea (Arabic) sweet
Kahlea, Kahleah, Kailea, Kaileah, Kallea, Kalleah, Kaylea, Kayleah, Khalea, Khaleah

Kalei (American) sweetheart
Kahlei, Kailei, Kallei, Kaylei, Khalei

Kaleigh (Sanskrit) energetic; dark
Kalea

Kalele (Hawaiian) pure

Kalena (Hawaiian) chaste
Kaleena

Kalet (French) beautiful energy
Kalay, Kalaye

Kaley (Sanskrit) energetic
Kalee, Kaleigh, Kalleigh

Kali (Greek) beauty
Kala, Kalli

Kalidas (Greek) most beautiful
Kaleedus, Kali

Kalila (Arabic) sweet; lovable
Cailey, Cailie, Caylie, Kailey, Kaililah, Kaleah, Kalela, Kalie, Kalilah, Kaly, Kay, Kaykay, Kaylee, Kayllie, Kyle, Kylila, Kylilah

Kalina (Hawaiian) unblemished
Kalinna, Kalynna

Kalinda (Hindi) mythical mountains;
goal-oriented
Kaleenda, Kalindi, Kalynda, Kalyndi

Kalindee (Indian) river
Kalindi

Kaliyan (Southeast Asian) excellent

Kallan (American) loving
Kall, Kallen, Kallun

Kallie (Greek) beautiful
Callie, Kali, Kalie, Kalley, Kally

Kalliope (Greek) beautiful voice
Calli, Calliope, Kalli, Kallyope

Kallista (Greek) pretty; bright-eyed
*Cala, Calesta, Calista, Callie, Callista,
Cally, Kala, Kalesta, Kalista, Kalli,
Kallie, Kally, Kallysta, Kalysta*

Kalota (Hawaiian) vivacious

Kalpana (Indian) dream

Kalyana (Indian) lucky

Kalyani (Indian) lucky
Kalni

Kalyn (Arabic) loved
*Calynn, Calynne, Kaelyn, Kaelynn,
Kalen, Kalin, Kalinn, Kallyn*

Kama (Sanskrit) beloved; Hindu god
of love
Kam, Kamie

Kamala (American) interesting;
(Arabic) perfection
*Camala, Kam, Kamalah, Kamali,
Kamilla, Kammy*

Kamaria (African) moonlike
Kamara, Kamaarie

Kambria (Latin) girl from Wales
Kambra, Kambrie, Kambriea, Kambry

Kambrin (American) form of
Cambria: the people

Kamea (Hawaiian) precious darling;
adored
Cammi, Kam, Kameo, Kammie

Kameko (Japanese) turtle girl; hides

Kamela (Italian) form of Camilla:
wonderful
Kam, Kamila, Kammy

Kameron (American) form of
Cameron: popular; crooked nose
*Cam, Cami, Cammie, Kamreen,
Kamrin, Kamren, Kamron*

Kamethia (American) divine

Kami (Italian) spiritual little one;
(Japanese) perfect aura
*Cami, Cammie, Cammy, Kammie,
Kammy*

Kamiah (Slavic) form of Kamila:
desires

Kamilah (Hindi) desires; (North
African) perfect

Kamila, Kamilla, Kamillah

Kamilia (Polish) perfect character; pure
Kam, Kamila, Kammy, Milla

Kamini (Indian) woman

Kamna (Indian) desired

Kamoya (Asian) focused

Kamyra (American) light
Kamera

Kanaka (Indian) golden child

Kanara (Hebrew) tiny bird; lithe
Kanarit, Kanarra

Kanda (Native American) magical

Kandace (Greek) charming; glowing
*Candace, Candie, Candy, Dacie, Kandi,
Kandice, Kandiss, Kandy*

Kandi (American) form of Kandace:
charming; glowing
Candi, Kandie, Kandy

Kandra (American) light
Candra

Kanear (American) talented

Kaneesha (American) dark-skinned
*Caneesha, Kaneesh, Kaneice, Kaneisha,
Kanesha, Kaneshia, Kaney, Kanish,
Nesha*

Kanel (Spanish) yellow hair

Kanesha (African American)
spontaneous
*Kaneesha, Kaneeshia, Kaneisha,
Kanisha, Kannesha*

Kanga (Australian) form of kangaroo: jumpy

Kanik (Egyptian) darkness

Kanisha (American) pretty
Kaneesha, Kanicia, Kenisha, Kinicia, Kinisha, Koneesha

Kannitha (Vietnamese) angelic

Kanoa (Hawaiian) freedom

Kansas (Place name) U.S. state
Kanny

Kanthi (Asian) angelic

Kanti (Indian) lovely

Kanya (Hindi) virginal
Kania

Kaori (Asian) free

Kaprece (American) capricious
Caprice, Kapp, Kappy, Kapreece, Kapri, Kaprise, Kapryce, Karpreese

Kapuki (African) first girl in the family

Kara (Danish) form of Cara: beloved friend
Carina, Carita, Kar, Karah, Kari, Karie, Karina, Karine, Karita, Karrah, Karrie, Kera

Karbie (American) energetic
Karbi, Karby

Karelle (French) joyful singer
Carel, Carelle, Karel

Karen (Greek/Irish) purehearted
Caren, Carin, Caron, Caronn, Carren, Carrin, Carron, Carryn, Caryn, Carynn, Carynne, Kare, Kareen, Karenna, Kari, Karin, Karina, Karna, Karon, Karron, Karryn, Karyn, Keren, Kerran, Kerrin, Kerron, Kerrynn, Keryn, Kerynne, Taran, Taren, Taryn

Karenina (Literature) purest

Karenz (English) form of Kerensa: lovable
Karence, Karens, Karense

Karhime (Arabic) giving

Kari (Scandinavian) pure
Cari, Karri, Karrie, Karry

Kariah (American) form of Mariah: sorrowful singer

Karian (American) daring
Kerian

Karianne (Scandinavian) pure
Kariane, Kariann, Kari-Ann, Karianna, Kerianne

Karida (Arabic) pure
Kareeda, Karita

Karima (Arabic) giving
Kareema, Kareemah, Kareima, Kareimah, Karimah

Karin (Scandinavian) kindhearted
Karen, Karine, Karinne

Karina (Russian) form of Karen: purehearted
Kare, Karinda, Karine, Karinna, Karrie, Karrina, Karyna

Karine (Russian) pure
Kaarrine, Karryne, Karyne

Karineh (Italian) form of Chiarina: clear

Karise (Greek) graceful woman
Karis, Karisse, Karyce

Karissa (Greek) longsuffering
Carissa, Karessa, Karisa

Karitina (Spanish) pure

Karizma (African) hopeful
Karisma

Karla (German) well-loved
Carla, Karlah, Karlie, Karlla, Karrla

Karlea (German) form of Karla: well-loved

Karlee (Slavic) form of Karla: well-loved

Karlin (American) winning; daring

Karlotta (German) form of Charlotte: little woman
Karlota, Karlotte, Lotta, Lottee, Lottey, Lottie

Karly (German) womanly; strength
Carly, Karlee, Karlie, Karlye

Karma (Hindi) destined for good things
Karm, Karmie, Karmy

Karmel (Hebrew) garden
Carmel, Karmela, Karmelle

Karmen (Hebrew) loving songs
Carmen, Karmin, Karmine

Karmiaso (Italian) garden girl

Karmilita (Spanish) form of Carmelita: in the garden

Karmille (Spanish) form of Carmel: garden

Karmit (Native American) nature

Karnesha (American) spicy
Carnesha, Karnisha, Karny

Karnit (American) gem

Karolina (Polish) form of Caroline: little; womanly
Karaline, Karalyn, Karalynna, Karalynne, Karla, Karleen, Karlen, Karlena, Karlene, Karli, Karlie, Karlina, Karlinka, Karo, Karolinka, Karolline, Karolyn, Karolyna, Karolyne, Karolynn, Karolynne, Leena, Lina, Lyna

Karoline (German) feminine form of Karl: forceful
Kare, Karola, Karolah, Karolina, Lina

Karolyn (American) friendly
Carolyn, Kara, Karal, Karalyn, Karilynne, Karolynn

Karre (English) form of Carrie: womanly; little

Karri (American) form of Karen: purehearetd
Kari, Karie, Karrie, Karry

Karrington (Last name as first name) admired
Carrington, Kare, Karring

Karryoun (American) form of Caroline: little; womanly

Karuenne (American) sweetness

Karwa (African) independent

Karwanna (African) independent

Karwey (African) independent

Karyn (American) sweet
Caren, Karen

Karynn (English) pure

Kasalya (Indian) clever

Kasandrae (English) shines

Kasandrah (English) shines

Kascade (Italian) water

Kasey (American) spirited
Casey, Kacey, Kasie, Kaysie

Kasha (Greek) form of Katherine: pure

Kashmir (Place name) a region near India and Pakistan; fertile
Cashmere, Cashmir, Kash, Kashmere

Kashonda (African American) dramatic
Kashanda, Kashawnda, Koshonda

Kashondra (African American) bright
Kachanne, Kachaundra, Kachee, Kashandra, Kashawndra, Kashee, Kashon, Kashondrah, Kashondre, Kashun

Kasi (American) form of Cassie: insightful
Kass, Kassi, Kassie

Kasia (Polish) form of Katarzyna: creative

Kasmira (Slavic) peacemaker

Kassandra (Greek) capricious
Cassandra, Kass, Kasandra, Kassandrah, Kassie

Kassidy (Irish) clever
Cassidy, Cassir, Kasadee, Kass, Kassie, Kassy, Kassydi

Kassie (American) clever
Kassee, Kassi, Kassy

Kat (American) outrageous
Cat

Katalin (American) pure heart; smart

Katana (English) form of Catina: pure

Kataniya (Hebrew) little girl

Katarina (Greek) pure
Katareena, Katarena, Katarinna, Kataryna, Katerina, Katryna

Katarzyna (Origin unknown) creative

Katarzina

Katchen (Greek) virtuous

Kat, Katshen

Katchi (American) sassy

Catshy, Cotchy, Kat, Kata, Katchie, Kati, Katshi, Katshie, Katshy, Katty, Kotchee, Kotchi, Kotchie

Kate (Greek) form of Katherine: pure

Cait, Caitie, Cate, Catee, Catey, Catie, Kait, Kaite, Kaitlin, Katee, Katey, Kathe, Kati, Katie, Katy, Kay-Kay

Katelyn ✪ (Irish) purehearted

Caitlin, Kaitlyn, Kaitlynne, Kat, Katelin, Katelynn, Kate-Lynn, Katline, Katy

Katera (Origin unknown) celebrant

Katara, Katura

Katherine ✪ (Greek) pure

Kat, Katharin, Katharine, Katherin, Kathy, Kathyrn, Katwin, Kaykay

Kathlaya (American) fashionable

Kathleen (Irish) brilliant; unflawed

Cathaleen, Cathaline, Cathleen, Kathaleen, Kathaleya, Kathaleyna, Kathaline, Kathelina, Katheline, Kathie, Kathlene, Kathlin, Kathline, Kathlyn, Kathlynn, Kathy

Kathryn (English) powerful and pure

Kathreena, Kathren, Kathrene, Kathrin, Kathrine, Kathryne

Kathy (English/Irish) form of Katherine: pure

Cathie, Cathy, Kath, Kathe, Kathee, Kathey, Kathi, Kathie

Katia (French) stylish

Kateeya, Kati, Katya

Katie (English) lively

Kat, Kate, Katy, Kay, Kaykay, Kaytie

Katina (American) form of Katrina: melodious

Kat, Kateen, Kateena

Katlynn (Greek) pure

Kat, Katlinn, Katlyn

Katrice (American) graceful

Katreese, Katrese, Katrie, Katrisse, Katry

Katrina (German) melodious

Catreena, Catreina, Catrina, Kaitrina, Katreena, Katreina, Katryna, Kay, Ketreina, Ketrina, Ketryna

Katrine (German/Polish) form of Kate: pure

Catrene, Kati, Katrene, Katrinna

Katy (English) lively

Cady, Katie, Kattee, Kattie, Kaytee

Kau (Indian) princess

Kaur

Kaulana (Hawaiian) well-known girl

Kaula, Kauna, Kahuna

Kaulene (American) famed

Kavinli (American) feminine form of Kevin: pretty; gentle

Cavin, Kaven, Kavin, Kavinlee, Kavinley, Kavinly

Kavita (Hindi) poem

Kaveta, Kavitah

Kavitha (Indian) poetic

Kavita

Kawana (African) certain

Kay (Latin/Welsh) happy; rejoicing

Cay, Caye, Kaye, Kaykay

Kaya (Native American) intelligent

Kaja, Kayia

Kaycie (American) merrymaker

CayCee, K.C., Kaycee, Kayci, Kaysie

Kaydence (American) in cadence

Kayla ✪ (Greek) pure

Cala, Cayla, Caylie, Kala, Kaela, Kaila, Kaylah, Kaylyn, Keyla

Kaylan (Irish) form of Caitlin: virginal

Kaylee ✪ (American) open

Cayley, Kaelie, Kaylea, Kaylie, Kayleigh

Kayleen (Hebrew/American) sweet

Kaileen, Kalene, Kay, Kaykay, Kaylean, Kayleene

Kayley (Irish) form of Kaylee: open
*Caleigh, Cayleigh, Cayley, Kaeleigh,
Kailee, Kaileigh, Kailey, Kaili,
Kaleigh, Kaley, Kaylea, Kaylee, Kaylie,
Kaylleigh, Kaylley*

Kaylin (American) form of Kaylee:
open
*Kailyn, Kaylan, Kaylanne, Kaylen,
Kaylinn, Kaylyn, Kaylynn, Kaylynne*

Kaylina (English) slim girl

Kaylon (Hebrew) crowned
*Kalonn, Kaylan, Kaylen, Kayln,
Kaylond, Kaylun*

Kayterly (American) delightful

Kazuya (Asian) lovely

Keahs (Unknown) optimist

Keane (American) keen
Kanee, Keanie, Keany, Keen

Keani (Asian) bold

Keanna (American) curious
Keana, Keannah

Keara (Irish) darkness
*Kearia, Kearra, Keera, Keerra, Keira,
Keirra, Kera, Kiara, Kiarra, Kiera, Kierra*

Kearney (Irish) winning
Kearne, Kearni, KeKe, Kerney

Keatha (American) feminine form of
Keith: witty

Kechia (African) determined

Kecia (American) focused

Keekee (American) dancing
Keakea, Kee-Kee

Keeley (Irish) noisy
*Kealey, Kealy, Keeley, Keeli, Keelia,
Keelie, Keely, Keighley, Keighly, Keili,
Keilie, Keylee, Keyley, Keylie, Keylley,
Keyllie*

Keelian (Irish) pretty

Keena (Irish) courageous
Keenya, Kina

Keenan (Irish) small
Keanan, Keen, Keeny

Keesee (American) joyous

Kefira (Hebrew) lioness
Kefeera, Kefeira, Kefirah, Kefirra

Kehohtee (Invented) alternate
spelling for Quixote

Kei (Japanese) respectful

Keidra (American) form of Kendra:
ingenious
Kedra, Keydra

Keija (Slavic) rapport

Keiki (Hawaiian) child

Keiko (Hawaiian) child of joy
Kei

Keila (Hebrew) crowned
Keilah

Keilani (Hawaiian) graceful leader
Kei, Lani, Lanie

Keira (Irish) dark-skinned
Keera, Kera

Keisha (American) dark-eyed
*Keasha, Keesha, Keeshah, Keicia,
Keishah, Keshia, Keysha, Kicia*

Keishla (American) dark

Keishonna (English) form of Keisha:
dark-eyed

Keita (Scottish) lives in the forest
Keiti

Keitha (Scottish) from the forest
Keithana

Kekoa (Hawaiian) happy

Kelby (English) lives in a farmhouse
Kelbea, Kelbeigh, Kelbey, Kellbie

Kelda (Scandinavian) spring of youth
Kellda

Keledi (African) sorrows

Kelila (Hebrew) regal woman
*Kayla, Kayle, Kaylee, Kelula, Kelulah,
Kelulla, Kelylah, Kyla, Kyle*

Kelinda (American) form of
Melinda: honey; sweetheart

Keller (Irish) daring
Kellers

Kellia (American) form of Kelly:
brave

Kelly (Irish) brave
Keli, Kellie, Kelley, Kellye

Kellyn (Irish) brave heart
Kelleen, Kellen, Kellene, Kellina, Kelline, Kellynn, Kellynne

Kelsey (Scottish) opinionated
Kelcey, Kelcie, Kelcy, Kellsey, Kellsie, Kelsea, Kelsee, Kelseigh, Kelsi, Kelsie, Kelsy

Keltoriah (American) brave

Kember (American) zany
Kem, Kemmie, Kimber

Kemeel (American) form of Camille: swift runner; great innocence

Kemeelah (American) form of Camille: swift runner; great innocence

Kemelah (American) form of Camille: swift runner; great innocence

Kemella (American) self-assured
Kemele, Kemellah, Kemelle

Kemicia (American) form of Kim: sharp

Kempley (English) from a meadowland: rascal
Kemplea, Kempleigh, Kemplie, Kemply

Kenda (English) aware
Kendi, Kendie, Kendy, Kennda, Kenndi, Kenndie, Kenndy

Kendall (English) quiet
Kendahl, Kendal, Kendell, Kendelle, Kendie, Kendylle

Kendella (English) form of Kendall: quiet

Kendra (American) ingenious
Ken, Kendrah, Kenna, Kennie, Kindra, Kinna, Kyndra

Kendrelle (English) rules quiet place

Kendry (English) rules quiet place

Kenia (African) giving; from the place name Kenya
Ken, Keneah

Kenichi (American) feminine form of Kenneth: good-looking

Kenine (Scottish) pretty

Kenith (American) feminine form of Kenneth: good-looking

Kenna (English) brilliant; (Scottish) creative
Kenina, Kennah, Kennette, Kennina, Kynna

Kennae (Irish) feminine form of Ken: good-looking
Kenae, Kenah

Kennedy (Irish) formidable
Kennedie, Kenny

Kenner (Scottish) feminine form of Kenneth: good-looking

Kennice (English) beauty
Kanice, Keneese, Kenese, Kennise

Kensington (English) brash
Kensingtyn

Kenta (English) feminine form of Kent: fair-skinned

Kentucky (Place name) U.S. state
Kentuckie

Kenya (Place name) country in Africa
Kenia, Kennya

Kenyatta (African) form of Kenya: country in Africa

Kenyetta (Place name) form of Kenya: country in Africa

Kenyie (Place name) form of Kenya: country in Africa

Kenzie (Scottish) pretty
Kensey, Kinsey

Keoshawn (African American) clever
Keosh, Keoshaun

Kerdonna (African American) loquacious
Donna, Kerdy, Kirdonna, Kyrdonna

Kerensa (English) lovable
Karensa, Karenza, Kerenza

Keri-Gee (English) awesome

Kerla (American) curly-haired

Kern (Irish) darkness

Kerra (American) bright
Cara, Carrah, Kara, Kerrah

Kerry (Irish) dark-haired
Carrie, Kari, Kera, Keree, Keri, Kerrey, Kerri, Kerria, Kerridana, Kerrie

Kerst (American) form of Kerstin:
a Christian

Kerstin (Scandinavian) a Christian

Kersten, Kerston, Kerstyn

Kerthia (American) giving

Kerth, Kerthea, Kerthi, Kerthy

Kesha (American) laughing

Kecia, Kesa, Keshah

Keshia (American) bouncy

Kecia, Keishia, Keschia, Kesia, Kesiah,
Kessiah

Keshon (African American) happy

Keshann, Keshaun, Keshawn, Keshonn,
Keshun

Keshondra (African American) joy-
filled

Keshaundra, Keshondrah, Keshundra,
Keshundrea, Keshundria, Keshy

Keshonna (African American) happy

Keshanna, Keshauna, Keshaunna,
Keshawna, Keshona

Kesi (African) baby born in hard
times

Kessie (African) fat baby cheeks

Kess, Kessa, Kesse, Kessey, Kessi, Kessia,
Kessiah

Ketrina (German) musical

Keturah (African) long-suffering

Katura, Ketura

Kevine (Irish) lively

Kevina, Kevinne, Kevyn, Kevynn,
Kevynne

Kevyn (Irish) form of Kevin: lovely
face

Keva, Kevan, Kevina, Kevone, Kevonna,
Kevynn

Kew (English) form of Cumale: open-
hearted

Keydy (American) knowing

Keydee, Keydi, Keydie

Keyla (Irish) form of Kelia: crowned

Keynny (American) feminine form of
Kenneth: good-looking

Keynshalli (Invented) form of
Keisha: dark-eyed

Keyonna (African American) energetic

Keyshawn (American) lively

Keyshan, Keyshann, Keyshaun,
Keyshaunna, Keyshon, Keyshona,
Keshonna, Keykey, Kiki

Kezettea (African) form of Kezia:
confident

Kezia (Hebrew) form of Cassis:
confident

Kazia, Kessie, Kessy, Ketzia, Ketziah,
Keziah, Kezzie, Kissie, Kizzie, Kizzy

Keziane (African) form of Kezia:
confident

Kezi, Kezian

Khadijah (Arabic) sweetheart

Kadija, Kadiya, Khadiya, Khadyja

Khai (American) unusual

Ki, Kie

Khaki (American) personality-plus

Kakee, Kaki, Kakie, Khakee, Khakie

Khali (Origin unknown) lively

Khalee, Khalie, Koli, Kollie

Khalida (Hindi) eternal

Khali, Khalia, Khalita

Khalilah (Arabic) friendly

Khalique (African) lasting

Kharol (American) form of Carol:
feminine; joyful song

Khasha (American) brash

Khawaja (American) excitable

Khawla (African) enthusiastic

Khiana (American) different

Kheana, Khianah, Khianna, Ki,
Kianah, Kianna, Kiannah

Khloe (English) form of Chloe:
flowering

Khonesa (Indian) able

Khorus (Greek) musical

Khyra (English) form of Kira: sunny;
lighthearted

Ki (Korean) born again

Kia (American) form of Kiana:
graceful

Keeah, Kiah

Kiana (American) graceful
Kia, Kiah, Kianna, Kiannah, Quiana,
Quianna

Kiani (Hawaiian) form of Kiana:
graceful

Kiantyne (Invented) laughs

Kiara (Irish) dark-skinned
Chiara, Chiarra, Keearah, Keearra,
Kiarra

Kibibi (African) small girl

Kidre (American) loyal
Kidrea, Kidrey, Kidri

Kiele (Hawaiian) aromatic flower;
gardenia
Kiela, Kieley, Kieli, Kielli, Kielly

Kienalle (American) light
Kieana, Kienall, Kieny

Kienna (Origin unknown) brash
Kiennah, Kienne

Kiera (Irish) dark-skinned
Keara, Keera, Kierra

Kiersten (Greek) blessed
Kerston, Kierstin, Kierstn, Kierstynn,
Kirst, Kirsten, Kirstie, Kirstin, Kirsty

Kiersty (American) spiritual

Kihae (Asian) fragrant

Kijana (American) form of Kiana:
graceful

Kiki (Spanish/American) form of
names beginning with K: vivacious
Keiki, Ki, Kiekie, Kikee

Kiko (Japanese) lively
Kiki, Kikoh

Kiku (Japanese) flower mum
Kiko

Kilday (American) pretty

Kiley (Irish) pretty
Kilea, Kilee, Kili, Kylee, Kyley, Kylie

Kiliki (Mythology) feminine

Killie (English) returns

Kim (Vietnamese) sharp
Kimey, Kimmi, Kimmy, Kym

Kima (American) bright

Kimalida (Spanish) hopes

Kimana (American) form of Kim:
sharp

Kimaya (Asian) golden child

Kimberly ✪ (English) leader
Kim, Kimber-Lea, Kimberlee,
Kimberleigh, Kimberley, Kimberli,
Kimberlie, Kimmy, Kimmie, Kymberly

Kimbra (English) fortified

Kimbrell (African American) smiling
Kim, Kimbrée, Kimbrel, Kimbrele,
Kimby, Kimmy

Kimeo (American) form of Kim:
sharp
Kim, Kime, Kimi

Kimetha (American) form of
Kimberly: leader
Kimeth

Kimi (Japanese) spiritual

Kimo (Asian) strong

Kimone (Origin unknown) darling
Kimonne, Kymone

Kimthy (Asian) form of Timothy:
reveres God

Kimula (Invented) strength

Kimya (American) form of Kim:
sharp

Kina (Hawaiian) girl from China

Kindrah (American) form of Kendra:
ingenious

Kineisha (American) form of
Keneisha: gorgeous woman
Keneesha, Kineasha, Kinesha, Kineshia,
Kiness, Kinisha, Kinnisha, Kinny

Kineta (Greek) energetic
Kinetta

Kini (American) form of Kenny:
formidable

Kinneta (Greek) kinetic energy

Kinsey (English) child
Kensey, Kinnsee, Kinnsey, Kinnsie,
Kinsee, Kinsey, Kinsie, Kinzee

Kinshasa (Asian) child

Kinsley (Origin unknown) familiar

Kingslea, Kingslee, Kingslie, Kinslea,
Kinslee, Kinslie, Kinsly, Kinzlea,
Kinzlee, Kinzley, Kinzly

Kintra (American) joyous

Kentra, Kint, Kintrey

Kinza (American) relative

Kioko (Japanese) happy baby

Kiyo, Kiyoko

Kiona (Native American) girl from
the hill

Kionea (Native American) interesting

Kip (Literature) naive

Kipling (Last name as first name)
energetic

Kiplin

Kippareen (American) humorous;
young

Kipple (American) form of Kipling:
energetic

Kira (Russian) sunny; light-hearted

Keera, Kera, Kiera, Kierra, Kiria,
Kiriah, Kirra, Kirya

Kiran (Irish) pretty; (Indian) light

Kiara, Kiaran, Kira, Kiri

Kirby (Anglo-Saxon) right

Kirbee, Kirbey, Kirbie

Kiriath (Biblical) place name

Kirima (Eskimo) hill child; high
aspirations

Kirsta (Scandinavian) Christian

Kirsten (Scandinavian) form of
Christine: follower of Christ

Karsten, Keerstin, Keirstin, Kersten,
Kerstin, Kiersten, Kierstin, Kierstynn,
Kirsteen, Kirstene, Kirsti, Kirstie,
Kirstin, Kirston, Kirsty, Kirstynn,
Kristen, Kristin, Kristyn, Krystene,
Krystin

Kirstie (Scandinavian) irrepressible

Kerstie, Kirstee, Kirsty

Kirti (Indian) famous

Kirtrina (American) form of Katrina:
melodious

Kischchan (American) tries hard

Kisha (Russian) ingenious

Keshah

Kishala (English) form of Kisha:
ingenious

Kishi (Japanese) eternal

Kishori (Indian) young

Kismet (Hindi) destiny; fate

Kismat, Kismete, Kismett

Kissa (African) a baby born after
twins

Kit (American) strong

Kitt

Kita (Japanese) northerner

Kithos (Greek) worthy

Kitten (English) form of Katherine:
pure

Kitty (Greek) form of Katherine: pure

Kit, Kittee, Kittey, Kitti, Kittie

Kiva (Origin unknown) bright

Keva

Kiwa (Origin unknown) lively

Kiewah, Kiwah

Kiya (Australian) form of Kylie:
graceful

Kya

Kizzie (African) energetic

Kissee, Kissie, Kiz, Kizzee, Kizzi, Kizzy

Klara (Hungarian) bright

Klari, Klarice, Klarika, Klarissa,
Klarisza, Klaryssa

Klarissa (German) bright-minded

Clarissa, Klarisa, Klarise

Klarybel (Polish) beauty

Klaribel, Klaribelle

Klaudia (Polish) lame

Klea (American) bold

Clea, Kleah, Kleea, Kleeah

Klementina (Polish) forgiving

Clemence, Clementine, Klementine,
Klementyna

Kleta (Greek) form of Cleopatra:
Egyptian queen

Cleta

Klotild (Hungarian) famous
Klothild, Klothilda, Klothilde, Klotilda, Klotilde

Klyra (Slavic) noble

Knoi (American) annoys

Koa (Hawaiian) seaside

Kobi (American) California girl
Cobi, Kobe

Kobra (Indian) form of cobra

Koche (American) bright

Koffi (African) Friday-born
Kaffe, Kaffi, Koffe, Koffie

Kogan (Last name as first name) self-assured
Kogann, Kogen, Kogey, Kogi

Koichi (Asian)

Kokan (American) real

Kokkie (Dutch) horn

Koko (Japanese) the stork comes

Kolleen (Irish) form of Colleen: young girl

Kona (Hawaiian) feminine
Koni, Konia

Konia (Hawaiian) bright light

Konki (American) constant

Konstance (Latin) loyal
Constance, Kon, Konnie, Konstanze, Stanze

Kora (Greek) practical
Cora, Koko, Korey, Kori

Koren (English) form of Corinne: maiden; protective

Kori (Greek) little girl; popular
Cori, Corrie, Koree, Korey, Kory

Korina (Greek) maiden
Corinna, Koreena, Korena, Korinna, Koryna

Kornelia (Latin) straight-laced
Cornelia, Kornelya, Korney, Korni, Kornie

Kortney (American) form of Courtney: domain of Curtis
Kortnee, Kortni, Kourtney, Kourtnie

Koshatta (Native American) diligent
Coushatta, Kosha, Koshat, Koshatte, Koshee, Koshi, Koshie, Koushatta

Koska (American) loose cannon

Kosta (Latin) form of Constance: loyal
Kostia, Kostusha, Kostya

Koto (Japanese) harp; musical

Koverne (Last name used as first name) homebody

Krenie (American) capable
Kren, Kreni, Krenn, Krennie, Kreny

Kresenz (German) crescent

Kris (American) form of Kristina: follower of Christ
Kaykay, Krissie, Krissy

Krishen (American) talkative
Crishen, Kris, Krish, Krishon

Krissa (German) form of Krista: follower of Christ

Krissen (American) feminine form of Christian: follower of Christ

Krissy (American) friendly
Kris, Krisie, Krissey, Krissi

Krista (German) form of Christina: follower of Christ
Khrista, Krysta

Kristanie (American) Christian

Kristeen (German) form of Christine: follower of Christ

Kristeenea (English) form of Christina: follower of Christ

Kristen (Greek) form of Christine: follower of Christ
Christen, Cristen, Kristin, Kristyn

Kristian (Greek) Christian woman
Kristiana, Kristianne, Kristyanna

Kristie (American) saucy
Christi, Christy, Kristi

Kristin (Scandinavian) high-energy
Kristen, Kristyne

Kristina (Scandinavian) form of Christina: follower of Christ
Krista, Kristie, Krysteena, Tina

Kristine (Swedish) form of Christine: follower of Christ
Kristee, Kristene, Kristi, Kristy

Kristy (American) form of Kristine: follower of Christ
Kristi, Kristie

Krysta (Polish) clear
Chrsta, Krista

Krystal (American) clear and brilliant
Cristalle, Cristel, Crysta, Crystal, Crystalle, Khristalle, Khristel, Khrystalle, Khrystle, Kristel, Kristle, Krys, Krystalle, Krystalline, Krystelle, Krystie, Krystle, Krystylle

Krystyna (Polish) Christian

Kuawanna (African) fragrant

Kubbae (American) wanderer

Kue (Biblical) place name

Kukan (Scandinavian) blossoms

Kumiko (Japanese) long hair in braids
Kumi

Kumud (Indian) lotus flower; Bright

Kundany (Indian) golden child

Kunday (Invented) form of Sunday: day of the week; sunny

Kurara (Japanese) peaceful

Kurene (American) monied

Kwanita (African) form of Juanita: believer in a gracious God; forgiving

Kyan (American) lively

Kyatana (American) vivacious

Kyishia (American) form of Keisha: dark-eyed

Kyla (Irish) pretty
Kiela, Kila, Ky

Kyle (Irish) pretty
Kyall, Kyel, Kylee, Kylie, Kyll

Kylee (Irish) form of Kylie: graceful
Kielie, Kiely, Kiley, Kye, Kyky, Kyleigh

Kyleighan (English) form of Kylie: graceful

Kylene (American) cute
Kyline

Kylera (English) feminine form of Kyler: peaceful

Kylern (English) feminine form of Kyler: peaceful

Kylie ☉ (Irish) graceful
Keyely, Kilea, Kiley, Kylee, Kyley

Kylynne (American) fashionable
Kilenne, Kilynn, Kyly

Kym (American) favorite
Kim, Kymm, Kymmi, Kymmie, Kymy

Kyna (African) diamond

Kynci (American) form of Kinsey: child

Kynthia (Greek) goddess of the moon
Cinthia, Cynthia

Kyoko (Japanese) sees herself in a mirror

Kyra (Greek) feminine
Kaira, Keera, Keira, Kira, Kyrah, Kyreena, Kyrene, Kyrha, Kyria, Kyrie, Kyrina, Kyrra, Kyry

Kyria (Greek) form of Kyra: feminine
Kyrea, Kyree, Kyrie, Kyry

L

Laarni (American) honest

Labe (American) slow-moving
Labie

Lace (American) delicate
Lacee, Lacey, Laci, Lacie, Lase

Lacey (Greek) cheery
Lacee, Laci, Lacie, Lacy

Lachelle (African American) sweetheart
Lachel, Lachell, Laschell, Lashelle

Lachesis (Mythological) one of the Greek Fates; the measurer

Lachina (African American) fragile

Lacole (American) sly
Lucole

Lacreta (Spanish) form of Lacretia: efficient
Lacrete, LaLa

Lacretia (Latin) efficient
Lacracia, Lacrecia, Lacrisha, Lacy

LaDaune (African American) the dawn
Ladaune, LaDawn

Ladda (American) open
Lada

Ladey (American) form of Lady: feminine

LaDorna (Spanish) adorned

Ladrenaan (Invented) likeable

Ladrenda (African American) cagy
Ladee, Ladey, Ladren, Ladrende, Lady

Lady (American) feminine
Ladee, Ladie

Laela (Hebrew) form of Leila: beauty of the night

Laetitia (Latin) joy
Lateaciah, Lateacya, Latycia, Leticia, Letisia, Letyziah

Laheelah (American) gifted

Laila (Scandinavian) dark beauty
Laili, Laleh, Layla, Laylah, Leila

Lainil (American) softhearted
Lainie, Lanel, Lanelle

Laitalin (American) secure

Laith (Scottish) princess

Lajean (French) soothing; steadfast
LaJean, Lajeanne, L'Jean

LaJoyce (English) combo of La and Joyce

Lakanel (American) hurt

Lake (Astrology) graceful dancer

Lakeisha (African American) the favorite; combo of La and Keisha

Lakeita (American) caring

Lakela (Hawaiian) feminine
Lakla

Lakendrae (American) great hopes

Lakeny (American) superb

Lakesha (African American) favored
Keishia, Lakaisha, Lakeesha, Lakeishah, Lakezia, Lakisha, LaKisha

Lakeyshia (African-American) crafty

Lakiesta (English) form of Lakesha: favored

Lakiya (English) form of Lakesha: favored

Lakya (Hindi) born on Thursday

Lakysha (English) form of Lakesha: favored

Lala (Slavic) pretty flower girl; tulip

Lalage (Greek) talkative
Lal, Lallie, Lally

Lalaney (American) form of Leilani: heavenly girl
Lala, Lalanee, Lalani

Laleema (Spanish) devoted
Lalema, Lalima

Lalena (Indian) girlish
Lalana

Lalita (Sanskrit) charmer
Lai, Lala, Lali, Lalitah, Lalite, Lalitte

Lalitha (Spanish) form of Lalita: charmer

Lally (English) babbling
Lalli

Lalmani (American) sociable

Lalya (Latin) eloquent
Lalia, Lall, Lalyah

Lama (Muslim) dark lips

Lamarian (American) conflicted
Lamare, Lamarean

Lambda (Greek)

Lamercie (French) forgiving

Lamia (Egyptian) calm
Lami

Lamiena (Spanish) calming

Lamika (African American) form of Tamika: lively

L'Amour (French) love
Amor, Amour, Lamore, Lamour, Lamoura

Lana (Latin) pretty; peacemaker
Lan, Lanna, Lanny

Lanai (Hawaiian) heavenly
Lenai

Lanalee (Invented) combo of Lana and Lee

Land (American) word as name; confident

Landd

Landa (American) blonde beauty

Landah

Landra (American) form of Landa: blonde beauty

Landry (American) leader

Landa, Landree

Landy (American) confident

Land, Landee, Landey, Landi

Lane (Last name as first name) precocious

Laine, Lainey, Laney, Lanie, Layne, Laynie

Lanee (Asian) graceful

Laneedy (English) form of Laney: precocious

Lanette (American) healthy

La-Net, LaNett, LaNette

Langley (American) special

Langlee, Langli, Langlie, Langly

Lani (Hawaiian) form of Leilani: heavenly girl

Lannie

LaNiece (Invented) form of Lenice: delightful

Lanigill (American) happy

Lanilee (American) heaven

Lanitia (Slavic) unique

Lanle (African) enriched

Lannea (American) mobile

Lannette (American) form of Lynette: small and fresh

Lanola (American) generous

Lanonre (American) of the sea

Lanora (Italian) form of Leonora: bright light

Lansing (Place name) hopeful

Lanseng

Lantana (Botanical) flowering

Lantanna

Laperonita (Spanish) upward

Laquanna (African American) outspoken

Kwanna, LaQuanna, LaQwana, Quanna

Lara (Russian) lovely

Larae (Slavic) form of Lara: lovely

Laraine (Latin) pretty

Lareine, Larene, Loraine

Larante (Last name used as first name) shares

Laray (American) form of Lara: lovely

Larby (American) form of Darby: a free woman

Larbee, Larbey, Larbi, Larbie

Larch (American) full of life

Lareina (Greek) seagull; flies over water

Larayna, Larayne, Lareine, Larena, Larrayna, Larreina

Larenya (English) form of Laraine: pretty

Laressia (English) form of Larissa: giving cheer

Lariesha (English) form of Larissa: giving cheer

Larinda (American) smart

Lare, Larin, Larine, Lorinda

Larissa (Latin) giving cheer

Laressa, Larisse, Laryssa

Lark (American) pretty

Larke

Larkin (American) pretty

Larken, Larkun

Larklee (Invented) combo of Lark and Lee; birdlike

Larkly (American) form of Larklee: birdlike

Larkspur (Botanical) tall and stately

Larla (American) deserving

Larlett (American) winner

Larni (American) form of Marni: storyteller

LaRobin (English) combo of La and Robin

Larrie (American) tomboyish

Larry

Larsa (Biblical) place name

Larsen (Scandinavian) laurel-crowned

Larson, Larssen, Larsson

Laruthenne (American) combo of La and Ruthenne

Lasa (American) complex

Lasalle (French) explorer

Lasea (Biblical) place name

Lasha (Spanish) forlorn

Lash, Lass

Lashanda (American) brassy

Lala, Lasha, LaShanda, LaShounda

Lashauna (American) happy

Lashona, Lashawna, Leshauna

LaShea (American) sparkling

Lashay, La-Shea, Lashea

Lashoun (African American) content

Lashaun, Lashawn, Lashown

Lassie (American) lass

Lass

Lastashtia (American) form of Latasha: born on Christmas

Lastenia (Spanish) lovely Christian girl

Lata (Hindi) lovely vine; entwines

Latash (American) form of Latasha: born on Christmas

Latasha (American) born on Christmas

Latacha, LaTasha, Latayshah, Latisha

LaTeasa (Spanish) tease

Latea, Lateasa, LaTease, LaTeese

Lateefah (African) gentle; pleasant

Lateefa, Latifa, Latifah, Lotifah, Tifa, Tifah

Latesha (American) form of Letitia: joy

Lateesha, Lateisha, Lateshah, Laticia, Latisha

Lathenia (American) verbose

Lathene, Lathey

Latice (American) form of Letitia: joy

Latifah (Muslim) gentle

Lateefa, Latifa, Latiffe, Latifuh

Latiki (Indian) small

Latika

Latina (Spanish) Spanish girl

Latisa (English) form of Latasha: born on Christmas

Latisehsha (African American) happy; talkative

Lati, Latise, Latiseh, Latisha

Latochia (English) form of Latasha: born on Christmas

Latona (Latin) goddess

Latonia (African American) rich

Latone, Latonea

Latosha (African American) happy

Latoyia (English) watchful

Latoyra (American) circumspect

Latreece (American) go-getter

Latreese, Latrice, Letrice, Lettie, Letty

Latrelia (Spanish) of the trellis

Latrelle (American) laughing

Lettie, Letrel, Letrelle, Litrelle

Latrice (Latin) noble

Latreece, Latreese

Latricia (American) happy

Latrecia, Latreesha, Latrisha, Latrishah

Latrisha (African American) prissy

Latrishe

Latroa (American) athletic

Latunga (African) athletic

Latunya (American) form of Latonya: birdlike

Latyffanie (American) combo of La and Tyffanie

Lauda (Latin) praised

Laudette (American) lauded

Laudomia (Italian) praiseworthy

Laufeia (Scandinavian) thriving

Launa (American) ideal

Launie (American) heavenly

Laura (Latin) laurel-crowned; joyous

Lara, Lora

Laurain (English) graceful

Laurdina (American) form of Laurinda: the laurel plant

Laureen (American) old-fashioned

Laurie, Laurine, Loreen

Laureens (Scandinavian) wins laurels

Laurel (Latin) the laurel plant

Laural, Laurell, Laurella, Laurelle,
Lorel, Lorell, Lorella, Lourelle

Lauren ✪ (Latin) laurel-crowned

Laren, Laurene, Lauryn, Laryn, Loren

Laurencia (Latin) laurel-crowned

Laurenciah, Laurens, Laurentana

Laurenne (Scandinavian) wins
laurels

Laurent (French) graceful

Laurente, Lorent

Laurentine (French) bright

Lauretta (American) graceful

Laureta, Laurettah, Lauritta, Lauritte,
Loretta

Laurette (American) form of Laura:
laurel-crowned; joyous; (English) form
of Laurita: victorious

Etta, Ette, Laure, Laurett, Lorette

Laurettean (English) form of
Laurita: victorious

Laurid (Welsh) form of Laura: laurel-
crowned; joyous

Laurie (English) careful

Lari, Lauri, Lori

Laurima (Spanish) form of Laura:
laurel-crowned; joyous

Laurinda (Spanish) the laurel plant

Laurissaa (Greek) pleased

Laurita (Spanish) victorious

Lavanda (Spanish) pure

Laveda (Latin) pure

Lavella, Lavelle, Laveta, Lavetta, Lavette

LaVeeda (Spanish) alive

Lavena (Celtic) joy

Lavi, Lavie, Lavina

Lavender (Latin) pale purple flowers;
peaceful

Laverne (Latin) breath of spring

Lavern, Lavirne, Verna, Verne

La Verta (American) truth

Laveta (American) vibrant

Lavette (Latin) pure; natural

Laveda, Lavede, Lavete, Lavett

Lavigne (French) vineyard

Lavilla (Spanish) gathers

Lavina (Latin) woman of Rome

Lavinia (Latin) cleansed; (Greek)
ladylike

Lavenia, Vin, Vina, Vinnie, Vinny

Lavita (American) charmer

Laveta, Lavitta, Lavitte

Lawanda (American) sassy

LaWanda, Lawonda

Lawenna form of Lawan: lovely

Lawrencetta (American) feminine
form of Lawrence: honored

Layce (American) spunky

Layine (Scandinavian) loves the sea

Layla ✪ (Arabic) dark

Laela, Laila, Lala, Laya, Laylah,
Laylie, Leila

Layli (American) form of Layla: dark

Layne (French) from the meadow

Laine, Lainee, Lainey

Laynn (American) form of Lane:
precocious

Layoce (American) form of Loyce:
delightful

Layouce (American) form of Loyce:
delightful

Laysha (American) form of Letitia:
joy

Lazette (American) form of Lizette:
lively

Lazine (Dutch) joyful

Lazina, Lazee

Lea (Hawaiian) goddess-like

Leacille (American) form of Lucille:
bright-eyed

Leaf (Botanical) hip

Leah ✪ (Hebrew) tired and burdened

Lea, Lee, Leeah, Leia, Lia

Leala (French) steadfast

Leandra (Greek) leonine

Leandrea, Leanndra, Leeandra, Leedie

Leanette (English) form of Lynnette:
small and fresh

Leanna (English) leaning

Leana, Leelee, Liana

Leanne (English) sweet

Lean, Leann, Lee, Leelee, Lianne

Leanona (English) form of Leona: bravehearted

Leanora (Greek) light

Lanora, Lanoriah, Lenora

Leanore (Greek) form of Eleanor: lighthearted

Lanore

Leatha (English) form of Alethea: truthful

Leatrice (American) charming

Leatrise

Leatricea (English) leader

Lebonah (Biblical) place name

Lecia (Latin) form of Letitia: joy

Leecia, Leesha, Lesha, Lesia

Lectricia (English) form of Leatrice: charming

Leda (Greek) feminine

Ledah, Lida, Lita

Lee (English/American/Chinese) light-footed

Lea, Leelee, Leigh

Leeannette (Greek) form of Leandra: leonine

Leann, Leeanett, Lee Annette, Lee-Annette, Leiandra

Leelee (American/Slavic) form of Leanne: sweet

Lee-Lee, Lele, Lelee

Leena (Latin) temptress

Lena, Lina

Leene (Scandinavian) form of Lena: siren

Leeo (American) sunny

Leo

Leesha (English) form of Lisha: God-loving

Le Etta (American) small

Leeuwen (Dutch) dear friend

Leeza (American) gorgeous

Leesa, Leeze, Liza, Lize

Legend (American) memorable

Legen, Legende, Legund

Legia (Spanish) bright

Legea

Lehava (Hebrew) flaming

Lei (Hawaiian) form of Leilani: heavenly girl

Leilei

Léi (Chinese) open; truthful

Leigh (English) light-footed

Lee, Leelee

Leila (Arabic) beauty of the night

Layla, Leela, Leilah, Lelah, Leyla, Lila

Leilani (Hawaiian) heavenly girl

Lanie

Leisa (English) form of Lisa: dedicated and spiritual

Leith (Scottish) from the river; nature-loving

Leithe, Lethe

Lejoi (French) joy

Joy, Lejoy

Leka (Indian) graphic proof

Lehka

Leland (American) special

Lelan, Lelande

Lelann (Greek) faithful

Lelia (Greek) articulate

Lee, Leelee

Lemetria (American) perfection

Leminda (American) mindful

Lemon (Botanical) zany

Lemtraia (American) sporty

Lemuela (Hebrew) loyal

Lemuelah, Lemuella, Lemuellah

Lena (Latin) siren

Leena, Lenette, Lina

Lendez (Spanish) form of Linda: pretty girl

Lendorah (English) form of Linda: pretty girl

Lendtra (English) form of Linda: pretty girl

Lenesha (African American) smiling

Leneisha, Lenisha, Lenni, Lennie,
Neshie

Lenetta (English) form of Lynette:
small and fresh

Lenice (American) delightful

Lenisa, Lenise

Lenikka (American) roving

Lenita (Latin) gentle spirit

Leneeta, Leneta, Lineta

Lenka (Slavic) cleansed

Lenkan (Slavic) excellent

Lenna (Hebrew) shy

Lenoa (Greek) form of Lenore:
lighthearted

Len, Lenor, Lenora

Lenore (Greek) form of Eleanor:
lighthearted

lighthearted

Leoda (German) popular

Leota

Leola (Latin) fierce; leonine

Lee, Leo, Leole

Leolan (Last name used as first name)
lionlike

Leolia (English) form of Leola:
leonine

Leoma (American) form of Leona:
bravehearted

Leona (Greek/American) bravehearted

Liona

Leonarda (German) lionhearted

Lenarda, Lenda, Lennarda, Leonarde

Leondrea (Greek) strong

Leondreah, Leondria

Leonetta (English) feminine form of
Leon: tenacious

Leonie (Latin) lionlike; fierce

Leola, Leonee, Leoney, Leoni, Leontine,
Leony

Leonila (Spanish) lioness

Leonora (English) bright light

Leanor, Leanora, Leanore, Lenora,
Lenore, Leonore

Leonore (Greek) glowing light

Lenore, Leonor, Leonora

Leonsio (Spanish) feminine form of
Leon: tenacious

Leo, Leonsee, Leonsi

Leopoldina (Invented) feminine
form of Leopold: brave

Dina, Leo, Leopolde, Leopoldyna

Leora (Greek) lighthearted

Leorah, Liora

Leoycey (Invented) sassy

Lequita (Spanish) bright; clear

Lera (Russian) strong

Lerae, Lerie, Lira

Leretta (American) form of Loretta:
large-eyed beauty

Lere, Lerie

Leria (Italian) brave

Lerita (Spanish) gives joy

Leritha (Spanish) gives joy

Lesha (Italian) kind

Leshia (Italian) feminine

Leslie (Scottish) fiesty; beautiful; smart

Les, Lesli, Lesley

Leslin (American) form of Leslie:
feisty; beautiful; smart

Lessie (Scottish) form of Leslie:
feisty; beautiful; smart

Lesstene (American) form of Leslie:
feisty; beautiful; smart

Lesvia (Slavic) spiritual

Leszlee (American) form of Leslie:
fiesty; beautiful; smart

Leta (Latin) happy

Leeta, Lita

Letai (Latin) glad

Letha (Greek) ladylike

Litha

Letian (Latin) glad

Letichel (American) happy;
important

Chel, Chelle, Leti, Letichell, Letishell,
Lettichelle, Lettychel

Leticia (Spanish) form of Letitia: joy

Letecia, Letisha, Lettice, Lettie, Letty,
Tiesha

Letina (Spanish) Latina

Letitia (Latin) joy

Leto (Greek) mother of Apollo

Letricia (Spanish) happy

Letsey (American) form of Lettie:
happy

Letsee, Letsy

Lettice (American) sweet

Letty

Lettie (Latin/Spanish) happy

Lettee, Letti, Letty, Lettye

Letycee (Invented) insightful

Leutricia (Spanish) form of Letricia:
happy

Leutu (Asian)

Levana (Hebrew) fair

Lev, Liv, Livana

Leverah (American) form of
Deborah: prophetess

Leverne (French) grove of trees

Levina (Latin) lightning

Levitt (American) straightforward

Levit

Levity (American) humorous

Levora (American) home-loving

*Levorah, Levore, Livee, Livie, Livora,
Livore*

Lewana (Hebrew) moon bright

Lexa (American) cheerful

Lex, Lexah

Lexandra (Slavic) bold

Lexi (Greek) helpful; sparkling

Lex, Lexie, Lexsey, Lexsie, Lexy

Lexine (Scottish) helper

Lexus (American) rich

Lexi, Lexorus, Lexsis, Lexuss, Lexxus

Lexy (Scottish) helper

Leya (Spanish) true blue

Leysa (Spanish) loyal

Lez (American) form of Leslie: feisty;
beautiful; smart

Lezena (American) smiling

Lezene, Lezina, Lyzena

Lez'lee (American) form of Leslie:
feisty; beautiful; smart

Li (Chinese) plum; strong

Lia (Greek/Russian/Italian) singular

Li, Liah

Liadin (Irish) sad

Lial (Italian) form of Leah: tired and
burdened

Lialeh (Italian) form of Leah:
tired and burdened

Lian (Latin/Chinese) graceful

Leane, Leanne, Liane

Liana (Greek) flowering; complicated

Leanna, Lee, Liane

Liani (Hawaiian) caressed

Lianna (Italian) sunny

Lianne (English) light

Leann, Leanne, Leeann

Libba (Biblical) place name; desired

Libby (Hebrew) form of Elizabeth:
God's promise

Lib, Libbi, Libbie

Liber (American) from the word
liberty; free

Lib, Libby, Lyber

Liberty (Latin) free and open

Lib, Libbie

Libnah (Biblical) place name; white

Librada (Spanish) free

Libra, Libradah

Libva (Biblical) place name; white

Liceth (American) form of Lysett:
pretty little one

Licia (Greek) outdoorsy

Lisha

Licona (Spanish)

Lida (Greek) beloved girl

Leedah, Lyda

Liddan (Irish) form of Liadin: sad

Lidia (Greek) pleasant spirit

Lydia

Lidiya (Russian) form of Lydia:
musical, unusual

Liese (German) given to God

Liesel (German) pretty

Leesel, Leezel

Lieselotte (Hebrew/French)
charming woman

Light (American) light-hearted
Li, Lite

Ligia (Greek) talented musician
Ligea, Lygia, Lygy

Lignon (French) clarity

Liguria (Greek) music lover

Likiana (Invented) likeable
Like, Likia

Lila (Arabic) playful
Lilah, Lyla, Lylah

Lilac (Botanical) tiny blossom
Lila

Lilah (Sanskrit) playful

Lila-Lee (American) lily

Lilavati (Hindi) goddess

Lileah (Latin) lily-like
Lili, Liliah, Lill, Lily, Lilya

Lilette (Latin) little lily; delicate
Lill, Lillette, Lillith, Lilly

Lilia (American) flowing
Lileah, Lyleah, Lylia

Lilian (Latin) pure beauty

Liliana (Italian) pretty
Lilianah, Lylianah

Lilias (Hebrew) night
Lilas, Lillas, Lillias

Liliash (Spanish) lily; innocent
Lil, Lileah, Liliosa, Lilya, Lyliase, Lylish

Lilith (Arabic) nocturnal
*Lilis, Lilita, Lill, Lilli, Lillie, Lillith,
Lilly, Lilyth, Lilythe*

Lillian ✪ (Latin) pretty as a lily
*Lila, Lileane, Lilian, Liliane, Lill,
Lilla, Lillah, Lillie, Lillyan, Lillyann,
Lilyanne, Liyan*

Lillias (Hebrew) night

Lily ✪ ✪ (Latin/Chinese) elegant
Lil, Lili, Lilie

Limor (Hebrew) myrrh; treasured
Leemor

Lin (English/Chinese) beautiful
Linn, Lynn

Lina (Greek/Latin/Scottish) light of
spirit; lake calm
Lena, Lin, Linah, Lynn

Linda (Spanish) pretty girl
Lind, Lindy, Lynda

Linden (American) harmonious
Lindan, Lindun, Lynden, Lynnden

Lindsay (English/Scottish) calming;
bright and shining
*Lindsee, Lindsey, Lindsi, Lindz,
Lyndsie, Lyndzee, Lynz*

Lindse (Spanish) form of Lindsay:
calming; bright and shining
Linds, Lindz, Lindze, Lyndzy

Lindy (American) music-lover
*Lind, Lindee, Lindi, Lindie, Linney,
Linnie, Linse, Linz, Linze*

Linette (French/English/American)
graceful and airy
Lanette, Linet, Linnet, Lynette

Ling (Chinese) delicate

Linga (American) form of Ling: delicate

Lingga (Scandinavian)

Linji (English) form of Linsey: bright
spirit

Lin-Lin (Chinese) beauty of a tinkling
bell
Lin, Lin Lin

Linna (Scandinavian) flower

Linnea (Swedish) statuesque
*Lin, Linayah, Linea, Linnay, Linny,
Lynnea*

Linnesh (American) form of Lindsay:
calming; bright and shining

Linnz (American) form of Lindsay:
calming; bright and shining

Lino (American) form of Lindsay:
calming; bright and shining

Linsey (English) bright spirit
Linsie, Linsy, Linzi, Linzie

Linsley (English) form of Lindsay:
calming; bright and shining

Linzetta (American) form of Linzey: calming; bright and shining
Linze, Linzette

Linzey (American) form of Lindsay: calming; bright and shining

Lio (Jewish) form of Liora: light

Liora (Hebrew) light
Leeor, Leeora, Lior, Liorit

Lioren (Jewish) form of Liora: light

Liotta (Italian) of the bay

Lioudmila (Slavic) loved

Lisa (Hebrew/American) dedicated and spiritual
Lee, Leelee, Leesa, Leesah, Leeza, Leisa, Lesa, Lysa

Lisanne (English/Dutch) God is my oath; favor; grace

Lisbet (Scandinavian) sweet

Lisbeth (Hebrew) form of Elizabeth: God's promise

Lise (German) form of Lisa: dedicated and spiritual
Lesa

Lisen (Dutch) form of Lisanne;: God is my oath; favor; grace

Lisette (French) little Elizabeth
Lise, Lisete, Lissette, Liz

Lisha (Hebrew) form of Elisha: God-loving
Lish, Lishie

Lissa (Greek) sweet
Lyssa

Lissandra (Greek) defends others

Lisset (French) form of Elizabeth: God's promise

Lisseth (Hebrew) form of Elizabeth: God's promise
Liseta, Liseth, Lisette, Lisith, Liss, Lisse, Lissi

Lissie (American) form of Elise: concecrated to God
Lis, Lissi, Lissey, Lissy

Liszt (Hungarian) musical

Lita (Latin) life-giving
Leta

Lithyia (Mythology) prepared

Litisha (Spanish) form of Letitia: joy

Litzy (Spanish) form of Letitia: joy

Liv (Latin/Scandinavian) lively
Leev

Livia (Hebrew) lively
Levia, Livya

Liviu (Spanish) lively

Livona (Hebrew) vibrant
Levona, Liv, Livvie, Livvy

Liya (Russian) lily; lovely
Leeya

Liz (English) form of Elizabeth: God's promise
Lis, Lissy, Lizy, Lizzi, Lizzie

Liza (American) smiling
Leeza, Liz, Lizah, Lizzie, Lizzy, Lyza

Lizabeth (English) abundant in God

Lizeth (Hebrew) ebullient
Liseth, Lizethe

Lizette (Hebrew) lively
Lizet, Lizett

Lizset (Spanish) form of Lysett: pretty little one

Lizzie (American) devout
Liz, Liza, Lizae, Lizette, Lizzee, Lizzey, Lizzi, Lizzy

Lizzine (American) form of Elizabeth: God's promise

Llewwllyn (Welsh) shines brightly

Lo (American) spunky
Loe

Loa (English) form of Louise: hardworking and brave

Loelia (Arabic) nocturnal
Leila

Loen (Spanish) lovely

Loey (Mythology) kind
Louhi

Logan (English) climbing
Lo, Logun

Logana (Scottish) form of Logan: climbing

Loganah (Scottish) form of Logan: climbing

Logred (Welsh) dedication

Loicy (American) delightful
Loice, Loisee, Loisey, Loisi, Loy, Loyce, Loycy, Loyse, Loysie

Loire (Place name) river in France; lovely wonder
Loir, Loirane

Lois (Greek) good
Lo, Loes

Loise (English) form of Louise: hardworking and brave

Lola (Spanish) pensive
Lo, Lolah, Lolita

Loleatha (Spanish) sad

Loleen (American) jubilant
Lolene

Loleta (Spanish) sad

Lo-Lin (Asian) sure

Lolita (Spanish) sad
Lo, Lola, Loleta, Lita

Lolly (English) candy; sweet

Loma (Spanish) lucky

Lomita (Spanish) good

Lona (Latin) lionlike; (Indian) lovely
Lonee, Lonie, Lonna, Lonnie

Londa (American) shy
Londah, Londe, Londy

London (Place name) calming
Londen, Londun, Londy, Loney, Lony

Loni (American) beauty
Loney, Lonie, Lonnie

Lonise (American) form of Denise: wine-lover

Lonjeana (Spanish) tall

Lonnecke (American) lone

Lonnette (American) pretty
Lonett, Lonette, Lonn, Lonnie

Lonzine (French) alone

Lopa (Spanish)

Loperena (Spanish)

Lora (Latin) regal
Laura, Lorah, Lorea, Loria

Lorain (English) sad

Loranden (American) ingenious
Lorandyn, Lorannden, Luranden

Lordena (Spanish) form of Lourdes: a girl from Lourdes, France; hallowed

Lordyn (American) enchanting
Lorden, Lordin, Lordine, Lordun, Lordynn

Loreen (American) variation on Lauren: laurel-crowned
Lorene

Lorel (German) tempting
Loreal

Lorela (German) attracts

Lorelei (German) siren
Loralee, LoraLee, Lorilie, Lurleen, Lurlene

Lorelle (American) lovely
Lore, Loreee, Lorel, Lorey, Lori, Lorie, Lorille

Loren (American) form of Lauren: laurel-crowned
Lorren, Lorri, Lorrie, Lorron, Lorryn, Lory, Loryn, Lourie

Lorena (English) form of Loren: laurel-crowned
Loreen, Lorene, Lorrie, Lorrine

Lorenia (English) form of Lorena: laurel-crowned

Loreniana (English) given laurels

Lorenza (Latin) form of Laura: laurel-crowned; joyous
Laurenza

Loreto (Italian) miraculous; honored

Loretta (English) large-eyed beauty
Lauretta

Lori (Latin) laurel-crowned and nature-loving
Laurie, Loree, Lorie, Lory

Lorinthe (American) form of Laura: laurel-crowned; joyous

Loris (Greek/Latin) fun-loving
Lorice, Lauris

Loriz (American) form of Loris: fun-loving

Lorna (Latin) laurel-crowned; natural
Lorenah

Lorola (Origin unknown) family

Lorraine (Latin/French) sad-eyed

Laraine, Lauraine, Lorain, Loraine,
Lorrie, Lors

Lorril (American) praise-worthy

Lorya (American) form of Laura:
laurel-crowned; joyous

Lotta (Swedish) sweet

Lottie (American) old-fashioned

Lottee, Lotti, Lotty

Lotus (Greek) flowery

Lolo, Lotie

Lou (American) form of Louise:
hardworking and brave

Loulou, Lu

Louella (English) elf

Loella, Loellah, Loelle, Luela, Luella

Louie (American) strong

Louisa (English) patient

Lou, Loulou, Lu, Luisa, Luizza

Louise (German) hardworking and
brave

Lolah, Lou, Loulou, Luise

Louiseine (American) intimidating

Louiselle (French) form of Louise:
hardworking and brave

Loura (Catalan) laurels

Louray (English) enchants

Lourdes (French) girl from Lourdes,
France; hallowed

Lordes, Lordez, Lourd

Louria (American) form of Laura:
laurel-crowned; joyous

Loutan (English) released

Love (English/American) loving

Lovey, Lovi, Luv

Loveada (Spanish) loving

Lova, Lovada

Lovella (Native American) soft spirit

Lovela

Lovely (American) loving

Lovelee, Loveley, Loveli, Lovey

Lovie (American) warm

Lovee, Lovey, Lovi, Lovy

Lovina (American) warm

Lovena, Lovey, Lovinah, Lovinnah

Lovisa (Scandinavian) aggressor

Loway (Last name used as first name)
wolf; free

Lowe (English) sly; pretty

Lowell (American) lovely

Lowel

Lowena (American) form of Louise:
hardworking and brave

Lowenek, Lowenna

Loy (English) adoring

Loyalty (American) loyal

Loyaltie

Loycie (English) adoring

Loydia (Spanish) form of Lydia:
musical; unusual

Ltanya (American) form of Latonya:
birdlike

Ltaya (American) form of Latonya

Lualla (American) adoring; graceful

Luba (Yiddish) dear

Liba, Lubah, Lyuba

Luberda (Spanish) light; dear

Luberdia

Luberta (Slavic) form of Luba: dear

Lubica (Slavic) form of Luba: dear

Lublain (Slavic) form of Luba: dear

Luca (Italian) light

Luka

Lucasta (Spanish) bringer of light

Luceil (French) light; lucky

Luce, Lucee, Lucy

Lucelle (French) sheds light

Lucellene (French) sheds light

Lucerne (Latin) born into the light

Lucerna

Lucero (Italian) light-hearted

Lucee, Lucey, Lucy

Lucetta (English) radiating joy

Lucette (French) pale light

Lucia (Italian/Greek/Spanish) light;
lucky in love

Chia, Luceah, Lucey, Luci

Luciana (Italian) fortunate

Louciana, Luceana, Lucianah

Lucie (French/American) lucky girl

Lucy

Lucienne (French) lucky

Lucianne, Lucien, Lucienn, Lucy-Ann

Lucilla (English) form of Lucille:
bright-eyed

Loucilah, Loucilla, Lucilah, Lucylla,
Lusyla, Luzela

Lucille (English) bright-eyed

Loucil, Loucile, Loucille, Lucyl, Lucie,
Lucile, Lucy

Lucillea (French) sheds light

Lucillet (French) sheds light

Lucina (American) happy

Lucena, Lucie, Lucinah, Lucy, Lucyna

Lucinda (Latin) prissy

Cinda, Cindie, Lu, Luceenda, Lucynda,
Lulu

Lucindia (English) form of Lucinda:
prissy

Lucine (Scandinavian) lucid

Lucinea (Spanish) lucid

Lucita (Spanish) light

Lusita, Luzita

Lucja (Polish) light

Luscia

Luckette (Invented) lucky

Luckett

Lucretia (Latin) wealthy woman

Lu, Lucrecia, Lucreesha, Lucritia

Lucy (Latin/Scottish/Spanish)
lighthearted

Lu, Luca, Luce, Luci, Lucie

Ludivina (Slavic) loved

Ludmilla (Slavic) beloved one

Lu, Ludie, Ludmila, Ludmylla, Lule, Lulu

Ludne (French) loved

Ludora (Spanish) loved

Lue (English) cheering

Lue-Ella (English) form of Ella:
beautiful and fanciful

Louel, Luella, Luelle

Luella (German) conniving

Loella, Louella, Lu, Lula, Lulah, Lulu

Luenetter (American) egotistical

Lou, Lu, Luene, Luenette

Lugene (American) form of Eugene:
blue-blood

Luicia (Spanish) light

Luisa (Spanish) smiling

Louisa

Luisana (Place name) from Louisiana

Luisanna, Luisanne, Luisiana

Luisito (Spanish) light

Luke (American) bouncy

Luc, Luka, Lukey, Lukie

Lula (German) all-encompassing

Lulu

Lulani (Polynesian) heaven-sent

Lula, Lani, Lanie

Lular (English) bounty of heaven

Lulu (German/English) kind

Lou, Loulou, Lu, Lulie

Lulua (English) comforts

Lulunena (German) comforts

Luminosa (Spanish) luminous

Luna (Latin) moonstruck

Loona

Luna-Coco (American) coconut moon

Lunan (Latin) moon

Lund (German) genius

Lun, Lunde

Lundria (Slavic) smart; from the
grove

Lundy (Scottish) grove by an island

Lundea, Lundee, Lundi

Lundyn (American) different

Lundan, Lunden, Lundon

Luned (Welsh) moonlike

Lunell (American) luminous

Lunette (French) of the moon

Lunwonda (African) moon child

Lupe (Spanish) enthusiastic

Loopy, Loopey, Lupeta, Lupey, Lupie,
Lupita

Luquitha (African American) fond

Luquetha, Luquith

Lur (Spanish) earth

Lura (American) loquacious
Loora, Lur, Lurah, Lurie

Luree (German) lures

Luretta (German) lures

Lurissa (American) beguiling
Luresa, Luressa, Luris, Lurisa, Lurissah, Lurly

Lurlaine (German) alluring

Lurlene (German) tempting
Lura, Lurleen, Lurlie, Lurline

Lushea (American) form of Lucia: light; lucky in love

Lutee (German) of the people

Lutherene (American) feminine form of Luther: reformer

Luticha (Spanish) form of Letitia: joy

Luvelle (American) light
Luvee, Luvell, Luvey, Luvy

Lu Verna (English) form of Laverne: breath of spring

Luvy (American) spontaneous
Lovey, Luv

Lux (Latin) light
Luxe, Luxee, Luxi, Luxy

Luz (Spanish) lighthearted
Lusa, Luzana, Luzi

Luzille (Spanish) light
Luz, Luzell

Lyanna (English) fierce

Lyanne (Greek) melodious
Liann, Lianne, Lyan, Lyana, Lyaneth, Lyann

Lyawonda (African American) friend
Lyawunda, Lywanda, Lywonda

Lycia (Biblical) place name

Lycoris (Greek) twilight

Lyda (American) unique

Lydda (Biblical) place name

Lydia (Greek) musical; unusual
Lidia, Lidya, Lyddie, Lydie, Lydy

Lydie (Slavic) girl of Lydia

Lyfe (American) life

Lyla (French) island girl
Lila, Lilah, Lile

Lyle (English) strident
Lile

Lymekia (Greek) form of Lydia: musical; unusual
Lymekea

Lynda (Spanish) form of Linda: pretty girl
Lindi, Lynde, Lyndie, Lynn

Lyndsay (Scottish) bright and shining
Lindsay, Lindsey

Lynelle (English) pretty girl; bright as sunshine
Linelle, Lynel, Lynie, Lynn

Lynette (French) small and fresh
Lyn, Lynet, Lynnet, Lynnie

Lynita (English) form of Lynette: small and fresh

Lynn (English) fresh as spring water
Lin, Linn, Linnie, Lyn, Lynne

Lynna (English) by the lake

Lynnaia (English) lake girl

Lynona (American) form of Wynona: firstborn girl

Lynsey (American) form of Lindsay: calming; bright and shining
Linzie, Lyndsey, Lynze, Lynzy

Lynzeen (American) form of Lindsay: calming; bright and shining

Lyonda (American) form of Lynda: pretty girl

Lyra (Greek) musical
Lyre

Lyric (Greek) musical
Lyrec

Lyrics (English) lyrical

Lyris (Greek) plays the lyre
Liris, Lirisa, Lirise

Lys (German) form of Elizabeth: God's promise

Lysa (Hebrew) God-loving
Leesa, Lisa

Lysalette (English) form of Lisette: little Elizabeth

Lysandra (Greek) liberator; she frees others
Lyse, Lysie

Lysanne (Greek) helpful
Lysann

Lysbeth (English) form of Elizabeth: God's promise

Lysett (American) pretty little one
Lyse, Lysette

Lysle (Spanish) pretty

Lyssan (Greek) form of Alexandra: defender of mankind
Liss, Lissan, Lissana, Lissandra, Lyss

Lyssette (English) form of Lisette: little Elizabeth

Lystra (Biblical) place name

Lytanisha (African American) scintillating
Litanisha, Lyta, Lytanis, Lytanish, Lytanishia, Nisa, Nisha

Lyttle (Last name used as first name) small

Lyudmilea (Slavic) beloved

M

Maacah (Biblical) place name

Maarath (Biblical) place name

Mab (Literature) Shakespearean queen of fairies

Mabel (Latin) well-loved
Mabbel, Mabil, Mable, Mabyl, Maybel, Maybie

Mabellee (Asian) beauty

Maben (Welsh) child

Mablee (Welsh) pretty

Macallister (Irish) confident

Macander (Biblical) place name

Macarena (Spanish) name of a dance; blessed
Macarene, Macaria, Macarria, Rena

Macaria (Spanish) blessed
Maca, Macarea, Macarie, Maka

Macey (American) upbeat; happy
Mace, Macie, Macy

Machelle (Hebrew) thinks of God

Mackenzie ✪ ✪ (Irish) leader
Mac, Mackenzee, Mackenzey, Mackenzi, Mackenzy, Mackie, Mackinsey, Mckenzie, McKinsey, McKinzie, MaKenzie

Macress (American) thankful

Mada (American) helpful
Madah, Maida

Madai (Biblical) place name

Madalena (Greek) form of Madeline: strength-giving
Madalayna, Madaleyna, Madelayna, Madelena, Madeleyna, Madelyna

Madalyn ✪ (Greek) high goals
Madelyn

Madchen (German) girl
Madchan, Madchin, Maddchen

Maddie (English) form of Madeline: strength-giving
Mad, Maddee, Maddey, Maddi, Maddy, Mady

Maddox (English) giving
Maddax, Maddee, Maddey, Maddie, Maddux, Maddy

Maddye (English) form of Madeleine: high-minded

Madeleine (French) high-minded
Madelon

Madeleinea (English) form of Madeleine: high-minded

Madeline ✪ (Greek) strength-giving
Madaleine, Maddie, Maddy, Madelene, Madi

Madelyn (Greek) strong woman
Madalyn, Madlynne, Madolyn

Madge (Greek/American) spunky
Madgie, Madg

Madgie (English) form of Madge: spunky; form of Margaret: treasured pearl; pure-spirited

Madhur (Hindi) sweet girl

Madina (Greek) form of Madeline: strength-giving
Mada, Maddelina, Maddi, Maddy, Madele, Madena, Madlin

Madine (American) form of Nadine: dancer

Madis (English) form of Madison: good-hearted

Madison ✿ ❂ (English) good-hearted
Maddie, Maddison, Maddy, Madisen, Madysin

Madlyina (English) form of Madeleine: high-minded

Madonna (Latin) my lady; spirited

Madora (Place name) from Madeira, Spain: volcanic
Madorra

Madrigal (Word as name)

Madrina (Spanish) godmother
Madra, Madreena, Madrine

Madrona (Spanish) mother; maternal
Madrena

Mae (English) bright flower
May

Maegan (Irish) a gem of a woman
Megan

MaElena (Spanish) light
Elena, Lena

Maeli (English) great
Maelee, Maeley, Maelie, Maely, Maylee, Mayley, Mayli, Maylie, Mayly

Maeve (Irish) queen
Maive, Mave, Mayve

Maevey (Irish) exciting

Mafe (Italian) strong

Magadan (Biblical) place name

Magali (French) treasured pearl

Magan (Greek) heavy-hearted
Mag, Magen, Maggie

Magany (Greek) doleful

Magda (Scandinavian) believer
Mag, Maggie

Magdala (Greek) girl in the tower
Magdalla

Magdalene (Greek/Scandinavian) spiritual
Mag, Magda, Magdalena, Magdaline, Magdalyn, Magdelin, Magdylena, Maggie

Magella (Slavic) starry-eyed

Maggie (Greek/English/Irish) priceless pearl
Mag, Maggee, Maggi

Magina (Russian) hardworking
Mageena, Maginah

Magli (French) treasured pearl

Maglie (French) treasured pearl

Magnolia (Latin) flowering and flourishing
Mag, Maggi, Maggie, Maggy, Magnole, Nolie

Magryta (Slavic) desired

Mahal (Filipino) loving woman
Mah, Maha

Mahala (Hebre/Native American) tender female
Mah, Mahalah, Mahalia, Mahla, Mahlie

Mahelia (Arabic) form of Mahala: tender female
Maheelia, Maheelya, Mahelya

Mahina (Hawaiian) moonbeam

Mahira (Hebrew) vibrant

Mahogany (Spanish) rich as wood
Mahagonie, Mahogony

Mahoney (American) high energy
Mahhony, Mahonay, Mahonie, Mahony

Mai (Scandinavian/Japanese) treasure; flower; singular
Mae, May

Maia (Greek) fertile; earth goddess
Maya, Mya

Maida (Greek) shy girl
Mady, Maidie, May, Mayda

Maidie (Scottish) maiden; virgin
Maidee, Maydee, Maydie

Maija (Scandinavian) form of Mary: star of the sea; sea of bitterness

Maike (German) form of Maria: desired child

Mailanna (Hawaiian) lei of Anna

Maileen (Hawaiian) lei

Mailene (Hawaiian) lei

Mailie (Scottish) virtuous

Mainan (American) guesses

Mair (Irish) form of Mary: star of the sea; sea of bitterness
Maire

Maira (Hebrew) bitter; saved
Mara, Marah

Maired (Irish) pearl; treasured
Mairead, Mared

Mairin (Irish) form of Mary: star of the sea; sea of bitterness

Maisha (Arabic) proud

Maisie (Scottish) treasure
Maesee, Maesey, Maesi, Maesie, Maesy, Maisee, Maisey, Maisi, Maisy, Maizie, Mazee

Maitland (American) form of Maitlyn: kind
Maitlande, Mateland, Matelande, Maytland, Maytlande

Maitlin (American) form of Maitlyn: kind
Matelin, Matelyn, Maytlin, Maytlyn

Maj (Slavic) star

Maja (Scandinavian) fertile

Majella (Slavic) star

Majidah (Arabic) slendid

Majula (Slavic) star

Maka (Hawaiian) face

Makala (Hawaiian) natural outdoors
Makal, Makie

Makani (Hawaiian) in the wind

Makay (American) charming

Makayla ✪ ✟ (American) magical
Makaila, Makala, Michaela, Mikaela, Mikayla, Mikaylah

Makeda (African) excellent

Makena (African) wisdom's child

Makkedah (African) lovely

Makula (American) exacting

Makyll (American) innovative
Makell

Makynna (American) friendly
Makenna, Makinna

Malah (Indian) garland
Mala

Malak (Arabic) angelic

Malatha (Biblical) place name

Malati (Indian) jasmine flower

Malay (Place name) from Malaysia; softspoken
Malae

Malaya (Filipino) free and open
Malea

Maleah (Hawaiian) sad

Malendita (Spanish) royal

Malene (Scandinavian) in the tower
Maleen, Maleene, Malyne

Malha (Hebrew) queenlike and regal

Mali (Thai) flowering beauty
Malee, Maley, Malie, Malley, Mallie, Maly

Malia (Hawaiian) thoughtful
Maylia

Maliaval (Hawaiian) peaceful

Malika (Hungarian) hardworking and punctual
Maleeka

Malikian (Hawaiian) of the queen

Malin (Native American) comfort-giver
Malen, Maline, Mallie

Malina (Scandinavian) in the tower
Maleena, Maleenah, Malinah, Malyna, Malynah

Malinda (Greek/American) honey
Melinda

Malinee (American) sweet

Malini (Indian) river

Malisa (English) loyal

Malissa (Greek) honey bee
Melissa

Maliyah (Hawaiian) form of Malia: thoughtful

Malla (Indian) adorned with necklace

Mallika (Indian) watchful; tending the garden
Malika

Mallory (French/German/American) tough-minded; spunky
Mal, Malery, Mallari, Mallery, Mallie, Mallorey, Mallori, Mallorie, Maloree, Malorey, Malori, Malorie, Malory

Malu (Hawaiian) peaceful
Maloo

Malvika (Slavic) darkness

Malvina (Scottish) romantic
Malv, Malva, Malvie, Melvina

Mame (American) form of Margaret: treasured pearl; pure-spirited
Maime, Mayme

Mamie (American) form of Margaret: treasured pearl; pure-spirited
Mamee, Mamey, Mami, Mamy

Manasa (Asian) lovely

Mancie (American) hopeful
Manci, Mansey, Mansie

Manda (American) form of Amanda: fit to be loved
Amand, Mandee, Mandi, Mandy

Mandana (African) combative

Mandeece (African) loved

Mandeen (American) form of Amanda: fit to be loved

Mandia (Indian) beloved

Mandisa (African) kind

Mandy (Latin) lovable
Manda, Mandee, Mandey, Mandi, Mandie

Mane (American) top
Main, Manie

Manee (Korean) peace giving
Mani, Manie

Manessa (Sanskrit) wise

Manilow (Last name as first name) musical

Manisha (Hindi) sharp intellect

Manju (Hindi) sweetheart

Manna (Hawaiian) perceptive
Mana, Manah, Mannah

Manolita (Spanish) girl who lives in God

Manon (French) exciting

Mantae (Slavic) form of Maria: desired child

Mantill (American) guarded
Mant, Mantell, Mantie

Manuela (Spanish) sophisticated girl
Manuella

Manya (Spanish) form of Maria: desired child

Manzie (Native American) flower
Mansi

Mappie (American) zany

Maquila (Spanish) stubborn

Mara (Greek) thoughtful believer
Marah, Marra

Maralys (American) devout

Maranda (Latin) wonderful
Marandah, Miranda

Marat (American) form of Merit: deserving

Marbell (American) pretty

Marbella (Spanish) pretty
Marb, Marbela, Marbelle

Marbury (American) substantial
Mar, Marbary

Marcelina (Latin) form of Marcella: dedicated to Mars
Marceleena, Marcelyna, Marcileena, Marcilina, Marcilyna, Marcyleena

Marceline (Latin) form of Marcella: dedicated to Mars
Marceleene, Marcelline, Marcelyne, Marcileene, Marcilyne, Marcyleene

Marcella (Latin) dedicated to Mars
Marce, Marcela, Marci, Marcie, Marse, Marsella

Marcellette (French) staunch

Marcellita (Spanish) desired; feisty
Marcel, Marcelita, Marcelite, Marcelle, Marcelli, Marcey, Marci

Marcellyn (English) form of Marceline: dedicated to Mars

Marcena (Latin/American) spirited
Marce, Marceen, Marcene, Marcie

March (American) month of March; spring girl

Marcia (Latin/American) dedicated to Mars
Marcie, Marsha

Marciana (Spanish) warring

Marcie (English) chummy
Marcee, Marcey, Marci, Marcy, Marsi, Marsie

Marcine (American) bright
Marceen, Marceene

Marconi (Italian) creates

Marcy (English/American) opinionated
Marci, Marsie, Marsy

Mardi (French) Tuesday

Mardjaneh (Indian) of the meadow

Mardonia (American) approving
Mardee, Mardi, Mardone, Mardonne, Mardy

Mare (American) living by the ocean

Mareane (Irish) form of Mary: star of the sea; sea of bitterness

Marelly (French) form of Mary: star of the sea; sea of bitterness

Maren (American) ocean-lover
Marin, Marren, Marrin

Marenz (Slavic) of the sea

Maret (English) form of Mary: star of the sea; sea of bitterness
Marett, Marit, Maritt, Maryt, Marytt

Marete (English) pearl girl

Marfelia (Spanish) form of Martha: lady

Marfo (Russian) form of Martha: lady

Marg (American) tenacious
Mar

Margaret (Greek/Scottish/English) treasured pearl; pure-spirited
Mag, Maggie, Marg, Margerite, Margie, Margo, Margret, Meg, Meggie

Margaretta (Spanish) pearl

Margarita (Italian/Spanish) winning
Marg, Margarit, Margarite, Margie, Margrita, Marguerita

Margarite (Greek/German) form of Margaret: treasured pearl; pure-spirited
Gretal, Marga, Margareeta, Margaryta, Margereeta, Margerita, Margeryta, Margit, Margot

Margaux (French) form of Margaret: treasured pearl; pure-spirited

Marge (English/American) form of Marjorie: bittersweet; pearl
Marg, Margie

Margery (English) form of Marjorie: bittersweet; pearl
Marge, Margie

Marghanita (Spanish) pearl

Margherita (Italian/Greek) form of Margaret: treasured pearl; pure-spirited
Marg

Margia (American) form of Margie: friendly
Marge, Margea, Margy

Margie (English) friendly
Margey, Margy, Marjie

Margina (American) centered

Margoletta (French) little Margo; spunky

Margot (French) lively
Margaux, Margo

Margrit (Spanish) treasured

Margrita (Spanish) treasure
Margreeta, Margrytaa

Margrite (Dutch) form of Margaret: treasured pearl; pure-spirited

Margrune (Slavic) form of Margaret: treasured pearl; pure-spirited

Marguerite (French) stuffy
Maggie, Marg, Margerite, Margie, Margina, Margurite

Margyd (Welsh) pearl-like

Mari (Japanese) ball; round

Maria ✿
(Latin/French/German/Italian/Polish/Spanish) desired child
Maja, Malita, Mareea, Marica, Marike, Marucha, Mezi, Mitzi

Mariah ✿ (Hebrew) God is my teacher
Marayah, Mariahe, Marriah, Meriah, Moriah

Marial (Spanish) embittered

Mariama (Hebrew) form of Mariam: bitter

Mariamne (French) form of Miriam: living with sadness
Mariam, Marianne

Marian (English) thoughtful
Mariane, Marianne, Maryann, Maryanne

Mariana (Spanish) quiet girl
Maryanna

Marianda (Invented) combo of Mari and Rianda

Maribel (French/English/American) star of the sea; beautiful
EmBee, Marabel, Maribela, Merrybelle

Maricruz (Spanish) Maria of the cross

Marid (English) form of Maria: desired child

Marie (French) form of Mary: star of the sea; sea of bitterness
Maree, Marye

Mariea (English) form of Maria: desired child

Mariel (German) spiritual
Mari, Mariele, Marielle

Mariella (Italian) form of Maria: desired child

Marielos (Spanish) form of Mariel: spiritual

Mariene (Spanish) devout
Mari, Marienne

Mariet (French) form of Marie: star of the sea; sea of bitterness
Mariett, Mariette, Maryet, Maryett, Maryette

Marigene (Dutch) embittered

Marigold (Botanical) sunny
Maragold, Marigolde, Marigole, Marrigold, Marygold, Marygolde

Marijana (Slavic) aggressive

Marijonna (Slavic) aggressive

Marika (Slavic/American) thoughtful and brooding
Mareeca, Mareecka, Mareeka, Marica, Maricka, Maryca, Marycka, Maryka, Merica, Merika, Merk, Merkie

Marikae (Slavic) bitter

Marilan (American) form of Marilyn: fond-spirited

Marilyn (Hebrew) fond-spirited
Maralynne, Mare, Marilin, Mariline, Marilinn, Marilynn, Marrie, Marrilyn, Marylyn, Marylynn, Merilyn, Merrilyn

Marin (Latin) sea-loving
Mare, Maren

Marina (Latin) lover of the ocean
Mareena, Marena, Maryna

Marinaea (American) form of Marin: sea-loving

Marinalla (American) of the sea

Marine (French) of the sea

Marinen (Mythology) sea

Marineuza (Spanish) sea child

Marioara (Indian) delicate

Marion (French) form of Mary: star of the sea; sea of bitterness
Mare, Marien, Marrion, Maryen, Maryian, Maryon

Mariposa (Spanish) butterfly
Mari, Mariposah, Maryposa

Mariquita (Spanish) form of
Margaret: treasured pearl; pure-spirited
Marikita, Marrikita, Marriquita

Maris (Latin) sea-loving
Mere, Meris, Marys

Marisa (Latin) sea-loving
*Marce, Maressa, Marissa, Marisse,
Mariza, Marsie, Marysa, Maryssa,
Merisa*

Marisela (Spanish) hearty
Marisella, Marysela

Mariska (American) endearing
Mareska, Marisca, Mariskah

Marisol (Spanish) stunning
*Mare, Mari, Marizol, Marrisol,
Marzol, Merizol*

Marisse (French) beloved

Maritala (Scandinavian) pearl

Maritel (Scandinavian) pearl

Maritza (Place name) for St. Moritz,
Switzerland

Marixa (Spanish) endearing

Marixbel (Spanish) pretty
Marix

Marizu (Spanish) blessed

Marjetta (Slavic) form of Margaret:
treasured pearl; pure-spirited

Marjie (Scottish) form of Marjorie:
bittersweet; pearl
Marji, Marjy

Marjolein (Dutch) spice

Marjorie (Greek/English/Scottish)
bittersweet; pearl
*Marg, Marge, Margerie, Margery,
Margorie, Marjie, Marjori*

Marketa (Slavic) form of Margaret:
treasured pearl; pure-spirited
Marketta

Marky (American) mischievous
Marki, Markie

Marla (German) believer; easygoing
Marlah, Marlla

Marlaina (American) form of
Marlene: child of light; bitter
Marlaine, Marlane

Marlake (Slavic) of the lake

Marlam (American) wanted

Marlana (Hebrew/Greek) vamp
Marlanna

Marleal (American) form of Mary:
star of the sea; sea of bitterness
Marle, Marleel, Marly

Marlee (Greek) guarded
Marleigh, Marley, Marli, Marlie, Marly

Marlen (American) desired
Marl, Marla, Marlin

Marlena (German) pretty; bittersweet
*Marla, Marlaina, Marleena, Marlina,
Marlyna, Marlynne, Marnie*

Marlene (German) child of light;
bitter
*Marlean, Marlee, Marleen, Marleene,
Marley, Marline, Marly, Marlyne*

Marlette (English) form of Merlette:
magical

Marley (English) form of Marlene:
child of light; bitter
Mar, Marlee, Marlie, Marly

Marliece (Spanish) desirable

Marlinn (German) form of Mary:
star of the sea; sea of bitterness

Marlise (English) considerate
Marlice, Marlis, Marlys

Marlo (American) vivacious
Marloe, Marloh, Marlow, Marlowe

Marlona (German) form of Mary:
star of the sea; sea of bitterness

Marlonene (German) form of Mary:
star of the sea; sea of bitterness

Marluce (German) form of Marlis:
religious

Marlycia (Spanish) desired
Lycia, Marly, Marlysia

Marlys (English) form of Marlis:
religious

Marna (French) form of Marlene: child of light; bitter

Marnelle (Hebrew) form of Marnie: storyteller

Marnie (Hebrew) storyteller
Marn, Marnee, Marney, Marni, Marny

Marnina (French) form of Marlene: child of light; bitter
Marneena, Marnyna

Marnita (American) worrier
Marneta, Marni, Marnite, Marnitta, Marny

Marolyn (Invented) form of Marilyn: fond-spirited
Maro, Marolin, Marolinne

Marqeen (American) form of Marquise: noble-spirited

Marquetisha (Spanish) form of Marquita: happy girl

Marquise (French) noble-spirited
Markeese, Marquees, Marquisa, Mars

Marquisha (African American) form of Marquise: noble-spirited
Marquish

Marquista (Spanish) form of Marquita: happy girl

Marquita (Spanish) happy girl
Marqueda, Marquitta, Marrie

Marquittaian (Spanish) form of Marquita: happy girl

Marrea (American) form of Maria: desired child

Marri (American) form of Mary: star of the sea; sea of bitterness

Marrie (American) form of Mary: star of the sea; sea of bitterness
Marry

Mars (Roman) warring

Marsala (Italian) seaport in Sicily
Marse, Marsela, Marsie

Marschelle (Scottish) form of Marsail: happy

Marselle (Spanish) happy

Marsha (Latin) form of Marcia: dedicated to Mars
Mars, Marsie

Marshay (American) exuberant
Marshae, Marshaya

Marshaye (French) difficult

Marshette (French) difficult

Marta (Danish) treasure
Mart, Marte, Marty, Merta

Martcia (Spanish) unmanageable

Marterrell (American) changeable
Marte, Marterill, Martrell

Martha (Aramaic) lady
Marta, Marth, Marti, Marty, Mattie

Marthe (Aramaic) ladylike

Marti (English) form of Martha: lady
Martee, Martey, Martie, Marty

Martijn (Dutch) unmanageable

Martina (Latin/German) combative
Marteena, Martene, Marti, Martinna, Martyna, Tina

Martine (French) combative

Martivanio (Italian) form of Martina: combative
Mart, Marti, Tivanio

Martonette (American) feminine form of Martin: warlike
Martanette, Martinette, Martonett

Martreece (American) unmanageable

Marty (English) form of Martha: lady
Marti

Maruja (Slavic) soft heart

Marusya (Slavic) softhearted

Marvel (French) astounding; marvelous

Marvella (French) marvelous woman
Marva, Marvelle, Marvie, Mavela

Marvis (American) form of Mavis: singing bird

Marwyn (Welsh) beautiful

Mary ✪ (Latin/Hebrew) star of the sea; sea of bitterness
Maire, Mara, Mare, Maree, Mari, Marie, Mariel, Marlo, Marye, Merree, Merry, Mitzie

Marya (Arabic) white and bright
Marja

Maryam (Arabic) form of Miriam: living with sadness

Maryann (English) form of Mary: star of the sea; sea of bitterness
Mariann, Marianne, Maryan, Maryanne

Maryina (Spanish) little Mary

Maryke (Dutch) kind; desired
Mairek, Marika, Maryk, Maryky

Mary-Marg (American) dramatic
Marimarg

Maryon (American) form of Marian: thoughtful

Marzel (Italian) form of Marzia: star of the sea; sea of bitterness

Marzia (Italian) form of Mary: star of the sea; sea of bitterness

Marzol (Spanish) form of Marisol: stunning

Masailda (American) supportive

Masha (Russian) child who was desired

Mashayl (Slavic) form of Mary: star of the sea; sea of bitterness; form of Masha: child who was desired

Mashella (Slavic) form of Mary: star of the sea; sea of bitterness; form of Masha: child who was desired

Mashonda (African American) believer
Masho, Mashonde

Masi (African) star

Masina (Last name as first) charming; delightful

Mason (French) diligent; reliable

Massey (German) confident
Massi, Massie

Massiel (American) giving
Masie, Masiel, Massey, Massielle

Massim (Latin) great
Massima, Maxim, Maxima

Matia (Hebrew) a God-given gift
Matea, Mattea, Mattie

Matild (Hungarian) strong

Matilda (German) powerful fighter
Mat, Mathilda, Mattie, Tilda, Tillie, Tilly

Matina (Scandinavian) morning child

Matney (American) born in the morning

Mattanah (Biblical) place name; God's child

Mattie (English) most honored
Matt, Matte, Mattey, Matti, Matty

Matus (Slavic) essential

Matusea (Slavic) essential

Matylda (Polish) strong fighter
Matyld

Maude (English) old-fashioned
Maud, Maudie

Maudeen (American) countrified
Maudie, Mawdeen, Mawdine

Maudella (English) mighty

Maudest (French) modest

Maudette (English) mighty

Maudisa (African) sweet
Maudesa, Maudesah

Mauline (English) strong

Mauna (American) attractive
Maune, Mawna, Mon

Maupassant (French) writes

Maura (Latin/Irish) dark
Moira, Maurie

Mauree (Spanish) dark

Maureen (Irish/French) night-loving
Maura, Maurene, Maurine, Moreen, Morene

Maureena (Irish) form of Mary: star of the sea; sea of bitterness

Maurelle (French) petite
Maure, Maurie, Maurielle

Mauricea (Spanish) form of Mary: star of the sea; sea of bitterness

Maurilia (Spanish) dark beauty

Maurise (French) dark
Maurice, Morise

Maurshia (Slavic) form of Marsha: dedicated to Mars

Mauve (French) gentle
Mauvey, Mauvie

Mave (French) bird; melodic

Mavi (French) sings

Mavis (French) singing bird
Mauvis, Mav, Mave

Maxcie (English) best

Maxcien (English) best

Maxeeme (Latin) form of Maxime:
maximum

Maxence (English) best

Maxie (Latin) fine
Maxee, Maxey, Maxy

Maxien (English) best

Maxilla (English) best

Maxime (Latin) maximum
Maxey, Maxi, Maxim

Maxine (Latin) greatest of all
Max, Maxeen, Maxene, Maxie, Maxy

May (English) the fifth month
Mae, Maye

Maya ☻ (Spanish/Hindi/Russian)
industrious; one of a kind; bitter
Maia, Maiya, Mayah, Mya, Myah, Mye

Mayada (English) form of May: the
fifth month

Maybelline (Latin) variation of
Mabel: well-loved
*Mabie, May, Maybeline, Maybie,
Maybleene*

Maybelyn (Spanish) form of Mabel:
well-lovedl

Mayeta (Native American) fruitful

Mayghaen (American) fortunate

Mayim (Origin unknown) special
Mayum

Maykaylee (American) ingenious
Maykayli, Maykaylie, Maykayly

Mayo (Place name) a county in
Ireland; vibrant
Mayoh

Mayphous (American) imaginative

Mayra (Spanish) flourishing; creative
Mayrah

Mayrallea (Spanish) form of May:
the fifth month

Mayrant (Spanish) industrious
Maya, Mayrynt

Maytra (English) form of Myra:
fragrant

Mayuri (Indian) hen

Mayya (Slavic) lovely

Mazeka (Slavic) form of May: the
fifth month

Mazel (Hebrew) luck
Masel, Mazil, Mazal

Mazella (English) form of May: the
fifth month

Mazen (English) form of May: the
fifth month

Mazie (Scottish) form of Maisie: treasure

Mazu (Chinese) goddess of the sea

McCanna (American) ebullient
Maccanna, McCannah

McCauley (Irish) feisty
Mac, McCauly, McCawlie

McCay (Irish) creative
Mackaylee, McCaylee

McCormick (Irish) last name as first
name
MacCormack, Mackey

McGown (Irish) sensible
Mac, MacGowen, Mackie, McGowen

McKenna (American) able
Mackenna, Makenna

McKenzie (Scottish) form of
Mackenzie: leader
Mackie, McKinzie, Mickey

McMurtry (Irish) last name as first
name
Mac, McMurt

Mead (Greek) honey-wine-loving
Meade, Meed, Meede

Meadhoh (Irish) joyful

Meador (Irish) righteous; form of the
meadow

Meadow (English) open land; calm

Meadoh

Meagan (Irish) joyous; precious

Maegan, Meaghan, Meegan, Meg,

Meganne, Meggie, Meggye, Meghan

Meagara (Mythology) first

Meanda (Invented) models

Meanne (American) models

Meara (Irish) happy girl

Meashley (American) charmer

Meash, Meashlee

Meatah (American) athletic

Mea, Mia, Miata, Miatah

Meatra (American) models

Meave (Irish) sings

Mecjhelle (Slavic) form of Michelle:
like the Lord

Mecoline (American) form of
Nicole: winning

Medal (Word as name)

Medalla (Spanish) lovely

Medalle (American) pretty

Medahl, Medoll

Medardo (Spanish) pretty

Medea (Greek) ruling; cruel

Medeia

Medeba (Biblical) place name

Medes (Biblical) place name

Media (Greek) form of Medea:
ruling; cruel

Mediatrix (Greek) ingenious

Medilyn (American) gift

Medina (Place name)

Medisyn (American) gift

Medusa (Greek) contriver; temptress

Medy (American) gift

Meeleen (Irish) excites

Meena (Hindi) fish

Meeno (Sanskrit) form of Meena: fish

Meera (Hindi) rich

Meg (Greek) able; lovable

Megs

Megan ♀ ♂ (Irish) precious; joyful

Meagan, Meaghen, Meggi, Meghan,

Meghann

Meggie (Greek) best

Meggey, Meggi, Meggy

Megha (Indian) cloudy; (Welsh)
pearl

Meghan (Welsh) pearl

Meghen, Meghyn

Mehetabel (Hebrew) won by faith

Mehitabel

Mehul (Hindi) rain girl

Meirion (Hebrew) light

Meissa (Hindi) form of Mesha: born
in lunar month; moon-loving

Meisa, Meysa, Meyssa

Mejia (Slavic) flowers

Mekeba (Invented) jubilant

Mel (Greek) sporty

Mell

Melada (Greek) form of Melanie:
dark; sweet

Mel, Melli

Melaina (Greek) dark; generous

Melana (Greek) giving; dark

Melancon (French) dark beauty; sweet

Mel, Melance, Melaney, Melanie,

Melanse, Melanson, Melonce,

Melonceson

Melangel (Welsh) darling angel

Melania (Italian) giving;
philanthropic

Mel, Melly

Melanie ♀ (Greek) dark; sweet

Melanee, Melaney, Melani, Melany,

Meleni, Melenie, Meleny

Melanna (Greek) dark

Melantha (Greek) dark-skinned; sweet

Melanthah

Melaynee (Greek) dark; sweet

Melb (Greek) mellow

Melba (Australian) talented; lighthearted

Melbah

Melbal (Greek) mellow

Melea (German) diligent

Melecio (Spanish) mild

Meleda (Spanish) sweet

Meleeda, Melida, Melyda

Melete (Greek) effective

Melezio (Spanish) mild

Melia (German) dedicated

Meelia, Meleea, Melya, Melyah

Melicent (English) form of

Millicent: soft-hearted

Melisent

Melina (Greek) honey; sweet

Meleena, Melena, Melinah, Melyna

Melinane (Greek) honey sweetness

Melinda (Latin) honey; sweetheart

Linda, Linnie, Linny, Lynda, Mellie,

Melynda, Milinda, Mindy, Mylinde

Melisande (French) strong

Melisenda

Meliss (American) honey bee

Melissa (Greek) honey

Melisa, Melysa, Melyssa, Melyssuh

Melita (Biblical) place name

Melitene (Biblical) place name

Melize (English) nymph; bee

Melizza (English) form of Melissa:

honey

Mellicent (German) form of

Millicent: soft-hearted

Melicent, Mellycent, Melycent

Mellie (Greek) bee; busy

Mellony (English) form of Melanie:

dark; sweet

Melnie (English) dark

Melody (Greek) song; musical

Mel, Mellie, Melodee, Melodey, Melodie

Melona (English) dark

Meloney (American) form of

Melanie: dark; sweet

Mel, Melone, Meloni

Melora (Latin) good

Meliora, Melorah, Melourah

Melosa (Greek) form of Melissa: honey

Melossa

Melotta (English) form of Melissa:

honey

Melrose (English) honey of roses;

sweet girl

Mellrose, Melrosie

Melua (Unknown) rising

Melusine (Mythology) honey bee

Melvia (American) leader; dark

Mel, Mell, Melvea

Melvina (Irish) prepared to lead

Malvina

Mena (Egyptian) pretty

Meenah, Menah

Menaka (Indian) heavenly girl

Mencina (Place name) serious

Mendee (American) form of

Melinda: honey; sweetheart

Meng (Asian) shines

Mengline (Asian) shines

Menon (French) form of Mariel:

spiritual

Menzalah (Biblical) place name

Meosha (African American) talented

Meeosha, Meoshe, Miosha

Merah (Biblical) abundant

Merary (American) merry

Marary, Meraree, Merarie

Mercadel (Spanish) mirth

Merce (Asian) merciful

Mercedes (Spanish) merciful;

rewarded

Mercedez, Mercides, Mersadez,

Mersaydes

Mercer (English) mercy

Mercia (English) form of Marcia:

dedicated to Mars

Mercilite (American) mercy

Mercy (English) forgiving

Merce, Mercee, Mercey, Merci, Mercie

Meredith (Welsh) protector

Mer, Meredithe, Meredyth, Merridith,

Merry, Merydith, Merydithe

Meredythe (English) excellent

Merel (Scandinavian) sea

Meri (Irish) by the sea

Merrie

Meria (Scandinavian) sea

Meribah (Biblical) place name

Meridian (American) perfect posture

Meredian, Meridiane

Merie (French) secretive; blackbird

Mer, Meri, Myrie

Meriel (Irish) girl who shines like the sea

Meri, Merial, Merri, Merriyl, Merry

Meris (Latin) form of Merissa: ocean-loving

Meriss, Merris, Merrys, Merys

Merissa (Latin) ocean-loving

Merisa, Meryssa

Merit (American) deserving

Merite, Meritt, Meritte, Meryt, Merytt, Mirit

Merithian (American) sea girl

Merka (Slavic) connives

Merle (Irish) shining girl

Merl, Murl, Murle

Merlette (English) magical

Merlin (English) magical

Merlina (English) magical

Merlyn (Spanish) sea child

Merney (American) form of Marnie: storyteller

Merolina (American) form of Carolina: well-loved

Merom (Biblical) place name

Meroth (Biblical) place name

Merribeth (English) cheerful

Merri-Beth, Merrybeth

Merridy (American) form of Meredith: protector

Merrience (American) merry child

Merrill (Irish) shines

Merril

Merry (English) cheerful

Mer, Meri, Merie, Merree, Merrey, Merri, Merrie, Mery

Mersaydes (Invented) form of Mercedes: merciful; rewarded

Mercy, Mersa, Mersy

Mersey (English) river Mersey; rich

Merce, Merse

Mersia (Hebrew) princess

Mercy, Mers, Mersea, Mersy

Mertha (American) joyful

Mertie (American) famed

Meryl (Irish) shining sea

Mer, Merel, Merri, Merrill, Merryl, Meryll

Meryletta (American) form of Mary: star of the sea; sea of bitterness

Merylette (American) form of Mary: star of the sea; sea of bitterness

Merynda (American) form of Marin: sea-loving

Merzi (American) mercy

Mesa (Place name) earthy

Mase, Maysa, Mesah

Mesembria (Biblical) place name

Mesha (Hindi) born in lunar month; moon-loving

Meshah

Meshalle (French) leader

Meshawnda (Invented) oblivious

Meshelle (French) leader

Messana (Biblical) place name

Meta (Scandinavian) form of Margaret: treasured pearl; pure-spirited

Metchie (Scandinavian) odd

Metta (Scandinavian) unique

Meverly (American) form of Beverly: beavers by the stream; friendly

Mexill (Invented) self-involved

Mhari (Scottish) form of Mary: star of the sea; sea of bitterness

Mhairi

Mi (Chinese) obsessive

My, Mye

Mia ✪ (Scandinavian/Italian) blessed; girl of mine

Me, Mea, Meah, Meea, Meya, Mya

Miaka (Japanese) influential

Mialinda (Italian) my sweet beauty

Miami (Place name)

Miano (Italian) my sweet

Micaela (Italian) form of Michael: like the Lord

Micah (Hebrew) religious
Mica, Mika, My, Myca

Micala (Hebrew) form of Michaela: God-loving
Micalah, Michala, Michalah, Mikala, Mikalah, Mycala, Mycalah, Mychala, Mychalah, Mykala, Mykalah

Michaela (Hebrew) God-loving
Meeca, Micaela, Micela, Michael, Michal, Michala, Michalla, Michela, Mikaela, Mikala, Mikela, Mycaela, Mycela, Mychaela, Mychela, Mykaela, Mykela

Michaele (Hebrew) loving God

Michaeleen (Italian) feminine form of Michael: like the Lord

Michaelena (Italian) feminine form of Michael: like the Lord

Michelin (American) lovable
Michalynn, Mish, Mishelin

Micheline (French) form of Michelle: like the Lord
Mishelinne

Michelle ☺
(Italian/French/American) feminine form of Michael: like the Lord
Machele, Machelle, Mechele, Mia, Michell, Michele, Mischel, Mischell,

Mischelle, Mish, Mishell, Mishelle

Mickellette (Slavic) feminine form of Michael: like the Lord

Mickey (American) quirky
Mick, Mickee, Micki, Micky, Miki, Mikie, Mycki

Mickley (American) form of Mickey: quirky
Mick, Mickaella, Micklee, Mickli, Miklea, Miklee, Mikleigh, Mikley, Myk, Mykkie

Mid (American) middle child
Middi, Middy

Middy (American) middle

Midge (English) form of Margaret: treasured pearl; pure-spirited

Midian (Biblical) place name

Mie (Dutch) form of Mary: star of the sea; sea of bitterness

Mienna (Dutch) form of Mary: star of the sea; sea of bitterness

Migdaluy (Spanish) form of Miguel; form of Michael: like the Lord

Mignon (French) cute
Migonette, Mim, Mimi, Minyon, Minyonne

Migon (American) precious
Mignonne, Migonette, Migonn, Migonne

Mika (Hebrew) wise and pious
Micah, Mikah, Mikie

Mikaela (Hebrew) God-loving
Mik, Mikayla, Mike, Mikhaila, Miki

Mikan (Slavic) child of God

Mikelle (Slavic) loves God

Mikenzi (American) form of Mackenzie: leader

Mila (Russian; Italian) form of Camilla: wonderful
Milah, Milla, Millah, Mimi

Milagros (Spanish) miracle
Mila, Milagro

Milana (Slavic) hospitable

Milandi (Italian) form of Milan: city in Italy; smooth

Milantia (Panamanian) calm
Mila

Milcah (Biblical) direct

Milda (Slavic) love goddess

Mildred (English) gentle
Mil, Mildread, Mildrid, Millie, Milly

Mildredena (Slavic) favorite

Milena (Greek) loving girl
Mela, Mili, Milina

Miley (Invented) form of Smiley: radiant

Miliani (Hawaiian) one who caresses
Mil, Mila

Milind (Slavic) favorite

Milinea (Slavic) favorite

Milissa (Greek) softspoken
Melissa, Missy

Miliulva (Slavic) loved

Milla (Polish) gentle; pure
Mila, Millah

Millay (Literature) for poet Edna St.
Vincent Millay; soft

Millea (English) mild

Millice (French) favored

Millicent (Greek/German)
softhearted
*Melicent, Melly, Milicent, Millie,
Millisent, Milly, Millycent, Milycent,
Missy*

Millie (English) form of Mildred:
gentle and Millicent: soft-hearted
Mil, Mili, Millee, Milley, Milli, Milly

Millimaci (Spanish) softhearted

Milu (Asian) lovely

Mim (American) form of Miriam:
living with sadness
Mimm, Mym, Mymm

Mima (Burmese) feminine

Mimi (French) form of Camilla:
wonderful
Meemee, Mim, Mims, Mimsie

Mimosa (Botanical) sensitive; tree

Min (Chinese) sensitive; softhearted

Mina (German/Polish) resolute
protector; willful
*Meena, Mena, Min, Minah, Myna,
Mynah*

Minal (German) kind

Minda (American) form of Melinda:
honey; sweetheart; (Hindi) wise

Minden (American) form of
Melinda: honey; sweetheart

Mindy (Greek) form of Melinda:
honey; sweetheart
*Mindee, Mindey, Mindi, Mindie,
Myndee, Myndi*

Minelle (English) pretty

Minerv (English) form of Minerva:
bright; strong

Minerva (Latin/Greek) bright; strong
Menerva, Min, Minnie, Myn

Minette (French) loyal woman
Min, Minnette, Minnie

Mineya (American) form of Minerva:
bright; strong

Ming (Chinese) shiny; hope of
tomorrow

Minhtu (Asian) light and clear

Mini (Scandinavian) mine

Miniver (English) assertive
Meniver, Minever, Miniverr

Minn (German) form of Minnie:
bright; strong

Minna (German) sturdy
Mina, Minnie, Mynna

Minnae (American) form of Minnie:
bright; strong

Minnie (German) form of Minerva:
bright; strong
Mini, Minni, Minny

Minnifer (American) form of
Jennifer: white wave

Minstie (American) amiable

Minsue (Asian) paradise

Minta (English) memorable
Minty

Mira (Latin/Spanish) wonderful girl
Meara, Mirror

Mirabel (Latin) marvelous; beautiful
reflection
Marabelle, Mira, Mirabell, Mirabelle

Mirabella (Italian) marvelous
*Mira, Mirabell, Mirabellah, Mirabelle,
Myrabell, Myrabelle*

Miracle (American) miracle baby
Merry, Mira, Mirakle, Mirry

Miraflor (Spanish) flower girl

Miranda (Latin) unique and amazing
*Maranda, Meranda, Mira, Mirrie,
Myranda*

Mirella (Spanish) wonderful
*Mira, Mirel, Mirela, Mirell, Mirelle,
Myrela, Myrella*

Mirelle (Latin) wonder
Mirell, Myrell, Myrelle

Mireya (Hebrew) form of Miriam: living with sadness

Mireyli (Spanish) wondrous; admirable
Mire, Mirey

Miri (Gypsy) bittersweet
Meeri, Miree, Mirey, Mirie, Miry

Miriam (Hebrew) living with sadness
Mariam, Maryam, Meriam, Miri, Miriame, Miriem, Mirriam, Miryam, Miryem, Mitzi, Myriam, Myriem, Myryam, Myryem

Mirinse (American) form of Marin: sea-loving

Mirit (English) form of Merit: deserving
Miritt, Miryt, Mirytt

Mirka (Polish) glorious
Mira, Mirk

Mirtha (Greek) burdened
Meert, Meerta, Mirt, Mirta

Mirthe (Dutch) mirth

Miryana (American) form of Mariana: quiet girl

Mischanna (Hebrew) form of Miriam: living with sadness
Misch, Mischana, Mish, Mishanna, Mishke

Miselsa (Spanish) form of Michael: like the Lord

Misha (Russian) feminine form of Michael: like the Lord
Mischa

Mishelene (French) form of Micheline: like the Lord
Mish, Mishlene

Mishna (Slavic) form of Misha; like the Lord

Missy (English) form of Melissa: honey
Miss, Missee, Missey, Missi, Missie

Misty (English) dreamy
Miss, Missy, Mistee, Mistey, Misti, Mistie, Mysti

Misty-Kyd (American) child in the mist

Mistyne (American) form of Misty: dreamy

Mita (Slavic) the day

Mitola (American) hopeful

Mitri (American) feminine form of Dimitri: fertile; flourishing

Mitten (American) cuddly
Mitt, Mittun, Mitty

Mittie (American) form of Matilda: fighter and Mitten: cuddly
Mittee, Mittey, Mitti, Myttie

Mitylene (Biblical) place name

Mitzi (German) dancer
Mitsee, Mitzee, Mitzie, Mitzy

Miya (Japanese) peaceful as a temple
Miyah

Mizpah (Biblical) place name

Mnemosyne (Greek) goddess of memory

Mo (Irish) form of Maureen: night-loving

Moana (Hawaiian) from the ocean

Mobley (Last name as first name) beauty queen
Moblee, Mobli, Moblie, Mobly

Mocha (Arabic) coffee with chocolate
Mo, Moka, Mokka

Modena (American) modest

Modesty (Latin) modest
Modesti, Modestie

Modestyne (French) modest
Modestine, Modie

Moema (Native American) sweetness

Moeshea (African American) talented
Moesha, Moeesha, Moeshia, Moisha, Mosha, Moysha

Mohana (Hindi) enchants; siren

Mohini (Indian) bewitches

Moina (Hawaiian) ocean-loving
Moyna

Moira (English/Irish) pure; great one

Maura, Moir, Moirah, Moire, Moyrah

Moire (Irish) great girl

Moirin (Irish) excellent

Mokysha (African American) dramatic

Kisha, Kysha, Mokesha, Mokey

Moladah (Biblical) place name

Moll (Literature) for Daniel Defoe's

Moll Flanders; outgoing

Mol, Molly

Mollo (Italian) form of Molly: jovial

Molly ✪ (Irish) jovial

Moli, Moll, Molley, Molli, Mollie

Momo (Japanese) peaches

Mona (Greek) form of Ramona:

beautiful protector

Monah, Mone

Monael (American) form of Monet:

artistic

Moncita (Spanish) alone

Monday (American) born on

Monday; hopeful

Mondae

Mondra (American) of the world

Monecha (English) alone

Moneek (Invented) form of

Monique: saucy; advisor

Moneeke

Monet (French) artistic

Mon, Monae, Monay

Monge (Spanish) thoughtful

Monica (Greek) seeking company of

others

Mon, Mona, Monicka, Monika,
Monike, Monique

Monicke (Spanish) form of

Monique: saucy; advisor

Monika (Polish) advisor

Monina (American) alone

Monique (French) saucy; advisor

Mon, Mone, Monee, Moneeqe,
Moneeque, Moni, Moniqe

Monita (Spanish) regal

Monroe (Last name as first) orderly

Monro, Monrow, Monrowe

Monserrat (Latin) tall

Monserat

Montana (Place name) U.S. state

Montayna, Montie, Monty

Montenia (Spanish) climber

Monte, Montenea, Montynia

Montoyia (Spanish) of the mountain

Monya (American) confident

Mon, Monyeh

Monyka (American) moon

Moon (American) dreamy

Monnie, Moone, Moonee, Mooney,
Moonny, Moonnye

Moon Unit (Invented) universal

appeal

Moon-Unit

Moonbeam (American) moon child

Moonbee (American) moon bee

Moonstone (American) gemstone

Mor (Irish) sweet

Mora (Spanish) sweet as a blueberry

Morag (Scottish) goddess

Morrag

Moraima (Spanish) forgiving

Mora, Morama

Moran (French) dark

Morayma (Spanish) lovely; forgiving

More (American) bonus

Moore, Morie

Moreen (English) good friend

Moreh (Biblical) place name

Morena (Irish) dark

Moreshath (Biblical) place name

Morettlia (American) royal

Morgan ✪ ♂ (Welsh) girl on the

seashore

Mor, Morey, Morgane, Morgannna,
Morgen, Morgyn

Morgander (American) soft-spoken;

divine

Moriah (French/Hebrew) dark girl; God-taught
Mareyeh, Mariah, Moorea, More, Moria, Morie, Morria, Morya

Morigan (Mythology) queenly

Morimasa (Asian) mermaid

Morimosa (Spanish) mermaid

Morine (American) form of Maureen: night-loving
Morri

Morinette (Irish) lush mane

Moritza (Place name) St. Moritz, Switzerland

Morla (American) form of Marla: believer; easygoing
Morley, Morly

Morna (French) dark

Morta (Mythological) one of the Roman Fates; the cutter

Morteza (Spanish) mortal

Morven (American) magical
Morvee, Morvey, Morvi

Morwenna (Welsh) seamaiden
Mo, Morwen

Morwyn (Welsh) maiden
Morwen, Morwenn, Morwynn, Morwynna

Moselle (Hebrew) uplifted
Mose, Mozelle, Mozie

Motumia (African) desirable

Mouna (Arabic) wanted

Moxie (American) determined

Moya (Scandinavian) mother
Moiya, Moy

Moyra (Irish) excellent

Mrina (Indian) lotus girl

Muadhnait (Irish) little noble girl

Mudeana (Spanish) glowing

Mudiwa (African) beloved
Mudewa

Muirne (Irish) affectionate

Muna (Arabic) hopes
Moona

Munashe (African) believer

Mundee (Irish) in demand

Munder (American) in demand

Mundy (Irish) in demand

Munira (Irish) wishful

Murali (Irish) seagoing

Murdina (Slavic) dark spirit
Murdi, Murdine

Mureann (Irish) pale

Mureen (Irish) form of Muriel: shining

Muriel (Celtic) shining
Meriel, Mur, Murial, Muriele, Muriell, Murielle, Muryel, Muryell, Muryelle

Murieliette (Irish) little Muriel; of the sea

Murieline (French) form of Muriel: shining

Murla (American) form of Merle: shining girl

Murle (American) form of Merle: shining girl

Murleance (American) blackbird; secretive

Murma (American) whispers

Murphy (Irish) spirited
Murphee, Murphey, Murphi, Murphie

Murray (Last name as first name) brisk
Muray, Murraye

Musa (African) child; muse

Musetta (French) instrument; musical
Museta

Musette (French) instrument; musical
Musett

Musique (French) musical
Museek, Museke, Musik

Mussie (American) musical
Muss, Mussi, Mussy

Muthanna (Biblical) gifted

Muyka (American) form of Michael: like the Lord

Mwazi (Israeli) type of fig

My (Scandinavian) dear

Myalinda (American) my beauty

Myana (American) my Ana

Myeshande (American) my Shande

Myeshia (African American) giving

Meyeshia, Mye, Myesha

Myfanwy (Welsh) water baby

Myisha (American) form of Moesha:

talented

Mykala (Scandinavian) giving

Mykaela, Mykela, Mykie

Mykelle (American) generous

Mykell

Mykenya (American) form of

Michaela: like the Lord

Myla (English) forgiving

Miela, Mylah

Mylee (American) forgives

Mylene (Greek) dark-skinned girl

Myleen

Mylie (German) forgiving

Miley, Mylee, Myli

Myliki (Mythology) changeable

Myna (English) talkative

Mina, Minah

Myndee (American) form of

Melinda: honey; sweetheart

Mynola (Invented) smart

Minola, Monoa, Mynolla, Mynolle

Myra (Latin) fragrant

Mira, Myrah

Myralette (American) form of Myra:

fragrant

Myreka (American) form of Myra:

fragrant

Myriam (French) bittersweet life

Myrisa (Spanish) fragrant

Myrischa (African American)

fragrant doll

Myresha, Myri, Myrish, Myrisha, Rischa

Myrna (Irish) loved

Merna, Mirna, Murna

Myrnatte (Irish) adored

Myrtle (Greek) loving

Mertle, Mirtle, Myrt, Myrtie

Mysha (Russian) form of Misha: like

the Lord

Mischa, Mish, Mysh

Mysta (Invented) mysterious

Mista, Mystah

Mystique (French) intriguing

woman

Mistie, Mistik, Mistique, Misty, Mystica

Myteen (American) girl

Mythi (American) loved

Mythiah (American) loved

Mythili (Slavic) most

N

Naama (Hebrew) sweet

Naamah, Naamit

Naamah (Biblical) sweet

Nanay, Nayamah, Naynay

Naarah (Aramaic) bright light

Naara

Naava (Hebrew) delightful girl

Naavah, N'Ava

Nabiha (Arabic) noble

Naihah

Nabila (Arabic) noble

Nabeela, Nabilah, Nabilia

Nabulungi (African) of nobility

Nacarena (Spanish) reborn

Nacey (Spanish) born

Nachaka (African) born leader

Naci (Spanish) born

Nada (Arabic) morning dew; giving

Nadaka (American) gives

Nadara (American) gives

Nadasen (American) gives

Nadelie (American) form of Natalie:

born on Christmas

Nadey

Nadeline (Invented) born on

Christmas

Nad, Nadelyne

Nadera (Indian) gives

Nadette (French) darling girl

Nadezda (Russian) hopeful
Nadeia

Nadia (Slavic) hopeful
Nada, Nadea, Nadeen, Nadene, Nadi, Nadie, Nadina, Nadine, Nady

Nadidaa (Slavic) hopes
Nadidah

Nadine (Russian/French) dancer
Nadeen, Nadene, Nadie, Nadyne, Naidyne

Nadinia (Slavic) optimist

Nadira (Arabic) precious gem
Nadirah, Nadra

Nadya (Russian) optimistic; life's beginnings

Nadyan (Hebrew) pond; reflective
Nadian

Nadzieja (Greek) water nymph
Nadzia, Nata, Natia, Natka

Naeemah (African) breathtaking

Nafisa (Arabic) treasure

Nafshiya (Persian) precious girl

Nagara (Indian) flourishes

Nagida (Hebrew) thrives
Nagia, Nagiah, Nagiya, Najiah, Najiya, Najiyah, Negida

Nagisa (Japanese) from the shore

Nahara (Aramaic) light
Nehara, Nehora

Nahida (Hebrew) rich
Nahid

Nahla (Arabic) succeeds

Nahtanha (African) warm

Nai (Japanese) intelligent
Nayah

Naia (Hawaiian) water nymph

Naida (Greek) nymph-like
Naiad, Naya, Nayad, Nyad

Nailah (African) successful
Naila

Naimah (Arabic) happy
Naeemah, Naima

Naimaina (American) sweet

Naja (Greek) form of Nadia: hopeful

Najat (Arabic) safe
Nagat

Najiba (Arabic) safe
Nagiba, Nagibah, Najibah

Najla (Arabic) large-eyed

Najwa (Arabic) confidante
Nagwa

Nakecia (American) pure

Nakeya (Arabic) pure

Nakeylia (American) pure

Nakia (Arabic) purest girl
Nakea

Nakita (Russian) precocious
Nakeeta, Nakeita, Nakya, Naquita, Nikita

Nala (African) loved
Nalah, Nalo

Nalani (Hawaiian) calming
Nalanie, Nalany

Nalin (Native American) serene maiden

Nalinee (Indian) lotus girl
Nalini

Nalini (American) form of Nalani: calming

Nallely (Spanish) friend
Nalelee, Naleley, Nallel

Nalukea (Hawaiian) sky girl

Nami (Japanese) rides a wave
Namiko

Namisha (African) content with life

Namono (African) twin

Nampeyo (Native American) female snake; sly
Nampayo, Nampayu

Namrata (Indian) demure

Nan (German/Scottish/English) bold; graceful
Na, Nana, Nannie, Nanny

Nana (Hebrew) form of Ann: loving; hospitable

Nanabah (Hebrew) form of Ann: loving; hospitable

Nanala (Hebrew) form of Ann: loving; hospitable

Nanalie (American) form of Natalie: born on Christmas
Nan, Nana, Nanalee

Nance (American) giving
Nans

Nancy (English/Irish) generous woman
Nan, Nancee, Nanci, Nancie, Nansee, Nonie

Nandana (Hindi) delightful; challenges
Nandini, Nandita

Nandini (Indian) gives happiness

Nanek (Hebrew) form of Nancy: generous woman
Naneka, Naneki, Naneta

Nanette (French) giving and gracious
Nanet

Nani (Greek) charming beauty
Nan, Nannie

Nanice (American) open-hearted
Nan, Naneece, Naneese, Naniece

Nanie (Hawaiian) charismatic beauty

Nanise (American) form of Nan: bold; graceful

Nanna (Scandinavian) brave
Nana

Nanon (French) slow to anger
Nan, Nanen

Nanvah (African) God's gift; an infant

Nao (Japanese) truthful; pleasing

Naola (American) form of Naomi: beautiful woman

Naoma (Hebrew) lovely

Naomi (Hebrew) beautiful woman
Naoma, Naomia, Naomie, Naomy, Naynay, Nene, Neoma, Noami, Noemi, Noemie, Noma, Nomah, Nomi

Naone (Hawaiian) fragrant

Naora (Native American) happy

Naoya (Asian) happy

Nara (Greek/Japanese) happy; dreamy
Narah, Nera

Narbata (Biblical) place name

Narbona (Spanish) place name

Narcedalia (Spanish) dark flower

Narcisista (Spanish) self-absorbed

Narcissa (Greek) narcissistic
Narcisa, Narcisse, Narkissa, Nars

Narcisse (French) self-absorbed

Narcissie (Greek) conceited; daffodil
Narci, Narcis, Narcissa, Narcisse, Narcissey, Narsee, Narsey, Narsis

Narcy (French) self-absorbed

Narda (Latin) fragrant

Narelle (Australian) of the sea

Narendara (Indian) form of Narendra, man of Indra: god of thunder and rain; powerful

Naresha (Hindi) ruler; wise

Nari (Japanese) thunders loudly

Narilla (Gypsy) boisterous
Narrila, Narrilla

Naroline (American) form of Caroline: little; womanly

Narses (American) self-absorbed

Nartlyn (American) self-conscious

Nasaria (Spanish) miracle

Nascha (Native American) owl; watchful

Naseem (Hindi) breezy

Nasha (Spanish) miracle

Nashae (American) miracle

Nashan (Origin unknown) miracle child

Nashota (Native American) second twin

Nasia (Hebrew) miraculous child
Naseea, Naseeah, Nasiah, Nasya, Nasyah

Nasnan (Native American) miracle child; mystical

Naspa (Hebrew) form of Nasia: miraculous child
Nasya

Nasrin (Hindi) wild rose
Nasreen

Nastasia (Greek/Russian) gorgeous girl
Nas, Nastasha, Natasie

Nasya (Hebrew) God's miracle
Nasia

Nat (American) form of Natalie: born on Christmas
Natt

Nata (Latin) saving

Natalia (Russian) form of Natalie: born on Christmas
Nat, Nata, Natala, Natalea, Natalee, Natalya, Nati, Nattie, Nattlee, Natty

Natalie ✿ ❂ (Latin) born on Christmas
Natala, Natalee, Natalene, Natalia, Natalina, Nataline, Natalka, Natalya, Natelie, Nathalia, Nathalie

Natane (Native American) daughter; giving

Nataniah (Hebrew) God's gift
Natania, Nataniela, Nataniella, Natanielle, Natanya, Nathania, Nathaniella, Nathanielle, Netana, Netanela, Netania, Netaniah, Netaniela, Netaniella, Netanya, Nethania, Nethanisah, Netina

Natarsha (American) splendid
Natarsh, Natarshah

Natasha (Russian) form of Natalie: born on Christmas
Nastasia, Nastassia, Nastassja, Nastassya, Nastasya, Natacha,

Natashah, Natashia, Natassia, Nitasha, Tashi, Tashia, Tasis, Tassa, Tassie

Natesa (Hindi) goddess

Nathadria (Hebrew) feminine form of Nathan: God's gift to mankind
Natania, Nath, Nathe, Nathed, Nathedrea, Natty, Thedria

Nathalie (French) form of Natalie: born on Christmas

Nathitfa (Arabic) unflawed
Nathifa, Nathifah, Natifa, Natifah

Nation (American) spirited; patriotic
Nashon, Nayshun

Natividad (Spanish) Christmas baby

Natka (Polish) hope for tomorrow; (Russian) wonders

Natosha (African American) form of Natasha: born on Christmas
Nat, Natosh, Natoshe, Natty

Natsu (Japanese) summer's child
Natsuko, Natsuyo

Nauasia (Latin) kind princess in *The Odyssey*

Navaira (Spanish) lovely girl

Naveen (Spanish) snowing

Navita (Hindi) new
Nava, Navite

Navy (American) daughter of a member of the Navy; dark blue

Nawal (Arabic) gifted

Nayana (Irish) form of Neala: spirited

Nayeli (African) of beginnings

Nayo (African) joy baby

Nazihah (Arabic) truthful

Nazira (Arabic) equality
Nazirah

Nazly (American) idealistic
Nazlee, Nazli, Nazlie

Neal (Irish) spirited
Neale, Neel, Neil

Neala (Irish) spirited
Neal, Nealie, Nealy, Neeli, Neelie, Neely, Neila, Neile, Neilla, Neille

Nealy (Irish) winner
Nealee, Nealey, Neali, Nealie

Neapolis (Biblical) place name

Neary (English) form of Nerissa: snail; movves slowly
Nearee, Nearey, Neari, Nearie, Neeree, Neerey, Neeri, Neerie, Neery

Neasa (Irish) sweet

Neata (Russian) born on Christmas
Neeta

Neba (Latin) misty
Neeba, Niba, Nyba

Necati (Spanish) sad

Necedah (Native American) yellow hair

Nechama (Hebrew) comforts others
Nachmi, Necha, Neche, Nehama

Neche (Spanish) pure

Nechona (Spanish) pure

Neci (Hungarian) intense

Necie (Hungarian) intense
Neci

Necolae (Spanish) form of Nicole:
winning

Necole (French) winning

Neda (Slavic) Sunday baby
Nedda, Neddie, Nedi

Nedaviah (Hebrew) generous girl
Nedavia, Nedavya, Nediva

Nedda (English) born to money
Ned, Neddy

Nedra (English) secretive
Ned, Nedre

Nedwyn (American) Ned's friend

Nedya (American) flourishes

Neeka (American) flourishes

Neelima (Indian) flourishes; sapphire
Neelam, Neela

Neely (Irish) sparkling smile
Nealy, Neelee, Neilie, Nelie

Neema (Hebrew) melodious

Neenah (Native American) flowing
water

Neevay (American) gives

Nefertari (Egyptian) beautiful queen

Nefris (Spanish) glamorous
Nef, Neff, Neffy, Nefras, Nefres

Neh (Hebrew) form of Nehara: light

Neha (Hindi) loves; rainy
Nehali, Nehi

Nehanda (Hebrew) comforter

Neia (African) promising

Neiana (Slavic) winning

Neidy (Spanish) winning

Neiley (Irish) winner
*Neelee, Neeley, Neeli, Neelie, Neely,
Neilee, Neili, Neilie, Neily*

Neilytta (American) winning

Neima (Hindi) growing; tree

Neith (Egyptian) feminine
Neit, Neithe

Neka (Native American) wild

Nekeisha (African American) bold
spirit
*Nek, Nekeishah, Nekesha, Nekisha,
Nekkie*

Nekia (Arabic) unblemished

Nekoma (Native American)
uninhibited; new moon

Neld (American) blonde

Nelda (American) friend
Neldah, Nell, Nellda, Nellie

Nelemita (Spanish) honest

Nelia (Spanish) form of Cornelia:
practical
Neelia, Neely, Nela, Nelie, Nene

Nelida (Spanish) honest

Nelka (Spanish) yellow hair
Nela

Nell (English) sweet charmer
Nelle, Nellie

Nellena (American) honest

Nellie (English) form of Cornelia:
practical; form of Eleanor:
lighthearted
Nel, Nela, Nell, Nelle, Nelli, Nelly

Nelliene (American) form of Nellie:
practical; lighthearted
Nell, Nelli, Nellienne

Nelvia (Greek) brash
Nell, Nelvea

Nelwynette (American) Nell's
friend

Nemera (Hebrew) leopard; exotic

Nemesis (Mythological) goddess of
justice and retribution

Nemoria (American) crafty
Nemorea

Nenan (American) sea child

Nenet (Egyptian) sea goddess

Nenita (Spanish) of the sea

Neola (Greek) new baby
Neolah

Nepa (Arabic) talented

Nera (Hebrew) candlelight
Neria, Neriah, Neriya

Nereida (Spanish) sea nymph
Nere, Nereide, Nereyda, Neri, Nireida

Neressa (Greek) coming from the sea
Narissa, Nene, Nerissa, Nerisse

Nerida (Greek) sea nymph
Nerice, Nerina, Nerine, Nerisse, Neryssa, Rissa

Nerissa (English) snail; moves slowly
Nerisa, Nerise

Nerizza (Spanish) slow

Nerthus (Scandinavian) masterful

Nerys (Welsh) ladylike
Neris, Neriss, Nerisse

Neshalinda (Spanish) peak of beauty

Nesiah (Greek) lamb; meek
Nesia, Nessia, Nesya, Nisia, Nisiah, Nisva

Nessa (Irish) devout
Nessah

Nessie (Greek) form of Vanessa: flighty
Nese, Nesi, Ness

Nest (Welsh) pure
Nesta

Nestora (Spanish) she is leaving
Nesto, Nestor

Neta (Hebrew) growing and flourishing

Netania (Hebrew) form of Nathaniel: God's gift

Netia (Hebrew) form of Neta: growing and flourishing

Netira (Spanish) flourishing

Netis (Native American) worthwhile

Netra (American) maturing well
Net, Netrah, Netrya, Nettie

Netta (Scottish) champion
Nett, Nettie

Nettie (French) gentle
Net, Neta, Netta, Netti, Nettia, Netty

Neva (Russian/English) the newest; snow
Neeva, Neve, Niv

Nevada (Spanish) girl who loves snow
Nev, Nevadah

Nevaeh ✪ ⚤ (American) heaven spelled backward

Neve (Irish) promising princess

Neviah (Irish) form of Nevina: she worships God
Nevia

Nevina (Irish) she worships God
Nev, Niv, Nivena, Nivina

Newlin (Last name as first name) healing
Newlinn, Newlinne, Newlyn, Newlynn

Neya (Spanish) wishful

Neyda (Spanish) pure
Ney

Neza (Slavic) form of Agnes: pure
Neysa

Ngabile (African) aware; knowing

Ngozi (African) fortunate

Ngu (African) peaceful

Nguyet (Vietnamese) moon child

Nia (Greek) priceless
Niah

Niabi (Native American) fawn; docile

Niamh (Irish) promising

Niandrea (Invented) form of Diandro: special
Andrea, Nia, Niand, Niandre

Niani (Spanish) icon

Nibal (Arabic) completed

Nibedita (Spanish) nubile

Nicaea (Biblical) place name

Nicelda (American) industrious
Niceld, Nicelde, Nicey

Nichole (French) light and lively
Nichol

Nichols (Last name as first name) smart
Nick, Nickee, Nickels, Nickey, Nicki, Nickie, Nicky, Nikels

Nick (American) form of Nicole: winning
Nik

Nicki (French) form of Nicole: winning
Nick, Nickey, Nicky, Niki

Nicks (American) fashionable
Nickee, Nickie, Nicksie, Nicky, Nix

Nico (Italian) victorious
Nicco, Nicko, Nikko, Niko

Nicola (Italian) lovely singer
Nekola, Nick, Nikkie, Nikola

Nicolasa (Spanish) spontaneous; winning
Nico, Nicole

Nicole ✿ (French) winning
Nacole, Nichole, Nick, Nickie, Nikki, Nikol, Nikole

Nicolette (French) a tiny Nicole; little beauty
Nettie, Nick, Nickie, Nicoline, Nikkolette, Nikolet

Nicolie (French) sweet
Nichollie, Nikolie

Nicomedia (Biblical) place name

Nicopolis (Biblical) place name

Nida (Greek) sweet girl

Nidhi (Indian) beloved gift

Nidia (Latin) home-loving
Nidie, Nidya

Niecy (Spanish) pure

Niemi (Origin unknown) beauty
Nyemi

Niesha (African American) virginal
Neisha, Nesha, Nesia, Nessie

Nieves (Spanish) snows; snow maiden
Neaves, Ni, Nievez, Nievis

Nihal (Greek) form of Nicole: winning

Nika (Scandinavian) God's child

Nike (Greek) goddess of victory; fleet of foot; a winner

Nikeesha (American) form of Nikita: daring
Niceesha, Nickeesha, Nickisha, Nicquisha, Nykesha

Niki (American) form of Nicole: winning and Nikita: daring
Nick, Nicki, Nicky, Nik, Nikki, Nikky

Nikita (Russian) daring
Nakeeta, Niki, Nikki, Niquitta

Nikithia (African American) winning; frank
Kithi, Kithia, Nikethia, Niki

Niko (Greek) form of Nikola: lovely singer
Neeko, Nyko

Nikole (Greek) winning
Nik, Niki

Nilana (Invented) combo of Nila and Lana

Nilanjana (Indian) girl of Nile

Nile (Biblical) place name; form of the Nile River

Niles (American) of the Nile River

Nili (Hebrew) plant; flourishes

Nilima (Indian) blue

Nilsine (Scandinavian) wine; ages well

Nima (Arabic) blessed
Neema, Neemah, Nema, Nimah

Nimfa (Spanish) blessed

Nina (Russian/Hebrew/Spanish) bold girl
Neena, Nena, Ninah

Ninel (Spanish) girlish

Ninelle (Spanish) girlish

Ninetta (American) form of Nanette: giving and gracious
Nineta

Ninette (American) form of Nanette: giving and gracious

Nineveh (Biblical) place name

Nini (Hungarian) forgiving
Ninee, Niney, Ninie, Ninnee, Ninney, Ninni, Ninnie, Niny

Ninon (French) feminine
Ninen

Ninoska (Russian) form of Nina: bold girl

Niobe (Greek) vain

Nipa (Hindi) stream

Nira (Hindi) night
Neera, Nyra

Niranjana (Hindi) full moon

Nirel (Hebrew) light of knowledge

Nirvana (Hindi) completion; oneness
with God
Nirvahna, Nirvanah

Nirveli (Hindi) water babe

Nisha (Hindi) nighttime
Nishi

Nishi (Japanese) from the west;
sincere
Nishie, Nishiko, Nishiyo

Nisibis (Biblical) place name;
feminine

Nissa (Hebrew) symbolic
Nisa, Niss, Nissah, Nissie

Nissie (Scandinavian) pretty; elf
Nisse, Nissee

Nita (Hebrew) form of Juanita:
believer in gracious God; forgiving
Neeta, Nitali, Nite, Nittie

Nitalooma (American) moral

Nitara (Hindi) well-grounded

Niteen (American) growing

Nitsa (Greek) form of Helen:
beautiful; light

Nituna (Native American) sweet
daughter

Niu (Chinese) girlish; confident

Niva (Spanish) form of Neva: the
newest; snow

Nivaeh (Spanish) form of Nieves:
snow maiden

Nivea (Spanish) reborn

Nixi (German) mystical
Nixee, Nixie

Niy (American) lively
Nye

Nizana (Hebrew) form of Nitzana:
budding beauty
Nitza, Zana

Noa (Hebrew) chosen
Noah

Noami (Hebrew) form of Naomi:
beautiful woman
Noamee, Noamey, Noamie, Noamy

Nobantu (African) able

Noel (Latin) born on Christmas
Noela, Noelle, Noellie, Noli

Noelan (Hawaiian) Christmas girl

Noelani (Hawaiian) Christmas child

Noelle (French) Christmas baby
Noel, Noell

Noemian (Spanish) pleases

Noga (Hebrew) light of day

Noheali (Hawaiian) Christmas

Nohelia (Hispanic) kind
Nohelya

Noicha (African) light heart
Nolcha

Noirin (Irish) form of Norin:
acknowledging others

Nokomis (Native American) moon
child

Noksu (African) princess

Nola (Latin) sensual
Nolah, Nolana, Nole, Nolie

Nolan (Latin) bell; form of Nola:
sensual
Nolen, Nolyn

Noleen (Irish) known

Noleta (Latin) reluctant
Nolita

Nolia (American) known

Nolina (Spanish) reticent

Nomalanga (Hawaiian) lingers

Nombeko (African) honored child

Nombese (African) wonder girl

Nomble (African) beautiful
Nombi

Nomita (Spanish) wins

Nomusa (African) goodhearted

Nona (Latin) ninth; knowing
*Nonah, Noni, Nonie, Nonn, Nonna,
Nonnah*

Noni (Latin) ninth child

Nonie (Spanish) ninth child

Noor (Hindi) lights the world
Noora

Nora (Greek/Scandinavian/Scottish)
light
Norah, Noreh

Norazah (Malaysian) light

Norberta (German) famous girl from
the north

Noreen (Latin) acknowledging others
Noreena, Norene, Noire, Norin, Norine,
Norinne, Nureen

Norell (Scandinavian) northern girl
Narelle, Norelle

Norena (American) leads

Nori (Japanese) normal

Norika (Japanese) athletic
Nori, Norike

Noriko (Japanese) follows tradition

Norita (Spanish) form of Nora: light

Norlaili (Asian) northern

Norlita (Spanish) knowing

Norma (Latin) gold standard
Noey, Nomah, Norm, Normah, Normie

Norna (Scandinavian) time goddess

Norrie (Asian) traditional
Nori

Norris (English) serious
Nore, Norrus

Nota (American) negative
Na, Nada, Not

Notaku (Asian) dealing with grief

Noula (Irish) form of Nuala: white
Noulah

Noura (Arabic) light girl
Nourah

Nourbese (African) wonderful

Nouvel (French) new

Nova (Latin) energetic; new
Noova, Novah, Novella, Novie

Novak (Last name as first name)
emphatic
Novac

Novella (Latin) new

Novena (Latin) blessing; prayerful
Noveena, Novina, Novyna

Novia (Spanish) sweetheart; girlfriend
Nov, Novie, Nuvia

Nowell (American) form of Noelle:
Christmas baby
Nowel, Nowele, Nowelle

Noyola (Spanish) knowing

Nu (Vietnamese) confident
Niu

Nuala (Irish) white

Nubia (Egyptian) white

Nudar (Arabic) golden girl

Nueva (Spanish) new; fresh
Nue, Nuey

Nuha (Arabic) great mind

Numa (Spanish) delightful
Num

Nuna (Native American) girl of the land

Nunia (Native American) girl of the
land

Nunu (Vietnamese) friendly

Nur (Arabic) bright light
Nura, Nuri, Nurya

Nura (Aramaic) light-footed
Noora, Noura, Nurrie

Nuria (Arabic) light
Noor, Noura, Nur, Nuriah, Nuriel

Nurit (Hebrew) form of Nurita:
flower
Nurice

Nurlene (American) boisterous
Nerlene, Nurleen

Nuru (African) light of day

Nusi (Hungarian) form of Hannah:
merciful; God-blessed

Nutan (Native American) heart

Nuvia (American) new
Nuvea

Nyasia (Greek) starts life

Nyckillan (American) form of
Nicky: smart

Nydia (Latin) nest-loving; home and
hearth woman
Nidia, Nidiah, Ny, Nydiah, Nydie,
Nydya

Nyla (Arabic) successful; astounding
Nila

Nylee (American) girl of Nile

Nylene (American) shy
Nyle, Nylean, Nyleen, Nyles, Nyline

Nyque (American) sea child

Nyra (American) sea child

Nyree (Asian) seagoing

Nysa (Greek) life-starting
Nisa, Nissa, Nissie, Nyssa

Nyura (African) light

Nyx (Greek) lively
Nix

O

Oak (Botanical) sturdy

Oakene (Botanical) sturdy

Oanna (Hawaiian) oceanic

Oba (Mythology) river goddess

Obala (African) form of Oba: river
goddess
Oballa, Obla, Obola

Obdulia (Spanish) comforts

Obede (English) obedient
Obead

Obedience (American) obedient
Obey

Obelia (Greek) needle; cautious
Obel, Obellia, Obiel

Obey (American) obedient

Obioma (African) kind

Oceana (Greek) ocean-loving; name
given to those with astrological signs
that have to do with water
Oceonne, Ocie, Oh

Ocin (Origin unknown) comes into
life

Octavia (Latin) eighth child; born on
eighth day of the month; musical
*Octave, Octavie, Octivia, Octtavia,
Ottavia, Tave, Tavi, Tavia, Tavie*

Oda (Hebrew) praises the Lord

Odalis (Spanish) humorous
Odales, Odallis, Odalous, Odalus

Oddrun (Scandinavian) secret love
Oda, Odd, Oddr

Oddveig (Scandinavian) woman with
spears

Ode (African) born on a road

Odeda (Hebrew) strength of
character

Odeen (Hebrew) praises

Odele (Hebrew/Greek) melodious
Odela, Odelle, Odie

Odelette (Greek) melodic; rich

Odelet, Odette

Odelia (Hebrew/Greek) singer of
spiritual songs
*Odele, Odelle, Odie, Odila, Odile,
Othelia*

Odelimpia (Spanish) melodic;
wealthy

Odelinda (Hebrew) praises

Odelita (Spanish) vocalist
Odelite

Odera (Hebrew) works the soil

Odessa (English) traveler on an
odyssey
Odessah, Odie, Odissa

Odette (French) good girl
Oddette, Odet, Odetta

Odhairnait (Irish) little and green;
elfin-like

Odile (French) sensuous
Odyll

Odilia (Spanish) wealthy
*Eudalia, Odalia, Odella, Odylia,
Othilia*

Odina (Native American) mountain
girl

Odine (Scandinavian) rules

Odiya (Hebrew) God's song

Odra (English) affluent

Odrenne (American) rich

Ofa (Polynesian) loving

Ofira (Hebrew) golden girl

Ogin (Native American) rose

Ohara (Japanese) meditative

Oh

Ohela (Hebrew) tent; nature-loving

Oheo (Native American) beauty

Oira (Latin) form of Ora: glowing

Okalani (Hawaiian) heavenly child

Okei (Japanese) form of Oki: born

mid-ocean; loves the water

Oki (Japanese) born mid-ocean; loves

the water

Oksana (Russian) praise to God

Oksanah, Oksie

Ola (Scandinavian) bold

Olah

Olabisi (African) joy

Olaide (American) lovely; thoughtful

Olai, Olay, Olayde

Olaug (Scandinavian) loves her

ancestors; loyal

Olda (Spanish) snow child

Oldriska (Czech) ruling noble

Olda, Oldra, Oldrina, Olina, Oluse

Oleda (Spanish) audacious

Oleia (Greek) smooth

Olena (Russian) generous

Olenya

Olenka (Russian) form of Helen:

beautiful; light

Olenta (Origin unknown) sweet

Olesia (Greek) regal

Oleta (Greek) true

Oletta

Olga (Russian) holy woman

Ola, Olgah, Ollie

Olgicia (Scandinavian) holy child

Oliana (Polynesian) oleander;

beautiful

Olida (Spanish) lighthearted

Oleda

Olidie (Spanish) light

Oli, Olidee, Olydie

Olina (Hawaiian) joy

Oleen, Oline

Olinda (Latin) fragrant

Oline (Hawaiian) happy

Olina

Olino (Spanish) scented

Olina, Oline

Olisa (African) loves God

Olive (Latin) subtle

Olyve

Olivia ♥ ⚧ (English) flourishing

Alivia, Olive, Olivea, Oliveah, Oliviah,

Ollie

Olubayo (African) resplendent

Olufemi (African) God loves her

Olva (Latin) form of Olivia:

flourishing

Olvyen (Welsh) footprint in white;

lasting impression

Olwen (Welsh) magical; white

Olwynn

Olwyn (Welsh) holy friend

Olya (Latin) perfect

Olyah

Olympia (Greek) heavenly woman

Olimpia, Ollie, Olympe, Olympie

Olynda (Invented) form of Lynda:

pretty girl

Lyn, Olin, Olinda, Olynde

Oma (Hebrew) reverant

Omah

Omana (Hindi) womanly

Omani (African) devout

Omanie (Origin unknown)

exuberant

Omanee

Omari (African) believer

Omayra (Latin) fragrant

Oma, Omyra

Omega (Greek) last is best

Omemee (Native American) dove;

peaceful

Omesha (African American) splendid

Omesh, Omie, Omisha

Omie (Italian) homebody

Omee

Ominotago (Native American) sweet sound

Omolara (African) birth timed well; welcome baby

Omora (Arabic) red-haired

Omorose (African) lovely

Omri (Arabic) red-haired

Omusa (African) adored

Omusupe (African) precious baby

Ona (Latin) the one
Oona

Onamwa (Native American) from the river

Onatah (Native American) earth child

Onawa (Native American) alert

Ondina (Latin) water spirit
Ondi, Ondine, Onyda

Ondrea (Czech) form of Andrea: feminine
Ondra

Ondreja (Czech) form of Andrea: feminine

Oneida (Native American) anticipated
Ona, Oneeda, Onida, Onie, Onyda

Oni (African) desired child

Onia (Latin) one and only

Onie (Latin) flamboyant
Oh, Oona, Oonie, Una

Onita (American) holy

Onora (Latin) honorable
Onoria, Onorine

Ontina (Origin unknown) an open mind
Ontine

Onyx (Latin) pretty shine

Oona (Latin) one alone
Oonagh, Oonah

Opa (Native American) owl; stares

Opal (Hindi) the opal; precious
Opale, Opalle, Opie

Opalina (Sanskrit) gem
Opaline

Ophelia (Greek) helpful woman; character from Shakespeare's *Hamlet*
Ofelia, Ofilia, Ophela, Ophelie, Ophlie, Phelia, Phelie

Ophira (Hebrew) fawn; lovable
Ofira

Ophrah (Biblical) place name; helpful

Opportina (Italian) sees opportunity; successful
Opportuna

Oprah (Hebrew) one who soars; excellent
Ophie, Ophrie, Opra, Oprie, Orpah

Ora (Greek) glowing
Orah, Orie

Orabel (Latin) believes in prayer
Orabelle, Oribel, Oribella, Oribelle

Oraleyda (Spanish) light of dawn
Ora, Oraleydea, Oralida

Oralie (Hebrew) light of dawn
Oralee, Orali, Orla

Orange (English) warm

Oranna (Australian) sought after

Orbelina (American) excited; dawn
Lina, Orbe, Orbee, Orbeline, Orbey, Orbi, Orby

Orchard (American) fruitful

Ordan (American) form of Jordan: excellent descendant

Ordella (Latin) form of Ora: glowing

Orea (Latin) form of Ora: glowing

Oreille (Latin) form of Oriole: golden light

Orela (Latin) form of Oriole: golden light

Orella (Latin) golden girl
Oralla

Orelle (Italian) feminine

Orenda (Place name) Orinda, California; lovely gold

Orene (French) nurturing
Orane, Orynne

Oresty (Greek) feminine form of Orestes: leader

Orestynna (Greek) feminine form of Orestes: leader

Oreun (Greek) star

Orfelinda (Spanish) pretty dawn
Orfelinde, Orfelynda

Orgina (Greek) origins

Orianettea (Italian) form of
Orianna: sunny; dawn

Orianna (Latin) sunny; dawn
Oria, Orian, Oriana, Oriane,
Oriannah, Orie

Orin (Irish) dark-haired
Oren, Orinn

Oringa (Invented) golden

Orino (Japanese) works outside
Ori

Oriole (Latin) golden light
Oreilda, Oreole, Oriel, Oriella, Oriol,
Oriola

Orit (Spanish) dawn

Orita (Spanish) dawn

Oritha (Greek) motherly

Orithna (Greek) natural

Orla (Irish) gold

Orlain (French) famed

Orlaith (Irish) golden lady

Orlanda (German) celebrity

Orlena (Russian) sharp-eyed

Orlenda (Russian) eagle-eyed
Orlinda

Orly (French) busy
Orlee

Ormanda (Latin) noble
Ormie

Ormey (German) sea child

Orna (Irish) dark-haired
Ornah, Ornas, Ornie

Ornice (Irish) pale face

Oropeza (Spanish) peaceful

Orpah (Hebrew) escapes; fawn
Ophra, Ophrah, Orpa, Orpha, Orphy

Orrilla (Spanish) gold

Orrine (French) golden

Orsa (Greek) form of Ursula: little
female bear

Orseline (Latin) bearlike

Orshan (American) of stars

Ortega (Spanish) nettles

Ortensia (Italian) form of Hortense:
caretaking the garden

Orthia (Greek) straightforward

Ortia (Spanish) golden child

Ortrud (Scandinavian) form of
Gertrude: beloved
Ortrude

Orva (French) golden girl
Or, Orvah, Orvan

Orwenn (Welsh) waves

Orya (Origin unknown) forthcoming

Osa (American) praises God

Osana (Latin) praises the Lord

Osarma (Origin unknown) sleek

Osbely (Spanish) lovely you

Osen (Japanese) one in a thousand

Oseye (African) happy

Osithe (Place name) form of Ostia,
Italy: together
Osyth

Osni (Spanish) bearlike

Osroene (Biblical) place name

Ostia (Biblical) place name

Osyka (Native American) eagle-eyed

Otellia (Spanish) form of Othelia:
singer of spiritual songs

Otha (Spanish) form of Othelia:
singer of spiritual songs; (German)
excels

Otilia (Slavic) fortunate

Otilie (Czech) fortunate girl

Otina (Origin unknown) fortunate

Ottavia (English) form of Octavia:
eighth child; born on the eighth day
of the month; musical

Otthild (German) prospers
Ottila, Ottilia, Ottilie, Otylia

Ottilie (Czech) lucky omen

Otylia (Polish) rich
Oteelya

Ouida (Literature) for the Victorian
author Ouida; romantic

Ourania (Greek) heavenly

Ovalia (Spanish) helpful
Ova, Ove, Ovelia

Ovanna (Italian) feminine form of
Ivan: believer in a gracious God;
reliable one

Ovida (Hebrew) worships

Ovidea (German) sheep herder; believer

Ovyena (Spanish) helps

Owen (Welsh) wellborn

Owena (Welsh) feisty
Oweina, Owina, Owinne

Oya (Africa) invited to earth

Oyama (African) called out

Oza (African) strong

Ozara (Hebrew) treasured
Ozarah

Ozelina (Spanish) strong

Ozera (Hebrew) of merit

Ozioma (Origin unknown) strength
of character

Ozmeen (American) prepared

Ozora (Hebrew) rich

P

Paavani (Hindi) purity of the river

Paavna (Hindi) pure

Pabiola (Spanish) small girl
Pabby, Pabi, Pabiole

Paca (Spanish) free girl

Pace (Last name as first name)
charismatic
Pase

Pacifica (Spanish) peaceful
Pacifika

Pacita (Spanish) free; peaceful

Paden (American) pious

Padgett (French) growing and
learning; lovely-haired
Padge, Padget, Paget, Pagett, Pagette

Padilla (Spanish) loving

Padma (Hindi) lotus blossom

Page ☺ (French) sharp; eager
Pagie, Paige, Paje, Payge

Pageant (American) theatrical
Padg, Padge, Padgeant, Padgent, Pagent

Paigene (American) youth

Paili (Irish) wished-for child

Paisha (Slavic) wise

Paisley (Scottish) patterned
Paislee, Pazley

Paiton (English) from a warring
town; sad

Paiva (Scandinavian) sun goddess

Paiz (Spanish) peaceful

Paka (African) kitty cat

Pal (American) friend; buddy

Pala (Native American) water

Palacia (Spanish) palace

Palakika (Hawaiian) much loved

Palanis (American) water child

Palcey (American) wise

Palemon (Spanish) kind
Palem, Palemond

Paley (Last name as first name) wise
Palee, Palie

Palila (Polynesian) bird; free flight

Palla (Greek) form of Pallas:
wise woman

Pallas (Greek) wise woman
Palace, Palas

Pallavi (Indian) new growth

Palma (Latin) successful
Palmah, Palmeda, Palmedah

Palmer (Latin) palm tree; balmy

Palmira (Spanish) palm-tree girl
Palmyra

Palom (Spanish) dove

Paloma (Spanish) dove
Palloma, Palometa, Palomita, Peloma

Palomaelle (Spanish) dove

Palomares (Spanish) dove

Pamela (Greek) sweet as honey
*Pam, Pamala, Pamalia, Pamalla,
Pamee, Pamelia, Pamelina, Pamelinn,
Pamella, Pamelyn, Pamilla, Pammee,*

Pammela, Pammi, Pammie, Pammy,
Pamyla, Pamylla

Pana (Native American) partridge; small

Panchett (American) freedom

Panda (Greek) all-knowing

Pandita (Hindi) learned

Pandora (Greek) a gift; curious
Pan, Pand, Panda, Pandie, Pandorah,
Pandorra, Panndora

Panea (Biblical) place name; open

Panfila (Greek) befriends all

Pang (Chinese) innovative

Panga (Native American) nature

Pangiota (Greek) all is holy

Panna (Hindi) emerald; knowing

Pannonia (Biblical) place name; friend of all

Panola (Greek) all

Panphila (Greek) all loving
Panfila, Panfyla, Panphyla

Panse (Greek) pansy flower

Pansee (Greek) pansy flower

Pansy (Greek) fragrant
Pan, Pansey, Pansie, Panze, Panzee, Panzie

Pantea (Indian) all-loving of gods

Pantelis (Greek) happy with all

Panthea (Greek) loves all gods

Panther (Greek) wild; all gods
Panthar, Panthea, Panthur, Panth

Panya (Greek) she is crowned

Panyin (African) the older twin

Paola (Italian) firebrand

Paolabella (Italian) lovely firebrand

Papina (African) vine; clings

Paradise (Word as name) dream girl

Parenth (American)

Parima (Indian) perfection

Paris (French) capital of France; graceful woman
Pareece, Parice, Parie, Parisa, Parris,
Parrish

Parissa (Spanish) form of Paris: capital of France; graceful woman

Pariste (American) of Paris

Paristeen (American) of Paris

Park (Last name as first name) of the park

Parker (English) noticed; in the park
Park, Parke, Parkie

Parminder (Hindi) attractive

Parnelle (French) small stone
Parn, Parnel, Parnell, Parney

Paronda (Indian) good

Parslee (Botanical) complementary
Pars, Parse, Parsley, Parsli

Partha (Greek) pure; full

Parthenia (Greek) from the Parthenon; virtuous
Parthania, Parthe, Parthee, Parthena,

Parthene, Parthenie, Parthina, Parthine,
Pathania, Pathena, Pathenia, Pathina,
Thenia

Parthenope (Greek) siren

Parthia (Biblical) place name; pure; full

Parvani (Hindi) full moon
Parvina

Parvati (Hindi) mountain child

Parvin (Hindi) star
Parveen

Pascale (French) born on a religious holiday
Pascal, Pascalette, Pascaline, Pascalle,
Paschale, Paskel, Paskil

Pascasia (French) born on Easter
Paschasia

Pascha (Slavic) Easter baby

Paschel (African) spiritual
Paschell

Pash (French) clever
Pasch

Pasha (Greek) lady by the sea
Passha

Pasionne (Spanish) passion

Pasqualina (Spanish) Easter baby

Passion (American) sensual
Pashun, Pass, Passyun, Pasyun

Pasua (French) Easter child

Pat (Latin) form of Patricia: woman of nobility; unbending
Patt, Patty

Patara (Biblical) place name

Paterekia (Hawaiian) patrician
Pakelekia

Pati (African) gathers fish

Patia (Latin) form of Patricia: woman of nobility; unbending

Patience (English) woman of patience
Pacience, Paciencia, Pat, Pattie

Patric (American) form of Patricia: woman of nobility; unbending

Patrice (French) form of Patricia: woman of nobility; unbending
Pat, Patreas, Patreece, Pattie, Pattrice, Trece, Treece

Patricia (Latin) woman of nobility; unbending
Pat, Patreece, Patreice, Patria, Patric, Patrica, Patrice, Patricka, Patrisha, Patrizia, Patsie, Patsy, Patti, Pattie, Patty, Tricia, Trish, Trisha

Patriena (Slavic) form of Patrice: woman of nobility; unbending

Patrika (Slavic) form of Patrice: woman of nobility; unbending

Patrina (American) noble; patrician
Patryna, Patrynna, Tryna, Trynnie

Patriz (Italian) noble

Patsy (Latin) form of Patricia: woman of nobility; unbending
Pat, Patsey, Patsi, Patsie, Patti, Patty

Patty (English) form of Patricia: woman of nobility; unbending
Pat, Pati, Patti, Pattie

Paula (Latin) small and feminine
Paola, Paolina, Paulah, Paule, Pauleen, Paulene, Pauletta, Paulette, Paulie, Paulina, Pauline, Paulita, Pauly, Paulyn, Pavla, Pavlina, Pavlinka, Pawlah, Pawlina, Pola

Paulee (American) small

Paulette (French) form of Paula: small and feminine
Paula, Paulett, Paulie, Paullette

Paulina (Latin/Italian) small; lovely
Paula, Paulena, Paulie

Pauline (Latin) form of Paula: small and feminine
Pauleen, Paulene

Paulisee (American) small

Pausha (Hindi) lunar month; moonlike

Pavana (Origin unknown) form of Paulina: small and feminine; (Indian) holy
Pavani

Pax (Latin) peace goddess

Paxton (Latin) peaceful

Pax, Paxten, Paxtun

Payton ⚥ ⓣ (Last name as first name) aggressive
*Pay, Paye, Payten, Paytun, **Peyton***

Paz (Hebrew/Spanish) sparkling; peaceful
Paza, Pazia, Paziah, Pazice, Pazit, Paziya, Pazya

Paza (Hebrew) golden child
Paz

Pazzy (Latin) peaceful
Paz, Pazet

Peace (English) peaceful woman
Pea, Peece

Peaches (American) outrageously sweet
Peach, Peachy

Peakalika (Hawaiian) happiness

Pearl (Latin) jewel from the sea
Pearla, Pearle, Pearaleen, Pearlena, Pearlette, Pearley, Pearlie, Pearline, Pearly, Perl, Perla, Perle, Perlette, Perley, Perlie, Perly

Pearlette (American) treasured pearl

Pearline (American) treasured pearl

Pecola (American) brash
Pekola

Pedzi (Origin unknown) gold

Pefilia (Spanish) profile

Pega (Greek) form of Peggy: pearl; princess

Peggy (Greek) pearl; priceless
Peg, Peggi, Peggie

Pegma (Greek) happy

Pehel (Biblical) place name

Pei (Place name) village; from Tang
Pei, China

Peigi (Scottish) pearl; priceless

Peigo (American) athletic

Peisha (American) lovely

Peke (Hawaiian) form of Bertha: bright

Pela (Polish) loves the sea; special

Pelagia (Polish) sea girl
Pelage, Pelageia, Pelagie, Pelegia, Pelgia,
Pellagia

Pelagla (Greek) girl of the sea
Pelagie, Pelagi, Pelagia, Pelagias, Pelaga

Pele (Hawaiian) volcano; conflicted;
(Polish) weaves dreams

Peleka (Hawaiian) strong; marvel

Pelham (English) thoughtful
Pelhim, Pellam, Pellham, Pellie

Pelia (Hebrew) marvelous
Peliah, Pelya, Pelyia

Pelika (Hawaiian) strong

Pelipa (African) loves horses
Phillipa

Pella (Biblical) place name; weaves
dreams

Pelulio (Hawaiian) sea treasure

Pelusium (Biblical) place name

Pemba (African) powerful

Pemelia (American) form of Pamela:
sweet as honey

Penda (African) beloved

Pendant (French) necklace; adorned
Pendan, Pendanyt

Penelope (Greek) patient; weaver of
dreams
Pela, Pelcia, Pen, Penalope, Penelopa,
Penina, Penine, Penna, Pennelope,
Penni, Pennie, Penny, Pinelopi, Popi

Peni (Greek) thinker

Peninah (Hebrew) pearl; lovely
Peni, Penie, Penina, Penini, Peninit,
Penny

Peninia (Biblical) precious girl

Penn (Last name as first name) loyal

Pennelle (American) loyal

Penny (Greek) form of Penelope:
patient; weaver of dreams
Pen, Penee, Penni, Pennie

Penthea (Spanish) orchid; lovely
Fentheam, Fentheas, Pentha, Pentheam,
Pentheas

Peony (Greek) flowering; giving
praise
Pea, Peoni, Peonie

Peoria (Place name) city in Illinois;
poised

Pepita (Spanish) high-energy

Pepa, Peppita, Peta

Pepper (Latin) spicy
Pep, Peppie, Peppyr

Peppy (American) cheerful
Pep, Peppey, Peppi, Peps

Pequita (Spanish) form of Pepita:
high-energy

Perach (Hebrew) flowering
Perah, Pericha, Pircha, Pirchia, Pirchit,
Pirchiya, Pirha

Perano (Spanish) wanders

Perciella (Greek) great excess

Perdita (Latin) wanders away

Perea (Biblical) place name

Perel (Latin) tested
Perele

Perfecta (Spanish) perfection
Perfekta

Perga (Biblical) place name

Peridot (Arabic) green gem; treasured
Peri

Peril (Latin) victor

Perita (Spanish) treasure

Periwinkle (Botanical) blue-eyed;
flower girl

Perla (Latin) substantial
Perlah

Perlace (Spanish) small pearl
Perl, Perlahse, Perlase, Perly

Perlette (French) pearl; treasured
Pearl, Pearline, Peraline, Perl, Perle, Perlett

Perlie (Latin) form of Pearl: jewel from the sea
Perli, Perly, Purlie

Perlina (American) small pearl
Pearl, Perl, Perlinna, Perlyna

Pernella (Scandinavian) rock; dependable
Parnella, Pernelle, Pernilla

Pernille (Scandinavian) rock; safe

Peron (Latin) travels

Perouze (Armenian) turquoise gemstone
Perou, Perous, Perouz, Perry

Perpetua (Spanish) lasting

Perri (Greek/Latin) outdoorsy; (English) wanderer
Peri, Perr, Perrie, Perry

Perrinada (American) generous

Persephone (Greek) breath of spring
Pers, Perse, Persefone, Persey

Persevera (Spanish) persevers

Pershella (American) philanthropic
Pershe, Pershel, Pershelle, Pershey, Persie, Persy

Persia (Place name) colorful
Persha, Perzha

Persis (Latin) form of Persia: colorful
Perssis

Perusia (Biblical) place name

Pesha (Hebrew) flourishing
Peshah, Peshia

Peshe (Hebrew) saved

Pessim (Native American)

Peta (English) saucy
Pet, Petra, Petrice, Petrina, Petrona, Petty

Petila (Slavic) adored

Petra (Slavic) glamorous; capable
Pet, Peti, Petrah, Pett, Petti, Pietra

Petri (Scandinavian) feminine form of Peter: dependable; rock

Petrine (Scandinavian) rock

Petrona (Italian) reliable

Petronilla (Greek) feminine form of Peter: dependable; rock
Petria, Petrina, Petrine, Petro, Petrone, Petronela, Petronella, Pett

Petru (Slavic) able

Petula (Latin) petulant song
Pet, Petulah, Petulia

Petunia (American) flower; perky
Pet, Petune

Pfeiffer (Last name as first name) lovely blonde; talented

Phaedra (Greek) bright
Faydra, Faydrah, Padra, Phae, Phedra

Phalba (American) offspring

Phalin (Asian) sapphire

Phan (Asian) shares

Phaselis (Biblical) place name

Phashestha (American) decorative
Phashey, Shesta

Pheakkley (Vietnamese) faithful

Pheba (Greek) smiling
Phibba

Phedella (American) lasting; loyal

Phedra (Greek) bright child
Faydra, Fedra, Phadra, Phaedra, Phedre

Phelisa (American) form of Felicity: friendly; happy

Phemia (Greek) language

Phenice (Origin unknown) enjoys life
Pheni, Phenica, Phenicia, Venice

Pheodora (Greek) God's gift to mankind

Pheresa (Spanish) form of Theresa: gardener

Phernita (American) articulate
Ferney, Phern

Phia (Irish) saint

Phila (Greek) loving
Phil, Philly

Philadelphia (Greek) loving one's fellow man
Fill, Phil, Philly

Philana (Greek) loving
Filana, Filly, Philly

Philantha (Greek) loves flowers

Philberta (English) intellectual

Philene (Greek) loving others

Philenet (American) loving

Philia (American) loving

Philida (Greek) loving others
Philina, Phillada, Phillida

Philippa (Greek) horse lover
Feefee, Felipa, Phil, Philipa, Philippe, Phillie, Phillipina, Phillippah, Pippa, Pippy

Philippitta (American) loves horses

Philise (Greek) loving
Felece, Felice, Philese

Philistia (Biblical) place name

Philly (Place name) from Philadelphia, Pennsylvania: loving one's fellow man
Filly, Philee, Phillie

Philma (Greek) loves others

Philomena (Greek) beloved
Filomena, Filomina, Mena, Phil, Phillomenah, Philomen, Philomene, Philomina

Philoteria (Biblical) place name

Philtherian (Greek) loving

Phiona (Scottish) form of Fiona: fair-haired
Phionna

Phira (Greek) loves music

Phoebe (Greek) bringing light
Febe, Fee, Feebe, Feebs, Pheabe, Phebe, Phebee, Pheby, Phobe, Phoeb, Phoebey, Phoebie, Phoebs

Phoenicia (Biblical) place name

Phoenix (Greek) rebirth
Fee, Fenix, Fenny, Phenix, Phoe

Phonsa (Origin unknown) jubilant

Phosa (Biblical) delicate girl

Photina (Origin unknown) fashionable

Phrgia (Biblical) place name

Phylicia (Greek) fortunate girl
Felicia, Phillie, Phyl, Phylecia

Phyllida (Greek) lovely; leafy bough
Filida, Phyll, Phyllyda

Phyllis (Greek) beautiful; leafy bough; articulate; smitten
Fillice, Fillis, Phil, Philis, Phillis, Philliss, Phillisse, Phyl, Phylis, Phyllys

Phynise (American)

Phyrus (Greek) form of Zephyrus: breezy

Pia (Latin) devout
Peah, Piah

Picabo (Place name) city in Idaho; swift
Peekaboo

Piedad (Spanish) devout

Pier (Greek) feminine form of Peter: dependable; rock
Peer

Pierette (Greek) reliable
Perett, Perette, Piere

Pierina (Greek) dependable
Peir, Per, Perina, Perine, Pieryna

Pierrette (French) little rock

Piers (French) little rock

Piki (Hindi) little cuckoo

Pilar (Spanish) worthwhile; pillar of strength

Pili (Spanish) pillar; strength

Pililani (Hawaiian) strong one

Pilisi (Hawaiian) simple life

Piluki (Hawaiian) little leaf; small

Pilvi (Italian) cheerful
Pilvee

Pineki (Hawaiian) peanut; tiny girl

Pinga (Hindi) dark

Pingjarje (Native American) shy; little doe

Pingla (Hindi) goddess

Pink (American) blushing
Pinkee, Pinkie, Pinky, Pinkye, Pynk

Pinquana (Native American) fragrant girl

Piper (English) player of a pipe; musical

Pippa (English) ebullient; horse-lover
Pip, Pipa

Pippi (English/French) blushing; loving horses
Pip, Pippie, Pippy

Pirene (French) rock; dependable

Pirouette (French) ballet term
Piro, Pirouet, Pirouetta

Pisidia (Biblical) place name; of the water

Pita (English) comforting

Pitana (Origin unknown) accented

Pitarra (American) interesting
Pitarr, Peta, Petah

Pity (American) sad
Pitee, Pitey, Pitie

Pixie (American) small; perky; (English) zany
Pixee, Pixey, Pixi

Placida (Latin) serenity
Plasida

Platinum (English) from the Spanish platinal; fine metal
Plati, Platnum

Platona (Spanish) good friend
Pleasance, Pleasant, Pleasants, Pleasence

Playla (Place name)

Pleshette (American) plush
Plesh

Pleun (Origin unknown) wordsmith

Plina (Spanish) full

Plum (Botanical) fruit; healthy

Po (Italian) effervescent
Poe

Pocahontas (Native American) joyful
Poca, Poka

Poe (Last name as first name) mysterious

Poetry (Word as name) romantic
Poe, Poesy, Poet

Polete (Hawaiian) small; kind
Poleke, Polina

Policia (Spanish) guards

Polina (Russian) small
Po, Pola, Polya

Poliquin (Last name as first name) all-encompassing

Polishia (Slavic) smooth

Polly (Irish) devout; joyous
Pauleigh, Paulie, Pol, Pollee, Polley, Polli, Pollie

Pollyanna (English) heroine of Eleanor Porter's novel
Polianna, Polliana, Pollie-anna, Polly

Polymnea (Mythology) songstress for all

Polyxena (Mythology) very hospitable

Pomona (Latin) apple of my eye; (Mythology) bears fruit
Pomonah

Pompa (Last name as first name) pompous
Pompy

Pompey (Place name) lavish
Pomp, Pompee, Pompei, Pompy

Poni (African) second daughter

Ponise (Spanish) sets aside
Pomice

Pony (American) wild west girl
Poney, Ponie

Poodle (American) sweet; curly-haired
Poo, Pood, Poodly

Poonam (Hindi) kind soul

Poppy (Latin) flower; bouncy girl
Pop, Poppi, Poppie

Poppy-Honey (American) sweet girl

Pora (Hebrew) fertile

Porsche (Latin) giving; high-minded
Porsh, Porsha, Porshe, Porshie, Portia

Porsha (German) giving
Porshea

Portia (Latin) a giving woman
Porcha, Porscha, Porsh, Porsha, Porshuh

Posala (Native American) good-bye to spring

Posh (American) fancy girl
Posha

Posy (American) sweet
Posee, Posey, Posie

Poupée (French) doll
Pou

Powder (American) gentle; light
Pow, Powd, Powdy, Powdyr, PowPow

Poweline (American) ready

Pragyata (Hindi) knowledgeable

Prancey (American) rambunctious

Prancine (American) form of Francine: beautiful

Prarthana (Hindi) prays

Prasanna (Indian) unswerving

Pratibha (Hindi) understanding

Precia (Latin) important
Preciah, Presha, Presheah, Preshuh

Preciliano (Spanish) precious

Precious (English) beloved
Precia, Preciosa, Preshie, Preshuce, Preshus

Predenita (Spanish) pretentious

Prema (Hindi) love

Premlata (Hindi) loving

Prentice (Last name as first name) learns
Prentiss

Prescilian (Hispanic) fashionable
Pres, Priss

Prescilline (Spanish) form of Priscilla: wisdom of the ages

Presencia (Spanish) presents well

Presley (English) talented
Preslee, Preslie, Presly, Prezlee, Prezley, Prezly

Prestha (Hindi) dearest girl

Pretice (American) form of Prentice: learns

Pribislava (Polish) glorifed; helpful
Pribena, Pribka, Pribuska

Price (Welsh) loving
Pri, Prise, Pry, Pryce, Pryse

Prima (Latin) first; fresh
Primalia, Primetta, Primia, Primie, Primina, Priminia, Primma, Primula

Primalia (Spanish) prime; first

Primavera (Italian) spring child

Primola (Botanical) flower; from primrose; first
Prim, Prym, Prymola

Primrose (English) rosy; fragrant
Prim, Primie, Rosie, Rosy

Princelle (American) princess

Princess (English) precious
Prin, Prince, Princesa, Princessa, Princie, Prinsess

Princy (American) form of Princess: precious

Prisca (Latin) old spirit

Prisciliana (Spanish) wise; old
Cissy, Priscili, Priss, Prissy

Priscilla (Latin) wisdom of the ages
Cilla, Precilla, Prescilla, Pricilla, Pris, Priscella, Priscila, Prisilla, Priss, Prissie, Prissilla, Prissy, Prysilla

Prisisima (Spanish) wise and feminine
Priss, Prissy, Sima

Prisma (Hindi) cherished baby

Prissy (Latin) form of Priscilla: wisdom of the ages
Prisi, Priss, Prissie

Pristina (Latin) pristine

Priti (Hindi) lovely

Priya (Hindi) sweetheart
Preeya, Preya, Priyah

Prizela (Spanish) form of Priscilla: wisdom of the ages

Prochora (Latin) leads

Promise (American) sincere
Promis

Proserpine (Mythology) queen of the underworld; secretive

Prospera (Latin) does well

Protima (Hindi) dancing girl

Prova (Place name) Provence, France
Pro, Proa, Provah

Pru (Latin) form of Prudence: wise; careful

Prudie, Prue

Prudence (Latin) wise; careful

Perd, Pru, Prudencia, Prudie, Prudince, Pruds, Prudu, Prudy, Prue

Prunella (Latin) shy

Pru, Prue, Prune, Prunie

Pryor (Last name as first name) wealthy

Prieyer, Pryar, Prye, Pryer

Psyche (Greek) soulful

Sye, Sykie

Pua (Hawaiian) flower

Pulcheria (Italian) chubby; curvy

Pulchia

Puma (American) cougar; wild spirit

Poom, Pooma, Poomah, Pumah, Pume

Punita (Indian) unblemished

Punsey (American) form of Pansy: fragrant

Purity (English) virginal

Puretee, Puritie

Purnima (Hindi) full moon baby

Pyera (Italian) sturdy; formidable; rock

Pyer, Pyerah

Pyllyon (English) enthusiastic

Pillion, Pillyon, Pillyun

Pyrena (Greek) fiery temper

Pyria (Origin unknown) cherished

Pyra, Pyrea

Pyrrha (Latin) fire

Pythia (Greek) prophet

Q

Qadira (Arabic) wields power

Kadira

Qamra (Arabic) moon girl

Kamra

Qing (Origin unknown) quick

Qitarah (Arabic) aromatic

Qiturah (Arabic) aromatic

Qeturah, Quetura, Queturah

Q-Malee (American) form of Cumale: open-hearted

Cue, Q, Quemalee, Quemali, Quemalie

Quan (Chinese) goddess of compassion

Quanda (English) queenly

Kwanda, Kwandah, Quandah, Qwanda

Quanella (African American) sparkling

Kwannie, Quanela

Quanesha (African American) singing

Kwaeesha, Kwannie, Quaneisha, Quanisha

Quantina (American) brave queen

Kwantina, Kwantynna, Quantinna, Quantyna, Tina

Qubilah (Arabic) easygoing

Queen (English) regal; special

Quanda, Queena, Queenette, Queenie

Queendiosa (American) queenly

Queenie (English) royal and dignified

Kweenie, Quee, Queen, Queeny

Queisha (American) contented child

Queshia, Queysha

Quenby (Swedish) feminine

Quenbee, Quenbey, Quenbi, Quenbie, Quinbee, Quinbie, Quinby

Quenna (English) feminine

Kwenna

Queosha (American) soulful

Querida (Spanish) dear one

Questa (French) looking for love

Kesta

Queta (Spanish) head of the house

Keta

Quiana (Origin unknown) form of Hannah: merciful; God-blessed

Qiana, Qianna, Quianna, Quiyanna

Quilla (English) writer

Kwila, Kwilla, Quila, Quillah, Quyla, Quylla

Quillee (Spanish) high spirits

Quina (African) fifth baby

Quinby (Scandinavian) living like royalty

Quenby, Quin, Quinbie, Quinnie

Quinceanos (Spanish) fifteenth child

Quin, Quince, Quincy

Quincy (French) fifth

Quince, Quincey, Quinci, Quincie, Quinsy

Quincylla (American) popular; fifth child

Cylla, Quince, Quincy

Quindelin (American) form of Gwendolyn: mystery goddess; bright

Quinella (Latin) a girl who is as pretty as two

Quinn

Quinetra (American) fifth baby

Quinise (American) fifth baby

Quinitka (American) fifth baby

Quinn (English/Irish) smart

Quin, Quinnie

Quinta (Latin) fifth day of the month

Quintana (Latin) fifth; lovely girl

Quentana, Quinn

Quintessa (Latin) essential goodness

Quintessen (American) fifth baby

Quintilla (Latin) fifth girl

Quintina

Quintina (Latin) fifth child

Quentina, Quintana, Quintessa, Quintona, Quintonette, Quintonice

Quintona (Latin) fifth

Quintwana (American) fifth girl in the family

Quintuana

Quinyette (American) likeable; fifth child

Kwenyette, Quiny

Quirina (Latin) contentious

Quisagna (Slavic) sister

Quisha (African American) beautiful mind

Keisha, Kesha, Key

Quita (Latin) peaceful

Keeta, Keetah

R

Raah (Greek) saved

Rabab (Origin unknown) different

Rabbah (Biblical) place name

Rabbit (American) lively; energetic

Rabit

Rabia (Arabic) wind

Rabiah (Arabic) breezy

Rachael (Hebrew) form of Rachel: peaceful as a lamb

Rach, Rachaele, Rachal, Rachel, Rachie, Rae, Raechal, Rasch, Ray, Raye

Rache (American) form of Rachel: peaceful as a lamb

Rachel ✿ (Hebrew) peaceful as a lamb

Rachelle (French) calm

Rach, Rachell, Rashell, Rashelle, Rochelle

Rachen (Slavic) peaceful

Rachene (French) peaceful

Rachna (Indian) organized

Racinda (Slavic) peaceful

Racquel (French) friendly

Racquelle, Raquel

Rada (Polish) glad

Radha (Hindi) successful; excels

Radhika

Radia (Slavic) happy

Radmilla (Slavic) glad; hardworking

Rae (English) raving beauty

Raedie, Raena, Ray, Raye

Raegan (French) delicate

Reagan, Regan, Regun

Raelan (American) simple beauty

Rafa (Arabic) joyful girl
Rafah

Rafaela (Hebrew) spiritual
Rafayela

Rafeline (French) happy

Raffaella (French) happy

Rafferty (Irish) prospering
Raferty, Raff, Raffarty, Rafty

Rageana (Spanish) form of Regina:
queen

Ragnild (Scandinavian) goddess of war
Ragnhild, Ragnhilda, Ragnhilde,
Ragnilda, Ranillda, Reinheld, Renilda,
Renilde, Reynilda, Reynilde

Raheel (Hebrew) form of Rachel:
peaceful as a lamb
Raheela

Rahela (Hawaiian) lamb

Rahil (Hebrew) form of Rachel:
peaceful as a lamb

Rahima (Pakistani) loving
Raheema, Raheema

Rain (English) falling water
Rainie, Reign

Raina (German) dramatic
Raine, Rainna, Rayna

Rainbow (American) bright
Rain, Rainbeau, Rainbo, Rainie

Raine (Latin) helpful friend
Raina, Rainie, Rana, Rane, Rayne

Rainey (Last name as first name) giving
Rainee, Rainie, Raney

Raisa (Russian) embraced
Rasa

Raissa (Russian) form of Rose: rose;
blushing beauty

Raja (Arabic) optimist

Rajani (Hindi) dark; hopeful

Rajata (Indian) silver; queen

Rajeana (Slavic) form of Regina: queen

Raji (Hindi) royal

Rajni (Hindi) dark night

Raka (Hindi) royal

Raleigh (Irish) admirable
Raileigh, Railey, Raley, Rawleigh,
Rawley

Ralphenne (American) feminine
form of Ralph: advisor to all

Ralphina (American) feminine form
of Ralph: advisor to all
Ralphine

Rama (Hindi) godlike; good

Ramah (Biblical) place name

Ramani (Indian) lovely

Ramba (African) high goals

Ramilia (Slavic) strong

Ramina (German) lovely

Ramona (Teutonic) beautiful
protector
Rae, Ramonah, Ramonna, Raymona

Ramonda (American) form of
Ramona: beautiful protector

Ramsay (English) from the isle of
rams; country girl
Ramsey

Ramsee (English) from the rams'
land

Ramsie (English) from the rams'
land

Rana (Hindi) royal

Ranchel (American) range girl

Randa (Latin) admired
Ran, Randah

Randall (English) protective of her own
Rand, Randal, Randi, Randy

Randella (American) sheltered

Randelle (American) wary
Randee, Randele

Randi (English) audacious
Randee, Randie, Randy

Rane (Scandinavian) queen-like
Rain, Raine, Ranie

Rani (Sanskrit) a queen
Rainie, Ranie

Rania (Sanskrit) regal
Ranea, Raneah, Raney, Ranie

Ranielle (French) royal; frank

Ranita (Hebrew) musical

Ranit, Ranite, Ranitra, Ranitta

Raoule (Spanish) feminine form of
Raoul: wild heart

Raoula, Raula

Rapa (Hawaiian) lovely by moonlight

Raphaela (Hebrew) helping to heal

Rafaela, Rafe

Raphenn (American) dreamy

Raphia (Biblical) place name

Raphina (German) exciting

Raquel (Spanish) sensual

Racuell, Raquelle, Raqwel

Raquita (Spanish) aggressive

Rasa (Slavic) morning dew

Rasheeda (Hindi) pious

Rashee, Rashida, Rashie, Rashy

Rashidah (Arabic) on the right path

Rashida

Rashinique (African American) rash

Rash, Rashy

Ratna (Indian) beauty

Raula (French) advises

Ravada (Spanish) raven

Raven (English) blackbird

Ravan, Rave, Ravin

Ravenna (English) blackbird

Ravette (English) special

Ravistene (American) raven

Rawn (American) ambitious

Rawnie (Slavic) ladylike

Rawani, Rawn, Rawnee

Ray (American) simplistic approach

Rae, Raymonde

Rayleen (American) popular

Raylene, Raylie, Rayly

Rayna (Scandinavian) strong girl

Raynee (Scandinavian) strong

Raynekka (Slavic) raven

Raynelle (American) giving hope;
combo of Ray and Nelle

Nellie, Rae, Raenel, Raenelle

Raynette (American) ray of hope;
dancer

Raenette, Raynet

Rayola (Spanish) hopeful

Razia (Hebrew) secretive

Razeah, Raziah

Raziella (Italian) graceful

Razina (African) nice

Rea (Polish) flowing

Raya

Reagan ✪ (Last name as first name)
strong

Regan, Reganne, Reggie

Reanika (American) happy

Reanne (American) happy

Reann, Rennie, Rere, Rianne

Reason (Word as name)

Reba (Hebrew) fourth-born

Rebah, Ree, Reeba

Rebazar (Spanish) fourth child

Rebecca (Hebrew) loyal

Becca, Becki, Beckie, Becky, Rebeca,
Rebeka, Rebekah

Rebi (Hebrew) friend who is steadfast

Reby, Ree, Ribi

Rebop (American) zany

Reebop

Redettea (American) righteous

Redita (Slavic) peaceful

Redonna (American) peaceful

Ree (Asian) mannered

Reed (English) red-haired

Read, Reade, Reid, Reida

Reem (Arabic) antelope; graceful

Reena (Arabic) antelope

Reenie (Greek) peace-loving

Reena, Reeni, Reeny, Ren, Rena

Reese (American) style-setting

Ree, Reece, Rees, Rere

Reeve (Last name as first name)
strong

Regan (Irish) queenly

Reagan

Reganean (American) form of
Regan: queenly

Regeana (American) form of Regina: queen

Rege, Regeanah, Regeane

Regene (Latin) queen

Regina (English/Latin) queen

Gina, Rege, Regena, Reggie, Regine

Regine (Latin) royal

Regene, Rejean

Reginia (American) queen

Regne (Slavic) leader

Rehema (African) well-grounded

Rehemah, Rehemma, Rehima

Reidee (American) red hair

Reidnilda (German) form of Reynalda: wise

Reiko (Japanese) appreciative

Rein (German) advises

Reina (Spanish) a thinker

Rein, Reinie, Rina

Reine (Spanish) form of Reina: a thinker

Reith (American) shy

Ree, Reeth

Rejena (Slavic) queen

Rejunda (Slavic) queen

Rekha (Hindi) focuses

Rela (German) everything

Reila, Rella

Relin (German) kind

Rella (Origin unknown) rogue

Remah (Hebrew) pale beauty

Rema, Remme, Remmie, Rima, Ryma

Remaliah (American) helps

Remata (German) helps

Remedios (Spanish) helpful

Remember (American) memorable

Remi, Remmi, Remmie, Remmy

Remi (French) woman of Rheims; jaded

Remee, Remie, Remy

Remille (French) helps

Remolda (Slavic) strong

Remonia (Slavic) strong

Ren (Asian) flower

Rena (Hebrew) joyful singer

Reena, Rinah, Rinne

Renae (French) form of Renee: born again

Renay, Rennie, Rere

Renard (French) fox; sly

Ren, Renarde, Rynard, Rynn

Renata (French) reaching out

Renie, Renita, Rennie, Rinata

Renatha (Slavic) born again

Rene (Greek) hopeful

Reen, Reenie, Reney

Renea (French) form of Renee: born again

Renny

Renee (French) born again

Rene, Rennie, Rere

Renetta (French) reborn

Ranetta, Renette

Renie (Latin) renewal

Renis (American) welcomed

Renita (Latin) poised

Ren, Renetta, Rennie

Renite (Latin) stubborn

Reneta, Renita

Reniti (English) upward

Renna (English) reborn

Rennyll (French) form of Renee: born again

Renelle

Renshaw (Last name as first name) directed

Renuka (Slavic) calm

Renzia (Greek) form of Renee: born again

Renze

Reonne (Welsh) maiden

Resa (Greek) productive; laughing

Reesa, Reese, Risa

Reseda (Latin) healing

Res, Reseta

Reseme (American) fragrant

Resenetta (Spanish) fragrant flower

Reshea (American) girlish

Reshma (African) compassionate; (Indian) sun

Reshma (Indian) sun

Resie (German) form of Theresa: gardener

Reta (African) shakes up
Reda, Reeda, Reeta, Rheta, Rhetta

Retanica (American) chaotic

Retha (German) form of Aretha: virtuous; vocalist

Retrola (American) retrospective

Reva (Hebrew) rainmaker
Ree, Reeva, Rere

Revada (American) revival

Reveca (Spanish) form of Rebecca: loyal
Reba, Rebeca, Reva

Revelina (American) revival

Reveriana (Spanish) of the river

Rew (Australian) of the spring

Rexie (American) confident
Rex, Rexi, Rexy

Reyna (Filipino) queen
Raina, Rayna, Rey

Reynalda (German) wise
Raynalda, Rey, Reyrey

Reynee (English) peaceful

Reynolds (Scottish) wispy
Rey, Reye, Reynells, Reynold

Reza (Czech) form of Theresa: gardenerl
Rezi, Rezka, Riza

Rezeda (Spanish) prayerful

Rhea (Greek) earthy; mother of gods; strong
Ria

Rheta (American) form of Rita: precious pearl

Rhiall (Welsh) nymph

Rhianna (Welsh) pure
Rheanna

Rhiannon (Welsh) goddess; intuitive
Rhian, Rhiane, Rhianen, Rhiann, Rhianon, Rhyan, Rhye, Riannon

Rhilla (Slavic) nymph

Rhoda (Greek) rosy
Rhodie, Roda, Rodi, Rodie, Rody, Roe

Rhodanthe (Greek) form of Rhodes: lovely
Rhodante

Rhodette (American) rose girl

Rhodora (Spanish) rose girl

Rhogean (French) form of Regine: royal

Rhola (Slavic) form of Rachel: peaceful as a lamb

Rhon (Welsh) blessing

Rhona (Scottish) power-wielding
Rona, Ronne

Rhonda (Welsh) vocal; quintessential
Rhon, Ron, Ronda, Ronnie

Rhondie (American) perfect
Rond, Rondie, Rondy

Rhonella (American) feminine form of Ronald: kind

Rhonetta (American) maximum

Rhonni (American) form of Ronnie: energetic

Rhonwen (Welsh) lovely
Rhonwenne, Rhonwin, Ronwen

Rhuenette (American) great

Rhyan (Welsh) magical

Rhyannah (Greek) nymph

Ria (Spanish) water-loving; river
Reah, Riah

Riah (Biblical) river

Riana (Irish) frisky
Reana, Rere, Rianna, Rinnie

Rianda (American) river

Riane (American) attractive
Reann, Reanne

Riannah (Irish) sweet

Riannon (Irish) free spirit
Rianna

Rica (Spanish) celestial
Ric, Ricca, Rickie, Rieka, Rika, Ryka

Ricarda (German) has power

Richelle (French) strong and artistic
Chelle, Chellie, Rich, Richel, Richele,
Richie

Richenda (German) rules

Richesse (French) wealthy
Richess

Richilda (American) sainted

Ricielle (African) beauty

Ricki (American) sporty
Rici, Rick, Rickie, Ricky, Rik, Riki, Rikki

Rickiann (Combo of Ricki and Ann)
sporty

Rickma (Hindi) golden

Rico (Italian) sexy
Reko, Ricco

Rida (Arabic) satisfied
Ridah

Rierla (Scandinavian) helpful

Rieshanda (American) nymph

Rihana (Irish) pretty

Rihanna (Scandinavian) nymph

Rijana (Slavic) nymph

Rikina (Hawaiian) Christian

Rilena (English) lively

Riley ♥ (Irish) courageous; lively
Reilly, Rylee, Ryleigh, Ryley, Rylie

Rilla (German) lives by the brook

Rima (Arabic) graceful; antelope
Rema, Remmee, Remmy, Rimmy, Ryma

Rimona (Hebrew) pomegranate;
small

Rina (Hebrew) joy
Renah

Rinda (Scandinavian) loyal
Rindah

Ring (American) magical
Ringe, Ryng

Riona (Irish) regal
Rina, Rine, Rionn, Rionna, Rionne

Ripley (American) unique
Riplee, Ripli, Riplie

Riquette (French) feminine form of
Richard: wealthy leader

Risen (Last name as first name) rysen
Ryzenne

Rish (American) born in religion

Risingsun (Native American) sun
child

Rissa (Latin) laughing
Resa, Risa, Riss, Rissah, Rissie

Rita (Greek) precious pearl
Reda, Reita, Rida

Ritsa (Greek) form of Alexandra:
defender of mankind

Ritz (American) rich
Rits

Riva (Hebrew) joining; sparkling
Reva, Revi, Revvy

River (Latin) woman by the stream
Riv

Rivernne (American) water child

Rivers (American) trendy

Riya (American) excited

Riza (Greek) dignified
Reza, Rize

Rizalin (American) form of Theresa:
gardener

Rizalina (American) form of
Theresa: gardener

Rizalinne (American) form of
Theresa: gardener

Rizalyne (American) form of
Theresa: gardener

Roanna (Spanish) brown skin
Ranna, Roanne, Ronni, Ronnie, Ronny

Roberta (English) brilliant mind
Robbie, Robby, Robertah, Robi

Robertia (English) feminine form of
Robert: brilliant; renowned

Robertz (French) feminine form of
Robert: brilliant; renowned

Robin (English) taken by the wind;
bird
Robbie, Robby, Robinn, Robinne, Robyn

Robina (Scottish) birdlike; robin
Robena

Robitaille (French) girl of grace

Rocheen (French) sturdy

Rochelle (French/Hebrew) small and strong-willed; dreamlike beauty
Roch, Roche, Rochel, Rochi, Rochie, Rochy, Roshelle

Rockella (Invented) rocker
Rockell, Rockelle

Rocky (American) tomboy
Rock, Rockee, Rockey, Rockie

Roda (Polish) intelligent

Roddy (German) well-known
Rod, Roddee, Roddey, Roddi, Roddie

Roderica (German) princess
Rica, Roda, Roddie, Rodericka, Rodrika

Roelina (German) famous

Rogelim (Biblical) place name

Rogeria (American) feminine form of Roger: famed warrior

Rogertha (American) feminine form of Roger: famed warrior
Rodge

Rohan (Hindi) sandalwood; pretty

Rohana (Hindi) sandalwood; textured
Rohanna

Roi Anne (American) royal

Roisin (Irish) rose

Roksana (Polish) dawn
Roksanna, Roksona

Rolanda (German) rich woman
Rolane, Rollande, Rollie

Rolandan (German) feminine form of Roland: renowned
Roland, Rolanden, Rollie, Rolly

Roldyn (Spanish) famed

Roline (German) destined for fame
Roelene, Roeline, Rolene, Rollene, Rolleen, Rollina, Rolline, Rolyne

Rolleen (Italian) famed

Rollettea (Italian) rolling

Roma (Italian) girl from Rome; adventurous
Romy

Romaine (French) daredevil
Romain, Romane, Romayne, Romi

Romalice (American) form of Rome: city in Italy

Roman (Italian) adventurous
Romi, Romie, Rommie, Rommye, Romyn

Romana (Italian) distinct; Roman

Romey (Latin) sea-loving
Romy

Romilda (Latin) striking
Romelda, Romey, Romie, Romy

Romilla (Latin) form of Rome: city in Italy
Romella, Romi, Romie, Romila

Romilly (Latin) wanderer
Romillee, Romillie, Romily

Romina (Spanish) form of Rome: city in Italy

Romney (Welsh) winding river

Romola (Latin) form of Rome: city in Italy

Romona (Spanish) form of Ramona: beautiful protector
Mona, Rome, Romie, Romy

Romy (French) form of Romaine: daredevil
Roe. Romi, Romie

Rona (Scandinavian/Scottish) powerful
Rhona, Ronne, Ronni

Ronallia (Scottish) smart

Ronat (Scandinavian) form of Rhona: power-wielding

Ronda (Welsh) form of Rhonda: vocal; quintessential
Ronni

Rondra (American) form of Rhonda: vocal; quintessential

Ronea (American) form of Rona: powerful

Roneathea (American) good face

Ronelle (English) winner
Ronnie

Ronette (English) form of Rona: powerful

Roney (Scandinavian) form of Rona: powerful
Roneye, Roni

Ronia (Scandinavian) lake

Ronis (English) image of beauty

Ronna (Slavic) image of beauty

Ronneta (English) go-getter
Roneda, Ronnete, Ronnette, Ronnie

Ronni (American) energetic
Ron, Ronee, Roni, Ronnie, Ronny

Rooki (American) sharp novice

Roopa (Hindi) beauty

Roquia (Spanish) royal

Rori (Irish) spirited; brilliant
Rory

Ros (English) form of Rosalind: lovely rose
Roz

Rosa (Italian/German) rose; blushing beauty
Rose, Rossah, Roza

Rosa-Adriana (Spanish) exotic rose

Rosaire (French) rosary

Rosalba (Latin) glorious as a rose
Rosalbah, Rosey, Rosi, Rosie, Rosy

Rosalia (Italian) hanging roses
Rosa, Rosalea, Rosaleah, Rosaliah, Roselia, Rosey, Rosi, Rosie, Rossalia, Rosy

Rosalie (English) striking dark beauty
Leelee, Rosa, Rosalee, RosaLee, Rosa-Lee, Rosie, Rossalie, Roz, Rozalee, Rozalie

Rosalind (Spanish) lovely rose
Lind, Ros, Rosa, Rosalyn, Rosalynde, Rosie, Roslyn, Roslynn, Roz

Rosalinda (Spanish) lovely rose
Rosa-Linda, Rosalynda

Rosaline (Spanish) a rose
Rosalyn, Rosalynne, Roslyn

Rosallie (Italian) fair rose

Rosalvo (Spanish) rosy-faced
Rosa, Rosey

Rosamond (English) beauty
Rosa, Rosamun, Rosamund, Rose, Rosemond, Rosie, Roz

Rosanna (English) lovely
Rosannah

Rosau (Spanish) rosary

Rosaura (Spanish) rosary

Rose (Latin) rose; blushing beauty
Rosa, Rosey, Rosi, Rosie, Rosy, Roze, Rozee

Rosebud (Latin) flowering

Roselle (Latin) rose

Rosellen (English) pretty
Roselinn, Roselyn

Rosena (American) form of Rose: rose; blushing beauty
Roze, Rozena, Rozenna

Rosenda (Spanish) rosy
Rose, Rosend, Rosende, Rosey, Rosie, Senda

Rosetta (Italian) longlasting beauty
Rose, Rosy, Rozetta

Rosette (Latin) flowering; rosy
Rosett, Rosetta

Roshall (African American) form of Rochelle: small and strong-willed; dreamlike beauty
Rochalle, Roshalle

Rosheen (Latin) rose

Roshell (French) form of Rochelle: small and strong-willed; dreamlike beauty
Roshelle

Roshi (Indian) bright
Roshni

Roshni (Sanskrit) light

Roshumba (African American) gorgeous
Rosh, Roshumbah

Roshunda (African American) flamboyant
Rosey, Roshun, Roshund, Rosie, Roz

Rosie (English) bright-cheeked
Rose, Rosi, Rosy

Rosina (English) rose

Rosita (Spanish) pretty

Roseta, Rosey, Rosie, Rositta

Ross (Scottish) peninsula is home

Rosse

Rossana (Italian) rose

Rosshalde (Welsh) rosary

Rossian (American) rosary

Roszl (Scottish) rose

Rotella (American) smart

Rotel, Rotela

Roth (American) studious

Rothe

Rotnei (American) bright

Rotnay

Roula (Scandinavian) secret

Rowan (Welsh) blonde

Rowanne

Rowena (Scottish) blissful; beloved
friend

Roe, Roenna, Rowina

Rowenta (Slavic) highborn

Roxanna (Persian) bright

Roxana, Roxie

Roxanne (Persian) lovely as the sun

Roxane, Roxann, Roxie, Roxy

Roxy (American) sunny

Rox, Roxi, Roxie

Royal (English) royal

Royale (English) of royal family

*Royalla, Royalene, Roayalina, Royall,
Royalle, Royalyn, Royalynne*

Royce (English) king's child

Roice

Roynale (American) motivated

Roy, Royna, Roynal

Roysee (English) royal

Roz (French) form of Rosalind: lovely
rose

Ros, Rozz, Rozzie

Rozanne (Slavic) rose

Rozen (Native American) rose

Rozettaline (American) rose

Rozina (Indian) pretty rose

Rozonda (American) pretty

Rosonde, Rozon, Rozond

Rubaina (Hindi) bright

Rube (Hawaiian) ruby; gem

Rubena (Hebrew) sassy

Rubyn, Rubyna, Rueben

Rubicela (Spanish) ruby

Rubina (Pakistani) gem

Rubi

Rubra (French) form of Ruby:
precious jewel

Rube, Rue

Ruby (French) precious jewel

Rubi, Rubie, Rue

Ruchi (German) brash

Rudelle (English) ruddy skin

Rudella

Rudy (German) sly

Rudee, Rudell, Rudie

Rue (English/German) looking back

Ru

Rufaro (African) happy

Rufina (Italian) red-haired

Rufeena, Rufeine, Ruffina, Ruphyna

Rujona (Slavic) form of Regina:
queen

Rujula (Indian) rich

Rujuta (Hindi) truthful

Rula (American) wild-spirited

Rue, Rulah, Rewela

Rulia (English) ruler

Rumah (Biblical) place name

Rumer (English) unique

Ru, Rumor

Rumiko (Asian)

Runa (Scandinavian) secret

Rupli (Hindi) beautiful

Ruri (Japanese) emerald

Rure, Rurrie, RuRu

Rusbel (Spanish) beautiful girl with
reddish hair

Rusbell, Rusbella

Ruselle (French) red hair

Rushenda (Slavic) red hair

Russine (French) red hair

Russo (American) happy

Russoh

Rusty (English) red-haired girl

Rustee, Rusti

Ruta (Lithuanian) practical

Rue, Rudah, Rutah

Rutanya (Slavic) friend

Ruth (Hebrew) loyal friend

Rue, Ruthie, Ruthy

Rutha (Hebrew) friend

Ruthian (American) friend

Ruthie (Hebrew) friendly and young

Ruth, Ruthey, Ruthi, Ruthy

Ryan (Irish) royal; assertive

Rian, Ryann, Ryen, Ryunn

Ryanna (Irish) leader

Rianna, Rianne, Ryana, Ryanne, Rynn

Ryba (Hebrew) traditional

Reba, Ree, Riba, Ribah

Ryenline (American) ruler

Ryenni (American) ruler

Rylee (Irish) brave

Rilee, Rili, Ryelee, Ryley, Ryli, Ryly

Ryleen (American) brave

Ryn (American) form of Wren: flighty girl; bird

Ren, Rynn

Ryne (Irish) form of Ryan: royal; assertive

Rynea, Ryni, Rynie

Rynie (American) loves the woods

Rinnie, Ryn

Rynn (American) outdoorsy woman

Rin, Rynna, Rynnie, Wren

Rynnea (American) sun-lover

Rynnee, Rynni, Rynnia

S

Saba (Arabic) morning star

Sabah

Sabella (English) spiritual

Bella, Belle, Sabela, Sabell, Sabelle, Sebelle

Sabeth (American) form of Elisabeth: God's promise

Sabina (Latin) desirable

Sabeena, Sabine, Sabinna, Sabyna, Say

Sabine (Latin) tribe in ancient Italy

Sabeen, Sabienne, Sabin, Sabyne

Sabirah (Arabic) young

Sabla (Arabic) young

Sable (English) chic

Sabelle, Sabie

Sablette (American) luxurious

Sable, Sablet

Sabra (Hebrew) substantial

Sabe, Sabera, Sabrah

Sabrina (Latin) passionate

Breena, Brina, Brinna, Sabe, Sabreena, Sabrinna

Sabrinus (English) princess

Sabry (American) worthwhile

Sacha (Greek) helpful girl

Sachie, Sachy

Sachen (Slavic) lucky

Sachi (Japanese) girl

Sachee, Sachey, Sachie, Sachy, Sashi, Shashie

Sachika (Japanese) happy

Sachin (Slavic) lucky

Sadawn (American) pure

Sadhana (Hindi) loyal

Sadiah (Arabic) good omen

Sadie (Hebrew) charmer; princess

Sade, Sadee, Sady, Sadye, Shaday

Safe (Word as name)

Safeenah (Muslim) ship at sea

Saffron (Indian) spice

Saffrone, Safron

Safia (Arabic) pure

Saga (Scandinavian) sensual

Sagah

Sagal (American) action-oriented

Sagall, Segalle

Sagartia (Biblical) place name

Sage (Latin) wise

Saige

Sahara (Place name) desert; wilderness

Saharra

Sahare (American) loner

Sahila (Hindi) guides others

Sahri (Arabic) giving

Saiby (American) gifted

Saida (Hebrew) happy girl

Sada, Sadie

Saige (English) wise

Sailor (American) outdoorsy

Sail, Saile, Sailer, Saylor

Sairsha (Indian) defends

Sajah (Hindi) meritorious

Sajie, Sayah

Sajida (Arabic) lady

Sakura (Japanese) wealthy

Sal (Spanish) savior

Salacia (Mythology) earthy

Salama (African) safe

Salamis (Biblical) place name

Salecah (Biblical) place name

Salena (Latin) needed; basic

Salene, Sally

Saletta (American) earthy

Salia (American) esoteric

Salih (Arabic) virtuous

Saliha (Arabic) correct

Salila (Indian) water child

Salima (Arabic) healthy; safety

Salma

Salina (French) quiet and deep

Sale, Salena

Sally (Hebrew) princess

Sal, Salli, Sallie

Salma (Hebrew; Spanish) peaceful; ingenious

Sal, Sali, Sallee, Salley, Salli, Sally, Salmah, Salwah

Salmone (Biblical) place name

Salome (Hebrew) sensual; peaceful

Sal, Salohme, Salomey, Salomi

Salonae (Biblical) place name

Saloni (Indian) peaceful

Salonna (American) peaceful

Salowmee (Invented) form of Salome: peaceful; sensual

Sal, Salomee, Salomie, Salomy, Slowmee

Salvadora (Spanish) saved

Sal, Salvadorah

Salvia (Spanish) healthy

Salwa (Indian) healthy

Sam (Hebrew) God leads

Samalyn (American) God-loving

Samantha (Hebrew) good listener

Sam, Samath, Sammi, Sammie

Samara (Hebrew) God-led; watchful

Sam, Samora

Samaria (Biblical) place name

Samatha (American) form of Samantha: good listener

Sami (Hebrew) insightful

Sam, Sammie, Sammy

Samia (Hindi) joyful

Sameah, Samee, Sameea, Samina, Sammy

Samimah (Hebrew) praised

Samine (Hindi) happy

Samira (Arabic) charismatic

Samona (Hebrew) form of Simone: wise and thoughtful

Samosata (Biblical) place name

Samothrace (Biblical) place name

Samuela (Hebrew) selected

Samm, Sammi, Sammy, Samula

Samyrah (African American) music-loving

Samirah, Samyra

Sana (Arabic) quintessential beauty

Sanaa (Arabic) excellent

Sancha (Spanish) sacred child

Sanchia

Sanchine (Italian) aware

Sandal (Word as name)

Sandhya (Indian) night

Sandhyn (Indian) night

Sandi (Greek) defends others

Sand, Sanda, Sandee, Sandie, Sandy

Sandip (Hindi) knowing

Sandra (Greek) helpful; protective
Sandrah, Sandy

Sandrea (Greek) selfless
Sandreea, Sandie, Sanndria

Sandreen (American) great
Sandrene, Sandrin, Sandrine

Sandy (American) playful
Sandee, Sandey, Sandi, Sandie

Sanella (Indian) golden

Saniata (Spanish) praised

Sanika (Spanish) old

Sanila (Indian) full of praise
Sanilla

Sanimora (Asian) good health

Sanita (Spanish) twilight

Saniyya (Hindi) a special moment in
time

Sanjuana (Spanish) God-loving
Sanwanna

Sanjuanita (Spanish) form of San
Juan; combo of San Juan and Juanita:
believer
Juanita, Sanjuan

Sanna (Scandinavian) truthful
Sana

Sanne (Persian) regal

Sanqueneta (Spanish) saint

Santa (Latin) saint

Santana (Spanish) saintly
San, Santanne, Santie, Santina

Sante (Spanish) healthy

Santeene (Spanish) passionate
*Santeena, Santene, Santie, Santina,
Santine, Satana*

Santi (Spanish) saint

Santia (African) lovable
Santea

Santina (Italian) loves life

Santine (Italian) loves life

Santonina (Spanish) ardent

Sanya (Slavic) dreamer

Sanyu (African) joy

Saper (American) dancer

Sapphira (Greek) blue gem

Sapphire (Greek) precious gem
Safire, Saphire, Sapphie, Sapphyre

Sapphireen (Greek) blue gem

Sappho (Greek) blue

Saqqarah (Biblical) place name

Sarafina (Hebrew) angelic
Seraphina

Sarah ☺ ☯ (Hebrew) God's princess
Sae, Sara, Saree, Sarrie

Sarai (Hebrew) contentious
Sari

Saraid (Irish) best

Saralyn (American) combo of Sara
and Lyn

Saree (Hebrew) woman of value
Sarie, Sary

Sarepta (Biblical) place name

Saretta (Indian) river
Sarita

Sari (Hebrew; Arabic) noble
Saree, Sarey, Sarie, Sarree, Sarrey, Sarri

Sariah (English) form of Sarah:
God's princess

Sarika (Hindi) thrush; sings

Sarilla (Spanish) princess
Sarella, Sarill, Sarille

Sarina (Hebrew) strong
Sareena, Sarena, Sarrie

Sarit (Hebrew) form of Sarah: God's
princess
Saritt, Saryt, Sarytt

Sarita (Spanish) regal
Sareeta, Sarie, Saritah

Sarmila (Indian) comforts

Sarolyn (English) form of Sharilyn:
dear

Sarria (Arabic) superb

Sarun (Indian) valued

Sarva (Indian) river

Sash (Indian) moon child
Sashhi

Sasha (Russian) beautiful courtesan;
helpful
Sacha, Sachie, Sascha, Sasheen, Sashy

Sashay (American) defends

Sasi-Ann (American) dramatic

Sasily (American) form of Cecile: blind

Saskia (Dutch) dramatic; armed with
a knife
Saskiah

Saskie (Dutch) Saxon girl

Sasmita (Hindi) laughter

Sassy (Irish) Saxon girl; flirtatious
Sass, Sassi, Sassie

Sata (Spanish) princess

Satchel (American) unusual
Satchal

Satha (Hindi) untruthful

Satin (French) shiny
Saten

Satomi (Indian) sweet

Saturine (American) from planet
Saturn; melancholy
Saturenne, Saturinne, Saturn, Saturyne

Satya (Arabic) lucky

Sauda (African) darkness

Saumet (French) good advisor

Saundra (Greek) defender
Sandi, Sandra, Sandrah

Saundrall (American) form of
Saundra: defender

Sauni (Arabic) genius
Sani

Sauri (Hebrew) princess

Savannah　　(Spanish) open heart
Sava, Savana, Savanah, Savanna, Seven

Savarne (Indian) ocean

Savea (Scandinavian) global view

Savedra (Indian) sun love

Saveen (Indian) morning

Savina (Latin) form of Sabina:
desirable
Saveena, Savyna

Savone (Italian) morning

Savonna (American) morning

Savy (American) morning

Sawyer (Last name as first name)
industrious
*Sawya, Sawyar, Sawyhr, Sawyie,
Sawyur*

Say (Asian) night

Sayde (American) form of Sadie:
charmer; princess
Saydey, Saydie

Sayleem (Arabic) safe haven

Saylem (Arabic) safe haven

Sayo (Japanese) born at night
Saio, Sao

Sayuri (Hindi) blooms

Sazana (African) princess

Scally (Last name as first)
introspective
Scalley, Scalli

Scarlett (English) red
Scarlet, Scarletta, Scarlette

Schae (Irish) variation of Shea: soft
beauty
Schay

Scharissea (American) form of
Cherise: cherry

Schelunda (American) invented

Schemika (African American) form
of Shameka: loving
Schemi, Schemike

Scheree (American) form of Sherry:
outgoing

Scherry (American) form of Sherry:
outgoing
Scherri, Scherrie

Schmoopie (American) baby; sweetie
*Schmoopee, Schmoopey, Schmoopy,
Shmoopi*

Schulyer (Dutch) form of Skyler:
protective; sheltering
Schulyar, Sky, Skye

Schunetta (American) invented

Schylar (Dutch) sheltering
*Schylarr, Schyler, Schylerr, Schylur,
Schylurr*

Scodra (Biblical) place name

Scooter (American) wild-spirit
Scooder, Scoot

Scottia (Scottish) form of Scotland

Scotty (Scottish) girl from Scotland
Scota, Scotti, Scottie

Scout (French) precocious

Scouts

Scully (Irish) strong

Scullee, Sculleigh, Sculley, Sculli, Scullie

Scupi (Biblical) place name

Scylla (Greek mythology) monstrous

Scyllaea (Greek) mythological

monster; menace

Cilla, Scylla, Silla

Scythian (Biblical) place name

Sea (American) sea-loving; flowing

Cee, See

Sealy (Last name as first name) fun-

loving

Celie, Seal, Sealie

Sean (Hebrew/Irish) God is giving

Seana (Irish) giving

Seane, Seanna, Suannea

Seandra (American) form of

Deandra: divine

Seandre, Seandreah, Seanne

Season (Latin) special; change

Seas, Seasee, Seasen, Seasie, Seasun,

Seazun, Seezun

Seaton (English) from the coast

Seaten, Seeten, Seeton, Seten, Seton

Sebaste (Biblical) place name

Sebastiana (French) respected

Sebastiane (Latin) respected female

Sebastian, Sebbie

Seely (English) bright

Sealee, Sealey, Seali, Sealie, Sealy, Seelee,

Seeley, Seeli, Seelie

Seema (Hebrew) treasured;

softhearted

Seem

Sehba (Indian) form of Shobha:

smart and pretty

Sehria (American) form of Sarah:

God's princess

Seine (French) river; flowing

Sane

Seire (Irish) form of Sierra: peaks;

outdoorsy

Sejal (Hindi) good character;

together

Sela (Hebrew) form of Cecilia: blind

Cela, Celia, Selah, Selia

Selahkiyah (Indian) girl of

mountain

Selame (Biblical) place name

Selanne (American) of the moon

Selannotta (American) of the moon

Selda (German) sure-footed

Seda, Seldah, Selde, Seldee, Seldey,

Seldi, Seldie

Selena (Greek) like the moon;

shapely

Celina, Sela, Seleene, Selene, Selina,

Sylena

Selene (Greek) goddess of the moon

Seleene, Seline, Selyne

Seleucia (Biblical) place name

Selfina (Spanish) moon child

Selima (Hebrew) peacemaker

Selema, Selemmah

Selin (Turkish) calm

Selina (Greek) moon

Celina

Sella (English) form of Selena:

like the moon; shapely

Sela

Selma (German) fair-minded female

Selle, Sellma, Selmah, Zele, Zelma

Selona (Greek) form of Selena: like

the moon; shapely

Celona, Sela, Seli, Selo, Selone

Selsa (Hispanic) enthusiastic

Sel, Sels

Sema (Greek) earthy

Semah, Semale, Semele

Semane (Biblical)

Semele (Mythology) needs proof;

(Latin) number one

Semilia (Latin) number one

Semilla (Spanish) earth mother

Samilla, Sem, Semila, Semillah,

Semmie, Semmy, Sumilla

Semira (Indian) divine

Semiramis (African) meets goals

Semone (American) sentimental

Semonne

Semora (English) form of Samara:
God-led; watchful

Semra (Arabic) earthy

Senay (Italian) happy

Sendy (American) form of Cindy:
moon goddess

Sendee, Sendie

Seneca (Native American) name of a
tribe that is part of the Iroquois
confederacy

Seneka

Senell (American) serene

Sennabis (Biblical) place name

Senone (Spanish) energetic

Senora (Spanish) old soul

Senorah (Spanish) old soul

Senovian (American) high-energy

Senta (German) crescent

Senza (Spanish) sensation

Senzala (Spanish) sensation

Seone (Scottish) sweet

Sephene (American) form of
Stephanie: regal

Sepphoris (Biblical) place name

September (Latin) serious; month

Seppie, Sept

Septima (Latin) seventh child

Septimma, Septyma

Sequoia (Cherokee) giant redwood;
formidable

Sekwoya

Serafina (Hebrew) ardent

*Serafeena, Serafeenah, Serafinah,
Serafyna, Serafynah, Seraphina,
Seraphine, Serifina*

Seraphina (Latin) angel

*Serapheena, Serapheenah, Seraphinah,
Seraphyna, Serphynah*

Seraphine (French) treasure

Seren (Latin) serene

Ceren, Seran

Serena (Latin) calm

Sarina, Sereena, Serenah, Serina

Serendipity (Invented) mercurial;
lucky

Sere, Seren, Serendipitee, Serin

Serene (American) word as name;
calm

Serenity (American) serene

Sera, Serenitee, Serenitie

Seriah (Spanish) smooth

Serida (Spanish) aggressive

Serpina (Mythology) form of
Proserpine: queen of the underworld;
secretive

Sesame (American) inventive

Sesamee, Sezamee

Sesha (Hindi) snake

Sesiti (Italian) sixth sextus

Seta (Hindi) form of Sita: divine

Seth (Hebrew) set; appointed; gentle

Sethe

Severia (Spanish) severe

Seville (Place name) from Seville, Spain

Sevill, Sevyll, Sevylle

Sevrea (American) severe

Sexton (English) church worker

Seymoura (Invented) feminine form
of Seymour: prayerful

Seymora

Shade (English) cool

Shadee, Shadi, Shady

Shadi (Iranian) happy

Shadow (English) mysterious

Shado, Shadoh

Shady (English) in shade

Shae (Hebrew) shy

Shay

Shaela (Irish) pretty

Shae, Shaelie, Shala

Shaelin (Irish) pretty

Shae, Shaelyn, Shaelynn, Shalyn

Shaeterral (African American) well-
shaped

Shatey, Shatrell, Shayterral

Shafiqa (Arabic) loves fellow man

Shahira (Arabic) famed

Shahla (Afghani) pretty girl

Shail (American) pretty

Shale

Shaila (Indian) laughter

Shailendra (Jewish) lovely

Shailesh (Jewish) lovely

Shaina (Hebrew) beauty

Shaine (Hebrew) pretty girl

Shanie, Shay, Shayne

Shainel (African American)

animated

Shainell, Shainelle, Shaynel

Shajara (Muslim) tree

Shajee (Muslim) brave

Shakila (Arabic) beauty

Shakira (Arabic/Spanish) grateful

Shak, Shakeera, Shakeerah, Shakeira,
Shakie, Shakyra, Skakarah

Shakonda (African American) lovely

Shalanda (African American) vivid

Shalande, Shally, Shalunda

Shaleah (Hebrew) weary

Shalea, Shalee, Shaleeah

Shaleina (Turkish) humorist

Shalina, Shalyna, Shalyne

Shalene (Hindi) giving

Shalimar (Polish) peace and glory

Shalina (Indian) form of Selena: like

the moon; shapely

Shalini (Indian) modest

Shallan (American) humorous

Shalonda (African American)

enthusiastic

Shalie, Shalondah, Shalonna, Shelonda

Shamara (Arabic) assertive

Shamarah, Shemera

Shamarie (American) form of

Shamara: assertive

Shameccah (American) form of

Shameka: loving

Shameena (Arabic) beautiful

Shamee, Shameenah, Shamina,
Shaminna

Shameka (African American) loving

Shameika, Shamekah, Shamika,
Shemeca

Shamica (American) form of

Shameka: loving

Shamilia (American) form of

Shameka: loving

Shamine (Hindi) pretty

Shamiyk (African) believer

Shamsa (Pakistani) adorable

Shan (Chinese) coral

Shana (Hebrew) pretty girl

Shaina, Shan, Shanah, Shane,
Shannah, Shanni, Shannie, Shanny,
Shayna, Shayne

Shanae (Irish) generous

Shan, Shanea, Shanee

Shanan (American) believes in a

gracious God

Shanasita (Spanish) wishful

Shanaye (American) form of Shay:

fairy place

Shanda (American)

Shandee (English) hopeful

Shandi, Shandie, Shandy

Shandel (American)

Shandilyn (American) not forsaken

Shandi, Shandy

Shandon (American)

Shandra (American) fun-loving

Chandra, Shan, Shandrie

Shane (Irish) soft-spoken

Shain, Shaine, Shanee, Shanie, Shayne

Shaneka (African American) perky;

pretty

Chaneka, Shan, Shanekah, Shanie,
Shanika

Shanelle (African American) form

of Chanel: fashionable; designer name

Shanel, Shannel, Shannell, Shanny

Shaney (African) fabulous

Shani (African) great

Shania (African) ambitious; bright-

eyed

Shane, Shaniah, Shanie, Shaniya,
Shanya

Shanian (American) form of Shania: ambitious; bright-eyed

Shanice (African American) bright-eyed

Chaniece, Shaneese, Shani, Shaniece

Shaniga (American) believer

Shanigan (Last name used as first name)

Shaniger (Last name as first name)

Shanika (African American) pretty; optimistic

Shan, Shane, Shanee, Shaneeka, Shaneika, Shaneikah, Shanequa, Shaney, Shaneyka

Shaniqua (African American) outgoing

Shane, Shaneekwa, Shaneequa, Shanequa, Shanie, Shanikwa, Shaniquah, Shanneequa

Shanique (African American) pretty; optimistic

Shanisha (African American) bright

Chaneisha, Chanisha, Shan, Shanecia, Shaneisha, Shanie

Shaniya (American) form of Shania: ambitious; bright-eyed

Shaniyer (American)

Shanna (Irish) lovely

Shanah, Shanea, Shannah

Shannon (Irish) smart

Shann, Shanna, Shannen, Shannyn, Shanon

Shanny (Irish) bubbly

Shannee, Shanni, Shannie

Shanta (French) singing; (Indian) peace

Shantah, Shante, Shantie

Shantara (French) bright-eyed

Shantay, Shantera, Shantie

Shante (French) form of Chantal: singer of songs

Shantae, Shantay

Shantell (American) bright singer

Chantel, Shantal, Shantel

Shanti (Hindi) calm

Shantinel (American) form of Shantell: bright singer

Shaphane (American)

Shaqi (American) form of Shaquan: fine

Shaquan (American) fine

Shak, Shaq, Shaquanda, Shaquanna, Shaquie, Shaquonda

Shaquita (African American) delight

Shaq, Shaqueita, Shaqueta, Shaquie

Shara (Hebrew) form of Sharon: open heart; desert plain

Sharah, Sharra, Sherah

Sharada (Indian) knowledge

Sharath (Slavic) protects

Shardae (Arabic) wanderer

Chardae, Sade, Shaday, Sharday, SharDay

Shar-Dae (African) generous

Sharee (American) dear

Sharie

Sharel (Spanish) princess

Shari (French) beloved girl

Shar, Sharee, Sharree, Sher, Sherri

Sharice (French) graceful

Cherise, Shar, Shareese, Shares

Sharif (Russian) mysterious

Shar, Shareef, Sharey, Shari, Sharrey, Shary

Sharil (American) form of Cheryl: beloved

Sharine (Hebrew) form of Sharon: open heart; desert plain

Shareen, Shareene, Sharyne

Sharissa (Hebrew) flat plain; quiet

Sharita (French) charitable

Shar, Shareetah, Shareta

Sharla (American) friendly

Sharlah

Sharlena (French) strong

Sharlene (German) form of Charlene: petite and beautiful

Charleen, Shar, Sharl, Sharleen, Sharline, Sharlyne

Sharlette (American) form of Charlotte: little woman

Sharlott (American) form of Charlotte: little woman

Sharmaine (American) form of Charmaine: bountiful orchard

Sharmanah (American) form of Sharmaine: bountiful orchard

Sharmeal (African American) exhilarating
Sharm, Sharma, Sharme, Sharmele

Sharna (Hebrew) broad-minded
Sharn, Sharnah

Sharnam (American) form of Sharmaine: bountiful orchard

Sharnea (American) quiet
Sharnay, Sharnee, Sharney

Sharnelle (African American) spiritual
Sharnel, Sharnie, Sharny

Sharnette (American) fighter
Chanet, Charnette, Shanet, Sharn, Sharnett, Sharney

Sharon (Hebrew) open heart; desert plain
Shar, Sharen, Shari, Sharin, Sharren, Sharron, Sharry, Sharyn, Sheron, Sherron

Sharona (Hebrew) form of Sharon: open heart; desert plain
Sharonah, Sharonna, Sharonnah

Sharonda (African American) open
Sharondah, Sheronda

Sharonett (American) form of Sharon: open heart; desert plain

Sharonetta (American) form of Sharon: open heart; desert plain

Sharr (Hebrew) vigilant

Sharrona (Hebrew) open
Sharona, Sharonne, Sherona, Shironah

Sharterica (African American) beloved
Sharter, Sharterika, Shartrica, Sharty

Sharuhen (Biblical) place name

Shashee (Hindi) luminous

Shashi (Indian) giving

Shasta (American) majestic mind
Shastah

Shatoya (African American) spirited
Shatoye, Shay, Shaytoya, Toya

Shauhna (Irish) form of Shauna: giving heart

Shauna (Hebrew/Irish) giving heart
Shauhna, Shaunie, Shaunna, Shawna

Shaundra (American) giving

Shaune (American) wide smile
Shaun, Shaunie, Shawn

Shauneice (American) excitable

Shaunelle (American) excitable

Shaunta (American) sings

Shauntee (Irish) dancing eyes
Shaun, Shawntey, Shawntie, Shawnty

Shauntrie (American) sings

Shavon (Irish) devout; energetic
Chavon, Chavonne, Shavaun, Shavon, Shavonne

Shawana (African American) dramatic
Shavaun, Shawahna, Shawanna, Shawnie

Shawandreka (African American) gutsy
Shawan, Shawand, Shawandrika, Shawann, Shawuan

Shawn (American) smiling
Shawne, Shawnee, Shawnie, Shawny

Shawna (Hebrew/Irish) feminine form of Sean: God is gracious
Shawnna

Shawnda (Irish) helpful friend
Shaunda, Shaundah, Shona

Shawneequa (African American) loquacious
Shauneequa, Shawneekwa

Shawnel (African American) audacious
Shaune, Shaunel, Shaunelle, Shawn, Shawnee, Shawnelle, Shawney, Shawni

Shawnet (American) feminine form of Sean: God is gracious

Shawnie (American) playful

Shaunie, Shawni

Shawyne (American) feminine form
of Sean: God is gracious

Shay (Irish) fairy place

Shaye

Shayla (Irish) fairy palace

Shayleen (Greek) moon

Shaylie (Latin) playful

Shaleigh, Shaylea, Shaylee, Shealee

Shayna (Hebrew) beauty

Shayne (Hebrew) form of Shane:
soft-spoken

Shaine, Shay, Sheyne

Shayni (Hebrew) beauty

Shayonda (African American) regal

Shay, Shaya, Shayon, Shayonde,
Sheyonda, Yona, Yonda

Shayter (American) friend of fairies

Shea (Irish) soft beauty

Shae, Shay

Sheaden (French) lovely

Sheba (Hebrew) form of Bathsheba:
beautiful; daughter of Sheba

Chebah, Sheeba, Sheebah

Sheconna (American) of fairies

Sheddreka (African American)
dynamo

Shedd, Sheddrik, Shedreke

Shedy (American) of fairies

Sheela (Hindi) gentle spirit

Sheelah, Sheeli, Sheila

Sheelyah (Irish) form of Shelia:
woman; gorgeous

Sheel, Sheil

Sheem (Native American) believer

Sheena (Hebrew) shining

Sheen, Sheenah, Shena

Shefalia (American)

Shehagh (Irish)

Sheila (Irish) vivacious; divine
woman

Shaylah, Sheela, Sheilia, Sheilya, Shel

Shelagh (Irish) fairy princess

Shelby (English) dignified

Chelby, Shel, Shelbee, Shelbi, Shelbie

Sheldon (English) farm on the ledge

Shelden

Sheleatha (American) shy

Shelia (Irish) woman; gorgeous

Shelya, Shelyah, Shillya

Shelita (Spanish) little girl

Chelita, Shelite, Shelitta

Shell (English) meadow

Shel

Shelley (English) outdoorsy;
meadow

Shelee, Shelli, Shelly

Shelline (French) form of Shelley:
outdoorsy; meadow

Shelton (English) farm on a ledge

Shelten

Shemari (American) sheltered

Shemelia (American) sheltered

Shemina (American) sheltered

Shemira (American) sheltered

Shena (Irish) shining

Shenae, Shenea, Shenna

Shenease (Hebrew) believer

Sheneda (Hebrew) believer

Sheneeka (African American)
easygoing

Shaneeka, Shaneka, Sheneecah, Sheneka

Shepard (English) vigilant

Shep, Sheperd, Shepherd, Sheppie

Shephelah (Biblical) place name

Shera (Hebrew) lighthearted

Sheera, Sheerah, Sherah

Sherael (American) form of Sherry:
outgoing

Sheraelle, Sherelle, Sherryelle

Sheray (French) saucy

Cheray, Sherayah

Sheree (French) dearest girl

Sheeree, Sher, Shere

Shereen (Indian) sheen

Shereitta (Spanish) effervescent

Sherele (French) bouncy

Sher, Sherell, Sherrie

Sheresa (American) dancer
Sher, Sherisa, Sherissa, Sherri

Shereth (American) loved

Sheretta (American) sparkling
Shere, Sherette

Sheri (French) sparkling eyes
Sher, Sherri, Sherrie

Sherice (French) artistic
Cherise, Sher, Shereece, Sherisse

Sheridan (Irish) free spirit;
outstanding
*Cheridan, Cheridyn, Sheridyn,
Sherridan*

Sherika (Arabic)

Sherine (American) shines

Sherita (French) stylish
Cherita, Sheretta

Sheritt (French) form of Sherry:
outgoing

Sherleen (American) easygoing
*Sherl, Sherlene, Sherline, Sherlyn,
Shirline*

Sherlie (English) form of Shirley:
bright meadow; cheerful girl

Sherlitha (Spanish) feminine
Sherl, Sherli

Sherlotta (American) form of
Charlotte: little woman

Sherolynna (American) lovely
Cherolina, Sher, Sheralina, Sherrilina

Sherrill (English) bright
*Cheril, Cherrill, Sherelle, Sheril,
Sherrell, Sheryl*

Sherrone (Hebrew) form of Sharon:
open heart; desert plain

Sherrunda (African American) free
spirit
*Sharun, Sharunda, Sherr, Sherrunde,
Sherunda*

Sherry (French) outgoing
*Sher, Sheri, Sherreye, Sherri, Sherrie,
Sherye*

Sheryl (French) beloved woman
*Cheryl, Sharal, Sher, Sheral, Sheril,
Sherill*

Shevonne (Gaelic) ambitious
Shavon, Shevaune, Shevon

Sheyenne (Native American) form
of Cheyenne: Native American tribe
*Shey, Shianne, Shyann, Shyanne,
Shyenne*

Sheyn (Hebrew) beauty

Shiaray (Native American)

Shibhan (Irish) variation of Siobhan:
believer; lovely
Shiban, Shibann, Shibhann

Shiela (Irish) blind

Shiffawn (American) pretty

Shifra (Hebrew) beautiful woman
Sheefra, Shifrah

Shikendra (African American)
spirited
Shiki, Shikie, Skikend

Shiloh (Hebrew) gifted by God
Shilo, Shy

Shilpa (Indian) in synch; rock

Shimchi (Asian) good

Shinae (American) shines

Shine (American) shining example
Shena, Shina

Shinea (Asian) good

Shinetta (American) shines

Shiney (American) glowing
Shine, Shiny

Shinikee (African American)
glorious
Shinakee, Shinikey, Shynikee

Shira (Hebrew) song; singer
Shirah, Shiree

Shireen (English) charmer
*Shareen, Shiree, Shireene, Shirene,
Shiri, Shiry, Shoreen, Shureen, Shurene*

Shirenzio (American) form of
Sharon: open heart; desert plain

Shirince (American) form of Sharon:
open heart; desert plain

Shirleen (American) nature-loving
Shirlene, Shirline

Shirlei (English) form of Shirley: bright meadow; cheerful girl

Shirleth (American) form of Shirley: bright meadow; cheerful girl

Shirley (English) bright meadow; cheerful girl
Sherlee, Sherley, Sherly, Shir, Shirl, Shirly

Shiyama (African) believer in God

Shlomith (Jewish) peaceful

Shlonda (African American) bright
Londa, Schlonda, Shodie

Shobby (American) smart

Shobha (Indian) smart and pretty

Shola (Hebrew) spirited
Sholah

Sholia (American) form of Salih: virtuous

Shon (Irish) form of Shona: open-hearted
Shonn

Shona (Irish) open-hearted
Shonah, Shonie

Shonda (Irish) runner
Shondah, Shonday, Shondie, Shounda, Shoundah

Shondra (Irish) pretty

Shonta (Irish) fearless
Shauntah, Shawnta, Shon, Shontie

Shony (Irish) shining
Shona, Shonee, Shoni, Shonie

Shoshana (Hebrew) beautiful; lily
Shoshanna, Shoshannah, Shoshauna

Shreya (Indian) good fortune

Shrill (American) word as name; ingenious

Shrilla (Hindi) beauty
Shrila

Shryl (American) ingenious

Shu Jane (Asian) kind

Shuchi (Hindi) pure

Shue (Asian) kind

Shula (Arabic) flaming

Shulamit (Hebrew) serene

Shulondia (African American) dynamic
Shulee, Shuley, Shuli, Shulonde, Shulondea, Shulondiah

Shumay (Muslim) eloquent

Shun (Irish) form of Jane: believer in a gracious God

Shuna (Irish) form of Jane: believer in a gracious God

Shunta (Irish) form of Jane: believer in a gracious God

Shuntay (African American; Irish) form of Shonta: fearless
Shuntae

Shuntele (Irish) energetic

Shura (Greek) protective

Shuranda (American) kind

Shurkela (American) kind

Shurla (American) fun

Shushan (Biblical) place name

Shyama (Native American) form of Cheyenne: Native American tribe

Shyanne (Native American) form of Cheyenne: Native American tribe
Shy

Shyla (English) creative
Shila, Shy, Shylah

Shyne (American) standout
Shine

Shyree (Native American) form of Cheyenne: Native American tribe

Sia (Welsh) calm; believer
Cia, Seea

Sian (Welsh) believer

Siana (Welsh) ebullient
Sian, Siane

Sianoee (Welsh) believer

Sib (Anglo-Saxon) form of Sibley: related
Sibb

Sibila (Greek) form of Sybil: future-gazing

Sibley (Anglo-Saxon) related
Siblee, Sibly

Sibmah (Biblical) place name

Sibyl (Greek) intuitive

Cibyl, Cyb, Cybil, Cybill, Cybyl, Sib, Sibbi, Sibbie, Sibby, Sibella, Sibil, Sibill, Sibyll, Sibylla, Sybela, Sybil, Sybyl

Sicily (Biblical) place name

Sid (Place name) form of Sidney: from Saint-Denis, France

Sidd

Sidelia (Spanish) stars

Sidhi (Indian) excels

Sidnah (American) form of Sidney: from Saint-Denis, France

Sidney (Place name) from Saint-Denis, France

Sidnee, Sidni, Sidny

Sidonia (French) spiritual

Sid, Sidoneah, Sydonya

Sidonie (French) appealing

Sidonee, Sidony, Sydoni

Sidra (Latin) star

Cidra, Siddey, Siddie, Siddy, Sidi, Sidrie, Sydra

Siely (American) form of Sealy: fun-loving

Sienna (English) delicate; reddish-brown

Siena, Siene

Sierra (Place name) peaks; outdoorsy

Cierra, Searah, Searrah, Siera, Sierrah, Sierre

Sigfrid (German) peacemaker

Sig, Sigfred, Sigfreid, Siggy

Signe (Latin) symbol

Sig, Signie, Signy

Signet (Scandinavian) form of Signe: symbol

Sigourney (English) leader who conquers

Sig, Siggie, Signe, Signy, Sigournay, Sygourny

Sigrid (Scandinavian) lovely

Segred, Sig, Siggy, Sigrede

Sigrun (Scandinavian) winning

Cigrun, Segrun

Sikita (American) active

Sikite

Sila (Native American) flowers

Sile (Turkish) misses home

Silenceia (Spanish) quiet

Siline (Greek) form of Selene: like the moon; shapely

Sileen, Sileene, Silyne

Silke (German) divine spirituality

Silvanna (Spanish) nature-lover

Sil, Silva, Silvana, Silvane, Silvanne, Silver

Silver (Anglo-Saxon) light-haired

Silva, Silvar, Sylver

Silvia (Latin) deep; woods-loving

Sill, Silvy, Siviah, Sylvia

Sima (Indian) wise

Simcha (Hebrew) joyful

Simchah

Simi (Lebanese) soft

Sim

Simica (American) tender

Sim, Simika, Simmy

Simoli (American) energy

Simona (American) form of Simone: wise and thoughtful

Sim, Simon, Sims

Simone (French) wise and thoughtful

Sim, Simonie, Symone

Simonetta (French) feminine form of Simon: good listener; thoughtful

Simonias (Biblical) place name

Sinaflor (Spanish) flowers

Sinai (Place name) Mt. Sinai

Sinclair (French) person from St. Clair; admired

Cinclair, Sinclare, Synclair, Synclare

Sinden (English) form of Cindy: moon goddess

Sindy (American) left behind

Cindy

Sine (Irish) God's gift

Sinead (Irish) singer; believer in a gracious God

Shanade

Sinforosa (Spanish) bad luck

Singrid (Scandinavian) form of
Sigrid: lovely

Sinope (Biblical) place name

Sinue (Spanish)

Siobhan (Irish) believer; lovely
Chevon, Chevonne, Chivon, Shavonne,
Shevon

Siphronia (Greek) sensible
Ciphronia, Sifronea, Sifronia, Syfronia

Sippar (Biblical) place name

Sirbonis (Biblical) place name

Siren (Greek) enchantress
Syren

Sirena (Greek) temptress
Sireena, Sirenah, Sirine, Sisi, Sissy,
Syrena

Sirene (Greek) enchantress
Sireen, Sireene, Siryne

Siri (Scandinavian) lovely

Siriny (Greek) spellbinding

Sirmium (Biblical) place name

Sirneicsa (Sanskrit) immortal

Siscia (Biblical) place name

Sisely (American) form of Cicely:
clever

Sisley (Last name as first name) able

Sissy (Latin) little sister; immature;
ingenue
Cissee, Cissey, Cissy, Sis, Sissi, Sissie

Sistene (Italian) spiritual
Sisteen, Sisteene

Sita (Hindi) divine
Seeta, Seetha

Sitiveni (Slavic) high esteem

Siv (Scandinavian) kinship; wife of
Thor
Sive

Sivana (Irish) form of Sivney: satisfied
Sivanah

Siwa (Biblical) place name

Siyona (Hindi) graceful

Sjanie (Scandinavian) energetic

Skayla (Slavic) smart

Skudra (Biblical) place name

Skye (Scottish) high-minded; head in
the clouds

Skyler (Dutch) protective; sheltering
Schuyler, Skieler, Skilar, Skiler, Skye,
Skyla, Skylar, Skylie, Skylor

Slane (Irish) form of Sloane: strong
Slaine

Slaney (Last name as first name)
selective

Slava (Russian) glory

Sloane (Irish) strong
Sloan, Slone

Sloni (Latin) clarity

Sly (American) form of Slyvestra:
forest-dweller; heavy duty

Slyvestra (American) feminine form
of Slyvester: forest-dweller; heavy duty

Smera (Hindi) smiles

Smiley (American) radiant
Smile, Smilee, Smiles, Smili, Smily

Smirna (American) refined

Smisha (American) feminine form of
Smith: crafty; blacksmith

Smita (Indian) grinning

Smyrna (Biblical) place name

Snooks (American) sweetie
Snookee, Snookie

Snow (American) quiet
Sno, Snowy

Snowdrop (Botanical) white flower

Sochia (American) form of Sasha:
beautiful courtesan; helpful

Socoh (Biblical) place name

Socorro (Spanish) helpful
Socoro

Socra (Greek) feminine form of
Socrates: philosophical; brilliant

Sofie (Greek) wise

Sofina (Spanish) form of Sophia: wise
one

Sofonias (Greek) form of Sophia:
wise one

Sofya (Russian) wise
Sofi, Sofie, Sofiya

Sohanne (Hindi) lovely

Soheila (Indian) sun

Sohella (Arabic) form of Saliha: correct

Sohni (Hindi) lovely

Sokan (Native American)

Solada (Asian) attentive

Solana (Spanish) sunny
Solanah, Soley, Solie

Solange (French) sophisticated
Solie

Soledad (Spanish) solitary woman
Saleda, Solada, Solay, Sole, Solee, Solie, Solita

Soleil (French) sun

Soli (Biblical) place name

Solida (Spanish) alone

Soline (French) solemn
Solen, Solenne, Souline

Solita (Latin) alone
Soleeta, Solyta

Soloma (Hindi) lunar

Somansh (Hindi) half-moon

Somayeh (Indian) moon

Somers (Last name as first name) summer girl

Somilla (Hindi) calm

Sommai (American) summer

Sommer (English) warm
Sommie, Summer, Summi

Sona (Hindi) form of Sonal: golden girl of the sun

Sonal (Hindi) golden girl of the sun

Sonali (Hindi) golden

Sonay (Asian) bright-eyed
Sonnae

Sondra (Greek) defender of mankind

Sonel (Hindi) form of Sonal: golden girl of the sun
Sonell

Sonesse (American) sings

Song (Chinese) independent

Songsira (American) sings

Sonia (Slavic) effervescent
Soni, Sonnie, Sonny, Sonya

Sonja (Scandinavian) bright woman

Sonnet (American) poetic
Sonnett, Sonni, Sonny

Sonnie (Slavic) wise

Sonoe (Asian) bright

Sonoma (Place name) city in California; wine-loving
Sonomah

Sonora (English) easygoing
Sonorah

Sonova (Spanish) nice

Sonseria (American) giving
Seria, Sonsere, Sonsey

Sonya (Greek) wise
Sonia, Sonje

Soo (Korean) gentle spirit

Soon-Yi (Chinese) delightful; assertive

Soozi (American) form of Suzy: lily; pretty flower
Soos, Sooz, Souz, Souze, Souzi, Soozy

Sophath (American) form of Sophie: wise one

Sophia (Greek) wise one
Sofeea, Sofi, Sofia, Sofie, Sophea, Sopheea, Sophie, Sophy

Sophia-Loren (Italian) namesake of movie star

Sophie (Greek) form of Sophia: wise one
Sophee, Sophey, Sophi, Sophy

Sophorn (American) form of Sophie: wise one

Sora (Native American) chirping bird
Sorra

Sorangel (Spanish) heavenly
Sorange

Soraya (Persian) royal

Sorayal (Russian) princess

Sorayalle (Russian) princess

Sorcha (Irish) bright
Shorshi, Sorsha, Sorshie

Sorek (Biblical) place name

Sorel (French) reddish-brown

Sorele (French) reddish-brown hair

Sorphal (Asian) speaks well

Sorrel (English) delicate

Sorel, Sorell, Sorie, Sorree, Sorrell, Sorri, Sorrie

Sosamma (Hindi) pretty

Sosannah (Hebrew) form of Susannah: gentle

Sosana, Sosanah, Sosanna

Soshana (Hebrew) lily

Soshanah

Sosy (Indian) health

Sotee (Greek) saved

Soulah (American) afire

Souza (Persian) fiery

Sowanna (Hindi) peaceful

Soynia (American) form of Sonya: wise

Sozos (Hindi) clingy

Sosos

Spaulding (English) divided field

Spalding

Spencer (English) sophisticate

Spence, Spenser

Spirit (American) lively; spirited

Spirite, Spyrit

Sprague (American) respected

Sprage

Sprandee (Invented) spry

Spring (English) springtime; fresh

Spryng

Sri (Hindi) glorious

Shree, Shri, Sree

Srikantha (Hindi) goddess

Srini (Hindi) feminine

Srinivas (Hindi) goddess

Srividya (Hindi) praised

Stacey (Greek) hopeful and spiritual

Stace, Staci, Stacie, Stacy, Staycee

Stacha (English) form of Anastasia: resurrection

Stacia (English) form of Anastasia: resurrection

Stace, Stacie, Stasia, Stayshah

Stahsha (Slavic) form of Stacia: resurrection

Stana (American) form of Stacia: resurrection

Stancie (American) adored

Stanise (American) darling

Stanee, Staneese, Stani, Stanice, Staniece

Star (English) a star

Starr

Starla (American) shining

Starlah, Starlie

Starlene (American) star

Starling (English) glossy bird

Starlite (American) extraordinary

Starlight, Starr

Starne (American) star

Stasia (Greek/Russian) ressurection

Stacie, Stasie, Stasya

Stefanie (Greek) form of Stephanie: regal

Stafanie, Stefannye, Stefany, Steff, Steffany, Steffie

Stefee (Greek) crowned

Steff (Greek) form of Stephanie: regal

Steffi (Greek) form of Stephanie: regal

Steffie, Steffy, Stefi

Stefnee (American) form of Stephanie: regal

Stef, Steffy

Stelanie (American) crowned

Stella (Latin) bright star

Stele, Stelie

Stephanie (Greek) regal

Stefanie, Steff, Steffie, Stephenie, Stephney

Stephel (American) crowned

Stephene (French/Greek) dignified

Steph, Stephie, Stephine

Stephine (French) crowned

Stephney (Greek) crowned

Stef, Steph, Stephie, Stephnie

Sterla (American) quality

Sterl, Sterlie, Stirla

Sterry (Dutch) star child
Sterree

Stevie (Greek/American) jovial
Steve, Stevee, Stevey, Stevi

Stevina (Slavic) crowned

Stina (Scandinavian) believer

Stockard (English) stockyard; sturdy
Stockerd, Stockyrd

Storelle (Invented) legend
Storee, Storell, Storey, Stori

Storm (English) powerful

Stormy (American) impulsive
Storm, Stormi, Stormie

Story (American) creative
Stori, Storie, Storee, Storey

Stuti (Hindi) goddess

Sua (Spanish) loved

Suazo (Spanish) loved

Subha (Indian) lucky

Sublime (Word as name)

Suchi (Indian) lovely

Sudha (Indian) nectar

Sue (Hebrew) form of Susan: lily;
pretty flower

Suelita (Spanish) comforts

Suez (Place name)

Suganda (Slavic) cedar

Sugar (American) sweet
Shug

Sugy (Spanish) form of Sugar: sweet
Sug, Sugey, Sugie

Suha (Indian) nectar
Sudha

Suhas (Hindi) jovial

Sujata (Indian) wellborn

Sujey (Asian) loved

Sukanya (Hindi) lovely

Sukhee (Asian) wise

Suki (Japanese) beloved
Suke, Sukie, Suky

Sula (Greek) sea-going
Soola, Sue, Suze

Sulafah (Muslim) best

Sulanie (American) sea

Sulay (Arabic) pleased

Sulema (Spanish) pleasant

Sullivan (Last name as first name)
bravehearted
Sulli, Sullie, Sullivin, Sully

Sumati (Indian) strong mind

Sumayah (Indian) good
temperament
Sumana, Sumaaya

Sumi (Asian) distinguished

Summer ♀ (English) summery; fresh
Somer, Sommer, Sum, Summie

Summerly (American) vivid summer

Sumona (Hindi) calm

Sun (Korean) obedient girl
Suna, Suni, Sunnie

Sunanda (American) sunny

Sunda (Slavic) form of Sandra:
helpful; protective

Sundancer (American) easygoing
Sunndance

Sunday (Latin) day of the week;
sunny
*Sun, Sundae, Sundaye, Sundee,
Sunney, Sunni, Sunnie, Sunny, Sunnye*

Sunil (American) sunny

Sunila (Hindi) blue sky

Sunita (Hindi) Dharma's child
Suniti

Sunna (American) sunny
Sun, Suna

Sunny (English) bright attitude
Sonny, Sun, Sunni, Sunnye

Sunshine (American) sunny

Supree (Indian) loved
Supriya

Suprema (Hindi) affectionate

Suprina (American) supreme
Suprinna

Suprita (Hindi) pleasant

Surbhi (Indian) sweet smelling

Surekha (Indian) fragrant

Suren (American) delivers

Surene (American) delivers

Suri (Hebrew) princess

Surina (Hindi) wise

Surrender (Word as name) dramatic
Surren

Suruchi (Hindi) pleasant

Surupa (Hindi) beauty

Surya (Indian) sun

Susa (Biblical) place name

Susan (Hebrew) lily; pretty flower
*Soozan, Sue, Susahn, Susanne, Susehn,
Susie, Suzan*

Susaneca (Hebrew) lily

Susannah (Hebrew) gentle
Sue, Susah, Susanna, Susie, Suzannah

Susene (French) pretty girl

Susette (French) form of Susan: lily;
pretty flower
Susett

Susha (Hindi) beauty

Sushma (Hindi) gorgeous

Sushmita (Indian) pretty smile

Susiana (Biblical) place name

Susie (American) form of Susan: lily;
pretty flower
Susey, Susi, Susy, Suze, Suzi, Suzie, Suzy

Susila (Hindi) sensual

Susita (Hindi) white

Susithah (Biblical) place name

Suszane (Slavic) form of Susan: lily;
pretty flower

Sutanu (Hindi) pretty

Sutapa (Hindi) follows God

Sutton (Last name as first name)
southern town
Suten, Sutten, Suton

Suvi (Hindi) excels

Suz (American) form of Susan; lily;
pretty flower
Suze

Suzan (American) form of Susan: lily;
pretty flower
Suzen

Suzanne (English) fragrant
Susanne, Suzan, Suzane, Suzann, Suze

Suzette (French) pretty little one
Sue, Susette, Suze

Suzy (French) form of Susan: lily;
pretty flower
Susy, Suze

Svana (Hindi) noisy

Svea (Swedish) patriotic
Svay

Svetlana (Russian) star bright
Sveta, Svete

Swaga (Hindi) gracious

Swan (Scandinavian) swan-like

Swanhildda (Teutonic) swan-like;
graceful
*Swan, Swanhild, Swann, Swanney,
Swanni, Swannie, Swanny*

Swarna (Hindi) lustrous

Swaru (Hindi) honest

Sweeney (Irish) young and
rambunctious
Sweenee, Sweeny

Sweetpea (American) sweet
Sweetie, Sweet-Pea

Swell (Invented) good
Swelle

Sweta (Hindi) fair

Swetha (Indian) light

Swift (word as name) bold
Swiftie, Swifty

Swoosie (American) unique
Swoose, Swoozie

Syama (Sanskrit) dark

Syantha (American) form of
Cynthia: moon goddess

Syb (Greek) form of Sybil: future-
gazing
Sybb

Sybil (Greek) future-gazing
Sibel, Sibyl, Syb, Sybill, Sybille, Sybyl

Syble (American) foresees

Syd (French) form of Sydney: enthusiastic
Sydd

Sydel (Hebrew) princess

Sydlyn (American) quiet
Sidlyn, Sydlin, Sydlinne

Sydne (French) enthusiastic

Sydney (French) enthusiastic
Sidney, Syd, Sydnee, Sydnie

Syene (Biblical) place name

Syfronia (Slavic) serious

Syka (Slavic) studious

Syl (Latin) loves the woods
Sill

Sylvah (Slavic) form of Sylvia: sylvan; girl of the forest

Sylvan (Latin) from the forest
Silvan, Silven, Silvyn, Sylven, Sylvyn

Sylvana (Latin) forest; natural woman
Silvanna, Syl, Sylvie

Sylvenita (Spanish) sylvan

Sylvestra (English) lives in the woods

Sylvia (Latin) sylvan; girl of the forest
Syl, Sylvea

Sylvie (Latin) sylvan; peacefulness
Sil, Silvie, Silvy, Syl, Sylvey, Sylvi, Sylvy

Sylwia (Polish) serene; in the woods
Silwia

Sylwia (Latin) form of Sylvia: sylvan; girl of the forest

Symira (American) enthusiastic
Sym, Symra, Syms, Symyra

Symone (Hebrew) good listener
Sym

Symphony (American) musical
Simphony, Symfonie, Symfony, Symphonee, Symphonie

Syna (Invented) sweet
Sina

Synde (American) form of Sydney: enthusiastic
Cindy

Synora (American) languid
Cinora, Sinora, Synee, Syni, Synor, Synore

Synov (Scandinavian) sun girl

Synpha (American) capable
Sinfa, Sinpha, Synfa

Syntiche (Biblical) shared goal

Syreeta (Hindi) orderly

Syreta (American) assertive
Sireta

T

Tabbath (Greek) gazelle

Tabea (German) lithe

Tabeen (American) pretty

Tabel (Biblical) happy

Tabia (African) talented girl

Tabina (Arabic) follower of Muhammed

Tabitha (Greek) graceful; gazelle
Tabatha, Tabbatha, Tabbi, Tabytha

Tabla (Native American) wears a tiara; regal

Tacey (American) precious
Tace, Tacita

Tacha (American) form of Tasha: born on Christmas
Tach

Tacho (American) form of Tasha: born on Christmas

Taci (American) strong

Tacie (American) healthy
Tace, Taci, Tacy

Tadewi (Native American) wind

Tadi (Native American) variation of Tadewi: wind

Tadit (Native American) fast

Tadita (Native American) runner
Tadeta

Taesha (American) sterling character
Tahisha, Taisha, Tisha

Taffese (Welsh) loved

Taffeta (American) shiny
Tafeta, Taffetah, Taffi, Taffy

Taffy (Welsh) sweet and beloved
Taffee, Taffey, Taffi

Tafin (American) loved

Taft (English) loved
Tafte

Tafta (American) loved

Taghrid (Arabic) singing bird

Tahcawin (Native American) doe

Tahira (Arabic) pure
Tahirah

Tahiyya (Arabic) welcome
Tahiyyah

Tahmeena (Arabic) form of Tamina: palms

Tahnee (English) little one

Tai (American) fond
Tie, Tye

Taima (Native American) thunder
Taimah, Taiomah

Tain (Native American) new moon

Taina (Spanish) form of Taima: thunder

Taipa (Native American) quail

Tairra (Irish) towers high

Taisha (American) form of Tasha: born on Christmas

Taiwo (African) firstborn of twins

Tajanan (American) regal bearing

Tajarah (Hindi) crowned

Tajie (American) highborn

Tajudeen (Spanish) clingy
Taj, Tajjy, Taju

Taka (Japanese) honorable

Takala (Native American) cornstalk
Takalah

Takara (Japanese) beloved gem
Taka, Taki

Takayren (Native American) commotion

Takeko (Japanese) child of the bamboo

Takenya (Native American) falcon in flight

Takeya (African American) knowing
Takeyah

Taki (Japanese) waterfall

Takia (Arabic) spiritual
Taki, Tikia, Tykia

Takiyah (Arabic) devout
Takeya, Takiya

Takona (American) special

Taku (Asian) worshipful

Takuhi (Armenian) queen

Tala (Native American) wolf

Talal (Hebrew) dew

Talasi (Native American) cornflower

Tale (African) green

Taleen (American) golden

Talent (American) self-assured
Talynt

Talesha (African American) friendly
Tal, Taleesh, Taleisha, Talisha, Tallie, Telesha

Tali (Hebrew) confident

Talia (Greek) golden; dew from heaven
Tahlia, Tali, Tallie, Tally, Talya, Talyah

Talian (American) golden girl

Talibah (African) intellectual
Tali, Talib, Taliba

Talila (Hebrew) dew

Talisa (African American) variation of Lisa: dedicated and spiritual
Telisa

Talise (Native American) beautiful creek

Talitha (African American) inventive
Taleetha, Taleta, Taletha, Talith, Tally

Taliyah (American) blooms

Tallis (English) forest

Tallulah (Native American) leaping water; sparkling girl
Talie, Talley, Tallula, Talula, Talulah

Talluse (American) bold
Talloose, Tallu, Taluce

Tally (Native American) heroine
Tallee, Talley, Talli, Taly

Talma (Hebrew) hill

Talou (American) saucy
Talli, Tallou, Tally

Talutah (Native American) red

Talya (Hebrew) lamb
Talia

Tam (Japanese) decorative
Tama

Tamah (Hebrew) marvel
Tama

Tamajer (American) palms

Tamaka (Japanese) bracelet; adorned
female

Tamaki (Japanese) bracelet

Tamala (American) kind
Tam, Tama, Tamela, Tammie, Tammy

Tamani (Hindi) desirable

Tamanna (Hindu) desire

Tamar (Hebrew) palm; breezy
Tama, Tamarr

Tamara (Hebrew) royal female
Tamera, Tammy, Tamora, Tamra

Tamas (Hindu) palm tree
Tamasa, Tamasi, Tamasvini

Tamasailau (Hawaiian) gem

Tamasine (English) twin; feminine
of Thomas
*Tamasin, Tamsin, Tamsyn, Tamzen,
Tamzin*

Tamatha (American) palms

Tamaura (American) palms

Tamay (American) form of Tammy:
sweetheart
Tamae, Tamaye

Tamaya (Native American) grounded

Tambara (American) high-energy
Tam, Tamb, Tambra, Tamby, Tammy

Tambra (American) palms

Tambre (American) high energy

Tambusi (African) frank
Tam, Tambussey, Tammy

Tame (American) calm

Tamefa (African American) form of
Tamika: lively
Tamefah, Tamifa

Tameria (Hebrew) palms

Tamesha (African American) open
face
Tamesh, Tamisha, Tammie, Tammy

Tamesis (Spanish) name for the
Thames River
Tam, Tamey

Tami (Japanese) people
Tamie, Tamiko

Tamia (Japanese) little gem
Tameea, Tamya

Tamiah (Hebrew) palms

Tamika (African American) lively
*Tameca, Tameeka, Tameka, Tamieka,
Tamikah, Tammi, Tammie, Tammy,
Temeka*

Tamiko (Japanese) the people's child
Tami, Tamico, Tamika

Tamina (Hebrew) palms

Tamirisa (Indian) night; dark
*Risa, Tami, Tamirysa, Tamrisa,
Tamyrisa*

Tammy (American) sweetheart
Tam, Tammie, Tammi, Tammye

Tamohara (Hindu) the sun

Tamony (Hebrew) form of Tamara:
royal female
*Tamanee, Tamaney, Tamani, Tamanie,
Tamany, Tamonee, Tamoney, Tamoni,
Tamonie*

Tamra (Hebrew) sweet girl
Tammie, Tamora, Tamrah

Tamrika (African) newly created
Tamreeka

Tamsin (English) benevolent
*Tam, Tami, Tammee, Tammey, Tammy,
Tammye, Tamsa, Tamsan, Tamsen*

Tamsinn (English) form of
Thomasina: twin

Tamula (American) giving

Tamyrah (African American) vocalist
Tamirah

Tamyren (Hebrew) form of Tamyrah:
vocalist

Tamzin (American) palms

Tana (Slavic) petite princess
Taina, Tan, Tanah, Tanie

Tanaga (American) form of Tanya: queenly bearing

Tanai (American) thorough

Tanaka (Japanese) swamp dweller

Tanay (African American) new
Tanee

Tanaya (Hindu) daughter

Tanda (English) altogether

Tanden (English) altogether

Tandra (English) altogether

Tandria (English) altogether

Tandy (English) team player
Tanda, Tandi, Tandie

Tane (Polynesian) fertile

Tanesha (African) strong
Tanish, Tanisha, Tannesha, Tannie

Tangelia (Greek) angel
Gelia, Tange, Tangey

Tangenika (American) form of former country Tanganyika
Tange, Tangi, Tangy

Tangerla (American) of the fairies

Tangi (American) tangerine
Tangee

Tango (Spanish) dance
Tangoh

Tangyla (Invented) form of Tangela: combo of Tan and Angela

Tange, Tangy

Tani (Slavic) glorious
Tahnie, Tanee, Tanie

Tania (Russian/Slavic) queenly
Tannie, Tanny, Tanya

Tanikella (American) of the fairies

Tanimu (American) of the fairies

Tanina (American) bold
Tan, Tana, Tanena, Taninah, Tanney, Tanni, Tannie, Tanny, Tanye, Tanyna

Tanis (Slavic) form of Tania: queenly
Taniss, Tanys, Tanyss

Tanise (American) unique
Tanes, Tanis

Tanish (Greek) eternal
Tan, Tanesh, Tanny

Tanisha (African American) talkative
Taniesha, Tannie, Tenisha, Tinishah

Tanit (American) goddess

Tanith (Irish) estate
Tanita, Tanitha

Taniyah (Slavic) form of Tanya: queenly bearing

Taniyen (Slavic) form of Tanya: queenly bearing

Tanja (American) queen of fairies

Tanjiela (American) queen of fairies

Tannelle (English) tans leather

Tanra (English) tans leather

Tanrik (Hindi) flowers

Tansy (Latin) pretty
Tan, Tancy, Tansee, Tanzi

Tanuneka (African American) gracious
Nuneka, Tanueka, Tanun

Tanvi (Hindu) young woman; fragile

Tanya (Russian) queenly bearing
Tahnya, Tan, Tanyie, Tawnyah, Tonya

Tanyav (Slavic) regal
Tanyev

Tanyette (Italian) talkative
Tanye, Tanyee, Tanyett

Tanze (Greek) form of Tansy: pretty
Tans, Tansee, Tanz, Tanzee, Tanzey, Tanzi

Tanzy (Greek) eternal

Tao (Vietnamese) apple

Tapa (Spanish) little snack
Tapas

Tapasya (Hindu) bitter

Tapia (Spanish) small

Tapice (Spanish) covered
Tapeece, Tapeese, Tapese, Tapiece, Tapp, Tappy

Tappuah (Biblical) place name

Tapus (Sanskrit) deliberate

Taquanna (African American) noisy
Takki, Takwana, Taquana, Taque, Taquie

Taquesha (African American) joyful
Takie, Takwesha

Taquilla (American) from the
Spanish word tequila; lively
*Takela, Takelah, Taque, Taquella, Taqui,
Taquile, Taquille*

Tara (Gaelic) towering
Tarah, Tari, Tarra

Tarafena (Biblical) gentle

Tarakini (Hindi) nighttime with stars

Taral (Hindu) rippling

Taralah (Biblical) place name

Taran (American) earthy
Taren, Tarran, Tarren, Tarryn, Taryn

Tarani (Hindu) light

Taree (Japanese) tree branch

Tarena (Slavic) melodic

Taricheae (Biblical) place name

Tarika (Hindu) star

Tarina (Slavic) kind

Tarita (American) starry

Tarla (American) flamboyant

Tarlam (Hindu) flowering

Tarlease (American) flamboyant

Tarleen (American) flamboyant

Tarmica (American) flamboyant

Tarnettia (American) from the lake

Taro (Invented) card name; farsighted

Tarona (American) form of Tara:
towering

Tarracina (Biblical) place name

Tarub (Arabic) cheerful

Taryn (English) county in Northern
Ireland
Taran, Taren, Tarran, Tarrin, Tarron

Tasha (Russian) form of Natasha:
born on Christmas
*Tacha, Tahshah, Tash, Tashie, Tasia,
Tasie, Tasy, Tasya*

Tashanah (African American)
spunky
Tash, Tashana

Tashanee (African American) lively
Tashaunie

Tashawndra (African American)
bright smiling
Tasha, Tashaundra, Tashie

Tashel (African American) studious
Tasha, Tashelle, Tochelle

Tashina (African American) sparkles
Tasheena, Tasheenah, Tashinah

Tashka (Russian) together
Tashca, Tashcka

Tashua (American) cherishes

Tashza (African American) form of
Tasha: born on Christmas
Tashi, Tashy, Tashzah

Tasia (American) Christmas baby

Tasida (Native American) rides a
horse

Taska (American) Christmas baby

Tasma (American) twin
Tasmah

Tasmin (Pakistani) twin

Tasmind (American) twin

Tasmine (English) twin
Tasmin

Tasni (Arabic) spring

Tassi (Slavic) bold
Tassee, Tassey, Tassy

Tassie (English) twin

Tatanika (Slavic) fairy queen

Tataren (Slavic) fairy queen

Tate (English) short

Tateeahna (Invented) form of
Tatiana: snow queen

Tatenda (Indian) fanciful

Tatiana (Russian) snow queen
*Tanya, Tatania, Tatia, Tatianna,
Tatiannia, Tatie, Tattianna, Tatyana,
Tatyanna*

Tatiyama (Asian) joyful

Tatjana (Slavic) vibrant

Tatrika (American) playful

Tatsu (Japanese) dragon

Tatum (English) cheery; high-spirited
Tata, Tate, Tatie, Tayte

Tauni (American) tawny; little

Taunja (American) form of Tonya:
queenly

Taunya (American) form of Tonya: queenly

Taura (Latin) bull-like; stubborn

Tauvia (American) form of Octavia: eighth child; born on the eighth day of the month; musical

Tavia (Latin) form of Octavia: eighth child; born on the eighth day of the month; musical
Tava, Taveah, Tavi

Tavina (American) form of Tavia; form of Octavia: eighth child

Tavishi (Hindi) brave

Tavonia (American) form of Tavia; form of Octavia: eighth child

Tawannah (African American) talkative
Tawana, Tawanda, Tawanna, Tawona

Tawanner (American) loquacious
Tawanne, Twanner

Tawanta (African American) smart
Tawan, Tawante

Tawia (African) born after twins

Tawn (English) small girl

Tawnida (American) small

Tawny (American) tan-skinned
Tawn, Tawnee, Tawni, Tawnie

Tawnya (American) form of Tanya: queenly bearing
Tawnie, Tawnyah, Tonya, Tonyah

Tawyn (American) reliable; tan
Tawenne, Tawin, Tawynne

Taya (English) tailor

Tayanita (Native American) beaver

Tayla (American) doll-like
Taila, Taylah

Taylor (English) tailor by trade; style-setter
Tailor, Talor, Tay, Taye, Taylar, Tayler

Tazmin (American) form of Jasmine: fragrant; sweet
Tazminn, Tazmyn, Tazmynn

Tazmind (American) form of Jasmine: fragrant; sweet

Tazu (Japanese) stork

Teagan (Irish) worldly; creative
Teague, Teegan, Tegan

Teague (Irish) creative
Tee, Teegue, Tegue

Teah (Greek) goddess
Tea

Teale (English) blue-green; bird
Teal, Teala

Tealisha (American) good heart
Tee

Teamhair (Irish) hill

Teamikka (African American) form of Tamika: lively
Teamika

Teana (American) form of Tina: little and lively
Teanah, Teane

Teasa (Slavic) calm

Techa (Greek) of God

Tecoa (American) precocious
Tekoa

Teddi (Greek) cuddly
Ted, Teddie, Teddy

Tedra (Greek) outgoing
Teddra, Tedrah

Teen (Spanish) form of Tina: little and lively

Tegin (Welsh) pretty

Tegvyen (Welsh) lovely

Tehara (Native American) darling
Tihara, Tyhara

Teishya (American) joyful

Tejuana (Place name) Tijuana, Mexico
Tijuana, T'Juana

Tekira (American) legendary
Tekera, Teki

Tekla (Greek) legend; divine glory
Tekk, Teklah, Thekla, Tikla, Tiklah

Tela (Greek) wise
Tella

Teleri (Welsh) variation of Eleri: smooth

Telery (Welsh) delight

Teletha (American) loving child

Teleza (African) slippery

Telina (American) storyteller

Teline, Telyna, Telyne, Tilina

Telma (Greek) ambitious

Telmah (American) capable

Telsa (American) form of Tessa:
reaping a harvest

Telly

Tema (Biblical) place name; orderly

Temetris (African American)
respected

Teme, Temi, Temitris, Temmy

Temika (American) form of Tamika:
lively

Temike (American) form of Tamika:
lively

Temira (Hebrew) tall

Temora, Timora

Temperance (Latin) moderation

Tempest (French) tempestuous;
stormy

Tempeste, Tempie, Tempyst

Templa (Latin) spiritual; moderate

Temp, Templah

Tenay (American) praised

Tendai

Tenday (African) praiseworthy

Tenesha (African American) clever

Tenesia, Tenicha, Tenisha, Tennie

Tenia (Spanish) tenuous

Tenika (American) cautious

Tennie (American) cautious

Tennille (American) innovative

*Tanielle, Tanile, Ten, Teneal, Tenile,
Tenneal, Tennelle, Tennie*

Tenuvah (Hebrew) fruit and
vegetables

Teo (Spanish) form of masculine name
Teodoro: God's gift

Teeo, Teoh

Teodomira (Spanish) important

Teodora (Scandinavian) God's gift

Teo, Teodore

Teodula (Spanish) gives

Tequila (Spanish) intoxicating

Tequela, Tequilla, Tiki, Tiquilia

Terah (Latin) earth's child

Tereena (American) earth

Terena (English) feminine version of
Terence

*Tereena, Terenia, Terina, Terrena,
Terrina, Teryna*

Teresa (Greek) gardener

*Taresa, Terese, Terhesa, Teri, Terre, Tess,
Tessie, Treece, Tressa, Tressae*

Terese (Greek) nurturing

Tarese, Therese, Treece

Teresille (American) earth

Teresita (Spanish) form of Teresa:
gardener

Tereso (Spanish) reaper

Tere, Terese

Teressa (English) reaps what she sows

Teri (Greek) reaper

Terre, Terri, Terrie

Terlah (Arabic) of the earth

Teronica (American) form of
Veronica: girl's image; real

Terra (Latin) earthy; name for
someone born under an astrological
earth sign

Tera, Terrie

Terrea (Spanish) earth

Terrell (Greek) hardy

Ter, Teral, Terell, Terrelle, Terrie, Teryl

Terrena (Latin) smooth-talking

Terina, Terrina, Terry

Ter-Ri (American) form of Terri: reaper

Terrian (American) earth

Terry (Greek) form of Theresa:
gardener

Teri, Terre, Terrey, Terri, Tery

Terson (Last name used as first name)
child of earth

Tertia (Latin) third

Ters, Tersh, Tersha, Tersia

Teshuah (Hebrew) reprieve

Teshua, Teshura

Tess (Greek) harvesting life

Tesse

Tessa (Greek) reaping a harvest

Tesa, Tessie, Teza

Tessella (Italian) countess

Tesela, Tesella, Tessela

Tessica (American) form of Jessica: rich

Tesica, Tess, Tessa, Tessie, Tessika

Tessie (Greek) form of Theresa: gardener

Tessey, Tessi, Tezi

Tetsu (Japanese) iron

Teuila (Spanish) young

Tevy (Cambodian) angel

Texie (American) form of Texas: U.S. state; cowboy

Tezuma (Spanish) form of the word Montezuma

Thada (Greek) appreciative

Thadda, Thaddeah

Thadyne (Hebrew) worthy of praise

Thadee, Thadine, Thady

Thalassa (Greek) sensitive

Talassa, Thalassah, Thalasse

Thalia (Greek) joyful; fun

Thalya

Thana (Arabic) happy; thanksgiving

Thandiwe (African) affectionate

Thanh (Vietnamese) brilliant

Thao (Vietnamese) respect

Tharamel (Invented) form of the word caramel: dedicated

Thara

The (Vietnamese) pledged

Thea (Greek) goddess

Teah, Teeah, Theah, Theeah, Theo, Tiah

Theadora (Greek) God's gift

Theadra (Greek) goddess

Thebes (Biblical) place name

Theda (American) confident

Thada, Thedah

Theia (Greek) divine one

Thekia (Greek) famous

Thekla (Greek) famous; divine

Tecla, Tekla, Thecla

Thel (American) opinionated

Thelia (Greek) form of Thalia: joyful; fun

Thelina (American) musical

Thelma (Greek) giver

Thel

Thema (African) queen

Themba (African) trusted

Themis (Greek) just

Themla (Greek) just

Theodora (Greek) sweetheart; God's gift

Dora, Teddi, Teddie, Teddy, Tedi, Tedra, Tedrah, Theda, Theo, Theodorah, Theodrah

Theola (Greek) excellent

Theo, Theolah, Thie

Theone (Greek) serene

Theona, Theonne

Theoni (Greek) God's child

Theonus (American) calm

Theophania (Greek) God's features

Theophanie

Theophila (Greek) loved by God

Theofila

Theora (Greek) God's gift

Theorah, Theorra, Theorrah

Theres (Greek) reaps what she sows

Theresa (Greek) gardener

Reza, Teresa, Terri, Terrie, Terry

Therese (Greek) bountiful harvest

Tereece, Terese, Terise, Terry

Theresia (Spanish) harvests

Theressa (Spanish) harvests

Therna (Greek) wild

Thera

Thersa (Hebrew) pleases

Therza, Thirza

Thesina (American) creates

Thessalonica (Biblical) place name

Thessaly (Biblical) place name

Theta (Greek) letter in Greek alphabet; substantial

Thayta, Thetah

Thetis (Greek) mother of Achilles

Theya (American) pleases

Thi (Vietnamese) poem

Thia (Greek) goddess

Thim (Thai) ice cream; sweet

Thirzah (Hebrew) pleasant

Thirza, Thursa, Thurza

Thoa (Asian) hopeful

Thocmetony (Native American) flower

Tocmetone

Thomasina (Hebrew) twin

Tom, Toma, Tomasa, Tomasina, Tomina, Tommie, Toto

Thomia (Hebrew) twin

Thonie (American) prepared

Thonne (American) prepared

Thora (Scandinavian) like thunder

Thorah

Thrixia (American) kindness

Thu (Vietnamese) autumn

Thuy (Vietnamese) gentle

Thyatira (Biblical) place name

Tiamat, Tiam, Tya

Thyra (Scandinavian) loud

Thira

Tia (Greek/Spanish) princess; aunt

Teah, Tee, Teia, Tiah

Tiama (Mythology) ocean-loving

Tian (Greek) lovely

Ti, Tiane, Tiann, Tianne, Tyan, Tyann, Tyanne, Tye

Tiana (Greek) highest beauty

Tana, Teeana, Tiane, Tiona

Tiandye (American) princess

Tianth (American) pretty and impetuous

Teanth, Tia, Tian, Tianeth

Tiara (Latin) crowned goddess

Teara, Tearra, Tee, Teearah, Tierah, Tira

Tiare (French) ornamented

Tiaret (French) wears a crown

Tiarna (American) tiara

Tiaura (American) form of Tiara: crowned goddess

Tibby (American) frisky

Tib, Tibb, Tybbee

Tiberia (Latin) majestic

Tibbie, Tibby

Tibisay (American) uniter

Tibi, Tibisae

Tichanda (African American) stylish

Tichaunda, Tishanda

Tiena (Spanish) earthy

Teena

Tierah (Latin) jeweled; ornament

Tia, Tiarra, Tiera

Tiernan (English) lord

Tierney (Irish) wealthy

Teern, Teerney, Teerny, Tiern

Tierra (Latin) tiara

Tifara (Hebrew) festive

Tiferet, Tifhara

Tifaya (Greek) form of Tiffany: lasting love

Tifayane, Tiff, Tiffy

Tiffa (American) holy trinity

Tiffany (Greek) lasting love

Tifanie, Tiff, Tiffanie, Tiffenie, Tiffi, Tiffie, Tiffy, Tiphanie, Tyfannie

Tiffin (American) form of Tiffany: lasting love

Tig (American) tigress

Tigerlilly (American) flower

Tigress (Latin) wild

Tigris, Tye, Tygris

Tigris (Biblical) place name; (Irish) tiger

Tija (Spanish) form of Tijuana, Mexico

Tijana (American) form of Tijuana, Mexico

Tiki (Polynesian) ancestor; image

Tekee

Tikoletta (American) frivolous

Til (American) form of Matilda: powerful fighter

Tilana (Spanish) truth

Tilda (German) form of Matilda: powerful fighter

Telda, Tildie, Till, Tylda

Tiliera (American) strong

Tilira (American) strong

Tilla (German) industrious

Tila

Tilly (German) cute; strong

Till, Tillee, Tillie

Timerra (American) timid

Timia (American) timid

Timmie (Greek) form of Timothie: honorable

Tim, Timi, Timmy

Timna (Biblical) Anah's sister

Timothea (Greek) honoring God

Timaula, Timi, Timie, Timmi, Timmie

Timothie (Greek) honorable

Tim, Timmie, Timothea, Timothy

Timsuh (Biblical) place name

Tina (Latin/Spanish) little and lively

Teena, Teenie, Tena, Tiny

Tinker (American) animated

Tinkette (American) form of Tinker: animated

Tinna (American) form of Tina: little and lively

Tinsia (American) form of Tina: little and lively

Tiofila (Spanish) friend

Tionne (American) hopeful

Tionn

Tiphanie (Spanish) form of Tiffany: lasting love

Tiphsuh (Biblical) place name

Tiponya (Native American) owl; watchful

Tippah (Hindi) form of Tipo: tiger; ferocious

Tipper (Irish) pourer of water; nurturing

Tip, Tippy, Typper

Tippett (American) giving

Tippie (American) generous

Tippi, Tippy

Tira (Hebrew) camp

Tirathana (Biblical) place name

Tiri (Welsh) sweet

Tirica (American) form of Erica: honorable; leading others

Tirion (Welsh) gentle

Tirrza (Hebrew) sweet; precious

Thirza, Thirzah, Tirza, Tirzah

Tirtha (Hindu) ford

Tirza (Hebrew) kindness

Thirza, Tirzah

Tisa (African) ninth child

Tesa, Tesah, Tisah

Tish (Latin) happy

Tysh

Tisha (Latin) joyful

Tesha, Ticia, Tishah, Tishie

Tishbe (Biblical) place name

Tishema (American) joyful

Tishka (American) joyful

Tishra (African American) original

Tishrah

Tishunette (African American) happy girl

Tish, Tisunette

Tita (Greek) giant; large

Titania (Greek) giant

Tivona (Hebrew) lover of nature

Tiwa (Native American) onion

Tobago (Place name) West Indies island; islander

Bago, ToTo

Tobarista (American) believer

Tobi (Hebrew) good

Tobie, Toby

Toblene (American) believer

Toffey (American) spirited

Toff, Toffee, Toffi, Toffie, Toffy

Tohuia (Polynesian) flower

Toinette (Latin) wonderful

Toin, Toinett, Toney, Tony, Toynet

Toireasa (Irish) strong

Treise

Toki (Japanese) chance

Tokiwa (Japanese) steady

Tolice (American) creative

Tolikna (Native American) coyote ears

Tollie (Hebrew) confident

Toll, Tollee, Tolli, Tolly, Tollye

Toloisi (French) ingenious

Tomazja (Polish) twin

Tomea (American) twin

Tomeka (African American) form of Tamika: lively

Tomeke

Tomiko (Japanese) wealthy

Miko, Tamiko, Tomi

Tomitria (African American) form of Tommie: sassy

Tomi

Tommie (Hebrew) sassy

Tom, Tomi, Tommy

Tomo (Japanese) intelligence

Tonaya (American) valuable

Tona, Tone

Tonesa (Greek) thriving

Tonet (French) form of Tony: meritorious

Tonetta (American) thriving

Toney (American) form of Tony: meritorious

Toni (Latin) form of Tony: meritorious

Tone, Tonee, Tonie

Tonia (Latin) a wonder

Toneah, Tonya, Tonyah, Toyiah

Tonia (Latin) daring

Tonni, Tonnie, Tony, Tonya

Tonicia (American) form of Tony: meritorious

Tonisha (African American) lively

Nisha, Tona, Toneisha, Tonesha, Tonie, Tonish

Tonla (American) form of Tonya: queenly

Tonna (American) form of Tony: meritorious

Tooka (Japanese) ten days

Topaz (Latin) gemstone; sparkling

Tophaz

Topher (Greek) feminine form of Christopher: the bearer of Christ

Tophery (Greek) form of Topher: the bearer of Christ

Tophie (Greek) form of Sophie: wise one

Topsy (English) topnotch

Toppie, Toppsy, Topsey, Topsi, Topsie

Tora (Scandinavian) thunder

Toranda (American) wins

Torborg (Scandinavian) thunder

Thorborg, Torbjorg

Tordis (Scandinavian) Thor's goddess

Tori (Scottish) rich and winning

Toree, Torri, Torrie, Torry, Tory

Torill (Scandinavian) loud

Toril, Torille

Torrance (Place name) town in California; confident

Torr, Torri

Torsha (American) wins

Torta (American) wins

Torunn (Scandinavian) loved by Thor

Toscha (Slavic) prepared

Tosha (Slavic) priceless

Tosh, Toshia

Toshala (Hindu) satisfied

Toshio (Japanese) year-old child

Toshi, Toshie, Toshiko, Toshikyo

Toski (Native American) bug

Tossia (Slavic) prepared

Toti (English) form of Charlotte: little woman

Totsi (Native American) moccasins

Toula (American) athletic

Tova (Hebrew) good woman

Tovah

Toxie (American) athletic

Toy (American) playful

Toia, Toya, Toye

Tozie (American) friendly

Trace (French) takes the right path

Traice, Trayce

Tracey (Gaelic) aggressive

Trace, Tracee, Traci, Tracie, Tracy

Tracinal (American) form of Tracy: summer

Tracy (English) summer
Trace, Tracee, Tracey, Traci, Tracie, Trasey, Treacy, Treesy

Traina (American) thinker

Trana (American) thoughtful

Trancine (American) form of Francine: beautiful

Tranell (American) confident
Tranel, Tranelle, Traney, Trani

Trang (Vietnamese) smart

Trangera (American) smart

Traniqua (African American) hopeful
Tranaqua, Tranekwa, Tranequa, Trani, Tranikwa, Tranney, Tranniqua, Tranny

Trava (Czech) grass

Traviata (Italian) woman who wanders

Travistene (American) feminine form of Travis: conflicted

Tray (American) feminine form of Trey: third-born; creatively brilliant

Trayceez (American) form of Tracy: summer

Traysha (American) form of Tricia: humorous

Trazanna (African American) talented
Traz, Trazannah, Traze

Treana (American) pure

Treann (American) pure

Treasah (American) pure

Treat (Word as name)

Trecia (American) form of Tricia: humorous

Tree (American) sturdy

Treece (American) form of Terese: nurturing
Treese, Trice

Treena (American) form of Trina: perfect; scintillating
Treen

Treesjie (American) distinctive

Trella (Spanish) star; sparkles
Trela

Tremira (African American) anxious
Tremera, Tremmi

Treneth (American) smiling
Trenith, Trenny

Trenia (American) form of Trina: perfect; scintillating

Trenica (African American) smiling
Trenika, Trinika

Trenise (African American) songbird
Tranese, Tranise, Trannise, Treenie, Treneese, Treni, Trenniece, Trenny

Trenllita (Spanish) form of Trina: perfect; scintillating

Trentine (American) pure

Trenyce (American) smiling
Trienyse, Trinyce

Tres (Greek) form of Theresa: gardener

Tresca (American) form of Theresa: gardener

Treseme (American) form of Theresa: gardener

Tressa (Greek) reaping life's harvest
Tresa, Tresah, Tress, Trisa

Tressel (American) form of Theresa: gardener

Tressem (American) form of Theresa: gardener

Tressie (American) successful
Tress, Tressa, Tressee, Tressey, Tressi, Tressy

Tressy (American) form of Theresa: gardener

Tresure (Invented) giving
Treasure, Tress

Treva (English) homestead by the sea

Trevei (American) wise

Trevina (English) variation of Treva: homestead by the sea

Treyvin (American) form of Trevin: strong

Tricia (Latin) humorous
Treasha, Tresha, Trich, Tricha, Trish, Trisha

Trido (American) threefold

Trilby (English) literary

Trilbie

Trill (American) excitable

Trin (American) pure

Trina (Greek) perfect; scintillating

Tina, Treena, Trine, Trinie

Trinda (American) pure

Trinesse (American) pure

Trinh (Vietnamese) virgin

Trinida (Spanish) trinity

Trinidad (Place name) island off of

Venezuela; spiritual person

Trini, Trinny

Trinity (Latin) triad

Trini, Trinita

Trinka (American) ideal

Trinlee (American) genuine

Trinley, Trinli, Trinly

Trionelle (Scottish) pure

Tripti (Hindi) content

Tris (American) form of Patricia:

woman of nobility; unbending

Trish (American) form of Patricia:

woman of nobility; unbending

Trysh

Trisha (American) form of Patricia:

woman of nobility; unbending

Tricia

Trishelle (African American)

humorous girl

Trichelle, Trichillem, Trish, Trishel, Trishie

Trishna (Indian) desired

Trissy (American) tall

Triss, Trissi, Trissie

Trista (Latin) pensive; sparkling love

Tresta, Trist, Tristie, Trysta

Tristen (Latin) bold

Tristan, Tristie, Tristin, Trysten

Tristica (Spanish) form of Trista:

pensive; sparkling love

Trist, Tristi, Tristika

Trixie (Latin) personable

Trix, Trixi, Trixy

Tru (English) form of Truly: honest

True

Truc (Vietnamese) desire

Trudin (American) form of Trudy:

hopeful

Trudis (German) optimist

Trudy (German) hopeful

Trude, Trudi, Trudie

True (American) truthful

Truee, Truie, Truth

Truette (American) truthful

Tru, True, Truett

Truffle (French) delicacy

Truff, Truffy

Trulea (American) honest

Trulencia (Spanish) honest

Lencia, Tru, Trulence, Trulens, Trulense

Truly (American) honest

True, Trulee, Truley

Trusteen (American) trusting

Trustean, Trustee, Trustine, Trusty,

Trusyne

Truth (American) honest

Truthe

Try (American) earnest

Tri, Trie

Tryna (Greek) form of Trina: perfect;

scintillating

Trine, Tryne, Trynna

Tsifira (Hebrew) crown

Tsomah (Native American) rose

Tsonka (American) capricious

Sonky, Tesonka, Tisonka, Tsonk

Tsuhgi (Japanese) second daughter

Tsula (Native American) fox

Tteirrah (American) form of Tara:

towering

Tua (Polynesian) outdoors

Tualau (Polynesian) outdoors

Tucker (English) tailor

Tukker

Tuenchit (Thai) mysterious

Tuesday (English) weekday

Tuhina (Hindu) snow

Tuki (Japanese) moon

Tula (Native American) moon

Tulasi (Indian) basil sacred

Tulia (Spanish) glorious
Tuli, Tuliana, Tulie, Tuliea, Tuly

Tuliki (Mythology) of the wind

Tully (Irish) powerful; dark spirit
Tull, Tulle, Tulli, Tullie

Tulse (Hindi) growing

Tulsi (Hindu) basil

Tunishua (American) place name
Tunisia

Tunisia (Place name)

Turin (American) creative
Turan, Turen, Turrin, Turun

Turney (Latin) wood worker
Turnee, Turni, Turnie, Turny

Turquoise (French) blue-green
Turkoise, Turquie, Turrkoise

Tursha (Slavic) warm
Tersha

Turush (Biblical) place name

Turya (Hindi) spiritual

Tusa (Native American) prairie dog

Tusti (Indian) peace

Tuwa (Native American) earth

Tuyen (Vietnamese) angel
Tuyet

Twaina (English) divided
Twayna

Twanda (African) dual

Tweetie (American) vivacious
Tweetee, Tweetey, Tweeti

Twiggy (English) slim
Twiggee, Twiggie, Twiggey

Twyla (English) creative
Twila, Twilia

Twynceola (African American) bold
Twin, Twyn, Twynce

Tyana (African American) new

Tyberia (Place name)

Tyce (American) Ty's child

Tye (American) talented

Tyeoka (African American) rhythmic
Tioka, Tyeo, Tyeoke

Tyesha (African American)
duplicitous
Tesha, Tisha, Tyeisha, Tyiesha, Tyisha

Tyisha (African American) sweet
Isha, Tisha, Ty, Tyeisha, Tyish

Tyla (American) form of Tyler: stylish;
tailor

Tyler (American) stylish; tailor
Tielyr, Tye

Tymitha (African American) kind
*Timitha, Tymi, Tymie, Tymith, Tymy,
Tymytha*

Tyndall (Irish) dark
Tyndal, Tyndel, Tyndell, Tyndyl, Tyndyll

Tyne (American/English) dramatic;
sylvan
Tie, Tine, Tye

Tynisha (African American) fertile
Tinisha, Tynesha, Tynie

Tyonia (American) of the river

Tyra (Scandinavian) assertive woman
Tye, Tyrah, Tyre, Tyrie

Tyrea (African American) form of
Thora: like thunder
Tyree, Tyria

Tyredda (American) form of Tyra:
assertive woman

Tyrina (American) ball of fire
Tierinna, Tye, Tyreena, Tyrinah

Tyrra (Scandinavian) aggressive

Tyson (French) son of Ty
Ty, Tysen

Tyzna (American) ingenious; assertive
Tyze, Tyzie

Tzadika (Hebrew) loyal
Zadika

Tzafra (Hebrew) morning
Tzefira, Zafra, Zefira

Tzahala (Hebrew) happy
Zahala

Tzeira (Hebrew) young

Tzemicha (Hebrew) in bloom
Zemicha

Tzeviya (Hebrew) gazelle
Civia, Tzevia, Tzivia, Tzivya, Zibiah,
Zivia

Tzigane (Hungarian) gypsy
Tsigana, Tsigane

Tzila (Hebrew) darkness
Tzili, Zila, Zili

Tzina (Hebrew) shelter
Zina

Tzipiya (Hebrew) hope
Tzipia, Zipia

Tziyona (Hebrew) hill
Zeona, Ziona

Tzofi (Hebrew) scout
Tzofia, Tzofit, Tzofiya, Zofi, Zofia,
Zofit

Tzuriya (Hebrew) God is powerful
Tzuria, Zuria

U

Uberta (Italian) bright

Uchechi (African) God's will

Udavine (American) thriving
Uda

Udele (English) prospering woman
Uda, Udela, Udell, Udella, Udelle

Uela (Unknown) dedicated to God
Uella

Ufrosinne (Mythology) jovial
Euphrosyne

Uganda (Place name) African nation

Ujhala (Hindi) shines

Ula (Celtic) jewel-like beauty
Eula, Ulah, Ule, Ulla, Ylla

Ulanda (American) confident
Uland, Ulandah, Ulande

Ulani (Hawaiian/Polynesian) happy
Ulanee

Ulatha (Biblical) place name; happy

Ulda (Unknown origin) prophetess

Ule (Unknown origin) burdens

Ulielmi (Unknown origin) intelligent

Ulima (Unknown origin) smart

Ulla (German) powerful and rich

Ulphi (Unknown origin) lovely
Ulphia, Ulphiah

Ulrika (Teutonic) leader
Rica, Ulree, Ulric, Ulrica, Ulrie, Ulry,
Urik

Ultima (Latin) aloof

Ulupi (Hindi) pretty

Ulva (German) wolf; courage

Ulyssia (Invented) feminine form of
Ulysses: forceful
Lyss, Lyssia, Uls, Ulsy, Ulsyia

Uma (Hebrew) nation; worldview
Umah

Umberlina (Unknown origin)
feminine form of Umberto: earthy

Umeko (Unknown origin) blossom

Umma (Hindi) mother
Uma, Umah

Umnia (Arabic) desirable
Umniah, Umniya, Umniyah

Una (Latin) unique
Ona, Oona, Unah

Unda (Scandinavian) water child

Undine (Latin) from the ocean
Ondine, Undene, Undyne

Undra (American) one; long-suffering

Unet (French) the one

Unette (American) the one

Unice (English) sensible
Eunice, Uniss

Unika (Slavic) different

Unique (Latin) singular
Uneek

Unity (English) unity of spirit
Unitee

Unn (Scandinavian) loving
Un

Ural (Place name) Ural Mountains
Ura, Uralle, Urine, Uris

Urania (Greek) universal beauty
Ranie, Uraine, Urana, Uraneah, Uranie

Urbai (Unknown origin) gentle

Urbana (Latin) born in the city
Urbani, Urbanna, Urbannai

Urbi (Egyptian) princess

Urena (Slavic) lights the way

Urgita (Hindi) energetic

Uria (Hebrew) God is my flame
Ria, Uri, Uriah, Urial, Urissa

Uridia (Slavic) light

Uriela (Hebrew) God's light
Uriella, Uriyella

Urit (Hebrew) candle

Urith (Hebrew) bright
Urit

Urmia (Biblical) place name

Ursa (Greek/Latin) star; bearlike
Urs, Ursah, Ursie

Ursula (Latin) little female bear
Ursa, Urse, Ursela, Ursila

Urta (Latin) spiny plant

Usha (Indian) dawn; awakening

Usher (Word as name) helpful
Ush, Ushar, Ushur

Usiana (Biblical) place name

Uta (Teutonic) battle heroine

Utas (Unknown origin) glorious

Ute (German) rich and powerful

Utica (Native American)

Uticas, Uttica

Utopia (American) idealistic
Uta, Utopiah

Uttasta (Unknown origin) from the homeland

Uzbek (Place name) for Uzbekistan
Usbek

Uzetta (American) serious
Uzette

Uzia (Hebrew) God is my strength
Uzial, Uzzia, Uzzial

Uzma (Spanish) capable
Usma, Uz, Uzmah

Uzoma (African) the right way

V

Vacla (Origin unknown) vain

Vaclava (Origin unknown) conceited

Vada (German) form of Valda: high spirits
Vaida, Vay

Vadnee (Origin unknown) gives

Vairie (Spanish) versatile child

Val (Latin) form of Valerie: robust

Vala (German) chosen one

Valaida (German) chosen

Valaine (French) chooses

Valarie (Latin) strong
Val, Valaria, Valerie

Valda (German) high spirits
Val, Valdah, Valida, Velda

Vale (English) valley; natural
Vail, Vaylie

Valecia (Spanish) form of Valencia: city in Spain; strong-willed

Valeda (Latin) strong woman
Val, Valayda, Valedah

Valencia (Place name) city in Spain; strong-willed
Val, Valecia, Valence, Valenica, Valensha, Valentia, Valenzia, Valincia

Valene (Latin) strong girl
Valaine, Valean, Valeda, Valeen, Valen, Valena, Valeney, Valina, Valine, Vallan, Vallen

Valensia (Spanish) strong

Valenteen (American) strong

Valentina (Latin) romantic
Val, Vala, Valantina, Vale, Valentin, Valentine, Valiaka, Valtina, Valyn, Valynn

Valeny (American) hard
Val, Valenie

Valera (American) form of Valerie: robust

Valeria ✿ ⊕ (Spanish) having valor
Valeri, Valerie, Valery

Valerie (Latin) robust
Vairy, Val, Valarae, Valaree, Valarey,
Valari, Valarie, Vale, Valeree, Valeri,
Valeriane, Valery, Vallarie, Valleree,
Valleri, Vallerie, Vallery, Valli, Vallie,
Vallirie, Valora, Valry, Veleria, Velerie

Valerta (Invented) form of Valerie:
robust
Valer, Valert

Valesca (Slavic) rules

Valeska (Polish) joyous leader
Valese, Valeshia, Valeske, Valezka,
Valisha

Valetta (Italian) feminine
Valettah, Valita, Valitta

Valida (Spanish) right

Valince (American) valiant

Valinda (American) valiant

Valindae (American) valiant

Valkie (Scandinavian) fantastic
Val, Valkee, Valki, Valkry, Valky

Valley (Word as name)

Vallie (Latin) natural
Val, Valli, Vally

Vallie-Mae (Latin) form of
Valentina and Mae: romantic
Valliemae, Vallimae, Vallimay

Valluri (Slavic) form of Valerie:
robust

Valma (Scandinavian) loyal

Valmay (American) spring

Valonia (Scandinavian) loyal
Vallon, Valona

Valora (Latin) intimidating
Val, Valorah, Valori, Valoria, Valorie,
Valory, Valorya

Valore (Latin) courageous
Val, Valour

Valoria (Spanish) brave
Vallee, Valora, Valore

Valrie (American) form of Valerie: robust

Value (Word as name) valued
Valu, Valyou

Valyn (American) perky
Valind, Valinn, Valynn

Vamia (Hispanic) energetic
Vamee, Vamie

Vanay (American) honor

Vanda (German) smiling beauty
Vandah, Vandana, Vandelia, Vandetta,
Vandi, Vannda

Vandan (American) honors

Vandana (Hindi) honor
Vandani

Vandeen (Sanskrit) prayerful

Vandyke (Dutch) lives by the water

Vaneecai (Slavic) form of Vanessa:
flighty

Vanessa ✿ ⊕ (Greek) flighty
Nessa, Van, Vanassa, Vanesa, Vanesah,
Vanesha, Vaneshia, Vanesia, Vanessah,
Vanesse, Vanessia, Vanessica, Vaniece,
Vaniessa, Vanisa, Vanissa, Vanita,
Vanna, Vannessa, Vanneza, Vanni,
Vannie, Vanny, Varnessa, Venesa,
Venessa, Veneza

Vani (Russian) form of Vania: gifted

Vania (Hebrew) gifted
Vaneah, Vanya

Vanille (American) simplistic
Vana, Vani, Vanila, Vanile, Vanna

Vanity (English) vain girl
Vanita, Vaniti

Vanna (Greek) golden girl
Van, Vana, Vanae, Vannah, Vannalee,
Vannaleigh

Vanniea (American) capricious

Vanora (Welsh) wave; mercurial
Vannora

Vantha (Greek) yellow hair

Vanthe (Greek) form of Xanthe:
beautiful blonde

Vantje (Scandinavian) blonde

Vanya (American) form of Vanna:
golden girl
Vani, Vanja, Vanni, Vanyuh

Vara (Greek) strange
Varah, Vare

Varaina (Invented) form of Lorraine: sad-eyed

Varda (Hebrew) rosy
Vadit, Vardah, Vardia, Vardice, Vardina, Vardis, Vardit

Varetta (American) methodical

Varina (Czech) form of Barbara: traveler from a foreign land

Varna (Origin unknown) no trace of vanity

Vasa (Slavic) pretty

Vashi (Slavic) pretty

Vashti (Persian) beauty
Vashtee, Vashtie

Vasta (Persian) pretty
Vastah

Vasteen (American) capable
Vas, Vastene, Vastine, Vasty

Vateyo (American) pious

Vatima (Slavic) form of Fatima: wise woman

Vaughan (Last name as first name) smooth talker
Vaughn, Vawn, Vawne

Veanetta (American) knowing

Veanu (American) knowing

Veata (Cambodian) smart; organized
Veatah

Veaunarda (Slavic) vineyard

Veda (Sanskrit) wise woman
Vedad, Vedah, Vedis, Veeda, Veida, Vida, Vita

Veddy (Slavic) jubilant

Vedea (Slavic) spirited child

Vedette (French) watchful
Veda, Vedett, Vedetta

Vedi (Sanskrit) wisdom

Vedis (Slavic) lively

Vedrana (Slavic) pleasant

Veena (Indian) musical instrument

Veera (Spanish) form of Vera: faithful friend

Vega (Scandinavian) star
Vay, Vayga, Vegah, Veguh

Velacy (Origin unknown) delicate

Velda (German) famous leader
Valeda, Veleda

Veleda (German) intelligent
Vel, Veladah, Velayda

Veletta (American) secretive

Velia (American) secretive

Velika (Slavic) wonder

Velina (American) secretive

Velinda (American) form of Melinda: honey; sweetheart
Vel, Velin, Velind, Vell, Velly, Velynda

Vell (American) form of Velma: hardworking
Vel, Velly, Vels

Vellamo (Mythology) attractive

Velma (German) hardworking
Valma, Vel, Vellma, Velmah, Vilma, Vilna

Velonne (Spanish) capable

Velore (Origin unknown) poised

Veltria (American) secretive

Velvet (French) luxurious
Vel, Vell, Velvete, Velvett

Vendy (American) respects

Venecia (Italian) girl from Venice; sparkles
Vanecia, Vanetia, Veneise, Venesa, Venesha, Venesher, Venesse, Venessia, Venetia, Venette, Venezia, Venice, Venicia, Veniece, Veniesa, Venise, Venisha, Venishia, Venita, Venitia, Venize, Vennesa, Vennice, Vennisa, Vennise, Vonitia, Vonizia

Veneradah (Spanish) honored; venerable
Ven, Venera, Venerada

Veneranda (Spanish) venerated; respected

Venetia (Latin) girl from Venice

Veney (American) respects

Venice (Place name) city in Italy; coming of age
Vanice, Vaniece, Veneece, Veneese

Venitia (Italian) forgiving
Esha, Venesha, Venn, Venney, Venni, Vennie, Venny

Venka (Indian) hunter

Venkata (Indian) hunter

Venke (Polish) form of Venice: city in Italy; coming of age

Vennita (Italian) form of Venice: city in Italy; coming of age
Nita, Vanecia, Ven, Venesha, Venetia, Venita, Vennie, Vinetia

Ventura (Spanish) fortunate

Venus (Latin) loving; goddess of love
Venis, Venise, Vennie, Venusa, Vinny

Veola (American) form of Viola: violet; lovely lady
Violet

Veoline (American) violet

Veonia (American) form of Venus: loving; goddess of love

Veonialle (American) form of Venus: loving; goddess of love

Vera (Russian) faithful friend
Vara, Veera, Veira, Veradis, Verah, Vere, Verie, Vira

Verbena (Latin) natural beauty

Verchema (American) honest

Verda (Latin) breath of spring
Ver, Vera, Verdah, Verde, Verdi, Verdie, Viridiana, Viridis

Verdad (Spanish) verdant; honest
Verda, Verdade, Verdie, Verdine, Verdite

Verdelina (American) verdant

Verdia (American) verdant

Verdie (Latin) fresh as springtime
Verd, Verda, Verdee, Verdi, Verdy

Verena (English) honest
Veren, Verenah, Verene, Verenis, Vereniz, Verina, Verine, Virena, Virna

Verenase (Swiss) flourishing; truthful
Ver, Verenese, Verennase, Vy, Vyrenase, Vyrennace

Verity (French) truthful
Verety, Verita, Veritee, Veriti, Veritie

Verla (Latin) truthful

Verlene (Latin) vivacious
Verleen, Verlena, Verlie, Verlin, Verlina, Verlinda, Verline, Verlyn, Verlynne

Verlita (Spanish) growing

Vermekia (African American) natural
Meki, Mekia, Verme, Vermekea, Vermy, Vermye

Verna (Latin) springlike
Vernah, Verne, Vernese, Vernesha, Verneshia, Vernessa, Vernetia, Vernetta, Vernette, Vernia, Vernice, Vernis, Vernisha, Vernishela, Vernita, Verusya, Viera, Virida, Virna, Virnell

Verneake (American) spring

Verneta (Latin) verdant
Verna, Vernita, Virena, Virna

Vernice (American) natural
Verna, Vernica, Vernicca, Vernie, Verniece, Vernique

Vernicia (Spanish) form of Vernice: natural
Vern, Verni, Vernisia

Vernita (Latin) of the spring

Verona (Place name) city in Italy; flourishes; honest

Veronica (Latin) girl's image; real
Nica, Ronica, Varonica, Veron, Verhonica, Verinica, Verohnica, Veron, Verone, Veronic, Veronice, Veronika, Veronne, Veronnica, Vironica, Von, Vonni, Vonnie, Vonny, Vron, Vronica

Veronican (American) form of Veronica: girl's image; real

Veronique (French) form of Veronica: girl's image; real
Veroneek, Veroneese, Veroniece

Veroniquea (French) form of
Veronica: girl's image; real
Vesna, Vezna

Versperah (Latin) evening star
Vesp, Vespa, Vespera

Vertrelle (African American)
organized
Vertey, Verti, Vertrel, Vetrell

Vesela (Origin unknown) open
Vess

Vesnah (Slavic) spring goddess

Vespera (Latin) evening star

Vesta (Latin) home-loving; goddess
of the home
Vess, Vessie, Vessy, Vest, Vestah, Vesteria

Veste (Latin) keeps home fires
burning
Esta, Vesta

Vetaria (Slavic) regal woman

Vevay (Latin) form of Vivian:
bubbling with life
Vevah, Vi, Viv, Vivay, Vivi, Vivie

Vevila (Irish) vivacious

Vevina (Latin) sweetheart

Vi (Latin) form of Viola: violet; lovely
lady
Vy, Vye

Viana (Italian) vital

Vianca (American) form of Bianca:
white

Vianey (Spanish) form of Vivian:
bubbling with life
*Via, Viana, Viane, Viani, Vianne,
Vianney, Viany*

Vianne (French) striking
Vi, Viane, Viann

Viara (American) vibrant

Vibeke (Hindi) vibrant

Vickay (American) form of Vicky:
winner

Vicky (Latin) form of Victoria:
winner
*Vic, Viccy, Vick, Vickee, Vickey, Vicki,
Vickie, Vikkey, Vikki, Viky*

Victoria (Latin) winner
*Vic, Vicki, Vicky, Victoriah, Victoriana,
Victorie, Victorina, Victorine, Victory,
Vikki, Viktoria, Vyctoria*

Victorine (French) winner

Victory (Latin) a winning woman
Vic, Viktorie

Vida (Hebrew) form of Davida:
beloved one
Veeda

Vidella (Spanish) life
Veda, Vida, Videline, Vydell

Vidette (Hebrew) loved
Viddey, Viddi, Viddie, Vidett, Videy

Vidonia (Portuguese) vine; winding

Vidrine (Last name as first name) life

Vie (American) competitor

Vienna (Place name) a city in Austria
*Veena, Vena, Venna, Viena, Vienette,
Viennah, Vienne, Vina*

Viennese (Place name) form of
Vienna: a city in Austria
Vee, Viena, Vienne

Viera (Spanish) smart; alive

Vieyra (Spanish) lively

Vigdis (Scandinavian) war goddess

Vigilia (Latin) vigilant

Vignette (American) special scene

Vijaya (Indian) wins

Vilhelmina (Scandinavian) form of
Wilhelmina: able protector
Velma, Vilhelmine, Vilma

Villa (American) of the village

Villette (French) little village girl
Vietta

Villian (American) form of Lillian:
pretty as a lilly

Villoria (Spanish) valor

Vilma (Spanish) form of Velma:
hardworking
Vi, Vil

Vilmean (American) form of Velma:
hardworking

Vimala (Hindi) attractive

Vina (Hindi) musical instrument
Veena, Vena, Vin, Vinah, Vinesha,
Vinessa, Vinia, Viniece, Vinique,
Vinisha, Vinita, Vinna, Vinni, Vinnie,
Vinny, Vinora, Vyna

Vinah (American) up-and-coming
Vi, Vyna

Vincentia (Latin) winner
Vicenta, Vin, Vincenta, Vincentena,
Vincentina, Vincentine, Vincenza,
Vincy, Vinnie

Vinci (Spanish) wins

Vincia (Spanish) forthright; winning
Vincenta, Vincey, Vinci

Vinee (Spanish) welcomed

Vineeta (Indian) modest

Vinefrida (Scandinavian) bold

Vinelle (English) wine

Vineta (Indian) modest
Vinata

Vinetae (English) wine

Vinia (Spanish) vineyard woman

Vinishia (English) wine

Vinita (Hindi) she comes home

Vinital (Indian) asks

Vinne (American) from the vineyard

Vinuela (Spanish) longsuffering

Viola (Latin) violet; lovely lady
Vi, Violah, Violaine, Violanta, Viole,
Violeine

Violanth (Latin) from the purple
flower violet
Vi, Viol, Viola, Violanta, Violante

Violet (English/French) purple flower
Vi, Viole, Violette, Vylolet, Vyoletta,
Vyolette

Violeta (Spanish) form of Violet:
purple flower

Violia (Italian) form of Violet: purple
flower

Violin (American) instrument

Violyne (Latin) form of Violet:
purple flower
Vi, Vio, Viola, Violene, Violine

Viorica (Spanish) views

Virendra (Spanish) alive

Virethal (American) vibrant

Virgilia (Latin) bears all; stoic
Virgillia

Virginia (Latin) pure female
Giniah, Verginia, Verginya, Virge,
Virgen, Virgenia, Virgenya, Virgie,
Virgine, Virginio, Virginnia, Virginya,
Virgy, Virjeana

Viridas (Latin) green; growing
Viridis

Viridis (Latin) green and verdant
Virdis, Virida, Viridia, Viridiana

Virjean (American) virginal

Virtue (Latin) strong; pure

Virzie (American) virginal

Visala (Indian) heavenly

Visidora (Spanish) clear view; strong

Vision (Word as name) visionary

Visitacion (Spanish) a visit

Vita (Latin) animated; lively; life
Veda, Veeta, Veta, Vete, Vitaliana,
Vitalina, Vitel, Vitella, Vitia, Vitka,
Vitke

Viv (Latin) form of Vivian: bubbling
with life

Viva (Latin) alive; lively
Veeva, Vivan, Vivva

Vivadell (Combo of Viva and Dell)
lively

Vivecca (Scandinavian) lively; energetic
Viv, Viveca, Vivecka, Viveka, Vivica,
Vivie, Vyveca

Vivi (Hindi) vital
Viv

Vivian (Latin) bubbling with life
Viv, Viva, Vive, Vivee, Vivi, Vivia,
Viviana, Viviane, Vivie, Vivien,
Vivienne, Vivina, Vivion, Vivyan,
Vyvyan

Vivianeth (American) form of
Vivian: bubbling with life

Vivianetta (American) form of
Vivian: bubbling with life

Vivianna (American) inventive
Viviannah, Vivianne

Vivilyn (American) vital
Viv, Vivi

Vivka (Slavic) form of Vivian:
bubbling with life

Vix (American) form of Vixen: flirt
Vixa, Vixie, Vyx

Vixen (American) flirt
Vix, Vixee, Vixie

Vlada (Slavic) admired

Vladmirea (Slavic) admired

Vlasta (Slavic) likeable

Voila (French) attention; seen
Vwala

Volante (Italian) veiled

Voletta (French) mysterious
Volette, Volettie

Volette (Greek) hidden; veiled

Volina (American) form of Violin:
instrument

Vona (French) pretty woman

Vonceil (Spanish) form of Yvonne:
athletic

Voncille (American) form of Yvonne:
athletic; form of Vonna: graceful

Vonda (Czech) loving; talented
Vondah, Vondi

Vondrah (Czech) loving
Vond, Vonda, Vondie, Vondra, Vondrea

Vonese (American) form of Vanessa:
flighty
Vonesa, Vonise, Vonne, Vonnesa, Vonny

Voni (Slavic) affectionate
Vonee, Vonie

Vonna (French) graceful
Vona, Vonah, Vonne, Vonni, Vonnie,
Vonny

Vonnala (American) sweet
Von, Vonala, Vonnalah, Vonnie

Vonzetta (American) form of
Yvonne: athletic

Voula (Greek) sly

Voyage (Word as name) trip;
wanderer
Voy

Vrant (American) truth

Vrenean (American) truth

Vyera (Spanish) form of Viera: alive

W

Wade (American) campy

Wafa (Arabic) loyal

Wakana (Japanese) plant; thriving

Wakanda (Native American) magical
Wakenda

Wakebia (African) strong

Wakeen (American) spunky
Wakeene, Wakey, Wakine

Wakeishah (African American)
happy
Wake, Wakeisha, Wakesha

Walburga (German) protective
Walberga, Wallburga, Walpurgis

Walda (German) powerful woman
Waldah, Waldena, Waldette, Waldina,
Wallda, Wally, Welda, Wellda

Waldeen (American) strong

Waleria (Polish) sweet

Waleska (Last name as first name)
effervescent
Wal, Walesk, Wally

Walker (English) active; mover
Wallker

Walkiria (Mythology) fantastic

Wallis (English) open-minded
Walis, Wallace, Walless, Wallie, Walliss,
Wally, Wallys

Walsie (American) form of Waltz:
graceful

Waltz (American) graceful

Wana (American) wandering

Wanakee (Native American)
innovative

Wanda (Polish) wild; wandering
Vanda, Wahnda, Wandah, Wandie,
Wandis, Wandy, Wannda, Wenda,
Wendaline, Wendall, Wendeline, Wendy,
Wohnda, Wonda, Wonnda

Wandelka (Slavic) praised

Wanetta (English) fair
Waneta, Wanette, Wanita

Wanicka (American) form of Juanita:
believer in a gracious God; forgiving

Wanita (American) form of Juanita:
believer in a gracious God; forgiving

Warda (German) guards her own
Wardia, Wardine

Warma (American) warmth-filled
Warm

Warna (German) defends her own

Warner (German) outgoing; fighter
Warna, Warnar, Warnir

Wasana (Native American) good
health

Washina (Native American) good
health

Waun (Native American) vocal

Wauneta (American) form of
Juanita: believer in a gracious God;
forgiving

Waverly (English) wavers in the
meadow of swaying aspens
Waverley

Wayla (African) young child

Waynette (English) makes wagons;
crafts wood
Waynel, Waynelle, Waynlyn

Waywan (Native American) little girl

Weeko (Native American) pretty

Wehilani (Hawaiian) heaven

Weinsia (American) of the heavens

Wenda (German) adventurer
Wend, Wendah, Wendy

Wendell (English) has wanderlust
Wendaline, Wendall, Wendelle

Wendy (English) friendly; childlike
Wenda, Wendaline, Wende, Wendee,
Wendeline, Wendey, Wendi, Wendie,
Wendye

Weneta (American) of the heavens

Wenetta (American) of the heavens

Weslee (English) girl from meadows
of the west
Weslea, Weslene, Wesley, Weslia, Weslie,
Weslyn

Weslia (English) meadow in the west
Wesleya, Weslie

Weslie (English) woman in the
meadow
Wes, Weslee, Wesli

Wheeler (English) inventive
Wheelah, Wheelar

Whitley (English) outdoorsy
Whitelea, Whitlea, Whitlee, Whitly,
Whittley, Witlee

Whitman (English) white-haired
Whit, Wittman

Whitney (English) white; fresh
Whit, Whiteney, Whitne, Whitnea,
Whitnee, Whitneigh, Whitni, Whitnie,
Whitny, Whittaney, Whittany, Whittney,
Whytnie

Whitson (Last name as first name)
white
Whits, Whitty, Witte, Witty

Whittier (Literature) for the poet
John Greenleaf Whittier; distinguished
Whitt

Whoopi (English) excitable
Whoopee, Whoopie, Whoopy

Whynesha (African American)
kindhearted
Whynesa, Wynes, Wynesa, Wynesha

Wibeke (Scandinavian) vibrant
Wiebke, Wiweca

Wiktoria (Polish) victor
Wikta

Wilda (English) wild-haired girl
Willda, Willie, Wylda, Wyle

Wildress (American) form of the
wilderness

Wile (American) coy; wily
Wiles, Wyle

Wilemma (English) determined

Wilene (English) determined

Wilfreda (English) goal-oriented
Wilfridda, Wilfrieda

Wilfrid (Spanish) willful

Wilhelmina (German) feminine
form of William: staunch protector
Willa, Willhelmena, Willie, Wilma

Willa (English) desirable
Will, Willah

Willette (American) open
Wilet, Wilett, Will, Willett

Willima (Spanish) protective

Willine (American) form of will:
willowy
Will, Willene, Willy, Willyne

Willis (American) sparkling
Wilice, Will, Willice

Willistine (French) form of Willis:
sparkling

Willough (American) form of Willow:
free spirit; willow tree

Willow (American) free spirit; willow
tree
Willo

Willsie (American) form of Willow:
free spirit; willow tree

Wilma (German) sturdy
*Willma, Wilmah, Wilmina, Wylm,
Wylma*

Wilmot (English) feminine form of
William: staunch protector

Wilona (English) desirable; desired
child
*Willone, Willonoa, Wilo, Wiloh,
Wilonah, Wilone, Wylona*

Win (German) flirty
Winnie, Wyn, Wynne

Winata (American) form of Juanita:
believer in a gracious God; forgiving

Wind (American) breezy
*Winde, Windee, Windey, Windi, Windy,
Wynd*

Winda (African) hunts for prey

Windy (English) likes the wind
*Windee, Windey, Windi, Windie,
Wyndee, Wyndy*

Winella (American) form of Juanita:
believer in a gracious God; forgiving

Winema (Native American) leader

Winesa (American) winning

Winetta (American) peaceful;
country girl
Winette, Winietta, Wyna, Wynette

Winifred (German) peaceful woman
*Win, Wina, Winafred, Windy,
Winefred, Winefride, Winefried,*

*Winfreda, Winfrieda, Winifryd,
Winne, Winnie, Winniefred,
Winnifreed, Wynafred, Wynifred,
Wynn, Wynne, Wynnifred*

Winkie (American) vital
Winkee, Winky

Winna (African) friendly
Winnah

Winner (American) outstanding

Winnie (English) winning
Wini, Winny, Wynnie

Winnielle (African) victorious female
Winielle, Winniele, Wynnielle

Winnien (American) saintly

Winola (German) vivacious

Winona (Native American) firstborn
girl
*Wenona, Wenonah, Winnie, Winnona,
Winoena, Winonah, Wye, Wynnona,
Wynona, Wynonah, Wynonna*

Winonia (American) oldest girl

Winsome (English) nice; beauty
Wynsome

Winter (English) child born in winter
Wynter

Wisdom (English) discerning

Wistar (German) respected
Wistarr, Wister

Wisteria (Botanical) vine; entangles
Wistaria

Witera (American) dramatic

Wonder (American) filled with
wonder
Wander, Wonda, Wondee, Wondy,
Wunder

Wonila (African American) swaying
Waunila, Wonilla, Wonny

Wood (American) smooth talker
Woode, Woodee, Woodie, Woody, Woodye

Woodett (English) of the woods

Woodine (English) of the woods

Worship (Word as name) religious

Wova (American) brassy
Whova, Wovah

Wowena (American) form of Rowena:
blissful; beloved friend

Wren (English) flighty girl; bird
Renn, Wrin, Wryn, Wrynne

Wrenny (American) wren

Wurei (American) combative

Wyanda (American) form of Wanda:
wild; wandering
Wyan

Wyanet (Native American) lovely
Wyanetta, Wyonet, Wyonetta

Wyetta (French) feisty
Wyette

Wyld (American) spirited

Wyldanen (American) spirited

Wyleen (American) spirit

Wylie (American) wily
Wylee, Wyley, Wyli

Wymette (American) vocalist
Wimet, Wimette, Wymet, Wynette

Wyna (American) oldest

Wynell (American) oldest

Wynelle (American) oldest

Wynndi (American) friend
Wendy

Wynne (Welsh) fair-haired
Win, Winne, Winnie, Winny, Winwin,
Wyn, Wynee, Wynn, Wynnie

Wynnika (American) friend

Wynstelle (Latin) chaste; star
Winstella, Winstelle, Wynnestella,
Wynnestelle

Wyntress (American) friend

Wyomie (Native American) horse-
rider on the plains
Why, Wyome, Wyomee, Wyomeh,
Wyomia

Wyoming (Native American) U.S.
state; cowgirl
Wy, Wye, Wyoh, Wyomia

Wyrene (American) helps

Wysandra (Greek) fair; protects

Wyss (Welsh) spontaneous; fair
Whyse

X

Xandra (Greek) protective
Xandrae, Zan, Zandie, Zandra

Xanthe (Greek) beautiful blonde; yellow
X, Xanth, X-Anth, Xantha, Xanthie,
Xes, Zane, Zanthie

Xanthippe (Greek) form of Xanthe:
beautiful blonde; yellow

Xara (Hebrew) form of Sarah: God's
princess

Xavia (Origin unknown) feminine
form of Xavier: familiar

Xaviera (French) smart
Zavey, Zavie, Zaviera, Zavierah, Zavy

Xena (Greek) girl from afar
Xenia, Zen, Zena, Zennie

Xeniah (Greek) gracious entertainer
Xen, Xenia, Zenia, Zeniah

Xianona (American) fragrant

Ximena (Greek) greets

Ximenia (Spanish) form of Serena:
calm

Xiomara (Spanish) congenial

Xloie (American) form of Chloe:
flowering

Xylene (Greek) outdoorsy
Leen, Lene, Xyleen, Xyline, Zylee, Zyleen, Zylie

Xylia (Greek) woods-loving
Zylea, Zylia

Xylophila (Greek) lover of nature

Y

Yacoa (American) form of Coco: coconut

Yadavendra (Indian) friendly

Yadira (Hindi) dearest

Yael (Hebrew) strength of God
Yaele, Yayl, Yayle

Yaffa (Hebrew) beautiful girl
Yafa, Yafah, Yaffah, Yapha

Yagna (Slavic) giving

Yahaira (Hebrew) precious
Yajaira

Yahnnie (Greek) giving
Yahn, Yanni, Yannie, Yannis

Yahsah (American) dear one

Yajaira (Spanish) dear one

Yaki (Japanese) tenacious
Yakee

Yakira (Hebrew) adored baby

Yalcin (American) violet

Yale (English) fertile moor
Yaile, Yayle

Yalonda (American) form of Yolanda: pretty as a violet flower

Yamayo (Asian) lovely

Yamileth (American) form of Yamila: beautiful

Yamilla (Arabic) form of Jamila: beautiful female; form of Camilla: wonderful
Yamila, Yamyla, Yamylla

Yamille (Arabic) beautiful
Yamill, Yamyl, Yamyle, Yamylle

Yamin (Hebrew) near to God

Yamini (Indian) nighttime

Yamya (Hindi) nighttime

Yan (Slavic) forgiving

Yana (Slavic) lovely
Yanah, Yanna, Yanni, Yannie, Yanny

Yancy (Native American) Yankee; sassy
Yancee, Yancey, Yanci, Yancie

Yanessa (American) form of Vanessa: flighty
Yanesa, Yanisa, Yanissa, Yanysa, Yanyssa

Yanet (Spanish) form of Janet: small; forgiving

Yaney (American) form of Janey: believer in a gracious God

Yanine (American) form of Janine: kind

Yanni (Australian) peaceful

Yaquelin (Spanish) form of Jacqueline: supplanter; substitute
Yackie, Yacque, Yacquelyn, Yaki, Yakie, Yaque, Yaquelinn, Yaquelinne

Yara (Spanish) expansive; princess
Yarah, Yare, Yarey

Yarai (African) modest
Nyarai

Yardena (Hebrew) flows naturally

Yardley (English) open-minded
Yardlee, Yardleigh, Yardli, Yardlie, Yardly

Yareli (American) grateful

Yarine (Russian) peaceful
Yari, Yarina

Yarita (Spanish) flashy

Yarkona (Hebrew) growing

Yas (Hindi) scented

Yasha (Indian) maternal

Yashita (Indian) famous

Yashona (Hindi) rich
Yaseana, Yashauna, Yashawna, Yeseana, Yeshauna, Yeshawna, Yeshona

Yasmina (Hindi) form of Jasmine: fragrant; sweet
Yasmeena, Yasmyna

Yasmine (Arabic) pretty
Yasmeen, Yasmen, Yasmin, Yasminn, Yasmyn, Yasmynn

Yati (Indian) careful

Yaura (American) desirous
Yara, Yaur, YaYa

YaVonne (Indian) beautiful girl

Yazith (Biblical) place name

Yazmin (Persian) pretty flower
Yazmen, Yazminn, Yazmyn, Yazmynn

Yeardley (English) home enclosed in meadow
Yeardlee, Yeardleigh, Yeardli, Yeardlie, Yeardly

Yebenette (American) little
Yebe, Yebey, Yebi

Yechiel (Spanish) helps

Yelba (Spanish) form of Melba: talented; light-hearted

Yelena (Russian) friendly

Yelisabeta (Russian) form of Elizabeth: God's promise
Yelizabet

Yemaya (African) smart; quirky
Yemye

Yenisey (French) spellbound

Yepa (Native American) traditional

Yeriel (Hebrew) God's child

Yesica (Hebrew) form of Jessica: rich

Yeskia (Spanish) yesida
Yesika

Yesmin (Spanish) jasmine flower

Yessenia (Spanish) devout
Jesenia, Yesenia

Yessi (Hebrew) God-loving

Yesun (Turkish) jade
Jesin, Yesim

Yetta (English) head of home

Yeva (Russian) lively; loving
Yevka

Yevettea (Slavic) form of Yvette: lively archer

Yevgeniya (Slavic) highborn

Yildiz (Spanish) star

Yilma (Spanish) form of Wilma: sturdy

Yilmalla (Spanish) form of Wilma: sturdy

Yina (Spanish) winning
Yena

Yinyin (Asian) silver hair

Yitta (Hebrew) lightness

Ynez (Spanish) form of Inez: lovely

Yoanna (Hebrew) feminine form of John: God is gracious
Yoana, Yoanah, Yoannah

Yochana (Indian) thoughtful

Yodelle (American) old-fashioned
Yode, Yodell, Yodelly, Yodette, Yodey

Yoella (Hebrew) loves Jehovah
Yoela, Yoelah, Yoellah

Yogee (American) bright

Yogeta (American) bright

Yogini (Indian) centered

Yogita (Indian) smart

Yohanna (Greek) violet; textured
Yohana, Yohanah, Yohannah

Yoka (Native American) bird song

Yokasta (Greek) form of Jocasta: light

Yoko (Japanese) good; striving
Yokoh

Yola (Spanish) form of Yolanda: pretty as a violet flower
Yolanda, Yoli

Yolada (Spanish) form of Yolanda: pretty as a violet flower

Yolanda (Greek) pretty as a violet flower
Yola, Yolana, Yolandah, Yolie, Yoyly

Yolia (Spanish) form of Julia: forever young

Yolie (Greek) violet; flower
Yolee, Yoley, Yoli, Yoly

Yomi (Spanish) sun child

Yon (Korean) lotus; lovely
Yonn

Yona (Hebrew) dove; calm
Yonah, Yonna, Yonnah

Yonaide (American)
Yonade, Yonaid

Yonina (Hebrew) dove; calm
Yonyna

Yonit (Hebrew) passive
Yonitt, Yonyt, Yonytt

Yorba (Place name)

Yordaine (French) form of Jordan:
excellent descendant
Yordane, Yordayne

Yordan (Hebrew) form of Jordan:
excellent descendant
Yorden, Yordyn

Yordana (Hebrew) humble
Yordanah, Yordanna, Yordannah

Yoreni (Place name)

Yori (Japanese) dependable
Yoree, Yorey, Yorie, Yory

York (English) forthright
Yorkie, Yorkke

Yoselin (Spanish) form of Joselin:
happy girl

Yosepha (Hebrew) form of
Josephine: blessed

Yoshe (Japanese) form of Yoshi: good
girl
Yoshee, Yoshey, Yoshi, Yoshie, Yoshy

Youhanna (Slavic) form of Johanna:
believer in a gracious God

Young (Korean) forever

Yousha (Indian) girl

Yousheika (Slavic) joyful

Youvet (French) form of Yvette: lively
archer

Youvone (American) form of
Yvonne: athletic

Yovana (Slavic) joy

Yovelle (Hebrew) joy

Yovona (African American) form of
Yvonne: athletic
*Yovaana, Yovanna, Yovhana, Yovhanna,
Yoviana, Yovianna*

Ysabel (Spanish) form of Isabel:
clever
*Ysabell, Ysabelle, Ysebel, Ysebell,
Ysebelle, Ysybel, Ysybell, Ysybelle*

Ysabella (Spanish) smart and witty
*Ysabela, Ysebela, Ysebella, Ysybela,
Ysybella*

Ysanne (English) graceful
Esan, Esanne, Essan, Ysan, Ysann

Yseult (Irish) prettiness
Yseulte

Yu (Asian) jade; a gem

Yue (Asian) happy

Yuette (American) capable
Yue, Yuete, Yuetta

Yuki (Japanese) snow child

Yukolina (Slavic) form of Julia:
forever young

Yulan (Spanish) splendid

Yuldene (Slavic) form of Juliana:
youthful; Jove's child

Yule (Spanish) competitive

Yulondita (Spanish) form of Juliana:
youthful; Jove's child

Yuna (African) gorgeous
Yunah

Yuri (Chinese) lily

Yuridia (American) lily

Yuta (American) dramatic
Uta

Yutaca (Spanish) dramatic

Yuti (Indian) united as one

Yuvati (Indian) girl

Yuventia (Spanish) archer

Yuvette (English) petite archer

Yuvrani (Indian) princess

Yves (French) clever

Yvette (French) lively archer
Yavet, Yevette, Yvete, Yvett

Yvonnda (American) form of
Yvonne: athetic

Yvonne (French) athletic
Vonne, Vonnie, Yavonne, Yvone, Yvonna

Yvonnig (Invented) athlete

Yzabel (Hebrew) form of Isabel:
God-loving
*Yzabell, Yzabelle, Yzebel, Yzebell,
Yzebelle, Yzybel, Yzybell, Yzybelle*

Z

Zabrina (American) form of Sabrina: passionate
Zabreena, Zabryna

Zac (American) God remembers her

Zachah (Hebrew) lord remembered; bravehearted
Zach, Zacha, Zachie, Zachrie

Zachree (Hebrew) loves God

Zada (Arabic) fortunate
Zaida, Zayda

Zadie (American) form of Sadie: charmer; princess

Zafira (Arabic) successful
Zafirah

Zahara (African) flower
Zahari, Zaharit

Zahavah (Hebrew) golden girl
Zahava, Zeheva, Zev

Zahidee (Arabic) white

Zahira (African) flower
Zahara, Zahirah, Zahrah, Zara, Zuhra

Zahra (African) blossoming
Zara, Zarah

Zaibunissa (Spanish) peaceful

Zaida (Spanish) peacemaker
Zada, Zai

Zaina (Arabic) lovely; beautiful girl

Zainab (Arabic) brave

Zaira (Arabic) flower
Zara, Zarah, Zaria, Zayeera

Zaire (Place name) country in Africa
Zai, Zay, Zayaire

Zakah (African) smart
Zaka, Zakia, Zakiah

Zakiya (Arabic) chaste
Zakiyah

Zakiyyah (Hebrew) pure

Zakria (Hebrew) pure

Zaky (Hebrew) pure

Zakya (Hebrew) chaste

Zale (Greek) strong force of the sea
Zaile, Zayle

Zalika (African) born to royalty

Zaltana (Native American) high mountain

Zaltene (American) highborn

Zambee (Place name) form of Zambia
Zambi, Zambie, Zamby

Zamilla (Greek) strong force of the sea
Zamila, Zamyla, Zamylla

Zamir (Hebrew) intelligent leader
Zameer, Zamyr

Zan (Greek/Chinese) supportive; praiseworthy
Zander, Zann

Zana (Greek) defender; energetic
Zanah

Zanabria (Greek) defends

Zandile (American) pure

Zandra (Greek) shy; helpful
Zan, Zondra

Zane (Scandinavian) bold girl
Zain

Zaneta (Spanish) God is good

Zanita (American) gifted
Zaneta, Zanetta, Zanette, Zanitt, Zeneta

Zanna (Hebrew) lily
Zana, Zanah, Zannah

Zanoah (Biblical) place name

Zanth (Greek) leader
Zanthe, Zanthi, Zanthie, Zanthy

Zara (Hebrew) dawn; glorious
Zahra, Zarah, Zaree

Zaray (Arabic) going strong

Zareen (Hebrew) form of Sareen: strong

Zarena (Hebrew) dawn
Zareena, Zarina, Zaryna

Zarephath (Biblical) place name

Zaria (Hebrew) form of Zara: dawn; glorious

Zarieh (Hebrew) form of Zara: dawn; glorious

Zarifa (Arabic) successful

Zarina (Hebrew) form of Sarika: thrush; sings

Zarita (Hebrew) form of Sarah: God's princess

Zarmina (Origin unknown) bright
Zar, Zarmynna

Zarney (American) progressive

Zarni (American) direct

Zarreta (American) form of Zara: dawn; glorious

Zarria (Arabic) splendid

Zavina (Spanish) flower

Zawadi (African) gift

Zayba (Muslim) lovely

Zayit (Hebrew) olive

Zaylee (English) heavenly
Zay, Zayle, Zayley, Zayli, Zaylie

Zayna (Arabic) wonderful; pretty girl
Zayne

Zaynab (Iranian) child of Ali
Zainab

Zaza (Hebrew) golden

Zazalesha (African American) zany
Lesha, Zaza, Zazalese, Zazalesh

Zazula (Polish) outstanding

Zdenka (Czech) one from Sidon; winding sheet
Zdena, Zdenicka, Zdenina, Zdeninka, Zdenuska

Zdeslava (Czech) present glory
Zdevsa, Zdisa, Zdiska, Zdislava

Zea (Latin) grain
Zia

Zeandrea (American) form of Deandra: divine
Zeandraea, Zeandraya, Zeandria, Zeandrya

Zeb (Hebrew) Jehovah's gift

Zebrine (American) form of Sabrina: passionate

Zecua (American) loyal

Zeezee (American) sunny

Zef (Polish) moves with the wind
Zeff

Zeffa (Origin unknown) breezy

Zefiryn (Polish) form of Zephyr: the west wind; wandering girl

Zehara (Hebrew) light

Zehava (Hebrew) gold
Zahava, Zehovit, Zehuva, Zehuvit

Zehira (Hebrew) careful

Zel (Persian) cymbal

Zela (Greek) blessed; smiling

Zelana (American) sunny

Zelda (German) practical
Zell, Zellie

Zeldia (Spanish) form of Zelda: practical

Zelenka (Czech) fresh

Zelfa (African American) in control

Zelia (Spanish) sunshine
Zeleah

Zella (German) resistant

Zelma (German) divine

Zelpha (American) confident

Zemira (Hebrew) song

Zemorah (Hebrew) tree branch
Zemora

Zena (Greek) holy

Zenae (Greek) helpful
Zen, Zenah, Zennie

Zenaida (Greek) daughter of Zeus

Zenana (Hebrew) woman
Zena, Zenia

Zenda (Hebrew) holy

Zeni (Slavic) gracious

Zenia (Greek) open
Zeniah, Zenney, Zenni, Zennie, Zenny, Zenya

Zenobia (Greek) strength of Zeus

Zenobietta (Spanish) form of Zenobia: strength of Zeus

Zenorina (Spanish) holy

Zenov (Slavic) gracious

Zenzi (German) crescent

Zephirin (English) form of Zephyr: the west wind; wandering girl

Zephirinia (English) form of Zephyr: the west wind; wandering girl

Zephyr (Greek) the west wind; wandering girl
Zefir, Zeph, Zephie, Zephir, Zephira, Zephyra

Zeppelina (English) beautiful storm

Zera (Hebrew) seeds

Zerafina (Greek) the west wind; zephyr
Zerafeena, Zerafyna

Zeraldina (Polish) spear ruler

Zerdali (Turkish) wild apricot

Zeredah (Biblical) place name

Zerel (Hindi) brave

Zerena (Turkish) golden woman
Zereena, Zerina, Zeryna

Zerlinda (Hebrew) dawn
Zerlina

Zerly (Hebrew) morning

Zerren (English) flower

Zesiro (African) first of twins

Zesta (American) zestful
Zestah, Zestie, Zesty

Zeta (Greek) born last
Zetah, Zetta

Zett (Hebrew) olive; flourishing
Zeta, Zetta

Zetulio (Spanish) from the rose

Zevida (Hebrew) current
Zevuda

Zezziska (Slavic) form of Jessica: rich

Zhane (African American) feminine of Shane

Zhanna (Slavic) form of Janet: small; forgiving

Zhen (Chinese) pure

Zhenia (Latin) bright
Zennia, Zhen, Zhenie

Zhi (Chinese) of high character; ethical

Zho (Chinese) character

Zhong (Chinese) honorable

Zhuo (Chinese) smart; wonderful
Zuo

Zi (Chinese) flourishing; giving

Zia (Latin) textured
Zea, Ziah

Zibah (Biblical) delights

Zibute (Lithuanian) shines

Zigana (Hungarian) gypsy

Zihna (Native American) spinning

Zila (Hebrew) shadowy
Zilah, Zilla, Zillah, Zylla

Zildjian (Slavic) God judges her

Zilias (Hebrew) shadow
Zillia, Zillya, Zilya

Zillah (Biblical) in the shade

Zilpah (Hebrew) dignity
Zillpha, Zilpha, Zulpha, Zylpha

Zilu (Biblical) place name

Zilvinas (Spanish) hidden

Zimbab (Place name) form of Zimbabwe
Zimbob

Zimriah (Hebrew) songs
Zimria, Zimriya

Zina (Greek) hospitable woman
Zena, Zinah, Zine, Zinnie

Zindi (Spanish) form of Cindy: moon goddess

Ziniah (Muslim) prepared

Zinnia (Botanical) flower
Zenia, Zinia, Zinny, Zinnya, Zinya

Zinzi (American) flower

Zinzida (African) gracious

Ziona (Hebrew) symbol of good
Zionah, Zyona, Zyonah

Zipory (Hebrew) bird

Zipporah (Hebrew) bird in flight
Ziporah, Zippi, Zippie, Zippora, Zippy

Ziracuny (Native American) water

Zirah (Hebrew) coliseum
Zira

Zisla (Slavic) rose

Zita (Greek) seeker; (Spanish) rose girl
Zeeta, Zitah

Ziv (Hebrew) radiant

Ziva (Hebrew) brilliant
Zeeva, Ziv

Ziz (Hungarian) dedicated
Zizz, Zyz, Zyzz

Zlata (Czech) golden

Zoa (Greek) life; vibrant

Zocha (Polish) wisdom

Zoe ✿ ⊕ (Greek) lively; vibrant

Zoee, **Zoey**, *Zoie*, *Zooey*

Zoelle (Spanish) form of Noelle:

Christmas baby

Zofia (Polish) skilled

Zofie (Czech) wise

Zoheret (Hebrew) shining

Zohreh (Hebrew) shines

Zoila (Italian) earthy

Zola (French) earthy

Zolah

Zolema (American) confessor

Zolem

Zona (Latin) funny; brash

Zonah, *Zonia*, *Zonna*

Zonia (English) flower

Zonice (American) form of Zona:

funny; brash

Zonta (Native American) honest

Zooey (Greek) life

Zoom (American) energetic

Zoomi, *Zoomy*, *Zoom-Zoom*

Zora (Slavic) beauty of dawn

Zara, *Zorah*, *Zorrah*, *Zorre*, *Zorrie*

Zoralle (Slavic) ethereal

Zoral, *Zoralye*, *Zorre*, *Zorrie*

Zore (Slavic) dawn of day

Zorina (Slavic) golden

Zorana

Zorka (Slavic) dawn

Zorke, *Zorky*

Zorna (Slavic) golden

Zorrie (American) gold

Zosa (Greek) lively

Zosah

Zosima (Greek) vibrant

Zowie (Irish) vibrant

Zowee, *Zowey*, *Zowi*, *Zowy*

ZsaZsa (Hungarian) wild-spirited

Zsa, *Zsaey*

Zuba (English) musical

Zubaida (Arabic) laborer

Zubaidah, *Zubeda*

Zubeen (American) excellent

Zubida (Spanish) singer

Zubinelle (Spanish) vocal

Zudora (Sanskrit) laborer

Zulah (African) country-loving

Zoola, *Zoolah*, *Zula*

Zulaila (African) smart

Zyan (Native American) everlasting

Zydeco (French) musical

Bibliography

"America's 40 Richest Under 40." Fortune Online. 16 Sept. 2002 www.fortune.com.

"The American States." Collin, P.H., ed. *Webster's Concise Desk Dictionary*. New York: Barnes & Noble Books, 2001.

"The Animal Kingdom." Collin, P.H., ed. *Webster's Concise Desk Dictionary*. New York: Barnes & Noble Books, 2001.

Baby Center Baby Name Finder Page. 1 Dec. 2002 www.babycenter.com/babyname.

Baby Chatter Page. 1 Dec. 2002 www.babychatter.com.

Baby Names/Birth Announcements Page. 1 Oct. 2002 www.princessprints.com.

Baby Names Page. 1 Dec. 2002 www.yourbabysname.com.

Baby Names Page. 1 Nov. 2002 www.babynames.com.

Baby Names Page. 1 Oct. 2002 www.babyshere.com.

Baby Names World Page. 15 Jan. 2003 www.babynameworld.com.

Baby Zone Page. "Around-the-World Names." 15 Jan. 2003 www.babyzone.com/babynames.

"Biographical Names." Collin, P.H., ed. *Webster's Concise Desk Dictionary*. New York: Barnes & Noble Books, 2001.

"Biographical Names." *The Merriam-Webster Dictionary*. Springfield, MA: Merriam-Webster, Inc., 1998.

"Books of the Bible." Collin, P.H., ed. *Webster's Concise Desk Dictionary*. New York: Barnes & Noble Books, 2001.

Celebrity Names Page. 1 Nov. 2002 www.celebnames.8m.com.

"Common English Given Names." *The Merriam-Webster Dictionary*. Springfield, MA: Merriam-Webster, Inc., 1998.

Death Penalty Info Page. 1 Feb. 2003. "Current Female Death Row Inmates."
    www.deathpenaltyinfo.org/womencases.html.

Dunkling, Leslie. *The Guinness Book of Names*. Enfield, UK: Guinness Publishing, 1993.

eBusinessRevolution Page. 1 Nov. 2002 www.ebusinessrevolution.com/babynames/a.html.

ePregnancy Page. 1 Dec. 2002 www.Epregnancy.com/directory/Baby_Names.

"Fifty Important Stars." Gove, Philip Babcock, ed. *Webster's Third New International Dictionary of the English Language Unabridged*. Springfield, MA: Merriam-Webster, Inc., 1981.

"Gambino Capos Held in 1989 Mob Hit." Jerry Capeci. This Week in Gangland, The Online Column Page. 1 Aug. 2002 www.ganglandnews.com/column289.htm.

Hanks, Patrick, and Flavia Hodges. *A Dictionary of First Names*. Oxford: Oxford University Press, 1992.

Hanley, Kate and the Parents of Parent Soup. *The Parent Soup Baby Name Finder: Real Advice from Real Parents Who Have Named Their Babies and Lived To Tell About It—with More Than 15,000 Names.* Lincolnwood, IL: Contemporary Books, 1998.

Harrison, G.B., ed. *Major British Writers.* New York: Harcourt, Brace &World, Inc., 1959.

HypoBirthing Page. "Baby Names." 1 Oct. 2002 www.hypobirthing.com.

Indian Baby Names Page. 1 Nov. 2002 www.indiaexpress.com/specials/babynames.

Irish Names Page. 15 Jan. 2003 www.hylit.com/info.

Jewish Baby Names Page. 15 Jan. 2003 www.jewishbabynames.net.

Lansky, Bruce. *The Mother of All Baby Name Books: Over 94,000 Baby Names Complete with Origins and Meanings.* New York: Meadowlark Press (Simon and Schuster), 2003.

Kaplan, Justin, and Anne Bernays. *The Language of Names: What We Call Ourselves and Why It Matters.* New York: Simon & Schuster, 1997.

"Months of the Principal Calendars." Gove, Philip Babcock, ed. *Webster's Third New International Dictionary of the English Language Unabridged.* Springfield, MA: Merriam-Webster Inc., 1981.

"Most Popular Names of the 1990s." Social Security Administration Online. 1 Nov. 2002 www.ssa.gov/OACT/babynames.

"Most Popular Names of the 1980s." Social Security Administration Online. 1 Nov. 2002 www.ssa.gov/OACT/babynames.

"Most Popular Names of the 1970s." Social Security Administration Online. 1 Nov. 2002 www.ssa.gov/OACT/babynames.

"Most Popular Names of the 1960s." Social Security Administration Online. 1 Nov. 2002 www.ssa.gov/OACT/babynames.

"Most Popular Names of the 1950s." Social Security Administration Online. 1 Nov. 2002 www.ssa.gov/OACT/babynames.

"Most Popular Names of 2001." Social Security Administration Online. 1 Nov. 2002 www.ssa.gov/OACT/babynames.

"Most Powerful Women in Business." Fortune Online. 14 Oct. 2002 www.fortune.com.

"Movie-Star Names." Internet Movie Database online. 1 Nov. 2002 www.imdb.com.

Norman, Teresa. *A World of Baby Names: A Rich and Diverse Collection of Names from Around the World.* New York: Perigee (Penguin Putnam), 1996.

Origins/Meanings of Baby Names from Around the World Page. 1 Nov. 2002 www.BabyNamesOrigins.com.

Oxygen Page. "Baby Names." 1 Nov. 2002 www.oxygen.com/babynamer.

Parenthood Page. 1 Nov. 2002 www.parenthood.com/parent_cfmfiles/babynames.cfm.

"The Plant Kingdom." Collin, P.H., ed. *Webster's Concise Desk Dictionary*. New York: Barnes & Noble Books, 2001.

Popular Baby Names Page. 1 Nov. 2002 www.popularbabynames.com.

"Presidents of the United States." Collin, P.H., ed. *Webster's Concise Desk Dictionary*. New York: Barnes & Noble Books, 2001.

"Prime Ministers of the U.K." Collin, P.H., ed. *Webster's Concise Desk Dictionary*. New York: Barnes & Noble Books, 2001.

Racketeering and Fraud Investigations Page. 4 Feb. 2003 www.oig.dol.gov/public/media/oi/mainz01.htm.

Rick Porelli's AmericanMafia.com Page. 21 June 2002 www.americanmafia.com/news/6-21-02_Feds_Bust.html.

Rosenkrantz, Linda, and Pamela Redmond Satran. *Baby Names Now*. New York: St. Martin's Press, 2002.

Rosenkrantz, Linda, and Pamela Redmond Satran. *Beyond Charles and Diana: An Anglophile's Guide to Baby Naming*. New York: St. Martin's Press, 1992.

Rosenkrantz, Linda, and Pamela Redmond Satran. *Beyond Jennifer and Jason*. New York: St. Martin's Press, 1994.

Ryan, Joal. *Puffy, Xena, Quentin, Uma: And 10,000 Other Names for Your New Millenium Baby*. New York: Plume (Penguin Putnam), 1999.

Schwegel, Janet. *The Baby Name Countdown*. New York: Marlowe & Company (Avalon), 2001.

Shaw, Jessica. *The Everything Baby Names Book*. Massachusetts: Adams Media Corporation, 1996.

"Signs of the Zodiac." Gove, Philip Babcock, ed. *Webster's Third New International Dictionary of the English Language Unabridged*. Springfield, Mass: Merriam-Webster Inc. Publishers, 1981.

Television-show credits. 1 Oct. 2002–25 Feb. 2003.

Texas Department of Criminal Justice Page. "Offenders on Death Row." 1 Feb. 2003 www.tdcj.state.tx.us/stat/offendersondrow.htm.

Trantino, Charlee. *Beautiful Baby Names from Your Favorite Soap Operas*. New York: Pinnacle Books, 1996.

20,000+ Names Page. "20,000+ Names from Around the World." 1 Nov. 2002 www.20000-names.com.

United Kingdom Baby Name Page. 15 Jan. 2003 www.baby-names.co.uk.

Wallace, Carol McD. *The Greatest Baby Name Book Ever*. New York: Avon, 1998.

About the Author

Diane Stafford

Author of the wildly popular books *40,001 Best Baby Names* and *50,001 Best Baby Names*, magazine editor (five times running) and book editor, Diane Stafford has 25 years of experience in writing and editing—but nothing has rivaled the indecent amount of fun involved in turning out a third edition, called *60,001+ Best Baby Names*, with 10,000 more names for readers.

Adding names from numerous sources, including radio talk-show listeners who called in when Stafford did first edition interviews, this high-energy author gamely enlarged the scope of a book already filled with great names, fun anecdotes, and baby-naming tips.

"Today people are more creative than ever when it comes to naming their babies," notes Stafford. "Though it may be hard to believe, the fact is, every name in this book belongs to someone out there—even ones as off-the-wall as Dijonaise, Zero, and Oddrun. Although the traditional favorites like Emma and Joshua still reign supreme, lots of people enjoy making up names for their kids, thus adding to the huge universe of options. While name inventing is controversial—people even talk about it at cocktail parties—my feeling is that you have every right to relish choosing a name for your baby. Sure, take it seriously, but not too seriously."

Stafford adds, "Having a baby is absolutely the most wonderful thing that can happen to a person, and I hope this book reflects my enormous respect for parents and my celebration of the special privilege of parenting."

Living with her husband, Civil Court judge Greg Munoz, in sunny Newport Beach, California, Stafford—a transplant from Houston, Texas—writes and edits books. Her published books include: *Migraines For Dummies, Potty Training For Dummies, The Encyclopedia of STDs, No More Panic Attacks, 1000 Best Job-Hunting Secrets, The Vitamin D Cure* (with Jim Dowd, MD), and her latest, *60,001+ Best Baby Names*. Four of these books were co-authored with Stafford's daughter, Jennifer Shoquist, MD; her job-hunting book co-author was Moritza Day.

Dad's Picks

_____

_____

_____

_____

_____

_____

_____

_____

_____

_____

_____

Mom's Picks

_____

_____

_____

_____

_____

_____

_____

_____

_____

_____

Our Picks

_____

_____

_____

_____

_____

_____

_____

_____

_____

_____

_____

Our Picks

Our Picks

Our Picks

_____

_____

_____

_____

_____

_____

_____

_____

_____

_____

_____

Notes

Notes

Notes

Notes

Notes

Notes

Notes